*tion of Knowledge*
*ern America,*
*50–1920*

# The Organization of Knowledge in Modern America, 1860–1920

*EDITED BY ALEXANDRA OLESON*
*AND JOHN VOSS*

*The Johns Hopkins University Press*
*Baltimore and London*

This collection of essays was prepared under the auspices of the American Academy of Arts and Sciences as part of a historical study of the organization of science and scholarship in the United States. It is a companion volume to *The Pursuit of Knowledge in the Early American Republic: American Scientific and Learned Societies from Colonial Times to the Civil War,* edited by Alexandra Oleson and Sanborn C. Brown, The Johns Hopkins University Press, 1976.

This volume is based upon work supported by the Mellon Foundation, the Division of Research Grants of the National Endowment for the Humanities, and the History and Philosophy of Science Division of the National Science Foundation (Grant No. SOC 74-12410). Any opinions, findings, and conclusions or recommendations expressed in this publication are those of the authors and do not necessarily reflect the views of the supporting foundations.

The Johns Hopkins University Press, Baltimore, Maryland 21218
The Johns Hopkins Press Ltd., London

Library of Congress Catalog Number 78-20521
ISBN 0-8018-2108-8
Library of Congress Cataloging in Publication data will be found on the last printed page of this book.

# Contents

# Introduction

ALEXANDRA OLESON AND JOHN VOSS

In the decades between 1860 and 1920, the organization of knowledge in America was transformed, and institutional patterns were established that persist to this day. Just as the United States evolved from a divided country with two-thirds of her territory largely unsettled into a politically united and economically powerful nation, so American science and scholarship, once fostered and sustained by regionally isolated learned societies, became centered in an expanding network of national organizations for the advancement of specialized knowledge. By 1920, Europe still overshadowed America in the significance of its contributions to knowledge, but the American order of learning excelled in the number and diversity of its institutions, the size of the community it served and employed, and the degree of financial support it received from public and private sources. Above all, an organizational structure had emerged that would provide the United States with the ability to achieve, within the next generation, a position of eminence in the intellectual world.

How did the modern organization of knowledge come into being? What were the principal factors underlying its development? Why did it assume the shape it did? What were the distinctive American features of the structure that emerged? At the most immediate level, the answers to these questions lie in the interaction of the ideas, individuals, and institutions actively involved in the transformation. But the organization of knowledge in this period was not a development set apart from American life. It was influenced by the tensions of a society in which forces of change were intruding upon, yet had not displaced, long-standing patterns of social life and thought. And it occurred against the background of factors that had contributed to the formation of a learned community in early America: the establishment in the New World of learned and scientific societies modeled on the academies of eighteenth-century Europe; the belief in the power of knowledge to solve practical problems and promote material well-being; the impact of Baconian philosophy on the American scientific tradition; and the desire of a new nation to gain a respected place in the international community of learned men.

To examine this complex development, the American Academy of Arts and Sciences invited scholars representing a range of historical fields and perspectives to contribute to a long-term study of the structure and organization of American science and scholarship. This volume, which covers the period from 1860 to 1920, consists of the work from the second phase of that inquiry. An initial volume focused on the origins and development of the principal institutions to promote and disseminate knowledge in early America: literary and philosophical societies, academies of arts and sciences, organizations to promote useful knowledge, and medical and agricultural societies. In the period before the rise of the university, these bodies sought to organize and encourage research; improve the practical arts; diffuse knowledge through lectures, writings, and natural history collections; and foster contacts with scholarly communities in England and on the continent. A third volume, now in preparation, will deal with the period from 1920 to 1970, when American science and scholarship came of age.

This second stage of the study was organized and directed by an American Academy advisory committee composed of Sanborn Brown, I. Bernard Cohen, A. Hunter Dupree, Neil Harris, John Higham, Alexandra Oleson, Nathan Reingold, Charles Rosenberg, Barbara Rosenkrantz, and John Voss. From the beginning, our intention was to break new ground in the study of institutionalized learning in the United States, rather than to produce a comprehensive or definitive history. In this second stage of the inquiry, we chose to commission a series of papers that would be selective, suggestive, and necessarily tentative. Case studies of representative disciplines, applied fields, and institutions constitute the main body of the book. Introductory essays synthesize the general themes of the inquiry, and concluding statements suggest further directions for research.

Following the pattern of our first phase, the authors presented their case studies in draft form at a symposium held in Cape Newagen, Maine, in the summer of 1975. Discussion at Newagen focused on points of comparison and contrast among fields and institutions and between the American organization of learning and other Western systems. The final versions of the papers published here incorporate many of the suggestions and comments set forth at those sessions.

The result is an attempt to present the first overview of the full breadth of American organized learning. The volume goes beyond the history of the university movement to examine the disciplines, applied fields, and institutional forms that provided the social and intellectual setting for learning, the vehicles for specialization and professionalization, employment opportunities, funds for research, and the means of communicating scientific and scholarly ideas to the wider public. Taken together, these essays illuminate the interacting forces that brought the American order of learning into existence at a critical time in the development of knowledge and American society.

In the first half of the nineteenth century, the expansion of science and scholarship, the elaboration of analytic methods appropriate to specific fields, and the concurrent need for new facilities and resources to advance research brought major structural changes to the learned institutions of Western Europe: the establishment of *grandes écoles* in France, the reforms at Oxford and Cambridge, the development of the modern German university. In America as well, this accretion of knowledge strained the boundaries of the old classical curriculum and overwhelmed the capacity of provincial academies and scientific societies to advance research. The American response to this challenge was a complex, diverse set of learned organizations that affirmed "the American talent for assimilating what seemed best, and inventing the rest."[1]

The growth of learning in nineteenth-century America was motivated and directed, in the first instance, by scientists, scholars, and institutional leaders who saw new organizations to promote knowledge as the fundamental instruments of material and cultural progress. As Charles Rosenberg has observed, only "through the antecedent creation of a group of would-be scholars and academic entrepreneurs, enthusiastic in their motivation, secure in their righteousness, and confident in their special knowledge"[2] could the American order of learning have come into being. Beginning in the 1820s, these individuals led pioneering, if often abortive, efforts to reform the colleges and launch graduate training programs. In the decades before the Civil War, they sought out academic and government posts that offered the opportunity—albeit limited—to carry out research. They provided the direction for the first government agencies to support and conduct scientific research, and they established the first specialized societies and journals in fields ranging from statistics to Oriental studies. As forums for discussion and publication, such organizations helped to establish a sense of community among American men of learning and between them and their peers in the much-admired European centers of culture. These beginnings were tentative and sporadic, yet they formed what Richard Storr has termed "a tradition of aspiration"[3] for those who would later succeed in transforming the institutions of American learning.

Creating a self-conscious group of scientists and scholars and an organizational structure to promote their work was not an easy task in a society imbued with a pragmatic, egalitarian spirit. However, in the antebellum period and to a much greater extent in the decades after the Civil War, men and women directly involved in the pursuit of knowledge found support and encouragement in a constituency of predominantly college-educated, middle-class Americans. This "cultivated" public was motivated by a variety of impulses: the legacy of the Puritans "to advance Learning and perpetuate it to Posterity;"[4] a sense that knowledge would lead to a better understanding of God's grand design; a romantic interest in the natural wonders of the continent and a curiosity about the new sciences, particularly geology and Darwinian biology, which were challenging accepted ways of thought; a regard for learning as a mark of respectability and social place—a bastion against Jacksonian vulgarity and later against the materialism and corruption of the Gilded Age; a widespread belief in the practical benefits of science; and a desire to equal, and perhaps surpass, the intellectual achievements of Europe.

As members of the cultivated elite, scientists, scholars, and academic reformers shared these concerns. At the same time, they recognized that the learned institutions of modern America would ultimately be shaped by two overriding factors: the commitment of the learned community to the promotion and dissemination of knowledge in a specialized field, and the dependence of an expanding, modernizing society on scientific and technological expertise.

The unplanned, indeed ad hoc, efforts to build a new order of learning were a product of the interaction between European intellectual traditions and the American social and cultural environment. One can scarcely overlook the imprint of the German ideal of scholarship—or, more properly, the American image of it. By the 1850s, German universities had begun to attract hundreds of American students. Their experience in German laboratories and seminars, their intense involvement in the objective analysis of a precisely defined area of study, and their affinity for the concept of the scholar in service to the nation were to have a marked effect on the organization of learning in the United States. Yet that influence was everywhere tempered by the circumstances and character of the American nation. The viability of American popular government, the primacy of the union, and the power of inventive technology and industrial organization had been confirmed by the Civil War. As the century progressed, economic expansion, coupled with the exploration and development of the vast resources of the continent, created a society that was increasingly dependent on trained experts to ensure its progress. In this context, provincial learned societies and colleges offering little more than the classical curriculum were anachronisms. What emerged in their place was an organizational complex so striking in its structure, scope, and size as to seem a uniquely American invention.

The keystone of that complex was the American university. Like its German counterpart, it combined advanced training and research; unlike the German university, it encompassed not only undergraduate and graduate instruction in the same institution but also professional training in such emerging technical specialties as agriculture, engineering, commerce, and social work. Moreover, to an increasing extent, American universities came to be characterized by the desire—indeed the economic necessity—to serve as many interests as possible. If the University of Wisconsin organized schools of agriculture and engineering in fulfillment of its land-grant award, by the 1890s it had established a graduate school for advanced training in the arts and sciences. If William Rainey Harper sought to make the University of Chicago a great center of scholarship, he also instituted a program of evening and correspondence courses.

The American university, as it emerged at the end of the nineteenth century, was Charles W. Eliot's elective principle writ large. Introduced by Eliot at Harvard in 1869 but anticipated by a number of earlier efforts, the elective system melded the pressures of specialization with the demands of American society. It made possible a college curriculum relevant to modern life, yet it also reflected American individualism and freedom of choice, as well as the scholarly insistence that the university promote education and research in all areas of learning, new and old. Against the claims of the prescribed classical studies for primacy in developing mental discipline, Eliot asserted the equal value of all fields of learning: "It cannot be said too loudly or too often that no subject of human inquiry can be out of place in the programme of a real university. It is only necessary that every subject be taught at the university on a higher plane than elsewhere."[5]

Adoption of the elective system opened the door to practical, vocational training in the university but was no less a stimulus to pure science and scholarship. As Frederick Rudolph states, "election permitted the professor to indulge his interests and the students to follow theirs; it encouraged the accumulation of knowledge and welcomed into the world of learning subjects that had been forbidden through an ill-considered belief that the ancients knew everything worth knowing."[6] Writing in 1908, Eliot declared: "The largest effect of the elective system is that it makes scholarship possible, not only among undergraduates but among graduate students and college teachers."[7]

Without sacrificing the German ideal to advance knowledge for its own sake, American academic reformers had thus managed to combine that goal with a broad and direct commitment to what they called "real life."[8] The mix of interests they professed to serve, from the study of Byzantine history to farm management, seemed incongruous, yet the new college presidents were aware that this variety would broaden the base of the financial support they needed to create centers of learning in a democratic society. The enterprising spirit of men like Eliot, Harper, Andrew D. White of Cornell, Daniel Coit Gilman of Johns Hopkins, James B. Angell of Michigan, and Charles R. Van Hise of Wisconsin can be measured by the number of dollars they garnered from new men of wealth, alumni, and state legislatures. More important for the future of American science and scholarship were the number of students they attracted to their institutions and the number of teaching positions they created for scientists and scholars.

The availability of large concentrations of surplus capital was a critical factor in the development of American higher education in the later decades of the nineteenth century. The diverse purposes of the universities matched the diverse impulses of the new industrial magnates. The stewardship of wealth, conceived as a religious obligation and a more secular social responsibility; the economic benefits promised by the new science and technology; public reputation as a defender of culture, acquired by patronizing rather than pursuing knowledge; penance for amassing great fortunes with ruthless tactics; and immortality for the family name—all could be expressed and realized by endowing a new or existing university. Noted tycoons, including Johns Hopkins, John D. Rockefeller, Andrew Carnegie, Leland Stanford, William Vanderbilt, even the likes of Daniel Drew, founded new institutions, but behind them stood a sizeable number of American millionaires (more than four thousand by 1900)[9] and a growing body of alumni, all eager and able to advance the financial cause of American higher education. In 1899, for example, the thirty-four largest gifts pledged to public causes totaled $80 million; of that sum, more than $55 million was given to institutions of higher learning, more than $5 million to libraries, and almost $3 million to museums.[10]

The comprehensive nature of the university, combined with the precedent for government support of higher education set by the Morrill Act, was also a factor in securing annual state appropriations for universities. As Van Hise of Wisconsin demonstrated, service to the state—notably in terms of agricultural research, advice on legislative programs, and the development of both technical and non-technical extension courses—could be financially rewarding.

Ultimately, however, it was the students who came to colleges and universities in expanding numbers who formed the principal economic base of American science and scholarship. By the early decades of the twentieth century, the gradual acceptance of the many versions of the elective system, the spread of coeducation, and the growing belief that higher education, particularly in its more practical and vocational forms, was the avenue to success in business and the professions resulted in a significant increase in college and university enrollments. The number of American undergraduates rose from approximately 52,300 in 1870 to 156,800 in 1890, 237,600 in 1900, and 597,900 in 1920.[11]

In the wake of this expansion came a corresponding demand for teachers trained in the specialized fields of chemistry, physics, modern languages, European history, and even the social sciences, which, under the elective system, had come to form a major part of the new college curriculum. In the mid-nineteenth century, however, prospective American professors had little choice but to go to Germany for advanced study in these disciplines.[12] Not until the post–Civil War decades did the aspirations of a substantial body of "Germany-returned," the ambitions of academic reformers, the philanthropic impulses of the wealthy, and the country's need for specialized expertise converge to establish the first true graduate schools in the United States. By the turn of the century, the number of students enrolled in American graduate programs had risen from fewer than fifty in 1870 to nearly six thousand.[13]

In practical terms, this marked increase reflected the expanding employment opportunities for M.A.s and Ph.D.s in colleges and universities. It should be noted, however, that American graduate schools were not teacher training institutions or normal schools; rather, their distinct purpose was to develop productive scholars and scientists.[14] If American graduate training provided the incentive to undertake research, college and university teaching afforded the opportunity. In this setting, the concept of what professors should be was transformed: they assumed a new identity as specialists aware of the inherent obligation of the scholar to advance as well as disseminate learning. Increasingly their promotion and status depended on their contribution to research, as judged by their disciplinary peers. By 1920, the spread of higher education and the identification of the college teacher with scholarship—in theory if not always in fact—provided America with a reservoir of manpower for research far larger than that of any European country.

Although the pursuit of knowledge in America came to be centered in the university, it was strengthened and extended by a variety of learned institutions that were more narrowly circumscribed in scope and function. To settle and farm the vast continent, to reap the economic benefits and cope with the complex problems of scientific and technological progress, the federal government expanded its work in the natural and social sciences, notably in the Department of Agriculture, the Geological Survey, the Bureau of American Ethnology, the National Bureau of Standards, and, with the onset of World War I, the National Research Council. The National Museum, incorporated into the Smithsonian Institution in 1855, became a major center for research in botany, zoology, geology, and anthropology, while the Library of Congress gained standing as the largest reference library in the nation.

With the aid of tax dollars and private philanthropy, museums and libraries for scholars and the public alike blossomed in the urban centers of late nineteenth- and early twentieth-century America. The industrial titans of the day displayed their enthusiasm for books, music, and art by endowing such institutions as the Field and Peabody museums, the Newberry and Morgan libraries, the Metropolitan Museum of Art, and the Boston Symphony Orchestra. Their desire to promote original research in science and scholarship was evidenced in the founding of the Rockefeller Institute for Medical Research and the Carnegie Institution of Washington at the turn of the century and a few years later in the establishment of the first private philanthropic foundations to support research: the Milbank Memorial Fund, the Russell Sage Foundation, the Carnegie Corporation of New York, and the Rockefeller Foundation.

By the early years of the twentieth century, industrial firms also were beginning to recognize the value of systematic research to test and improve existing products and processes and to develop new means of competitive advantage. Prophetically, it was Thomas Edison, the personification of the self-taught tinkerer, who founded the first important industrial laboratory in Menlo Park, New Jersey, in 1876. By the outbreak of World War I, pioneering research programs had been organized by General Electric, Westinghouse, DuPont, Standard Oil of Indiana, Eastman Kodak, and American Telephone and Telegraph.

Finally, the growth of knowledge in ever-narrowing fields, coupled with improvements in transportation and communication, produced a proliferation of national associations of specialists. By 1920, national societies had been formed in all of the major disciplines of the sciences, social sciences, and humanities, and in an increasing number of subfields as well; indeed, specialization had advanced so far that a movement toward federation had begun with the formation of the American Council of Learned Societies in 1919.

Many of these organizations drew strength in their formative years from "amateur" as well as "professional" members who shared an interest in raising the cultural standards of the nation; by the early twentieth century, however, leadership was firmly in the hands of professional scientists and scholars concerned with formalizing, standardizing, and advancing research in their fields. Through annual meetings and the publication of journals and monographs, learned societies and professional associations promoted the exchange of ideas about new research and new methods of investigation; gradually, they assumed the function of a clearing house for information on employment opportunities. Analogous organizations of experts in the "useful arts" of agriculture and engineering and in the traditional professions of law and medicine were also in existence by 1900. In the American order of learning, the displacement of regional societies of "generalists" by these national associations of specialists signaled the coming of age of self-conscious communities of peer groups, intent on securing for themselves and their branch of learning an identity and status that transcended institutional boundaries.

The complex and interrelated development of America's learned institutions is the central theme of the papers that follow. The overview essays by John Higham and Edward Shils explore the major structural and intellectual factors that shaped American science and scholarship in the decades after the Civil War. Higham points to specialization as the motive force underlying the reordering of American intellectual life, but, as he explains, it was specialization in a uniquely American form. The concept of specialized inquiry seemed to contradict the values of an open, egalitarian society. The tension was resolved by the development, "in an apparently ad hoc way," of a flexible, diverse institutional matrix that widened "the opportunity to specialize," restricted "the opportunity to dominate," and thus enabled America to "erect a great decentralized democracy of specialists."

In an analysis of the nature and composition of this matrix, Edward Shils focuses on the major structural development of the period: the ascendancy of the universities over an expanding body of dependent or supplementary institutions for the advancement of learning and the emergence, in turn, of a "constellation" of universities at the center of the national academic order. By comparing the purpose and structure of various classes of learned institutions, Shils illustrates the particular strengths of the university: its capacity to combine specialization and breadth and its concern with practical study as well as pure science and scholarship. Above all, the university's dual commitment to teaching and research represented an "unsurpassed arrangement" for the discovery and diffusion of knowledge and ensured the perpetuation of the university and, indeed, all intellectual institutions.

These introductory statements show that the growth of knowledge, like the development of American society, was marked by a number of sometimes contradictory and sometimes complementary dualisms: teaching and research, abstract learning and the practical arts, liberal culture and specialized research, amateurism and professionalism, the push for centralized intellectual leadership and the pull of decentralized authority. The most striking of these "biformities," to use Michael Kammen's term,[15] was clearly the fragmentation of knowledge into specialized units, coupled with the standardization of the institutional forms established to advance and transmit knowledge. In his essay, Lawrence Veysey characterizes the coexistence of specialization and standardization as "the basic paradox embodied in Herbert Spencer's famous formula of an evolution from 'indefinite incoherent homogeneity' toward a new state of 'definite coherent heterogeneity'; the latter phrase might well describe the tendency of organizational life in America as it blossomed in the decades prior to 1920.'' This paradox underlies the two-fold division of the case studies in this volume.

The first group of case studies focuses on the development of disciplines and applied fields and illustrates various ways to approach and interpret the transformation of American science and scholarship. The humanities—the oldest subjects in the curriculum, yet the last to develop a sense of identity as a concrete grouping of academic disciplines—are examined in a wide-ranging essay by Laurence Veysey. His analysis extends beyond the university to encompass the "multiple organized worlds" of the humanities: museums, libraries, professional associations, the Chatauqua, women's clubs, art galleries, and local literary, history, and music societies. As Veysey states, the very existence of these organizations confounds any "neat polarity between the amateur and the professional." Dorothy Ross charts the emergence of the social sciences as separate, academic, professionalized, and increasingly "scientistic" disciplines by distinguishing three distinct groups of intellectuals concerned with the development of these fields: the advocates of political, social, economic, and educational reform in the 1870s; the academic pioneers who in the same decade introduced the social sciences into the college curriculum as independent subjects; and the German-trained generation of the 1880s who ultimately took the lead in defining the new professions. Drawing on extensive statistical data, Daniel Kevles presents a comparative study of the physics, mathematics, and chemistry communities. He takes into account the level of training required in each field; the employment opportunities in government, industry, and academia; the relative quality and rate of research productivity; and the impact of developments such as the organization of professional societies and the mobilization of scientists during World War I.

In conception and content, Garland Allen's essay on the reorientation of the biological sciences in this period represents a deliberate departure from the broader analyses that precede and follow it. In a volume of this kind it is important, indeed essential, that the pursuit of knowledge as a personal activity not be lost. Allen illuminates this perspective by examining the career of one of America's earliest Nobel laureates, Thomas Hunt Morgan, and his role in the formation of the new field of genetics, the first scientific discipline in which the American contribution equaled that of Europe. Allen's description of Morgan's work places the generalized concepts of specialization and professionalism in a highly specific personal context: that of the individual scientist engrossed in solving an intellectual problem. The essay demonstrates the interaction between the evolution of scientific ideas and the social, economic, and institutional factors that transformed biology from a largely descriptive to an increasingly experimental science.

The essays on the applied fields show that specialization was as compelling a force in the growth of the useful arts as it was in the development of academic disciplines. Margaret Rossiter's study of American agriculture deals with an applied science experiencing "rapid and governmentally force-fed specialization." In agriculture as in no other area of science and learning, the political power of interest groups (organized by farmers and scientist-administrators alike) was coupled with a generalized belief in the efficacy of science to improve productivity. This interaction produced substantial federal appropriations for research on a guaranteed annual basis, as well as a vast infrastructure comprised of colleges in every state, experiment stations across the country, and a federal agency with a large staff of specialists in Washington, D.C.

To a far more limited degree, the government also used science to promote other aspects of the economy through the work of such agencies as the Bureau of Standards. However, as John Rae points out, the major stimulus to specialization in engineering and industry-related science was the expansion of the American economy and the accompanying growth in the complexity of its technical needs. Before 1920, organized research was just beginning to take hold in the newer, science-based industries; nonetheless, the link between scientific advance and economic gain was apparent in the vast accumulation of technological innovations produced by a range of entrepreneurial talent: ingenious inventors, university professors, government investigators, and the scientists and engineers employed in growing numbers to meet the technical and managerial challenges faced by American industry.

If the knowledge produced in the specialized fields of applied science was impressive, its immediate impact on the American economy was not. As Louis Galambos observes in the concluding essay of this section, American economic growth in the nineteenth century was stimulated largely by new inputs of capital, land, and people and by developments in machine technology that were easily adopted by farms and firms. In the early decades of the twentieth century, however, productivity became increasingly dependent on modern science and advanced technology. Paradoxically, the reorganization of the sources of knowledge in the period 1860 to 1920 produced an abundance of ideas with significant potential for agriculture and industry, yet the application of those ideas to the economy was delayed by farmers who resisted innovations until unusual market conditions prompted them to act and by businessmen preoccupied with the problems of consolidating and then solidifying their new corporate empires. Not until the 1920s did the American economy successfully exploit the reorganized sources of knowledge.

By 1920, the organizational structure that would govern the production of knowledge in America was in place. The second group of case studies focuses on the principal components of that framework: the university, the private research organization, the library, the national and regional learned society. In his overview of new private and state universities and transformed traditional colleges, Hugh Hawkins assesses the conflicts and opportunities inherent in the university's dual commitment to diffuse knowledge through teaching and to increase knowledge through research. Since the leading universities that emerged in this period never proposed "scholarship in isolation from instruction," Hawkins maintains that "the ability to shift the balance between these functions was part of the flexibility that helped win support for universities in a nation that often seemed too democratic and too utilitarian to nurture the life of the mind."

The tension between teaching and research is also underlined in Nathan Reingold's study of the Carnegie Institution of Washington. Established to advance basic research at a time when the federal concern with science was limited and intermittent, the Carnegie Institution necessarily dealt with such policy issues as the support of individuals, the allocation of funds among intellectual fields, and the relationship between a private research organization and institutions of higher education. Its decisions were highly influential, constituting what Reingold terms a "de facto national science policy."

In contrast to the Carnegie Institution, the National Academy of Sciences had, in A. Hunter Dupree's view, an anomalous role in the late nineteenth and early twentieth centuries. Dupree maintains that as the flow of specialized knowledge became channeled through individual disciplines and as research was concentrated in universities and government agencies, the National Academy was left with no clear purpose. Its sole function in this period was "to exist" and, by its structure and membership, to serve as a symbolic definition of the boundaries of the scientific community.

The ability of American learned institutions to adapt to changing circumstances is illustrated in John Cole's analysis of American libraries and Sally Kohlstedt's study of the Boston Society of Natural History. Cole examines how "the growth of a new American faith in the power of knowledge and its specialized uses" brought a marked change in the functions of public and private libraries, exemplified by the transformation of the Library of Congress from a "storehouse" in 1880 to a "workshop" in 1912. Kohlstedt discusses the struggle of the Boston Society of Natural History to redefine its goals and sustain itself over a century of social and professional change. "In the process," she observes, "the Society lost much of its relevance for the productive, scientific community, but it pioneered in the development of a science museum and other activities designed to educate the public."

As these essays show, the organization of learning in America has so many different dimensions that our effort can represent only a first approximation of the topics scholars might pursue. Even a volume of this size has not touched on a number of significant areas of knowledge needing study: medicine and public health, statistics and social work, to name only a few. The concluding essays by Fritz Ringer, Neil Harris, and Charles Rosenberg suggest directions for further research.

One pervasive theme of this volume is the influence of German scholarship and the German university on American intellectual life. In reality, however, the German academic environment differed significantly from American perceptions, and translations, of it. Ringer's analysis of how German scientists and scholars dealt with the rapid advance of specialization, the pressures of an increasingly technological society, and the tension between teaching and research helps the reader identify parallels and differences in the response of German and American academic communities to comparable social and intellectual challenges. Ringer suggests that "one can say very little about the modern university in general; one can talk intelligibly only about the German university or the American university, recognizing that each has been thoroughly rooted in its own social and cultural system."

If the contrast between the German model and the American concept of the American university merits consideration, so too does the relationship between the structure of the learned community and popular expressions of knowledge. In an essay meant to serve as commentary and counterpoint to this volume's principal concern with science and scholarship, Neil Harris surveys the extent to which popular institutions influenced, reflected, or diverged from the organized world of "high culture." He points out that occupational and special interest groups from retail merchants to stamp collectors formed societies, established journals, and produced encyclopedias and treatises that paralleled those of the disciplines and the professions. Even folk-healing sects and spiritualists sought the legitimacy conferred by association with, and sometimes mimicry of, the institutions of the learned world. Moreover, the public concern with knowledge covered a wide spectrum of expression, from the enthusiasm that greeted the world's fairs in Philadelphia, Chicago, and St. Louis to the outrage leveled at concepts of modern science that threatened long-held religious beliefs.

Harris's discussion of the popular reaction to knowledge and its institutions, along with the cross-national comparison suggested by Ringer, illuminate promising yet little explored dimensions of the growth of knowledge in America. In the final essay of the volume, Charles Rosenberg considers the still-tentative quality of our understanding of the relationship between knowledge and its social setting. Rosenberg asserts that if historians are to explain and describe the patterns of social and institutional change, they must look beyond such superficial and overschematized concepts as modernization and professionalization to examine the "fine structure" of specific developments. In every area of knowledge, attention must be given to the interaction of social needs and values, the norms and ideas of a given discipline or profession, and the varying institutional contexts in which that intellectual activity is pursued. As Rosenberg explains and as these essays indicate, only by analyzing the many elements involved in this complex process can an understanding of the "ecology" of knowledge be achieved.

By 1920, knowledge in America was being transmitted and advanced within an institutional network as vast and heterogeneous as American society itself. No Royal Commission seeking to bring Britain into the mainstream of modern science and scholarship, no French or German minister of education charged with the direction of higher education and research, not even a group of American scientists or scholars with sufficient authority and wealth would have deliberately set out to create such a decentralized, pluralistic structure. Yet implicit in this structure were the sources of strength and vitality that would distinguish the American organization of learning: the opportunity to borrow selectively from European institutions of higher education and research; the flexibility to change organizational forms, invent new structures, and incorporate emerging fields; the refusal to erect barriers between pure and applied research, between the discovery and the application of knowledge; the openness to recruit and reward excellence without regard for the traditional social hierarchies that constrained European intellectual life; the need to rely on a multiplicity of patrons and constituencies and thereby to cultivate broad public support; and the inevitable impulse among regions, institutions, and individuals to compete for recognition.

If the American order of learning was diverse in size, purpose, and fields of study, its institutional forms displayed a uniformity that was all the more remarkable in the absence of centralized direction. Universities, whether private or public, came to resemble one another in their methods of training, departmental organization, and administrative systems. Graduate schools established common requirements for advanced degrees, and professional associations adopted common objectives and modes of operation. Libraries, foundations, research laboratories, and institutes followed standard organizational patterns.

This uniformity of structural arrangements was rooted in elusive elements that remain open to further analysis and interpretation. Many European observers have been struck by the sameness of the "external aspects" of life in the United States. One of the most perceptive of these commentators, Lord Bryce, asserted that the uniformity of America's cities, factories, and farms, as well as "its institutions and social habits," could be ascribed "above all, to the newness of the country."[16] Americans were neither constrained by long-standing cultural traditions nor encumbered by long-established institutions. Through adaptation and innovation, they established the basic pattern of their learned organizations in less than a human life span. In a highly mobile and competitive society, innovations that proved successful in one field or institution were swiftly duplicated and implemented elsewhere.

American institutions of learning, like industrial corporations, also have been seen as part of a trend toward nationally oriented, impersonal, hierarchical organizations. Emerging in the latter part of the nineteenth century, these bodies manifested the distinctive features of specialization: the acceptance of objective criteria for judging individual ability, a division of labor among experts, and a coordination of effort achieved through rational methods of control and communication. At the same time, they mirrored the democratic insistence on equal access, at some level, to all areas of knowledge—from the most esoteric to the most technical. As John Higham shows in his essay, the American order of learning reconciled egalitarian values with the elitist nature of specialization by adopting standardized institutional devices: the formal requirements of the Ph.D. degree, the academic department as a "society of equals," reference tools to promote communication among fields, even the concept of the multipurpose organization. The result was a standardization of form amid a diversity of interests.

But if structure was the most visible uniformity in the American pursuit of learning, there was also a unity of spirit. Americans retained a deep-rooted faith in knowledge and education as a means of advancing the welfare of the country. They believed that the empirical science and critical scholarship of the nineteenth century were creating an objective, rational conception of nature and human history. They were confident that the new nation would make its mark in the world of learning. "Fundamental, systematically acquired knowledge," writes Edward Shils, "held out the prospect of the transfiguration of life by improving man's control over the resources of nature and the powers that weaken the body; it offered the prospect of a better understanding of society that would lead, it was felt, to the improvement of society. It was thought that the progress of mankind entailed the improvement of understanding simply as a state of being and not solely as an instrument of action. The honor and the glory of a country that promoted the acquisition of such knowledge was assured; its power and influence would grow proportionately and deservedly."

## Notes

1. Roy MacLeod, "Science and the Social Relations of Scholarship, 1870–1918: An Anglo-American Perspective" (Paper prepared for the 1975 Newagen Conference sponsored by the American Academy of Arts and Sciences).

2. Charles E. Rosenberg, *No Other Gods: On Science and American Social Thought* (Baltimore: Johns Hopkins University Press, 1976), p. 17.

3. Richard J. Storr, *The Beginnings of Graduate Education in America* (Chicago: University of Chicago Press, 1953), p. 129.

4. Quoted in Oscar Handlin and Mary F. Handlin, *The American College and American Culture: Socialization as a Function of Higher Education* (New York: McGraw-Hill, 1970), p. 6.

5. Charles W. Eliot, "The New Education: Its Organization," *Atlantic Monthly* 23 (February 1869): 215.

6. Frederick Rudolph, *The American College and University* (New York: Alfred A. Knopf, 1962), p. 305.

7. Charles W. Eliot, *University Administration* (Boston: Houghton Mifflin Co., 1908), p. 150.

8. For an analysis of the various concepts of "real life" used by academic reformers in the period 1865–1910, see Laurence R. Veysey, *The Emergence of the American University* (Chicago: University of Chicago Press, 1965), pp. 61–68, 69–120 passim.

9. Merle Curti, Judith Green, and Roderick Nash, "Anatomy of Giving: Millionaires in the Late Nineteenth Century," *American Quarterly* 15 (Fall 1963): 418.

10. John Morton Blum, *The Promise of America: An Historical Inquiry* (Boston: Houghton Mifflin Co., 1965), p. 72.

11. U.S. Department of Health, Education, and Welfare, *Biennial Survey of Education in the United States, 1956–1958*, chapter 1, A Statistical Survey of Education (Washington, D.C.: U.S. Government Printing Office, 1963), p. 27.

12. Americans were drawn to Germany in the first instance because it was the intellectual center of the world; moreover, its universities, unlike Oxford and Cambridge, imposed few admission requirements. Until the 1870s, German universities were virtually the only institutions in the world to provide advanced training in specialized scientific and scholarly research. In the same period, as Lord Bryce observed, English universities were "so much occupied in preparing men to pass undergraduate examinations as to give . . . but little advanced training." (See James Bryce, *The American Commonwealth* [New York: Macmillan Co., 1910], pp. 729–30.) Scientific research and teaching were not undertaken in British universities until the 1850s, and all religious tests were not removed at

Oxford and Cambridge until 1871. Advanced training in France was even less attractive to Americans. The French system of higher education consisted of independent professional and technical schools directed toward preparing students for state examinations. There was no attempt to link research and teaching until the establishment of the *Ecole practique des hautes études* in 1868. For differing perspectives on the American attitude toward European and particularly German higher education in the nineteenth century, see Burton Bledstein, *The Culture of Professionalism* (New York: W. W. Norton, 1976), pp. 310–31; John S. Brubacher and Willis Rudy, *Higher Education in Transition* (New York: Harper and Row, 1968), pp. 175–79; Richard Hofstadter and Walter T. Metzger, *The Development of Academic Freedom in the United States* (New York: Columbia University Press, 1955), pp. 367–83, 391–407; Charles Franklin Thwing, *The American and the German University, One Hundred Years of History* (New York: Macmillan Co., 1928); and Laurence Veysey, *The Emergence of the American University*, pp. 125–133. For an analysis of the incorporation of research in European higher education, see Joseph Ben-David, *Centers of Learning: Britain, France, Germany, United States* (New York: McGraw-Hill, 1977), pp. 15–24, 93–113; MacLeod, "Science and the Social Relations of Scholarship, 1870–1918" and Henry Paul, "The Growth of the Learned Community in France" (Papers prepared for the 1975 Newagen Conference sponsored by the American Academy of Arts and Sciences); and the article by Fritz Ringer in this volume.

13. Walter C. John, *Graduate Studies in Universities and Colleges in the United States*, U.S. Department of Education, Bulletin no. 26 (Washington, D.C.: U.S. Government Printing Office, 1935), pp. 12–13.

14. In this respect, the American graduate schools were similar to the German philosophy faculties. Although the majority of German Ph.Ds were destined to become teachers in the Gymnasien and other higher schools (see the essay by Fritz Ringer in this volume), they were not trained as teachers or professional educators but as scientists and scholars. As Friedrich Paulsen stated, "preparation to become a teacher is simply synonymous with the equipment of a scholar. The philologists and historians, mathematicians and natural scientists conduct their department lectures and exercises as if to continue scientific investigations was the future destiny of all of their students." (See Paulsen, *The German Universities and University Study*, trans. Frank Thilly and William W. Elwang [New York: Charles Scribner's Sons, 1906], p. 416.) Given this concept of instruction, not only those students who became university professors but those who eventually taught in the Gymnasien—and in American colleges—came to regard themselves as members of the scientific and scholarly community. For a discussion of the German concept of university instruction, see Paulsen, *The German University*, pp. 189–226, 416–419.

15. See Michael Kammen, *People of Paradox: An Inquiry Concerning the Origins of American Civilization* (New York: Alfred A. Knopf, 1972), especially chapter 4.

16. Bryce, *The American Commonwealth*, p. 887.

# Acknowledgments

In a real sense, this study is a product of the complex network it describes. Its contributors are men and women from universities, libraries, government agencies, and learned societies. The work was supported by public and private foundations, organized by an academy at the time of its bicentennial, and published by this country's oldest university press in continuous operation. The American Academy is proud to have been associated with these individuals and institutions in this collaborative undertaking.

For our part, we would like to express special thanks to the members of the American Academy advisory committee who guided the study from its inception: Sanborn Brown, A. Hunter Dupree, Neil Harris, John Higham, Nathan Reingold, Charles Rosenberg, Barbara Rosenkrantz, and particularly I. Bernard Cohen. Harvey Brooks, former president of the Academy, encouraged and aided the effort to develop a series of studies on the history of learned institutions in America. Peter Buck was an unfailing source of ideas throughout the project and a helpful, if insistent, critic.

The final form of the volume, and indeed the substance of the essays, owes much to discussions at a summer workshop held at Cape Newagen, Maine, in 1975. Among those who contributed papers, memoranda, commentaries, and criticism on that occasion were Saul Benison, Seymour Cohen, Donna Haraway, James Hobbins, Morton Keller, Roy MacLeod, Ronald Overmann, Henry Paul, Carroll Pursell, and Douglas Sloan.

Members of the Academy staff offered invaluable assistance. Alice Agoos performed a variety of editorial tasks. Bernice Khouri cheerfully agreed to spend endless hours at the Xerox machine. Florence Perry typed many more versions of the essays than she probably cares to remember. Jane Lucey was helpful in innumerable ways, not least in assuming some of our administrative duties at the Academy while the editing was in progress.

The financial resources that made the study possible were provided at various stages by the Mellon Foundation, the National Endowment for the Humanities, and the National Science Foundation. For their generosity and understanding of the value of this effort, we are immensely grateful.

*Overview*

# The Matrix
# of Specialization

## JOHN HIGHAM

The essays in this volume deal with the period in which the modern organization of knowledge came into being. It is true that some foundations for wide collaboration in sustained, self-correcting research were laid before the Civil War—the Smithsonian Institution, for example, under Joseph Henry's inspired direction, and the American Association for the Advancement of Science which provided after 1848 a general clearing house for scientific reports. Also, in the first half of the nineteenth century a few professors had won the right to be judged primarily on their original investigations.[1] Yet these were mere beginnings. In 1860 there was no American university fully worthy of the name. The United States had no libraries of national or international renown, no industrial laboratories or great private foundations, no widely based learned societies devoted exclusively to the advancement of knowledge within a single limited field. In the late nineteenth and early twentieth centuries all these agencies took shape. Interlocking with one another, they constituted a matrix for research that has survived to this day.

Efforts to account for this enormous and complex reordering of intellectual life have characteristically viewed it from outside, as a change in conditions of employment. Amateur scholars and gentlemen-scientists gave way to professionals. A "professional outlook" thereupon reshaped the production and conservation of knowledge.[2] Accordingly we now have a growing literature, with its own internal controversies, on the history and sociology of the academic and scholarly professions. Historians, while differing in their definitions of "professionalization," have largely agreed in assigning it preeminent importance.

Undeniably central though it is, the theme of professionalization does not go to the heart of this great transition. As Laurence Veysey reminds us in his essay, the professions already comprised an influential sector of American society before scholarly disciplines became professionalized. The reorganization of the professions in such a way as to vest new authority in emerging academic groups must have been an effect of antecedent changes as well as a cause. It is necessary therefore to ask: what distinctive characteristic of nineteenth-century knowledge impelled its creators and custodians to turn their particular competences into professions? The obvious answer is specialization. The multiplication and differentiation of bodies of esoteric knowledge made the new professions possible. Indeed, the rampant growth of specialization pervades, as no other theme does, the history of knowledge in the period under examination. It is so ubiquitous that historians have taken it for granted, as if it were one of the constants of nature, like the speed of light, rather than one of the riddles of history.

The essays in this volume may be read, therefore, not only as separate chapters in the variegated history of science and scholarship but also as contributions to a still unwritten general history of specialization. What such a history might embrace—what illumination it might give to the most fundamental problems of modern society—we can only begin to guess. But the materials before us do yield some clues to one aspect of the topic—they tell us something about the shape intellectual specialization has assumed in the United States. Most particularly, the essays gathered herein compel attention to an extraordinary reversal in American attitudes toward specialization.

Before looking at attitudes and institutions, something should be said about specialization as a process that would bring about a greater division of intellectual labor, a process that went on continuously throughout the nineteenth century. Before the Civil War, a professor of natural philosophy in the smaller colleges might have taught all the sciences, but in the larger ones the responsibility was more and more divided. Thus Yale created a professorship of mathematics in 1836, separated chemistry from natural history in 1853, and eleven years later divided natural history between a professor of botany and a professor of geology. Some "men of science" hailed the trend. Others regretted it.[3] Until after mid-century, however, these reactions seem to have done little to shape or direct the process. In the second half of the century specialization acquired a programmatic thrust. The institutional matrix, which had earlier accommodated increasing specialization, was now transformed by it. This happened as effective resistance to specialization markedly declined.

In the early nineteenth century, specialization went against the grain of American culture. To parcel out segments of work or knowledge, so that the responsibility of each person contracts while his dependence on others increases, violated the American ideal of the untrammeled individual and its corollary, the jack-of-all-trades. Moreover the intellectual specialist affronted egalitarian values: he dealt in secrets only a few could share. In Jacksonian America, disdain for esoteric knowledge and hostility toward any narrow delimitation of competence flourished. Both the learned professions and the colleges were distrusted as bastions of privilege. Under the pressure of populistic criticism both lowered their standards. Commencement speakers assured their audiences, as Gulian C. Verplanck did at Union College in 1836, that science was no longer "a thing mysterious and solitary . . . but . . . familiar and popular to a degree which the recluse scholar of former days could never imagine."[4] The true American scholar, as described by Ralph Waldo Emerson a year later, was not the learned specialist cut off from life but the active, unbounded individual.[5] These sentiments struck contemporary European observers forcefully because they were so very American. More than one foreign traveller marvelled that "every man you meet [in America] thinks himself capable of giving an opinion upon questions of the most difficult kind."[6]

Yet the last third of the nineteenth century saw the virtual overthrow of effective resistance to specialization. 1869 may serve as a turning point. Harvard that year inaugurated an elective system. Simultaneously the American Medical Association officially resolved "that this Association recognizes specialties as proper and legitimate fields of practice."[7] The elective system, by shattering the classical curriculum, opened every aspect of higher education to the incursion of specialists. Within the medical profession the official recognition of specialized practices soon led to the subordination of the general practitioner in income and prestige, as many of them had feared. Rural spokesmen in backward areas of the country continued to complain about the high costs of specialized services and the self-importance of those who provided them. But libraries swelled to bursting, the Ph.D. Octopus (as William James called it) reached out to every reputable college, and the number of occupations listed in the United States Census multiplied time and time again. "In all of our large cities and densely populated districts," a writer marvelled in 1880, "specialism revels in tropical luxuriance."[8]

A large part of this transformation was unavoidable. It flowed in good measure from modernizing tendencies that penetrated all advanced societies. Yet the American case was exceptional in the extent to which established norms were seemingly reversed. Of the leading countries in the western world, the United States in 1830 was perhaps the least specialized and surely the most committed to the omnicompetence of the ordinary citizen. By 1920, however, America had embraced the specialist and sanctified the expert with an enthusiasm unmatched elsewhere. For European critics and imitators alike, the American assembly line with its minute subdivision of labor and the American university with its cafeteria style of education were becoming emblems of the future. Literature reinforced the lessons of experience when Sinclair Lewis produced in Martin Arrowsmith the most compelling literary hero of the 1920s: a scientist whose narrow, ruthlessly focused intelligence was as distinctively American as Emerson's Scholar had once seemed.[9]

While American opinion shifted from one extreme to another—often repudiating specialization in the early nineteenth century and embracing it uncritically in the late nineteenth century—European intellectuals displayed a persistent ambivalence. The Scottish philosophers of the eighteenth century grasped the contradiction specialization posed. They acclaimed it as the prime cause of the rise of civilization, while, at the same time, they feared it as a profound threat to civic virtue and social solidarity.[10] Without using the term specialization, Adam Ferguson was perhaps the first to comment on its incursion into intellectual life. Ferguson's *Essay on the History of Civil Society* (1767) observed that "a continued subdivision," already so productive in the mechanical arts, could extend to every art and profession, "and thinking itself in this age of separations may become a peculiar craft."[11]

Adam Smith a few years later welcomed "this subdivision of employment in philosophy." As in every other business, Smith said, each individual "becomes more expert in his own peculiar branch, more work is done upon the whole, and the quantity of science is considerably increased by it." But no one has written a more searing commentary than Smith's on the brutalizing effects industrial specialization was having on the masses. Although stimulating the minds of the few to an extraordinary degree, specialization according to *The Wealth of Nations* was reducing the great body of the people to mental torpor and moral flaccidity.[12]

The warnings of the Scottish philosophers swelled into a more immediate and pervasive concern in the "synthetic philosophy" of Auguste Comte. It was he who apparently minted the word *spécialisation;* from him it passed into English. Comte accepted a division of labor among scholars and scientists as essential to intellectual progress. For him the crux of the problem was not (as for Smith) increasing inequality but rather the "dispersive" tendency of empirical research, and the consequent fracturing of intellectual authority.[13] Comte's entire system may be understood as a strategy for harnessing the energies of specialization while overcoming its disintegrative effects.

In England, Comte's line of thought was taken up by John Stuart Mill and Thomas Huxley—champions of science who were nevertheless distressed over the narrowness of mind that seemed likely to result from the runaway growth of research.[14] In the United States, however, the criticism of specialization during the late nineteenth and early twentieth centuries came from other quarters. It came from outside the scientific culture. Among American intellectuals it was a lament, a protest, and a rear-guard action, usually associated with the Genteel Tradition and mounted by those who sought to preserve as the central purpose of higher education the making of gentlemen. These proponents of "liberal education" complained unceasingly of a "dissevering of sympathy and dehumanizing of scholarship, the lowering of tone which comes from losing one's view of knowledge in its unified grandeur."[15]

In shaping American colleges the power of the gentlemanly ideal was substantial and lasting, but it worked largely to protect a certain jurisdiction. Instead of bringing a larger dimension into specialized thought, the champions of liberal education for the most part concentrated on holding their own within the setting in which they felt at home: the undergraduate college. In doing so, they conceded to specialists the control of graduate and professional studies. Although we customarily regard American universities of the late nineteenth century as forums of conflict between opposing educational ideals, it may be more accurate to observe how a doctrine of two spheres inhibited an effective challenge of one to the other. In 1898, William T. Harris, a leading theoretician of "liberal education," placed his blessing on this historic compromise: "Higher education seeks as its first goal the unity of human learning. Then in its second stage it specializes. . . . The first part of higher education, that for the B.A. degree . . . shows how all branches form a connected whole and what each contributes to the explanation of the others. . . . After . . . comes the selection of a specialty. . . . We accordingly rejoice in the fact of the increasing popularity of the university in both of its functions—that of culture and that of specialization.''[16]

If the beleaguered defenders of gentility were somewhat compromised, outside their ranks the trend toward intellectual specialization in the late nineteenth and early twentieth centuries provoked little serious discussion of any kind. No American who identified with the scientific culture seems to have published a book on the subject. The few articles that I have discovered were content with declaring that specialization is an inviolable law of nature, or at least an inescapable condition of modern life, and man should take full advantage of it. In 1882 a young graduate student at Johns Hopkins, in a letter to a friend, caught the euphoric note of the time: '' . . . vive la specialization! Go to, let us centrifugate.''[17]

For many Americans Herbert Spencer provided all the explanation that was desired. Among the nineteenth-century system builders, Spencer stands out for his comforting faith in specialization as the universal law of progress. All structures, according to Spencer, are organic. All organisms evolve by a more and more complex differentiation of their parts. Specialization, therefore, is a beneficent necessity making for ever greater articulation and interdependence.[18] There is nothing to worry about. The unique enthusiasm for Spencer's philosophy in late-nineteenth-century America fits neatly with the American proclivity for specialization.

When the spell of Spencerian determinism was broken at the end of the nineteenth century, one might have thought that a significant reappraisal of specialization would arise. No one was better prepared for the task than John Dewey. His whole cast of mind worked against the separation of one realm of experience from another, against the compartmentalization and fragmentation of culture. Throughout a long life, Dewey circled warily around the question of specialization; yet he touched it only in glancing ways. Intellectual specialization, he believed, could and should be compatible with breadth. ''Over-specialization,'' on the other hand, is ''unnatural.'' Dewey never made the difference between the two altogether clear. But he always associated over-specialization with institutional barriers that separate thought from practical activity.[19] Faced with the problem of intellectual differentiation, Dewey spoke of social divisions. He relied so heavily on scientific inquiry as the means of integrating experience that when it failed, the blame had to lie somewhere outside the scientific enterprise—among those who resist inquiry rather than those who practice it.

Spencer and Dewey—one of them at the beginning and the other at the end of the era we are examining—illustrate the intellectual strategies that shielded America's proliferating specialists from probing self-appraisal and criticism. Both of these leaders of opinion offered assurance that scientific inquiry, in demonstrating the interrelatedness of all things, was rendering obsolete the profound theoretical questions that had engaged men in the past. Otherwise very different from one another, Spencer and Dewey alike encouraged a cheerful outreach of research in every direction, with a minimum of theoretical guidance.

The degree to which that actually happened is hard to judge. For many decades foreign critics contended that American scholars and scientists were bypassing broad conceptual issues and plunging instead into concrete applications or trivial particulars. One version of the indictment, a version Americans often echoed, charged that pure science was neglected in this country because of an excessive concentration on practical applications.[20] Another version alleged that American scholars sacrificed theoretical breadth and coherence because of their addiction to a narrow factuality. In a lecture delivered in 1929, the outstanding Anglo-American sociologist Robert MacIver described the antitheoretical bent of his American colleagues with detachment and elegance:

It might be maintained that one thing which American and German sociologists have in common is a preoccupation with method. But method means an entirely different thing to American and to German investigators. To the American, method means preeminently research technique, a device for collecting, recording, sorting, classifying, tabulating or counting facts. To the German, method is a principle in terms of which he arranges facts in categories, determines the relation of the categories to one another, analyses a social situation or a large-scale social movement into its essential factors, and offers a synthetic interpretation to the world. In a word, the American is eager for new facts and new verifications, whereas the German seeks new formulations and new thought-constructions. It is not that the German is careless of facts; it is certainly not that he is less thorough. It is that his main objective is different. His voyage of exploration seeks the far horizon of new principles whereas the American does coasting voyages from facts to facts. Consequently, the German is often more preoccupied with the interpretation of old facts than with the discovery of new ones, while the American is often so keen for new facts that he is apt to neglect the established ones.[21]

There seems little doubt that MacIver's characterization applied in a rough way to some fields, notably history, political science, and sociology. Where it did apply, the conclusion might plausibly follow that "coasting voyages" scattered the explorers and therefore promoted specialization. Yet caution must be exercised in attributing a high degree of specialization in the late nineteenth century to habits of mind (such as an antitheoretical bias) that have persisted in one form or another throughout American history.

An indifference or hostility to the role of theory and hypothesis in the formulation of knowledge was actually most blatant and presumptuous during the early nineteenth century. Far from encouraging specialized inquiry, this naive empiricism validated egalitarian resistance to specialists. In Jacksonian America reliable knowledge was widely believed to be immediately available through the direct observation of surface appearances. This was the meaning of the "Baconian method" celebrated in the magazines of the period; it was the upshot of the common-sense philosophy propagated in all the colleges. Both taught that science is nothing more than a classification of the evidence of the senses. Anyone, therefore, could participate in the scientific enterprise.[22] Science, as Verplanck said, had become "familiar and popular."

The leading American scientists were never altogether comfortable with the belief that Everyman can trust his senses, that science is everybody's business. Looking enviously to Europe, scientific leaders complained more and more loudly, as the century progressed, of the mediocrity of American science and the dispersion of scientific resources. The rapid advance of specialization never figured in their complaints; that was not part of the problem, it was part of the solution.[23]

The matrix of specialization was built by people who were deeply dissatisfied with the status of science and scholarship in America and who set out deliberately to remodel their own situation along European lines. Their object was partly to elevate men of science and men of letters to the dignity of a European elite. At the same time they sought to purify science and scholarship (as well as art and literature) by making those enterprises more rigorous and sophisticated and thus removing them from common understanding and participation. Intellectual specialization inevitably challenged egalitarian values by conferring new authority on technical elites. Accordingly it assisted the strong post–Civil War reaction among the cultivated classes against the alleged excesses of the democratic revolution. Outraged by the corruption and materialism that democracy had spawned, and rallying around the watch words "civilization" and "culture," the "better sort" of Americans—upholders of education and respectability—mounted a counteroffensive in the late nineteenth century to recoup some of the authority they had lost in preceding decades. Over and over again, one finds a common idealistic and elitist motive among the leading scholars and scientists of the late nineteenth century: a zeal to make "a higher order of things" prevail over "the base votaries of Mammon," a determination (as another young aspirant said) to tread "the path of science, though alone and exposed to the sneers of the vulgar and ignorant."[24] Men and women of this persuasion were implicitly redefining science. Explicitly they were detaching themselves from the loosely structured, nontheoretical, community-based culture of Jacksonian America. Specialization, entrenched in newly created professional guilds, provided a means to those ends.

Yet the outcome was not European. It was different in ways that have become intelligible only in retrospect. However much American scholars and scientists aspired to transplant the structure of authority they observed abroad, egalitarian traditions could not be swept aside. Nor could the empirical and pragmatic temper that infused those traditions be altogether reversed. A new set of relations between intellectual elites and the social order would have to be worked out.

A crucial incompatibility between the European pattern and the American milieu is revealed in the ill-starred attempts of American intellectuals to group themselves into national academies like the Royal Society of London or the French Academy of Sciences. These were quasi-official bodies, their membership sharply limited to a fixed number of supreme experts drawn from various fields of learning and supposedly capable of setting standards for all the lesser authorities. Thus the national academy in European countries constituted a pinnacle of eminence, through which intellectual leadership was recognized, reinforced, and consolidated. In this volume, A. Hunter Dupree reviews the ineffectual career of the first American venture along these lines, the National Academy of Sciences.[25] Laurence Veysey sketches other efforts to create centralized academies in the humanities in the 1880s and 1890s. Margaret Rossiter shows how the Society for the Promotion of Agricultural Science functioned as an academy during the same period. In medicine, the Congress of Physicians and Surgeons, founded in 1888, tried to play a similar role.[26] Without exception, these enterprises failed to flourish, if they survived at all.

When Lord Bryce, who was then the British Ambassador to the United States, suggested in 1907 a new attempt to set up an honorific body that would preside over the destinies of the humanities, J. Franklin Jameson wisely discouraged him. "I told him," Jameson later recalled, "that I did not believe such a plan was consistent with American ways, and that what such an Academy might accomplish was being achieved well enough by our various humanistic societies, with their broad membership, and the representative and elect quality of their guiding officers."[27]

Broad membership . . . representative and elect! Jameson saw that organized specialization in the United States needed to conform to the national style. The European centralist approach disqualified itself by emphasizing the vertical dimension of specialization. It made the hierarchical structure of intellectual authority overt by setting an apex on the pyramid. As the experience of the late nineteenth century demonstrated, the best strategy for American specialists was to play down vertical relationships, expand horizontally, and thereby erect a great decentralized democracy of specialists. The conflict between a Jacksonian distrust of privileged elites and the advance of specialization was resolved by widening immensely the opportunity to specialize and restricting the opportunity to dominate. The way to overcome resistance to specialization, Americans discovered, was to create a superabundance of it. That may explain why, in the second half of the century, a sharp reversal of attitudes occurred.

To resolve the apparent contradiction of a democracy of specialists called for major innovations. Learned societies with "broad membership" and "representative" officers were necessary but not sufficient. The institutional matrix would have to be flexible and polycentric, yet capable somehow of coordinating an infinite variety of research activities. The pattern that developed between 1870 and 1910, in an apparently ad hoc way, was one of the remarkable achievements of American civilization. It had these features:

1. *A standard entrance requirement.* In transplanting the German Ph.D. to the United States, Americans altered it to suit their own needs. The doctor's degree in Germany meant two things: that a student had received a broad education and imbibed a love of pure "science", and that he had at some point probed the

frontiers of knowledge—an attainment characteristically (but not quite universally) demonstrated in the form of a dissertation. Americans downplayed the first aspect of the Ph.D. and accentuated the second. The Ph.D. became in effect a certification that the candidate was an academic specialist and thereby sanctified specialization as the supreme object of American higher education.

American educational historians have never quite realized that the Ph.D. in a German university was not the highest on an ascending scale of academic degrees, as it proudly became in America. It was the basic and almost the only degree the philosophical faculty (i.e., arts and sciences) awarded. There was no B.A., no graduate school, and no clear differentiation between the few students who hoped for a career in science or scholarship and the many students who were simply preparing themselves for secondary school teaching or for some other profession. The German Ph.D., though it was the first requisite for appointment to a professorship, was really designed to serve this much wider constituency: most students who took the degree were destined to be *gymnasium* teachers. In addition to writing a brief dissertation, candidates underwent examination in three broad subjects, such as history, geography, and mathematics. Neither the dissertation nor the examinations were very concentrated or demanding.[28] Rather, they partook of the encompassing spirit of *Wissenschaft,* which Fritz Ringer describes in his essay.

The Americans converted the Ph.D. into an advanced degree for students already committed to a career of research in a single field. Consequently, when Johns Hopkins formalized requirements in 1877/78, it stipulated two years of study beyond the baccalaureate in "one main subject" and "one subsidiary subject." Moreover, the Hopkins authorities demanded "an elaborate thesis" requiring "labor for the greater part of an academic year" and showing "powers of independent thought as well as of careful research.[29] Subsequently, standards were further raised, so that the doctorate became a three-year rather than a two-year degree prior to World War I.[30] William James could see no serious purpose in all of this—he called it "a sham, a bauble, a dodge whereby to decorate the catalog of schools and colleges."[31] Actually it was a conscientious rational means of ensuring that a decentralized system would produce fully qualified specialists in every field of knowledge.

As a regulative mechanism in America, the academic degree had a very serious limitation, however. In the absence of governmental supervision, degrees could be altered, multiplied, and debased by any institution to serve any purpose. As the importance of degrees increased in the second half of the nineteenth century, their number and variety passed all bounds. The Commissioner of Education counted fourteen different degrees in use in 1872. Fifteen years later the first American handbook on degrees complained of more than sixty. To attach a uniform meaning to the Ph.D. and to fight off alternative degrees required a sustained struggle. In the 1890s graduate students at the leading universities organized clubs, which affiliated as the Federation of Graduate Clubs and pressed for the adoption of uniform requirements. In 1900 the Association of

American Universities was founded "to protect the dignity" and secure "greater uniformity" in the American doctorate. Gradually the awarding of honorary Ph.D.'s was stamped out. The rival degree, doctor of science (D.Sc.), which Harvard introduced in 1872, was converted into an honorary degree.[32] The doctor of philosophy prevailed in this welter of multiple possibilities because it signified the ability to do original work of a scientific order in any field.[33]

2. *The university department as a society of equals.* Once certified, the Ph.D.'s needed an institutional setting in which each could pursue his own specialty with a maximum degree of independence. Americans assumed that every academic person should not only have his own distinct specialty but be able to aspire to his own sphere of influence. Every Ph.D. who chose to teach should be able some day to become a professor. That was not the case in continental European universities. In Europe, one professor represented a whole field. Professors were few, and each was likely to have his own research institute staffed by apprentices and assistants. To become a professor, therefore, was not a normal career expectation but a sacred calling reserved for a very few exceptional individuals. So jealously were professorial prerogatives guarded that provision for new fields of study usually came slowly and reluctantly. Specialization was confined within strict limits.

The formation of departments in American universities permitted an entirely different set of relationships.[34] In a department, several relatively autonomous teachers shared responsibility for a field of knowledge. Every one of them could have unchallenged control of his own little subdivision of the field. By the 1890s departments were developing a busy, independent life which they conducted for the most part on a collegial basis. The department could easily expand to accommodate new specialties, it facilitated the coexistence of a considerable number of full professors and its self-governing procedures acknowledged the juridical equality of all specialists. As the departments rose in importance after 1900, they acquired power that had earlier belonged to the university presidents. The age of strong presidents passed, and that too promoted specialization.[35]

3. *Multipurpose agencies to sponsor research.* Another way to promote specialization without concentrating authority was to give the sponsoring institutions a mixture of purposes and a multiplicity of constituencies. Here again the universities were a model. They loudly proclaimed an allegiance to ideals of public service and cultural conservation as well as research. They catered to gentlemen, aspiring accountants, civil reformers, and girls escaping from the farm, while nourishing every species of scientist and scholar. Astounded by this variety, French observers thought it wasteful and chaotic.[36] Yet it made possible a profusion of specialists inconceivable elsewhere. And by intertwining their work with other objectives, the American "multiversity" neutralized opposition.

Similarly, the libraries on which scholars depended made themselves accessible to everyone while, at the same time, amassing the resources specialists required. In his chapter, John Cole describes how American libraries turned from the mere acquisition and preservation of books to a new policy of actively stimulating and facilitating their use. This popular outreach did not for a moment divert the libraries from accumulating materials that specialists wanted. On the contrary, the widening utility of American libraries to the whole community justified the ever-increasing appropriations that book-loving librarians lavished on their research collections. Even the rare-book libraries, which guarded their holdings from indiscriminate use, did not restrict themselves entirely to a scholarly clientele—they functioned also as museums, appealing to a larger public by displaying their treasures under glass.

The great private foundations that appeared in the early twentieth century at first seemed to resist the heterogeneous intermixture of purposes that transfigured universities and libraries. Customarily, charitable trusts were set up for a narrowly defined object, as in the case of the Rockefeller Institute for Medical Research (1901) and the Carnegie Foundation for the Advancement of Teaching (1905). Nathan Reingold points out in his essay that the Carnegie Institution of Washington (1902), although breaking new ground in its commitment to fundamental research in a wide variety of fields, followed European precedent in becoming strictly a research center without any practical or pedagogical objective. It was not until John D. Rockefeller in 1909 earmarked fifty million dollars to promote ''any and all of the elements of human progress'' that the distinctive flexibility and many-sidedness of the modern American foundation began to emerge. From this grant developed the Rockefeller Foundation (1913), which gradually learned to avoid fixed and limited goals by making outside agencies responsible for executing the projects it funded.[37] The very word ''foundation'' came to signify a new kind of institution with exceptional latitude in disbursing its funds.[38]

4. *Rule by reference works.* The problem of specialization is inevitably one of communication among fields. In America this difficulty was aggravated by the diffusion of authority throughout a horizontal system. Since all of the above arrangements tended to obscure the visibility of leaders, only an experienced insider could say with reasonable accuracy where the influential ideas and investigators within a discipline were to be found. The crucial challenge to the American system, therefore, was to coordinate specialized knowledge and to give outstanding scholars and ideas a wider hearing. The challenge was met with a new panoply of reference tools. Instead of vesting leadership in an academy, Americans called on the neutral services of bibliographers and librarians.

Certain types of reference works were done better in Europe than in the United States. The great nineteenth-century encyclopedias were European. Americans also lagged far behind the French and Germans in the production of comprehensive guides to a single specialized field, like the *Quellenkunde der deutschen Geschichte,* which was first published in 1830 and enlarged and improved under a succession of editors. Works of this kind, surveying a large subject and evaluating the leading materials for it, expressed the stability and concentration of intellectual authority that existed in a European research institute. By contrast, Americans excelled in producing open-ended reference works designed to acquaint a miscellaneous variety of users with what was current outside their own specialties. The notable American achievements in the organization of knowledge were indexes, catalogs, and directories.

The model of American reference tools was the public card catalog. Today we take it so much for granted that we have forgotten how revolutionary a dictionary catalog of loose cards was when introduced at the Harvard Library in 1861. Infinitely flexible, it could accommodate any degree of specialization. In the next half century improvements in the organization and cataloging of printed matter came with increasing rapidity, the most notable being the Dewey decimal system of classifying books (1876) and the sale of printed cards by the Library of Congress (1901).[39] Card catalogs have facilitated the distribution of specialized knowledge by permitting anyone, starting either with the name of an author or with a topic, to acquaint himself with the current authorities on any subject a library encompasses. At the same time, card catalogs have added to the prestige of specialized knowledge by guiding readers to the most up-to-date and specific works. Because the card catalog is so obviously designed for quick inclusion of new publications, it confirms the premium on contemporaneity that is inherent in the specializing process.

While Melvil Dewey and Charles A. Cutter worked out the modern principles of book classification in the 1870s, other Americans developed similar controls over the vast literature of medicine and law. Publications in both law and medicine were proliferating in so many directions that they posed, in an acute form, the problem of communication between specialties. In the field of law, perhaps the outstanding achievement was the modern digest, essentially an elaborate subject index to law reports. The *American Digest: Century Edition* (fifty volumes, published between 1897 and 1904) established a uniform classification of the law which became the recognized standard for all subsequent indexes and digests. For its contribution to indexing techniques and for its sheer magnitude—a half million cases assimilated to one topical arrangement—the *Century Digest* was hailed as "the magnum opus of American law."[40]

Meanwhile, John Shaw Billings, librarian of the Surgeon General's Library in Washington, was building the largest collection of medical literature in the world and devising an index to all of the books, pamphlets, theses, and journal articles the Library held and was receiving. The result was the monumental *Index-Catalogue of the Surgeon General's Library* (1880–1955) for which Billings and his successor, Dr. Robert Fletcher, are said to have indexed, by subject, 168,000 books and more than one-half million articles before Fletcher's death in 1912.[41] This they supplemented with a monthly bulletin, the *Index-Medicus* (1879–1926).

What Billings and Fletcher accomplished for medical literature, a former farm boy and bookseller did for other current publications. Following in the footsteps of several less successful predecessors, Halsey William Wilson launched in 1900 the *United States Catalog,* a trade list of books in print. The following year he inaugurated the famous *Readers' Guide to Periodical Literature.* By 1900 American libraries were so numerous and avid for reference services that current, ongoing bibliographies could be produced for a profit. Wilson proved himself a master in articulating detailed subject entries. One project reinforced another and his efforts expanded rapidly. Incorporating as the H. W. Wilson Company in 1902, he absorbed rivals, created such new serials as the *Book Review Digest* (1906) and the *International Index to Periodicals* (1907), and built a staff that filled a five-story plant in New York City. By the 1930s the Wilson publications indexed, reviewed, and catalogued more than 1,200 periodicals and all books printed in the English language in all countries of the world.[42] Nothing approaching this bibliographical empire existed anywhere else.

What remained teasingly unanswered, after the indexes and catalogs were on hand, was the elusive issue of individual merit and importance. Who matters? What counts? These were questions no reference work could objectively arbitrate, but it is suggestive that one of the foremost American scholars of the early twentieth century tried to produce just such an instrument. James McKeen Cattell was a psychologist with a special interest in measuring individual mental differences and a passion for organizing and promoting science. In 1906 he combined both objects by creating *American Men of Science: A Biographical Directory*. "There is here given for the first time," Cattell announced, "a fairly complete survey of the scientific activity of a country at a given period." Cattell hoped that the directory's main service would be to make scientists better acquainted with each other.[43] To that end he starred the names of the most notable figures in twelve principal sciences, as determined by an elaborate analysis of the rank orderings that leaders in each field supplied. Cattell's directory began publication in the same year that Wilson launched the *Book Review Digest,* and the stars in the former correspond functionally to the plusses and minuses in the latter.

A new edition of *American Men of Science* appeared every few years. Its total number of biographies grew from 4,000 in 1906 to 34,000 in 1943. To be starred in its pages gave a scientist dramatic visibility and benefited his career and his university alike. According to some admirers, Cattell's directory not only opened a window into the compartmentalized life of specialists but also provided a major incentive to the advance of American science.[44] The grandiose nature of the idea takes us beyond the obvious hunger for recognition felt by thousands of obscure specialists. The belief that a handbook of classified information could exercise a significant influence in organizing and inspiring the march of science bespeaks a trust that bordered on piety. It suggests that reference works were the icons of a redemptive empiricism.

In reviewing the peculiarly American institutions called forth by specialization, I have not tried to be exhaustive. Further analysis should uncover others.[45] The four I have touched upon present a most miscellaneous appearance: a strengthened Ph.D. degree, the departmentalization of universities, the funding of research by agencies with nonresearch purposes, and the development of reference tools designed to open the latest specialties to outsiders. What could these oddly assorted devices have in common? What linked the American doctorate, the American academic department, the American foundation, and the American card catalog? On close inspection the answer seems clear. Each provided a means of reconciling the elitist tendencies of intellectual specialization with the egalitarian requirements of American society. Together they demonstrate that Americans, while failing to *discuss* the deeper problems of specialization in the late nineteenth century, nonetheless *reacted* with vigor and inventiveness. Not in ideas but in institutions did the onrush of specialization produce a creative response.

## Notes

1. Sally Gregory Kohlstedt, *The Formation of the American Scientific Community: The American Association for the Advancement of Science, 1848–1860* (Urbana, Ill.: University of Illinois Press, 1976); Robert A. McCaughey, "The Transformation of American Academic Life: Harvard University, 1821–1892," *Perspectives in American History* 7 (1974): 246–74.

2. See the illuminating discussion of these issues in Laurence Veysey's essay in this volume and in Nathan Reingold's valuable corrective to the canonical distinction between professional and amateur: "Definitions and Speculations: The Professionalization of Science in America in the Nineteenth Century," in *The Pursuit of Knowledge in the Early American Republic,* eds. Alexandra Oleson and Sanborn C. Brown (Baltimore: The Johns Hopkins University Press, 1976), pp. 33–69.

3. George H. Daniels, *American Science in the Age of Jackson* (New York: Columbia University Press, 1968), pp. 27–38; Howard S. Miller, "Science and Private Agencies," in *Science and Society in the United States,* eds. David D. Van Tassel and Michael G. Hall (Homewood, Ill.: Dorsey Press, 1966), p. 198. The advance of specialization in the first half of the century is ably treated in Stanley M. Guralnick, *Science and the Ante-Bellum American College,* Memoirs of the American Philosophical Society, vol. 109 (Philadelphia: American Philosophical Society, 1975).

4. "The Advantages and Dangers of the American Scholar," in *American Philosophic Addresses, 1700–1900,* ed. Joseph L. Blau (New York: Columbia University Press, 1946), p. 125. See also, Merle Curti, *American Paradox: The Conflict of Thought and Action* (New Brunswick, N.J.: Rutgers University Press, 1956), pp. 40–56; James McLachlan, "The *Choice of Hercules:* American Student Societies in the Early 19th Century," in *The University in Society,* 2 vols., ed. Lawrence Stone (Princeton: Princeton University Press, 1974), 2:468, 485; Samuel Haber, "The Professions and Higher Education in America: A Historical View," in *Higher Education and the Labor Market,* ed. Margaret S. Gordon (New York: McGraw-Hill, 1974), pp. 246–52.

5. Emerson's address, "The American Scholar," is reprinted in Blau, ed., *American Philosophic Addresses,* pp. 153–70.

6. Quoted in Kohlstedt, *Formation of the American Scientific Community,* p. 134. See also, Alexis de Tocqueville, *Democracy in America,* 2 vols., ed. Phillips Bradley (New York: Alfred A. Knopf, 1945), 2:3–5.

7. George Rosen, "Changing Attitudes of the Medical Profession to Specialization," *Bulletin of the History of Medicine* 12 (July 1942): 343–54; Hugh Hawkins, *Between Harvard and America: The Educational Leadership of Charles W. Eliot* (New York: Oxford University Press, 1972), p. 288.

8. Quoted in William G. Rothstein, *American Physicians in the Nineteenth Century: From Sects to Science* (Baltimore: The Johns Hopkins Press, 1972), p. 211. For typical complaints about the cost of specialized education, see Clifford S. Griffin, *The University of Kansas: A History* (Lawrence, Kansas: Regents Press, 1974), especially pp. 118–19.

9. Charles E. Rosenberg, "Martin Arrowsmith: The Scientist as Hero," *American Quarterly* 15 (Fall 1963): 447–458.

10. J. G. A. Pocock, *The Machiavellian Moment: Florentine Political Thought and the Atlantic Republican Tradition* (Princeton: Princeton University Press, 1975), pp. 498–503.

11. Adam Ferguson, *An Essay on the History of Civil Society,* 8th ed. (Philadelphia: A. Finley, 1819), p. 330.

12. Adam Smith, *An Inquiry into the Nature and Causes of the Wealth of Nations* (New York: Modern Library, 1937), pp. 10, 734–35.

13. Auguste Comte, *Cours de philosophie positive,* 2d ed., 6 vols. (Paris: Bachelier, Imprimeur-Libraire, 1864), 1:26–29, 6:384–89. See also Paul Robert, *Dictionnaire alphabétique et analogique de la langue francaise,* 6 vols. (Paris: Societe du nouveau Littre, 1964), 6:523.

14. John Stuart Mill, *Collected Works of John Stuart Mill,* 13 vols. (Toronto: University of Toronto Press, 1969), vol. 10, *Auguste Comte and Positivism,* pp. 312, 314; "Wordsworth and Professor Huxley on the Narrowness of Specialists," *Spectator* 58 (5 December 1885): 1611–12. See also *Oxford English Dictionary,* s.v. "speciality," "specialization."

15. Laurence R. Veysey, *The Emergence of the American University* (Chicago: University of Chicago Press, 1965), pp. 161, 200. See also Hawkins, *Between Harvard and America,* pp. 69–70, 272–77.

16. W. T. Harris, "The Use of Higher Education," *Educational Review* 16 (September 1898): 153–54, 161.

17. Elizabeth Donnan and Leo F. Stock, eds., *An Historian's World: Selections from the Correspondence of John Franklin Jameson,* Memoirs of the American Philosophical Society, vol. 42 (Philadelphia: American Philosophical Society, 1956), p. 22. See also S. W. Williston, "Specialization in Education," *Science,* n.s., 18 (31 July 1903): 129–38; W. A. Kellerman, "The Specialist," *Science* 19 (18 March 1892): 161–63; Henry Calderwood, "Risks and Responsibilities of Specialism," *Presbyterian Review* 6 (1885): 91–100; Henry J. Philpott, "Social Sustenance," *Popular Science Monthly* 31 (1887): 612–25.

18. Herbert Spencer, *Essays on Education and Kindred Subjects* (London: Everyman's Library, J. M. Dent, n.d.), pp. 163–75; Herbert Spencer, *The Study of Sociology* (Ann Arbor, Mich.: University of Michigan Press, 1961), pp. 301–6.

19. John Dewey, *The Early Works 1882–1898,* 3 vols. (Carbondale, Ill.: Southern Illinois University Press, 1969), vol. 3, *Early Essays and Outlines of a Critical Theory of Ethics,* pp. 319–20; idem. *Experience and Nature* (Chicago: Open Court, 1925), pp. 205, 409–10. A helpful chapter, "John Dewey and the Unity of Knowledge," with an emphasis somewhat different from mine, is in Jean B. Quandt, *From the Small Town to the Great Community: The Social Thought of Progressive Intellectuals* (New Brunswick, N.J.: Rutgers University Press, 1970), pp. 102–25.

20. The case is reexamined and qualified in I. Bernard Cohen, "Science and the Growth of the American Republic," *Review of Politics* 38 (July 1976): 370–84. For a thorough, convincing critique, see Nathan Reingold, "American Indifference to Basic Research: A Reappraisal," in *Nineteenth Century American Science: A Reappraisal,* ed. George H. Daniels (Evanston, Ill.: Northwestern University Press, 1972), pp. 38–62.

21. Robert M. MacIver, "Sociology," in *A Quarter Century of Learning, 1904–1929,* Lectures delivered at Columbia University at the 175th Anniversary (New York: Columbia University Press, 1931), pp. 70–71. See also David A. Hollinger, *Morris R. Cohen and the Scientific Ideal* (Cambridge, Mass.: MIT Press, 1975), pp. 147–48.

22. I have profited especially from Thomas Bender, "Science and the Culture of American Communities: The Nineteenth Century," *History of Education Quarterly* 16 (Spring 1976): 70–71; but see also Daniel Howe, *The Unitarian Conscience: Harvard Moral Philosophy, 1805–1861* (Cambridge, Mass.: Harvard University Press, 1970), pp. 30–38, and Daniels' chapter, "The Reign of Bacon in America," in his *American Science,* pp. 63–85.

23. For an early assault on popular empiricism, and an appeal for "a minute subdivision in the pursuit of science" to overcome the evils of "charlatanism," see Alexander Dallas Bache's presidential address, *Proceedings of the American Association for the Advancement of Science,* August 1851, pp. xliii–liii. Subsequent complaints are quoted in Cohen, "Science," pp. 379–82.

24. Quoted in Charles Rosenberg's illuminating article, "Science and Social Values in Nineteenth-Century America: A Case Study in the Growth of Scientific Institutions," in *Science and Values,* eds. Arnold Thackray and Everett Mendelsohn (Atlantic Highlands, N.J.: Humanities Press, 1974), p. 25.

25. See also Daniel J. Kevles, "On the Flaws of American Physics," in Daniels, ed.*Nineteenth-Century American Science,* pp. 148–51.

26. Rothstein, *American Physicians,* pp. 214–15.

27. J. F. Jameson to Edward C. Armstrong, 21 July 1926, "A.C.L.S. Correspondence," American Historical Association Archives, Division of Manuscripts, Library of Congress, Washington, D.C.

28. James E. Russell, *German Higher Schools: The History, Organization and Methods of Secondary Education in Germany* (New York, London: Longman's Green, 1916), p. 358. See also Friedrich Paulsen, *The German Universities and University Study,* trans., Frank Thilly and William

W. Elwang (New York: Charles Scribner's Sons, 1906), pp. 334–35, 408–28; Matthew Arnold, *Higher Schools and Universities* (London: Macmillan, 1882), pp. 145–50.

29. Francesco Cordasco, *The Shaping of American Graduate Education: Daniel Coit Gilman and the Protean Ph.D.* (Totawa, N.J.: Rowman and Littlefield, 1973), pp. 85–88.

30. Walton C. John, *Graduate Studies in Universities and Colleges in the United States,* U.S. Department of Education, Bulletin no. 20 (Washington, D.C.: U.S. Government Printing Office, 1934), pp. 46–52.

31. Sol Cohen, ed., *Education in the United States: A Documentary History,* 5 vols. (New York: Random House, 1974), 5:2755.

32. A few exceptions lingered. See John, *Graduate Study,* pp. 24–31, 201–2; Stephen H. Spurr, *Academic Degree Structures: Innovative Approaches* (New York: McGraw-Hill, 1970), pp. 16–17, 148–49; Walter Crosby Eells, *Degrees in Higher Education* (Washington, D.C.: Center for Applied Research in Education, 1963), pp. 6–7.

33. Richard J. Storr, *The Beginning of the Future: A Historical Approach to Graduate Education in the Arts and Sciences* (New York: McGraw-Hill, 1973), p. 48.

34. Joseph Ben-David, "The Universities and the Growth of Science in Germany and the United States," *Minerva* 7 (Autumn-Winter 1968–69): 1–35. See also Terry Nichols Clark, *Prophets and Patrons: The French University and the Emergence of the Social Sciences* (Cambridge, Mass.: Harvard University Press, 1973), pp. 84–89.

35. Veysey, *Emergence,* pp. 304, 320–22. The resurgence of liberal culture in the early twentieth century, under the leadership of two strong university presidents (Woodrow Wilson and A. Lawrence Lowell), may perhaps be understood as a reaction against the increasing autonomy and parochialism of the departments. See also Hawkins in this volume.

36. Delaye Gager, *French Comment on American Education* (New York: AMS Press, 1925), pp. 2–3.

37. Raymond B. Fosdick, *The Story of the Rockefeller Foundation* (New York: Harper, 1952), pp. 15, 27–29.

38. F. Emerson Andrews, "Growth and Present Status of American Foundations," *Proceedings of the American Philosophical Society* 105 (1961): 158. See also Commission on Foundations and Private Philanthropy, *Foundations: Private Giving and Public Policy* (Chicago: University of Chicago Press, 1970), pp. 39–41.

39. In addition to John Cole's essay in this volume, see Arthur E. Bestor, "The Transformation of American Scholarship 1875–1917," *Library Quarterly* 23 (July 1953): 175–77.

40. Roger W. Cooley, *Brief Making and the Use of Law Books,* 2 vols., 4th ed. (St. Paul, Minn.: West, 1924), 1:67–68. See also Frederick C. Hicks, *Materials and Methods of Legal Research* (Rochester, N.Y.: Lawyers' Cooperative, 1923), pp. 250, 271.

41. I am indebted to an unpublished paper by Saul Benison on the Army Medical Corps, presented at the 1976 Newagen Conference sponsored by the American Academy of Arts and Sciences.

42. *The National Cyclopaedia of American Biography,* Current Series, vol. E:361. See also John Lawler, *The H. W. Wilson Company: Half a Century of Bibliographic Publishing* (Minneapolis, Minn.: University of Minnesota Press, 1950).

43. J. McKeen Cattell, ed., *American Men of Science: A Biographical Directory* (New York: Science Press, 1906), p. v. See also Dorothy Ross's biography of Cattell in *Dictionary of American Biography,* Supplement Three, s.v. "Cattell, James McKeen."

44. Stephen Sargent Visher, "J. McKeen Cattell and American Science," *School and Society* 13 (December 1947): 450–52.

45. Since writing this essay I have shown how the distinctive features of the American university press may be understood in the same terms. See "University Presses and Academic Specialization," *Scholarly Publishing* 10 (October 1978): 36–44.

# The Order of Learning
# in the United States: The Ascendancy
# of the University

*EDWARD SHILS*

I

The history of the order of learning in the United States from the end of the Civil War to the end of World War I may be seen largely as the history of a fundamental change in institutional structure. One particular class of institutions, the university, gained ascendancy over other institutional forms for the discovery and diffusion of knowledge, and specific universities within that newly dominant class came to be recognized as the central elements in the academic order. The ascendancy of the universities was based on superiority in productivity, both qualitative and quantitative, and in prestige—a prestige acknowledged not only within the order of learning but by the wider public as well.

In a sense, the history of learning in this period is characterized by two important developments. First, the amateur scientists and scholars were displaced by those who earned their living by studying and teaching within an elaborate institution. Second, those institutions whose members regarded study and teaching as their major obligation came to be recognized as the primary instruments for the cultivation of learning in America. In the decades following the end of the Civil War, the productive scholars and scientists of the United States increasingly became members of academic institutions. Instead of relying on their own financial resources and carrying out their work at home or in the private libraries of learned societies, the new scholars and scientists gained their livelihood primarily through employment by a college or university, using the books, journals, laboratories, and equipment provided by these institutions. Far less common and prominent were scholars and scientists who had no obligation to concern themselves with the discovery and communication of truths to their peers and juniors through learned papers, classes, and seminars—the men of learning who lived from their own privately amassed or inherited fortune or conducted their intellectual activities avocationally while earning their living as administrative civil servants, diplomats, journalists, private businessmen or practitioners of a learned profession, sacred or secular.

This important change in the life of the scholar was graphically depicted by Max Weber in *Wissenschaft als Beruf*. Weber did not, however, lay equal stress on the concomitant ascendancy of the university, perhaps because a similar transition had already occurred in Germany and Weber thus took for granted the preponderance of the university in the order of learning. It is true that during this period amateur scientists and scholars were also being absorbed by governmental research institutions, such as agricultural experiment stations, the Geological Survey (including the Bureau of Ethnology), and, following the turn of the century, by such private research organizations as the Carnegie Institution of Washington, the Rockefeller Institute for Medical Research, the Bell Telephone laboratories, and the General Electric Laboratory. Nonetheless, in the midst of this more pervasive incorporation of scholars and scientists in institutions, the growing dominance of the universities within the cosmos of American learning appears in retrospect to have been the most significant feature of the time.

In 1865 most of the serious and productive intellectual life of the country was still carried on outside the universities. Of the most famous scholars and scientists alive in the early part of the period, Henry Adams, J. H. Motley, George Bancroft, Joseph Henry, and Henry C. Lea were not university teachers, although both Adams and Bancroft briefly held posts at Harvard. J. W. Powell taught for five years at Illinois Wesleyan University and at the Illinois Normal University. Charles S. Peirce taught at The Johns Hopkins University for five years. The tradition of private and avocational learning in the United States persisted but it was unable to maintain the dominance it had once enjoyed, largely because it could not meet the demand for greater opportunities for scientific and scholarly research and training that led to the institutionalization of learning in the universities. Even in the time of its greatest prominence, the American amateur tradition lagged behind its European counterpart, particularly that of France and Great Britain, in both scale and achievement. The striking difference between the United States on the one side and Great Britain and France on the other was that the United States did not produce that closely serried sequence of geniuses that made British and French science and scholarship of the eighteenth and much of the nineteenth centuries so distinguished. The United States never attained the great height of amateur learning of Great Britain's mighty mountain chain that linked together peaks like William Harvey, Robert Boyle, Joseph Priestly, John Dalton, Humphrey Davy, Charles Darwin, Edward Gibbon, David Hume, Thomas B. Macaulay, George Grote, David Ricardo, and James and John Stuart Mill.

Indeed, American scholars and scientists were very conscious of their peripherality with respect to Europe and this probably influenced their level of aspiration; they seem not to have thought that it lay within their power to produce works of the quality of their European contemporaries. It is clear that America lacked sufficient concentration of talent in a center; the intellectual community that existed was too attenuated to produce the necessary self-confidence. In addition, the reservoir of persons sufficiently educated and wealthy to devote themselves to learned pursuits was probably too small. Even in cities like Philadelphia, Boston, and New York, persons with a high degree of concentration of purpose and energy were too few in number to embody and express, in a sufficiently compelling way, standards that could compete with the immediate, practical, and highly absorbing professional, political, and commercial preoccupations of the time. The local and state academies did not have enough prestige to compel individuals without very strong intellectual character to live up to the highest standards. Perhaps the original mental endowment was lacking; perhaps family traditions and the informal, local intellectual communities and academies in the United States were neither dense enough, intense enough, nor stringent enough to call forth the exertions and the accomplishments that emerged in Great Britain. Perhaps there were just not enough geniuses who were sufficiently committed to scientific or scholarly studies to give an immediately apprehensible form to the mode of proceeding and the ethos needed for outstanding accomplishment. Undoubtedly, there was a circularity of effect. In any case, in no field, except perhaps historical studies, did the United States have clusters of eminent amateur scholars and scientists of the quality attained at the higher reaches in Europe.

Yet is unlikely that either a larger number of practitioners or greater accomplishments would have saved the tradition of amateur scholarly and scientific research in the United States. More young persons wanted to do research than were able to support themselves from their own private means, and the knowledge of how German universities had turned such aspirations into reality increased the number of American aspirants to careers in college and university teaching. Thus the amateur tradition was bound to yield, just as a much more productive amateur practice in Europe had yielded, to competing academic institutionalization, or—as Max Weber would have called it—academic bureaucratization.

## II

Prior to the opening of The Johns Hopkins University in 1876, the learned world in the United States was rather inchoate. It had no center and no hierarchy, yet it was somewhat differentiated. There were colleges, universities (at least in name), governmental scientific bureaus, and the bare beginnings of industrial research enterprises. A few learned associations and scientific and scholarly journals had been established. One national quasi-governmental academy, two old academies that purported to be national, and a number of academies of local jurisdiction were also in existence, as were museums and several large libraries. The result was an amorphous agglomeration of institutions and activities that were scant in number and widely dispersed territorially; the connections between them were infrequent and of marginal importance.

With the retreat of amateur research, the cognate institutions of amateur research, namely, the local scientific and scholarly academies, went into decline. The avidity of intellectual desire could not be satisfied by the occasional meetings of academies or by the limitations of private means nor could local academies attract more specialized audiences. What they offered was too slight in comparison with the opportunities for intercourse and investigation offered by universities and especially university departments and laboratories that were the most fundamental elements of the emerging translocal scientific and scholarly communities.

The few outstanding individuals who dominated science and scholarship in this period—among them Asa Gray, Joseph Henry, and Simon Newcomb—did not plan for or foresee the ascendancy of the academic order. Insofar as they thought that a single institution or institutional order should predominate, they looked to the National Academy of Sciences or the Smithsonian Institution to perform that role. It was felt that these bodies should give advice to the government on matters that involved science and technology, recognize and honor past achievements in science, and guide and encourage scientists toward the study of certain fields and problems.

The establishment of Johns Hopkins, Clark, and the University of Chicago changed the intellectual environment in unpremeditated ways. Governmental scientific institutions lost their previous position of relative predominance as their work was exceeded in volume and at least equaled or surpassed in quality by the products of academic research. There were, moreover, many areas of scientific endeavor that lay beyond the concern of the government; here the universities had a free hand.

Yet the close link between science and the universities that emerged might not have developed had the American government chosen to promote science as the French government had done in the seventeenth century through the honors granted and the resources allotted by the Paris Academy of Sciences, or as the Soviet government has deliberately done by elevating the Academy of Science above the universities and giving it control over all research except that carried on by the various ministries. Despite widespread confidence in progress through the "arts and sciences," the government of the United States was not inclined to establish a comprehensive program to promote such endeavors because it was believed that the "arts and sciences," like economic life, would develop from the initiative of private persons. Instead, governmental scientific institutions became complementary or ancillary to the universities, providing practical services, conducting surveys, and offering employment to university graduates and facilities for publication of their research.

The American government's scientific interests were limited to specific areas, as evidenced in its support of the Coast Survey, the Geological Survey, and the Permanent Commission of the Navy Department. The Smithsonian Institution could have been used for the furtherance of scientific research but the government never attempted to develop it in this way. Until the end of the period, the National Academy of Sciences performed little more than honorific functions. Since it had no resources for the support of research, the NAS could do little to advance science in general, or even in particular directions. Unlike the Royal

Society of London or various German academies, the National Academy could not even function as a meeting place because its members were separated by large distances. Until the creation of the National Research Council, the NAS did not even carry out functions for which it had been expressly founded—to serve as advisor to the federal government. In a sense, the fact that the National Academy of Sciences was not promoted to a position in which it could exercise influence by its accomplishments, example and prestige left the way open for the academic order to attain ascendancy.

In agriculture, the field in which governmental science reached it peak, colleges and experiment stations had to await the ascendancy of the universities before they could become effective. The founding of the first agricultural experiment stations more or less coincided with the establishment of the Johns Hopkins University; the first land grant colleges preceded Hopkins by about a decade. Both institutions were in some measure the result of the same ideals that had inspired the creation of the new universities—ideals that were embodied, or were thought to have been embodied, in German practices. Even before the Civil War, these ideals were being advocated by young men like Evan Pugh and Samuel Johnson, two American chemists who studied in Germany in the 1850s. They maintained that scientific results comparable to those achieved in the German universities could contribute to the improvement of the quality of agriculture in the United States, and they went on to take leadership roles in the development of America's agricultural colleges and experiment stations.

Yet until the new type of university was well established, agricultural institutions scarcely advanced. In the agricultural schools of the land grant colleges and state universities, teaching was the primary function, leaving little time for research. Prior to the passage of the Hatch Act in 1887, the few existing experiment stations conducted only limited research activities. Neither the staff members of the early colleges and stations nor their public "believed" in science with the ardent conviction that led to its application. The farmers who formed the lay constituency of these institutions had no understanding of how fundamental scientific research could improve their productivity: they wanted information about the quality of the seeds they purchased and the fertility of the soil they tilled; they were interested in testing by specific and reliable methods; and they thought that agricultural colleges should provide practical training in farming.

In the 1880s, enterprising deans of agricultural colleges and directors of experiment stations tried to create among farmers an appreciation of the results of scientific agriculture that they were not in a position to deliver, partly because trained agricultural scientists were still in short supply and partly because money was not available either to employ scientists or to provide them with the resources needed for research. When funds were forthcoming after 1887, these administrators turned to the universities in search of scientists. What they found were individuals infused with the new ethos of the American academic order and determined to do more than conduct tests and analyses and manage model farms. The young agricultural scientists shared the values of the pious pioneers, Pugh and Johnson. They were offended by both the contemptuous attitude expressed toward them by teachers of the humanities and sciences at their own state universities and by the layman's belief that they were simply analysts. The ideal of the university as a place of fundamental learning impelled them and they wanted to conform to its implicit demands.

The entry of the United States Department of Agriculture into the promotion of agricultural research and the bonds established among the younger scientists on the staffs of the agricultural experiment stations—through the formation of sections of the American Association for the Advancement of Science and of specialized scientific societies and through the creation of journals—reinforced the pressure of this ideal and the determination of the better-trained "station men" to be regarded as scientists. For these individuals who felt themselves cut off from the academic center, the Department of Agriculture provided the experience of solidarity and consensus with like-minded persons and embodied the ideal to which they were devoted.

The agricultural scientist's conception of himself as a scientist was further strengthened by attending conferences and reading scientific journals, which in turn fortified his attachment to the scientific ideal. Yet the presence of the university remained the essential element for agricultural scientists seeking professional identity. In the first instance, they could not establish a system of science wholly separate from that cultivated in the universities. They were trained in universities; some of them had taught in universities; the basic sciences on which they drew were developed in universities; and the universities presented to them the realization of the scientific ideal. Their principal achievements in genetics and plant pathology were offshoots of the science of the universities and they wanted the approbation of their colleagues within their own scientific disciplines. Passage of the Adams Act (1906), which allocated federal funds for "original" scientific research, bore witness to the ascendancy of the standards of the university over the scientific activities of extra academic institutions. As Charles Rosenberg has observed elsewhere, in the end, the significant contributions of agricultural experiment stations to both the improvement of farming practices and the advancement of biological sciences can be attributed to their "willing adherence" to the values of the academic order.

The agricultural experiment stations remained in a dependent and supplementary position to the university in part because they adopted the principle of specialization; in this sense, their status was analogous to that of the independent research institutions, such as the Rockefeller Institute for Medical Research and the Carnegie Institution of Washington, which appeared early in the twentieth century. The prestige of specialization was great in America during this era, but it was not unequivocal. Despite the respect accorded specialization as a form of moral self-discipline and a more efficient way of conducting research, the older ideal of breadth of perspective was still vital and the standing of research institutions suffered accordingly. The university was unique in that it covered the entire range of learning. There was always an opportunity for a specialist whose interest impinged on an adjacent or occasionally remote field to seek guidance from a colleague in that field. Moreover, because the universities were able to reincorporate their most distinguished graduates, they came to form an intellectually self-sustaining order. In contrast, research institutions, both private and governmental, were designed to cover a narrower range of topics and often proved to be less attractive to the best university graduates. Even in those specialized fields in which they carried out important work, their accomplishments were never imposing enough for them to represent an alternative dominant order to the universities.

The dependent relationship between the universities and private research institutions in this period is exemplified by the development of an institution that did not become an independent research center—the Marine Biological Laboratory at Woods Hole established in 1888. As in the case of the universities, a German model was chosen. The pattern was sketched by Karl Vogt who organized the first summer classes in marine biology in 1844; it was established in a more elaborate and stable form by German zoologist, Anton Dohrn, who founded the *Stazione Zoologica* in Naples in 1872. Charles Otis Whitman, the first director of the Marine Biological Laboratory, had taken his Ph.D. degree at Leipzig and had worked at the *Stazione Zoologica;* he argued that if a comparable American institution were not established and supported, American work in the pertinent subjects would remain permanently inferior to that of Germany.

Unlike Carnegie and Rockefeller, the Marine Biological Laboratory was not intended to be an autonomous institution with its own permanent staff of investigators and completely independent financial resources. The model on which it was based emerged from a situation in which the academic order had become dominant; the institution in Naples was conceived as an indispensable *auxiliary* in certain fields of science. In America, the MBL depended on the universities to provide the investigators, young and old, who worked at Woods Hole during the summer months. The leading American biologists of the period before the First World War came to the MBL—but their sojourns there were interludes in their academic careers.

The dependence of the Marine Biological Laboratory on the universities is illustrated by the career of Whitman. When he was young and not yet famous, he thought of the Laboratory as an institution that would compensate for the deficiencies of research in the universities. After he became a famous professor at the University of Chicago, he viewed it as ancillary or complementary to the work of the universities. It acquired a dual function that postulated the prior existence of the universities; it had the characteristics of a three-month meeting of a set of closely related professional scientific societies, yet it was also a laboratory where university teachers could turn their attention to specialized topics difficult to work on elsewhere, while also engaging in a continuous informal exchange of information and interpretation. The MBL became a unique part of the academic world—an interuniversity institution that established a precedent for the consortia that developed after the Second World War around the accelerators at Brookhaven and Weston.

Just as the MBL, the Rockefeller Institute and the Carnegie Institution were dependent on the prior and continuing existence of the universities to sustain their composite of activities, bodies such as the New York Museum of Natural History, the Field Museum, and the American Geographical Society lived alongside the universities but did not form a national system for the organization of learning. They sponsored important research and publications by members of their staff who were also custodians of their collections; they maintained serial publications of scholarly monographs and developed their collections. Their work, however, was marginal and supplementary to the large volume of high-quality research carried out in the same fields at the universities. If they were rivals of the universities, they were rivals only in the relatively narrow ranges of learning that they covered. At the same time, their dependence on the universities was inevitable. Unless they were to rely largely on learned amateurs, they had to recruit their staff from persons who had been trained in universities and who continued to look to universities as the centers of learned production. In addition, the main audience for the publications of the most important of the autonomous research institutes was to be found in the universities.

There was yet another reason why the private research institutions could not compete effectively with the universities—they were simply too few in number. When the Rockefeller Institute for Medical Research and the Carnegie Institution of Washington were established at the turn of the century, there were practically no similar institutions with which to form an alliance and create a sense of community; the two together were not enough to serve as a point of crystallization. Independent research institutions as constituencies of an autonomous and dominant order within the whole order of learning had no precedent. The Kaiser-Wilhelm-Gesellschaft was not established until 1911. The Physikalisch-technische Reichsanstalt was largely governmental, as was Britain's National Physical Laboratory. The Royal Institution, distinguished though some of its associates were, never presented a pattern that was recognized by public opinion as an example of how scientific research and training should be organized. At the same time, there were already many universities and their very existence challenged and supported those who sought to reform them. To be sure, the universities had to be reformed before they could ascend to a dominant position, but their prior existence in considerable numbers gave substance to the belief that they were endowed with the power of endurance. For all these reasons, the autonomous research institutes, however distinguished their accomplishments in specialized areas of research, were compelled to function as somewhat peripheral parts of the academic order.

The industrial research laboratories were even less well qualified to compete with the universities. Not only were they very few in number, relatively small in size, and specialized within a narrow range, but they did not accord freedom of publication to their scientists and were, for the most part, devoted to applied or practical research. They were considered to serve the standard of profitability rather than an ideal of the selfless pursuit of truth and were regarded in public opinion as less worthy of deference than were the universities.

In a different way, libraries were also confined to a peripheral position. From the beginning, university libraries were clearly subsidiary. The great public and private libraries performed invaluable functions but mainly as adjuncts to the academic order. Libraries in this period were no longer collections assembled primarily for the sake of giving a permanent resting place to the results of human creativity; having ceased to be ends in themselves, they became instrumental to the desires of their users. Nonetheless, neither the Library of Congress nor the Library of the Surgeon-General, any more than the Bibliothèque Nationale, the British Museum, or the Preussische Staatsbibliothek, could become centers of a national system of learning. The tasks of a library are principally curatorial and hence auxiliary to the use of the books, manuscripts, etc., that it houses. A library does not teach; the training and formation of a staff of librarians, archivists, and paleographers, whether they are engaged in full-time research or whether their research is supplementary to their curatorial functions, does not approximate the teaching in universities.

Independent and specialized professional schools, particularly those concerned with the study of medicine, were also largely overpowered by the universities over the course of this half century. Advanced technological institutions like the Massachusetts Institute of Technology and the California Institute of Technology were the only ones in their category that approached the eminence and centrality of the leading universities and they did so by approximating the broad functions and interests of the university. Despite the promise of their early beginnings, independent engineering colleges like Rensselaer fell by the wayside. Once entry into the legal profession became conditional on systematic study, independent law schools, apart from universities, never emerged from a rather lowly obscurity. By the end of our period, only a few independent medical colleges survived without incorporation into universities. Again, it was the German model that showed the way. The growing recognition that education for the learned professions required systematic and fundamental training in scientific subjects made it imperative that professional schools be associated with universities. The alternative was to wither.

Independent liberal arts colleges that provided education for undergraduates were the only institutions that managed to withstand the tentacular dominance of the universities—an achievement that can be attributed mainly to their decision to concentrate on the instruction of younger students and to eschew research. For many years their proponents fought a rear-guard action that was partly successful, partly unsuccessful. They became subsidiaries of the universities by sending many of their graduates on to postgraduate and professional studies and by drawing some of their teaching staff from the universities. Those that grew into universities, as did Harvard, Princeton, Yale, and Columbia, were able to retain some of their identity, largely by resistance and concessions.

III

After examining the various classes of learned institutions in some detail, the general question remains: Why, in this period, did the universities succeed in establishing and maintaining dominance over the American order of learning? The main part of the answer lies in the universities' dual function of teaching and research. An institution that produced both its own *Nachwuchs* and the staff of other learned institutions assured itself of centrality in the system of learning. It aroused identifications and loyalties that later experience did not extinguish. It fostered parochial traditions that provided the motive for more widely acclaimed achievements. By teaching, the universities guided the future of their subjects; they infused their influence into members of the next generation, encouraging students to go beyond what they had been taught and to do so in the tradition in which they themselves had discovered and learned. Teachers were enlivened by their relations with students. Teaching maintained identification with a wider discipline yet it did not prevent specialized research.

The American university's dual commitment to teaching and research was not evident when the leading state universities of the Midwest were founded in the period before the Civil War. Both the legislatures and the wider public thought of these state institutions primarily as agents for the spread of an "improving" knowledge, as disseminators of the best of inherited knowledge and only secondarily as the creators of new knowledge. The concept of improvement was vague and comprehensive, signifying not only improvement of a practical sort but spiritual improvement as well. Moreover, an interest in practical improvement was not identical with an interest in research; rather, it reflected the work undertaken by the schools of agriculture and mechanical arts that came to be associated with these universities as a result of the Morrill Act.

An indisputable place for research in American higher education did not come until the later decades of the nineteenth century. As the reflux of young men from the German universities began in earnest, complaints were heard that American universities did not conduct research, that they were reluctant to demand that professors undertake research, and that they did not give due reward, in terms of appointment and promotion, to past and prospective accomplishments in research. It was only with the founding of The Johns Hopkins University in 1876, Clark University in 1887, and the University of Chicago in 1892 that a pronounced shift occurred in the nature of the American higher education. The establishment of Johns Hopkins was perhaps the single, most decisive event in the history of learning in the Western hemisphere. It was the impact of competition from Johns Hopkins and the embarrassment of comparison with it that led academic leaders including Charles Eliot of Harvard to respond to demands from some of their teachers to provide in various ways for ongoing research.

In the second half of our period, American universities sought to make research an integral and major part of their program, while never abandoning the teaching function that had enabled them first to attain, and then to maintain, their dominance in the world of learning. They were determined to uphold the expectation that everyone in the university would engage in research. They did not succeed. Then as now, there were some who did a great deal of research, many who did a little, and others who did none. There were also some who protested plaintively or vehemently against the effort to reward accomplishments in research. At universities like Harvard, Columbia, Princeton, and Yale, large groups of professors regarded the teaching of undergraduates as the primary obligation and viewed with unease the precedence in fame and salary accorded to their colleagues who were more productive in research. Their criticisms were sometimes intertwined with the resentment of humanistic scholars toward the natural scientists—a resentment that seemed to be the epitome of all that was most detrimental to the preservation of the traditional culture of the educated man.

In some respects a compromise was attained through division of labor. There was first a division between the universities, which did both research and teaching with a marked emphasis on the former, and the liberal arts colleges, which concentrated mainly on teaching and neither encouraged the practice nor provided support for research. Second, within the universities, there emerged a division of labor between the younger teachers who were assigned the more elementary courses and their older colleagues who taught the advanced courses that were more directly related to research. (This dichotomy had been observed by Max Weber when he travelled in the United States in 1904.) While the junior faculty had heavier teaching responsibilities, they were also expected to engage in research, especially at the midwestern state universities and the new private universities. At the same time, the more established, senior scholars had less teaching to do and their teaching was more congenial to research.

Except for this division of labor, the balance between teaching and research was never free from stress. It was a delicately poised equilibrium in which each part appeared to be ready to fly off centrifugally. Yet the break never occurred. Fragile and distressing though it often was, the equilibrium was held within the institutional vise of the university as an institution, and sustained by the German ideal of what a university should be.

The advantage which the universities had over other organizations in securing funds to support research was another factor contributing to their ascendancy within the order of learning. Again the importance of the pedagogical function is evident. Little financial support was obtained by the universities explicitly and exclusively for research. Nonetheless, despite what might appear from the perspective of today as an arduous round of teaching responsibilities, scientists and scholars who wanted to do research, especially those above the rank of instructor, could find time for it. They were paid to teach but they also could do research "in the interstices" of teaching. Financial requirements for research were not large and there were few projects for which many assistants were required.

Although the two decades between 1880 and 1900 were years of praise for science, that praise was not accompanied by a readiness to spend much money on research, particularly fundamental research. As noted earlier, industrial enterprises moved very slowly to establish laboratories; they still counted on purchasing inventions offered to them by individual inventors. The federal and state governments recognized the value of research but they usually thought of it as survey, assay, testing, and routine analysis; the "users" in agriculture or mining wanted exactly such services. The state and local academies of science, and the three national academies—the American Philosophical Society, the American Academy of Arts and Sciences, and the National Academy of Sciences—had very little money for research; they sought mainly to give honors to those who had done research without their aid. The universities were in an advantageous position because their relatively large staffs were paid to devote themselves professionally to activities which were close to research in a place where libraries and laboratories existed. The universities, moreover, were increasingly committed to an ethos which held that scientific and scholarly research was essential to the advancement of knowledge.

While the tradition of "pure research" was adopted from the German universities, its successful institutionalization in the United States can be attributed largely to the structure of the universities that cultivated it. In the American universities, research was what later came to be called a "spin-off" of the provision for teaching. The money spent on research might not have been as great as was desired by the academic scientists—although one does not encounter many complaints about its paucity—but because it was hidden in an "unvouchered" budget, the resulting arrangements allowed academic scientists to pursue their own interests and follow their own convictions as to what was scientifically important. Scientists in agricultural experiment stations had to respond to a public of "users," demanding immediately practical but often scientifically insignificant results. Scientists in government and industrial enterprises could not choose their research subjects nor were they always free to publish their results. Academic scientists, however, had no masters who prescribed practical or routine research; they were limited only by their own capacities and imaginations and the demands of teaching which did not by any means consume all their time and energy.

Those who carried out research in the university benefited in yet another way. With a public consisting of university teachers in their own field, they could become famous in that field throughout the whole academic order—a distinction that was more difficult to achieve for those without the advantage of a preestablished public and the means of communicating with it. The plurality of the universities gave the impression of a mighty concourse which was reinforced by the linkages and interchanges between the members of various learned institutions. A translocal identification was strengthened in the minds of those who experienced this plurality of connections and thus felt themselves to be engaged in a vast, national, and international movement of the spirit. Despite the growing specialization in research, the coexistence of the practitioners of disciplines within faculties and of faculties themselves within universities created a density and radius of intellectual intercourse which supported the general conviction that the advancement of knowledge was an end of the highest value.

The universities dominated the institutionalized system of learning for still another reason, namely, their comprehensiveness. They taught and investigated over the entire range of learning. This multitude of diverse, specialized interests enabled the universities to receive the deference that had hitherto been accorded to the churches. In addition, they could focus their attention on fundamental problems; they were not circumscribed by practical necessities. At a time of faltering theological conviction, the university scholar or scientist assumed the role of an earnest seeker after fundamental truth.'

In the allegedly practical and "materialistic" American society of the period after the Civil War, there was still a deep piety that had ceased to be monopolized by the doctrines of ecclesiastical Christianity. The seriousness with which fundamental knowledge was pursued by universities aroused the admiration of those possessed by this enduring piety. By their concern with fundamental learning, the universities were able to become, in a sense, the heirs of the churches. More specialized, more practical institutions could claim neither that vital inheritance nor the consequent support of private patrons and state legislatures.

Finally, pervading all the factors contributing to the dominance of the university was the decisive element—the love of learning. It is said, quite frequently, that the scientific side of the American academic order, particularly chemistry, developed in response to the needs of industrial capitalism in the United States; that is not, in fact, the case. As late as 1900, only a small fraction of the chemists in the United States were employed full-time in the chemical industry. In an era when most firms were still operated by single owners or partnerships, the individual units were simply too small to support research. By the first decade of the century, there was much talk of the positive contribution of scientific research to industrial progress. Publicists and ceremonial orators repeatedly praised the practical powers of scientific knowledge. Academic scientists themselves began increasingly to legitimate their scientific research by reference to the practical benefits it would produce. Enthusiastic discussions about the introduction of Frederick Taylor's "scientific methods" into management became common. Nonetheless, even in the large firms, Taylor's ideas were not seriously implemented until after the First World War. Had industry been more insistent on the utilization of the results of scientific research, industrial laboratories attached to particular firms and independent laboratories working on scientific problems would have been more common. As it turned out, the motive force of scientific research lay within the university—in the interest of the scientists themselves and in the willingness, if not the active desire, of strong university presidents to reserve a portion of the academic budget for research. The situation was no different in the other disciplines. In the case of the social sciences, the desire for social improvement was a supplementary factor. However, in all areas of learning the primary motivation for growth was intellectual curiosity—an irrepressible desire to understand.

Through its various endeavors the university managed to accommodate specialization as well as breadth, practicality as well as fundamental enquiry. The university was, moreover, self-reproductive and self-extending. The combination of research and teaching might have been adventitious; however, once it was put into practice, the result was an unsurpassed arrangement for promoting the discovery, diffusion, and influence of knowledge. Taken together, these factors resulted in the increased visibility of academic research, a mutual awareness on the part of members of the academic order, and a sense of community among academic scientists and scholars across institutional and disciplinary boundaries as well as within them. Universities had long been visible to the educated and to some sections of the governing classes, but as science grew in prestige, they were recognized and given increasingly more prominence by organs of public opinion. Science and the universities became almost identical for the broader public; scholarship in the humanistic and social science disciplines gained from the association. When the "demand" for science increased, as it did in the early decades of this century and especially during the First World War, the universities were in the first line to satisfy this demand, thus ensuring and increasing their ascendancy within the order of learning.

## IV

One of the principal elements of the German tradition—and a major factor in the triumph of the university within the American order of learning—was the emergence of specialization as a requirement of scientific and scholarly achievement. Systematic training in the universities, especially at the postgraduate level, was more conducive to specialization than was the self-education of the amateur. The specialized academic was in regular contact with his specialized colleagues and he was expected to demonstrate both a detailed mastery of numerous minute details and an acquaintance with a large number of publications dealing with these details. The amateur, following some other occupation and proceeding at a more leisurely pace, could not cover the same ground at the speed required by specialization. As the number of persons working on a limited range of closely linked or similar problems increased, the results of scientific experiments and other types of research could not be allowed to lie about in drawers. The need to achieve, manifested in the desire for recognition, loyalty to a department and university, personal ambition, and the scientific ethos all pressed for publication as rapidly as possible. The more productive specialists became, the more imperative specialization became—it was impossible for any one person to master more than a narrow sector of the expanding body of scientific literature. The increased number of specialists and the creation of new journals greatly enlarged the body of literature on particular topics; the expanded holdings of university libraries likewise made the task of "keeping up with the literature" more demanding and possible only at the cost of general reading.

Specialization displayed both lights and shadows. Its lights were a seriousness of purpose and an intention to make a contribution—the desire to win recognition from those qualified to judge whether a given piece of work added to the body of significant knowledge in a field and made further progress possible. The growing conviction that "truth always lies in the details" meant that the details had to be explored with increasing thoroughness. As the word dilettante became a term of scorn, the American academic order increasingly turned to the German model of *Fachmenschentum*. (To be a serious scientist or scholar required that one be a *Fachmann*.) There was a stern moral overtone to specialization. It meant no trifling, no self-indulgence. It was unsympathetic to false pride and omniscience. In sum, specialization was consistent with the secularized Protestant puritanism of the quarter century preceding World War I.

To be sure, the ideal of *Bildung* was not wholly vanquished by the concept of *Fachmenschentum*. It should be noted that many of the scholars and scientists who entered American academic life in the 1880s and 1890s were widely read in philosophy and literature. Despite the praise of the specialist that was heard everywhere in Germany, the breadth of reading of the German professors appeared overpowering to the young Americans studying in Germany. William James' description of Dilthey in one of his letters home in 1867 spoke for the thousands who came after him. Many of the young Americans themselves had already studied modern literature and classics as well as scientific subjects. In Germany they sometimes became intoxicated with reading not just in their own subjects but over a wide range. The aftermath of religious doubt deepened their philosophical interests. In later years, many of those who had studied in Germany retained their knowledge of German; this too kept them from exclusive concentration on a single subject.

Nonetheless, specialization was making its way under the shadows of a narrowing range of attention. Its progress was aided by the departmental system that permitted a measure of specialization in teaching. Still, the degree of specialization in teaching was never as pronounced as it was in research where it went hand in hand with the extension of the radius of the academic's interest beyond the boundaries of his own college or university. The individual investigator who wished to follow closely the most recent literature in his field inevitably became part of a national and international academic community. And since the names of universities were never completely severed from the names of individuals, the deference accorded to individuals for their respective achievements was diffused onto their universities, producing an institutional hierarchy based on distinction in science and scholarship. By requiring the academic to direct his attention outward, specialization in research contributed to the definition of the centers of the academic order—those institutions that provided the models of topics to be studied, observations and interpretations to be examined, and standards of achievement to be built upon.

Yet specialization did not result in the fragmentation of the academic order, although it did reduce the magnitude of a culture common to most academics. The reputation of the leading universities was not based on achievement in a single area but in many different fields of research. By supporting the translocal elements of the scientific and scholarly community, specialization served to consolidate the academic order and its hegemony over the amateur and other intellectual institutions.

## V

From the 1880s onward, the holders of doctorates from American universities and those who had studied in German universities—in outlook and status, they were increasingly identical—became aware of the qualities and interests they shared as practitioners of particular disciplines. The result was the growing prominence of national scientific and scholarly associations and their journals. Before the Civil War and in the two decades immediately following it, the activities of the American Association for the Advancement of Science, like the efforts of the earlier established *Verein deutscher Naturforscher und Artzte* and the British Association for the Advancement of Science, had provided occasions for intellectual intercourse. Contact within the boundaries of loosely defined disciplines was eagerly sought, and for this reason the special sections of these societies multiplied. The disciplinary learned societies, formed in the last quarter of the nineteenth century, were expressions of a desire for a more regular and intense intellectual interchange that would link men of learning who had been dispersed throughout a burgeoning national territory.

For many, the desire for such contact had been quickened by their intense intellectual experiences in small Germany university towns or in university quarters of larger towns, where they found themselves in the company of other young men equally passionate in their devotion to enhancing their understanding and improving their knowledge, and where the "professor" appeared to be the embodiment of learning in its most exalted form. This close contact among intellectuals was evident not only in tightly knit university communities but also at the national level in the existence and activities of national scientific and scholarly associations such as the *Verein fur Sozialpolitik*. American scholars had never been exposed to such intense intellectual activity at home and the experience left an indelible mark.

For these young men, returning to the United States in the years immediately following the Civil War meant reentering a life where the intellectual air was very thin. Those who found employment in colleges and universities felt isolated. The older generation of teachers was neither accustomed to nor interested in engaging in serious scholarly discussions at a local or national level. In most colleges and universities, departments, which first emerged as administrative conveniences attendant on the system of electives, were small, and thus there was little opportunity to encounter like-minded colleagues. Students as serious about the pursuit of learning as these young scholars had been were rare. The "Germany-returned"—to use a term parallel to the "England-returned" which became current in India—had a sense of being cut off from a vital source of intellectual substance. Unlike the "England-returned" Indians, however, the Americans were in a more invigorating environment. They felt a need not only to teach and to do research in their chosen fields but also to create a sense of intellectual community. Rather than repining or losing themselves in feelings of impotence, they set about to stimulate American intellectual activity by pursuing their own scholarly and scientific labors and by founding societies and journals that helped to fill the empty, isolating space around them.

In contrast with the older academies, the scientific and scholarly societies that began to emerge in the 1880s were formed around specialized disciplines and were relatively independent of universities. They represented an effort by amateurs and scientific and scholarly organizers to break out of the boundaries set by locality and to reach across space into national communities. Increasingly they were taken over by academics, in consonance with the ascendancy of the universities, and became the periodic gathering place of scientists and scholars from various universities.

In terms of the "Germany-returned" Americans, the establishment of these societies was more than an effort to confer legitimacy on and to elevate the status of the new academic professions while increasing their public influence. Both the organizations and their publications were intended at least as much to uphold the intellectual morale of the young generation of academics who were not wholly at ease in the sparsely settled intellectual domain of their own country. By providing the conditions of intellectual community, young academics gave a sense of their ability to influence scientific and scholarly progress. The journals that they founded were, of course, a means of communication but more important they and the learned societies served to sustain the faith of young scientists and scholars in the value of their undertaking by bringing more impressively into their consciousness the similar interests and activities of others.

These academics were fortunate to live in a period when the larger movements of society, before and during their own time, were favorable to their goals. At the very foundation of their good fortune was the widespread persistence of a firm Christian belief. Their own falling away from the basic theological and historical tenets of Christianity in their literal form did not dissolve the more general bearing and active force of character that such belief engendered. These academics adhered to the value of exertion for the purpose of seeking an ultimate truth and of subsequently transfiguring the earth in accordance with that truth—in whatever sphere—and they believed that exertion brought commensurate reward. They had ceased to believe in a literal Christian interpretation of the universe and of human existence, yet they were determined to repair that loss by replacing it or shoring it up with scientific and scholarly knowledge, which if it did not disclose God's design, would at least reveal the lawfulness of some of the workings of nature and society.

They were fortunate too in returning to the United States at a time when universities and colleges were beginning to look favorably on "modern subjects," at least to the extent of employing young scholars who had studied them. The departmental organization of universities had not been designed to create local intellectual communities, but it made their formation easier by bringing together in circumscribed spaces persons of overlapping and sympathetic interests. Moreover, the departmental pattern of organization gave scholars the opportunity to undertake specialized investigations, which had been emphasized in their German training as one of the decisive requirements of intellectual progress. The fact that research could be launched with small grants or none at all was another fortunate element. As active researchers, young academics were able to consolidate their identification as scientists and scholars working in particular disciplines. It is true that they did not have the leisure and freedom of the German *Privatdozent;* they had to teach elementary courses and they had to teach more hours weekly but they also had the advantage of being paid. Although unsteadily poised on the lowest rungs of the academic ladder, they were at the beginning of an academic career. The increased number of posts in a department and the gradation of ranks offered the promise—not certain but at least possible—of advancement. A young scholar or scientist was no longer a school teacher or an assistant master serving at the pleasure of the head master or president—a "hand" taken on at short notice and dismissed at equally short notice. He was beginning to become a "college teacher" or a "university teacher." There was a new dignity in the status of "college" and "university teacher," a new conception of the powers, privileges, and obligations of the position. "Practical men" might have spoken disparagingly of such an occupation but university teachers themselves often felt that they had embarked on a lofty calling.

Yet this new image of the university scientist and scholar would not have emerged without another closely allied change. Before the Civil War, presidents of colleges had been imperious and autocratic; they were the chief agents of their governing bodies; all their teachers were their "assistants." Powerful though the presidents were, they had not been influential in advancing the cause of learning; they had regarded themselves largely as administrators of schools in which the moral character of selected youths was formed. About 1870 onward, a major change occurred. College and university presidents remained powerful, but a small influential group of them emerged to exercise their power on behalf of learning. Daniel Coit Gilman of Johns Hopkins was the first and foremost; followed by Andrew White of Cornell, G. Stanley Hall of Clark, William Rainey Harper of Chicago, and Charles Eliot of Harvard, all of whom moved in the same direction. Like their junior faculty, they were persuaded that the life of learning had become one of the highest vocations of man.

Just as the young teacher could feel himself at the beginning of an academic career, full of potentialities, so too did the presidents of the colleges and universities acquire a sense of their potentialities. At the end of the nineteenth century it was the great magnates of industry and commerce who, despite the roughness of their methods, represented in the eyes of the educated public the forward surge of the country toward greatness. Yet university and college presidents were not insignificant figures in this powerful wave of moral progress and national eminence. They shared the confidence of leading businessmen, politicians, and publicists in the grandeur of what was a collective national undertaking. Their particular jurisdiction was the world of learning and they benefited from the approbation that was accorded to it by many of the leading figures of American society. A spectrum of "anti-intellectual" elements including fundamentalist Christian sects, rough and vulgar politicians, Gradgrind-like businessmen, cultural philistines, and the ebbing reservoir of the genteel tradition persisted in the United States, but they did not dominate the newly forming and reforming universities. The receptivity of state legislatures in the Midwest and on the Pacific coast and the philanthropic largesse of great businessmen assured university presidents, and in turn university teachers, that the currents of public opinion were running in their direction.

Thus the "Germany-returned" young American scientists and scholars did not come home to a barren waste. Even the hindrances to their progress were in flux and they were encouraged by evidence of like minds and situations. They knew that there were others facing similar problems and possessing a similar resolve to prove themselves in the world of learning and to bring that learning to bear on the shortcomings of their society. They gravitated toward the universities led by presidents whose ideals and goals they admired—universities where they saw the lamps of the German tradition burning, dimly in some, more brightly in others.

## VI

Accompanying the ascendancy of the universities over the American order of learning was the ascendancy of a few universities within the national academic order. Important scientific papers and distinguished learned dissertations were not produced at every university, and the audience for scholarly work was as unevenly distributed as those who addressed it. At the same time, it was rare that a given university could point to a complete concentration of intellectual talent and production in a particular subject. One university might exceed another in the number of its eminent teachers and investigators and in the number of Ph.D's granted in a given field, but it never held a monopoly. Thus what emerged was not a single intellectual center, but a constellation of centers that were in competition with one another and were, at the same time, infusing their ideals on the peripheral institutions.

The greatest concentration of scientific and scholarly activity was to be found in a relatively small number of institutions: the new universities like Johns

Hopkins, Chicago, and Stanford; the slowly self-transforming, older universities of the East; and the state universities of the Midwest and California. The work undertaken at these centers helped to create an intellectual consensus about what was true and important in a given field, in terms of both substantive issues and methodological problems.

The research and publications of individual faculty members were the basis for the distinction achieved by those institutions that comprised the central constellation. The importance of a given department was frequently the result of the towering accomplishments of one person. The simultaneous elevation of four or five departments within a major branch of learning or eight or ten in a university as a whole made that university into a center sought out by graduate students and professional academics alike.

Columbia University was one such center. In anthropology, for example, it took the lead because the figure of Franz Boas towered above all his colleagues. The department of anthropology at Columbia produced a steady stream of learned publications and distinguished research students. Boas' work was not only an enduring contribution to knowledge; it was also a model for other investigators in the field. Anthropology had existed in the United States before Boas, but the emergence of a department that trained future anthropologists and brought forth men like Kroeber, Lowie, and Sapir, each of whom in his turn became a point of crystallization of anthropological study, transformed the loose "consciousness of kind" into a sense of being part of a discipline of universal validity. Moore and Seligman in economics, Burgess in political science, Dewey in philosophy, Morgan in genetics, Beard and Robinson in history were a few of those who made their departments and Columbia University into an important center of learning.

The University of Chicago was another such center. Moore in mathematics, Michelson and Millikan in physics, Loeb in physiology, Manley in English, Thomas and Park in sociology, Freund and Merriam in political science, Shorey in classics were the individuals whose light was diffused over the rest of their institution. Sociology at Chicago illustrates the role of a leading center of research and training. Sociology was a "movement" of the mind before it became a discipline. As it grew academically a substantive body of literature developed, consolidating the subject and strengthening the sense of identity of its practitioners. The department of sociology of the University of Chicago was a crucial element in the process. Yet "Chicago sociology," like "Columbia anthropology," never monopolized all the activity in its field. It did, however, draw out and emphasize certain themes and techniques, thereby providing a common conception of the substance and methodology of a field through the works that its members produced.

Johns Hopkins University and Harvard University in historical studies, Johns Hopkins, Harvard, Chicago, Columbia, and Wisconsin in economics performed similar roles. In the social sciences as in other subjects, the development of academic departments transformed heterogeneous and somewhat inchoate bodies of intellectual activities and beliefs into disciplines.

Of course, centers did not always remain centers. Within the central constellation particular institutions waxed and waned, while some of the lesser universities became independent centers in their own right, each sharing and reinforcing the common culture of a field and developing its own distinctive features. The important element was not the specific composition of the constellation but rather its very existence. Its emergence helped to make the academic order into a community—a necessary condition of the ascendancy of academia in the order of learning.

The sense of community was nurtured by movements within the central constellation and between the central and the concentric peripheral circles. An American student seldom pursued his graduate studies at the same institution at which he had taken his bachelor's degree. If he succeed in entering the academic profession, he rarely began his career at the same university at which he had taken his advanced degree; as he progressed, he moved from one university to another. American universities did not have the degree of "inbreeding" that was characteristic of the British universities; the greater egalitarianism of American society permitted a young man trained at the center to settle more easily into an institution a little removed from it than appears to have been the case in Britain at that time. The movement of academics among universities was further facilitated by the fact that student bodies, the number of available teaching posts, and the number of universities themselves were growing more rapidly in America than elsewhere.

These movements consolidated the collective self-image of the academic order and the position of the central constellation within it. Academics came to believe that they were part of a mighty regiment, somewhat distinct from the rest of American society—contributing to it, criticizing it, supported by it, and harassed by it. They also saw themselves as separate from the other intellectual institutions of the learned and the literary worlds—from industrial laboratories and governmental scientific service with which they had only irregular contact and from the world of artists and literary men with whom they had very little interchange, even in New York and Chicago. Finally, they were united by a common universe of discourse that was sustained, in large measure, by the preponderance of scholarly work emanating from the central constellation. Although separated by fields and specialization within fields, by the end of the century, scientists and scholars could still be bound together across institutional boundaries by reading common bodies of scientific and scholarly literature which originated primarily from within the university.

Moreover, it was the universities themselves that increasingly became the source of most scientific and scholarly publications. In the last years of the nineteenth century, universities that had already achieved a position at the center of the academic order further strengthened their ascendancy by establishing scholarly publishing houses. The presses of The Johns Hopkins University, the University of Chicago, Cornell University, Columbia University, Harvard University, and the University of California were initially organs for the publication of works, including multi-volumed series and journals, written and edited by teachers at these institutions. Series such as the Johns Hopkins Studies in History and Political Science, the Columbia University Studies in Public Law and Political Science, and the Harvard Oriental Series offered the newer members of the various disciplines a ready opportunity to bring their research results to a wider audience; they also underscored the identification of these younger scholars with the institutions where they were trained and where some held appointments. By coupling the scholarly and scientific eminence of the institutions and departments with the names of particular scholars, these publications thickened the lines that defined the centers and linked them to the periphery.

The academic press was also an important element in making the university the focal point of scientific and scholarly communications. The transactions and proceedings of those academies that managed to survive in this period could not compete with the specialized learned journals emanating from the universities and published by university presses, scientific and scholarly societies, and sometimes by commercial enterprises under academic editorship. Industrial research, insofar as it existed, likewise contributed little to the flow of learned communications. In the particular fields in which they specialized, independent museums such as the Field Museum and the American Museum of Natural History produced works which were read and respected. Some of the governmental scientific services, such as the Bureau of Ethnology, published reports which became part of the standard literature of their subjects.

Taken as a whole, however, it was the publications arising in the universities and produced by university publishing houses that dominated the network of scientific and scholarly communication. In short, the universities were not only filling up much of the world of learning; they were also expanding its space.


## VII

Beneath the widespread recognition of the legitimacy of disciplines as universally valid bodies of knowledge, there remained a sensitive institutional parochialism within the American academic profession. Like all loyalties to a collectivity, allegiance to a scholarly institution was not an emotion expressed with equal force by all academics. Young, recently recruited teachers could not be expected to feel the same degree of loyalty to their university as those who had long been members of the faculty and had risen to prominence by office, seniority, and accomplishment attained in ''their'' university or college. Although an emulative pride and sensitivity about the reputation and good name of a college or university had existed even before the ''cognitive revolution'' that spread and deepened after the Civil War, sentiments of loyalty on the part of a president and faculty were heightened by the standing of their university as a center of scientific and scholarly endeavor.

When William Rainey Harper was founding and presiding over the University of Chicago, his aim was to establish an institution that while specifically "American," would be in the same class as the German universities. Daniel Coit Gilman set a similar goal for Johns Hopkins. The presidents bore the responsibility for making their universities as "great" as they could be while the professors wanted to make their own departments "the best." For the former, "greatness" meant not only intellectual accomplishment but also public reputation and the financial benefits of such a reputation. The desire of a group of professors to build a great department might have been intertwined with personal vanity and corporate pride. It was clear, however, that their aspirations could be realized only through the production of distinguished scientific and scholarly work addressed to other scientists and scholars in the United States and abroad, most of whom were by then associated with universities. In these circumstances, self-awareness of the academic status of the intellectual world and of the hierarchy of center and periphery became acute.

Ultimately, eminence in the larger academic order was based on the achievements of departments: for individual teachers, this meant their own departments; for the president and some professors, it meant many departments within the university. Yet great departments could not be created without financial support. Before the First World War, the largest portion of funds for research came not from patrons outside the universities but from the internal budget of the university. As university presidents came to recognize the extent to which intellectual achievement aided them in building their institutions, they became increasingly willing to support the appointment of distinguished faculty. Of course, many scholars and scientists who were less than eminent had to be hired to provide for the routine teaching of various subjects, but at the level of professorships, proud and aspiring presidents placed resources at the disposal of their more ambitious and successful departments to enable them to attract the best scholars and scientists available. Departments and universities that were content to do more than "fill the slots" allotted to them sank in the hierarchy; such was the fate of institutions with more limited resources or those in which emulative institutional patriotism was weak. Although these universities were not necessarily devoid of outstanding departments, they "contracted out" of the race and accepted their peripherality.

Only a small number of universities had both the individuals and the resources needed to bring them to the forefront of the American academic order. These few were determined to live up to the German standard, not only to benefit students who would be instructed and inspired by the most outstanding workers in their respective fields, not only to stimulate faculty through contacts with distinguished colleagues, but also to satisfy the personal pride of the president and the leading professors who sought the distinction of association with a "great" department and a "great" university.

The effort to be among the best of institutions or departments was spurred by the growing prominence of research. As long as universities and colleges confined themselves to teaching, to the formation of character and the "molding of men," they were visible only locally and to those who had direct contact with them. Few easily and widely recognized marks of accomplishment resulted from such pedagogical activities. However, achievements in research were discernible not so much by the general public as by the public consisting of other workers in the same or related fields. Colleagues at other universities were more effectively present in the minds of those academics who did research than was the case with those whose affections were given in the first instance to teaching. The audience of the latter was the student body, locally circumscribed; the audience for the former was national and international.

Indeed the emergence of central and peripheral universities was conditional on the existence of translocal scholarly and scientific communities. These national communities and the organizations and organs through which they were given form aided the comparison and assessment of scientific and scholarly production. Through publication of the results of research, academics and their works were placed on a stage that enhanced their visibility. Evaluations of individual works and their authors were consolidated into assessments of departments and entire institutions. The result was a stratification of works, individuals, departments, and institutions. Some individuals withdrew from the competition and some never entered it. Others, at or nearer to the center, were sensitive to their reputation and were close enough to distinction to believe in the value of such prominence. This belief was especially apparent when appointments were about to be made, and there was an opportunity to raise the prestige of one's university by attracting a distinguished scientist or scholar.

The ranking of universities in a national hierarchy was affected by the deliberate efforts of university presidents and professors to maintain or raise the status of their institution. It was in this period that American university teachers and administrators developed the policy of "going after" a man, of making a deliberate effort to bring to their universities the best, or prospectively best, scholars and scientists. The practice of *Berufung* had long been in use in Germany when it was taken up in the United States. The new universities tried to win to their service the best of the newer men at the older universities. It was relatively easy for Johns Hopkins, Chicago, and Stanford to leap to the forefront while other universities in the country were slumbering and ambitious and talented younger persons were suffering from the restraints imposed upon them by their more traditional institutions. But the older universities rallied; they made efforts to satisfy those who wished to do research and to bring back the best of those they had lost.

The dynamics of American universities determined to enhance their reputation and hence to build their intellectual and material fortunes stood in marked contrast to the practice of the older English universities that were so confident of their superiority that they had no need to exert any effort to attract the leading scientists and scholars. In Great Britain the pattern of an academic career from the 1870s to the First World War was relatively simple: graduate from Oxford, Cambridge, or London; obtain an appointment for a time at one of the provincial universities like Manchester or Liverpool; and then, for those who reached the highest eminence, return as professors to Oxford, Cambridge, or London. The provincial universities could compete only for scholars or scientists who had not yet reached the peak of accomplishment; in attracting persons of great distinction, all the advantages lay with the three universities in the South. The vice-chancellors of Britain's modern universities either did not have or did not choose to exercise the powers of American university presidents.

No such predetermined path or unchanging hierarchy existed in the United States. In this sense, the American academic order more closely resembled that of Germany. The Prussian Minister of Education, Friedrich Althoff, was much like an American university president in his solicitous intrusiveness. In some of the German states, the initiative was borne by a few senior professors who sought to attract to their universities the best men available anywhere in Germany. (They were the beneficiaries of a tradition inherited from the time of the princely states when rulers vied with one another for the greater glory of possessing an eminent university.)

There was nothing comparable to the American or German system in France, where the Sorbonne so far outdistanced the universities of the provinces that the latter could do little more than reconcile themselves to their inferior status. Only the University of Toulouse once sought to break out of that condition and, in the end, its efforts were unsuccessful. As a consequence—and despite the fact that the national university system was a legal reality—the stimulus of institutional emulation was absent. The preponderance of the *grandes écoles,* the Collège de France, and the Ecole pratique des hautes études prevented the universities from attaining the ascendancy in France that they secured in the United States, Germany, and to a lesser extent, the United Kingdom.

Emulation was an essential motivating force in the shifting status of American academic institutions. Yet none of the emulative actions of the American universities would have occurred had presidents and professors not expressed both a passionate attachment to their universities and departments and a jealous concern for their personal reputations. Here was a parochiality that was perfectly compatible with intellectual attachment to scientific and scholarly communities extending far beyond the boundaries of individual universities.

## VIII

The story of the ascension of the universities is not one of even and unimpeded progress along a single front. There were contrary movements in public opinion and within the learned world against the dominance of the universities, and against the major universities that were the most visible parts of the academic dominance. The universities were criticized by radicals for being too subservient to the earthly powers and by conservatives for being too critical of them; they were criticized by "practical" men for concentrating on interests too remote from the ordinary business of daily life and by men of letters for being too close to it. Members of more rustic universities criticized the universities of the Eastern seaboard. Specialization and narrowness, utilitarianism, triviality and the "ivory tower," the reactionary support of capitalism and irresponsible radicalism, and excessive secularism and piety were among the charges leveled against the universities.

There was a kernel of truth in all these accusations. The American universities were sometimes subservient to external powers who charged that university teachers taught doctrines subversive of existing institutions and arrangements. The cases of Edward Ross at Stanford, Scott Nearing at Pennsylvania, Louis Levine at Montana, and Charles Beard and James McKeen Cattell at Columbia indicate that these criticisms were not baseless. At the same time, the universities were also hospitable to stringent critics of the existing order, such as John Dewey, Richard Ely, Simon Patten, and their numerous intellectual progeny, whose ideas contributed markedly to the collectivist transformation of American society in the half-century following World War I. Those businessmen and publicists who thought that "the universities" were preaching "socialism" exaggerated, but they were not wholly off the mark. In addition, the American universities performed a variety of trivial activities ranging from semicommercial football spectacles and numerous practical programs with little respectable intellectual content to worthy but distracting activities in extramural teaching and service. Yet in the half-century between the Civil War and the end of the First World War, these criticisms and diversions did not deflect the universities from the course on which they had been launched by the zeal for learning of the "Germany-returned" generation and by attendant circumstances in the structure of knowledge and society. They withstood critics, opponents, and rivals and developed, among other things, economic theory, oriental studies, sociology, genetics, theoretical physics, and the most recondite branches of mathematics.

Successful as the universities were in gaining intellectual dominion over alternative modes of organization for the cultivation—both discovery and transmission—of learning, they were less successful in their relation with alternative modes of thought and expression. Whereas their organizational rivals fell into the places "to which they had been called by God," their intellectual rivals did not readily accept the preeminence of the universities. Academics, amateurs, librarians, officials of learned societies, directors of independent research institutions, and scientists employed by the government took the ascendancy of the universities with good grace. Priests and clergy, bohemians, socialists, literary men and artists, mystics, and devotees of the occult were not so easily reconciled. However, the opposition was never unified, even within each of its constituent currents. Neither the fundamentalist Christian nor the populist rivals could forge a united front because their numbers were so prevalent within the universities. The radicals and bohemians were held at arms length, discouraged from entering the universities or extruded from them if they did succeed in gaining entrance. A few novelists and poets could be found on university faculties, although their tasks were to do research and to teach from the general body of learning. Likewise the mystics and pantheists in the university were directly engaged in science and scholarship. Artistic expression and communion with the deity did not fall within the terms of reference of the university; those who practiced them had to do so avocationally.

The profession of letters would have been in more severe conflict with the universities but for a spontaneously achieved division of labor. Academics studied literature historically and philologically, in a scholarly way; they edited texts and wrote historical works about genres, traditions, epochs and authors of the past. Men of letters were primarily concerned with contemporary authors and their writings. As long as men of letters, such as Ellery Sedgwick of the *Atlantic Monthly* and Paul Elmer More of Princeton, were still predominantly devoted to the genteel tradition, there was a truce or alliance. Novelists seldom treated the subjects dealt with by university faculties. The break came first in the outer areas of the republic of letters. But by 1920 the members of university departments of English and modern languages and literature had begun to turn their attention to contemporary works. Men of letters, particularly H. L. Mencken, became aggressively scornful of universities and of university teachers. The result was a conflict between the academics who generally disdained "modern" literature and the men of letters who generally supported it. Students of literature within the universities, although much criticized from outside, were themselves critical of specific features of the universities. Some of them bitterly attacked the scientific and scholarly side of university activity.

At Harvard, Irving Babbitt was a scholar who belonged to the ascendant academic order, but he was hostile toward the scientism and utilitarianism that he saw in the universities. He shared his antiutilitarianism with the exponents of the genteel tradition who did not approve of the research activities of the graduate schools and who were committed to the undergraduate schools. It was the survivors of the genteel tradition who became the defenders of "the humanities" within the universities and continued their defensiveness against science, technology, and the social sciences.

In literature, unlike religion, the external critics of the university were ultimately victorious—although not in the period before World War I. First, scholarship triumphed over the genteel tradition and then after the Second World War, scholarship itself was shaken by "modernism," which ended by bringing the bohemian outlook into the universities. But that story belongs to a later chapter.

In the end, the severity of their critics, internal and external, did not deter the universities from the course set by Johns Hopkins and the University of Chicago. Columbia and Harvard regrouped their forces and moved in the same direction as did Yale. They were joined by Stanford University, the University of Michigan, and the University of California; the Universities of Illinois, Wisconsin, and Indiana were scarcely behind their sister institutions in the Midwest and West.

What propelled the university movement was a drift of opinion toward the appreciation of knowledge, particularly knowledge of a scientific character. There was general agreement that knowledge could be accepted as knowledge only if it rested on empirical evidence, rigorously criticized and rationally analyzed, and that this kind of knowledge was worthy of all the effort and resources required to attain it. Great businessmen, leading state politicians as well as a few major national politicians, important publicists and, in a vague way, much of the electorate joined in the appreciation of this kind of knowledge and of the university as its proper organ. The universities were supported because they performed a dual function: they infused knowledge into the young who would apply it in their professions and whose lives would be illuminated by its possession, and they contributed to the improvement of the stock of knowledge, penetrating further and further into the nature of reality. The knowledge that was appreciated was secular knowledge which continued the mission of sacred knowledge, complemented it, led to it, or replaced it; fundamental, systematically acquired knowledge was thought in some way to be a step toward redemption. This kind of knowledge held out the prospect of the transfiguration of life by improving man's control over the resources of nature and the powers that weaken his body; it offered the prospect of a better understanding of society that, it was felt, would lead to the improvement of society. It was thought that the progress of mankind entailed the improvement of understanding simply as a state of being and not solely as an instrument of action. The honor and the glory of a country that promoted the acquisition of such knowledge was assured; its power and influence would grow proportionately and deservedly.

It was this movement of belief that carried forward the universities—a movement to which both leading academics and the leading university administrators subscribed. There were, of course, disagreements on particular points—on the emphasis to be given to theoretical and fundamental knowledge in comparison with practical, useful discoveries, or on the value of immediate intervention into practical affairs as against the postponement or avoidance of intervention until knowledge was sufficiently reliable. Certain studies were sometimes more favored than others because they attracted more financial support or at least did not discourage it. There were other disagreements too, and not all institutions and subjects moved with equal speed in the same direction. Nonetheless, the movement went on: the centers spreading their influence over the peripheries; the centers competing with each other and sometimes changing places. The universities at the center moved into new spiritual terrain, drawing the rest of the intellectual order with them.

The universities were vouchsafed this vocation because they appeared to be the best imaginable instrument for the performance of the dual cognitive function. They could not only produce more knowledge more reliably and more continuously than any other learned organization, but they could also transmit it, thus making provision for the persistence of that progress. No other arrangement of intellectual activities could approximate their success in this regard. Universities moved forward over the whole of the legitimate cognitive front. They worked in a way that drew most fruitfully on the cooperation and contributions of numerous individuals and institutions in many countries. Libraries became their instruments, industrial and governmental laboratories their executants. Within the ascendancy of the university community, order was maintained and kept in movement by the ascendancy of a central constellation of universities over most of the others.

This was the situation at the end of the First World War. Traditions of thought and loyalty had been founded and reinforced in the preceding half century. In the ensuing half century, these traditions and loyalties were to bear fruit, but they were also to be subjected to unprecedented strains precisely because they had been so successful.

*The Specialization of Science and Scholarship*

# The Plural Organized
# Worlds of the Humanities

LAURENCE VEYSEY

Like other areas of knowledge, the humanities in the period between 1865 and 1920 may be viewed from three quite different perspectives, each of them equally valid in its own terms. First, there is a sense of burgeoning variety as these subjects were taken over by the universities and underwent a rapid process of intellectual segmentation, dividing into a large array of departmental and subdepartmental fields. Perhaps the entire range of what became known as the humanities had never possessed any intrinsic intellectual coherence; but the structure of American academia, emphasizing the equality of all departments regardless of their nature, gave this incoherence striking new visibility. When we inspect the humanistic landscape from about the year 1880 onward, the map-maker's unifying label nearly disappears in the vista of separate kingdoms and principalities—the most important of which were termed "classics," "modern languages," "history," "philosophy," "art," and "music." These grander divisions in turn disguised a myriad of subentities. The movement toward specialization proceeded no less within the humanities than within the sciences, despite great resistance to it in some humanistic circles.

Second, on the organizational level, the humanities and fine arts fell prey to a somewhat contrary process. Standardization and uniformity characterized the new external forms (such as the academic departments) that came into being to sustain each field. Here one encounters all the phenomena linked to the much discussed concept of professionalization, and indeed the arrival of firmly planted notions of structural hierarchy and bureaucratic procedure in all respects. The kingdoms may have been separate and diverse, but nearly all of them came to be governed by the same kinds of rules.

Finally, both the intellectual and organizational evolution occurred within a stable, homogeneous social context. Those who played out roles within these realms, both as leaders and as followers, were members of a single, quite well-defined cultivated elite. In the widest sense this elite was drawn from professors, schoolmasters, authors, lawyers, clergymen, artists, and performers. (It was certainly far less inclusive than the 3.78 percent of the American population aged twenty-five to sixty-four who were counted by the census of 1890 as members of professions, or the 4 percent of the college-age group who in 1900 were actually attending college.)[1] The academic department, along with the museum, symphony, and opera house, became newly secure bastions for such an elite, which was marked as much by social identity as by learning. The isolation of this elite from the mainstream of American life changed surprisingly little during the entire period, though toward the end an avant-garde faction of artists and writers beyond the universities began identifying itself in principle with the "common man."

None of these three perspectives should be lost from view while each is being explored. One cannot choose among them, seeking an ultimate fundamental insight, because the study of intellectual, institutional, and broadly social history is equally legitimate. To focus alone on one dimension is to fall into the myopia all too characteristic of subdisciplinary historical pursuits. And, as we shall see, despite their logical distinctness, each focus has important connections with the others.

But what, from these diverse points of view, was peculiar about the humanities? If in large part they illustrate changes occurring more universally in the realm of knowledge, nonetheless they carried a peculiar burden. On the plane of thought, they claimed to represent the heritage of higher "civilization." Thus, in a time of rapid academic transformation marked by strongly progressive assumptions, the humanities stood for an important degree of continuity. While participating to some extent in the pervasive onward and upward mood, their spokesmen insisted that an acquaintance with the literary and artistic remains of the long-term past still ought to furnish the hallmark of the truly educated man or woman. Toward the end of the period their position faced a new internal challenge on this score from avant-gardism, but for most of this time, and for all of it inside the universities, the humanities and the fine arts were the special bulwarks of an orientation toward the past.[2]

Of course the past the humanists invoked was highly selective, tending to center on a few Greek, Roman, and Renaissance aristocrats, artists, and politicians, and in more modern times on the creators of what were confidently termed "masterpieces."[3] Certain individuals, stretching from Plato to Emerson, were placed on pedestals as the carriers of a single worthy civilized tradition. Their output, interpreted as embodying a timeless morality, came to be taught as a kind of substitute for the now partly discredited religious scriptures. Potentially, the new Germanic style of historical and philological research might subvert these oversimplified pseudohistorical formulas, just as it had already undermined the sacred position of the Bible, but in the period before 1920 such probing skepticism only seldom entered into the motivation of humanistic scholars. In the main, scholarship pressed its searchlight into further corners of the agreed civilization, not challenging the ethical generalizations of the recently formed Western

European and Northern American upper-middle class which had created the very notion of civilization itself. The humanities existed to uphold "standards."[4]

The intellectual peculiarities of the humanities were subtly interrelated with questions of social status. Knowledge of "civilization," transplanted here from Europe and long symbolized by mastery of the classic tongues, guarded the entrances into the cultivated elite.[5] Humanists were very rarely pluralists. Instead, with absolutistic assurance they asserted the continued universal need for their tradition-based recipe for learning—and for social respectability. This placed them in a highly awkward position within a society that increasingly claimed to espouse democracy. American humanists could not be as unreservedly hostile to the forces of modern democratic change as their late-nineteenth-century counterparts in Germany.[6] Though they nurtured would-be aristocratic pretensions more noticeably than other American academics, thus embodying an exclusivist tone that especially characterized the humanities on their social side, these men did not dare press their inclinations beyond a certain point. Predisposed in varying degree toward the state of mind that led Henry James to emigrate to England, casting uneasy glances alike at homegrown utilitarian populism and at the influx of immigrant millions mainly unconcerned with Anglo-Saxon cultural standards, cultivated humanists inside the new universities had to assert their claims to hierarchy—which they identified with such values as reason and order—in a climate that made it appear the times were heavily against them.

On another front, they felt deeply challenged by their minority position within the universities. What intellectual stance should they take with regard to the rising thrust of science? In the growing atmosphere of specialization, it was no longer possible even to maintain a common standpoint. Younger scholars were appearing in their own fields who accepted a scientific vocabulary and model for intellectual endeavor. Thus in a double sense, involving campuses and disciplines, the enemy was already inside the gates.

In this situation, in which intellectual qualms could intermingle with somewhat less freely spoken social fears, academic humanists had split by the end of the 1880s into two distinct persuasions. One camp, identified with the term "culture," resisted the new tendencies toward specialization and scientistic imagery.[7] Composed of classicists and a fraction of men from such fields as English literature and the history of art, and further able to count upon philosophical idealists as somewhat standoffish allies, the advocates of culture espoused the values of the older college-trained elite, though updating these values away from a defense of Christian orthodoxy. In their view, the main aim of education continued to be the training of future leaders for the whole society, directly inculcating them with a moral viewpoint that sought to rise above materialism. The outlook of such professors remained one of cultivated generalism. From within the universities they preached the same gospel of civilization as did their friends who upheld the so-called genteel tradition on the outside—editors of the nation's leading literary monthlies and organizers of the fine arts in America's major cities. Professors of this type—and they continued to reproduce themselves in significant numbers down through later decades—in effect embraced the role of the man of letters.[8]

Thanks in part to their nonacademic allies, such men had greater power and élan than their minority position within the new universities would indicate. Their social connections made them formidable, as when Andrew F. West single-handedly secured the vast benefaction for Princeton that pushed Woodrow Wilson into exile. In terms of broad outside status, these men were preeminent; intellectually, they were now underdogs. It was thus very often hard to tell whether they spoke from strength or weakness. Speak they did, and their stridently insistent rhetoric further helped to compensate for their paucity of numbers in the academic world. As the years went on, their jeremiads became increasingly aggressive-defensive, sometimes downright shrill. A negative militancy of tone—present in the writings of Charles Eliot Norton, Paul Shorey, Andrew F. West, and even to some degree in those of Woodrow Wilson—came to be regarded as the single most glaring symptom of the culture-oriented standpoint. But by 1890 or 1900, these generalists could scarcely pretend to speak for all the humanities and fine arts.

A second persuasion had taken firm root by the end of the 1880s—the advocacy of advanced research.[9] To the generalists, research meant submergence in arcane dry-as-dust materials located within subfields they could scarcely comprehend, along with the acceptance of a dubious and pretentious scientistic posture. The Ph.D. and the entire Germanic style of graduate training threatened liberal education. Did it threaten the existence of the cultivated social elite as well? This was the crucial point at which intellectual and social considerations intermingled. A Ph.D. degree was to be won on merit. In this respect, it might seem to undermine ascribed social standards, the role of "good family" in managing the nation's cultural life. But the generalists couched their reservations about it in intellectual terms. One may only infer, from their frequent commitment to a style of teaching centered on contacts with socially favored undergraduates who lacked well-defined academic ambitions, the part played in their intellectual preferences by adherence to a gentlemanly social role. Meanwhile, the researchers who had sprung up alongside them were, by upbringing, members of the same overall cultivated elite. The impact of their acceptance of intellectual specialization on the survival of the social elite, as distinct from the generalists' fears in this connection, will merit exploration later.

The consequences of the growing trend toward specialization within the humanities were in any event profound, both in terms of ideas and the organization of scholarly endeavor. Indeed it should be made clear at the outset that the very term "humanities" changed its meaning fundamentally during a long process that began in the 1870s and continued into the 1940s. The stages through which this suggestive verbal transformation passed mark first, the resistance of classicists to the rapid diversification of subject matter inside the universities;

second, the rather sporadic adoption of the word "humanities" by spokesmen for a number of the younger disciplines; and third, the conversion of it by a new minority around 1940 into a rallying cry for an intensive interdisciplinary campaign in more modern dress, one that disguised its increasing use as a covering label adopted for sheer administrative convenience.

In the days of the old-time college, the idea of the humanities was invoked to defend the entire existing prescribed curriculum which centered on Greek, Latin, and mathematics. Enforced study of the ancient languages would discipline, that is, sharpen, the various faculties of the human mind. It would also provide culture through exposure to the highly regarded thoughts of the classic authors. The cultural argument gained prominence after 1890, but among classicists who came of age in this entire period, the conception of mental discipline was never wholly abandoned. "*Humanitas* was the word by which the Roman designated . . . manhood in its broadest sense," wrote a youthful defender of the old regime when he sought to define the humanities, "—the full, symmetrical, many-sided human character, not highly polished at one point, rough elsewhere, but with every part developed to the extent of its capacity."[10]

In the 1870s such rhetoric justified the whole traditional collegiate establishment. Thirty years later, thanks to the fast-sweeping tide of change that produced the elective system and the departmentalization of learning, it amounted to the special plea of a single vested interest among two or three dozen others. Not surprisingly, the universalist claims of classicists grew more anguished as the reality of the new institutional situation closed in upon them. In this spirit a professor of Greek at Brown University insisted in 1903 that the future fate of his own field was "more than an academic question. It is in the last analysis an issue of civilization."[11] For Paul Shorey and Andrew F. West, so rapid a demotion of the subject's educational status proved almost unbearably hard to live with, and down to their deaths in the 1920s they continued to invoke the term "humanities," along with such synonyms as "culture studies" and "the liberal arts," in the older sense of Greek and Latin language training, to the virtual exclusion of all else.[12]

But the word "humanities" saw relatively infrequent use in America either by these classicists or by members of the younger humanistic disciplines until the end of the 1930s. It surfaces in print on scattered occasions, but far less often than the phrases "culture" or "liberal education." More than these alternatives, one suspects, it was handicapped by musty connotations in an era when most men were anxious to appear up-to-date.[13] These overtones came forth when Felix E. Schelling played with the term during a Phi Beta Kappa address at the University of Pennsylvania in 1902:

The humanities, the liberal arts: I suppose that these words call up to the minds of many of us, who are not wholly unlettered, a thing in some manner connected with the study of the classics, a something opposed to science and to the study of nature, a something very impractical and very desirable to possess, if you do not lose bread and butter by it; a thing much talked of at commencements, and, happily, for the most part, forgotten meanwhile. Indeed, the popular conception of the humanities is . . . not so much a definite conception as an ineffaceable impression that there really are such tongues, and that it is a very disagreeable thing to have much to do with them. The humanities! the very term is redolent of times long gone and smacking of generations before the last. Beside glittering, new-minted epithets like "sociology," "criminology," and "degeneracy," the very word "humanities" looks dim and faded in this new century.[14]

"In America," wrote a young student of John Dewey's in 1910, "the once all-powerful humanities have been reduced to a somewhat humble and apologetic role."[15] Such a statement implies that the humanities still might mean primarily the classics, since by then departments of English, history, philosophy, the modern foreign tongues, and often art and music had become well-established inside the universities. Taking these studies in sum, one would have to view them as vigorous and expanding, scarcely as "humble and apologetic." The key question, then, is how early and how self-consciously the phrase "humanities" came to be attached to this entire range of disciplines. The answer, so far as it can be gleaned, is that the shift came about slowly and in piecemeal fashion.

Certain advocates of culture, not excluding classicists, had given the humanities this broader meaning as early as the 1890s.[16] What becomes striking is their unconcern with the problem of linking their ideals to a precise grouping of concrete disciplines. Instead, these men appear surprisingly often to have become victims of the spirit of specialization against which they so often preached in their rhetoric. That is, if they talked of "the humanities" at all, it was to assert that their own study—be it history, philosophy, English, or the history of art—was one of them, but without going on to develop a broader conception of what "they" after all encompassed.[17] Occasionally it was implied that the humanities comprised all nonscientific areas of study, or again all areas that were not utilitarian in function.[18] But the same speakers might also inconsistently assert that their own subject—even if it be Greek or Latin—was truly practical. Polemical volumes were devoted to testimonials of just this kind from lawyers, doctors, scientists, and engineers. Meanwhile, within their own disciplines, such men faced the continual opposition of those other figures who embraced a scientistic conception of learning.

In sum, the six decades before 1940 may be seen as a period of groping, confusion, and sharp divisions, both within single departments and as regards their mutual relations. General rhetoric about culture seldom connected to any well-defined range of subject matter broader than the spokesman's own. The result was unguided drift. The constitution of the American Council of Learned Societies was drafted in 1919 with the phrase, "devoted to humanistic fields," included in the organization's title. But the ACLS promptly issued invitations to all the professional associations concerned with the study of man from any point of view.[19] On the other hand, in *The Higher Learning in America,* published in 1918, Thorstein Veblen had already matter-of-factly used language that implied the three-fold division of subjects into natural sciences, social sciences, and humanities that has since become familiar.[20]

By implication, the definition of the humanities greatly clarified itself when several organizations seceded from the ACLS to form the Social Science Research Council in 1923. The humanities were what was left. But this does not necessarily suggest a strong sense of group identity. In fact, not until the 1940s does one discover a sudden outpouring of books and manifestoes with "the humanities" in their titles, using the word with an entirely new frequency and insistence.[21] Only then does the phrase gain the wide resonance it has since retained. In this chronology there is the interesting implication that "the humanities," in their modern meaning of a concrete grouping of academic disciplines rather than their older meaning of classical language study, took on a more or less clear shape *after* the self-conscious arrival of the social sciences, not before.

The prolonged confusion over the term directly reflects the realities of intellectual segmentation during the last hundred years. It is a point that can scarcely be overstated. We are left with the possibility that the grouping of the fields of history, English, classical and modern languages, philosophy, art, and music may at bottom be nothing more than a growing convenience—perhaps especially for deans and university presidents in neatly structuring their organizations. It appears plain that, at least since the 1920s, the disciplines that constitute the social sciences have had far more awareness of their interrelatedness than have those that are said to form the humanities. This is quite understandable. For in our century what Dorothy Ross elsewhere in this volume calls a scientistic orientation has alone retained any shred of the capacity to unify learned men in intellectual terms. Those who reject the dominant scientific conception of the pursuit of knowledge can only wander off in a score of mutually unrelated directions. It is easy to see these as amounting to no more than a mixed bag of random leftovers. In particular, when such fields as history, English, foreign languages, and the history of art and music rejected science and yet invoked the past, there was the grave danger that they would run around in a spirit of sheer antiquarianism—calling attention to anything merely because it has existed, with no self-conscious principle of selection, no concept of the logical relationship between evidence and larger hypothetical generalizations. Of course none of this matters if one stops dreaming of intellectual unification and rests content with the celebration of particular achievements in art, music, poetry, literary criticism, or philosophy. But these symptoms of confusion, drift, and retreatism deserve emphasis in dealing with a rubric that to outsiders often appears far more coherent than it is.[22]

The disparate fields that became known as the humanities took part in the organizational proliferation that was the second dominant tendency of the period. They shared in the movement toward what is commonly termed "professionalization," affecting the entirety of American learning, and they can therefore furnish important illustrations of this process. However, their relevance to the study of the growth of the organized professions does not end there. In significant ways the humanistic fields turn out, on close inspection, to violate the usual

historical descriptions of professionalization and the sociological models that
have been created to account for its rise. The humanistic disciplines are not
among the most typical exemplars of professional evolution. For this very reason, they deserve careful attention from the standpoint of the history of professionalization, as they forcefully call attention to the ambiguities of this very
concept, which too often has been seized upon in isolation from broader social
and intellectual contexts.

We need to begin by recalling the pattern that is often taken to explain the
history of the professions in the United States. Historians and sociologists frequently write as if professionalization has followed a standard evolutionary
course.[23] A professional association is established to exclude the unqualified; a
code of ethics is adopted, emphasizing the social utility of the service being
performed; the protection of a legal status is commonly sought; and training
facilities are created under some degree of control by the professional society,
further to enforce minimal qualifications of expertise and to guard the gates of
entry. Historical accounts of the "rise" of professions in America, following this
model, are generally presented from within the standpoint of the younger, rapidly
growing, technically oriented professions of the mid-twentieth century. They
repeatedly stress such aspects as prolonged formal training, a "social mission"
(surely a cloudy notion with respect to the humanities), and a sense of colleague-
ship and "professional culture" based upon functionally specific, work-oriented
considerations.

The humanities present us with a major historical example that cannot be fitted
into so neat a mold. Theirs is the story, not so much of the creation of professions
from scratch, as of the transition from an older, long existing professional outlook and mentality to newer, more specialized versions of it at the end of the
nineteenth century. In their case, the use of such words as "lay" or "amateur,"
to contrast with "professional," is at least partly misplaced. The earlier cultivated elite, set apart by its study of the ancient languages, was composed of
persons almost entirely drawn from the most traditional and honored of the
professions, some of them labeled as such for hundreds of years. What is too
simply called amateurism actually represented the generalized monopoly of
learning among the members of the older professions. In an embryonic way, the
profession of college teacher already existed, though as the role was then defined
it largely resembled that of the schoolmaster, and it fitted inconspicuously into
the broader reservoir of cultivation that marked this elite as a whole. Resistance
to newer forms of professionalization, after they appeared in the 1870s and
1880s, was thus the response of certain professionals to others, all of them still
sharing the same underlying genteel social code.

A substantial caveat deserves to be entered here against the abuse of the
concept of professionalism by recent scholars, even at the risk of some digres-
sion.[24] Much of what the phenomenon is said to involve—in the mid-twentieth-
century version too routinely employed as the norm for definitions—turns out on
closer inspection to reflect much broader tendencies in American life, not at all

peculiar to the far more limited occupational sector in question. Take, for instance, the central idea of specialization. No other trend has entered so fully into discussions of professional evolution.[25] Yet in fact a great many zones of the occupational structure have become more highly specialized in the last hundred years. (Who could be more minutely narrowed in terms of function than an automobile assembly line worker?) Again, the existence of a particular lore or technical vocabulary—greatly emphasized by George Daniels in his account of professionalization—is widely found among religious movements and, for that matter, hobby groups. Such carefully hoarded knowledge is apt to surround any intensely pursued interest, not necessarily a formal occupation, creating a special intellectual universe of insiders. Nor does it help to specify that the specialization must ensue from a prolonged training involving nonmanual skills. Such training characterizes many facets of the business community, yet business (despite some recent blurring of the lines) is still excluded from consideration as a profession by the U.S. Census Bureau because it involves the buying or selling of material goods. Such an exclusion can only be a significant carry-over of traditional distinctions based upon social prestige. Even the nonmanual demarcation, itself honorific, is occasionally violated, for instance in the cases of athletes, dentists, and surgeons, all of whom are indeed recognized as professionals by the census.

These ambiguities should make us leery of the further suggestion that professional training is inevitably conducted in university settings, even in the present day.[26] Actors, a group relevant to the humanities, have consistently been classified as professionals by the census since 1880, yet their preparation is not characteristically academic. On the other hand, the arduous and extensive training undergone by artisans and craftsmen does not entitle them to cross over the magic boundary, once again for reasons of inherited social prejudice.[27] It is small wonder that some sociologists throw up their hands and speak of a "continuum" of occupations with respect to professional status, rather than insisting on a neat separation of them into sheep and goats.[28] Yet to take this drastic step is to ignore the great significance historically attached to professional status by men and women keenly aware of the enhanced standing the label does provide.

If specialization and prolonged training are not peculiar to the professions, neither is another trait emphasized in particular by the historian Robert Wiebe—the tendency to identify oneself primarily in terms of one's occupation.[29] Such a characteristic is indeed probably fairly specific to the middle class, but again it is no monopoly of professionals, nor, in all likelihood, of Wiebe's somewhat broader "new" middle class. A small-town businessman may well think of himself continually as a newspaper owner or a used car dealer, purely in the context of his local associations. So for that matter may a farmer, whose physical surroundings are not likely to permit him to forget. Nor can the issue of an occupational self-identification be crucially sealed by the act of attending an annual convention of fellow experts or subscribing to their journals. In the pre-1920 period, only a small minority of the members of such groups as the American Historical Association and the Modern Language Association actually showed up at annual meetings, while on the other hand many kinds of businessmen traveled routinely to regional or national conferences and so did the members of hobby clubs. What is specifically professional about these forms of activity, and indeed about the role played by an occupation in one's waking life, remains indistinct.

In still another direction, professionalism is occasionally confounded with managerialism, a trend that stems from the unique requirements of large-scale organizations and has turned the managers of such entities into members of a would-be profession of its own. But management has nothing to do with the tasks of most other kinds of professional persons, except insofar as they must learn (somewhat like factory workers) to submit to aspects of it when they labor inside organizations. Symptoms of managerialism, centering upon such goals as organizational efficiency, affected the humanities in the period before 1920, both in universities and in the major art museums, but these must be recognized as a distinct phenomenon. The tension that arose between the professor's commitment to his discipline and to his university campus in fact mirrored this very contrast between professionalism and managerialism. Managerialism was at best tolerated by academics who, in the humanities, might respond either with resistance or enthusiasm to changing conceptions of professional life itself.

Sometimes the professions are distinguished from all other occupations by their supposed link with an ideal of social service. Thus Bernard Barber saw as essential to them "a primary orientation to the community interest rather than to individual self-interest," and Alma S. Wittlin spoke of how "a profession enshrines the meaning of a calling and an avowal to a higher purpose."[30] Such language makes us aware of the powerful tendency for academics to read their own undoubtedly high sense of mission into the life-choices of what is actually a very miscellaneous sector of the population. Moreover, among academics, it is usually social scientists—with their specially developed rationale for self-legitimization by means of defining abstract "social needs" and then stepping in to fill them—who construct definitions of professionalism along these lines. In the humanities, and for that matter in the natural sciences, there is more of a tradition of unashamedly regarding one's special intellectual interests as their own sufficient end. As the ideology of universal cultural "standards" has gradually evaporated, an artist or a professor of Sanskrit—indeed very often an historian who spends his energies in the pre-modern period—finds himself put in an awkward position by the notion of social service. The connection can always be rhetorically forged, but it seems oddly abstract and artificial, even as the sense of the overall "professionalization" of norms in such occupations grows stronger.

Missing from the dichotomy between self-interest and social or community interest, as proposed by Barber, is recognition of a third independent source of interest that may frequently be the most compelling of all—the fascination with a particular kind of subject matter. Among automobile mechanics as well as academics, this may easily develop to the point that it becomes an all-consuming obsession, no different in its psychological basis from compulsive participation in tournament bridge playing or political or religious sectarianism. Like divine grace, it is something from the outside that takes over one's mind and from which there is afterward no appeal, short of an effort at "deprogramming." It sweeps the individual—if he is an academic—into a preexisting, enclosed intellectual world, perhaps called American history, Byzantine painting, or the poetry of the Romantics. Mastery of the lore, then some degree of displayed championship at interpreting it before the small, knowing audience of insiders, become the goals lending purpose to one's daily labors.[31] The most important boundary may well be not the formalistic one between so-called amateurs and professionals but the line that divides those whom William James called the once- and twice-born, between those persons of all backgrounds who have become converted to a profoundly sustaining intellectual allegiance of this kind and those others (possibly laboring alongside them in the same academic departments) who have not. The university may be unique for the opportunity it offers to devote a lifetime to such sharply delimited intellectual obsessions in a setting that simultaneously provides high social prestige and relatively generous financial reward. Meanwhile, some drifting academics (content more largely with the external emblems of such prestige or with the psychic rewards of organizational gamesmanship) lead lives of a basically different texture. So perhaps do the members of certain other entire professions; at least a stereotype of this kind, no doubt unfortunate, fastens upon dentists and funeral directors.

When the basic satisfactions one may gain as an adult are seen in the form of this triad of alternatives—centering on personal prestige and income, social mission, or attachment to an absorbing predefined intellectual subuniverse—the vagueness of the concept of professionalism as it applies to motives becomes apparent. Some of the most notoriously venal occupations are counted as professions. So are some of the most markedly anti-social callings—in the sense that they whisk their members away for endless hours into the solitude of the laboratory or the library stacks, usually to work on "problems" of interest only to a handful of the similarly initiated. Then, finally, a number of professions do contain elements—frequently subsections within them—oriented primarily toward a vision of social change. But altruism is a splintery reed on which to fasten the concept of the professions as a whole.

Unrecognized in the recent model for the rise of the professions is a continuing tension between the intellectual life and what is called the professional life. If the image of the professions often conjures up the notion of a trained expert placing his skills at the service of a client, this conception ultimately collides with the ideal of research itself as a free-wheeling activity of the mind that may lead in entirely unpredictable, and not particularly useful, directions. Again, both the humanities and the natural sciences have always contained strong pockets of resistance to the supposition that they must justify themselves in terms of client-centered vocational utility. No doubt for this reason, the circular that announced the first graduate programs at the newly established Johns Hopkins University deliberately spoke of them as offering "advanced (not professional) study."[32] And to this day in the humanities, the word "professional" is not the preferred label of self-identification for a share of intellectuals to whom it connotes an at least faintly undesirable image of technicality, routinization, and above all, divorce of job from self.

At bottom the professions have existed most clearly as a status group. What they offer is enhanced social prestige—a secure position somewhere near the high end of the social pyramid or diamond.[33] Moreover, this remains as true now as in the era of the cultivated generalists over a century ago. This is in fact the great unspoken thread of continuity in the history of the professions. To define their role on some other basis is to exaggerate the degree of rationality in the social order. Acknowledging this, one may then turn to observe the ways in which the professions have participated in the trends toward specialization of activity and the growth of various kinds of insider knowledge, intellectual or technical.

As an overall sector of the society, the professions grew only slightly during the decades before the First World War—rising from 3.78 percent of the mature working-age population in America in 1890 to 4.44 percent in 1920.[34] To gain a more precise understanding of how changes in the professional occupations in this period affected the humanities, one naturally wants to probe beneath this total picture and begin examining particular groups. Unfortunately the Census Bureau labels for them (for instance, professors, teachers, and authors) often make it impossible to discern the humanistic share of their aggregates—a fact that again hints at the tenuousness of the humanities as a unified conception. However, if we look at all the professions relevant either to the cultivated elite of generalists or to the younger, more specialized humanistic fields, we find that in our period only the number of college and university professors and librarians was spectacularly rising as a fraction of the mature working-age population in America. Several other professions partly or entirely humanistic—actors, architects, artists and teachers of art, authors, musicians and teachers of music, and finally, elementary and secondary teachers as a whole—were gaining, but at a much slower rate, while it is notable that the older learned professions—clergymen, lawyers, and doctors—were all static or slightly declining. (See tables 1 and 2.)[35]

In terms of gross statistics, the rise of a new academic sector alongside the older occupations relevant to humanistic learning or expression is the most striking development within the period. The academic boom forms a strong contrast to the undynamic picture revealed elsewhere. While college professors grew to become 0.07 percent of the mature working-age population by 1920, the combined total of clergymen, lawyers, and doctors fell from 1.12 percent of it in 1880 to 0.81 percent forty years later. As one can see, this academicization still produced only a very minor direct share of the overall aggregate within the most relevant professions. Indirectly, as the universities increasingly took over training for a wide variety of prestigious occupations, the impact was undeniably much larger.

What the figures most clearly tell us is that, at least before 1920, great internal

Table 1
Growth of Professions Most Relevant
to the Humanities: Raw Figures

| Professionals | Number of Persons | | |
|---|---|---|---|
| | *1880* | *1920* | *1960* |
| Actors | 4,812 | 28,361 | 9,217 |
| Architects | 3,375 | 18,185 | 30,028 |
| Artists and teachers of art | 9,104 | 35,402 | 101,689 |
| Authors[a] | 1,131 | 6,668 | 27,476 |
| Clergymen | 64,698 | 127,270 | 199,701 |
| Lawyers | 64,137 | 122,519 | 208,696 |
| Librarians | [b] | 15,297 | 84,332 |
| Musicians and teachers of music | 30,477 | 130,265 | 191,004 |
| Physicians and surgeons | 85,671 | 144,977 | 229,671 |
| Professors | [c] | 33,407 | 191,433[d] |
| Teachers[e] | 227,710 | 752,055 | 1,670,810 |
| Engineers | 8,261 | 136,121 | 859,547 |

[a] In 1880 the category also included lecturers and literary persons.
[b] Not separately listed until the 1910 census.
[c] Not separately listed until the 1890 census.
[d] Census classifications in 1960 required adding those persons listed as natural and social scientists (but employed in educational institutions) to those listed as professors, in order to obtain this total.
[e] In 1880 the category also included scientific persons.

changes were occurring within a surprisingly static sector of the American population. The word "growth" may appropriately be used to describe the new organizations that came into being, and of course the population as a whole, but not apparently the share of American energy that was being poured in humanistic directions. Much the same proportion of people, from the same favored social and ethnic backgrounds, were organizing themselves as never before.

The rise of academia encouraged a new style of specialization, such as was occurring in many other professional and nonprofessional areas of American life. The social effect of intellectual specialization was to transfer cultural authority, most crucially over the printed word and over what was taught in colleges to sons and daughters of the elite—away from the cultivated professions considered as an entirety and toward a far smaller, specially trained segment within them, those who now earned Ph.D. degrees (and, eventually, those who gained similar kinds of recognition in the fine arts). Concretely, this meant vesting such authority in a group that, as of 1900, numbered only a few hundred persons spread across the humanistic fields. The immediate effect was thus the intensification of elitism as it was transferred to a new academic basis. A double requirement was now imposed—intellectual merit, at least of a certain kind that was defined far more rigorously, as well as a continuing expectation of social acceptability. The history of the new-style academicization (or, if one insists, the professionalization) of humanistic learning should not be mistakenly confounded with its democratization. At least until the great growth of universities after the Second World War, something like the reverse was true.[36] It is small wonder, then, that some others who did not hold the Ph.D. were made to feel uncomfortable by the new trend which meant, for instance, that no longer would a clergyman or lawyer seem the equal of the graduate-school-trained historian when it came to discussing or writing history.

What from the outside might seem an alarming concentration of intellectual authority appeared to insiders as an exhilarating liberation from past custom. The creation of The Johns Hopkins University in 1876 unleashed extravagant hopes among a small circle of young men who had caught sight of a far more intense version of the intellectual life already under way in Germany and who began to dream that it might now be transplanted into the raw soil of the United States. National pride and an expanding trickle of resources made the transfer possible. A quarter-century later America boasted a dozen academic institutions with first-rate graduate schools. Far more widespread was the transformation of the undergraduate curriculum into departmentalized units, allowing history, English, philosophy, and the most important foreign languages to become recognized as independently legitimate fields of endeavor. (Art and music lagged behind but were well established at most of the better universities and colleges by 1920.)[37] In every one of these disciplines there came into existence a critical mass that could support the founding of specialized scholarly journals, national and regional associations with annual meetings for the reading of papers and convivial contact among the small band who had similar interests, and an advanced teaching apparatus in the form of the seminar. The seminar crucially gained and trained converts for the transmission of the precise lore of the specialty to new generations thereafter.

*Table 2*
*Growth of Professions Most Relevant*
*to the Humanities: Percentages of American*
*Population Aged 25 to 64*

|  | *Percentage of Population* | | |
|---|---|---|---|
| *Professionals* | *1880* | *1920* | *1960* |
| Actors | 0.03 % | 0.06 % | 0.01% |
| Architects | 0.02 | 0.04 | 0.04 |
| Artists and teachers of art | 0.05 | 0.07 | 0.12 |
| Authors[a] | 0.006 | 0.014 | 0.03 |
| Clergymen | 0.34 | 0.26 | 0.24 |
| Lawyers | 0.33 | 0.25 | 0.25 |
| Librarians | [b] | 0.03 | 0.10 |
| Musicians and teachers of music | 0.16 | 0.27 | 0.23 |
| Physicians and surgeons | 0.45 | 0.30 | 0.28 |
| Professors | [c] | 0.07 | 0.23 |
| Teachers[d] | 1.19 | 1.56 | 2.01 |
| Engineers | 0.04 | 0.28 | 1.04 |

[a] In 1880 the category also included lecturers and literary persons.
[b] Not separately listed until the 1910 census.
[c] Not separately listed until the 1890 census, when they formed 0.02% of the population aged 25 to 64.
[d] In 1880 the category also included scientific persons.

The university, beyond doubt, was the single most central institution affecting the humanities in our period.[38] The fact that all the various forms of collective organization fostered by the university—from departments and seminars to study clubs—could gain standing so rapidly and surefootedly, along lines that by the 1890s were already remarkably standardized, revealed the existence of an appetite for the newly defined version of the intellectual life in advance of the concrete containers that were created to house it.[39] (On a far larger scale, we are familiar today with this situation in a reverse sense, when a leveling off in the apparent demand for scholarship once more brings about a disparity between the basic desire to lead such a life and the opportunities provided by society to enter into it.)

These cravings sparked the energies of only a few thousand young men, and a scattering of young women, during the 1880s and 1890s. That they led to such tangible results, solid and self-perpetuating over the next century, in contrast to the burning hopes of the slightly greater number of American socialists at the same moment in time, had much to do with the confidence these particular dreamers were able to inspire among men of great political and financial influence, stemming from the fact that they comprised an only mildly deviant segment of the existing cultivated professional elite. When the degree of deviance suddenly deepened, as among the Greenwich Village Bohemians after 1910, a far more skeptical response developed to the ensuing demands for attention and legitimacy.

The universities immediately began to form the solid backbone of humanistic endeavor in America. But the new academic scene did not monopolize humanistic activity. If we look at what was going on in the relevant fields at all levels, from Chautauqua and the rapidly spreading women's clubs upward into the graduate schools, we glimpse a far more complicated organizational picture. If we add the publishing and performance networks and the public and private school systems, we compound it further. Within each field of effort we find not one world of participation among insiders, but multiple worlds, curiously isolated from each other. The period 1870 to 1920 marks the first great flowering of an organized network of structures involving the humanities in their every phase.

Four major types of organizations may be discerned, coming into existence in profusion. The first group was educational—comprising not just universities, but schools, elementary and advanced, public and private, general and highly specialized (as in the case of art schools and conservatories of music).[40] The second group may be called custodial—consisting of physical repositories for valued objects, such as museums, archives, and libraries. The third group constituted voluntary associations primarily oriented toward meetings or publications, in a few cases devoted to general cultural uplift but more often to particular intense specialties of interest. The fourth might be thought of as the media—the agencies of publication and performance, including publishers of books and magazines, art societies that held exhibitions, art dealerships and galleries, operatic, symphonic, and choral music societies, and theatrical and other booking agents who controlled the distribution of particular cultural events. Of course these several forms of organization were in practice often mixed. A museum might run an art school, a voluntary association such as an historical society might publish learned articles on a regular or an occasional basis as well as hold meetings, and a university might shelter all types of activity simultaneously, though primarily devoting itself to teaching. But this four-fold distinction is highly useful for analysis.

Organizations of all four types had existed before the Civil War, though without the university (as more than an occasional beginning) to spur them on. Except for schools, colleges, and impermanent lyceums, societies with a distinctly cultural purpose were then few and far between. Starting around 1870, the small number of blinking dots across the map of the American high-cultural landscape began to be joined at a rapid pace by much thicker clusterings. The lights continue to flash on with unabated momentum to the year 1920 and beyond. If we mentally assign four different colors to these lights, representing the different kinds of culturally relevant organizations we have identified, the picture of unvarying growth in the numbers of the new foundings is scarcely changed. Only with respect to schools, colleges, and universities after 1910 do we note a diminishing of brand-new creations. An odd fact is that although many of the most prominent learned societies of our own time were established in the period from 1880 to 1905, it turns out that exactly half of the total number of national organizations of this kind in the area of the humanities that were conspicuous in 1960 were founded before 1920.[41]

Such growth is impressive, especially in contrast to the relatively static picture we encountered in viewing the overall place of the professions in American society before 1920. But, keeping in mind that it occurred within a privileged demographic enclave, what were its social effects? At first sight, what stands out is the way in which the cultivated were drawn off into increasingly fragmented channels for the spending of their time. Such Balkanization might operate in the long run to undermine the cohesiveness of the cultivated elite, thereby at least potentially reducing its collective power. The occasions would progressively become fewer when learned men and women would confront the larger public with a single voice. But a deeper look might reveal another, contrary implication. By emphasizing intellectual merit as a necessary further ingredient for success, a section of the elite redefined itself in a way that made its role appear more widely justifiable. However much one might resent the exclusivist claims of Ph.D. holders, the requirements for the degree had been established on a disarmingly rational basis. The new form of advanced academic training thus threw up a facade of democratic opportunity, relatively agreeable to outsiders, whereas in practice such a demanding, prolonged course of study was all but unavailable to the great masses of the population who depended upon the earning power of their sons.

Of course it would be wrong to impute too deliberate a motive of this kind to humanists who accepted specialization. For one thing, it must seldom have crossed their minds that these effects were built into the situation.[42] Only in our present day have these issues of truly open access assumed a clearer shape, at least among ourselves as academics. In those earlier decades, humanists might often speak of the need for greater outreach, for an "uplifting" of the population, but in the context of the gradual trickling down of culture through various forms of education. Among a few of the cultivated generalists in particular, such a message was preached in a style not dissimilar from that of the religious evangelists.[43]

But at the same time, especially in the 1880s and 1890s, humanists of both sorts revealed their underlying appetite for exclusiveness by turning with ever greater enthusiasm to the continental European model of centralized cultural institutions. Indeed in that period they became transfixed by such a model as never before or since.[44] The model suggested a need for creating organizations with a national scope, leading to unity and system rather than to fragmentation. Efforts to implement it could be found in every field except philosophy. In literature, leading New Englanders of an earlier day, including Charles Sumner and Ralph Waldo Emerson, had already dreamed of establishing a national academy along European lines in 1864. It failed in Congress.[45] A body of this kind, the National Institute of Arts and Letters, limited to 250 members, was actually established in New York in 1898 without congressional blessing.[46] Meanwhile, in 1892, Congress did actually establish a National Academy of Art, headquartered in New York, with J. P. Morgan as its president.[47] This academy, not to be confused with the National Academy of Design, led a shadowy existence until it helped sponsor the formation of the American Federation of Arts in 1909. The AFA, in its early years, aggressively embodied these same centralizing hopes, basking briefly in a climate of benign recognition by the federal government.[48] During the 1890s some leading members of the American Historical Association likewise dreamed of turning it into a quasi-official agency, enjoying close relationships with the national government and locating itself at the scene of power in Washington, D.C.[49] Hopes for a centralization of cultural authority lingered as late as 1920, when a committee of the American Oriental Society was studying the formation of a "National Academy of the Humanities."[50] All these organizations would impose "standards," hence offer a kind of cultural equivalent to orderly monopolies in business.

But in fact the peak of such efforts had been reached in the late 1890s with the major push toward the creation of a national university, again in Washington, and when, at the same time, the attempts among language teachers and historians to impose uniform curricula upon the nation's schools (for the benefit of the college-bound segment of their students) reached their height.[51] This was a decisive moment in the history of humanistic organization—and perhaps of academic organization more generally—in the United States. The national university scheme collapsed amid the opposition of existing universities, which by this time could defend themselves as established, effective institutions. Shortly afterward the nation's school systems, increasingly in the grip of a leadership

committed to administrative empire—building and registering open hostility to
cultivation as a major pedagogical ideal—turned away from the recommended
standard curricula and reasserted their own decentralized authority. In the world
of art, the AFA tried to impose standards through its traveling exhibitions but
found itself increasingly bypassed and ignored after the Armory Show of 1913. A
European-style National Conservatory, established in New York in 1892 for the
training of musicians, collapsed after a few years. As the hopes for a unified
cultural establishment crumbled during the Progressive era, it became apparent
that the multitude of cultural organizations would simply go on leading separate
lives of their own—at most sometimes choosing to federate along lines that
emphasized local home rule. When the American Council of Learned Societies
was formed in 1919, it acted as the servant of its component scholarly organizations, not as their director or master.

The centrifugal forces in American cultural life were to win a clear victory by
1920, as measured against the intentions prevalent within the elite around 1895.[52]
At most, an uneasy balance emerged between centralism and decentralism inside
particular fields, and this balance remained a frozen feature of the organizational
landscape thereafter. Only in the 1970s did the new role of the federal government in tne humanities appear to promise a long-delayed movement back in the
direction of centralization.

A large measure of decentralism did not necessarily mean diversity. From
some points of view, the standardized form of these organizations is what seems
most highly striking about them. Whether they were university departments or
faculties, professional associations, or ''amateur'' societies devoted to some
phase of history or the arts, almost invariably they followed the model of a
formal parliamentary democracy, involving reliance upon Robert's rules of order
as interpreted by gentlemen. Their style was the product of the pervasive
liberalism of the nineteenth century, oriented especially toward the concept of a
free marketplace for the display of relevant ideas. Within these terms, the mode
of operation was often tilted toward quasi-aristocratic clubbishness, thereby permitting both the evolution of long-term cliques and their occasional challenge by
factions, personal or ideological, representing interests not given sufficient recognition by the official leadership. But most of the time, the all-important quality
of dignity prevailed. Ritualized internal partisanship, i.e., the flourishing of a
party system, was not thought to be in keeping with the tone appropriate to such
societies, not even to universities as a whole where persistent standpatter and
insurgent groups often suggested incipient informal tendencies in such a direction.

Such standardization of organizational form and style, and such homogeneity
of social background and status of the membership, could easily coexist, as we
have had occasion to emphasize, with intellectual specialization and insulation.
This is the basic paradox embodied in Herbert Spencer's famous formula of an
historical drift from ''indefinite incoherent homogeneity'' toward a new state of
''definite coherent heterogeneity.'' In fact, the latter phrase could well describe

the tendency of organizational life in America as it blossomed in the decades before 1920. Definiteness and coherence pertained to the standardized external forms that came into being, while heterogencity marked the subject matter and, to some extent, the vocational composition of the membership. Segmentation and a certain uniformity thus seemed to go hand in hand.

The impression of uniformity is enhanced by the fact that organizational growth occurred simultaneously in all sectors, from universities and art museums to specialized and nonspecialized voluntary associations and performance agencies. It is sometimes thought that an academic, cosmopolitan world of scholarship was replacing the local, "amateur" world within each field. Actually, both worlds were organizing themselves in proliferating fashion side by side at much the same moment in time. Indeed, the "amateur" (or intellectually less abstract) world was probably growing at a faster rate. A greater number of local historical societies, for instance, were formed after the creation of the American Historical Association, not before.

The organized worlds of participation within the humanities do not in fact always lend themselves very well to classification based on the distinction, originated by Robert K. Merton and emphasized by Robert Wiebe, between the cosmopolitanism of a "new" middle class and the localism of provincial "island" communities. Organizations could be national in scope, as were the federated women's clubs, Chautauqua, and the Daughters of the American Revolution, without thereby acquiring an academic or abstruse image. Yet such societies could share more attitudes in common with professors' groups than is sometimes realized. Consider briefly the DAR, founded in 1890. It was indeed divided into local chapters, though everywhere it possessed a uniform historical orientation of a strongly nationalist kind. But this was an age when most academic professors of history likewise were glad to celebrate the nation's past. The professors and the DAR ladies embraced a common commitment to nationalism and to domestic law and order; indeed the two groups generally came from the same social and ethnic background. If the DAR honored the lineage of individuals, "professional" historians emphasized the collective roots or "germs" that permitted the same kind of pride in an Anglo-Saxon past. Facing forward, both the DAR and the AHA, with their antisectional outlooks, offered a tone basically congenial to modernization. It is far from obvious who had a national perspective, who a local one. Too often we inject our own value preferences into these basic definitions, using such words as amateur and local to brand ideas (such as fervent patriotism) that we presently find distasteful.[53]

In viewing the trend over time, we should remind ourselves that the older cultivated generalists represented the cosmopolitanism of their own day—though they looked toward the Germany of Goethe rather than that of Wundt or Helmholtz. Ralph Waldo Emerson thought of himself not primarily as a resident of Concord, but as a figure aspiring to international prominence in the fields of literature and philosophy. His activities, even on their external side, revealed that local "islands" were already being bridged in the 1860s and 1870s, and in a more concrete way than by the mere spread of books. On his extensive lecture tours, Emerson personally visited with admirers in Midwestern towns and cities, creating cross-regional networks of enthusiasts that sometimes endured for twenty years.[54] All this suggests that a less formal, national cultural configuration predated the American university in its research-oriented form.

In the other direction, at a much later date, academia could go on fostering its own varieties of antiquarian pursuits. The reverence ultimately accorded the Adamses and other prominent New England families approached the genealogical. One guesses that most professors themselves retained a mixture of cosmopolitan and local identities. Only a minority of them published anything more in their lifetimes than their appointments initially required. (It was estimated as late as 1926 that only about 150 persons were actively keeping the entire profession of historical scholarship in America alive through habitual publication.)[55]

Embodying these last realities, a further self-contained network of organizations took shape in the years before 1920, one that has been all but forgotten in accounts of the intellectual life of the period. It consisted of societies—national, regional, or local—catering to teachers in particular disciplines at the high school or college level or both combined. Oriented toward the same subject matter as the well-known associations of academic specialists, these teacher groups were indeed academic—and often, as with the classicists who spawned several such regional bodies, quite convincingly learned—yet not so actively concerned with the advancement of fresh scholarship. They cannot be dismissed as mere educationist groups, however, for they were concerned only with the subject matter of individual humanistic fields.

*Table 3*
*Membership Figures in Several Prominent Humanistic*
*Learned Societies*

| Year | American Oriental Soc. | American Philological Assn. | Modern Language Assn. of America | American Historical Assn. | American Philosophical Assn. |
|------|------------------------|------------------------------|-----------------------------------|----------------------------|-------------------------------|
| 1870 | 192[a] | 163 | . . . . . | . . . . . | . . . . . |
| 1880 | 199[b] | 190 | . . . . . | . . . . . | . . . . . |
| 1890 | 202 | 356 | 312 | 632 | . . . . . |
| 1900 | 288 | 483 | 538 | 1,550[c] | 115[d] |
| 1910 | 285 | 640 | 997 | 2,755[e] | 175 |
| 1920 | 462 | 635 | 1,631 | 2,074[f] | 257 |
| 1960 | 1,022 | 1,400 | 11,000 | 8,400 | 1,718[g] |

[a]Figures are for 1864.
[b]Figures are for 1878.
[c]Approximate.
[d]APA figures are for 1902; there were also fifty-three members of the Western Philosophical Association in 1902.
[e]Figures are for 1911.
[f]No one has adequately explored the reasons for this striking decline; see Higham, *History*, p. 27 (full citation in note 2, p. 90). The start of a transition away from such a heavy nonacademic membership and the appeal of the Mississippi Valley Historical Association for Midwestern Americanists may have been responsible.
[g]The former American and Western associations have since merged into a new APA.

Table 4
Percentage of Members in Several Prominent
Humanistic Learned Societies Who Can Be Identified
as Academics Above the Secondary Level

| Year | American Oriental Soc. | American Philological Assn. | Modern Language Assn. of America | American Historical Assn. | American Philosophical Assn. |
|------|------------------------|-----------------------------|----------------------------------|---------------------------|------------------------------|
| 1870 | 34[a]% | 60% | .... | ..... | ..... |
| 1880 | 43[b] | 60 | ..... | ..... | ..... |
| 1890 | 53 | 70 | 78% | 24% | ..... |
| 1900 | 44 | 79 | 81 | 21 | 90[c]% |
| 1910 | 46[d] | 81 | 83 | 29[e] | 89 |
| 1920 | 46[d] | 80 | 87 | [f] | 92 |

*Note:* Entire memberships were tabulated except for the MLA in 1910 and 1920 (50 percent sample used) and for the AHA in all years (50 percent sample used in 1890, 25 percent sample thereafter). Members were counted as academic if they listed a college or university address (except for librarians, etc.), or if they were shown with "Prof." beside their name, regardless of address (other than identifiable preparatory school addresses). Thus graduate students are counted as academics when listing a university address but cannot be so identified when living at a residential street address. Particularly in later years, therefore, the true percentage of academics is no doubt slightly higher than the figures given. Those listing the title "Dr." or "Ph.D." after their name, but not professor, and with a residential address, are not ordinarily counted as academics. Colleges and universities have been broadly defined to include technical institutes, theological schools, etc., but not private schools of languages. Museum addresses are not counted as academic.
[a]Figure is for 1864.
[b]Figure is for 1878.
[c]Figure is for 1902; in 1902, 83 percent of the members of the Western Philosophical Association are identifiable as academics.
[d]Perhaps one-half the academic membership of the AOS in later years was composed of professors in theological seminaries.
[e]Figure is for 1911.
[f]AHA directories in this period do not permit accurate identification of the members' occupations.

At the same time, the major humanistic learned societies offered no common pattern when it came to the exclusion of nonacademic ("amateur") persons from membership, or indeed with respect to the overall size and scope of the organization. (See tables 3 and 4.) Nor was the trend toward professionalization uniform among them in the period between 1880 and 1920. Generally speaking, the earlier a society was founded, the smaller the percentage of its members who held academic posts, though the percentage gradually rose in all societies. Philosophers, organizing last, were the most close-knit in terms of their academic composition, yet they alone failed to join in a single nationwide association.

Naturally, the rank-and-file membership furnishes only one clue regarding the extent to which these societies were run by academic specialists. Attendance at annual meetings reveals participation at a far more active level of engagement. (See table 5.) No doubt, with the possible exception of the Orientalists and historians, the members who gathered for these affairs were overwhelmingly academic. But, as will be seen shortly, this did not prevent them from interacting in a style that often partook of a gentleman's club. The smallness of all these conventions, even those of the conspicuously larger AHA, as late as the year 1920, must inevitably impress us from our distance. Though the assemblages usually grew somewhat as the decades went on, in this whole period expansion proceeded within easily manageable bounds. At their biggest, these national gatherings were smaller than the freshman lecture classes already being held at Harvard around 1900 in such fields as geology, government, and the fine arts.

Yet, because these learned societies were democracies only in a formal sense, one cannot stop at the level of meeting attendance in the effort to gain a realistic understanding of their character. To be sure, a mistake of the opposite kind can be made by confining ourselves too exclusively to the handful of men, such as J. Franklin Jameson, who were editing their journals. These men were apt to be the most scholarly-minded of the entire spectrum of participants, hence unrepresentative at the farther end. But it is proper to give special weight to the entire group of men who operated perennially behind the scenes, pushing certain policies as they steered their organizations forward. And there is no doubt that, in the main, these men represented the mood of the new academic specialization, placing its imprint upon these societies to a far greater degree than gross membership figures would in some cases indicate.

Nonetheless, a perusal of organizations that developed within the several humanistic fields at the end of the nineteenth century reveals a multiplicity of newly thriving worlds rather than a neat polarity between the amateur and the professional.[56] A rapid tour of these fields, from the point of view of their organization, also demonstrates the way in which specialized expertise appeared within an unchanging elitist social context.

The esoteric subject of Asian languages and literature was the first to achieve something like a "modern" national organization: the American Oriental Society, founded in Boston in 1842.[57] The field was atypical in that it lacked sufficiently wide appeal to spawn diversified popular imitations or teachers' groups. Yet its membership for many decades included figures from high society (Mrs. van Rensellaer was a member in 1920), clergymen and other amateurs (such as

*Table 5*
*Attendance at Annual Meetings in Several Prominent*
*Humanistic Learned Societies*

| Year | American Oriental Soc. | American Philological Assn. | Modern Language Assn. of America | American Historical Assn. | American Philosophical Assn. |
|---|---|---|---|---|---|
| 1870 | ? | ? | ..... | ..... | ..... |
| 1880 | ? | 24 | ..... | ..... | ..... |
| 1890 | 35[a] | 53 | 61 | 108 | ..... |
| 1900 | 49 | 35 | ? | 200[b] | 50[c] |
| 1910 | 45 | 131 | ? | 290 | ? |
| 1920 | 29 | 114 | 145 | 360[d] | ? |

*Note:* These figures appear in the journals of the organizations concerned. Leaders indicate an organization was not in existence at the date indicated. Question marks show it existed, but the figure is unknown.
[a]In 1892; the 1890 figure is not available.
[b]In 1899 and approximate; the 1900 figure is not available.
[c]In 1903 ("over 50").
[d]In 1915, 430 persons attended the AHA meeting, the largest pre-1920 figure I have uncovered.

Ralph Waldo Emerson), along with a surprisingly high proportion of academics even as early as 1864. Except for the religiously oriented Society of Biblical Literature and Exegesis, founded in 1880, the field remained unmarked by further proliferative development.[58]

It was natural that classicists, as a strongly established interest, should begin to organize very early. The AOS created a Classics Section in 1848, and a Greek Club existed among New York laymen who wished to continue reading authors in the original in their spare time. Both antecedents led to the formation of the American Philological Association in 1869.[59] From the first, the APA had a more squarely academic tone than the AOS and an emphasis upon scholarship, often in a somewhat scientistic vein, established itself without challenge.[60] However, though the APA was dominated by classics scholars, it was open to "any lover of philological studies" (there were many papers on American Indian dialects in the early years). So broad an umbrella led to a later subdivision of the field with the APA narrowing itself more clearly to Greek and Latin in the process. Though scholarly, it remained relatively small, clublike, and complacent; by the mid-1880s it was already open to charges of excessive intellectual narrowness. The related field of archaeology was organized into the Archaeological Institute of America, a considerably larger and livelier body.

Classicists were unusually prone to organize as teachers on a regional basis. Far more vigorous and extensive than the APA, these classics associations published journals with considerable scholarly content and brought high school and college teachers together more effectively than was the case in most other disciplines. By the early twentieth century, organization was moving one notch further down into the realm of high school classics clubs, designed to spark enthusiasm among students for what so often seemed a dreary aspect of the curriculum.[61]

The great spread of classics club activity represented the conscious counterattack of a group seeing itself engaged in a fight for survival. Latin was a widely loathed subject, largely confined to a captive audience. (Altogether one finds very few groups of laymen in later life voluntarily banding together to continue study of the texts.)[62] It seems paradoxical at first to encounter such a further proliferation of organizations in such a static corner of the intellectual landscape, even on into the 1920s.[63] But organization may in fact serve a special function when an interest conceives itself to be threatened with hostility and decline. Such a strategy helps foster solidarity and renewed willingness to carry on the campaign. One teacher, "wearied by the heated struggle to defend his subject among unbelievers," found that to arrive at one of the meetings of the Classical Association of the Middle States and Maryland—simply to be in "an assembly where Greek and Latin are in good repute—" was like entering "a cool breeze on a stifling morning. Conference and co-operation," this person added, "have in the last ten years been bringing teachers of the Classics some results.'"[64] It is not inconceivable that these tactics helped Latin study to long avoid a precipitous decline.

The claims of the modern languages, especially English, German, and French, to parity with Latin and Greek go back long before Charles Francis Adams, Jr.

made his famous address attacking the value of the classics, under the title of ''A College Fetish'' in 1883. Professorships of English had been common in American colleges since the 1860s, and of French and German since the late 1870s.[65] The changing general climate in education, as much as Adams's widely publicized speech, encouraged the banding together of about forty modern language teachers, nearly all academics, to found the Modern Language Association of America during the autumn following Adams's bombshell.[66] A motive for its creation was the desire to convince the educated public, nurtured in classicism, that high standards of training and expertise now existed in the modern languages as well as the ancient, and thereby to create the confident climate that would allow modern language study to spread much farther in universities and schools.[67] Thus from the beginning the MLA aimed itself at internal academic goals, avoiding an uncertainty that would long haunt the historians. Its affairs were run by a small number of professors, mainly from Harvard and Johns Hopkins.[68]

Shrewdly, the MLA founders avoided a direct confrontation with classicists. Sensing their growing strength, they took the line that what the curriculum needed was more language study of all kinds. And yet, with classicists breathing heavily upon them, the MLA leaders tended initially to emphasize the arduous character of their disciplines in order that they might seem truly equal with the older ones. It was somewhat the same battle that art and music were to face, though not history or philosophy. Anxieties of this kind, along with very real and apparently unending classroom teaching problems, no doubt contributed to the heavily pedagogical tone of the papers read at the early MLA conventions. By 1903 enough security had been gained to let the MLA define itself as a research-oriented organization, pure and simple. The Pedagogical Section was then disbanded.

The early MLA was cliquish. Informal custom and private initiatives from the officers reigned in place of codified rules to an unusual extent.[69] The eminent habitually attended the small annual meetings and therefore dominated the event with their presence. From almost the first, camaraderie was relished far more than the official program which was put together in a haphazard fashion. Members recalled ''such an air of sociability . . . that the crowd in the lobbies vastly outnumbered the little company of serious-minded persons who dutifully listened to the reading of the papers.''[70] In the very early years, discussions had followed each paper, though much time was spent in them on elaborate, harmlessly courteous, or irrelevant remarks.[71] Eventually the sheer lack of discussion after a paper had been read became painfully conspicuous.[72] A band of bright younger members would regularly cut the president's address to gather in a tavern. Old-timers later recalled ''the venerated smoke talks, the abundant free lunches, the punch bowls, and the free cigars . . . all the new evening dresses, the genial toastmaster and his array of talent, the music and the songs.''[73] The social tenor of the gatherings was elegant to the point of exclusiveness.[74]

In all this, there is much suggestion of a growing slackness of tone, an open awareness that personal relationships and social amenities counted for more than did attempts at intellectual problem-solving. The MLA publications quickly assumed a bulky appearance; it was easy to publish an article or a briefer "note" in them. For long stretches the secretaries would complacently report that the affairs of the Association were "for the most part quiet and uneventful."[75] A professionally based membership clearly meant nothing automatic in the way of work-oriented zeal.

In 1920 John M. Manly of the University of Chicago shook the association with a call to a new style of seriousness, team-work, and specialization, directly imitating the natural sciences. Under his leadership, an array of new, smaller research groups blossomed within the organization. In the next few years, membership and meeting attendance suddenly mushroomed. Some kind of a turning point had been reached in terms of energy, though not in terms of basic intellectual perspective, for the philological direction was now for a time pursued more earnestly than ever before. Seemingly the only choice had been between torpor and scientism.

The unconcern of the MLA with teaching after 1903 and natural desires for a more accessible organizational life led to the proliferation of second-tier societies in the same field as the MLA, for instance, locally in Ohio and in New England. Subject-area specialization then arrived, when the National Council of Teachers of English was founded in 1911. As of 1913, some forty local associations for the study of French were known to exist, mainly in college or university towns, and perhaps consisting of those learning the language as well as their teachers.[76] The more purely pedagogical groups combined to form the National Federation of Modern Language Teachers Associations in 1916.

Literature was a field with far greater popular appeal than Oriental studies or classics. Thus it became one of the major focal points for the simultaneous rise of nonacademic societies and movements. These blossomed on both a local and a national basis, sustaining a series of worlds divorced from the MLA and from the various teachers' organizations. The situation is complicated by the fact that some of the largest "uplift" movements—Chautauqua and the women's clubs, for instance—were broadly interdisciplinary in scope, including all the eventual humanistic subjects, the arts, and civic interests allied to the social sciences.

Strictly literary societies were numerous, however.[77] Enthusiasm for the study of high culture caught fire among a visible segment of the middle class in American cities and small towns during the 1870s and 1880s. Culture on this level was very largely pursued by women. Some were, of course, school teachers; others were the wives of locally prominent professional men. The share of the overall adult American population that engaged in these cultural studies cannot be precisely known, but a reasonable guess places it at between one and three precent. Purely literary endeavors commonly took the form of Shakespeare and Browning societies. Among the liveliest of these organizations—which varied greatly in their aims and tenor—was the Browning Society of Philadelphia. This group rapidly broadened itself into a general literary study organization, meeting every two weeks with a format of oral readings from chosen texts, a musical interlude, a paper, and then a discussion or debate. More intensive study sessions followed these general meetings. While in 1903 debate topics tended to be dutifully mundane ("Was Tennyson justified in his wide departures from the early chronicles"), by 1906 they had become intriguingly bold ("Platonic love, so-called: is it possible between men and women?"; "Would life be meaningless without a belief in personal immortality?"; "Can the puritanical distrust of art be justified?").[78] One has the sense that the Browning Society of Philadelphia in these years represented the spirit of so-called amateurism at its best.

National associations for the study of folklore and dialects were established in the late 1880s, and in the case of the American Folklore Society, gradually won marginal academic respectability. A curious phenomenon was the appearance of a rash of "book clubs," mainly in the larger Eastern cities but eventually in Chicago and Milwaukee as well. A first wave of these organizations had occurred between 1854 and 1869; a second one followed from 1881 into the next century. As organizations these were extremely small and exclusive; the members' wealth must have been great. Their main function was to reprint literary and historical documents in limited fancy editions.[79] Perhaps the same impulse fed into the creation of the Bibliographical Society of America, founded in 1899. Though at first it bridged the book collector world and the institutional nexus of the librarians, as time went on it became increasingly dominated by the former—in a movement contrary to professionalization—and fell into a thoroughly genteel pattern.[80]

The array of literary organizations that mushroomed in late-nineteenth-century America had no common focus, aside from the basic fact that almost all of them drew their members from various sectors of the Protestant upper-middle class. Perhaps no other area of humanistic engagement so well illustrates the variety of impulses that could enter into the creation of similarly structured organizations.

By contrast, the realm of organized historical effort was a good deal more clear-cut, even if it became almost as large numerically.[81] In comparison with English or German, history was a bit slower to arrive as an academic subject, establishing itself in some leading universities only at the end of the 1880s. But it rode the crest of a mounting wave of public interest and support, located within the familiar cultivated elite. By 1889—one year before the DAR was founded— enthusiasm for history, almost invariably in a context of American nationalism, had become potent enough to allow the American Historical Association to receive semiofficial status by an act of Congress.

After its creation in 1884, the AHA rapidly became a far larger organization than the MLA, and for a long time it was quite different in character.[82] Although Herbert Baxter Adams, its original leading promoter, was also located at The Johns Hopkins University, his mind ran to outreach rather than to exclusiveness.[83] Thus, throughout the early history of the AHA, professors were expected to mingle with large flocks of well-heeled laymen inside the organization.[84] Indeed, even at the initial founders' meeting, only a minority of those present were academics.[85] Until after 1907, professors were rarely chosen president. In 1895 a revolt headed by J. Franklin Jameson began to move the AHA onto a more academic course and away from the Washington-centered milieu of Adams. But it was a long wait until the change affected the nature of the rank-and-file membership. Meanwhile, the AHA gained the kind of financial support that was unique for a humanistic learned society—a grant from the Carnegie Institution awarded annually for a period after 1903. The AHA thrived in an atmosphere of unusual security and beneficent recognition. The question was whether enough intellectual vitality entered into the recipe to allow it to live up to its potential.

Genuine issues were indeed at stake in the effort of trained specialists to give direction to the AHA, yet the organization served just as well to illustrate the fundamental compatibility on many levels between the older- and newer-style professional. The MLA, though dominated by scholars, had after all fallen into a complacency of its own from which it had to be rescued. Within the AHA, one finds the same complaints over the dull and perfunctory nature of many of the papers read before it and of the lack of response by the audiences who listened to them.[86] There is the same enthusiasm for the convivial side of the annual meetings.[87] If anything, a greater degree of lavishness marked the AHA entertainments. A purely social "committee of one hundred" was formed to arrange the extensive after-hours receptions held for the members when the group met in New York in 1896. In 1920 we still find the French ambassador playing host to the entire assemblage. That same year the secretary, John S. Bassett, complacently observed that "historical writing has never been a poor man's pursuit, but always a pursuit of the well-to-do or the endowed." His only lament was that so few young men of independent means were studying history in the nation's graduate schools.[88]

In this atmosphere, quite apart from the mix of academics and laymen, an affirmative, agreeable mood prevailed, deeply affecting the intellectual tone. Seemingly nothing was said that would grate against the ears of a comfortably entrenched national elite. When the AHA's official link to the federal government was questioned, the fear was not that it would inhibit adequate intellectual freedom, only that it might dampen the role of the Europeanists. Critical free-ranging debate over interpretations appears seldom to have occurred in the course of AHA meeting programs, though a few voices calling for it could be discerned. Even Frederick Jackson Turner's Midwestern regional chauvinism scarcely ruffled the AHA waters, and, as a result, a separate Mississippi Valley Historical Association was formed in 1907 to harbor plainer (but often still narrower) tastes. Whatever its faults, Charles A. Beard's *An Economic Interpretation of the Constitution of the United States* (1913) is now regarded as the intellectual bombshell of the period. But the papers, discussions, and addresses at the several AHA conventions following its publication gave it almost no attention. Instead they continued serenely to discuss the Revolutionary era—and the whole of American history—from long-established points of view.[89] The outbreak of war in 1914 did occasion a brief flurry of rather vigorous discussion about nationalism, though it was treated as a safely European topic.[90] All in all, the notion of the historian as the soberly noncontroversial balancewheel of the existing social order remained dominant, to the point that the distinct flavor of Progressivism scarcely invaded the proceedings on any level.[91] A few years earlier Woodrow Wilson was reported as declaring from the floor: "A man might as well quarrel with his own nature and that of his ancestors as for the true historian to find fault with the people he attempts to describe.'"[92] Given such a determined avoidance of the open-ended examination of ideas, tensions between so-called amateur and professional in the organization might seem rather beside the point.

If this was the AHA, then one may well imagine the nature of the local historical societies—some four to five hundred of them by 1904.[93] Though a few of them amassed important archival collections and many more maintained museums of a rather haphazard sort, their main tendency was to commemorate nearby ancestral monuments, emphasizing military sites or the dwellings of once prominent families. The scholarship they fostered shaded off rapidly into genealogy. In some Midwestern states, where the societies were run by the government rather than as private voluntary bodies, the tone was more congenial to that of the academic historians. In still other areas, such as the byways of upstate New York, an "historical society" might be nothing more than a group of farmers conducting an annual picnic to swap pioneering reminiscences.[94]

A somewhat distinct impulse produced the great flowering of historically oriented patriotic organizations, most of which came into existence during the one decade of the 1890s. The special character of these groups lay in their fusion of historical interest with an active patriotic ideology and even more in the explicit use of historical criteria to mark off their members as a unique social elite. In theory, anyone could join a local history society, but the patriotic groups made the act of joining the real hurdle. One had to give proof that one's own ancestors had been in America at a given earlier time, or, in some cases, had fought on the American side in one of the wars. The Daughters of the American Revolution became by far the largest of these groups. In these years its political tone was not conspicuously extremist; its similarities with the AHA on some important levels have already been noted. All these organizations, founded so closely together in time, flourished amid the great popular upsurge of interest in American history that became so noticeable in the years just before 1900.[95]

Historical interests, whether engaged in as a profession or a pastime, appeared widely comprehensible, involving little in the way of arcane jargon or intense mental effort aside from drudgery. Among the humanities, philosophy stood at the opposite extreme. As an academic subject, it was not taught below the college level. It labored under an image of forbidding difficulty, but of another kind than was faced by the classic tongues, for it dealt with abstractions at a level that surpassed those of the natural sciences. Closely allied with theology in the longer British and American past, philosophy by the 1880s had become an elaborate effort to deal with religious doubts. Yet few Americans who were struggling with these doubts took the further step of immersing themselves in the writings of Plato, Aristotle, Kant, or Hegel. Only a very small chosen band spent their lives in this peculiarly severe form of intellectual isolation, mastering arduous terminologies that prepared them to embark upon an unending round of mutual disagreements. Paradoxically, to want to think about reality in the most comprehensive and general way was a highly specialized acquired taste.

And yet in 1895 philosophy enrolled 18 percent of all American graduate students as compared with 25 percent in the natural sciences as a whole. The field had become a standard academic department, on a par with history or English. Philosophy departments then included psychology as well. The union of these subjects seemed irksome even in 1900, inasmuch as psychology was already laboratory-oriented and physiological in its approach to the functioning of the human mind. Perhaps the combination resulted from a desire to place such daring empirical thrusts, enormously controversial in their implications, under some degree of control by other men, the true philosophers, who would maintain a framework of reassuring idealism surrounding the psychologists' results.[96] In any event, after a long delay, by 1920 the formal divorce of the two fields had usually taken place.

One might expect that philosophers, as befits those who are committed to an all-absorbing quest for truth, would shrug their shoulders both at high society and at the details of their own external organization. To some considerable extent, this in fact seems to have been the case. A small number of eventually famous Cambridge academics met quietly for private discussion under such labels as the Metaphysical Club in the 1860s and 1870s.[97] There was a long gap between these early unpublicized local gatherings and the appearance of an impersonal professional organization along more or less standard lines. This occurred, though only on a regional basis, with the establishment of the American Philosophical Association in 1901.[98] Membership in the APA was confined to the Northeast; similar regional bodies were founded in the West in 1900 and in the South in 1904. From then on, at least some philosophers became quite willing to think of themselves as members of a profession and lamented the continuing absence of a single national organization to bring them all together on that basis.[99] At the time of the First World War, one member even expressed open disappointment that "no philosopher in his official capacity has been called to the nation's councils."[100]

On the intellectual plane, the elusive promise of the annual APA meetings, at least as late as 1917, was that they might actually bring about agreement on the nature of ultimate truth through deliberation by a committee.[101] Of course in actuality, philosophy had developed into a field characterized by peculiarly deep-seated internecine disputes, mitigated only by genteel norms of address.[102] What groups such as the APA truly offered was a forum for the individual display of intellectual manifestoes. As George Santayana, briefly a member of the APA, shrewdly observed at the time, "professional philosophers are usually . . . absorbed in defending some vested illusion or some eloquent idea. Like lawyers or detectives, they study the case for which they are retained, to see how much evidence or semblance of evidence they can gather for the defense, and how much prejudice they can raise against the witnesses for the prosecution. . . . They do not covet truth, but victory and the dispelling of their own doubts."[103] Beneath their hefty layers of insider technicalities, philosophers could indeed function like other men. But what set them apart from historians and linguists was their passionate self-identification with highly abstract thought. In large measure they were still the heirs of the nineteenth-century theological tradition.

From the printed abstracts of papers and from the absence of any descriptions of social events, one imagines that the philosophers' annual meetings were quite unlike those of the AHA or MLA—not only much smaller but far more solemn.[104] And yet from the retrospect of a quarter-century, a participant could phrase his judgments of their value along surprisingly familiar lines. "We should have to admit that the papers have not always added greatly to our insight and that discussion has at times seemed footless and fruitless. We have frequently been more bewildered than illuminated and sometimes, I have no doubt, we have felt frankly bored or irritated." And yet, this writer went on to assert, the lone individual and the social group have a "reciprocally stimulating and beneficial influence. If so, the Association has measurably filled its function. Something, too, I am sure, has been gained by the cultivation of friendly personal relations . . . ; we are far from all thinking alike, but our coming together has conduced to understanding, to tolerance, to liking and to respect."[105] Perhaps this last statement in its own way disguised a wish.

In philosophy there was no vast laymen's realm of participation such as sprang up around the other disciplines, unless one counts certain sectors of organized religion. What did exist followed a very different timetable from the one in history. In a few scattered locations—notably St. Louis; three Illinois sites, Jacksonville, Quincy, and Chicago; Osceola, Kansas; and later, Concord, Massachusetts—philosophical study clubs or "schools" came into existence. But these tended to appear early, often before the Civil War, and to die out by the 1890s. Usually they centered around a single magnetic leader—in various instances a doctor, a lawyer, an army general, the wife of a land speculator, a laborer turned politician, and the unclassifiable Bronson Alcott. The entire group would be pulled in the direction of the leader's consuming interest, usually in Hegel or Plato. In this context, "study" verged on a quasi-religious commitment. Some laborious scholarship arose from these circles, but it tended to be pedestrian from a later academic standpoint—even though so many of the first generation of academic philosophers were committed to a version of Hegelianism in much the same near-religious spirit.[106] The so-called St. Louis movement, which actually involved a long succession of clubs in that city from the 1850s until the last survivor expired in the 1930s, was by far the most important manifestation of this kind.

If philosophy comprised the most austere world within the humanities, the fine arts—by the close of our period—represented an arena of unusually wide participation. From rather small beginnings at the time of the Civil War, art and music grew to occupy a highly visible, or audible, place in American life. The realm of art alone became exceedingly complex, offering another major illustration of the multiplicity of mutually separated worlds that could coexist under a single commonly accepted covering label. Art reached out to touch a whole variety of American institutions. It was in part an academic study, a business, an activity of government (as in city planning), a widespread component of elementary and secondary school curricula, a preserve of museums and private collectors, a focal point for enthusiastic lay participation analogous to that in literature and history, and, finally, a vocation requiring arduous training, often in distinctive schools established solely for that purpose. Further, it was subdivided into several major forms of expression—painting, drawing, sculpture, and architecture—that led quite different lives. In some sense, every American was a consumer of it when he bought a china cup at Woolworth's or tacked a calendar on his wall. History and literature (beyond the Bible) were far easier to avoid.[107]

In the 1860s the paucity of art, even in the sense of consciously intended design, much less of paintings, exhibitions, and museums, was a marked feature of life in the United States.[108] Yet the 1870s—the same decade that brought the initial decisive moves toward the American university—saw a sudden art boom in the urban centers.[109] Several of the most important museums were founded between 1869 and 1879. Art schools instantly multiplied in answer to a new demand. Original paintings began to become popular for the first time in striking contrast to the indifference shown them even in New York just a few years earlier. The Philadelphia Centennial exhibition of 1876 played an important role in developing this appetite, which should be understood as almost totally uninformed in qualitative terms. However, within the next twenty years a distinct version of "good taste" developed, solidly in alliance with the values of the genteel tradition and producing a new certainty about "standards." Meanwhile, no doubt due to the improvements in trans-Atlantic travel and the consequent rise of tourism among the wealthy, the European art of earlier centuries began to be discovered, and its collection, both by museums and by private individuals, quickly became a major enthusiasm.[110] Starting in the 1880s, and to a full degree in the 1890s, such "great" art acquired an extraordinary degree of prestige, establishing itself as a secure component of high culture alongside the literary traditions preached in the colleges. At the very top of the pinnacle, J. P. Morgan sought to "corner" the art market in exactly the same way as he did railroads and steel. The Metropolitan Museum of New York became his creature.

By the opening of the twentieth century, the upper reaches of the American art world took on the tone of an entrenched establishment. There was the same sense as in Europe, only somewhat milder, of an array of powerful organizations enforcing conventional standards, blocking upstarts who might have unfashionable ideas.[111] In New York the National Academy of Design tried to control the scene, not just by choosing its own members (125 recognized painters, 25 sculptors, and 25 architects or engravers, who were called "academicians"), but by enforcing a jury system for the all-important decisions as to whose work would be hung in public exhibitions.[112] After 1909 the American Federation of Art in Washington stood for the same academistic values.[113]

Irving K. Pond, president of the American Institute of Architects in 1911, provided one of the most clear-cut statements of the philosophy underlying this entire artistic establishment. Art must represent the spirit of "the race," that is, the nation. "The traits of [individual] personality are of the accidentals or incidentals which art ignores." A genuine artist will not "search for something outside of his time and environment, something which shall startle the race and give it a thrill, but for some deep sentiment, for some characteristic note, which, being sounded, the race shall by sympathetic vibration recognize as its own and receive to its heart, for, like the Lord, the race is mindful of its own!"[114] The American race evidently vibrated to the Roman. Official art was civic, classical. Radical art was individual, romantic. Despite some who wavered or compromised, the stage was set for a sharp polarization.

It might seem that the quiet world of museums was immune to such emerging conflicts. Their story appeared to be one of simple if rather amazing growth. Where practically none had existed in 1870, by 1920, some 120 art museums were listed in the *American Art Annual*. A small number of these had become true giants. Organization of the museum managers inevitably ensued; the American Association of Museums was formed in 1906, claiming 263 members ten years later.[115] These men struggled to establish their dignity against the threat of trustees who might ignorantly intervene in basic decisions about the kind of art objects to collect, the often imperious demands of wealthy donors, and the somewhat different expectations of city governments that provided a degree of tax support to all but a few of the large museums. Local industrialists also had an interest in museums, linked to their utilitarian efforts to improve the design of products. These were the most conspicuous outside forces affecting the daily lives of the museum staffs, beyond the tide of visitors on the day or two per week when, according to usual arrangements with the cities, admission was free.[116]

Museums, like state universities, were forced to pay frequent obeisance to the rhetoric of democracy. In general, a utilitarian and civic orientation developed among the managers, who dedicated themselves less to art than to the running of a certain kind of service institution. (Thus those associated with both science and art museums joined the same professional organization, resisting efforts at separation even after a new Association of Art Museum Directors was founded in 1917.)[117] The "treasure-house" concept of a museum repelled these managers; it smacked of European effeteness and conjured up the still worse image of the mausoleum.[118] Instead, these men regarded high attendance figures as a basic measure of achievement and contrived all sorts of devices for luring ever greater numbers of the public. Educational programs, such cultural events as concerts deliberately held within the museums, classes for children—all had such a function. In Chicago the major museum went so far in this direction as to threaten to become a kind of circus.[119]

If in all these respects the art museums oddly remind us of public school systems, their contrary pull was toward the ostentation and frequent preciosity of high culture. Thus museum ideals could become the focus of lively controversy, carried on not by the broad specturm of managers but by articulate spokesmen at the extremes. Benjamin Ives Gilman, director of the Boston Museum of Fine Arts, forthrightly expressed a devotion to culture in a form that elevated aestheticism, defiantly endorsed the "treasure-house" image, and registered quite open contempt for the ordinary public. It is curious how automatically, in Gilman's thinking, an unashamed primary regard for artistic beauty went along with unabashed social snobbery. "Fine art has always been associated with the lives of those who have had exceptional opportunities . . . for seeking to make themselves personally agreeable one to another," he declared. "Our museums are right in allying themselves to Society spelled with the capital S."[120] At the opposite extreme, John Cotton Dana of Newark poured scorn on the standard assumptions of art collecting and display that dominated the period. American museums were gloomy palaces, set off in parks distant from the urban masses. "Their buildings are remote and are religious or autocratic or aristocratic in style; their administrators . . . are inclined to look upon themselves as high priests of a peculiar cult . . . and the trustees are prone to think . . . more of preservation than of utilization." Daring to attack the fashion of importing art works from abroad, Dana identified himself with the struggles of young contemporary American artists and craftsmen whose pictures he proudly hung. Museums, he said, must relate themselves closely to "life."[121]

Contrary as they might seem, Dana and Gilman shared a fundamental commitment to some of the central assumptions of the cultivated elite. Dana paused in his diatribe to remark that "a certain refinement of daily life is worth all its costs," and that museums should help the people "to appreciate the high importance of manners, to hold by the laws of simplicity and restraint, and to broaden their sympathies and multiply their interests."[122] The difference was that Dana would genuinely crusade for culture among the people—to be sure, also somewhat redefining its content toward the contemporary—while Gilman represented the same ideal on its inward-turning side. And no matter how the museum managers may have been divided in their attitudes, all of them could be found taking part in the expected rituals of their social peers.[123]

The varying worlds within art could embrace civic or vocational utilitarianism as well as liberal high culture.[124] The independent art schools were narrowly vocational, though appealing to a genteel kind of student.[125] Inside the universities, research aspirations became added to the mix. A scientist orientation in art study was not unknown.[126] Though the history of art, as an academic field, was somewhat hampered by its dispersion among departments of fine arts, classics, or archaeology at different institutions, and by continuing vagueness as to method, it had gained a distinct toehold on leading campuses by 1920.[127] No national scholarly organization came into existence in the realm of art comparable to the MLA or the AHA, but the College Art Association of America was founded in 1912 to serve undergraduate teachers in the subject. Although it gave voice to diverse viewpoints and was recalled as lively, its leadership spoke in the usual tone of the high cultural establishment, saying their mission was to supply "an authoritative voice" in an age when "new cults arrive . . . and opinions change with bewildering swiftness." Against these unsettling challenges, it would endeavor to hold the line.[128] The CAAA counted 220 members in 1919. Below it, some forty local high school art teachers' associations were known to exist in 1912.[129]

Professional artists ultimately found it logical to organize themselves along specialized lines—no doubt in part for solid business reasons. Thus by the teens we find not only the Association of American Painters and Sculptors, but an American Water Color Society, a National Association of Portrait Painters, a National Association of Women Painters and Sculptors, a National League of Handicraft Societies, and a Society of Illustrators. These groups only begin to exemplify the list of societies attempting to achieve national status.

On a broader level, the proliferation of art societies was considerable, even if one counts only those holding regular meetings as distinct from the purely formal corporations that ran local museums. Around 260 of the active kind found their way into the *American Art Annual* for 1908–1909, which attempted a comprehensive list.[130] By the mid-teens, college campuses were spawning a number of art clubs formed by students, instructors, and interested nearby laymen.[131] In addition, a 1910 study showed that about one fifth of the women's clubs throughout the nation devoted some degree of special attention to art among their other activities. Twenty-one statewide art committees owned travelling galleries to carry art to the hinterlands.[132] The AFA tried to incorporate the local art societies all over the nation as chapters; by 1914 it had 200 of these. The indifference of 1860 had been transformed into a beehive of complex activity. For all this, the organized art world remained smaller than the mushrooming world of historical societies, but it was far more complicated and a good deal livelier. Even though it partook of the nature of a genteel establishment, confining itself to the same segment of the population that might also choose to study history or literature, the very visibility of art may have given it a more active role in the imaginations of those who pursued it, engaging the emotions more easily on a continuing basis.

In music the identification of cultural organizations with high social status reached its peak. Extra-musical considerations loomed large in the consumption of music, whether in the worship of the star performer, the conversational distractions of the hall (which in these decades could reach noisy levels during a concert), or the social importance attached to the act of attending any of the hundred symphony orchestras or handful of opera companies founded in America by the end of 1919.[133] The music world was keyed to a narrower base of support, at least at its top end, than the world of art. Though less dependent upon philanthropy (or upon local government subsidy), in view of the far greater potential for income from the daily box office, musical organizations were if anything more firmly under the control of high society in the various cities.[134] Already by the 1860s the New York Philharmonic had become socially fashionable, though from the 1880s until at least the teens it was overshadowed in these terms by the opera. The Metropolitan Opera fell under the unrelenting grip of the reigning social elite in the narrowest sense. J. P. Morgan vetoed a performance there of the supposedly risqué *Salome* in 1907, and influential ladies were able to banish Wagner on the nights when they would attend. The very design of the opera house maximized the space available for boxes owned by the wealthy at the expense of the working needs of the performers. When Judge Elbert H. Gary died, his box was sold in 1924 for two hundred thousand dollars.[135]

And yet musical organizations, as they developed in this period, revealed the familiar shift toward technicalized insiderism that is often called professionalism. The dominance of the symphony signaled its advance, since the earlier popular choral societies had usually offered an outlet to lay participation, not so clearly distinguishing between the roles of performer and audience. The shift from choral singing to symphony listening never became complete, but by 1920 there was an absolute diminishing of the choral groups.[136] In practice, a relatively small world of high-quality music performance was sharply divorced from the far vaster worlds of music education and of small-town talent and private lesson-giving.[137]

Musical organizations grew to become by far the most numerous within any of the humanistic fields. By 1924 the National Federation of Music Clubs counted 1,934 member societies, along with 718 "junior" groups. Even without the preadult segment, this was several times the number of art societies existing at roughly the same time.[138] At the college level, music had frequently been introduced but not without controversy. Many institutions were willing to give credit for theoretically or culturally oriented music courses, but not for so-called "applied" courses—that is, in the learning of an instrument. In 1919 at least 203 universities and colleges offered a special Bachelor of Music degree. As of 1908, only about half the students in these programs, or in the independent music schools that flourished alongside them, had completed three years of high school before entering.[139] Thus the same split developed, as in art, between the academic, or culturally motivated, kind of study and the narrow technical training for pursuing a vocation. The only broad organization that tried to bind the diverse world of music education together was the Music Teachers National Association, founded in 1876 with initial strength in the Midwest.

This tour of the various fields can no more than suggest some of the principal forces at work during the great spread of humanistic organizations in the half century before 1920. It was a proliferation that proceeded simultaneously on many levels—involving academic fields of scholarship, college teacher organizations, societies of practicing artists and music lovers (themselves often formed along minutely specialized lines), and laymen's groups reflecting widely differing degrees of sophistication. And yet we must again remind ourselves that the whole of it took place within a basically unchanging minor fraction of the total American population, encompassing probably well under 3 percent of the American adults who were then alive.[140]

This elite had attempted to gain cultural hegemony throughout the United States. It had sought to impose its own sense of "standards"—moral, academic, and social—upon the vast remainder of the citizenry, at the very time when three-quarters of the inhabitants of major American cities were first-generation immigrants or their children. We saw that its efforts to found a centralized network of organizations geared to such a role met with decreasing success after the 1890s. But it remains to be seen how the elite weathered certain larger challenges to its authority toward the close of the period.

In *The End of American Innocence,* Henry May portrays these challenges in vivid terms. He pictures the cultural establishment, guarding its fortresses so diligently as late as 1910, as then being rapidly overthrown in the years between 1912 and 1917 by a whole new cultural wave.[141] The wave is epitomized by the sudden eruption of a highly rebellious younger generation, surfacing in Greenwich Village and more briefly in Chicago, which announced its liberation from the norms imposed by the existing custodians of high culture.

As seen by its protagonists, this episode indeed amounted to a revolution—in more recent vocabulary, the launching of a counter-culture, on a par with similar movements that occurred in the 1830s among Transcendentalists and again in the 1960s on a far greater though more short-lived scale. All three upheavals were centered intellectually in the humanities, though all involved a tone of political and moral radicalism that went beyond them. All displayed an intense hostility toward established institutions and organizations, which were believed to be drenched in corruption. Yet, despite the lure of a nonattached, free-lance vision of life, this mood was balanced by a frequent willingness to create alternative organizations, often far more mundane than utopian communities.[142] In each case, a share of the well-educated elite broke away from its elders to embrace values that were abstractly democratic, while continuing to function in many respects as a segment of the elite itself.[143]

Though innovation and creative freedom of expression were among the central values promoted by the rebels, such ideals were scarcely brand-new; ultimately they stemmed from the European romanticism of the early nineteenth century. Whitman and Emerson became the saints of a local American tradition of this kind, but, as Henry May has abundantly shown, the transmission of a new cultural wave from Europe, centered in such figures as Nietzsche and Freud, was an extremely important source of Greenwich Village ferment in the early decades of the twentieth century. In the fine arts even more than in literature, the focus at the time of the Armory Show was one of proclaiming the latest European styles rather than promoting a new movement among American artists. (American painting did not gain world stature until the 1940s, roughly a century after the same degree of achievement in literature.)

The key counter-cultural organization in this transmission process was a small art gallery on lower Fifth Avenue in New York, named Photo-Secession, begun in 1905 by the photographer Alfred Stieglitz; it was listed thereafter alongside all the staid art societies in *American Art Annual* directories. From the standpoint of the artistic avant-garde, Photo-Secession was for a few years the most important cultural organization in America, eclipsing in significance the entire range of establishment institutions, including even the universities. It was here that radical contemporary European art, of the kind that has since shaped the sensibilities of most educated people, was first displayed publicly in the United States.[144] Stieglitz in turn was among the major promoters of the Armory Show, which in 1913 brought on something like a civil war within the American artistic community.[145]

The opening guns on the conservative side had been sounded in 1909 by Sir Caspar Purdon Clarke, J. P. Morgan's hand-picked director of the Metropolitan Museum, who declared: "There is a state of unrest all over the world in art as in all other things. It is the same in literature as in music, in painting, and in sculpture. And I dislike unrest." To which Stieglitz replied that the Metropolitan exuded the atmosphere "of a cemetery dedicated to the dead rich."[146] When Adeline Adams visited the Armory Show to report on it for the American Federation of Arts, she used such adjectives as "blasphemous," "barbaric," and "decadent," maintaining that American art had "no place whatever for antique corroding neurasthenias spewed out of European capitals."[147] Four years later the AFA was still fuming editorially at the likes of Picasso and Matisse, calling them "a group of madmen who . . . willingly and deliberately chose to interpret ugliness rather than loveliness, deformity instead of perfection. That some of these men were really insane was no secret and yet even so they found followers."[148] Never before had antagonisms within the American cultivated elite grown so shrill, not even in Paul Shorey's laments over the decline of the classics. The world of taste was torn asunder into two sharply defined parties, with little blurring of the lines between them until after the Second World War.[149]

The modernist camp mounted other organizations of its own, apart from Stieglitz's circle. A new rebel group, the Association of American Painters and Sculptors, seceded from the National Academy of Design in 1912. Its members, though diverse, registered a common impatience with museums, dealers, and critics, and it became the official sponsor of the Armory Show the next year. The AAPS melted away thereafter, but in 1915 a group of socialist artists founded the People's Art Guild, and in 1917 a Society of Independent Artists was formed to try to keep alive the innovating spirit. It announced that it would abandon juries, award no prizes, and hang paintings at its exhibitions democratically—in alphabetical order.[150]

In a broader sense, the ferment of the teens brought a new awareness of a fundamental division in the American cultural landscape. Previously there had been only the forces of uplift versus the counter-tendencies of ignorance and indifference. Now for the first time some of the most sophisticated and well-educated people began to use "academic" as a term of reproach. The arrival of an avant-garde provided the altered perspective that enabled such concepts as "highbrow" and "lowbrow" to come into being, implying that a certain detachment was possible from both of them.[151] The more pedantic forms of humanistic scholarship would thereafter have to defend themselves not simply against the genteel amateurism of Charles Eliot Norton or Barrett Wendell but against an antitraditional outlook that elevated literary and artistic expression as a contemporary, perhaps even spontaneous, act, while reserving for Germanic facthunters in graduate schools much the same imagery that Stieglitz applied to museums.

The rebellion was aggressive; it was real. But it masked more of a capacity of the older world of high culture to survive, and indeed numerically to keep on growing, than is allowed by the metaphor of assaults upon fortresses. In a literal sense, though key magazines were taken over by forces friendlier to innovation,[152] the institutions that symbolized the older cultural establishment lived on and on. The historian of the highly conservative National Academy of Design writes that long after the First World War its exhibitions and its art school continued "as if nothing had happened to disturb their serenity."[153] The same might be said of a great variety of agencies of genteel humanism as the twentieth century unrolled. Per capita, there would be quite a bit more attention paid to classical music, to Shakespeare, and to the earlier masters of European painting in 1960 than in 1910.

Thus, if the pre–World War I establishment of polite culture and humane scholarship did not triumph in the manner expected by its centralizing leadership of the 1890s, neither did it disappear. Rather, it clung to life—in some areas vigorously thrived—inside the universities and to a lesser extent in the museums and the various learned societies. For its part, the avant-garde world moved ahead in fits and starts; in the 1920s, for instance, it ran into unexpected doldrums in the fine arts.[154] The result was a curious standoff, characteristic of the twentieth-century climate so often vaguely labeled "pluralistic." There was room enough for everyone. No one gained a clear-cut victory. Neither the optimists nor the pessimists of the teens were quite capable of imagining this undramatic outcome, whereby the several cultural miniworlds—ultimately joined by such popular new forms as jazz—would simply go on existing side by side, marked by compartmentalized isolation and intermittent mutual disdain. Culture shifted away from the realm of public, would-be national institutions, housed in buildings with Roman columns and openly claiming a superior status that was as much social as intellectual. It moved into the far more private stamping ground of individual taste and free choice—though invidious socioeconomic and ethnic distinctions quietly survived as such choice was exercised. A certain degree of grudging tolerance was slowly emerging from a situation, resembling the much earlier one in American religious history, when men of traditionally hostile ideologies were forced to live in close mutual proximity.

In the process, the well-established position of the universities immeasurably strengthened the continuities, blurring the impact of the changes. At the same time the role of the universities on their humanistic side somewhat altered, primarily because they failed to change as rapidly as the larger scene around them. Before the First World War, the European traditionalism of their humanistic subject matter had been somewhat disguised by the ethos of innovation arising from the very act of creating these institutions. Starting in the 1920s, the universities emerged more nakedly as the guardians of tradition in these disciplines. No matter that the classics had been so largely lost. There was suppleness in the universities' maneuvering, registering itself in the shift to translations that was achieved when a survey course in Western civilization was inaugurated at Columbia during World War I, setting a pattern that became widely imitated from then on. This change signaled an ability to adjust where absolutely necessary while holding onto the main goal—the communication of what were believed to be the essentials of European high cultural values.[155] By the mid-twentieth century, the universities would remain the most prominent fortresses of high culture, even if they moved to incorporate some elements of the avant-garde as well, as that too became a more accepted part of the grand tradition.

If this, very broadly, was where the cultural elite was heading, one wants finally to ask questions about its basic intellectual achievement. In particular, what did American humanistic scholarship of this era, the fruit of the new style of specialization, actually add up to? How major were its successes in these decades before the First World War? Would the body of this scholarship be greatly missed if it were suddenly to vanish from our library shelves? From some points of view the last question may seem inpossibly audacious. Can one generation judge another without imposing its own equally arbitrary biases?[156] Yet there are strategies whereby such an appraisal can be attempted on a basis more objective than random impression.

First, it is clear that, both quantitatively and structurally, American humanists of the period had laid an indispensable foundation for further development of their fields. This base did not merely consist of the universities, museums, and all the specialist organizations that have been alluded to previously; in a more precise sense, as regards scholarship, it was embodied in the fifty-eight or more learned journals that were founded in the area of the humanities and fine arts through the year 1920.[157] These publications comprised an available, dramatically visible series of repositiories for the best thinking that future generations of scholars could muster. Thus their very existence as permanent outlets counted for something important, quite apart from whatever value one chooses to place upon their pre-1920 contents.

The same might be said of those agencies established to foster humanistic research, independent of particular universities. Research institutes relevant to the humanities actually date from the founding of the American School of Classical Studies at Athens in 1882, at Rome in 1895, and (temporarily) at Jerusalem and Baghdad in 1900. These organizations very early allowed advanced students in classics, art history, and archaeology the opportunity to spend a year of full-time study amid the material remains of the ancient world.[158] At the close of the period, the creation of the American Council of Learned Societies, albeit on a hastily improvised and rather uncertain basis, promised some degree of comprehensive support for humanistic scholars in the future.[159] A start had been made, at least, toward recognizing such needs, though the days of major foundation grants for fellowships still lay ahead.

But what of the quality of humanistic scholarship in this era? One way of assessing it is to try to determine its impact upon the international scholarly community of the day. In the field of classics, such a yardstick is conveniently available. In 1908 John Edwin Sandys, an Englishman, produced a conscientious compendium summarizing the contributions made to classical scholarship on a country-by-country basis. In a volume of 470 pages, the American contribution was accorded 20 pages. In a condensed table of important scholarly names, Germany and Austria together received half the space, and France and England 15 percent each; Italy and the United States then followed with about 5 percent each, and other countries had still lesser amounts.[160] Such concrete allocations of notable results in national terms are unfortunately lacking in most other fields. But as regards English philology, Harrison Ross Steeves found it sufficient in 1913 to append a single thirteen-page chapter on American scholarly organizations to a 217 page book that otherwise dealt entirely with their English equivalents. As Steeves asserted: "It is not to be expected that the activities of learned societies in the United States should produce results to be compared in a large way with those secured by such societies in Great Britain." Pointing to the geographical isolation of Americans from the textual sources, and to their much more indirect identification with "English literary activity," he concluded that American groups worked "along lines subordinate to or collateral with the labors of European scholars." Further, he detected a recent decline in the interest shown among American professors in the history of the English language.[161] A similar unfavorable judgment of American historical societies was made by Waldo G. Leland in 1909, on the basis of a look at their European counterparts. "A striking difference between the foreign societies and those of America," wrote Leland rather wistfully, "is the greater part played by the national Governments in their direction. In wealth and membership the American societies are perhaps rather better off than those of Europe, but in the production of useful material systematically planned and edited with a high degree of scholarship they are undoubtedly far behind."[162] From these several observers, we receive an impression that American humanistic scholarship, while it certainly counted for something, was as yet a rather minor element on the larger world stage. By 1920 America had become a newly flourishing province of Europe in these terms, though with the capacity for eventual independence and leadership.

A second quite different avenue toward an assessment is offered in the treatment of pre-1920 scholarship by later American researchers in the same disciplines. Such appraisals may be divided chronologically into two kinds: those made not long after the end of the period, looking backward; and those made from the vantage point of roughly our own time. The former are noteworthy for their negativism. Writing in 1931, Dixon Ryan Fox was impressed by the general mediocrity of American scholarship in the early twentieth century.[163] Frederic A. Ogg, surveying the scene broadly in 1928, declared:

The meagerness of first-rate American contributions to philosophy, philology, political science, and even history and economics—although the showing is somewhat better in these two fields—plainly reveals the immaturity of our culture. Plenty of research work, of a kind, is all the time in progress. Quantitatively, there is little ground for complaint. But a considerable proportion of the studies undertaken are ill-planned, crudely executed, and barren of significant result. Serious and competent scholars notoriously lack time and means for carrying out important projects. Methods of investigation are imperfectly developed, and fields capable of contributing richly to one another are not adequately linked up. The public has little appreciation.[164]

It is possible to discount these opinions as stemming in part from the frustration inevitable among earnest idealists. They can be balanced by cheerful onward-and-upward accounts written of the development of particular disciplines and departments. But sweepingly optimistic assessments of the academic scene rather than of single fields are notably rare.[165] Instead, it is the sense of letdown after the high hopes surrounding the initial creation of the American university that predominates as one moves into the years after the First World War.[166]

There is no doubt, however, that a half-century interval allows for a somewhat cooler measure to be taken. In this regard, it is fortunate that the series of Princeton Studies in Humanistic Scholarship, published in the mid-1960s, provides abundant source material for such a retrospective impression.[167] The key question is how many pre-1920 American names are still found worthy of mention by later scholars reviewing achievements in the same fields. The answer is surprisingly uniform, especially in view of the diversity of approaches taken by the different authors. A handful of pre-1920 names nearly always appears, regardless of the subject, and in only a single field (Russian literature) are there none at all.[168] These names may sometimes be mentioned with great respect; at other times they are slipped in condescendingly as barely worthy of citation from a later vantage point. But again and again, in small numbers, they recur.

In broader terms, the dozen or so authors in the Princeton series commonly leave us with a strong sense of satisfaction over recent improvements in their fields. Regarding English literary scholarship, for instance, David Daiches declares that "the work done on all three authors [whom he has reviewed, namely, DeQuincey, Pope, and Gray] by American scholars and critics in the last thirty years or so is altogether more substantial and more interesting than that done in the preceding thirty or forty years. . . . On the whole, the books and articles on the three authors that were produced in the earlier period are both duller and less central."[169] Similar judgments are made, though often less explicitly, by a number of other authors in the series.[170] Only in Oriental literature (particularly Sanskrit) does one gain the impression that American scholarship may actually have been stronger and more meritorious around the turn of the century than later on.

Viewed in the long run, the value of pre-1920 American humanistic scholarship appears to center upon fifty or sixty names.[171] These, at the least, comprise the figures from the earlier period who are still remembered for their broad contribution to creative activity in the various relevant disciplines. Naturally, the list would be greatly expanded if it took into account the scholars who remain valued for their incidental contributions to highly specialized research topics.[172] But, in the other direction, it would doubtless be narrowed further if it were confined solely to those people whose books or essays one could now confidently assign as reading in a typical undergraduate course (excluding, of course, authors treated as primary sources in history courses). So perhaps it represents a tolerable median yardstick of appraisal.

It will be interesting to compare this number of names against a similar list for the period 1920–70, a task that should be feasible not too long after the turn of the twenty-first century. Meanwhile, such a figure at least permits us to conclude that in the decades before the First World War, the humanities did establish themselves in a modern academic sense on more than a flimsy or marginal basis. If the collective trend toward a newer style of professionalism in the humanities was in some respects ambiguous, being so highly colored by its ties to a mood of exclusivist social pretension, the narrower effort to attain first-rate individual scholarly achievement was far from a total loss.

Finally, one might ask whether there would have been these fifty or sixty names without the existence of the organizations that had sprung into being alongside them. One such organization, the university, paid the salaries of nearly all of these individuals. The learned societies and their journals offered almost indispensable stage settings for the display of talent, regardless of their diluted memberships and their frequent lack of collective intellectual vitality in the highest sense. Even the avant-garde counter-culture rapidly organized itself, if on a less stable basis. The most highly innovative individual transcends the scene around him but gains his initial impetus from its presence. Quietly he measures himself against it during his productive period, and he counts upon its long-term existence in order to be remembered later on. George Santayana, the arch-example of the man who regarded himself as above the academic crowd, said ultimately, ''my life in the 1890s [when he was teaching at Harvard] . . . seems to be, in retrospect, the vital period in it.''[173] From the attic retreat in his Pennsylvania farmhouse, Charles S. Peirce, who is generally considered the most brilliant intellect to become engaged in a humanistic field during this period of time in America and who had desperately hoped to be retained on the faculty of Johns Hopkins, might well have uttered a similar judgment about the utility of organizations.

## Notes

This essay was researched and first written while the author held a Senior Fellowship from the National Endowment for the Humanities and was concurrently a fellow of the Charles Warren Center at Harvard University.

1. I have calculated the statistics on professions from U.S. Census Bureau data; see below, n. 35. Another relevant figure is the approximately 1.9 percent of the population aged 14 to 21 who in 1890 were studying Greek or Latin, a statistic I have indirectly calculated from data in U.S. Bureau of Education, *Report, 1900–1901* (Washington, D.C: U.S. Government Printing Office, 1901), 2: 1625, table 8.

2. See Willystine Goodsell, *The Conflict of Naturalism and Humanism* (New York: Teachers College, 1910), p. 4; Thomas Fitz-Hugh, *The Philosophy of the Humanities* (Chicago: University of Chicago Press, 1898), p. 40; John Higham, *Writing American History* (Bloomington, Ind.: Indiana University Press, 1970), p. 13. In art and music instruction the historical approach collided continually with an alternative emphasis on sheer training in technique, which had an analogue in elementary courses in English composition. Purely aesthetic approaches in any of these fields were notably absent, making it impossible to define their meaning in terms of a conscious attempt to explicate a single autonomous realm of "culture." Of course, in this era, the social sciences were also very often characterized by an historical approach, but it was oriented toward progressive stages of evolution in contrast to the more timeless and static view of the past prevalent (outside the discipline of history) in the humanities.

3. An exception to the exclusive focus on Western and Near Eastern civilization was the interest that developed in Chinese and Japanese art on the part of a few museums and collectors by 1900.

4. No example can adequately illustrate such a widely pervasive assumption in the pedagogical literature of the several fields. However, a professor of Latin at Lafayette College captured the common mood on its more rhapsodic side when he spoke of liberal studies as containing "the record of human achievement full of inspiration and power; the noble thoughts of great thinkers, living truths wrought out of human experience, and all shaped into beautiful expression under the creative imagination of gifted men—the humanities, indeed, the inspiration and the nutriment of living souls." William Baxter Owen, *The Humanities in the Education of the Future* (Boston: Sherman, French, 1912), pp. 30–31. Another comprehensive statement is William T. Harris, "The Study of Art and Literature in Schools," U.S. Bureau of Education, *Report, 1898–99*, 2: 696–700; and see also Harry W. Desmond, "By Way of Introduction," *Architectural Record* 1 (1891): 6.

5. In fact, the barriers were more truly ethnic than those defined by learning, for some Roman Catholics in this country were also studying Latin, while not thereby gaining welcome into the charmed circles.

6. See Fritz K. Ringer, *The Decline of the German Mandarins* (Cambridge, Mass.: Harvard University Press, 1969).

7. Along with Dorothy Ross in this volume, I adopt the word *scientistic* to describe thought that claims or aspires to be scientific, so as to withhold judgment on whether such thought is or is not "truly" scientific.

8. See John Gross, *The Rise and Fall of the Man of Letters* (New York: Macmillan, 1969); Laurence Veysey, *The Emergence of the American University* (Chicago: University of Chicago Press, 1965), pp. 180–251.

9. See Veysey, *Emergence,* pp. 121–79. William Morton Payne, ed., *English in American Universities* (Boston: D.C. Heath, 1895), provides invaluable information about the relative strengths of the two factions within this crucial field on twenty leading campuses. A literary perspective, congenial to the generalists, could be said to dominate at perhaps eight of the twenty institutions. However, philologists, representing the research ideal, comprised a large minority at no fewer than fifteen of them and clearly saw themselves as riding a growing wave of strength. Some enthusiastic philologists in this period actually advocated the mass teaching of the Anglo-Saxon language in the nation's elementary schools.

10. Clement L. Smith, *Address on the Use of Language in Education* (Philadelphia; J. B. Lippincott, 1873), p. 23.

11. J. Irving Manatt, "The Future of Greek Studies," *Leader* (Boston, March 1903), p. 195.

12. See *Classical Weekly* (New York, 1907- ); Francis W. Kelsey, ed., *Latin and Greek in American Education: With Symposia on the Value of Humanistic Studies* (New York: Macmillan, 1911); Andrew F. West, ed., *Value of the Classics* (Princeton: Princeton University Press, 1917); Paul Shorey, *The Assault on Humanism* (Boston: Atlantic Monthly, 1917), perhaps unequaled in its tone of passionate sectarian isolation; *The Classical Investigation Conducted by the Advisory Committee of the American Classical League: Part One: General Report* (Princeton: Princeton University Press, 1924), especially p. 67. For the use of the term "humanities" in this unchanged definition as late as 1929, see Herbert Weir Smyth in *The Development of Harvard University, 1869–1929,* ed.

Samuel Eliot Morison (Cambridge, Mass.: Harvard University Press, 1930), p. 61. Classicists tended to exaggerate the immediate threat of decline in their discipline. Though Greek lost ground rapidly as a field of classroom instruction by 1900, Latin slowly gained until the mid-1930s, when it could be estimated that 5.4 percent of the American population aged 14 to 21 was studying it. Internally, however, literary classicists faced a threat from archaeology, which they often saw as undermining their own interpretation of the ancient world. See *Classical Weekly* 10 (October 1916): 2, 7.

13. Yet even such euphemisms could bear the same stigma during the upsurge of utilitarian thinking in the Progressive Era, one that had certain parallels with the widespread popular mood of the 1970s. "I know that the term 'culture courses,' in connection with college work, is now provocative of a sneer or a smile," opined Edgar Robinson in "The Relation of the University to Fine Arts," *Columbia University Quarterly* 14 (1911): 33.

14. Felix E. Schelling, *Humanities Gone and to Come* (Philadelphia: Phi Beta Kappa Society, 1902), pp. 3–4. In this context, note the perhaps deliberately careful use of the term "culture studies," primarily to defend Greek and Latin, by R. M. Wenley, "The Nature of Culture Studies," *School Review* 13 (1905): 441–57. See also Kelsey, *Latin and Greek in American Education*, where the many contributors use the term "humanities" very seldom.

15. Goodsell, *Conflict of Naturalism and Humanism*, p. 161.

16. In 1898 a professor of Latin at the University of Texas had already begun defining the humanities as the whole range of study of religion, law, art, and science, unifying them under the concept of "civilization" in a way that anticipates Arnold J. Toynbee. Fitz-Hugh, *Philosophy of the Humanities*, pp. 9–11. See also Owen, *Humanities in the Education of the Future*, passim, one of the very few books written between 1870 and 1940 with the word "humanities" in the title. It is interesting that, so far as I can tell, the word appears only twice in the *text* of the entire book.

17. Thus Charles H. Handschin announced in 1913: "The study of the modern languages constitutes the new humanism. In them is incorporated the culture of the race since the fall of the Roman Empire." Charles Hart Handschin, "The Teaching of Modern Languages in the United States," U.S. Bureau of Education, *Bulletin,* no. 3 (1913), p. 7. Similarly Charles Eliot Norton was content to boost the history of art as "this great branch of the humanities" in 1895, seemingly not caring to go beyond the promotion of his own special field. "The Educational Value of the History of the Fine Arts," *Educational Review* 9 (1895): 344. Again, a statement of definition by a committee of the AHA declared that history "belongs to the humanities, for its essential purpose is to disclose human life," but argued for its disciplinary independence rather than its close relationships with other fields (aside from government). The Committee of Seven, *The Study of History in Schools: Report to the American Historical Association* (New York: Macmillan, 1899), p. 32. Finally, the only statement I have found referring to the humanities at an annual meeting of the American Philosophical Association before 1920, by Norman Kemp Smith, runs parallel to the above: "Philosophy is not science. . . . It is humanistic, and finds its chief tasks in the realm of the value problems." *Philosophical Review* 22 (1913): 175.

18. E.g., see Veysey, *Emergence,* p. 181; Schelling, *Humanities Gone and to Come,* p. 10.

19. For a good contemporary account, see *Journal of the American Oriental Society* 40 (1920): 78.

20. Thorstein Veblen, *The Higher Learning in America* (New York: Hill & Wang, 1957; 1st published 1918), p. 129. See also Goodsell, *Conflict Between Naturalism and Humanism,* pp. 175–77, where social science in effect mediates between natural science and the humanities. Andrew C. McLaughlin, "American History and American Democracy," *American Historical Review* 20 (1915): 255, refers to the "natural sciences" and to the "social sciences" but does not think to mention "the humanities."

21. The catalyst for this sudden explosion of the word in educational writings may have been a symposium held at Princeton in 1938 called "The Meaning of the Humanities." See Patricia Beesley, *The Revival of the Humanities in American Education* (New York: Columbia University Press, 1940), p. 69. However, she notes that "some thirty American colleges in the past dozen years have boldly revived the name Humanities for new comprehensive courses in literature, language, art, philosophy, religion, and history, to complement or balance the broad courses in Social Sciences and Natural Sciences which sprang up immediately after the first World War as outgrowths of 'War Aims' courses." Ibid., pp. ix–x.

22. For a recent argument that, on these grounds, the term *humanities* ought to be straightforwardly abandoned, see William Riley Parker, "The Future of the 'Modern Humanities,'" in *The Future of the Modern Humanities,* ed. J. C. Laidlaw (n.p.: Modern Humanities Research Association, 1969), p. 107.

23. E.G., see Theodore Caplow, *The Sociology of Work* (Minneapolis: University of Minnesota Press, 1954), pp. 139–40; George H. Daniels, "The Process of Professionalization in American Science: The Emergent Period, 1820–1860," *Isis* 58 (1967): 151–66. For a far more historically accurate and stimulating overall treatment of the subject, see Samuel Haber, "The Professions and Higher Education in America: A Historical View," in *Higher Education and the Labor Market*, ed. Margaret S. Gordon (New York: McGraw-Hill, 1974), pp. 237–80; and see also Mary O. Furner, *Advocacy and Objectivity: A Crisis in the Professionalization of American Social Science, 1865–1905* (Lexington, Ky.: University Press of Kentucky, 1975), p. 3, n. 3. For further thoughts on this question, see Laurence Veysey, "Who's a Professional? Who Cares?" *Reviews in American History* 3 (1975): 419–23.

24. This abuse has not ended in the still more recent attempts to turn the notion of professionalism around and make it serve as a whipping-boy for everything evil in American life. See Burton J. Bledstein, *The Culture of Professionalism: The Middle Class and the Development of Higher Education in America* (New York: Norton, 1976). In both the celebration of professionalism and the attack upon it, there is the same undiscriminating magnification of the process, lacking in alertness to its precise historical dimensions and to its varying internal meanings. In particular, Bledstein greatly exaggerates the role of the graduate schools as upward mobility mechanisms in the entire period, as well as the quantitative proliferation of the professions before 1920 (see especially p. 36).

25. For instance, the components of one recently constructed "index" of professionalization nearly all directly relate to specialization. Robert A. McCaughey, "The Transformation of American Academic Life: Harvard University, 1821–1892," *Perspectives in American History* 8 (1974): 315. Yet some professions, like the clergy, stubbornly remain unspecialized; see James M. Gustafson, "The Clergy in the United States," *Daedalus* 92 (1963): 743.

26. See Bernard Barber, "The Sociology of the Professions," *Daedalus* 92 (1963): 674.

27. Alfred North Whitehead attempted to defend this distinction on the grounds that a profession, unlike a craft, involves activitieś that depend on theoretical analysis. "Preface," *Daedalus* 92 (1963): 647. But it is hard to see how this applies to such professions as dentists or funeral directors, any more than to masons or mechanics. Again, Everett C. Hughes maintains that "the essence of the professional idea and the professional claim" is that professionals "profess to know better than others the nature of certain matters, and to know better than their clients what ails them or their affairs." "Professions", *Daedalus* 92 (1963): 656. But what description could be more applicable to the role of automobile mechanic? Indeed these examples make us realize that it is socially more honorable to perform mechanical operations upon the human body than upon inanimate objects, even in an age when automobiles are about equally central to our lives. Such ultimately irrational distinctions becloud the entire concept of professionalism.

28. Howard M. Vollmer and Donald L. Mills, eds., *Professionalization* (Englewood Cliffs, N.J.: Prentice-Hall, 1966), pp. 10, 34; Barber, "Sociology of the Professions," pp. 671–72.

29. See Robert H. Wiebe, *The Search for Order, 1877–1920* (New York: Hill and Wang, 1967), especially pp. 112, 131.

30. Barber, "Sociology of the Professions," p. 672; Alma S. Wittlin, "The Teacher," *Daedalus*, 92 (1963): 746.

31. An extreme example of these enclosed intellectual worlds in the humanities is unwittingly provided by *The Classical Weekly*, widely circulated among classics teachers in the Northeast, during the spring of 1917. A thorough perusal of the issues of April, May, and June of that year reveals utterly no mention that the United States had entered the First World War. Instead, the discussion of Latin grammatical forms continues apace, as do enthusiastic notices for classicists' gatherings in various cities. There is no recognition whatever that times around them have abruptly changed.

32. Quoted in Veysey, *Emergence*, p. 149.

33. Of course, some professions confer less prestige than some nonprofessional (e.g., business and political) roles. There is an overlap. Yet as a general promise of social reward, professional status carries with it an unequaled degree of security.

34. These percentages result from comparing the figures of professionals, according to the Census Bureau's generous definition, with the entire population in America between the ages of 25 and 64, the span that best captures all those who have settled into any kind of long-term calling or occupation and are still active in it. A major curve of growth among the professions does begin after 1920, producing an 8.70 percent figure in 1960 and a 12.99 percent figure in 1970. As an overall status group, wives (most of whom were then nonworking) and children living at home should also be included, making it necessary to triple or quadruple these figures, at least for the earlier years.

Descriptions of the great growth of the professions often fail to point out that it is largely a post-1920 phenomenon; see Barber, "Sociology of the Professions," p. 671; Bledstein, *Culture of Professionalism,* passim.

35. In tables 1 and 2 I have included engineers for contrast. By "spectacularly rising" I mean more than doubling in a forty-year period (1880–1920) as a share of the mature working-age population. I have also included 1960 figures in the tables (to create a second forty-year period), enabling us to see which trends were peculiar to the pre-1920 decades and which were longer term. Of course, in absolute numbers all the professions were gaining steadily at all times (with but minor exceptions). But, especially after an initial critical mass is reached, at a level which might comprise only a few hundred persons, the proportional share of the population would seem a far more meaningful measure of any occupation's position within the evolving society.

36. Democratization has two main aspects—the proportional growth in the number of favorable slots that are potentially open to a given population, and the social spectrum from which they are in fact filled. The first has received attention in table 2. Regarding the second, Robert H. Knapp, in *The Origins of American Humanistic Scholars* (Englewood Cliffs, N.J.: Prentice-Hall, 1964), emphasizes the sociological continuities in recruitment into these fields even in the 1950s. Impressionistically, it seems likely that a certain degree of democratization did occur in the late 1940s, when it suddenly became somewhat easier for persons from a lower-middle-class or non-Protestant background to rise into academic positions, with the humanities somewhat lagging behind other areas in these respects. However, statistics recently gathered for all academic fields show that there has been remarkably little change in the social origins of professors even in the most contemporary years. See Everett C. Ladd, Jr., and Seymour Martin Lipset, *The Divided Academy* (New York: McGraw-Hill, 1975), p. 173, table 53.

37. In a survey taken in 1914, 60 percent of the 149 colleges and universities that responded were giving art instruction. (Unfortunately, 251 institutions did not return the questionnaire.) "The College Art Association of America," *School and Society* 4 (1916): 335. In a similar poll taken in 1919, 55 percent of the 419 colleges and universities that responded were giving music instruction for credit. (Only 167 did not return the questionnaire.) "Present Status of Music Instruction in Colleges and High Schools, 1919–1920," U.S. Bureau of Education, *Bulletin* (1921), no. 9, pp. 5–6. The smaller, weaker colleges tended not to have these subjects, so the proportion of college students to whom they were available was much higher.

38. Its centrality in the realms of art and music would seem hard to establish in the years before 1920, though of course becoming somewhat more important thereafter. As of 1908, music students in America were about evenly divided between those in independent schools and those in music departments of colleges and universities. Arthur L. Manchester, "Music Education in the United States," U.S. Bureau of Education, *Bulletin* (1908), no. 4, pp. 44–45.

39. At a meeting held in Poughkeepsie to found the American Philological Association in 1869, "Dr. S. H. Taylor of Andover, Mass., spoke of the desire he had felt for many years of conventions and associations among the teachers of linguistic science. He gave an account of some meetings which have been held by the professors of language in Massachusetts, and closed by expressing his great gratification at now seeing face to face so many professors of national reputation whom he had never before had an opportunity of meeting." *American Philological Association Transactions,* 1 (1870): 10. See also Veysey, *Emergence,* pp. 149–50.

40. One notes that schools and universities were either broadly comprehensive, beyond the scope of the humanities alone, or else were devoted entirely to some particular subject within them, most often art or music. No organizations devoted to instruction appeared that were confined to the whole of the humanities and nothing else. This confirms our earlier suggestion that the humanities is an artificially imposed term, rather than an organic division of knowledge-seeking with resonance at the time. Even the numerous small colleges rhetorically devoted to the liberal arts felt compelled to offer a good deal of natural and social science in their curricula, usually as early as the 1880s.

41. Joseph C. Kiger, *American Learned Societies* (Washington: Public Affairs Press, 1963), pp. 18–21, 256–66.

42. Though they were reminded of precisely these inequities by Edward Bellamy in his popular novel of 1887, *Looking Backward* (New York: New American Library, 1960), p. 101.

43. In an article planned for publication elsewhere, I shall discuss the intentions of the crusaders for high culture in America in this period and the quite limited audience they actually reached.

44. As late as 1911 an enthusiastic promoter of the new Drama League of America—which aimed to be a highly centralized "uplift" organization—called for "the evolution of an American drama,

which shall conceive America not as a New England, North or South, but as a New Europe from coast to coast.'' William Norman Guthrie, ''Editorial,'' *Drama* 1 (1911): 165.

45. See Daniel Aaron, *The Unwritten War* (New York: Alfred A. Knopf, 1973), pp. 35–36.

46. The American Academy of Arts and Letters was founded in 1904 as a still more exclusive ''interior organization'' of the NIAL. The Academy chose thirty (later increased to fifty) of the most outstanding writers, artists, and musicians for academician status, allowing them to pick their successors as vacancies occurred. The annual *Proceedings* of the AAAL reveal what one might suspect— that it was a dull mutual admiration society limited to the established and the elderly; more than this, it was strongly hostile to forces of innovation. Though it still exists, the Academy was never able to gain anything like the prestige of its European equivalents. In 1916 its Chancellor, William M. Sloane, openly admitted, ''Primarily we exist for ourselves as a mutual-benefit society.'' *AAAL Proceedings* (1916), p. 6.

47. ''Address of the Hon. Elihu Root, Senator from New York, at the Convention at which the American Federation of Arts was Organized, May 11, 1909'' (undated mimeograph, from the AFA), p. 1.

48. Theodore Roosevelt and Elihu Root had encouraged the formation of the AFA, which aimed to offer national direction to the uplifting of civic taste. See *Proceedings of the Convention at Which the American Federation of Arts was Formed* (Washington: Byron S. Adams, 1909); *Proceedings of the First Annual Convention of the American Federation of Arts* (1910); and ''It is Difficult to Imagine Doing without the American Federation of Arts'' (1959), especially pp. 11–12. The attempt to impose centralized standards in the fine arts had already taken the form of the jury system for the judgment of new works in painting and sculpture and, at the ultimate level, the election of certain artists to academician status by the National Academy of Design in New York. But in fact successful revolts were mounted against the NAD in the 1870s and again after 1909. See Eliot Clark, *History of the National Academy of Design, 1825–1953* (New York: Columbia University Press, 1954), especially pp. 96–99, 102, 106–8, 162.

49. See John Higham et al., *History* (Englewood Cliffs, New Jersey: Prentice-Hall, 1965), pp. 14–15.

50. *Journal of the American Oriental Society* 40 (1920): 217.

51. See David Madsen, *The National University* (Detroit: Wayne State University Press, 1966). The Committee of Twelve, organized to promote a standard curriculum in the modern languages, issued its widely read report in 1898, and the Committee of Seven, representing the historians, issued theirs a year later. There was perhaps a second weaker wave of effort in this overall direction around 1909–1911.

52. For further discussion of this outcome in broader cultural terms, see the next to last section of this chapter, pp. 82–86.

53. It is thus not surprising that the Secretary of the AHA explicitly praised such societies as the DAR: ''No one could listen to the report of [their work] . . . without being deeply impressed with the merit of their activities, the fine spirit of patriotism animating them, and the possibilities and prospects of their achievement in historical lines.'' AHA, *Annual Report* (1916), p. 42.

54. See Paul R. Anderson, *Platonism in the Midwest* (New York: Temple University Publications, 1963), especially pp. 122–23. It is possible to argue that the well-known lyceums of the 1830s and 1840s were more of a regional phenomenon.

55. Higham, *History,* p. 58. This was, however, one-quarter of the then-existing number of persons holding a Ph.D. in history, a larger fraction than popularly quoted figures of a similar kind in recent years.

56. No effort will be made here to describe comprehensively the foundings and growth of individual societies and associations. Succinct accounts of the most important learned societies may be found in Kiger, *American Learned Societies,* pp. 14–53. A very useful work of reference is J. David Thompson, ed., *Handbook of Learned Societies and Institutions: America* (Washington, D.C.: Carnegie Institution of Washington, 1908), though it contains some omissions. For reasons that now seem purely arbitrary, most organizations in the fine arts were not regarded as learned societies and are not listed in Thompson's directory. But a rather full directory of art associations appears in various issues of the *American Art Annual* (Washington: American Federation of Arts). There seems to be no equivalent directory in music.

57. For an overview of the AOS, see Nathaniel Schmidt, ''Early Oriental Studies in Europe and the Work of the American Oriental Society, 1842–1922,'' *Journal of the American Oriental Society* 43 (1923), part 1, pp. 10–14. See also W. D. Whitney's untitled printed statement to the members of the AOS, New Haven, April 1891, Widener Library.

58. It may be possible that such groups as the Theosophical Society and the Vedanta Society of America are considered relevant on the more popular level of philosophical interest in Eastern ideas. But these had only very small memberships—a few thousand in the case of Theosophy, a few hundred in that of Vedanta. See Laurence Veysey, *The Communal Experience* (New York: Harper and Row, 1973), pp. 208–20. There was an independent Oriental Club in Philadelphia after the 1890s.

59. For an overview of the APA, see Frank Gardner Moore, "A History of the American Philological Association," *American Philological Association Transactions* 50 (1919): 5–32. See also *APA Proceedings,* 1 (1869): 5–7, and 2 (1870): 4–7, for the founding and early sense of scope and purpose, aiming for a breadth and depth it never satisfactorily achieved.

60. E.g., see Martin L. D'Ooge, "The Historical Method and Purpose in Philology," *American Philological Association Proceedings* 16 (184): xiii.

61. Hints exist of a strong atmosphere of incipient student rebellion against the dull rote learning that commonly prevailed in the Latin classroom and increasingly set limits on what even a good teacher could demand in the way of work. See *Classical Weekly* 2 (1909): 107.

62. A Classical Reading League existed in 1917, enrolling 227 in correspondence courses, but it was entirely intended for teachers; *Classical Weekly* 10 (1917): 133. The only genuine layman's amateur groups appear to have been in the Philadelphia area and in Essex County, New Jersey. Even the latter was a mixed club of laymen and teachers; *Classical Weekly* 1 (1908): 159. The earlier New York Greek Club had long since expired, and there is no mention of successors.

63. American Classical League *The Classical Investigation,* pp. 106–7. The League itself was a merger in 1918 of the previously strong regional organizations.

64. Susan Braley Franklin, "First Year Latin," *Classical Weekly,* 1 (108): 98, for some reason referring to herself as "he."

65. The scattered beginnings of American academic recognition of these fields go back all the way into the eighteenth century. On English, see Parker in Laidlaw, *Future of the Modern Humanities,* pp. 108–112; on German, L. Viereck, "German Instruction in American Schools," U.S. Bureau of Education, *Report,* 1900–1901, 1: 531–708; and on the modern foreign languages in general, Handschin, "The Teaching of Modern Languages," pp. 17–37, 84–86. Most major universities had at least a joint professor of Italian and Spanish by the mid-1890s. The Spanish-American War gave a definite boost to the study of Spanish, though it remained minor in extent until the great collapse of German in the First World War. Only a few universities offered Russian or Portuguese until the 1940s.

66. The best account of early MLA history is William Riley Parker, "The MLA, 1883–1953," *Proceedings of the Modern Language Association* 68 (1953): 3–39. See also MLA, *Proceedings at New York, December 29, 30, 1884* (Baltimore: Modern Language Association, 1885), 1–vii; Carleton Brown, "A Survey of the First Half-Century," *PMLA* 48 (1933), Supplement, p. 1411; Percy W. Long, "The Association in Review," *PMLA* 64 (1949), Supplement, part 2, pp. 1–12; John M. Manly, "The President's Address: New Bottles," *PMLA* 36 (1921): xlvi–lxx.

67. Parker, "The MLA, 1883–1953," pp. 25–26. Another motive was the direct desire to imitate a similar organization recently founded in Germany.

68. Ibid. Indeed the original plan of the organization in 1883 would have restricted membership to college-level faculty, plus those lower-level teachers specifically invited, *Proceedings of the Modern Language Association* (1884), p. vi. The MLA was probably the first learned society in America to begin in such an academically exclusivist atmosphere. The nonacademic members that were in fact accepted thereafter were no doubt courted for their dues, perhaps in some instances for their prestige.

69. Parker, "The MLA, 1883–1953," p. 31; Long, "The Association in Review," p. 4. In 1911 one cabal resulted in a rare floor fight. The association had been promised a $5,000 gift from Andrew Carnegie if it would adopt simplified spelling, a fad of the era. A trainload of members under Brander Matthews' direction was brought into the convention, helping tip the scales in favor. Ibid., p. 2; Brown, "A Survey of the First Half-Century," pp. 1413–14. Though it was then the height of the Progressive era, only a minority seem to have regarded this episode as a shameful scandal.

70. Brown, "A Survey of the First Half-Century," pp. 1419–20.

71. Stenographic transcripts of the floor discussions at early conventions were printed in the *Transactions* and convey in detail the ponderous, very often wandering, but sometimes mildly witty flow of discourse.

72. Manly, "New Bottles," p. lv.

73. Long, "The Association in Review," pp. 3, 5.

74. E.g., see *PMLA* (1889), pp. iii–iv.

75. Parker, "The MLA, 1883-1953," p. 33.

76. Viereck, "German Instruction," pp. 576-77, 586-87; Handschin, "Teaching of Modern Languages," pp. 21, 49.

77. For a worthwhile attempt to cover them comprehensively, see Harrison Ross Steeves, *Learned Societies and English Literary Scholarship* (New York: Columbia University Press, 1913), pp. 204-17.

78. Yearbooks of The Browning Society of Philadelphia, 1902-1910, in Widener Library.

79. See Adolf Growoll, *American Book Clubs: Their Beginnings and History* (New York: Dodd, Mead, 1897).

80. Henry B. Van Hoesen, "The Bibliographical Society of America—Its Leaders and Activities, 1904-1939," *Papers of the Bibliographical Society of America* 35 (1941): 177-202.

81. Comparisons as to size are difficult, because the share of attention given to cultural study in the vast assortment of women's clubs was declining at the same time that local history societies were greatly expanding. Within the realm of what were recognized as learned societies, the historical organizations were always enormously larger.

82. On the AHA, see Higham, *History,* pp. 6-51; J. Franklin Jameson, "The American Historical Association, 1884-1909," *American Historical Review* 15 (1909): 1-20; idem, "Early Days of the American Historical Association, 1884-1895," *American Historical Review* 40, (1934): 1-9, a more relaxed reminiscence. However, Jameson's version should be balanced by the accounts of the early annual meetings, written by Herbert Baxter Adams and appearing at the start of each year's *Annual Report,* since Jameson and Adams represented conflicting tendencies within the organization.

83. Higham, *History,* p. 12, presents evidence that this attitude was coldly calculated on Adams' part, but the psychological truth may be more complicated. The annual reports and an enthusiastic account written by Adams of Chautauqua reveal a man genuinely unable to resist the pleasures of conviviality with all and sundry of an appropriate social status.

84. It was a calculated policy of early AHA leaders such as Adams to promote memberships among nonacademics. This was sometimes frankly justified on the basis of the income and support such cultivated and powerful citizens could provide. But it also suggests some degree of fundamental congeniality across this dividing line. See *History,* pp. 12-18, for Higham's extended discussion of the compatibility of so-called amateur and professional outlooks on many levels among the historians of that day.

85. Jameson, "Early Days," p. 3.

86. See AHA, *Annual Report* (1911), p. 25; (1914), p. 40; (1916), p. 45.

87. "But others . . . found agreeable variations to the monotony of the regular proceedings by strolling about the museum and talking with old friends. . . . Historical conventions in Washington serve many profitable purposes, social, educational, and scientific. It is perhaps safe to say that some good and useful work was done at luncheons and dinner parties and at the Cosmos Club." Herbert B. Adams, in AHA, *Annual Report* (1890), p. 6.

88. AHA, *Annual Report* (1897), pp. 3-4; (1920), I, 35, 37.

89. Writing in 1917, William A. Dunning utterly ignored Beard in his summary of American historiography during the preceding thirty years. See Dunning, "A Generation of American Historiography," in AHA, *Annual Report* (1917), pp. 347-54. *An Economic Interpretation* did receive a brief sympathetic review by William E. Dodd in the *American Historical Review* 19 (1913): 162-63. It was attacked at length by O. G. Libby in the *Mississippi Valley Historical Review* 1 (1914): 113-17, where Beard was accused of giving support to agitators and contributing to popular unrest, beside receiving some cogent criticism of his argument. An unsigned review of Beard's book, *Contemporary American History, 1877-1913,* in the *American Historical Review* 20 (1914): 179-80, was extremely hostile. Andrew C. McLaughlin's presidential address to the AHA of 1914, "American History and American Democracy," *American Historical Review* 20 (1915): 260, 265, spent one paragraph deploring the materialism inherent in economic interpretations of constitutional history, clearly referring to Beard, then gingerly skipped over the Constitution in a later section devoted to a broad review of recent interpretations of various chronological periods.

90. See AHA, *Annual Report* (1915), pp. 37-38, and Henry Morse Stephens's presidential address of 1915, "Nationality and History," *American Historical Review,* 21 (1916): 225-36.

91. The sole exception was an open floor discussion in 1913 on "social and industrial" versus political history. Several Progressively oriented speakers raised their voices, but the majority was heard to urge that the political framework for understanding American history be kept foremost. AHA, *Annual Report* (1913), pp. 32-33. Theodore Roosevelt was given a warm but distinctly nonpolitical welcome when he became president of the AHA at the end of 1912.

92. AHA, *Annual Report* (1896), p. 17. The context was the interpretation of Southern history.

93. College and high school history teachers' groups did exist, but not on a scale of development comparable to the linguists'. All in all, there was far less pedagogical ferment in history than in English, though more than in philosophy.

94. For a sympathetic account of these societies, see Walter Muir Whitehill, *Independent Historical Societies* (Boston: Boston Athenaeum, 1962). For candid contemporary characterizations, see Frank H. Severance, the secretary of the Buffalo Historical Society, "Historical Museums," American Association of Museums, *Proceedings* 4 (1910): 66–67; also *American Historical Review* 15 (1910): 487–88, and AHA, *Annual Report* (1904), pp. 115–27; (1913), p. 30.

95. See AHA, *Annual Report* (1900), pp. 3–4.

96. And yet some psychologists themselves were reluctant to identify their field too exclusively with a scientistic world-view. For a good symposium on the status of psychology in relation both to philosophy and natural science, see *Philosophical Review* 15 (1906): 173–77.

97. For an immensely detailed study of philosophy at Harvard in this period, see Bruce Kuklick, *The Rise of American Philosophy: Cambridge, Massachusetts, 1860–1930* (New Haven: Yale University Press, 1977). Far less geared to the institutional milieu is Elizabeth Flower and Murray G. Murphey, *A History of Philosophy in America*, 2 vols. (New York: G. P. Putnam's Sons, 1977).

98. For its founding and early history, see H. N. Gardiner, "The First Twenty-Five Years of the American Philosophical Association," *Philosophical Review* 35 (1926): 145–58.

99. See *Philosophical Review* 28 (1919): 178–81. Nor were the philosophers so unworldly as not to appeal to the Carnegie Foundation for money in 1908; *Philosophical Review* 17 (1909): 165–66. For a plea on behalf of the benefits of association and collective identity, see J. E. Creighton, "The Purposes of a Philosophical Association," *Philosophical Review* 11, (1902): 219–37. However, Creighton expressed a scientistic frame of reference (on all but the most ultimate intellectual level) that was then uncongenial to a majority of philosophers, hence in its own way divisive.

100. *Philosophical Review* 27 (1918): 132.

101. "The difficulties in the communication of philosophical ideas and reasonings from one mind to another are notorious. . . . Your committee accordingly believes that one of the principal functions of this society is to bring about a genuine meeting of minds upon actually *identical* points of the logical universe, or to come as near to that result as is possible; in other words, to promote the coherent, methodical, mutually intelligible, and constructive discussion of common problems. It is not, indeed . . . the committee's opinion that this object should exclude other matters from the program. . . . But an especially important part of the business of such a body as this is concerned with . . . the conversion of the spontaneous *apercus* of individual minds into rigorously tested, adequately explicated and properly correlated philosophical insights." A.O. Lovejoy *et al.*, *Philosophical Review* 27 (1918): 167; and cf. *Philosophical Review* 19 (1910): 180–82, and especially 22 (1913): 172–78. Yet this position was clearly controversial in itself. Any expression of a desire for unity immediately raised the further question—on whose terms?

102. For open recognition of this problem as one stemming from the theological origins of much recent philosophical speculation, see Creighton, "Purposes," p. 225.

103. George Santayana, "The Genteel Tradition in American Philosophy" (1911) in *The Genteel Tradition: Nine Essays by George Santayana*, ed. Douglas L. Wilson (Cambridge, Mass.: Harvard University Press, 1967). p. 49. Santayana was here voicing a skeptical viewpoint by no means confined to himself; cf. Alexander T. Ormond, "Philosophy and Its Correlations," *Philosophical Review* 12 (1903): 113–15.

104. At the outset, J. E. Creighton nonetheless expressed a fear that the social side of the gatherings would dominate too much. "One not infrequently hears it said that the main purpose of these gatherings [of professional societies] is social, to meet one's colleagues personally, to renew old friendships and to form new ones. This is certainly a feature of the meetings which no one will be inclined to underestimate, and the indirect results of such personal intercourse are often of genuine scientific importance. There is a danger, however, if the social advantages are exclusively emphasized . . . the members may come to feel that they are in no way responsible for the programme, which is after all unimportant, furnishing as it does only an excuse for meeting. And, in consequence of this feeling, they may, when it is not perfectly convenient to attend the meetings, resolve to remain at home." "Purposes," p. 220. This last assumption reveals the greater austerity of the philosophers (or at least of Creighton) as compared with language professors and historians, and all of Creighton's remarks appear to involve a negative judgment upon organizations like the AHA and MLA.

105. Gardiner, "The First Twenty-Five Years," pp. 157–58.

106. On these groups and movements, see Flower and Murphey, *A History of Philosophy in*

*America* 2: 463–76, 482–509; Henry A. Pochmann, *New England Transcendentalism and St. Louis Hegelianism* (Philadelphia: Carl Schurz Memorial Foundation, 1948): Anderson, *Platonism in the Midwest,* passim. Less scholarly work has been done on an unknown number of laymen's clubs (such as the Boston Radical Club) that reflected an interest in the empiricist rather than the idealist tradition in philosophy. But Spencerians, for example, tended to identify themselves with social science rather than with the humanities, requiring careful definition of the boundary between these two regions in the lay philosophical sector.

107. It is extremely difficult to impose narrower limits on the definition of art without falling into the pattern of the advocates of high culture, whose own conception of "good" art faced rising challenges before 1920 and withering criticism thereafter. Seemingly one can discuss literature without comprehending the daily newspaper, while to draw a similar line in art is at once to become partisan with respect to some segment of the diverse interests identifying themselves with the word. The safest course, therefore, is at the outset to try to be as comprehensive in viewing the subject as possible.

108. See James Jackson Jarves, *The Art-Idea: Sculpture, Painting, and Architecture in America,* 2d ed. (New York: Hurd and Houghton, 1865), pp. 175–77.

109. On the art boom, see Russell Lynes, *The Tastemakers* (New York: Harper, 1954), pp. 45–48; G. W. Benjamin, *Art in America: A Critical and Historical Sketch* (New York: Harper, 1879), pp. 178–87; S. R. Koehler, *Art Education and Art Patronage in the United States* (Philadelphia: Edward Stern, 1882), pp. 4–6, 11. For a good survey of the American art scene in this take-off period, replete with statistics, see Edwards Clarke, "Drawing in Public Schools," U.S. Bureau of Education, *Circular of Information,* 1874, no. 2, which is far broader than its title indicates. On the Philadelphia exhibition and its importance, see Oliver W. Larkin, *Art and Life in America* (New York: Rinehart, 1949), p. 242, and Lynes, *The Tastemakers,* pp. 112–17. Americans were far from unique in their aesthetically uninformed taste at the time; Larkin, *Art and Life,* p. 316, declares that the bad paintings of all the major countries displayed a remarkable similarity of themes.

110. On the mixture of motives that spurred collection, see Daniel M. Fox, *Engines of Culture: Philanthropy and Art Museums* (Madison, Wis.: State Historical Society of Wisconsin, 1963), especially pp. 7, 18–24, 28; Rene Brimo, *L'évolution du Goût aux Etats-Unis* (Paris: James Fortune, 1938), especially pp. 78–79, 101–2, 118, 124, 174, 191–92; Aline B. Saarinen, *The Proud Possessors* (New York: Random House, 1958); Marie A. Sahm, "Private Art Collections in the United States," College Art Association of America, *Bulletin,* no. 4 (September 1918), pp. 16–17. Lynes, *Tastemakers,* p. 198, gives us the wonderful picture of Henry Clay Frick sitting on his genuine Renaissance throne in Pittsburgh, listening to an organist play his favorite "Silver Threads Among the Gold," while he reads *The Saturday Evening Post.*

111. Larkin, *Art and Life,* pp. 324–25, 354, sees the American art world in this period as similar to the political world, with die-hard standpatters, mild progressives, radical secessionists—its "trusts and its trust-busters." Innovators faced "an academism less official in its monopoly than in European countries, but none the less powerful." Cf. Lynes, *Tastemakers,* pp. 151, 196. Brimo, *L'évolution,* p. 168, emphasizes that there was less organized resistance to new art in the United States than in France.

112. The conservatism and alleged favoritism of the NAD has been an issue periodically since the 1870s, when younger artists seceded from it to found a rival art school, the Arts Students League, and a rival "academy," with its own juries, the Society of American Artists. By 1900 the SAA had itself become nearly as conservative as the NAD, and in 1906 it rejoined it. See above, n. 48. The NAD voted academician status to Robert Henri in 1906 and to George Bellows in 1913, despite their "ash-can" realism. Other painters further to the "left" ceased submitting their work to the NAD after about 1909. Clark, *History of the National Academy of Design,* pp. 177–78.

113. Their own account admitted that at their first convention in 1910 "there was, perhaps, nothing very radical in the addresses delivered.... From first to last a spirit of unanimity and harmony characterized the meetings." *Art and Progress,* 1 (1910): 268. The annual AFA conventions brought together "artists and teachers of art, museum directors, members of art commissions, collectors and critics." *Art and Progress* 5 (1914): 335. The AFA sent out traveling exhibitions to uplift taste and simultaneously sought to sell the paintings of its members. Its sales were highest in Texas.

114. Irving K. Pond, "Art and Individuality," *Art and Progress* 2 (1911): 328. Yet Pond also attacked the overuse of trite formulas in the arts, such as Roman columns, ibid., p. 361. Earlier another architectural spokesman had declared: "No effective work can be done by cutting adrift from

what is. Reformation must be *from* what is and not *against* what is. Artificial progress, there is enough of it.'' Desmond, ''By Way of Introduction,'' p. 6. These statements offer a thematic parallel to the attack upon individualism in literature and art by William T. Harris; see above, n. 4.

115. For an overall view of American museums of all kinds, see Paul M. Rea, ''Condition and Needs of American Museums,'' American Association of Museums, *Proceedings,* 10 (1916): 9–15, 24–26. Though art museums were only 10 percent of the total number of museums in the country at that time, they were about half the giants. Art museums and science museums had generally followed the same chronological course of growth. For other general treatments of the rise of the American art museum, see Brimo, *L'évolution,* pp. 171–87; Fox, *Engines of Culture,* which is full of insights but pitched on a very general plane; and the bland article by Robert C. Smith, ''The Museum of Art in the United States,'' *Art Quarterly* 21 (1958): 297–316. Neil Harris, ''The Gilded Age Revisited: Boston and the Museum Movement,'' *American Quarterly* 14 (1962): 545–66, unearths the forgotten earliest years of what became a major museum. Interestingly, when it was proposed to open up the AAM to interested laymen, the idea was resoundingly rejected. AAM, *Proceedings* 11 (1917): 22–23. See also Brimo, *L'évolution,* p. 185.

116. In Boston and other cities, museums in this period were practically empty when admission (usually 25¢) was charged, but thronged when it was not. Walter Muir Whitehill, *Museum of Fine Arts, Boston: A Centennial History* (Cambridge, Mass.: Harvard University Press, 1970) 1: 40, 83.

117. See AAM, *Proceedings* 2 (1908): 29–33.

118. E.g., see AAM, *Proceedings* 6 (1912): 56.

119. See Lynes, *Tastemakers* p. 149. A few museums embraced the research ideal. See AAM, *Proceedings* 5 (1911): 84.

120. Benjamin Ives Gilman, *Museum Ideals of Purpose and Method,* 2d ed. (Cambridge, Mass.: Harvard University Press, 1923; 1st published 1918), especially pp. xii, xviii, 6–8, 274, 379–81, 390–91 (the quotation). It is interesting that Gilman nonetheless was willing to accept the idea of government tax support and free admissions, and that he enthusiastically endorsed the professionalization of museum management (''The Day of the Expert,'' ibid., pp. 347–62, 382–86). For a similar display of open elitism, see John Pickard, a professor at the University of Missouri, ''Message of Art for the Collegian,'' *Art and Progress* 7 (1916): 148.

121. John Cotton Dana, *The Gloom of the Museum* (Woodstock, Vt.: Elm Tree Press, 1917), especially pp. 5–8 (where his debt to Veblen is explicit), 12–13, 17 (quotation), 22. Cf. AAM, *Proceedings* 9 (1915): 80–88, where Dana presents his ideas on the floor and is strongly put down by the others. Dana's views were attacked in an editorial in the AFA's *American Magazine of Art* (formerly *Art and Progress*) 8 (1917): 416–17. On Dana, see also Larkin, *Art and Life*, p. 360.

122. Dana, *Gloom,* pp. 20, 30.

123. Thus, when the AAM met in San Francisco in 1915, not only did political notables entertain them, but so did Mrs. Spreckels and other social figures. At the 1913 AFA convention in Washington, Woodrow Wilson threw a garden party for the members at the White House. *Art and Progress* 4 (1913): 1042. Federal recognition of the arts occurred in 1910 when Congress established a national Commission of Fine Arts. History was the only other field to receive such a token nod from officialdom in this period.

124. Cf. Charles G. Leland, ''Industrial Art in Schools,'' U.S. Bureau of Education, *Circulars of Information,* no. 4, 1882, especially pp. 30–33, a populistic attack upon high culture, with Thomas Davidson, *The Place of Art in Education: A Lecture* (Boston: Ginn, 1885).

125. The *American Art Annual* counted 102 such schools in 1910, enrolling 31,710 students in the 81 that reported figures. Of these, 57 offered life-drawing, setting them apart as an elite. Additionally, 7,751 students were taking studio courses in the 130 colleges and universities that taught them during 1909–1910. (This compared with 5,877 students in college courses in the history of art at the same time.) In 1913, there were 3,767 painters, sculptors, and illustrators in the United States who had exhibited their work within the last twelve months. *Art and Progress,* 6 (1915): 281. The *Annual* listed 274 art schools in 1920. For a vivid account of the atmosphere inside one of these schools, see Cecilia Beaux, ''Professional Art Schools,'' *Art and Progress* 7 (1915): 3–8. Students were recruited ''largely from the classes where, if the circumstances are not actually easy, the way is open for the young person to choose what would have been called in old times 'One of the Polite Professions.' '' Yet such students she found unable easily to identify with the great works of art. ''The chasm between the Greek fragment and the street outside is too great . . . to bridge over.''

126. See Veysey, *Emergence,* p. 174. Oddly enough, if one knows the universities of the period, art study at Yale stressed utilitarian vocational training, at Princeton research, and at Harvard

cultural appreciation. As time went on, the cultural orientation noticeably lost ground both in universities and public schools. See Walter Sargent, "The Value of Art Education in Colleges," CAAA, *Bulletin*, no. 4 (September 1918) 84; William G. Whitford, *An Introduction to Art Education*, rev. ed. (New York: D. Appleton-Century, 1937), pp. 12–13, where a graph traces the back and forth movement of aims between utility and culture from 1821 to 1936 (culture dominating only from the 1880s until about 1905); and Royal Bailey Farnum, "Art Education: The Present Situation." U.S. Bureau of Education, *Bulletin*, no. 13 (1923), pp. 4–5, where in a poll of leaders in art education regarding the recent trend in aims, twenty-nine saw them moving in the industrial direction and only fourteen in the direction of "taste and culture."

127. For a comprehensive history of the history of art as a scholarly field, see Priscilla Hiss and Roberta Fansler, *Research in Fine Arts in the Colleges & Universities of the United States* (New York: Carnegie Corporation, 1934). The chief emphasis was on Greek and Roman art, and after 1900 the Italian Renaissance. As of 1918, nine American universities offered a Ph.D. in the Fine Arts. For a survey of undergraduate instruction in the nonstudio side of the fine arts, see E. Baldwin Smith, *The Study of the History of Art in the Colleges and Universities of the United States* (Princeton: Princeton University Press, 1912).

128. *College Art Journal* 1 (1942): 100–104; Holmes Smith, "Problems of the College Art Association," CAAA *Bulletin*, no. 1 (1913) 6–10. Cf. Edward Dickinson, *Music and the Higher Education* (New York: Scribner's, 1915), pp. 47–48, 54. Controversy at CAAA meetings centered around the split between historical and studio approaches to teaching. There was some interaction between the CAAA and the AAM.

129. Royal Bailey Farnum, "Present Status of Drawing and Art in the Elementary and Secondary Schools of the United States," U.S. Bureau of Education, *Bulletin*, no. 13 (1914), pp. 223–26, lists and describes them.

130. As to the completeness of this directory, one might note that it lists under Providence, Rhode Island, only the long established Providence Art Club and the Water Color Club, whereas a local Providence guide of the same date also shows a Handicraft Club of 170 women and a Providence Ceramic Club (the *American Art Annual* included many crafts and ceramics clubs in other cities). In addition, in Providence, "smaller clubs, circles for listening to lectures on art, or for studying art without a teacher, are formed from time to time." William Kirk, ed., *A Modern City: Providence, Rhode Island, and Its Activities* (Chicago: University of Chicago Press [*sic*], 1909), pp. 268–70. Art clubs continued rapidly to proliferate. In 1924 it was said that there were 485 art associations in America, excluding museums, libraries, and schools, and another 400 women's clubs devoting their "entire efforts to art." *Office Memorandum on Adult Education*, 2 vols., (New York: Carnegie Corporation of New York, 1925–26), ser. 2, pp. 46, 48. On an unusually aggressive art society of the 1890s in Chicago, the Central Art Association, see Lynes, *Tastemakers*, pp. 151–56.

131. Dickinson, *Music*, p. 55.

132. *American Art Annual* 8 (1910–11): 337–38.

133. See John H. Mueller, *The American Symphony Orchestra: A Social History of Musical Taste* (Bloomington, Ind.: Indiana University Press, 1951), pp. 286, 295–96; Helen M. Thompson, "The American Symphony Orchestra," in *One Hundred Years of Music in America*, ed. Paul Henry Lang, (New York: Grosset and Dunlap, 1961), p. 41. Exactly one symphony orchestra, the New York Philharmonic, had existed in 1860. The founding dates are in Margaret Grant and Herman S. Hettinger, *America's Symphony Orchestras and How They are Supported* (New York: W. W. Norton, 1940), p. 24. As of 1900, four symphonies—those of Boston, Chicago, Cincinnati, and Pittsburgh—had become first-rate; twenty years later, the select list would include a dozen.

134. See Fox, *Engines of Culture*, p. 82. Baltimore alone gave municipal funding to its symphony, starting in 1915. Grant and Hettinger, *America's Symphony Orchestras*, p. 200; see also pp. 35–37, and Mueller, *The American Symphony Orchestra*, pp. 294, 334–38, concerning the role of private philanthropy.

135. Mueller, *The American Symphony Orchestra*, pp. 43–44. For an excellent account of the relationship between high society and the opera in New York, see Irving Kolodin, *The Metropolitan Opera, 1883–1966: A Candid History* (New York: Alfred A. Knopf, 1966), especially pp. 4, 49–52, 55–77. Only thirty-five of the most highly prestigious boxes at the opera were available. Jews were excluded from them until after 1920. The peak of high society's involvement in the opera was between 1893 and 1913, though the tone did not entirely fade until 1933.

136. See Mueller, *American Symphony Orchestra*, pp. 19–29, 28–29; Louis C. Elson, *The History of American Music* (New York: Macmillan, 1925), pp. 73 93; Hermann Klein, *Unmusical*

*New York* (London: John Lane, 1910), pp. 83–86, an invaluable insider's view of the contemporary New York music scene.

137. However, in the instance of music, professionalism failed to involve an examination system for the bestowal of approval by recognized experts (Klein, *Unmusical New York,* pp. 110–11, 116–17, laments this in comparison with Europe). There were no juries for the evaluation of composition or performance, akin to those of the National Academy of Design in art (above, n. 48). The conservatories that sprang up had to rest content with supplying their students with degrees—and in no field were degrees more chaotic, more uncertain of their meaning, than in music. Advanced scholarly study of music (which became known as musicology, leading to the Ph.D.) did not get underway in America until the 1930s. The best account of the history of music education is in Willis J. Wager and Earl J. McGrath, *Liberal Education and Music* (New York: Teachers College, 1962).

138. Carnegie Corporation, *Office Memorandum,* p. 48. For the musical life of a medium-sized city in 1910, see Kirk, *Providence,* pp. 259–62.

139. Manchester, "Music Education," p. 42.

140. I have calculated, on the basis of Thompson's 1908 directory (see above, n. 56), that 0.39 percent of American adults, or roughly 1 out of every 300, was then a member of a learned society with humanistic interests. To derive this estimate, the average membership figure for the large number of organizations actually providing such data in the directory was counted in each case where no membership total was given. Organizations that embodied mixed humanistic and scientific aims were generally counted one-half. It should be recalled that organizations in the fine arts were not included in this directory, nor were the numerous women's clubs. The overwhelming bulk of the learned societies in the realm of the humanities were local history societies.

141. Henry F. May, *The End of American Innocence: A Study of the First Years of Our Own Time, 1912–1917* (New York: Alfred A. Knopf, 1959).

142. The best overall history of Bohemianism in America is still Albert Parry, *Garrets and Pretenders* (New York: Covici Friede, 1933). It is, of course, enormously more complicated than this brief sketch allows. However, there is unmistakable cyclical continuity from the era of Walt Whitman and the circle that met at Pfaff's Restaurant in New York in the 1850s, or from Thoreau and the Concord Transcendentalists, down through the Village explosion of the teens and ultimately the counter-culture of the 1960s. See Veysey, *Communal Experience,* pp. 34–44. On the Bohemianism of the teens specifically, the best brief account is Kenneth S. Lynn, "The Rebels of Greenwich Village," *Perspectives in American History,* 8 (1974): 335–77, though its pervasively Freudian interpretation offers no substitute for the complex portrayal of ideas in May's book.

143. A great many of the Bohemians of the teens had come from advantaged families and had attended the "right" colleges, a fact emphasized by Lynn.

144. The name *Secession* was clearly imitated from the Viennese rebel movement of the late 1890s. See Carl E. Schorske, "Cultural Hothouse," *New York Review of Books* 22 (December 11, 1975): 39. Stieglitz's art exhibits were first held in 1908. A small number of critics reacted favorably to them from the first. The first one-man Picasso exhibition in America was held there in 1911, and the first exhibit of African art in 1914. By then the gallery had been renamed "291," after the street address. It was actually three small rooms on the top floor of an old brownstone. A proto-Dadaist magazine, *291* was briefly published, 1915–1916, and at least sixty-eight people formed a definite circle around Stieglitz in 1914. See Dorothy Norman, *Alfred Stieglitz: An American Seer* (New York: Random House, 1973), especially pp. 68, 72–73, 80, 107–8, 144, 122; Waldo Frank et al., *America & Alfred Stieglitz: A Collective Portrait* (New York: Literary Guild, 1934), especially pp. 83, 108, 112, 236, 275, 277–78, 314; Larkin, *Art and Life,* pp. 354–55. The gallery closed in 1917.

145. There are various accounts of the behind-the-scenes maneuvering that resulted in the Armory Show. E.g., see Lynes, *Tastemakers,* pp. 200–204; Larkin, *Art and Life,* p. 361; Norman, *Stieglitz,* p. 118.

146. Quoted in Norman, *Stieglitz,* pp. 75, 109.

147. Adeline Adams, "The Secret of Life," *Art and Progress* 4 (1913): 925–32.

148. "Frightfulness in Art," *American Magazine of Art* 8 (1917): 244. On this controversy, see also Larkin, *Art and Life,* pp. 351–54.

149. Lynes, *Tastemakers,* p. 222. In contrast the French impressionists had been received with relatively little determined opposition in the United States—indeed, much less than in France—during the period between their first exhibit here in 1885 and their ultimate enshrinement in the Museum of Modern Art in 1929. See Brimo, *L'évolution,* pp. 158–59. By 1915 the art critics for several major magazines, such as *Forum, Century,* and *Harper's,* had gone over to the rebel side. It

is this kind of rapid surrender that forms the basis for Henry May's image of the crumbling of the fortresses of the established culture.

150. Larkin, *Art and Life,* pp. 360, 366–67.

151. These words were coined by Van Wyck Brooks in *America's Coming of Age* (New York: Huebsch, 1915), taking off from remarks by Santayana in "The Genteel Tradition in American Philosophy." The most satisfactory attempt to diagram the entire American cultural landscape from the more complicated twentieth-century perspective is, I believe, that of Dwight Macdonald, "A Theory of Mass Culture," in *Mass Culture in America,* ed. Bernard Rosenberg and David Manning White (New York: Free Press, 1964), pp. 59–73.

152. Not, however, *The Atlantic Monthly,* which has always remained faithful to the values of the turn-of-the-century cultivated elite.

153. Clark, *History of the National Academy of Design,* p. 169.

154. See Larkin, *Art and Life,* p. 375.

155. See Walter R. Agard, "Classical Scholarship," in *American Scholarship in the Twentieth Century,* ed. Merle Curti (Cambridge, Mass.: Harvard University Press, 1953), pp. 164–65.

156. "It is hardly fair to make our tastes and aesthetic ideologies retroactive, unless we accord the right of future critics to prepare analogous obituaries for us." Mueller, *American Symphony Orchestra,* p. 43.

157. These journals are individually listed in ACLS, *Bulletin,* no. 8 (October 1928), pp. 22–54. The list does not include journals that suspended publication before 1928. It is a generously defined list, containing a number of titles not strictly academic (especially in the fine arts).

158. On these institutions, see L. E. Lord, *History of the American School of Classical Studies at Athens* (Cambridge, Mass.: Harvard University Press, 1947); *Classical Weekly* 1 (January 25, 1908): 105–106; *American Magazine of Art* 11 (1920): 92; Hiss and Fansler, *Research in Fine Arts,* p. 54; Agard, "Classical Scholarship," pp. 150, 154–57.

159. Concerning the founding of the ACLS, see Higham, *Writing American History,* p. 16.

160. John Edwin Sandys, *A History of Classical Scholarship* (Cambridge: University Press, 1908), 3: 48–49, passim.

161. Steeves, *Learned Societies,* pp. 204–205. Compare this with the opposite verdict reached by René Wellek, "Literary Scholarship," in Curti, *American Scholarship,* p. 116, concerning the situation in the field by 1950.

162. AHA, *Annual Report* (1909), p. 31.

163. Dixon Ryan Fox, "Editorial Introduction," in *A Quarter Century of Learning, 1904–1929* (New York: Columbia University Press, 1931), p. 7. Still, his criteria were more appropriate to the sciences than to the humanities, as he emphasized the paucity of Nobel prizes awarded to Americans.

164. Frederic A. Ogg, *Research in the Humanistic and Social Sciences: Report of a Survey Conducted for the American Council of Learned Societies* (New York: Century, 1928), pp. 16–17. Ogg's intellectual standpoint may have been more that of the social sciences than the humanities as he ranged over all these disciplines. But for an even gloomier assessment of the contemporary scholarly situation, purely from a humanistic perspective, see A. Kingsley Porter, "Problems of the Art Professor," *Scribner's Magazine* 65 (1919): 125–28, a lament more broadly general than the title indicates. For further negative assessments in this general period, see Curti, *American Scholarship,* p. 15, n. 29.

165. At an earlier date, the 1903 Phi Beta Kappa address at Northwestern University by William Morton Payne, *The American Scholar of the Twentieth Century* (Burlington, Vt.: by the author, 1903), constitutes a good specimen of the balanced, inoffensive, self-congratulatory kind of statement agreeable to the internal esteem of the academic community and written from a humanistic standpoint. See p. 9. Complacency of tone pervades the accounts of individual departments in Morison, ed., *The Development of Harvard University, 1869–1929.*

166. Elsewhere I have argued that the universities, and perhaps especially the humanities, endured doldrums from roughly 1910 to the late 1930s, fulfilling their original promise only much more tardily, beginning about 1950. Laurence Veysey, "Stability and Experiment in the American Undergraduate Curriculum," in *Content and Context: Essays on College Education,* ed. Carl Kaysen (New York: McGraw-Hill, 1973), pp. 9–10.

167. The series is marred by unevenness. A number of the authors arbitrarily begin their surveys of particular scholarly areas in the 1920s or the 1930s, though this is a significant decision in itself. On the contrary, John Higham's volume *History* had to be excluded from consideration, due to its avowedly historical approach, short-circuiting the presentist evaluations of earlier work that in this

context have meaning. Volumes on the classics and on Chinese painting were apparently never published, and those on religion were not consulted. Still, the remaining volumes provide no less than twelve appraisals of particular humanistic fields by as many individual authors.

168. My count of pre-1920 names is as follows: Italian literature, 1; Spanish literature, 1; Oriental literature, 8; German literature, 3; Russian literature, 0; English literature, 5; Linguistics, 2; Literary criticism, 4, plus several poets active in the teens whose sensibility had great impact upon later academic criticism; Musicology, 4; Philosophy (combining several separate essays into one count), 5; Art history, 7; Archaeology, 1. I do not claim that my reading of these lengthy volumes was perfectly accurate in this respect. Names were considered to be pre-1920 if they had done any significant publishing before that date.

169. David Daiches, *English Literature* (Englewood Cliffs, N.J.: Prentice-Hall, 1964), pp. 4–5. A similar, more forcibly stated rejection of early scholarship in the same field may be found in Welleck, "Literary Scholarship," in Curti, *American Scholarship,* pp. 11–18, though it is presented partly as an argument against philology regardless of time.

170. Lying outside the series, though equally relevant, is the predominantly negative assessment of earlier classical scholarship, apart from the area of archaeology, in Agard, "Classical Scholarship," pp. 151–54.

171. The total obtained from n. 168 should at the very least be slightly revised upward to account for such fields as history and classics, which for arbitrary reasons do not appear there.

172. In literature, a retrospective survey along these more inclusive lines was conducted by the MLA in 1958. Jurists were asked to nominate what they considered to be the outstanding articles of all time in the *PMLA* addressed to various subfields of scholarship. In the list of the most outstanding articles of all, 3 of the 16 were published before 1920. Of the 217 articles either nominated or given honorable mention in all the various categories, 22.6 percent were published before 1920. This suggests a rather favorable verdict upon the value of pre-1920 scholarship, though in some cases the jurists were clearly distributing their choices along the entire timespan out of a sense of historical fealty, and there was an air of apologetic barrel-scraping about some of the names mentioned. Maynard Mack et al., "A Mirror for the Lamp," *PMLA* 73 (December 1958), part 2, pp. 45–71.

173. Santayana to Mrs. M. T. Richards, February 7, 1952, quoted in Veysey, *Emergence,* p. 421.

# The Development
# of the Social Sciences

*DOROTHY ROSS*

Let me begin by admitting that discussion of the formation of five disciplines—psychology, anthropology, economics, sociology, and political science—within the compass of a single essay and under the rubric of the "social sciences" not only lacks prudence but risks historical anachronism. At the beginning of this period in 1865, these disciplines had little independent existence in America. Although recognized traditions of thought existed in each subject, they were generally the concern of men and women of affairs debating the practical problems of government and education and of gentlemen scholars and clergymen discussing history, morals, philosophy, and natural history—the larger humanistic traditions from which these subjects branched. In American colleges, where religious considerations still controlled faculty and curriculum, many of the topics that later constituted the social sciences were treated within senior courses in moral and mental philosophy.

With the expansion of universities in the 1870s and 1880s, these five subjects began to forge separate intellectual and social identities, but they still lacked a common sense of themselves as branches of social science. Psychologists and anthropologists, for example, often felt more closely allied to biology, and political scientists to history and jurisprudence, than to any other of the five disciplines. It was only after World War I that a more common identity emerged.[1]

As before and after the 1920s, this common identity was hardly cohesive. The Social Science Research Council (SSRC), the umbrella organization formed in 1923, included history and statistics, disciplines that were linked to the social sciences yet maintained independent roots in other traditions.[2] Even within the core subjects, diversity reigned. Both anthropology and psychology maintained strong ties with the natural sciences. A major part of psychology has never been "social." And if one attempts to find a deeper conceptual unity than the generic tag of sociality, the social sciences appear even more diverse. The focus on culture and its links to personality and social structure, which George Stocking has described as an increasingly pervasive paradigm for the social sciences since the 1920s, has had to share the field with a behavioral viewpoint, more closely linked to biology and to quantitative methods. Indeed today the five disciplines would be better described as "social and behavioral sciences" than by the former term alone. And large segments of these subjects are not essentially related to either the cultural or behavioral viewpoints, but have roots in older systematic traditions.[3]

If we keep in mind the mixed identities of the social sciences during their formative decades and still today, it is possible without anachronism to discern similarities in the way these five disciplines developed after the Civil War. All of them became separate disciplines. All became firmly established in academic institutions. All underwent a process of professionalization. And all five disciplines attempted to establish themselves as sciences.

The first three of these characteristics the social sciences shared with many other subjects in America during the post–Civil War period. The natural sciences had organized professionally in the American Association for the Advancement of Science before the Civil War. After the war, the natural sciences found new bases of support in the universities and formed separate professional organizations. Before any of the social sciences had organized, the formation of the American Philological Society in 1869, the Modern Language Association in 1883, and the American Historical Association in 1884 marked the entry into American colleges and universities of other groups of scholars with professional ideals.[4] Four of the five social science subjects formed their first graduate departments and professional journals in the 1880s, and sociology followed in the early 1890s. Economics was the first to form a national professional association in 1885; psychology followed in 1892; and the others were organized just after the turn of the century—anthropology in 1902, political science in 1903, and sociology in 1905.

To some extent, the humanistic disciplines that emerged in the decades after the Civil War shared the scientific aspirations of the social scientists as well. Philologists and historians were also intent on making their disciplines empirical sciences. By about 1920, however, the social sciences had diverged from these older historical subjects. Social scientists focused their attention on the regularities underlying social phenomena and accepted an ideal of science that stressed objectivity of method and technical manipulation of contemporary social processes.

Several aspects of these developments have been the subject of intense investigation by recent historians.[5] Drawing heavily on this work, as well as on my own,[6] I have outlined below some of the factors that led the social sciences to take form as separate, academic, professional, and scientific disciplines. Part I below identifies a number of groups of scholars concerned with social science during the 1870s and 1880s and discusses the emergence of academic and scientific disciplines in this area. Part II describes the generation of young academics who appeared after 1880 and analyzes their impulse toward professionalization. Part III discusses some of the processes of conflict and compromise within the new professional institutions that helped shape the disciplines. Finally, part IV deals specifically with the scientific aspirations of the social sciences and notes some of the factors that led to the appearance of a more rigorous scientism[7] after 1912.

I

Among social thinkers active in America during the 1870s, those with the longest heritage were the clerical professors of moral and mental philosophy in the American colleges. Since the early nineteenth century, the college curriculum had been organized to culminate in courses in mental and moral philosophy, where aspects of social life were studied as subdivisions of man's moral behavior in a natural world governed by God. Those subdivisions that rested on subjects already well-developed in British thought, like political economy and philosophical psychology, often became areas of interest and writing for these scholars. The proper principles of political action and the moral bases of social behavior were seldom given extended treatment, and topics later recognized as part of anthropology rarely appeared. Regarding themselves as preservers of the moral heritage of Protestant Christianity, these clerical professors were already fading from view in the 1870s.[8] Their place was being taken by new groups who played a more direct role in the emergence of the social sciences.

One such group were independent scholars and reformers employed in the older professions who began to take an avocational or public interest in social science reform. Such, for example, were Frank B. Sanborn, an author, abolitionist, and leader in the charity-organization movement; George W. Curtis, editor and advocate of civil service reform; and Lester Frank Ward, a government botanist whose cosmic social theory advocated the rational control of social evolution by educated experts. Other such men, largely self-taught, were already employed by the government in areas related to social science, among them the economist Carroll D. Wright, director of the Massachusetts Bureau of Statistics of Labor and later director of the Federal Bureau of Labor Statistics, and John Wesley Powell, geologist and ethnologist who founded and directed the Smithsonian's Bureau of Ethnology from 1880 until his death in 1902.

Except for workers in the area of anthropology, whose chief institutional tie was with the American Association for the Advancement of Science, many advocates of political, social, economic, and educational reform, like Wright, Curtis, and Sanborn, found an institutional locus in the American Social Science Association (ASSA). Modeled on the British National Association for Promotion of Social Science, the ASSA had been founded in 1865 to extend social knowledge and provide a more authoritative basis for dealing with contemporary social problems. Besides reformers and workers in practical social services, the ASSA drew its leadership from two important sections of the New England cultivated elite: natural scientists like Benjamin Peirce and Louis Agassiz, who had been trying for decades to raise the standard of competence in scientific investigation, and university reformers like Charles W. Eliot and Daniel Coit Gilman who held similar goals for the American colleges and universities.

The ASSA divided its work into four departments: education, public health, social economy, and jurisprudence, a division that reflected both the definition of the older professions of education, medicine, and law and the lack of definition in the "social" category. The ASSA proved to be an important catalyst in the development of a secular social science, as both reformers and a newer generation of academic social scientists temporarily joined its ranks in the 1870s and 1880s. As each group of social investigators defined its problems and its methods more clearly, however, they seceded from the Association. The ASSA has gone down in history as the "mother of associations;" its most permanent function was to provide institutional auspices for the founding of specialized organizations like the National Conference of Charities and Corrections and the American Economic Association.[9]

For a time, however, the ASSA leadership hoped to remain at the center of social science development. As colleges adopted the elective system, members of the social science movement began to give courses to undergraduates. The courses were oriented toward social problems and took students into the cities and institutions to actually see the "delinquent, defective and dependent classes." Indeed, such "problems" courses have persisted as a feature of sociology.[10] However, both the colleges and some leaders of the ASSA were reluctant to become too closely identified. From Ralph Waldo Emerson's rebuke of Harvard's isolation from the world in 1837 to Wendell Phillips's in 1881, American colleges had not been conspicuous for their support of reform activities. The expanding universities, with their dependence on the respectable class for students and financial support, were also wary of the social science movement. When some of the ASSA leaders urged the affiliation of the association with Johns Hopkins University, President Gilman replied that the desire of the ASSA not only to study but to advocate reforms made it incompatible with university education.[11]

Meanwhile, the separate disciplines that would later constitute the social sciences were making their independent appearance in the colleges under more scholarly auspices. A number of men who had started in the older clerical or public milieus began to devote their full energies to teaching these subjects in the 1870s and to teaching them as independent subjects free from religious constraint.[12] Under pressure from groups of trustees and alumni to introduce modern knowledge into their curricula, the colleges were beginning to make openings for this new group. William James, for example, introduced physiological psychology, and Charles Dunbar, political economy, at Harvard. William Graham Sumner taught sociology at Yale; Francis A. Walker, political economy at Yale's Sheffield Scientific School; and Andrew D. White introduced political science at Cornell. While the Philadelphia anthropologist Daniel Brinton taught briefly at the University of Pennsylvania, the main anthropological development in the 1870s occurred under Powell at Washington, or in the museums as under Frederic Ward Putnam at Harvard's Peabody Museum of American Archaeology and Ethnology.

In each of the five disciplines, the academic pioneers of the 1870s worked within systematic traditions that had been developed abroad and explored in limited ways by their clerical and secular predecessors in America. Except for classical political economy, these systematic traditions were taking form in the 1870s along evolutionary lines: British associationist psychology was being recast on evolutionary, biological assumptions; a universal theory of evolution was taking shape in anthropology; in sociology there were positivistic theories of social evolution propounded by Comte and Spencer; and in political science, theories of the historical evolution of Anglo-American political institutions. The American academics were also sometimes alert to still newer developments abroad. William James, for example, incorporated into his thinking some of the new physiology and experimental psychology. In economics, Francis Walker accepted into the classical tradition some insights from German historical economics. Simon Newcomb, an astronomer and mathematician employed in government and at the early Johns Hopkins, quickly took up the idea of marginal utility that was being formulated within the classical tradition and suggested the possibility of developing it in mathematical terms. While some members of the next generation would regard these developments in method and theory as the bases for major reorientations of their fields, for the pioneer groups of the 1870s, these developments did not so much challenge the older systematic traditions as extend them.

The new academics tended to define science in the manner common among humanistic subjects earlier in the nineteenth century—as a body of systematic principles resting on empirical evidence. Consistent with this view, the reform purpose of the new sciences was cast in the tradition of general edification. Although influenced by the mounting evidence of conflict in the public arena, the academics of the 1870s were unhurried in their solution. Rational scientific principles would be disseminated in the new courses to the future leaders of society; they would promote reasoned discourse and encourage the adoption of correct practices in the society at large.[13] The desire to train an expert civil service, which motivated some of the early work in political science, and the experience of some economists in advising government and men of affairs on economic questions were half-steps beyond this traditional approach, related both to the concept of public leadership and the newer concept of professional expertise.

Why this new body of interest in the social sciences emerged among reformers and academics in the 1870s is one of the major questions facing historical inquiry. To some extent, the appearance of the social sciences in the 1870s reflected the internal growth of knowledge in each field that had occurred in Europe over the preceding century and that had hitherto been underutilized in America. But it would be difficult to attribute the new attention given these subjects to the state of intellectual development they had reached. The advent of evolutionary concepts is one intellectual development that occurred in several fields at roughly this period. For example, Spencer's evolutionary theories had a galvanizing effect on American sociology, providing perspectives on historical comparative analysis that dramatically increased the sense of scientific identity. Yet sociologists quickly discovered that beneath these broad conceptions, they had no established subject matter and few clues as to how to analyze what subjects they addressed. In psychology, while evolutionary concepts were providing some synthetic perspectives during the 1870s, it is arguable that the physiological psychology and laboratory experimentation developed in Germany were more central to the perception of growth in the field held by its American practitioners and, in this case, provided the core around which the field formed. In economics, evolutionary concepts played virtually no role as yet in America; indeed, classical economics, though far better developed intellectually than sociological theory, was in some quarters on the defensive, and the impact of historical methods and marginal analysis was hardly felt. The fact that these fields all took on similar institutional identities in the 1870s, despite the varying state of momentum, coherence, and complexity in their subject matters, suggests the importance of sociocultural factors in the timing of this early crystallization.

The post–Civil War decades were a time of substantial social change resulting from industrialism and the growth of cities, and sociologists have linked these social changes to profound changes in cultural attitudes. That a scientific view of the world is an essential element in the increasingly rational character of modern society has been a fundamental premise of sociological theory since it first emerged in the early nineteenth century. Historians have only recently begun to explore that linkage more carefully and to explain the particular kinds of social scientific explanations that developed in these decades by reference to the particular kinds of sociocultural needs felt at the time.[14]

It is clear, however, that the concatenation of declining religious authority, growing urban problems, and the prolonged depression and labor conflict of the 1870s was beginning to create a sense of crisis among some intellectuals. The men who responded to the call of the ASSA and who sought to develop in the colleges a more worldly and effective kind of knowledge were particularly sensitive to the need for intelligent leadership and social order. Like many of their contemporaries in various fields discussed in this volume, the social scientists thought of themselves as members of a social and cultural elite who represented the dominant line of American development; as the heirs of the republican tradition, they sought to assume the moral authority befitting their station. Generally the sons of native Protestant families, they had been taught in college that they constituted an elite of learning and virtue whose leadership American society should follow. Thus they regarded themselves, often quite explicitly, as a natural aristocracy generated by and in some ways identified with the "people," but yet a class apart. In the general social crisis, the authority of their class was seen as synonymous with intellectual order in the society at large—the assertion of the one being a guarantee of the other.[15]

## II

During the 1870s, the social sciences began to take root as separate, academic, and scientific disciplines. Before we can follow these processes further and examine the professional character these disciplines displayed, we must introduce another and younger group of social scientists who appeared around 1880. The older scholars were educated and certified, if at all, in one of the traditional branches of knowledge. The younger group had received its training, and often Ph.D. degrees, from German universities or from such pioneer American universities as Johns Hopkins.[16] It was the younger generation who took the lead in establishing the new courses and graduate training programs and who founded the journals and national associations that ultimately defined the new professions.

Within the generation of the 1880s, we can discern two different types of scholars. In each of the five disciplinary areas, there were scholars whose attitudes toward science and reform were close to that of the older, traditional generation. Among the younger traditionalists were classical political economists like J. Laurence Laughlin of Cornell, later chairman of the Department of Economics at Chicago; psychologists of a philosophical inclination like James Mark Baldwin of Princeton and John Dewey of Michigan and Chicago; anthropologists like W J McGee, an evolutionary formalist who succeeded Powell as Director of the Bureau of Ethnology; political scientists like Herbert Baxter Adams of Johns Hopkins and Albert Bushnell Hart of Harvard, who were loyal to history and its traditions of political discourse; and sociologists like Thomas Nixon Carver of Harvard who worked within the older positivist tradition, and C. R. Henderson of Chicago, an heir to the meliorative, problem-oriented social science of the 1870s.[17]

Although the traditionalists composed quite substantial groups in all the disciplines, there were also scholars with a different outlook and more militant professional ideals. In economics, the militant group was composed of men trained in German historical economics, like Richard T. Ely of Johns Hopkins. In psychology, it consisted of laboratory men trained in the new German physiological psychology, like G. Stanley Hall, founding president of Clark University. In anthropology, Franz Boas of Columbia led a group of allies and students who desired a more historical and critically scientific anthropology. In sociology, Albion W. Small, chairman of the department at Chicago, E. A. Ross of Stanford, and Franklin Giddings of Columbia spearheaded the search for theoretical and professional identity. In political science, a group of men oriented toward historical and administrative problems took the lead in establishing professional institutions. The pioneer in the group was John W. Burgess, who introduced political science at Amherst College in the 1870s and at Columbia College in 1880; although an enterprising advocate of political studies, Burgess shared many of the scientific and social attitudes of the older traditional scholars.[18]

The single most striking similarity in the attitudes of these militant groups was their conception of modern science as a product of empirical investigation.

Whether from their exposure to German *Wissenschaft,* then in its most empirical phase, or from the stunning achievement of Darwin in biology, and generally from both, they argued that "real" science or the "newer" science built its theories closely on empirical observation. To some extent, this empirical thrust in the social sciences may have echoed the Baconian empiricism that dominated inquiry in the natural sciences in ante-bellum America. But many spokesmen attempted to define a more sophisticated position. Those with philosophical inclinations and training, like Franz Boas and G. Stanley Hall, felt the need to link their empirical stance in science to contemporary epistemology. Like William James, they were under the influence of neo-Kantian idealism and worked out an empiricist epistemology that incorporated substantial elements of idealism. In all the social sciences, many spokesmen also drew support for empirical science from a new historical consciousness. If knowledge emerged only from the intimate fusion of mind and object; if social objects changed constantly over time and in complex interaction, only a social science dedicated to close and continuous observation of social objects could hope to understand them.[19]

In turning to empirical science, the militant groups were consciously diverging from the conceptions of science held by their more traditional academic precursors and colleagues. While traditionalists and militants recognized that both deduction and induction played some necessary role in science, they differed in emphasis. In psychology, anthropology, and economics, the reigning schools of systematic knowledge were vulnerable to the charge of being unduly deductive in character. Militants were quick to show that at critical points in their theories, the traditionalists had deduced conclusions regarding the nature of the will, or economic motivation, or the evolutionary sequence of culture from theoretical premises rather than from empirical observation. In effect, the younger militants had perceived a serious disjunction between the theories of their elders and the nature of reality as disclosed by their own empirical observations; in all three cases they emphasized empirical investigation as the chief criterion of science.

The division was not as clear-cut in the less-developed subjects. In political science the principal parent tradition in America was a nominalist historiography; thus the younger political scientists urged that empirical investigation become scientific, chiefly by use of the comparative method. In sociology, where precursors were split between positivistic theorists and practical reformers, the militants stressed the need to be both more empirical than the theorists and more theoretical than the reformers.[20]

Besides their empirical conception of science, the militant groups also generally shared a desire to use their knowledge more directly in the solution of social problems than had their academic precursors. Their sense of urgency undoubtedly arose from the fact that they grew to maturity during the 1870s and 1880s, when industrialization had generated the first major wave of depression and labor violence in America. During that period, the revival of democratic sentiment and the appearance of socialism as an alternative course for modern industrial society accentuated their sense of social crisis. Many of them also came from family backgrounds in which the Protestant evangelical tradition had been a powerful influence. In part the failure to believe literally in Christianity any longer, or the failure to achieve the religious experience some evangelical sects demanded led them to pour their energy into the fervor for moral betterment. The organic religious values and idealistic worldview of the evangelical social scientists made the social conflict they saw around them particularly painful and led them to seek ways to use their scientific knowledge to restore social harmony.[21]

The active reform concern of these militant groups was expressed in social values that were generally different from the values of their traditional precursors and contemporaries, in most cases further left on the political spectrum toward greater social equality and governmental responsibility.[22] The conflict in social values was particularly fierce in economics, where the historical economists were influenced by socialism and desired to expand the role of the state in economic activity as a means of moderating the harsh consequences of industrialization. Militants took a more liberal or radical position on such issues as government ownership or regulation of the economy, support of labor unions, labor's claim to a greater share of profits and control of industry, and government welfare legislation. Their overtly ethical conception of economics conflicted sharply with that of the traditionalists, who had been trying to separate their subject from moral philosophy by asserting that economics, as a science, had nothing to do with ethics.

In sociology, the militants' organic social values—their desire to secure moral integration in a society that displayed increasing moral fragmentation—led them in the direction of reformist programs that were quite consciously left of the rigid laissez-faire stance of their academic precursor, William Graham Sumner, but were nonetheless varied. Indeed, the differences among the sociological reformers were almost as visible as their common difference from Sumner. In anthropology, Boas's left-liberal political stance differed from that of many of the traditionalists in the field, but his reform interest was more muted than that of economists and sociologists. His egalitarian ethos worked its way gradually into the profession by means of his empirical findings.

In political science the difference in social values was also less severe than in economics. While the militant political scientists agreed on the need for a more positive role for the state in modern society, their views occupied a more conservative range on the political spectrum, probably because scholars concerned with pressing social issues of the day naturally gravitated to economics and sociology. Burgess's interest in the state had emerged from Civil War nationalism and conservative concern for order; in the context of the new economic and social issues, he advocated a limited role for the state as protector of property rights. Most others in the group saw the state as an agent of liberal, stabilizing reform.

In psychology, the conflict in values was again sharply drawn. Far more than their traditional precursors, the new experimental psychologists wanted to divorce themselves altogether from religion and metaphysics and to shift the ground on which moral and existential issues were to be solved. These secular values involved them from the start in conflicts over religious belief and educational practice, with the new psychologists siding generally against the soul and with some form of progressive education.

Thus, during the 1880s many of the new generation of social scientists conceived of their scientific stance and their social task in distinctly different terms than did the traditional generation of the 1870s. It may also be that social differences between these groups augmented the sense of scientific and moral difference between them. Among the militant leaders, probably four could be seen as outsiders to the gentlemanly tradition of social science that existed within the traditional generation: Boas as a German-Jewish immigré; Hall and Ely as farm boys who felt on the margins of the wealthier and more cultured traditions they discovered in Cambridge and New York; and Burgess as a deracinated Southerner. These kinds of social differences, however, had earlier been absorbed into the scholarly milieus of the colleges and cities. What is most striking about the new groups was their unwillingness to enter under the old terms of a clerical vocation or an apprenticeship to approved traditions.[23]

The militants turned instead to professionalization. They recognized that professional development—in the form of graduate programs, journals, and national associations—was the means by which they could force entry for their new programs into the American colleges and universities.[24]

In economics, psychology, and anthropology, the militants' professionalizing efforts involved them in sharp conflicts with the traditionalists. In economics, where the classical laissez-faire school of political economy had virtually usurped the title of "economist," the historical school felt it was fighting for its right to exist when it organized the American Economic Association around its own reformist tenets. In psychology, where philosophical psychology still carried the status conferred upon it by its ties with the old mental philosophy, the new generation aggressively established laboratories and a new professional journal to capture for themselves a comparable position in the universities. In anthropology, Boas, after his initial brash attack on the evolutionary formalism of the anthropological establishment, set out on a long campaign to build a department at Columbia University and research ties with museums that supported his own conception of anthropology; in the process, he became a powerful force in professionalizing the discipline.

In political science and sociology, the efforts toward professionalization did not result in clear-cut conflicts between militants and traditionalists. Burgess's program of political science based on history and law was not at first sharply differentiated from the aspirations of a traditional figure like White, or from the program of history-including-political science that Herbert Baxter Adams was establishing at Johns Hopkins. Given his position at the still unreformed Columbia College, Burgess's aggressive professional efforts were initially directed against the conception of the older college and narrow legal training rather than against history per se, which he usurped by appointment. In the course of the

1880s and 1890s, however, the distinctly scientific aims and contemporary statist concern of Burgess's program became more sharply delineated from the historical focus of a figure like Herbert Baxter Adams. A member of the empirical, professionalizing wing of the new historical profession, Adams was soon associated with the traditionalists in political science, while the institutional development Burgess secured at Columbia grew through the efforts of his lieutenants into a professional journal and association for the whole discipline.

In sociology, neither the laissez-faire Sumner nor the practical social reformers had the academic standing to challenge the leadership of the militants. But the new sociologists found that they had laid claim to the true science of society through the development of professional institutions before they could make good on the promise. Instead of facing a sharp-edged enemy in the traditional camps, the professionalizing sociologists were surrounded by a sea of academic doubters who questioned the substance of their new field.[25]

The social scientists of the 1880s had to exert their authority not only against other academics but also against popular claimants to science and social usefulness. This second front was not very important where disciplinary expertise was already well developed, as in economics, or where popular practitioners made no claim to science, as in politics. But the new psychologists had to counter popular spiritualists and psychic researchers, and the sociologists tried to displace the growing number of clerical and lay social reformers. For the insecure and amorphous subject of sociology, popular counter-claims were a major threat, particularly since popular reformers often advocated more radical reforms than the academic sociologists could approve. In the 1890s, Small and his colleagues regarded the reformers as their chief competitors, and Small apparently rushed to start his *American Journal of Sociology* to prevent the formation of a reformist journal for "Christian sociology."[26]

The conditions and motives behind the professionalizing activity of the 1880s is a major question for historical inquiry. We have seen that the younger militant social scientists had a powerful motive for the formation of professional institutions: they lacked a firm footing in the colleges and educated communities for their new conceptions of social science, and thereby for themselves. But their turn to professionalism also reflected fundamental changes in modern society.

Sociologists and historians have long seen the development of industrialism in the nineteenth century, with its increased specialization of labor, as the seed-bed for professionalism.[27] Professionalism can be defined as a form of occupational control, one form among others (guilds, patronage, state regulation) that historically have attempted to regulate the problematical relationship between producer and consumer arising from the specialization of labor. Two aspects of that relationship create the possibility of professionalization. One is the degree of uncertainty in the relationship, which increases with the degree of specialization in production; the other is the potential for autonomy that an occupational group has—the degree to which it can exert its power over the producer-consumer relation. Professionalism is a form of collegial occupational control in which the producer's expert knowledge creates a high degree of uncertainty in the relationship and thus a high need for control, and in which the historically high status of its practitioners and the fragmentation of its consumers has enabled the occupation to press and enforce its claims for collegial autonomy.[28]

All the groups of social scientists we have discussed here—the reformers of the ASSA, the academic pioneers of the 1870s, and the younger generation of the 1880s—were subject alike to the underlying process of modernization, and all showed some interest in professional development. As industrialization proceeded and society became more complex, a greater degree of uncertainty entered into the relationship between the producers and consumers of social knowledge, an uncertainty that increased as thinkers and reformers began to propound unfamiliar explanations. In addition, the social base of many of the social scientists in the patrician class or in the genteel professions—and the claim they made to scientific expertise at a time when the authority of science was rising dramatically—augmented the power of the social scientists to enforce their claims to autonomy.

The tempo of professionalizing activities, however, was markedly quickened by the generation of the 1880s and the kind of professionalism they espoused came to dominate their disciplines. There appears to have been at least three professional ideals at work among the early social scientists—that of the practitioner, that of the college based teacher-scholar, and that of the research-oriented scholar-scientist. If we examine more closely the differing claims to professional status put forward by these early social scientists, we can see why the attitudes of the academics of the 1880s led more directly toward professionalizing activity and why the institutions and norms they established prevailed.

There were a number of groups of practitioners in the area of social science, many of them active in the ASSA, who felt the need to develop expert knowledge, vocational careers, and organizational bases for professional advancement; these included particularly workers in the area of charity and corrections and government workers in the areas of labor and statistics. Carroll D. Wright is perhaps the best example of such a practitioner who attempted to develop a scientific professional base in government civil service. Had American social science developed in that mold, as it did partially in Britain, it might have fallen heir to the large amount of private funding for social welfare activities available after 1900 and particularly after 1920. The ASSA, as some academics and practitioners originally contemplated, might then have served as a bridge between expert practitioners and academics, bringing together both theory and practice in the investigation of social problems.[29]

However, in late-nineteenth-century America, the practical vocations offered limited opportunities for people interested in developing social scientific knowledge. Government service offered very few jobs above a routine level. The Social Gospel, Chautauqua, and urban reform movements that supported some of the early economists, sociologists, and political scientists offered equally meager support for a career, as did the politically influenced and erratically funded public school systems. Only in anthropology did museums and government seem to provide any basis for a sustained career. Moreover, neither charity work nor government service offered the kind of status that could support claims to professional autonomy.[30] The younger social scientists therefore saw more opportunity in the scholarly vocation and semipatrician status of the college professor than in the practical vocations.[31]

The academic pioneers in social science subjects during the 1870s also had professional goals, but they were already members of a profession, that of college teacher, which had generally been in America a marginal adjunct to the clerical profession. Their professional aims were oriented toward strengthening the traditional conception of the college professor as a teacher and as a member of an elite community. In that multifaceted ideal, competence and scholarship in a special field were important but remained imbedded in duties to the community and the institution that related to personal character and class status. Traditional scholars, like William Graham Sumner and William James, were joined by university reformers based in the ASSA, such as Charles W. Eliot and Andrew D. White, in this desire to establish academic careers for teacher-scholars who could speak with authority to the problems and anxieties of the respectable community.

Rooted in a long-standing genteel and community-based professional culture, the teacher-scholars believed that their systematic knowledge could be shared with an enlightened public, its principles taught and grasped in classrooms and public journals alike. Thus they felt less strongly the growing uncertainty in the relationship between producers and consumers of social knowledge. Moreover, they enjoyed a firm base in their institutional communities through personal, family, or class ties and could hope to strengthen their professional roles through the kinds of alliances with trustees, alumni, journalists, and philanthropic capitalists through which they had already begun to reform the colleges.[32] This mentality informed the Political Economy Club, a social and professional club for academic economists and men of affairs established in the early 1880s by younger and older traditionalists. The Club foundered on the members' relative disinterest in strengthening their purely functional identification and their lack of collegiality—characteristics possessed more fully by the younger militants.[33]

Finally, there was the professional ideal the younger social scientists of the 1880s learned chiefly in Germany: that of the university professor whose prime commitment was to the advancement of knowledge in his own discipline. While the example of the flourishing German universities had influenced American intellectuals intermittently throughout the nineteenth century, the social scientists of the 1880s participated in the upsurge of migration to German universities. Many of them, impressed by the scientific success and the relatively high status of German university professors, adopted the German ideal of the research-oriented professor.[34] The first professional institutions the Americans so quickly fashioned, from graduate seminars and Doctor of Philosophy degrees to journals and associations, were adaptations of the institutional framework of their respected German models. These institutions were at once professional and research-oriented. Their research function—to provide the kind of exchange of information and peer review that was necessary to stimulate and monitor advanced scholarship—was itself a collegial exercise of autonomy.

Moreover, in Germany, the younger social scientists studied at first hand the specialized bodies of knowledge that had developed in the universities during the nineteenth century. In degree of technical elaboration as well as in language, these scholarly traditions offered a kind of social knowledge more esoteric and distant than the social scientists possessed before and thus increased the need and opportunity for professional control.[35] While to some extent the German model of professional status and specialized knowledge influenced all the new social scientists of the 1880s, it appeared to influence those in the militant groups most strongly. Many of the younger traditionalists either studied only in this country or were critical of their German mentors. But the militants were more impressed by their German hosts and more immersed in German scholarship.[36] They thus sought entrance to the university in a manner that utilized the collegiality of their German-based reserach ideal and gave maximum power to the professional credentials attached to that ideal.

The desire of these academics of the 1880s to establish their disciplines as academic professions would not have met with success, however, had it not been for one timely development—the modernization and expansion of the universities.[37] There were already by the early 1880s more social science aspirants than there were academic jobs for them. Ely and Hall, for example, had been nearly destitute for a time on their return from Germany. Hall and Burgess had rushed at the chance to teach at their unreformed collegiate alma maters, and had university reform not allowed them to move to more promising institutions, they may well have remained where they were and been forced to modify their aims.

The social scientists followed in a long line of scholars who had tried to establish an ideal of scholarly research in American colleges. Earlier in the nineteenth century some of the natural science fields, and then philology and modern languages, had felt the impact of the research ideal. Intermittently scholars in these fields had forced the colleges to accept their demands for less elementary teaching and more time and facilities for research. But in a few cases in the 1870s and increasingly in the 1880s, college presidents and trustees became willing partners in this process.

In general, college presidents recognized research as part of a professor's scholarly function and one that brought distinction to him and his institution, but prior to the 1880s they tended to subordinate the advancement of knowledge to the functions of teaching and of usefully bringing knowledge to bear on the enlightenment and progress of the community. Thus Eliot at Harvard in the 1870s sought men not with academic credentials but with energy and character, men who had a lively interest in current issues and public problems; for some time thereafter, Eliot gave little recognition to the academic research ideal. But the presidents of new and ambitious institutions—like Gilman at Johns Hopkins, Hall at Clark, and Harper at Chicago—recognized that their institutions lacked roots among the local elite and had to build their prestige on the basis of the new scientific and professional ideals. Increasingly forced to compete in a national arena for funds, faculty, graduate students, and recognition, even the more traditional college presidents began to impose functional standards on people seeking employment and responded to the research-oriented professional standards of their new faculties.[38]

Thus the professional ideal of the young research-oriented scholars gained prominence in American universities as the position of the cultivated elite gradually weakened, even in its locus of greatest strength—the college community. In England, the traditional ideal of the teacher as moral guide and member of a broadly literate community of gentlemen commanded far greater resources, in the nation and the universities, and thus was able to subordinate the demand for specialized research-oriented disciplinary communities. In American academe, however, the professional ideal of the genteel culture could not withstand the inroads made by the aggressive, competitive, professionalizing activities of the research-oriented newcomers.[39]

Connected to the rise of the new university, and stretching out from it, was the power of a respectable and literate middle class. Ultimately, the ability of the militant social scientists to sustain their claims for a place in the universities and for professional standing rested on the willingness of the educated public to accept those claims. It may be that their functional orientation, their empirical scientific stance, and the specific vocabularies they applied to the problems of industrial society carried greater credibility and authority in the new industrial world than did the genteel norms and knowledge.[40] But once established in the universities, the professionals fell heir to an important source of authority. As Veblen showed, the democratization of culture resulted in wide acceptance through the middle class of genteel respectability and its canons of intellectual and moral hierarchy. Although the professional academics had to fend off popular rivals, what is perhaps most striking is the rapidity with which their role was accepted and their knowledge sought. With relative ease—and sometimes hearing little change in content—the middle class public turned from the moral advice of the clergy to the expert advice of the university social scientists, from the old elite's conception of society as hierarchically ordered by virtue to the new elite's conception of society as a meritocracy, hierarchically ordered by competence.[41]

III

Let us now turn to some of the conflicts, compromises, and variations that affected the social science professions from the 1880s through the early years of the century. If separate, academic, and professionalizing social science disciplines existed by the 1880s and 1890s, they still needed to consolidate their new identities. Some agreement on distinctive areas of subject matter had emerged among the academics of the 1870s, but by the 1880s, as different groups of social scientists began to converge in professional organizations, very different conceptions of scientific methodology and purpose, as well as different substantive traditions of inquiry, were joined together. What kinds of consensus came to operate within each discipline to permit them to cohere as disciplines and as professions?[42]

We have as yet only partial answers to that question. To some extent professional motivations themselves promoted disciplinary unity. Once formed, professional institutions acted as moderators and neutralizers of the conflicting views of disciplinary advance. In every discipline, the older and younger traditionalists were brought together in the new professional institutions to augment their strength. Except in anthropology, where Boas's intellectual strength secured his position, the aggressive leaders of the militant groups were soon removed from leadership positions and replaced by others who were anxious to promote professional unity and raise professional standards.[43]

Professional institutions presumably could not override all substantive differences. Professional motivations appear rather to have drawn upon and interacted with important areas of intellectual consensus. The most obvious was an agreement to take an agnostic attitude toward fundamental principles. In economics, for example, classical economists and empiricists quickly realized that they had much common ground; both were willing to use the classical model of the market and empirical investigation of how the market actually worked in their studies of the economy. The principles on which they rationalized this joint work were quite different, however. Their agreement to live and let live presupposed a conception of knowledge in which systematic principles were not grounded in metaphysical and religious principles, as they had been for many earlier theorists in the nineteenth century. Most were willing to overlook the fact that different systematic orientations would ultimately lead to divergent interests and fragmenting bodies of knowledge. The processes of scholarly and scientific verification could presumably be trusted to exert control in the end.[44]

Where the future could not be trusted was in those areas that implicated controversial values in the society at large. With regard to such matters, disagreement within the discipline aroused public opposition and jeopardized the professional's claim to expert knowledge. In psychology, the debate over empiricism carried overtones of irreligion to combatants on both sides and therefore was longer and more heated. The empiricists appeared to carry the day in psychology, but only with the understanding that empiricism presupposed an agnostic attitude toward philosophical and religious questions generally. When William James in 1895 decided that those questions required answers, he took formal leave of the new profession of psychology.[45]

In the area of reformist social values, the social scientists were treading on particularly dangerous ground. The dependence of the universities on the support of the respectable public for funds and students made them anxious both to demonstrate the usefulness of their faculties and to avoid public criticism. College presidents urged their social science faculties to display their vital contributions to democracy. Yet identification with a controversial reform cause or service in the government under political appointment were frowned upon because they risked partisan identification.[46]

Not only was political respectability called for by the university in this period of social and political conflict, but standards of personal morality were imposed that reflected the late-nineteenth-century Victorian milieux more closely than the loosening moral standards of the twentieth-century city. The enforcement of both political and moral standards was intermittent, but together their toll among the most creative social scientists of this period was heavy. By 1920, William I. Thomas, the Chicago sociologist; John B. Watson, professor of psychology at Johns Hopkins and the founder of behaviorism; James McKeen Cattell, a leading scientific psychologist and university reformer at Columbia; Charles Beard, the Columbia historian; and Thorstein Veblen of Chicago and Stanford had left their universities under pressure.[47]

The professions also enforced public standards of political respectability. Furner has shown how political pressure and the series of late-nineteenth-century academic freedom cases led the economists to formulate implicit professional standards that proscribed political advocacy on the far left and right. Rather than risk their status as objective scientists, a status on which their places in both university and profession rested, they limited their political advocacy to the liberal center, where their values were less conspicuous. After 1900, when centrist Progressive politics offered them opportunities to exert influence, they perfected the role of the academic expert who carried out the political goals of society rather than led society to reformulate its goals. By 1905, when the last national association formed, the strategy of the economists was well understood by the sociologists and political scientists.[48]

But again, this centrist compromise was not a permanent solution to the conflict between advocacy and objectivity so much as a temporary truce. A study of similar depth for a later period may disclose an analogous cycle of heterodox advocacy followed by centrist compromise when conservative pressure, greatly augmented by World War I and postwar reaction, narrowed the limits of political action. At the same time, the war suggested to social scientists, as the Progressive period had earlier, the possibilities of power and usefulness inherent in technical expertise.[49]

As the debate over political ideologies suggests, consensus within the social science professions and public attitudes toward them varied considerably over time and widely among the different social science disciplines. It is important to recognize that although the social sciences during this period were all undergoing processes that led in the direction of separate, academic, and professional organization, these processes did not act on each field in a uniform or even mutually reinforcing fashion.

The university setting, in which separate departmental status brought increased rewards in funds and power, provided a powerful impetus to the distinct subjects that were emerging from under the religious umbrella. The limited resources and elementary teaching needs of many of the colleges, however, worked against this separatism. Even in 1920, sociology and political science were still often sub-groups within departments of economics or history.

While the academic base provided the primary support for professional development, it also to some extent hindered it. Teaching requirements often interfered with the research activities that conferred professional status, and it was a token of the increasing strength of the social science professions that teaching loads, at least for those who had gained professional recognition, were reduced over the course of this period. The degree of professional orientation varied widely, then as today, between the larger universities and colleges that drew upon and contributed to the major graduate schools, and the smaller colleges and local institutions that were oriented to more special or provincial needs.

The staggered timing of professional development had a significant effect on the nature and direction of the social science disciplines. Once the American Historical Association had formed in 1884 and the American Economic Association in 1885, both sociologists and political scientists met as members of these groups and were at first little differentiated from them. From about 1890 to 1905 the critical discussions in which both the earlier- and later-forming disciplines mutually defined their boundaries took place at these association meetings. As economics came to define itself more narrowly, those with primarily social and political concerns tended to be drawn into the newer subjects. As history narrowed into the strictly empirical and contextual study of the past, the more analytic and scientific concerns of the social scientists drew off as well. The result of these processes was not only an emergent separatism, but much interaction and the movement of early social scientists from field to field.[50]

In addition, particular institutional alliances often had substantial effects on the kind of social science that developed. At Columbia, for example, where Burgess had taken the lead, economics and sociology developed as part of his graduate faculty of political science and were often spoken of as part of the group of "political sciences." Psychology and anthropology, in part because of Burgess's conservative control, remained in the philosophical division of the university. At Chicago, where all the social sciences were early subject to the strong influence of the functionalist psychology department, and where the absence of entrenched traditions encouraged interaction, a cooperating "social science group" that encompassed all the social science disciplines had formed by 1916. It is not surprising that a Chicago political scientist, Charles E. Merriam, took the lead in forming the Social Science Research Council in 1923. At Harvard, in contrast, Eliot's early appointment of traditional figures in the 1870s helped to establish strong autonomous departments in anthropology, psychology, economics, and history. It took political science until 1911 to gain departmental independence from history, and sociology until 1931 to become separate from economics. Social psychology, with its strong interdisciplinary leanings, eventually seceded from the psychology department.[51]

By the 1920s the social science disciplines in America appear to have entered upon a new stage of development. Although internal conflict over the nature of scientific methods and reform would recur, the disciplines themselves were well established. The experience of economists in statistical work and psychologists in mental testing during World War I greatly strengthened their professional positions. After the war, academic social scientists in these more fully developed disciplines could demand leaves of absence for government and consulting positions, thus securing a greater degree of independence from university constraint. But even the more backward political scientists and sociologists were able to attract to themselves sizeable foundation funds for research, further strengthening their professional position and their base in academia.[52] The formation of the Social Science Research Council (SSRC) in 1923 can serve as a convenient symbol of the substantial, if uneven, development of the social science disciplines.

Even heterodox social scientists now had greater room for maneuver. In contrast to the situation at the turn of the century, when censured social scientists had to retract or curtail their activities to remain in the university or were forced out into marginal jobs, such exiles from academia as Veblen, Thomas, Watson, and Beard managed without retraction to retain or regain their professional status and were able to develop institutional ties and sources of support—though often fragile ones—outside academia. The formation of the New School for Social Research in 1918, which provided refuge for many of the academic casualties of the previous decade, was for this heterodox group a landmark of professional development comparable to the SSRC for the centrist social science tradition.[53]

## IV

The basic conditions that led to the development of separate, academic professions provided the basis for their scientism as well. The social sciences formed under the banner of science. The competitive university and professional contexts in which they grew required that they constantly prove and solidify their status as sciences. Given these underlying factors and the failure of the social sciences actually to achieve the kind of agreement that characterized the natural sciences, it is understandable that social scientists would continually try to reformulate and strengthen their methodological programs.[54]

The social scientists began, however, with very diverse conceptions of science. Methods and models continued to be drawn from parent humanistic disciplines as well as from natural science. The natural sciences themselves presented different models of scientific authority ranging from astronomy and physics, the reigning natural sciences of the eighteenth century, to physiology and biology, the rising sciences of life during the nineteenth century. Moreover, the heavy influence of German historicism on the social scientists of the 1880s led to the definition of scientific method as much in historical as in natural science terms. Among the historically oriented economists, sociologists, and political scientists—like Ely, Small and Burgess—scientific method meant in large part historical method. However, many of them were methodologically unsophisticated (Small was an exception) and rhetorically linked their conception of social science methodology to the more scientifically prestigious fields of physiology or physics. Members of these idealistic historical schools, recognizing that their reformist goals involved not only scientific determination of facts but ethical judgments regarding values, believed it possible to include both those functions within the domain of science. Thus when Veblen asked in 1898, ''Why Is Economics Not a Darwinian Science?,'' he was not only urging a more rigorous scientism on his colleagues but a Darwinian model of economics whose scientific authority neither the ethical historical school nor the classical market economists would accept.[55]

The first generation of professional social scientists also had rather loose conceptions of empirical scientific method. In psychology, for example, empiricism initially denoted laboratory experimentation and direct observation but specified little else regarding how these procedures were to be carried out. In the other social sciences, little distinction was initially made between empiricism as the gathering of historical evidence from books and documents and empiricism as direct observation under systematic conditions.[56] From the 1890s onward, however, efforts were made to achieve more rigorous scientific methods. Psychologists showed an increasing concern for rigor in laboratory investigation, and economists were attracted to statistical methods and theories capable of mathematical formulation, such as marginal utility theory. After the turn of the century, political scientists and sociologists displayed increasing concern over the development of techniques of observation that would enable them to understand the actual functioning of social and political processes.[57]

Around 1912, however, a distinctly new voice appeared in the social science literature, and it swelled to a powerful chorus after World War I. Social scientists began to call for a more objective version of empiricism and social intervention. The new program was more quantitative and behavioristic and urged that social science eschew ethical judgments altogether in favor of more explicit methodology and objective examination of facts. While the call for objectivity sometimes expressed itself as a renewed commitment to empiricism, it also was apparent in efforts to revise general theory.

In psychology, the subject with the deepest roots in American collegiate philosophy, and therefore the strongest impulse to disengage from it, this scientistic impulse was profound and far-reaching. Enunciated first in 1912 and 1913 by John B. Watson, behaviorism sought to eliminate from psychology any dealings with subjective consciousness. Psychology was to observe and record only objective behavior, behavior that could be seen in, and understood entirely as, biological response. Although few followed Watson's attempt to reduce thought wholly to muscular behavior, his theory, his objectivist attitude, and his emphasis on achieving total prediction and control deeply influenced psychology and, more superficially, the other social sciences.[58]

In economics, the interest in basic statistical data was augmented after the war by a more self-conscious group of younger institutionalists, such as Wesley C. Mitchell of Columbia. They were successors to the old historical school, but they were influenced by Veblen's scientific stance and behaviorist psychology to call for a closer empirical study of the actual working of the economic institutions of capitalism.[59] In sociology, Robert Park, who had early been disillusioned with reformers and attracted to direct investigation of social facts, dominated Chicago sociology during the 1920s with his program of urban research seen as basic science. More radical than Park was a group of objectivist sociologists, including his Columbia colleagues, Luther Lee Bernard and William F. Ogburn, who called for a behaviorist attitude and research program.[60] In political science, Charles Merriam led the movement for a more systematic collection of data, exact methods, and the incorporation of the advances of neighboring sciences. Merriam also had in his camp younger colleagues who urged a more stringently behavioristic approach to the study of political processes.[61] All of these groups hoped that the development of an objective science would eventually provide social scientists with the tools to exercise "social control."

In anthropology, a "scientific reaction" against cultural anthropology appeared late, during the war years and after, and was perhaps the weakest of any in the social science disciplines—a token, perhaps, of Boas's strength in the profession and of anthropology's historic scientific identity. The pressures that were applied to anthropology from biology found some allies, but Boas was largely able to absorb these pressures and contain the biological concern within his own cultural framework.[62]

The conditions that led to the emergence of this more rigorous scientism have only begun to be investigated by historians. One factor appears to have been the increasingly aggressive influence of biology, and then of behaviorist psychology, on the other social sciences after about 1905. From about 1880 to 1905 the social sciences did not appear to feel that their free borrowings placed them under threat, either institutional or intellectual, from the natural sciences or from the more rapidly advancing psychology. After 1905, however, there is evidence of greater sensitivity to, and defensiveness against, both biology and psychology in the face of new currents within these subjects—Mendelian genetics, the mechanistic philosophy of Jacques Loeb, behaviorism. The social sciences thus had to disengage from their old roots in an outmoded biology, protect their social spheres from total absorption by a mechanistic biology or behavioristic psychology, and prove by the more rigorous standards of these schools the genuine character of their own sciences.[63]

Another level of explanation for the particular kind of scientism espoused by American social science lies in the political-institutional context. The political and professional pressures that had pushed social scientists toward a centrist political stance from 1880 to 1905 could feed into scientism. When Richard Ely and E. A. Ross were attacked for their political heterodoxy, they made it clear to their colleagues that they would henceforth do only genuinely scientific work.

Many in the growing political center of Progressive reform appeared to believe that in accepting the goals set by the society at large they were eschewing ethics for science. The later cycle of political heterodoxy and postwar reaction appeared to produce similar results. Whether social scientists wished to retreat from the public arena altogether or only to hide the political implications of their work, a program of basic quantitative or behavioral science and such scientistic euphemisms as "social control," "adjustment," or "social reconstruction" were appropriate shields.[64]

Not only on a political level did conflicts in values lead toward scientism. In late-nineteenth-century America, the breakup of Protestant village culture by the industrial economy and the rise of the heterogeneous city precipitated a profound crisis in values. While there had been different and competing value systems in America before, there had not been a large class of educated people whose allegiance was so deeply divided. The division of intellectual authority itself between village and religious sources on the one hand and more modern and scientific sources on the other created, in the minds of people shaped by both, severe conflicts in values.[65]

In the waning light of natural law conceptions, science could appear to resolve these conflicts by making value decisions itself. The most popular solutions in late-nineteenth-century America were attempts to root values directly in scientific evolutionary laws. Within an evolutionary framework, the disparate ideals of the older, agrarian and commercial society and the newer heterogeneous, urban one, and the countercurrents of emotional expression and rational control that the Victorian culture had organized into sexual and class roles—all these could be hierarchically arranged and pinned down on a scale of races, classes, sexes, and historical stages, rooted in nature itself and organized to display the future triumph of traditional virtues.

Explicitly or implicitly many of the new social scientists shared all or part of this evolutionary viewpoint. Yet for many, the empiricist program and its reformist values implied contrary hierarchies. Exposure to the complex life of modern society and the insistent exploration of irrationality in human nature led many to grapple more directly with the problem of values. No one described the resulting sense of crisis more tellingly than Albion Small in 1902. The problem, he said, was the breakdown of the older Protestant standard of values, the fragmentation of society into a multiplicity of ethnic groups and functional roles, each of which provided a different framework of values and viewpoints from which to understand the world. More than that, these conflicting values had polarized around a set of fundamental problems:

We are dealing in modern society with certain radical questions; e.g., Shall we aim for physical enjoyment, or for extinction of sensuous desire? Shall we posit an ideal of government or no government? Shall we plan for private property or communism, for monopoly or competition, for freedom of thought or for perpetual social chaperoning of mind and conscience? These are not questions of biology, or civics, or economics, or theology. They are not questions of ways and means. They are not problems of how to do things. They are questions of what is fit to do.[66]

Small, rooted as he was in the older moral philosophy, argued that the only solution was for sociology to discover the totality of relations that composed modern society and, on the basis of that scientific knowledge, to construct a hierarchy of values.

Other social scientists, perhaps those less deeply and personally rooted in the older morality, could not face that task with equanimity. For these people science offered an alternative solution to the conflict of values: it enabled value decisions to be avoided altogether. For example, Robert Park, Small's successor at Chicago, was early immobilized by the painful problem of value judgment and sought to escape in the distance of objective science. "There is only one thing I can do," Park had concluded, "understand." The program for sociology he developed urged scientists not to make value judgments but only to exercise their insight and empathy in understanding the values of their subjects.[67] Some behaviorists went further. John B. Watson, raised and educated in a rural, provincial, and religious South Carolina milieu, was thrown suddenly into the midst of Chicago, the subtleties of philosophy, and the power of the irrational exposed by Freud, and he reacted violently. Watson apparently escaped the strange and threatening panoply of conflicting values by urging scientists to avoid the consciousness of their subjects altogether, to deal with them wholly externally, as objects.[68]

It may be that the emergence of this fiercely objective social science reflected in part the appearance of a distinctly new generation of social scientists. Among the leadership, at least, Watson, Mitchell, and Merriam were all born in the 1870s and had received their training in the United States, under the first professional generation. Imbued with the scientific hopes of their teachers, they could nonetheless easily perceive—as each new generation has been able to do—the values that lay just below the surface of their mentors' claimed objectivity.[69] Yet the accelerating crisis in values affected them as sharply as their elders, indeed more so, for they were without the unconscious legacy of the old moral idealism. Such a generational experience could have been involved in the attempt of these social scientists to form an objective, value-free social science.

Finally, from an institutional point of view, the war and the greater centralization of science it inaugurated augmented the contacts between the social sciences and the natural sciences and increased the vulnerability of the social sciences to their standards. The federal government's organization of science and its control of research funds were still meager during this period, but in the following years they constituted an ever more powerful magnet, drawing the social sciences toward the development of their disciplines along apolitical and value-free scientific lines acceptable to the natural sciences and to the government.[70]

The wave of scientism launched before and after World War I did not wholly prevail. Older methods and models persisted and scientific aspirations considerably outran scientific capabilities. Moreover, scientism set in motion substantial countercurrents in defense of social science methods that took into account the uniquely human attributes of subjectivity and choice. And when reformist attitudes arose in the society at large, as they did again in the 1930s and 1960s, they stimulated reactions against scientism in the name of a more explicitly value-oriented social science.

The result of these interacting processes is the imposition of a cyclical pattern upon the search for more sophisticated methods, as waves of scientism recede under the impact of political activism and the failure of scientific results to match scientistic rhetoric, and as conservative political pressures and the recognition of scientific inadequacy send social scientists again into a renewed commitment to the development of an objective science.[71] These recurrent cycles of scientism appear to be rooted in the political and institutional contexts and bifurcated aims of the social sciences—contexts and purposes that were firmly established during the formative decades of the social sciences in America.

## Notes

In addition to the members of the Academy conference, I would like to thank Professors John C. Burnham, Vernon Dibble, Fred I. Greenstein, Nathan G. Hale, Jr., David Hall, David Hollinger, Bruce Kuklick, James McLachlan, and Arnold Thackray and his colleagues in the University of Pennsylvania seminar on the history of science for their challenging comments on earlier drafts of this paper.

1. John Higham, *Writing American History: Essays on Modern Scholarship* (Bloomington, Ind.: Indiana University Press, 1970), pp. 3–24.

2. The SSRC also included geography. I have not included geography in this essay, nor statistics and history, in order to focus on what appears to be the central line of social science development. As it is, the pattern of similarities I construct is strained by the inclusion of anthropology, whose central derivation was from nineteenth-century natural history, and whose nineteenth-century practitioners had no involvement with college education. The other four disciplines had strong roots in philosophical and historical subjects pursued in American colleges. My references to anthropology are meant to point up similarities between its development and that of the other social sciences that the current literature discloses, and not to suggest that its history can be mainly defined by those similarities.

3. A number of basic works on the history of the social science disciplines provide a general orientation to their institutional and intellectual development: in psychology, Gardner Murphy, *An Historical Introduction to Modern Psychology* (London: Kegan Paul, Trench, Trubner, 1929); Edwin G. Boring, *A History of Experimental Psychology* (New York: Appleton-Century-Crofts, 1957); in anthropology, George W. Stocking, Jr., *Race, Culture and Evolution: Essays in the History of Anthropology* (New York: Free Press, 1968); Regna Darnell, ed., *Readings in the History of Anthropology* (New York: Harper & Row, 1974); Frederica DeLaguna, ed., *Selected Papers from the American Anthropologist, 1888–1920* (Evanston, Ill.: Row, Peterson, 1960); in economics, Joseph Dorfman, *The Economic Mind in American Civilization,* 5 vols. (New York: The Viking Press, 1946–59); in political science, Albert Somit and Joseph Tanenhaus, *The Development of American Political Science: From Burgess to Behavioralism* (Boston: Allyn and Bacon, 1967); Bernard Crick, *The American Science of Politics: Its Origins and Conditions* (Berkeley: University of California Press, 1960); Dwight Waldo, "Political Science: Tradition, Discipline, Profession, Science, Enterprise," in *The Handbook of Political Science,* ed. Fred I. Greenstein and Nelson W. Polsby (Reading, Mass.: Addison-Wesley, 1975), pp. 1–130; and in sociology, L. L. Bernard and Jessie Bernard, *Origins of American Sociology: the Social Science Movement in the United States* (New York: Thomas Y. Crowell, 1943); Anthony Oberschall, "The Institutionalization of American Sociology," in *The Establishment of Empirical Sociology,* ed. Anthony Oberschall (New York: Harper & Row, 1972), pp. 187–251; Don Martindale, *The Nature and Types of Sociological Theory* (Boston: Houghton, Mifflin, 1969).

4. Ralph S. Bates, *Scientific Societies in the United States,* 3d ed. (Cambridge, Mass.: MIT Press, 1965), chap. 3; idem, "Preliminary Meeting," *Transactions of the American Philological Association, 1869–70* (1871), pp. 5–7; Rene Wellek, "American Literary Scholarship," in *Concepts of Criticism* (New Haven: Yale University Press, 1963); John Higham, *History* (Englewood Cliffs, N.J.: Prentice-Hall, 1965).

5. Laurence R. Veysey, *The Emergence of the American University* (Chicago: University of Chicago Press, 1965); Mary Furner, *Advocacy and Objectivity: A Crisis in the Professionalization of American Social Science, 1865-1905* (Lexington, Ky.: University Press of Kentucky, 1975); Stocking, *Race, Culture and Evolution;* idem, ed., *The Shaping of American Anthropology, 1883-1911: A Franz Boas Reader* (New York: Basic Books, 1974); idem, "Some Problems in the Understanding of Nineteenth Century Cultural Evolutionism," in *Readings,* ed. Darnell, pp. 407-25.

6. Dorothy Ross, *G. Stanley Hall: The Psychologist as Prophet* (Chicago: University of Chicago Press, 1972); idem., "James McKeen Cattell," *Dictionary of American Biography,* supp. 3, pp. 148-51; idem, "The 'New History' and the 'New Psychology': An Early Attempt at Psychohistory," in *The Hofstadter Aegis: A Memorial,* ed. Stanley Elkins and Eric McKitrick (New York: Alfred A. Knopf, 1974); idem, "Socialism and American Liberalism: Academic Social Thought in the 1880s," *Perspectives in American History,* 11 (1977-1978): 5-79.

7. By scientism I mean the belief that the objective methods of the natural sciences should be used in the study of human affairs; and that such methods are the only fruitful ones in the pursuit of knowledge. This formulation leaves open the definitions of "objective methods," "natural science," and "knowledge," which changed over time.

8. On moral philosophy, see Norman S. Fiering, "President Samuel Johnson and the Circle of Knowledge," *William and Mary Quarterly* 28 (April 1971): 199-236; Wilson Smith, *Professors and Public Ethics: Studies of Northern Moral Philosophers before the Civil War* (Ithaca, N.Y.: Cornell University Press, 1956); Donald Harvey Meyer, *The Instructed Conscience* (Philadelphia: University of Pennsylvania Press, 1972); Daniel Walker Howe, *The Unitarian Conscience: Harvard Moral Philosophy, 1805-1861* (Cambridge, Mass.: Harvard University Press, 1970); and Gladys Bryson, "The Emergence of the Social Sciences from Moral Philosophy," *International Journal of Ethics* 42 (April 1932): 304-8. On mental philosophy, see Herbert W. Schneider, *A History of American Philosophy* (New York: Columbia University Press, 1946), chap. 4, p. 439.

9. On the formation of the ASSA and the history of the social science movement, see Furner, *Advocacy and Objectivity,* intro., chaps. 1, 2, 13; Thomas L. Haskell, *The Emergence of Professional Social Science: The American Social Science Association and the Nineteenth Century Crisis of Authority* (Urbana, Ill.: University of Illinois Press, 1977); Bernard and Bernard, *Origins,* pt. 8; and Gunther Brandt, "The Origins of American Sociology: A Study in the Ideology of Social Science, 1865-1895," (Ph.D. diss., Princeton University, 1974). On the contemporaneous British development, see Philip Abrams, *The Origins of British Sociology: 1834-1914* (Chicago: University of Chicago Press, 1968), p. 1. On anthropology, see Curtis M. Hinsley, Jr., "The Development of a Profession: Anthropology in Washington, D.C., 1846-1903," (Ph.D. diss., University of Wisconsin, Madison, 1976); George G. MacCurdy, "Twenty Years of Section H, Anthropology," *Science,* n.s. 15 (4 April 1902): 532-4; W. M. Davis, "John Wesley Powell 1834-1902," *Biographical Memoirs of the National Academy of Sciences* 8 (1915): 9-83.

10. Bernard and Bernard, *Origins,* pt. 9; Oberschall, "Institutionalization," pp. 212-14; David B. Potts, "Social Ethics at Harvard, 1881-1931," *Social Sciences at Harvard, 1860-1920,* ed. Paul Buck (Cambridge, Mass.: Harvard University Press, 1965), pp. 91-128.

11. Haskell, *Emergence of Professional Social Science,* chap. 7; Furner, *Advocacy and Objectivity,* pp. 313-20; Ralph W. Emerson, "The American Scholar" (1837) and Wendell Phillips, "The Scholar in a Republic" (1881), both delivered as Phi Beta Kappa addresses at Harvard.

12. For material on the pioneer social scientists of the 1870s, see Robert Church, "The Development of the Social Sciences as Academic Disciplines at Harvard University, 1869-1900," 2 vols. (Ph.D. diss., Harvard University, 1965); Ralph Barton Perry, *The Thought and Character of William James,* 2 vols. (Boston: Little Brown, 1935), vol. 2, pt. 4; Sheldon M. Stern, "William James and the New Psychology," in *Social Sciences at Harvard,* ed. Buck, pp. 175-222; Dorfman, *Economic Mind,* vol. 3, chap. 4; Furner, *Advocacy and Objectivity,* chap. 2; Anna Haddow, *Political Science in American Colleges and Universities, 1636-1900* (New York: Octagon Books, 1969); Robert C. Bannister, Jr., "William Graham Sumner's Social Darwinism: A Reconsideration," *History of Political Economy* 5 (Spring 1973): 89-109; Harris E. Starr, *William Graham Sumner* (New York: Henry Holt, 1925); Regna Darnell, "The Emergence of Academic Anthropology at the University of Pennsylvania," *Journal of the History of the Behavioral Sciences* (hereafter cited as *JHBS*) (January 1970): 80-92. Powell and his colleagues in Washington anthropology shared these attitudes; see Hinsley, "Development of a Profession," pt. 2.

13. In an excellent discussion of the economists of the 1870s who absorbed marginalism into their eclectic systems, Goodwin notes that they "saw economics not as a collection of analytical tools but

as a body of established principles which were crucially important only when applied to public policy." Craufurd D. W. Goodwin, "Marginalism Moves to the New World," in *The Marginal Revolution in Economics,* ed., R. D. Collison Black, A. W. Coats, and Craufurd D. W. Goodwin (Durham, N.C.: Duke University Press, 1973), pp. 295–97. In psychology, too, preservation of the concepts of a spiritual soul and of free will were the critical principles of the older tradition; early psychologists like William James, George Trumbull Ladd, and James McCosh tried to incorporate the new physiological methods without altogether abandoning those principles.

14. For suggestive discussions of the social and cultural roots of the rising authority of science in late-nineteenth-century America, see Haskell, *Emergence of Professional Social Science*; David A. Hollinger, "American Cultural Critics and the Search for a Scientific Conscience: From Andrew Dickson White to Robert K. Merton" (Paper delivered to the Social Science History Association, Philadelphia, October 1976); and David Hall, "The Victorian Connection," *American Quarterly* 27 (December 1975): 561–74.

15. See Bannister, "William Graham Sumner's Social Darwinism;" John Tomsich, *A Genteel Endeavor* (Stanford: Stanford University Press, 1971); Haskell, *Emergence of Professional Social Science,* chap. 4.

16. Among the social scientists about whom I have thus far been able to gather data, no one in the traditional generation is born later than 1842 nor holds a Ph.D. degree. The professional generation, born after 1844, nearly all hold Ph.D.s in subjects closely related to their new disciplines. Anthropology was an exception to this generalization; here there appeared to be a younger group of government- and museum-based anthropologists without professional degrees. See Hinsley, "Development of a Profession."

17. The existence of younger groups of traditionalists can be most clearly seen for economics in Furner, *Advocacy and Objectivity,* chap. 2; for psychology, in Ross, *G. Stanley Hall,* chaps. 10, 13, 14; for sociology, in Oberschall, "Institutionalization," and Robert L. Church, "The Economists Study Society: Sociology at Harvard, 1891–1902," in *Social Sciences at Harvard,* ed. Buck; for political science, in Church, "The Development of the Social Sciences;" Somit and Tanenhaus, *Development of Political Science,* pp. 36–37; for anthropology, in Stocking, "Franz Boas and the Founding of the American Anthropological Association," *American Anthropologist* (hereafter cited as *AA*) 62 (February 1960): 1–17; Robert H. Lowie, "Reminiscences of Anthropological Currents in America Half a Century Ago," *AA* 58 (December 1956) pp. 996–1003. The relation of the younger traditionalists to the professionalization process varied somewhat in each discipline. In anthropology, traditional figures like Putnam and the younger McGee contributed substantially to institutional development, but according to Stocking, their professionalism was the general one of natural science and was not "specific to anthropology." See also, Hinsley, "Development of a Profession," pt. 4, p. 516.

18. The existence of these militant groups and their early professional thrust is best seen for economics in Furner, *Advocacy and Objectivity,* chaps. 2, 3; A. W. Coats, "The First Two Decades of the American Economic Association," *American Economic Review* (hereafter cited as *AER*) 50 (September 1960): 555–74; Richard T. Ely, *Ground Under Our Feet, An Autobiography* (New York: Macmillan, 1938); and idem, "Report of the Organization of the American Economic Association," *Publications of the AEA* 1 (March 1886); for psychology, in Ross, *G. Stanley Hall,* pt. 2; Frank M. Albrecht, "The New Psychology in America; 1880–1895," (Ph.D. diss., Johns Hopkins University, 1960); Michael M. Sokal, "The Education and Psychological Career of James McKeen Cattell, 1860–1904," (Ph.D. diss., Case Western Reserve University, 1972); for anthropology, in Stocking, *Race, Culture and Evolution,* chap. 11; idem, ed., *The Shaping of American Anthropology,* pts. 1, 2, 9; idem, "Franz Boas and the Founding of the AAA," in *AA,* volume 62, pp. 1–17; for political science, in R. Gordon Hoxie, *A History of the Faculty of Political Science, Columbia University* (New York: Columbia University Press, 1955); John W. Burgess, *Reminiscences of an American Scholar: The Beginnings of Columbia University* (New York: Columbia University Press, 1934); Thomas Le Duc, *Piety and Intellect at Amherst College* (New York: Columbia University Press, 1946), chap. 4; *Proceedings of the American Political Science Association* 1 (1904); Furner, *Advocacy and Objectivity,* chap. 12; for sociology, in Albion W. Small, "Fifty Years of Sociology in the United States (1865–1915)," *American Journal of Sociology* (hereafter cited as *AJS*) 31 (May 1916): 721–864; "Organization of the American Sociological Society. Official Report," *AJS* 11 (January 1906): 555–69; "The ASS," *AJS* 12 (March 1907): 579–80.

19. On Baconian empiricism, see Theodore Dwight Bozeman, *Protestants in an Age of Science:*

The Baconian Ideal and Antebellum American Religious Thought (Chapel Hill, N.C.: University of North Carolina Press, 1977), chaps. 1, 8. On James' revision of empiricism, see Bruce Kuklick, *The Rise of American Philosophy, Cambridge, Massachusetts: 1860–1930* (New Haven: Yale University Press, 1977). For a general account of the empirical stance and neo-Kantian and historicist roots of the militant groups, see Jurgen Herbst, *The German Historical School in American Scholarship: A Study in the Transfer of Culture* (Ithaca, N.Y.: Cornell University Press, 1965); Fritz R. Ringer, *The Decline of the German Mandarins* (Cambridge: Harvard University Press, 1969), pp. 295–315; in relation to psychology, Ross, *G. Stanley Hall*, chaps. 5, 6, 9; in relation to anthropology, Stocking, *Race, Culture and Evolution*, chap. 7. Interestingly, Hinsley, "Development of a Profession," p. 501, suggests that the identifying characteristic of a group of younger, professionally oriented anthropologists who emerged from Washington institutions was their recognition of the importance of "subjectivity in field observations" and "the interrelatedness of cultural phenomena," a recognition apparently gained from long experience in the field rather than from philosophical and historical sources.

20. For polemical statements of the militants' empirical programs, see Ely, "The Past and Present of Political Economy," *Johns Hopkins University Studies in Historical and Political Science,* 2d ser., no. 3 (March 1884); the debate between the historical school and the classical economists in *Science,* reprinted as Henry C. Adams, et al., *Science Economic Discussion* (New York: Science Co., 1886); Ross, *G. Stanley Hall,* chaps. 9, 10, 13; James McKeen Cattell, "Mental Tests and Measurements," *Mind* 15 (1890): 373–81; "The Progress of Psychology," *Popular Science Monthly* 43 (1893): 779–85; Boas's early programmatic statements in *Science* and his address at the St. Louis Congress in 1904, "The History of Anthropology," reprinted in Stocking, ed., *Shaping of American Anthropology;* Albion Small and George E. Vincent, *An Introduction to the Study of Society* (New York: American Book, 1894); Small, "The Era of Sociology," pp. 1–15; idem, "Free Investigation," pp. 212–13; and idem, reviews, pp. 219–28, *AJS* 1; Burgess, "The Study of the Political Sciences in Columbia College," *International Review* 12 (April 1882): 346–51; "Political Science and History," *American Historical Review* 2 (April 1897): 401–8.

21. Ross, "Socialism and American Liberalism"; A. W. Coats, "Henry Carter Adams: A Case Study in the Emergence of the Social Sciences in the United States, 1850–1900," *Journal of American Studies* 2 (October 1968): 177–97; William R. Hutchison, "Cultural Strain and Protestant Liberalism," *American Historical Review* 75 (April 1971): 386–411; Richard T. Ely, *Ground Under Our Feet,* pp. 16, 65, 72.

22. Furner, *Advocacy and Objectivity,* chap. 2, has discovered a strong correlation between membership in the group of German historical economists, evangelical background, and left-liberal political sympathies. In the other social science disciplines, my evidence is impressionistic. See Hoxie, *A History of the Faculty of Political Science;* Munroe Smith, "Introduction. The Domain of Political Science," *Political Science Quarterly* 1 (March 1886): 1–8; Small and Vincent, *Introduction to the Study of Sociology;* Stocking, *Race, Culture and Evolution,* chap. 7, 8; Hinsley, "Development of a Profession," p. 505; Ross, *G. Stanley Hall,* chaps. 10, 15–17.

23. Current evidence of any class difference between the two groups is inconclusive. P. M. G. Harris found a slightly rising curve in the class origin of scholars after the Civil War, as did Higham in history at the very end of the century. Harris, "The Social Origins of American Leaders: The Demographic Foundations," *Perspectives in American History* 3 (1969): 206; Higham, *History,* pp. 62–64. However, Furner, *Advocacy and Objectivity,* chap. 2, is able to differentiate the militant group of economists on the basis of "social location," a category that includes class status, religion, rural-urban background, and other variables.

24. While these social scientists had the components of the concept of professionalization clearly in mind, they sometimes spoke of their aims as being specifically "professional," and other times, reacting to the narrower practical connotations of the term, defined their aims as "non-professional specializations." For an example of the former, see Ely, "American Colleges and German Universities," *Harper's New Monthly Magazine* 61 (July 1880): 253–60; for the latter, see John W. Burgess, *The American University* (Boston: Ginn, Heath, 1884), reprinted in idem, *Reminiscences,* p. 365.

25. Ely, *Ground Under Our Feet,* p. 132; Ross, *G. Stanley Hall,* pt. 2; Stocking, *The Shaping of American Anthropology,* pp. 283–86; Burgess, *Reminiscences,* chap. 5; Somit and Tanenhaus, *Development of Political Science,* pp. 34–48; Furner, *Advocacy and Objectivity,* pp. 278–91; Small, "Fifty Years," pp. 781, 796–804.

26. Ross, *G. Stanley Hall,* pp. 162–64, 170–71; Small to Ward, 25 May 1895, in Bernhard J.

Stern, "The Letters of Albion W. Small to Lester F. Ward," *Social Forces* 1 (December 1933): 171–72.

27. See, for example, Haskell, *Emergence of Professional Social Science,* chaps. 1, 2; and Robert Wiebe, *The Search for Order, 1877–1920* (New York: Hill and Wang, 1967), chap. 5.

28. My understanding of professionalism is drawn primarily from Terence J. Johnson, *Professions and Power* (London: Macmillan, 1972); Henrika Kuklick, "The Organization of Social Science in the United States," *American Quarterly* 28 (Spring 1976): 124–41; and idem, "Boundary Maintenance in American Sociology: Limitations of the Concept of 'Professionalization'" (Paper delivered to the Social Science History Association, Philadelphia, October 1976); William R. Johnson, "Professions in Process: Doctors and Teachers in American Culture," *History of Education Quarterly* 15 (Summer 1975): 185–200; and Samuel Haber, "The Professions and Higher Education in America: A Historical View," in *Higher Education and the Labor Market,* ed. Margaret S. Gordon (New York: McGraw-Hill, 1974), pp. 237–280. A new and important work on this subject is Magali Sarfatti Larson, *The Rise of Professionalism: A Sociological Analysis* (Berkeley: University of California Press, 1977).

29. James Leiby, *Carroll Wright and Labor Reform: The Origin of Labor Statistics* (Cambridge, Mass.: Harvard University Press, 1969); Abrams, *The Origins of British Sociology,* chap. 7; Barry D. Karl, *Charles E. Merriam and the Study of Politics* (Chicago: University of Chicago Press, 1974).

30. Darnell, "The Emergence of Academic Anthropology at the University of Pennsylvania"; Stocking, *Race, Culture and Evolution,* chap. 11; Michael B. Katz, "The 'New Departure' in Quincy, 1873–1881: The Nature of Nineteenth Century Educational Reform," *New England Quarterly* 40 (March 1967): 1–30; Oberschall, "Institutionalization," pp. 200–3; David M. Grossman, "Professors and Public Service, 1885–1925: A Chapter in the Professionalization of the Social Sciences," (Ph.D. diss. Washington University, St. Louis, 1973), pp. 27–28, 33–38, 43, 57–60, 274.

31. Burgess, *Reminiscences;* E. A. Ross, *Seventy Years of It* (New York: D. Appleton-Century, 1936), p. 90; Ross, *G. Stanley Hall,* p. 136; Ely, *Ground Under Our Feet,* pp. 35, 41, 60, 124; Higham, *History,* pp. 6–25, 64.

32. Stern, "William James and the New Psychology"; William Graham Sumner, "The 'Ways and Means' of Our Colleges," *Nation* 11 (8 September 1870): 152–54; Hugh Hawkins, *Between Harvard and America: The Educational Leadership of Charles W. Eliot* (New York: Oxford University Press, 1972). Furner, *Advocacy and Objectivity,* intro. and chap. 1, distinguishes between the functionally oriented professionalism of the academic social scientists and an older conception of professionalism, typical of the ASSA, in which expert function is subordinated to class status. This distinction is systematically explored in Larson, *Rise of Professionalism,* chaps. 1, 2. For an illuminating discussion of the triumph of the professional ideal of the teacher-scholar at Oxford, see Arthur Engel, "The Emerging Concept of the Academic Profession at Oxford, 1800–1854," in *The University and Society,* 2 vols., ed. Lawrence Stone, vol. 1: *Oxford and Cambridge from the Fourteenth to the Early Nineteenth Century* (Princeton: Princeton University Press, 1971), pp. 305–51.

33. Furner, *Advocacy and Objectivity,* pp. 65–67; A. W. Coats, "The Political Economy Club: A Neglected Episode in American Economic Thought," *AER* 51 (September 1961): 624–37.

34. Herbst, *The German Historical School,* chap. 1; Veysey, *Emergence of the American University,* pp. 125–33; Ringer, *Decline of the German Mandarins;* Joseph Ben-David and Abraham Zloczower, "Universities and Academic Systems in Modern Societies," *European Journal of Sociology* 3 (1962): 48–62.

35. A number of the most militant professionalizers, like Ely and Hall, expressed their new ideas in popular tracts despite the criticism of their professional peers, but this strident popularizing can be seen as a complementary response, in men with deep roots in the traditional culture, to the increased distance between expert social knowledge and public understanding. Eventually Ely succumbed to the professional pressures toward a scientific consensus.

36. Furner, *Advocacy and Objectivity,* pp. 48–57, describes the more positive response to Germany of the economists I have called "militant professionalizers." My evidence for the other disciplines is impressionistic. For historian-political scientists like H. B. Adams and Hart, Germanophile professionalizing activity was oriented toward the discipline of history.

37. Veysey, *The Emergence of the American University;* and for important individual histories, Hugh Hawkins, *Pioneer: A History of the Johns Hopkins University, 1874–1889* (Ithaca, N.Y.: Cornell University Press, 1860); Merle Curti and Vernon Carstensen, *The University of Wisconsin,*

*1848–1925*, 2 vols. (Madison, Wis.: University of Wisconsin Press, 1949), vol. 1; Richard J. Storr, *Harper's University: The Beginnings* (Chicago: The University of Chicago Press, 1966).

38. Robert A. McCaughey, "The Transformation of American Academic Life: Harvard University, 1821–1892," *Perspectives in American History* 8 (1975): 239–332, presents a valuable, detailed analysis of modernization at Harvard. However, it defines professionalism exclusively in research-oriented terms.

39. Engel, "Academic Profession at Oxford;" Abrams, *Origins of British Sociology,* pp. 136–53; Larson, *Rise of Professionalism,* pp. 16, 81 ff., esp. p. 103: "The English case shows with clarity that the internal characteristics of professionalization and of the professional model are subordinate to broader social and economic structures."

40. Haskell, *Emergence of Professional Social Science,* presents an analysis of the sources of authority commanded by the new social science professions.

41. The degree to which the new language of social science harbored the old concepts of Protestant village culture needs considerably more exploration. Ross, *G. Stanley Hall,* chaps. 7, 15–18; C. Wright Mills, "The Professional Ideology of Social Pathologists," *AJS* 49 (September 1943): 165–80.

42. The degree of consensus within professions is a major issue in the sociological literature. See William J. Goode, "Community within a Community: The Professions," *American Sociological Review* 22 (April 1957):194–200; Rue Bucher and Anselm Strauss, "Professions in Process," *AJS,* volume 66 (January 1961), pages 325–34; and the discussion in Furner, *Advocacy and Objectivity,* introduction. The problem of consensus is also central to the work of Thomas Kuhn. Kuhn has argued that the critical point in the formation of a natural science—and that usually prior to its professional institutionalization—is the acceptance of a paradigm of scientific practice in the field, a consensus on what the science is about and how to go about solving problems in it. See T. S. Kuhn, *The Structure of Scientific Revolutions*, 2d ed., rev. (Chicago: University of Chicago Press, 1970) and M. D. King, "Reason, Tradition, and the Progressiveness of Science," *History and Theory* 10 (1971): 3–32. It appears, however, that social sciences have not generally conformed to the model of normal science Kuhn has constructed for the natural sciences. For an ambivalent account of the differences, see Cornelis J. Lammers, "Mono- and Polyparadigmatic Developments in Natural and Social Sciences," in *Social Processes of Scientific Development,* ed. Richard Whitley, (London: Routledge and Kegan Paul, 1974), pp. 123–47.

43. Furner, *Advocacy and Objectivity,* chaps, 4, 5; Coats, "First Two Decades of the AEA"; Ross, *G. Stanley Hall,* chaps. 13, 14. In political science and sociology, professional leadership drifted away from Burgess and Small and by the time their professional organizations were formed in 1903 and 1905, the initial militancy of the founders had abated, all groups were brought into the associations from the start, and control was firmly in the hands of the younger professionals. In some respects, the "scientific reaction" against Boas after World War I was a belated, though similar, response among anthropologists. Stocking, *Race, Culture and Evolution,* chap. 11.

44. Furner, *Advocacy and Objectivity,* chaps. 3–5, describes the quick decision of the economists to cease quarreling in public over methods and their implicit agreement on the possible value of both empirical and theoretical work. See also Henry C. Adams et al., *Science Economic Discussion.* Haskell, *Emergence of Professional Social Science,* argues that the conflicts in economics were superficial and that from the start a consensus on state intervention, the moral role of economists, and overriding professional aims was present.

45. Ross, *G. Stanley Hall,* chaps. 9–14.

46. Veysey, *Emergence of the American University;* Furner, *Advocacy and Objectivity,* chaps. 6–10; Metzger, *Academic Freedom,* pt. 4; Grossman, "Professors and Public Service." Such pressures may have had a particularly retarding effect on political science, where more formalistic studies of institutions persisted longest. Sociologists had a license from the beginning to investigate society's outcasts, but direct observation of the real workings of politics was a particularly dangerous undertaking. For indications of this situation, see Somit and Tanenhaus, *Development of Political Science,* pp. 69–76; Grossman, "Professors and Public Service," pp. 212–20; Small, "Fifty Years," p. 760; Karl, *Charles E. Merriam,* pp. 45–46.

47. Joseph Dorfman, *Thorstein Veblen and His America* (New York: Augustus M. Kelley, 1966), p. 295; Morris Janowitz, *W. I. Thomas on Social Organization and Social Personality: Selected Papers* (Chicago: University of Chicago Press, 1966), Intro.; David Bakan, "Behaviorism and American Urbanization," *JHBS* 2 (January 1966): 13: Hoxie, *The Faculty of Political Science,* pp. 105–9; Carol S. Gruber, *Mars and Minerva: World War I and the Uses of the Higher Learning in*

*America* (Baton Rouge, La.: Louisiana State University Press, 1975); Gruber, "Academic Freedom at Columbia University, 1917–1918: The Case of James McKeen Cattell," *American Association of University Professors Bulletin* 58 (Autumn 1972): 297–305.

48. Furner, *Advocacy and Objectivity;* Bari Watkins, "The Professors and the Unions: American Academic Social Theory and Labor Reform, 1883–1915," (Ph.D. diss., Yale University, 1976), places the process of professional conformity in the larger context of secularization, specialization, and bureaucratization. See also Watkins, "Review Essay, *Advocacy and Objectivity," History and Theory* 15 (1976): 57–66. Robert Church, "Economists as Experts: The Rise of an Academic Profession in America 1870–1917," *The University in Society,* 2 vols., ed. Lawrence Stone, vol. 2: *Europe, Scotland, and the United States from the Sixteenth to the Twentieth Century* (Princeton: Princeton University Press, 1974) pp. 571–610, describes the development of the academic expert in economics, but takes no notice of the external political situation.

49. For indications of this cycle, see James Weinstein, *The Corporate Ideal in the Liberal State: 1900–1918* (Boston: Beacon Press, 1968); Graham Adams, *Age of Industrial Violence, 1910–15* (New York: Columbia University Press, 1966); *Proceedings of the ASS* 9 (December 1914); Hoxie, *The Faculty of Political Science,* pp. 105–9; Grossman, "Professors and Public Service," pp. 107–13, 127, 249; Joseph Dorfman, ed., "The Seligman Correspondence," *Political Science Quarterly* 56 (September 1941): 404–5; Gruber, *Mars and Minerva;* Karl, *Charles E. Merriam,* chaps. 4, 5, 6. For the impact of the war on the conception of technical expertise, see Herbert Heaton, *A Scholar in Action: Edwin F. Gay* (Cambridge, Mass.: Harvard University Press, 1952), chaps. 3–5; and Grossman, "Professors and Public Service," pp. 152–94.

50. For a discussion of this process in relation to economics, see Furner, *Advocacy and Objectivity,* chaps. 11, 12; in relation to history, Higham, *History,* pp. 106–10. For an example of this critical debate in sociology, see Small, "Fifty Years," pp. 806–15; Franklin H. Giddings, "A Theory of Social Causation," and "Discussion," *Publications of the American Economic Association,* 3d ser., 5 (1904): 383–443.

51. On Columbia, see Hoxie, *A History of The Faculty of Political Science.* Seymour Martin Lipset, "The Department of Sociology," in Hoxie, pp. 284–304, points out the political emphasis and relative lack of influence from psychology that has since characterized Columbia sociology. On Chicago, see Small, "Fifty Years"; Wesley C. Mitchell, "Research in the Social Sciences," in *The New Social Science,* ed. Leonard D. White (Chicago: University of Chicago Press, 1930), pp. 4–15; Karl, *Charles E. Merriam,* chaps. 3, 6, 7; on Harvard, *Social Sciences at Harvard,* ed. Buck, and Church, "Development of the Social Sciences."

52. Karl, *Charles E. Merriam,* chap. 7; Grossman, "Professors and Public Service," pp. 338–40, passim; Grossman, "Philanthropy and Social Science Research: The Rockefeller Foundation and Economics, 1913–1929" (Paper delivered to the Social Science History Association, Ann Arbor, October 1977); Heaton, *A Scholar in Action;* Daniel Kevles, "Testing the Army's Intelligence: Psychologists and the Military in World War I," *Journal of American History* 55 (December 1968): 565–81.

53. The position of the heterodox social scientists was still highly precarious, however, and the surrounding context of professionalization soon forced the New School to change its character. But compare the abortive attempt of early dissident social scientists like Edward Bemis, John R. Commons, and Frank Parsons to form a university for economic and social research as an "academic refuge," *Arena* 22 (October 1899): 472–81; Howard H. Quint, *The Forging of American Socialism* (Columbia: University of South Carolina Press, 1953), pp. 264–66; Ross E. Paulson, *Radicalism and Reform: The Vrooman Family and American Social Thought, 1837–1937* (Lexington, Ky.: University of Kentucky Press, 1968), pp. 138–46. An account of the origins of the New School is in Lucy Sprague Mitchell, *Two Lives: The Story of Wesley Clair Mitchell and Myself* (New York: Simon and Schuster, 1953) pp. 333–43.

54. Speaking for the militants in sociology, Small later remarked: "It was strategically necessary for these innovators . . . to gain ground by playing the academic game under the existing rules. Their instincts . . . prompted them to speak for a 'science' in the old uncritical sense, and having announced themselves as the exponents of a 'science,' they were under bonds to make good. . . . I have certain persuasive reasons for believing that the academic beginnings of all social sciences in this country were in this respect substantially like those of sociology." Small, "Fifty years," pp. 801–802 n.

55. *Quarterly Journal of Economics* 12 (1898): 373–97.

56. For discussions of early methods, see Albrecht, "The New Psychology"; and Ross, *G.*

*Stanley Hall,* chap. 9; Somit and Tanenhaus, *Development of Political Science,* pp. 69–76; Small and Vincent, *Introduction to the Study of Society,* chap. 3.

57. Ross, *G. Stanley Hall,* chap. 14; James McKeen Cattell, "Address of the President Before the APA, 1895," *Psychological Review* 3 (1896): 134–48; "The Conceptions and Methods of Psychology," in *Congress of Arts and Sciences: Universal Exposition, St. Louis, 1904,* 8 vols., ed. Howard J. Rogers (Boston: Houghton Mifflin, 1906), 5: 593–604; Heaton, *Edwin F. Gay,* chaps. 2, 3; Dorfman, *Economic Mind,* 3: 241, chap. 20; Goodwin, "Marginalism Moves to the New World," and George J. Stigler, "The Adoption of the Marginal Utility Theory," in *Marginal Revolution,* ed. Black, et al., pp. 305–20; Somit and Tanenhaus, *Development of Political Science,* pp. 69–76; A. Lawrence Lowell, "The Physiology of Politics," *American Political Science Review* 4 (February 1910): 1–15; Oberschall, "Institutionalization," pp. 232–35; Robert E. L. Faris, *Chicago Sociology 1920–1932* (Chicago: University of Chicago Press, 1967), pp. 12–19.

58. John C. Burnham, "On the Origins of Behaviorism," *JHBS* 4 (April 1968): 143–51; Thomas M. Camfield, "The Professionalization of American Psychology, 1870–1917," *JHBS* 9 (January 1973): 71–73.

59. Dorfman, *Economic Mind,* 4: 133–35, chap. 13; Paul T. Homan, "An Appraisal of Institutional Economics," *AER* 22 (March 1932): 10–17; Charleton H. Parker, "Motives in Economic Life," and "Discussion," *AER* 8, supp. (March 1918): 212–38, reprinted in *Proceedings of the ASS* 12 (1918): 131–57; J. M. Clark, "Economic Theory in an Era of Social Readjustment," and Walton H. Hamilton, "The Institutional Approach to Economic Theory," and "Discussion," *AER* 9, supp. (March 1919): 280–90, 309–24.

60. Faris, *Chicago Sociology,* chaps. 2, 3; Fred H. Matthews, "Robert E. Park and the Development of American Sociology," (Ph.D. diss., Harvard University, 1973), pp. 163 ff.; L. L. Bernard, "The Objective Viewpoint in Sociology," *AJS* 25 (November 1919): 298–325; J. L. Gillin, "Report of the Committee on the Standardization of Research of the ASS," *Proceedings of the ASS* 15 (1920): 231–41; idem, "Report of the Research Committee of ASS," *Proceedings of the ASS* 16 (1921): 243–48.

61. Somit and Tanenhaus, *Development of Political Science,* chap. 9; Crick, *American Science of Politics,* chap. 8; Karl, *Charles E. Merriam,* chaps. 6–8; "The Present State of the Study of Politics," *American Political Science Review* 15 (May 1921): 173–85.

62. Stocking, *Race, Culture and Evolution,* chap. 11.

63. For some indications of this new relationships between biology, psychology, and the social sciences after 1905, see Brunham, "On the Origins of Behaviorism," p. 147; Hamilton Cravens and John C. Burnham, "Psychology and Evolutionary Naturalism in American Thought, 1890–1940," *American Quarterly* 23 (December 1971): 635–57. My impression is that the sociologists who were anxious before 1905 to base their science on psychological rather than biological principles were not primarily concerned with establishing their professional autonomy vis-à-vis biology, but with establishing the psychological, and hence reformist bases of their subject. For a contrary view, see Hamilton Cravens, "The Abandonment of Evolutionary Social Theory in America: The Impact of Academic Professionalization upon American Sociological Theory, 1890–1920," *American Studies* 12 (1971): 5–20. Brian MacKenzie, "Darwinism and Positivism as Methodological Influences on the Development of Psychology," *JHBS* 12 (October 1976): 330–37, traces the rising scientism in psychology to the dominance of positivism in physics.

64. The scientism induced by the war needs considerable research. The motives expressed in Merriam, "Present State of the Study of Politics," suggest that for him, science served as a kind of liberal detour that would avoid the violent ideological conflict that had overrun political discourse, make good the defeat of Progressivism, and lead back ultimately to greater social usefulness. For evidence of concern with the political advantages of an objective scientific stance, see Karl, *Charles E. Merriam,* pp. 131–32; Grossman, "Philanthropy and Social Science Research."

65. See Vernon Dibble, *The Legacy of Albion Small* (Chicago: University of Chicago Press, 1975), pp. 73–74. The rise of social science in Europe has been associated with a crisis in values. See Robert A. Nisbet, "The French Revolution and the Rise of Sociology in France," *AJS* 49 (September 1943): 156–64; Alvin Gouldner, *The Coming Crisis of Western Sociology* (New York: Basic Books, 1970), pp. 88–108.

66. Small, *The Significance of Sociology for Ethics,* University of Chicago Decennial Publications no. 4 (Chicago: University of Chicago Press, 1902), pp. 5–6, 23–24.

67. Matthews, "Robert E. Park," pp. 55–56, 59, 216–18, 258–60.

68. Bakan, "Behaviorism and American Urbanization," pp. 5–28.

69. Charles Merriam recalled how as a graduate student he had surprised his mentor at Columbia, William A. Dunning, by telling him that he could detect beneath Dunning's studied objective prose, his preference in political philosophy. Merriam, "Dunning," in *American Masters of Social Science,* ed. Howard W. Odum, (Port Washington, N.Y.: Kennikat Press, 1965), p. 137.

70. Stocking, *Race, Culture and Evolution,* chap. 11; Charles W. Heywood, "Scientists and Society in the United States, 1900–1940: Changing Concepts of Social Responsibility," (Ph.D. diss., University of Pennsylvania, 1954), pp. 49–51, 100. On the post-1945 trend toward behaviorism influenced by foundation and government control of research money, see Somit and Tanenhaus, *Development of Political Science,* p. 185; James G. Miller, "Toward a General Theory for the Behavioral Sciences," in *The State of the Social Sciences,* ed. Leonard D. White (Chicago: University of Chicago Press, 1956), pp. 29–30.

71. General accounts of these subjects take note of two major waves of scientism, following World War I and II, as well as heightened reformist interest in the 1930s and 1960s. The cyclical pattern is explicitly discerned by Waldo in "Political Science."

# The Physics, Mathematics, and Chemistry Communities: A Comparative Analysis*

## DANIEL KEVLES

Not long before the nation's centennial, the astronomer Simon Newcomb lamented that the United States stood embarrassingly behind the leading scientific countries of Europe in the practice of physics, mathematics, and chemistry.[1] Around 1870, the three disciplines were part of a prescribed undergraduate curriculum designed to produce not scientists or mathematicians but the generally cultivated man. Together, physics, mathematics, and chemistry accounted for less than one quarter of a typical undergraduate's studies. Allowed so little time in the curriculum, courses in these subjects rarely went far beyond the elementary level, and physics as well as chemistry, with a few institutional exceptions, was inculcated without laboratory instruction.[2] Of course, students might pursue advanced work with an occasional research-minded professor. At Harvard there was the mathematician Benjamin Peirce and the chemist Wolcott Gibbs; the Yale faculty included the physicist Arthur W. Wright, who held the first Ph.D. granted in the United States. Still there were no good graduate schools in the country, certainly none offering high-quality training in physics, mathematics, or chemistry. Students eager for advanced study in these fields usually went to Europe, especially Germany.

Regardless of their training, physicists, chemists, and mathematicians had only limited employment opportunities in the United States. Chemists might set themselves up as independent consultants or actually find employment in business firms as analysts and assayists. But there was no significant industrial demand for practitioners in any of the three fields. In the burgeoning electrical industry, the technological innovator of the day was, of course, Thomas Edison, the self-taught genius whose spectacular success was generally taken as proof that in business, college training was not only unnecessary but a liability. Andrew Carnegie recalled that in the early 1870s chemistry was "almost an unknown agent in connection with the manufacture of pig iron." The blast furnace manager was usually "a rude bully, who was supposed to diagnose the condition of the furnace by instinct."[3] In ceramics, pulp and paper, or sugar refining, just

*This chapter should be read in conjunction with the tables on pp. 161–72.

as in iron and steel, there were scarcely any chemists either. In the governmental sector, chemists were somewhat better off than mathematicians, for whom virtually no posts existed save in the Nautical Almanac or the Naval Observatory, or physicists, whose only significant place of federal employment was the U.S. Coast Survey. State geological surveys hired chemists; so did local gas commissions, assay offices, and the U.S. Department of Agriculture. But the vast majority of practicing physicists, chemists, and mathematicians were employed in the academic world where they were largely occupied with teaching rather than with research.

A count of research papers appearing in the 1870s indicates that about thirty chemists, twenty physicists, and probably still fewer mathematicians pursued and published research with any regularity.[4] Much of the research reflected the indigenous circumstances of the respective disciplines. More a servant than a queen of the sciences, mathematical investigations in America were mainly concerned with astronomical problems. Much of chemistry dealt with the analysis of minerals, waters, and soils, or involved simple inorganic investigations, often of practical utility.[5] An important part of American physics was meteorology and geophysics. No small portion of European scientific work covered the same fields, but Europeans also explored the more "abstract" branches of each discipline—in mathematics, the emerging areas of analysis; in physics, heat, light, electricity, and magnetism; in chemistry, the structure and properties of inorganic and, especially, organic materials. In the abstract branches of mathematics, Americans could point to the accomplishments of Benjamin Peirce; in physics, of Joseph Henry; in chemistry, of Wolcott Gibbs. But the arena of abstract science and mathematics was largely dominated by Europeans.

In the United States, as in most European nations, neither physicists, mathematicians, nor chemists had a professional society devoted to their discipline. While members of all three disciplines participated in the affairs of the American Association for the Advancement of Science, where there were separate sections in each field, the AAAS did little for any branch of science between its annual meetings. The National Academy of Sciences was even more ineffectual. Simon Newcomb, a member, noted, "The contrast between the eminent name of the Academy and the celebrity of its members on the one hand and its means of doing either harm or good on the other, is ridiculous in a degree of which the members themselves can hardly help being conscious. It is too suggestive of eminent respectability out at the elbows."[6]

From time to time, mathematicians and chemists had created special journals of their own but all had been short-lived. Chemists, physicists, and occasionally mathematicians published their work in the *American Journal of Science* or in local organs of equally broad disciplinary scope. Expressing their own accurate estimate of the quality and prestige of domestic journals, the practitioners in the three fields tended to send their best work abroad for publication. All things considered, like other scientists and scholars, they were naturally concerned about the status of their disciplines within the United States.

In the late 1830s, Joseph Henry had returned from Europe and announced to Alexander Dallas Bache: "the real working men . . . of science in this country should make common cause . . . to raise their own scientific character."[7] In the early 1870s, not least for reasons of cultural nationalism, the leaders of American physics, mathematics, and chemistry were eager to improve the practice of their respective disciplines and to enlarge productivity in research, especially productivity in the abstract branches dominated by Europeans. Like their brethren in Europe, practitioners in all three disciplines were becoming more specialized, more ambitious to make their mark in professional scientific advancement rather than to contribute to the enlargement of general scientific culture. Reflecting the trend, in Des Moines, Iowa, in 1874, Joel E. Hendricks, a self-trained mathematician, founded *The Analyst,* the first American journal to publish original mathematical papers regularly and the first in some time, perhaps the first ever, to be abstracted in the *Jahrbuch über die Fortschritte der Mathematick.* A few years before, in 1870, Charles F. Chandler, professor of analytical chemistry at Columbia College, and his brother William H. Chandler, who was connected with a scientific school, established the *American Chemist,* an organ for the publication of abstract as well as practical research in that discipline. And in 1874, a group of chemists meeting at Northumberland, Pennsylvania, to celebrate the 100th anniversary of Joseph Priestley's discovery of oxygen were stimulated to call for the creation of a national chemical society. The move failed that year because of objections that the country was too large for a national society to be workable, and that no society so specialized could flourish. But in 1876, despite the objections, chemists in New York City led by Charles Chandler did create an American Chemical Society, with fifty-three resident and eighty nonresident members; it soon ambitiously began publishing the *Journal of the American Chemical Society.*[8]

The Chandlers hoped that the *American Chemist* would find support among industrial and commercial as well as among academic interests. Given the prevailing attitudes of indifference if not hostility toward science in industrial circles, their hopes were doomed. In any case, the leaders of physics, mathematics, and chemistry in the United States tended to the posture expressed earlier by the chemist T. Sterry Hunt. While Hunt did not underrate the many practical benefits of chemistry, he believed that "science for the millions is a humbug! True science, like true nobility, is essentially aristocratic."[9] It was in the post–Civil War decades that the phrase "abstract science" was replaced in the language of the scientific community by the phrase "pure science," which meant less purity of subject than purity of motive. Much of the scientific leadership of the day disdained the pursuit of science for profit, not least because profit-makers had little use for them. To the leadership of American science, physics, mathematics, and chemistry were worth studying because they raised the cultural standing of the nation, ennobled and enriched the mind, and encouraged well-disciplined habits of thought.

Espousing these purposes, the scientific community may not have found much support among the industrial entrepreneurs of the day, but it did find enthusiastic patrons among a special group of college-educated Americans consisting of predominantly upper-middle-class, well-to-do professionals, businessmen of a mercantile cast, and landed gentry. Often described as "cultivated" Americans, they formed a supportive audience for the post–Civil War popularization of science manifest in the lectures of a John Tyndall or Thomas Henry Huxley and in the vogue of the new *Popular Science Monthly*. Their interest in science was stimulated in part by the chief subjects of the popularizers—notably the theory of evolution, the mechanical theory of heat, the theory of the conservation of energy—all of which were intellectually exciting and accessible to the lay mind. No less important, their interest was strengthened by their affinity for the expressed values of the scientific community, which they found especially appealing amid the business and political corruption of the era of Ulysses S. Grant.[10]

Cultivated America included a group of new college presidents who, in the post–Civil War decade, joined with their scientific faculties to reform the American system of higher education. Led notably by Charles William Eliot at Harvard, they assumed that by encouraging students to develop scientific habits of thinking, they would inculcate in them disinterested, noble habits of mind. Introducing the elective system in college studies, they encouraged the teaching of science by the laboratory method and established degrees in scientific subjects. To raise the nation's cultural standing, they also established graduate programs in scientific and nonscientific fields. By the mid-1870s, some twenty-five institutions awarded the Ph.D. in the United States, but the pacesetter in the movement for graduate training and research was the new Johns Hopkins University under the presidency of Daniel Coit Gilman.

When Johns Hopkins opened its doors in 1876, Gilman's stellar faculty included, in mathematics, James J. Sylvester, in chemistry, Ira Remsen, in physics, Henry Rowland. Sylvester, sixty-two, a leading British mathematician who had never gained an appropriate academic post at home, was an eccentric enthusiast of his discipline with a special zeal for promoting research in the newer fields of abstract mathematics. In contrast, Remsen, twenty-nine, a native American with a Ph.D. from Göttingen, was stiff and formal but also energetic, productive, and an ambitious advocate of organic chemistry. Rowland, a twenty-seven-year-old product of Rensselaer Polytechnic Institute, had no graduate training, but he had taught himself Faraday, embarked on a program of independent research, and had already won the accolade of the great British physicist, James Clerk Maxwell, for his experimental work in electromagnetism.[11] Both Remsen and Rowland promptly established two of the finest research laboratories in the country for chemistry and physics. And all three professors gave thought to establishing journals to help promulgate the gospel of advanced research in their respective disciplines.

To Sylvester, *The Analyst* was no doubt an inadequate organ for his type of original mathematical research because the bulk of its articles dealt with applied topics. Not long after he joined the Hopkins faculty, Sylvester queried American mathematicians on whether they would support a new journal. All but one of the forty respondents voted for the venture, though some did express the hope that the subject matter would not be so erudite as to intimidate American readers. In 1878, Sylvester inaugurated the *American Journal of Mathematics* with a subsidy from the Hopkins trustees. Meanwhile Remsen, who had embarked on a prolific program of research in organic chemistry, found himself with nowhere to publish. The *American Chemist* was failing and the *Journal of the American Chemical Society* appeared only intermittently. When Remsen submitted a long article to the *American Journal of Science,* the editor, James Dwight Dana, rejected it on grounds that it would overwhelm his periodical. Eager to have the work of his laboratory properly recognized and granted its due priority, Remsen prevailed upon Gilman and the Hopkins trustees in 1878 to sponsor a new *Notes from the Chemical Laboratory,* which in 1879 became the *American Chemical Journal.* In physics, Rowland did not try until 1884, and then unsuccessfully, to establish his own journal, perhaps because the output of the Hopkins laboratory was initially rather limited. He failed in 1884 because Dana pleaded with Gilman not to permit the venture. Dana's *American Journal of Science* already had to do without chemistry. If it lost physics as well, the bulk of its pages would be devoted to geology, and Dana was sure that a purely geological journal could not command a sufficient number of subscribers to pay for itself.[12]

In the thirty years following the outbreak of the Civil War, American universities, led by Hopkins, produced twenty-three Ph.D.'s in mathematics, thirty-three in physics, and forty-one in chemistry.[13] During this period, first-degree graduates and Ph.D.'s in chemistry especially found expanding employment opportunities in the public sector, notably at the local level where the public health movement created a rising demand for water and soil analysts, milk inspectors, and control technicians for the manufacture and sale of kerosene. At the state level, chemists also found posts in the growing number of agricultural experiment stations which were authorized in every state and were made financial wards of the federal government by the Hatch Act of 1887. At the federal level, the Department of Agriculture hired more chemists after the 1880s, while at least some new posts became available for chemists and physicists too in the new U.S. Geological Survey and the U.S. Weather Service. In industry, some chemists found jobs in drug firms, coal and oil distilleries, cottonseed oil plants, metal smelting enterprises, and gas works; a number continued to strike out successfully as independent entrepreneurs or consultants.

But the number of governmental positions for physicists, chemists, and mathematicians remained comparatively small, and there was hardly any industrial demand to speak of for Ph.D.'s in the three fields. In chemistry, industrial firms wanted mainly analysts, not organic chemists. Insurance companies needed only actuarial calculators, not mathematicians. And in 1884 the trade journal *Electrical World* succinctly expressed the attitude of its constituency: "Edison's mathematics would hardly qualify him for admission to a single college or university . . ., but we would rather have his opinion on electrical questions than

[that] of most physicists.''[14] In the post–Civil War decades, Ph.D.'s in physics, mathematics, and chemistry tended overwhelmingly to make their careers in the academic world.

There, professors of physics, chemistry, and mathematics significantly increased the output of research in their respective disciplines. Between 1870 and 1893, 236 American physicists published 899 articles in European and American journals; 82 mathematicians published 272 articles; 327 chemists published 1186 articles. At home, the large majority of chemical research found its way into Remsen's *American Chemical Journal,* while the results of mathematical research were published mainly in Sylvester's *American Journal of Mathematics.* Physicists continued for the most part to rely upon the *American Journal of Science,* though the Harvard faculty published part of its work in the *Proceedings of the American Academy of Arts and Sciences.*

More important than the enlargement in the output of research during this period was the increase in the number of practitioners in each discipline who were producing work of significance. Along with Remsen in chemistry were Frank W. Clarke, H. S. Hill, Charles Loring Jackson, A. R. Leeds, Arthur Michael, Albert A. Michelson, Alfred M. Mayer, Carl Barus, and of course Josiah Willard Gibbs, a genius for any age. In mathematics, Sylvester returned to England in 1884 but there remained T. Craig, George Bruce Halstead, W. W. Johnson, Simon Newcomb, D. Stone, and William E. Story.[15] However despite the rise in the quantity and quality of American physical, chemical, and mathematical research at the opening of the 1890s, the practitioners of all three disciplines in America still felt themselves—and probably actually remained— less accomplished than their counterparts in the leading scientific nations of Europe.

The productivity of American physicists lagged behind that of Europeans; so evidently did that of American mathematicians and probably that of American chemists. Thirty percent of the articles in Sylvester's journal were published by foreigners, but that was the result of a deliberate editorial policy to acquaint American mathematicians with the work of Europeans. More significant, a disproportionately large fraction of the articles by productive American authors in both Sylvester's journal and Remsen's *American Chemical Journal* were contributed by Johns Hopkins faculty or graduates.[16] Outside the Hopkins orbit in late-nineteenth-century academia, the encouragement of graduate training and research was more honored in rhetoric than in reality. A growing number of scientists, their ambitions fired by the model of the German university, might hunger for recognition in the world research community, but academic administrators were more concerned with their faculty's pedagogical accomplishments. "Our aim," president Francis Amasa Walker of MIT put it, "should be: *the mind of the student,* not scientific discovery, not professional accomplishment.''[17]

No less important, university presidents tended to discourage research on grounds that it would lead to narrow specialization, to the fracture of a general culture that they believed could and should be preserved. If late-nineteenth-century universities were thus arenas of conflict between teaching and research, they were in a deeper sense a battleground between ideals of purpose—between the diffusion as against the advancement of knowledge, between the education of widely literate citizens as against the training of professionals, between the preservation of a general culture as against the encouragement of specialization to a degree that would make general culture impossible.

In this conflict, the late-nineteenth-century university president held the more powerful hand. Lord Bryce observed that he exercised virtually autocratic powers; he controlled salaries, appointments, promotions—in short, the entire system of academic rewards and incentives.[18] The president used his powers to stress teaching over research in the use of faculty time, university resources, and even the design of laboratories. Of course, the professors complained that they had too little time and support for research, but the professors of the day lived in a buyers', not a sellers', market. Unable to brandish offers from other universities, they had no leverage with which to force their presidential superiors to modify policies, either for them as individuals or for their departments. If American physicists, chemists, and mathematicians were less productive than their European counterparts, it was because their academic circumstances and incentives simply discouraged the pursuit of research.

Outside the academic world, research remained unheard of in industry. In federal agencies it was always in a precarious position, especially if it was the kind of research vulnerable to charges of impracticality. "We are not fomenting science," the director of the Coast and Geodetic Survey typically had to assure a congressional investigating committee, "We are doing practical work for practical purposes."[19] At state agricultural experiment stations, chemists faced the difficulty of doing any research at all amid the demands of their agrarian constituencies. In 1886, the soil scientist E. W. Hilgard complained of the California State Experiment Station: "There is no rest here for anyone, wicked or otherwise, least of all for a man who, like myself, is in a position which authorizes everyone from the shock-haired and hayseed-bestrewn granger to the justices of the supreme court to ply me with questions on their private business."[20] Nevertheless, like Frank W. Clarke, W. O. Atwater, or Harvey Wiley; like Simon Newcomb or Charles Saunders Peirce; like Carl Barus or Thomas C. Mendenhall—some of the more productive chemists, mathematicians, and physicists were employed in federal agencies and agricultural experiment stations.[21] Government chemists produced enough research to help make viable the new *Journal of Analytical and Applied Chemistry,* which was founded in the 1880s as a private venture by Edward Hart, one of the first chemistry fellows at Johns Hopkins.

If most government-sponsored research was understandably of a practical type, so was some academic work. But critics then and later who accounted for the inferior standing of American science by singling out its applied tendencies implicitly idealized the situation abroad. In chemistry, European practitioners also paid considerable attention to applied subjects. While in mathematics the percentage of articles published abroad in the field of abstract analysis increased rapidly, some 30 percent of world research output dealt with such applied subjects as geodesy or physical theory or astronomy.[22] In any case, applied work could lead to fundamental results. The American mathematical astronomer, G. W. Hill, hit upon the idea of infinite determinants in the course of analyzing the relative motions of the earth, sun, and moon. Josiah Willard Gibbs earned a place in the mathematical history books for his work on quaternions, during which he invented the modern notation of vector analysis and to which he had come via the route of electromagnetic theory. Agricultural experiment station scientists contributed to fundamental knowledge of, among other things, plant chemistry, and in physics, Edison of course stumbled upon the Edison effect. More important, whatever the attention to applied research, a large part of the work published by Americans in mathematics and chemistry, and virtually all of it in physics, was in "pure," or fundamental subjects.[23]

The trouble with physics, mathematics, and chemistry in late-nineteenth-century America was not so much in the subject matter as in the quality of the research, and particularly its relation to the kind of research likely to win accolades and reputations among the more abstract scientific community of Europe. One is at hazard in attempting to specify what constitutes quality in science no less than in literature or art, but certain general features of merit do suggest themselves. Whether in theoretical or experimental science, quality frequently lies in explorations that throw light on a general category of phenomena or the development of techniques that permit practitioners to deal with a wide variety of problems. In late-nineteenth-century chemistry, one would set high on the scale of quality the structural theory of the benzene ring and low on it the analysis of the constituents of an arbitrary organic compound. Similarly in mathematics, the more general—and rigorous—the proof or the more widely applicable the analytic technique, the higher the quality. On the scale of quality, the Pythagorean theorem, of course, stands far higher than the mere calculation of the sides of a particular right triangle. Late-nineteenth-century American mathematics seems to have consisted too much of mere calculations. American physics and chemistry in the same period lacked a meaningful theoretical side, and too much of the experimental work consisted of mere fact-gathering as opposed to the gathering of important facts or the invention of significant experimental techniques.

In part, the emphasis on fact-gathering revealed the degree to which American science derived from the idea that science proceeds merely by the accumulation of empirical data. If this naive reading of Baconian instruction was strong in the United States, it was vigorous in Britain, too, but the British produced more high-quality science without, it seems, having significantly more physicists, chemists, or mathematicians. A more important influence than the American version of Baconism was the democratic assumption that lay implicitly beneath it—since all data were of equal importance, so by extension were all data gatherers. But as the Nobel laureate Luis Alvarez once said, "There is no democracy in physics. You can't say that some second rate guy's opinion should count as much as [Enrico] Fermi's."[24] Even in late-nineteenth-century American physics, 85 percent of the research articles were published by 21 percent of the practitioners; in mathematics, 75 percent were published by 35 percent; in chemistry, 69 percent were published by 21 percent.[25] And within this productive group, a still smaller number—the disciplinary elite—produced the important work. The fundamental difficulty in American physics, mathematics, and chemistry of the day was that this disciplinary elite operated in an institutional framework that was more democratic in initiative than elitist in control, a system that offered the practitioners of the first rank little opportunity to set high quality standards for the research of the much larger second-rank group.

Standards of significance could have been set in first-rate centers of research and training, where members of the disciplinary elite, concentrated in sufficient numbers, might have stimulated each other and instilled in students a taste for the significant type of research. However, apart from Johns Hopkins, the university system's commitment to graduate training in the late nineteenth century was, like its commitment to research, generally weak. A physics student recalled that he went to Princeton for graduate work, "browsed in the library, played in the laboratory, and deteriorated intellectually." Felix Klein, the great German mathematician, whose institute in Göttingen was a magnet for advanced students everywhere, declared the preparation of Americans—presumably he included those who came with college degrees—for his higher courses "entirely inadequate."[26] The low quality of American graduate schools drove students in physics and chemistry as well as those in mathematics to study abroad, not only for doctoral but for postdoctoral training. For the three disciplines, the productive group in physics was twice as likely as the less productive to have studied in Europe; in mathematics, almost three times as likely; in chemistry, almost four times.[27]

At home, the majority of Ph.D.'s in each discipline were trained at a handful of schools. In physics, the schools were Hopkins, Harvard, and Yale; in mathematics, Hopkins and Yale; in chemistry, Hopkins, Harvard, Yale, and Columbia.[28] Yet, save for Hopkins in mathematics and Harvard in chemistry, none of these schools had a concentration of any fraction of the respective disciplinary elites. The best organic chemist in the United States was Arthur Michael, but he was on the faculty at Tufts which had no graduate program. Other chemists of merit, including Edgar F. Smith at the University of Pennsylvania and Charles F. Mabery at Case Institute of Technology, taught no graduate students either. The physicist Albert A. Michelson was also at Case, and his highly capable colleague, Alfred M. Mayer, was at the Stevens Institute in Hoboken. In mathematics, G. W. Hill spent most of his professional life at the Nautical Almanac in Washington, D.C. before retiring to his birthplace in upstate New York. More generally, the productive, as opposed to the elite, group in physics was scattered throughout some twenty-five academic institutions; in mathematics, throughout fourteen; in chemistry, throughout twenty-nine.[29]

In short, in late-nineteenth-century physics, mathematics, and chemistry, the small disciplinary elite and the larger productive groups were generally situated outside of the graduate training network. True, in physics there was a slight concentration of the productive, as distinct from the elite, group at Harvard, but most of its members were like John Trowbridge, whose research fell squarely in the fact-gathering tradition. The only outstanding physicist at Yale was Willard Gibbs who had a mere handful of students throughout his career. Hopkins' sole source of strength in physics was Rowland, who did train a generation of able spectroscopists. In mathematics Hopkins, which had an able staff gathered by Sylvester and graduated fully 43 percent of the mathematics Ph.D.'s published between 1878 and 1890, served students in that discipline exceptionally well.[30]

In chemistry, the productive practitioners at Yale and Columbia fell into the fact-gathering school. Harvard students might receive capable training in inorganic and even organic chemistry from Wolcott Gibbs, Henry B. Hill, and Charles Loring Jackson. But here, too, Hopkins commanded the field, graduating a full 36 percent of the chemistry Ph.D.'s or as large a fraction as Harvard, Yale, and Columbia combined.[31] In chemistry as in physics, the Hopkins department was really little more than one man deep; the majority of students took their Ph.D.'s under Ira Remsen. Yet for all of Remsen's energetic evangelism for organic chemistry, his own research was largely in the fact-gathering tradition, which in organic chemistry meant the fabrication of new compounds and the analysis of their constitution. Of course, organic chemistry was in a stage when the accumulation of new compounds served a certain useful purpose, much the same as did Rowland's accumulation of more accurate spectroscopic data. Nevertheless, Remsen tended to encourage too much the conduct of descriptive chemistry and too little the pondering of the more fundamental problems of chemical structure.[32]

Graduate schools aside, standards of quality in research could have been set by the journals in the respective disciplines. Physicists, still without an organ of their own, continued to publish in Dana's *American Journal of Science,* but Dana, eager to maintain the disciplinary diversity of his journal and thus to keep a financially viable list of subscribers, was evidently willing to publish even mediocre studies by established physicists. In mathematics, *The Analyst,* and its successor after 1883, the *Annals of Mathematics,* continued to devote its pages largely to applied work; it was not a salient forum for research in the newer abstract areas of the discipline. In contrast, the *American Journal of Mathematics,* with its large percentage of foreign authors and high editorial standards, seems to have done an excellent job both in introducing American mathematicians to key problems in abstract mathematics and in displaying models of what constituted high-quality work.

In chemistry, virtually no one respected the *Journal of the American Chemical*

*Society,* which, with its intermittent publication, was by common acknowledgment a forum for the weakest work. By contrast, Remsen's *American Chemical Journal* ably promulgated the gospel of organic chemistry, yet it also tended to uphold Remsen's fact-gathering style of research as the model of meritorious effort in the field. Indeed, the glamor attached to Remsen's organic chemistry annoyed many inorganic chemists, including Frank W. Clarke, who in 1878 chided his American colleagues for making their "chief aim to discover immense numbers of new compounds, and to theorize upon their constitutions. . . . These chemists have devoted nine-tenths of their energy to the compounds of a single element, carbon." In Clarke's mind, three great problems in chemistry warranted considerably more attention than they were receiving: "First, what laws govern the transformations of energy that occur during chemical changes? Second, how do the properties of compounds stand related to those of the elements contained in them? Third, what is the nature of the chemical union?"[33] Clarke's critique of organic chemists in America was unfair; most were only following part of the program underway in Europe. But he was right to call his colleagues to account for paying so little attention to the emerging field of physical chemistry which was given almost no space in Remsen's *Journal,* the chief organ for the publication of American chemical research.

The end result was that, in the late nineteenth century, American scientists continued to send their papers to European journals. The productive group of American chemists published 16 percent of its work abroad; the productive group of American mathematicians, 19 percent; and the productive group of physicists, 21 percent.[34] And in all three disciplines, these articles tended to report on the most significant work.

Apart from journals, standards of quality could also have been set by professional societies. But physics and mathematics remained without a professional society, and the American Chemical Society was hardly worthy of its name. Although officers of the Society were slightly more likely than members of the productive group in their discipline to hold Ph.D.'s, and almost as likely to have studied abroad, their publication rate was 25 percent lower than that of the productive group, and only 57 percent belonged to the productive group itself. No less important, 22 percent of their employment was in business or industry.[35] In short, the leadership of the Society was by most measures less involved in research than was the productive group of American chemists. Then, too, for a dozen years after the Society's founding in 1876, all its directors were residents of New York City and vicinity. Chemists elsewhere, quite accurately perceiving the Society as more local than national in character, resented its claim to represent all of American chemistry. In 1881, the nonresident membership reached a peak of 124, then declined to 76 by 1889. Even the resident New York membership, after rising to an 1884 peak of 119, fell to 91. Some of the nation's best chemists had never joined the Society, and many of those who did, including Frank Clarke, Ira Remsen, and William H. Chandler, resigned. In 1884, dissidents in the capital added to the Society's difficulties by forming the Chemical

Society of Washington, which was largely dominated by government chemists and doubtless connected with analytical rather than with organic subjects.[36]

Of course, members of all three disciplines could still rely upon the American Association for the Advancement of Science and the National Academy of Sciences. But the AAAS continued without a regular journal or much activity between its annual meetings. Besides, to the dissatisfaction of some scientists, the AAAS made no distinction between average and superior practitioners of any discipline. Advocates of an elite scientific organization that might set standards of excellence in research looked to the National Academy of Sciences, yet the Academy published no regular journal either, held poorly attended and infrequent meetings, and had only a limited endowment income to parcel out for research. In addition, since over half its membership came from federal scientific agencies, non-Washington scientists regarded the Academy with the same kind of geographical resentment that chemists from outside New York City displayed toward the American Chemical Society.

By 1890, physics, mathematics, and chemistry in the United States were unquestionably more advanced than in 1870. Neophytes in each field could obtain first degrees in their subject and a nominal graduate training that often prepared them for work in the important areas of organic chemistry, abstract mathematics, and spectroscopic physics. The graduate pilgrimage to Europe increased their contact with these important areas of research and also helped sensitize them—more than they might have been otherwise—to what constituted quality work in their disciplines. So to an extent did the new journals at home, especially in mathematics. And the emergence of universities and the enlargement of governmental science provided not only rhetorical but in some cases real institutional possibilities for the pursuit of research. But while a solid foundation had been laid for the practice of the three disciplines in America, their rise to first rank awaited a greater concentration of means and able men in institutions devoted to research and training, publication, and professional activities. It awaited, in short, the accommodation of the elitism inherent in high-quality science to the democratic assumptions and geographical pluralism characteristic of science in the United States.

Yet by 1890, economic and technological forces were changing the status and opportunities of physicists, mathematicians, and chemists in America. The electrical industry was beginning to shift from direct to alternating current. Posing more complicated technical challenges than direct current, alternating current rapidly moved the design of electrical circuits, machinery, and appliances beyond the capacity of the self-trained technician. About the same time, such chemically related industries as iron and steel, fertilizer, and sugar were finding it advantageous to employ analytic chemists. Even more important, manufacturers in the newer areas of drugs and petroleum products, and especially coal tar dyes, increasingly felt a need for chemists in organic fields. By the early twentieth century, William McMurtrie, president of the American Chemical Society, happily observed: "We cannot yet boast with the Germans that single works employ more than 100 thoroughly educated chemists . . . , yet many of the more important works have corps of chemists numbering from 10 to 50, while very many more have smaller numbers."[38]

While many of the chemists were at first put to such routine tasks as the improvement of the production process, a growing number eventually addressed themselves to product development or applied research. And in the first decade of the twentieth century, a few firms in the more technologically intensive sectors of the electrical and chemical industries—notably DuPont, AT&T, Westinghouse, General Electric, and Standard Oil of Indiana—opened genuine research laboratories. As Professor Marston T. Bogert of Columbia University noted, in the chemical industry, research helped to prove true the "old joke about the Chicago packing-houses using every part of the pig, including the squeal. . . . In modern abattoirs and packing-houses, the hides are used for leather; the grease is converted into soap, candles, oleo, and glycerin; the blood and scrap into blood albumen, fertilizers, and potassium cyanide; the horns and hoofs into jelly, buttons, knife handles, etc.; the feet, bones, and heads, into glue, bone oil and bone-black."[39]

The economic advantages of research in the physical sciences were recognized in the federal government when, at the turn of the century, Congress responded to the demands of a coalition of scientists and manufacturers by creating the National Bureau of Standards. Established to determine standards not only of weight and length but of electrical and chemical quantities, the Bureau was authorized to conduct research in all pertinent areas of the physical sciences. At the same time, spurred ahead by the assumption that chemical research would benefit agriculture, the chemical agencies in the Agriculture Department expanded their budgets and personnel, while the Adams Act of 1906 provided funds for the conduct of original research at state experiment stations. In the area of regulation, scientists like Harvey Wiley in the Agriculture Department's Bureau of Chemistry joined forces with social reformers to prompt the passage of laws protecting Americans from adulterated products. After passage of the Pure Food and Drug Act of 1906, Wiley's Bureau of Chemistry was given additional duties in the regulatory sphere. Soon, the National Bureau of Standards enlarged its range of activities by embarking on a crusade for honesty in weights and measures. By 1915, the combination of economic development and regulation for reform had substantially increased the number of places for physicists and especially chemists in governmental agencies.[40]

Responding to the rising industrial and governmental demand, an increasing number of young Americans went to college to study science and engineering. Once introduced to advanced courses in physics, mathematics, and chemistry, many remained in school to pursue doctorates. In the decade after 1895, physics became a field of rich intellectual excitement as a result of the discovery of X-rays, radioactivity, and the electron, as well as the theories of special relativity and quanta. The advent of the electron also added luster to chemistry by rendering more answerable the questions Frank Clarke had posed about the dynamics of chemical bonding and transformations. Mathematics was proceeding at a rapid pace in the fields of topology, groups, abstract algebra, and function theory, and in 1900 the great German mathematician David Hilbert set out his celebrated list of twenty-three research problems that would prove difficult enough to occupy more than one mathematical generation. Between 1890 and 1915, American universities granted about 200 doctorates in mathematics, 300 in physics, and 500 in chemistry—approximately ten times as many in each discipline as they had awarded in the previous quarter century.[41]

The more American scientists and mathematicians went into advanced work in electrons, organic structure, or mathematical groups, the more specialized they tended to become. Not only did chemists speak less to physicists, and members of the two disciplines hardly at all to mathematicians, but the disciplines themselves became increasingly fragmented. Expressing the trend, early in the century, workers in two different branches of chemistry founded the *Journal of Physical Chemistry* and the *Journal of Biological Chemistry*. Even more objectionable to some lay critics was the fact that, whatever the discipline, science was rapidly leaving the arena of general culture. In 1906 the *Nation* complained: "Today, science has withdrawn into realms that are hardly [intelligible].... Physics has outgrown the old formulas of gravity, magnetism, and pressure; has discarded the molecule and atom for the ion, and may in its recent generalizations be followed only by an expert in the higher, not to say the transcendental, mathematics.... In short, one may say not that the average cultivated man has given up science, but that science has deserted him."[42]

But there was hardly any stopping the trend to specialization as long as science remained an open, internationally competitive enterprise. Either scientists specialized or they failed to keep pace with the advances in their respective fields. In each discipline, the subject matter was growing increasingly complicated, beyond the accessibility of mere commonsense expositions. In addition, the academic studies offered in each tended increasingly to be not so much education as professional training, even at the undergraduate level. And the elective system made specialization all the more likely in an academic environment that encouraged the view that higher education was essential in preparation for a career. In industry and government, as in the respective professions at large, the demand was for specialists, no matter what the cultural cost.

In the context of the day, the specialists themselves celebrated less the ennobling, cultural values of science and more its utilitarian benefits. Rapidly disappearing was the disparagement of money-making typical of Rowland and Simon Newcomb. The chemists, for whom the industrial and governmental demand was considerably greater than for physicists and mathematicians, led the way toward the utilitarian rationale. As early as 1892, Albert B. Prescott, the retiring president of the American Association for the Advancement of Science, told his fellow chemical practitioners: "The advancement of chemical science is not confined to discovery, nor to education, nor to economic use. All of those interests it should embrace. To disparage one of them is injurious to the others. Indeed they ought to have equal support.''[43] In 1909, eager to please its industrial constituency,the American Chemical Society established the *Journal of Industrial and Engineering Chemistry*.

Despite the new opportunities in utilitarian science, probably the bulk of Ph.D.'s in chemistry, and certainly the vast majority of them in physics and mathematics, made their careers in the academic rather than in the industrial or governmental sectors of research. If there was virtually no industrial or governmental demand for mathematicians, in both areas electrical engineers were much preferred to Ph.D.'s in physics. McMurtrie estimated that 80 percent of the working chemists in the country were connected with industry, but he might have added that it was not likely that 80 percent of chemistry Ph.D.'s were so employed. While the industrial trend might be toward hiring trained chemists, the experience of Otto Eisenschiml, the product of a Vienna technical institute, was not atypical. When Eisenschiml joined an American industrial firm, he found that he was the only employee among twelve with any training in chemistry and he was told by the chief of his laboratory, a former water-pail carrier who had worked his way up, that there was to be "no university nonsense around here.''[44] Of course, attitudes toward highly trained chemists or physicists varied from one sector of the industry to another. But even at the new research laboratory of Western Electric, only a small fraction of the staff was given the liberty to pursue the research it desired. The bulk of employees did applied work, much of it of a routine nature. Scientists in government laboratories remained under the watchful eye of attentive congressional administrators, who were wary of permitting their staffs to explore subjects too remote from evident practical purposes.

By contrast, in the academic world the argument that basic scientific research served both economic development and social reform was rapidly taking hold, and presidents in the leading public and private universities were transforming their rhetorical genuflections to research into the reality of budgetary and administrative commitments. Prevailing arguments aside, with the influx of undergraduates into courses to prepare them for careers in science and engineering, the demand for professors of physics, chemistry, and mathematics climbed to an unprecedented height. Endowed with the considerable bargaining power generated by the market demand, professors in the three fields joined with their colleagues in other disciplines to wrest from the president's office concessions affecting their professional lives. They won greater control over appointments, salaries, and promotions, and they used their new power to stress accomplishment in research as an important criterion in the assessment of academic merit.[45]

The increased incentives for research combined with the growth of practitioners in each discipline to produce a remarkable expansion of research output. Compared to the earlier period, in the quarter-century after 1890, over three times as many physicists—64—published research; as did over four times as many mathematicians—338; and almost seven times as many chemists—2219. A related, though considerably less spectacular, development was the enlargement of the productive groups, which in each discipline just about doubled, reaching 91 as compared to 49 in physics, 74 as compared to 29 in mathematics, 155 as compared to 68 in chemistry.[46] In chemistry, the productive group was no doubt substantially larger, since much of its research output was masked by industrial secrecy, a practice deplored by governmental and academic chemists alike. In any case, in the open literature, about 14 percent of the physicists published 53 percent of the articles in their field; about 7 percent of the chemists published 46 percent in theirs; about 21 percent of the mathematicians published 69 percent in their discipline.[47] In each field, too, not only did the productive group increase in size but so did the disciplinary elite. The physics community included Percy W. Bridgman, Karl T. Compton, William Duane, Robert A. Millikan, Robert W. Wood, and Richard Tolman. The mathematicians included H. Bateman, Garrett D. Birkhoff, Gilbert A. Bliss, Maxime Bôcher, Leonard E. Dickson, George A. Miller, Eliakim H. Moore, Oswald Veblen, Edward B. Van Vleck, and Ernest J. Wilcynski. The chemists included Marston T. Bogert, Moses Gomberg, Charles Loring Jackson, T. B. Johnson, E. P. Kohler, Irving Langmuir, Arthur Michael, Arthur A. Noyes, Theodore W. Richards, Julius Stieglitz, and H. L. Wheeler.

There was no institutional concentration of the disciplinary elite, with the exception of the mathematics group at the University of Chicago. There Eliakim H. Moore built a remarkable department with Oskar Bolza and H. Maschke. Gilbert A. Bliss assessed the enterprise: "Moore was brilliant and aggressive in his scholarship, Bolza rapid and thorough, and Maschke more brilliant but sagacious and without doubt one of the most delightful lecturers on geometry of all times. These three supplemented one another perfectly, and they promptly obtained for the Department of Mathematics at the University of Chicago a place among the recognized leaders."[48] Yet if there was no other concentration of disciplinary elites, a number of other departments in each of the three fields acquired depth, with three or more of their staff members among the productive groups. In physics, the departments included those at Harvard, Cornell, Michigan, Chicago, Illinois, Princeton, Wisconsin, Ohio State, and Minnesota, which together had some 36 percent of the employment positions in the field. In chemistry, the prominent departments were at Yale, MIT, Cornell, Harvard, Columbia, Chicago, Berkeley, Bryn Mawr, Illinois, Michigan, and Wisconsin, which together accounted for 26 percent of the employment positions. Chicago, Harvard, Princeton, Columbia, Hopkins, Illinois, Cornell, Pennsylvania, and Yale had the leading mathematics departments, with a combined total of 49 percent of the employment positions.[49]

The significantly productive departments drew a large fraction of graduate students. In chemistry, 72 percent of Ph.D.'s publishing in the period took their doctorates at seven schools, five of which had productive staffs in some depth. In physics, 71 percent earned their doctorates at seven schools, five of which had substantial productive staffs. In mathematics, 86 percent took their doctorates at eight schools, seven of which enjoyed productive depth; Chicago alone, with its stellar department, accounted for 24 percent of the doctorates in mathematics.[50] After the turn of the century, there was a steady decline in the number of

Americans who went abroad for doctoral study. Between 1898 and 1915, Americans earned 38 Ph.D.'s in physics at European universities, compared to 44 from 1852 to 1897. In mathematics they earned 21 compared to 29; in chemistry, only 32 compared to 116. It could be said of all three fields, as an American Subcommittee of the International Commission on the Teaching of Mathematics declared of its own: "The increase in the number of strong men in mathematics is resulting in added strength in an increasing number of institutions. . . . In those universities in which within the past ten years three or more doctorates have been awarded, there is a degree of uniformity in the requirements which probably indicates and establishes a standard for the United States . . . "[51]

At the same time, the practitioners of the three disciplines were establishing new and more effective professional societies. In 1888, the young mathematician, Thomas S. Fiske, returned to New York City from studying in England, where he had been stimulated by meetings of the London Mathematical Society. Eager to develop a stronger feeling of comradeship in mathematics at home, Fiske and two other recent graduates of Columbia, all of them twenty-three years old, initiated the formation of the New York Mathematical Society. By 1894, the organization, which had begun publication of a bulletin to review advances in the field, had a membership of 225 people and was renamed the American Mathematical Society.[52] Five years later, in 1899, Arthur Gordon Webster of Clark University invited his colleagues elsewhere to join in the formation of an American Physical Society; the inaugural meeting of the organization was held at Columbia in the spring. Meanwhile, activists in the Washington Chemical Society, notably Harvey W. Wiley and Frank W. Clarke, had grown increasingly eager for the creation of a genuinely national society in their discipline. New York chemists, eager to preserve the existing American Chemical Society, agreed to revise the charter so that residence in New York was no longer a requirement of office. In 1891, the Society was reconstituted as a truly national organization.[53]

The American Chemical Society was made workable as a national organization by the establishment of local sections, with each section having the right to elect one councilor for every 100 members. By 1901 the American Chemical Society had thirteen local sections, all of them active; at least six held monthly meetings. The membership of the national society was close to 2,000 and its finances were in sound condition. In a similar vein, the American Mathematical Society established a local section in Chicago in 1896, another in San Francisco in 1902, and a third in the southwestern United States in 1906.[54] While the American Physical Society formed no local sections before World War I, it arranged to hold meetings, often three or four times a year, in different cities throughout the northeastern and midwestern United States.

While local interests were accommodated, each of the societies was centrally governed by a popularly elected council. It was the council that nominated candidates for office (including positions on the council itself), selected administrative committees, and guided the society's professional activities. More republican than directly democratic, this system of governance increased the likelihood that officers and councilors would be selected from among the better-qualified practitioners in the respective disciplines. In each of the societies, the average productivity rate of the officers tended to be lower than the average of the entire productive group, yet it was far higher than the average productivity of all producers in the discipline. In the American Chemical Society, about 50 percent of the officers came from the productive group; in the Physical Society, about 56 percent; in the Mathematical Society, about 60 percent. Whereas in the Mathematical Society the distribution of employment among the officers tended to match the distribution among the publishing members of the discipline at large, in the Physical Society there was a disproportionately large representation of government physicists, and in the Chemical Society there was a similarly large group of chemists from business and industry. The societies themselves, in short, expressed and advanced the degree to which the respective disciplines were becoming not only abstract and academic but involved in the utilitarian institutions of the day.[55]

When the American Chemical Society was reformed in the 1890s, President Harvey Wiley acted to revitalize its journal by inviting Edward Hart to become the editor. Hart's own *Journal of Analytical Chemistry* was incorporated into the *Journal of the American Chemical Society,* which soon began appearing on a regular basis in healthy competition with the *American Chemical Journal*. About the same time, 1893, Professor Edward L. Nichols of Cornell founded *The Physical Review,* which was subsidized by the university's trustees. And at the end of the 1890s, officers of the American Mathematical Society proposed to Johns Hopkins a change in control of the *American Journal of Mathematics*. The reformers, convinced that the publication gave too much space to foreigners and too little to the competent work of Americans, wanted the periodical to be managed by editors representing the Society, who would have all submissions promptly refereed by competent specialists. The university refused to approve the change. Undeterred, at a meeting in New York City, the reformers persuaded supporters of the *Journal* that the Society could certainly publish the record of its own activities, including the papers presented at its own meetings. To this end, in 1900 the first issue appeared of the *Transactions of the American Mathematical Society*.[56]

But the founding of new journals, even journals sponsored by professional societies, did not necessarily make for high standards of publication. The *Journal of the American Chemical Society* still had its critics. "If I were editing a journal, not a Society journal," Edward Hart explained in 1899, "I should undoubtedly reject some of the articles we have published, but under the present condition, and especially with the local sections as centers of disaffection, I think it is wiser to publish them than to reject them and have a row . . . , especially while the Society is growing. We should accept and print everything of the least value, for we must try to avoid disputes and disaffection in the Society in order to secure a larger membership, without which, and the money obtained from it, we can do nothing, and with which we can do everything that should be done." But in the meantime, the *Journal's* editorial policies remained weak.[57] In 1907,

225 papers were submitted; Hart published 171 straightaway, another 31 after revision. Only 23, or less than 10 percent, were rejected, a rather low rate for a journal of high quality. In the case of *The Physical Review,* four out of five articles published before about 1910 concerned the old physics of the nineteenth century rather than the new physics of X rays, radioactivity, or electrons, not to mention relativity and quanta. More important, a disproportionately large fraction of articles in the journal were published by Cornell graduates or faculty.[58]

Quite in contrast, the quality of the *Transactions of the American Mathematical Society* began and remained at a decidedly high level. Guaranteed in its first ten years a healthy subvention by a consortium of universities, it did not have to cope with the financial problems that plagued Hart. Moreover, it was edited by E. H. Moore, Thomas Fiske, and E. W. Brown, and Moore was a far better mathematician than either Nichols or his coeditor Ernest Merritt was a physicist. Moore did most of the refereeing himself for the first three years, but all three editors, in the recollection of Brown, "wrestled with our younger contributors to try and get them to put their ideas into good form." After July 1902, Moore and his associates relied on seven cooperating editors, all of high standing in the American mathematical community. In 1908, Moore was succeeded as chief editor by Maxime Bôcher, who was in turn followed by L. E. Dickson. In all, the *Transactions of the American Mathematical Society* set an inspiringly high standard for the discipline of its day.[59]

Gradually, the *The Physical Review* improved, too, becoming increasingly a forum for the new physics, especially the physics of electrons. And in 1913 the *Review* was shifted from the sponsorship of Cornell to that of the American Physical Society, which made it an instrument of the national community in the discipline and endowed it with standards as high as those of the discipline's best practitioners who were appointed to the editorial board. Perhaps the journals of chemistry also improved as more practitioners entered the field, but in 1909 William A. Noyes was still voicing the traditional critique of his discipline: "It seems possible that if we directed our thoughts more toward fundamental problems instead of towards the accumulation of compounds and of facts which are little more than permutations of compounds and of facts already known, more real progress could be made."

Even though a committee of distinguished American mathematicians declared that too much trivial work passed for an original contribution in American journals, on the eve of World War I, mathematics was probably the best developed of the three disciplines practiced in the United States.[60] But whatever their relative standings, the condition of all three was sharply different from what it had been in 1860. Each was solidly established in the universities, while physics and especially chemistry were rapidly making their way in industry and government. Each had an exponentially increasing number of practitioners supplied with the ambition, incentives, and means to produce research at a rapidly rising rate. Each also had emerging within itself a disciplinary elite, productive in research and respected across the Atlantic. No less important, these elites commanded an institutional framework—the centers of graduate training and research, the national societies, the journals—that had grown up since the Civil War. A common development in the world of learning, such institutional elements were essential for setting standards of quality in scientific disciplines. Thus, by the eve of World War I, physics, mathematics, and chemistry in America operated under an institutional system of recruitment and training, of employment and research, of governance and guidance that would contribute mightily to their ultimate ascendancy in the world scientific arena.

## Notes

In writing this chapter, I have benefited from the comments of my fellow participants in the American Academy symposium. I also want to thank Jeffrey Sturchio, who is writing his doctoral dissertation on American chemistry in this period, for his advice on sources; D. Stanley Tarbell and Ann Tracy Tarbell for making available to me their draft study of Ira Remsen; Roy MacLeod for his acute criticisms of the penultimate draft of this paper; and especially Carolyn Harding for her untiring and reliable aid in the gathering and analysis of the statistical data.

1. Simon Newcomb, "Exact Science in America," *North American Review* 119 (1874): 290. Except for Daniel J. Kevles, *The Physicists: The History of a Scientific Community in Modern America* (New York: Alfred A. Knopf, 1978), there are no comprehensive studies of the three disciplines in the United States for the period covered by this chapter. Edward H. Beardsley, *The Rise of the American Chemistry Profession, 1850–1900,* University of Florida Monographs, Social Sciences no. 23 (Gainesville: University of Florida Press, 1964) is an able pioneering work that requires revision. The same must be said of David E. Smith's much older *History of Mathematics in America Before 1900,* Carus Mathematical Monographs no. 5 (Chicago: Mathematical Association of America, 1934), and of Florian Cajori, *The Teaching and History of Mathematics in the United States,* Bureau of Education, Circular Information no. 3 (Washington, D.C.: U.S. Government Printing Office, 1890).

The arguments and interpretations herein advanced rest heavily on a statistical survey of the American physics, mathematics, and chemical communities from 1870 to 1915. The survey was conducted by compiling a list of everyone who published at least one article in physics, mathematics, or chemistry in in the leading American journals for these fields during this period. This method led to some omissions or underrepresentations, e.g., the mathematician G. B. Halstead or the chemist John U. Nef, but the statistical patterns nevertheless seem to be indicative. For the presentation and analysis of the resulting data, the subject was divided into two periods separated in the 1890s, when two of the disciplines acquired professional societies and the third developed a much stronger one and when all three communities also began to expand at a rapid rate. The resulting data are presented in tables 1 through 11. For a full discussion of the statistical study, see Daniel J. Kevles and Carolyn Harding, "The Physics, Mathematics, and Chemical Communities in America, 1870–1915: A Statistical Survey," California Institute of Technology, Social Science Working Paper no. 136, March 1977 (copies available upon request).

It should be pointed ᴄut that statistical assessments of scientific productivity take no account of the relative intellectual significance of what was published. Any attempt to assess the merits of a scientific community clearly requires an analysis of the quality of the work done. However, it would seem useful at the start to determine who the practitioners were, including not only the practitioners whom the scientific textbooks have starred as significant but also those who earned scientific prominence among their contemporaries. It would also seem useful to know as much as possible, if only in a statistical manner, about patterns of graduate training, employment, and officeholding in professional societies. Such statistics provide an essential point of departure for understanding in a discipline the relationship among scientific quality, institutional structure, and patterns of training and employment. Since they are only a point of departure, the conclusions herein advanced are intended to be tentative and suggestive of further work.

2. Stanley M. Guralnick, "Science and the American College, 1818–1860" (Ph.D. diss., University of Pennsylvania, 1969), passim. The Yale curriculum typically devoted 0.71 academic years out of 4.0 to science. *Catalogue of Yale College, 1866–67.*

3. Quoted in Beardsley, *Rise of the American Chemistry Profession,* p. 62.

4. Robert Siegfried, "A Study of Chemical Research Publications from the United States Before 1880" (Ph.D. diss., University of Wisconsin, 1952), p. 99. The number of physicists is taken from publishers in the *American Journal of Science* who contributed at least five articles from 1870–72

onward. Thomas Fiske, "Mathematical Progress in America," *Bulletin of the American Mathematical Society* 11 (1904–5): 238.

5. G. D. Birkhoff, "Fifty Years of American Mathematical Research," *Science* 88 (November 18, 1938): 462; C. G. Caldwell, "The American Chemist," *Journal of the American Chemical Society* 14 (1892): 331.

6. Newcomb, "Abstract Science in America, 1776–1876," *North American Review* 121 (January 1876): 104.

7. Henry to Bache, August 9, 1938, quoted in Nathan Reingold, ed., *Science in Nineteenth Century America: A Documentary History* (New York: Quadrangle, 1964), p. 85.

8. Charles Albert Browne and Mary Elvira Weeks, *A History of the American Chemical Society* (Washington, D.C.: American Chemical Society, 1952), pp.10–21.

9. Quoted in Margaret W. Rossiter, *The Emergence of Agricultural Science: Justus Liebig and the Americans, 1840–1880* (New Haven: Yale University Press, 1975), p. 123.

10. Kevles, *The Physicists,* pp. 14–24.

11. Hugh Hawkins, *Pioneer: A History of the Johns Hopkins University, 1874–1889* (Ithaca, N.Y.: Cornell University Press, 1960), pp. 34–35, 57–58, 47–48; D. Stanley Tarbell and Ann Tracy Tarbell, "Remsen Revisited: The Influence of the Johns Hopkins School on the Development of Organic Chemistry in the United States" (unpublished manuscript), pp. 1–5; Daniel J. Kevles, "Henry Augustus Rowland," in *Dictionary of Scientific Biography,* 12 vols., American Council of Learned Societies (New York: Scribners, 1975), 11: 577–59.

12. Hawkins, *Pioneer,* pp. 74–76; Dana to Gilman, June 20, 1884, Dana Family Papers, Stirling Library, Yale University, New Haven, Connecticut.

13. See table 4. The figure for chemistry may be some 50 percent too low, according to the results of the Chemical Indicators Project, recently completed under the direction of Arnold Thackray at the History and Sociology of Science Department, University of Pennsylvania. The discrepancy may be attributed to the fact that while the figures in this essay are drawn from a survey of publishers, the Chemical Indicator figure is drawn from a count of Ph.D.'s actually awarded.

14. *Electrical World* 4 (20 September 1884): 96.

15. Tables 1 and 2. See also Judith V. Grabiner, "Mathematics in America—the First Hundred Years," unpublished manuscript, 1976, pp. 17–21.

16. Russell McCormmach, ed., *Historical Studies in the Physical Sciences,* 6 vols. (Princeton, N.J.: Princeton University Press, 1965–1975), vol. 5: *Personnel Funding, and Productivity in Physics Circa 1900* (1975), by Paul Forman, John Heilbron, and Spencer Weart, pp. 123, 184, 188, 190; Fiske, "Mathematical Progress in America," p. 239. Of the sixty-eight productive chemists published in Remsen's journal, the six (8 percent) associated with Hopkins contributed 18 percent of the articles. Of the twenty-nine productive mathematicians published in Sylvester's journal, the eleven (37 percent) associated with Hopkins published 53 percent of the articles. Table 8.

17. Francis A. Walker to Alpheus Hyatt, August 29, 1889, Alfred M. Mayer-Alfred G. Mayer-Alpheus Hyatt Papers, Rare Book Room, Princeton University Library, Princeton, New Jersey.

18. On Bryce see George W. Pierson, *Yale: College and University, 1871–1937,* 2 vols. (New Haven: Yale University Press, 1952), 1:129.

19. U.S. Congress, Senate, Joint Commission to Consider the Present Organization of the Signal Service, Geological Survey, Coast and Geodetic Survey, and the Hydrographic Office of the Navy Department . . . , *Testimony,* Sen. Misc. Doc. 82 (Ser. 2345), 49th Cong., 1 sess., March 16, 1886, p. 54.

20. Quoted in Charles Rosenberg, "Science, Technology, and Economic Growth: The Case of the Agricultural Experiment Station Scientist, 1875–1914," in *Nineteenth-Century American Science,* ed. George H. Daniels (Evanston, Ill.: Northwestern University Press, 1972), p. 198.

21. The portion of employment positions, i.e., posts occupied for a reasonable time, in government agencies held by productive physicists was 17 percent; by productive mathematicians, 16 percent; by productive chemists, including those at experiment stations, 12 percent. Table 7.

22. Florian Cajori, *A History of Mathematics,* 2d ed. (New York: Macmillan, 1919), pp. 278–79; Aaron J. Ihde, *The Development of Modern Chemistry* (New York: Harper and Row, 1964), pp. 254, 363–64.

23. Typically, the physics articles in the *American Journal of Science* in 1882–85 were mainly concerned with dynamical electricity, light, spectra, heat, geophysical subjects, and meteorology.

24. Alvarez is quoted in Daniel S. Greenberg, *The Politics of Pure Science* (New York: New American Library, 1967), p. 43. There were about seventy physicists in British higher education in 1890. Russell Moseley, "The Growth of Physics and Its Emergence as a Profession in Britain, 1870–1939" (M.Sc. paper, University of Sussex, 1971).

25. Table 1.

26. The Ph.D. student was Henry Crew, quoted in William F. Meggers, "Henry Crew," *Biographical Memoirs of the National Academy of Sciences* 37 (1964): 36; Felix Klein, *Lectures on Mathematics: The Evanston Colloquium* (New York: American Mathematical Society, 1911), p. 97.

27. Table 1.

28. Table 4.

29. Table 7.

30. Table 4.

31. Ibid.

32. Tarbell and Tarbell, "Remsen Revisited," pp. 2, 9, 19–20.

33. Quoted in Siegfried, "A Study of Chemical Research Publications," pp. 110–11.

34. Table 1.

35. Table 11.

36. Browne and Weeks, *History of the American Chemical Society,* pp. 21–31.

37. Daniel J. Kevles, "On the Flaws of American Physics: A Social and Institutional Analysis," in *Nineteenth-Century American Science,* ed. Daniels, pp. 147–51.

38. Williams Haynes, *American Chemical Industry: Background and Beginnings,* 6 vols. (New York: Van Nostrand Press, 1945–54), 1:245, 395–96; Beardsley, *The Rise of the American Chemistry Profession,* p. 65; McMurtie, "The Condition, Prospects and Future Educational Demands of the Chemical Industries," *Journal of the American Chemical Society* 23 (February 1901): 79–80.

39. Marston T. Bogert, "The Function of Chemistry in the Conservation of Our Natural Resources," *Journal of the American Chemical Society* 31 (1909): 139.

40. Rexmond G. Cochrane, *Measures for Progress: A History of the National Bureau of Standards* (Washington, D.C.: National Bureau of Standards, Department of Commerce, 1966), pp. 1–87; Oscar E. Anderson, J., *The Health of a Nation: Harvey W. Wiley and the Fight for Pure Food* (Chicago: University of Chicago Press, 1958), pp. 85, 103–5, 113–14; Rosenberg, "Science, Technology, and Economic Growth," pp. 200–204.

41. Table 4.

42. "Exit the Amateur Scientist," *Nation* 83 (August 22, 1906): 160.

43. Prescott, "The Immediate Work in Chemical Science," *Journal of the American Chemical Society* 14 (1892): 200.

44. Quoted in Beardsley, *The Rise of the American Chemistry Profession,* p. 63.

45. Joseph Jastrow, "The Academic Career as Affected by Administration," *Science* (April 13, 1906): 567; James McKeen Cattell, *University Control* (New York: Science Press, 1913), pp. 20, 24; Maurice Caullery, *Universities and the Scientific Life in the United States,* trans. James Haughton Wood and Emmet Russel (Cambridge, Mass.: Harvard University Press, 1922), p. 52.

46. Tables 1, 2.

47. Ibid.

48. Quoted in Smith, *A History of Mathematics in America,* p. 142.

49. Table 7.

50. Table 4.

51. Table 10; "Preparation for Research and the Doctor's Degree in Mathematics," *Bulletin of the American Mathematical Society* 17 (March 1911): 305.

52. Raymond Clare Archibald, *A Semicentennial History of the American Mathematical Society, 1888–1938* (New York: American Mathematical Society, 1938), p. 4.

53. Webster to Carl Barus, 1 May 1899, John Hay Library, Brown University, Providence, Rhode Island; Browne and Weeks, *History of the American Chemical Society,* pp. 32–33, 36–38, 52.

54. Browne and Weeks, *History of the American Chemical Society,* p. 53: William McMurtrie, "The Condition, Prospects, and Future Educational Demands of the Chemical Industries," *Journal of the American Chemical Society* 23 (February 1901): 74; Archibald, *A Semicentennial History,* pp. 8–9.

55. Table 11.

56. Archibald, *A Semicentennial History,* p. 58.

57. Hart to Edward W. Morely, August 1, 1899, Edward W. Morley Papers, Box 33, Library of Congress, Washington, D.C.

58. *Journal of the American Chemical Society* 30 (1980): 14–15; table 8. The subject distribution of articles in the *Physical Review* is from an analysis by the author.

59. Brown, quoted in Archibald, *A Semicentennial History,* pp. 60–61.

60. Noyes, "Molecular Rearrangements," *Journal of the American Chemical Society* 31 (1909): 1368; International Commission on the Teaching of Mathematics, Committee 12, "Graduate Work in Mathematics in Universities and in Other Institutions of Like Grade in the United States," *Bulletin of the American Mathematical Society* 18 (December 1911): 133.

Table 1

Productive Physicists, Mathematicians, and Chemists

| | First Period | | | | | | Second Period | | | | | |
| | Physicists 1870–1893 | | Mathematicians 1878–1890 | | Chemists 1879–1891 | | Physicists 1894–1915 | | Mathematicians 1891–1915 | | Chemists 1892–1914 | |
| | N | % | N | % | N | % | N | % | N | % | N | % |
|---|---|---|---|---|---|---|---|---|---|---|---|---|
| Total People | 49 | | 29 | | 68 | | 91 | | 74 | | 155 | |
| Total Articles | 757 | | 203 | | 813 | | 1098 | | 1137 | | 2884 | |
| Foreign Articles[a] | 144 | (19) | 39 | (19) | 134 | (16) | 372 | (34) | 303 | (27) | 403 | (14) |
| Average Productivity Rate[b] | 1.02 | | 0.90 | | 1.03 | | 1.12 | | 1.13 | | 1.33 | |
| Ph.D.'s[c] | 18 | (37) | 15 | (52) | 31 | (46) | 70 | (77) | 69 | (93) | 110 | (71) |
| Foreign Ph.D.'s[d] | 6 | (33) | 4 | (27) | 17 | (55) | 15 | (21) | 22 | (32) | 35 | (32) |
| Foreign Study[c] | 14 | (29) | 9 | (31) | 35 | (51) | 35 | (38) | 34 | (46) | 63 | (41) |

[a] As percentage of total articles.
[b] Articles per person per year; rates of 1.00 or more are omitted from calculation if based on three years or less.
[c] As percentage of entire disciplinary group.
[d] As percentage of total Ph.D.'s.

Table 2

Less Productive Physicists, Mathematicians, and Chemists

| | First Period | | | | | | Second Period | | | | | |
| | Physicists 1870–1893 | | Mathematicians 1878–1890 | | Chemists 1879–1891 | | Physicists 1894–1915 | | Mathematicians 1891–1915 | | Chemists 1892–1914 | |
| | N | % | N | % | N | % | N | % | N | % | N | % |
|---|---|---|---|---|---|---|---|---|---|---|---|---|
| Total People | 187 | | 53 | | 259 | | 560 | | 266 | | 2064[a] | |
| Total Articles | 142 | | 69 | | 373 | | 813 | | 480 | | 3296 | |
| Average Productivity Rate[b] | 0.15 | | 0.17 | | 0.21 | | 0.20 | | 0.18 | | 0.15 | |
| Ph.D.'s[c] | 40 | (21) | 17 | (32) | 47 | (18) | 278 | (50) | 176 | (66) | 472 | (23) |
| Foreign Ph.D.'s[d] | 18 | (45) | 5 | (29) | 19 | (40) | 46 | (17) | 19 | (11) | 72 | (15) |
| Foreign Study[c] | 29 | (16) | 6 | (11) | 38 | (15) | 93 | (18) | 54 | (20) | 176 | ( 9) |

[a] Absolute figures in this column obtained by multiplying sample figures by 8.
[b] Articles per person per year; rates of 1.00 or more are omitted from calculation if based on three years or less.
[c] As percentage of entire disciplinary group.
[d] As percentage of total Ph.D.'s.

Table 3
Distribution of Domestic Doctorates: Productive Groups

| | First Period | | | | | | Second Period | | | | | |
|---|---|---|---|---|---|---|---|---|---|---|---|---|
| | Physicists 1870–1893 | | Mathematicians 1878–1890 | | Chemists 1879–1891 | | Physicists 1894–1915 | | Mathematicians 1891–1915 | | Chemists 1892–1915 | |
| Institution | N | % | N | % | N | % | N | % | N | % | N | % |
| Berkeley | | | | | | | 1 | (1) | | | 1 | (1) |
| Brown | | | | | | | | | | | | |
| Bryn Mawr | | | | | | | | | | | | |
| Chicago | | | | | | | 4 | (5) | 16 | (33) | 5 | (6) |
| Clark | | | | | | | 2 | (3) | 2 | (4) | | |
| Columbia | | | 2 | (18) | 2 | (15) | 4 | (5) | 1 | (2) | 9 | (12) |
| Cornell | | | | | | | 21 | (28) | 6 | (13) | 4 | (5) |
| Harvard | 1 | (9) | 1 | (9) | 3 | (23) | 16 | (21) | 6 | (13) | 9 | (12) |
| Hopkins | 3 | (27) | 5 | (45) | 3 | (23) | 8 | (11) | 6 | (13) | 21 | (27) |
| Illinois | | | | | | | 2 | (3) | | | 1 | (1) |
| Iowa | | | | | | | 2 | (3) | | | | |
| Lafayette | | | | | | | | | | | | |
| MIT | | | | | | | 1 | (1) | | | 3 | (4) |
| Michigan | | | | | | | 3 | (4) | 1 | (2) | 3 | (4) |
| Minnesota | | | | | | | 2 | (3) | | | 1 | (1) |
| Missouri | | | | | | | | | | | | |
| Nebraska | | | | | | | | | | | | |
| NYU | | | | | | | | | | | | |
| N. Carolina | | | | | | | | | | | 1 | (1) |
| Penn | | | | | | | 1 | (1) | 1 | (2) | 6 | (8) |
| Princeton | | | 1 | (9) | | | 5 | (7) | 1 | (2) | 1 | (1) |
| Stanford | | | | | | | | | 1 | (2) | | |
| Wisconsin | | | | | | | 1 | (1) | | | 2 | (3) |
| Yale | 5 | (45) | 1 | (9) | 3 | (23) | 3 | (4) | 3 | (6) | 8 | (10) |
| Others[a] | 2 | (18) | 1 | (9) | 2 | (15) | | | 4 | (8) | 2 | (3) |
| Totals | 11 | | 11 | | 13 | | 76 | | 48 | | 77 | |

Note: Percentages do not always total 100 because of rounding.
[a]Others are American, Boston, Catholic, Cincinnati, Colorado, Cumberland, George Washington, Georgia, Hillsdale, Illinois Wesleyan, Indiana, McGill, Marietta, Ohio State, Ohio Wesleyan, Omaha, Purdue, Stevens, Syracuse, Tulane, Virginia, Washington and Jefferson, Western Reserve, and unknown.

Table 4

Distribution of Domestic Doctorates

| | First Period | | | | | | Second Period | | | | | |
|---|---|---|---|---|---|---|---|---|---|---|---|---|
| | Physicists 1870–1893 | | Mathematicians 1878–1890 | | Chemists 1879–1891 | | Physicists 1894–1915 | | Mathematicians 1891–1915 | | Chemists 1892–1915 | |
| Institution | N | % | N | % | N | % | N | % | N | % | N | % |
| Berkeley | | | | | 1 | ( 2) | 5 | ( 2) | 1 | | 17 | ( 4) |
| Brown | | | | | | | 2 | ( 1) | | | | |
| Bryn Mawr | | | | | | | 2 | ( 1) | 2 | ( 1) | | |
| Chicago | | | | | | | 31 | (10) | 49 | (24) | 54 | (11) |
| Clark | | | | | | | 11 | ( 4) | 14 | ( 7) | 8 | ( 2) |
| Columbia | 1 | ( 3) | | | 4 | (10) | 23 | ( 7) | 11 | ( 5) | 51 | (11) |
| Cornell | 5 | (15) | 2 | ( 9) | | | 59 | (19) | 17 | ( 8) | 36 | ( 8) |
| Harvard | 12 | (36) | 1 | ( 4) | 5 | (12) | 27 | ( 9) | 20 | (10) | 57 | (12) |
| Hopkins | | | 10 | (43) | 15 | (37) | 47 | (15) | 29 | (14) | 69 | (15) |
| Illinois | | | | | | | 11 | ( 4) | 2 | ( 1) | 9 | ( 2) |
| Iowa | | | | | 1 | ( 2) | 2 | ( 1) | | | 11 | ( 2) |
| Lafayette | | | | | 1 | ( 2) | | | 2 | ( 1) | 11 | ( 2) |
| MIT | 1 | ( 3) | | | 2 | ( 5) | 2 | ( 1) | | | 1 | |
| Michigan | | | | | | | 12 | ( 4) | 1 | | 16 | ( 3) |
| Minnesota | | | | | | | 6 | ( 2) | | | | |
| Missouri | | | | | 1 | ( 2) | | | | | 8 | ( 2) |
| Nebraska | | | | | | | 2 | ( 1) | 3 | ( 1) | | |
| NYU | | | | | 1 | ( 2) | | | | | 9 | ( 2) |
| N. Carolina | | | | | 1 | ( 2) | | | 4 | ( 2) | | |
| Penn | | | | | | | 12 | ( 4) | 10 | ( 5) | 38 | ( 8) |
| Princeton | | | 2 | ( 9) | | | 19 | ( 6) | 1 | | 9 | ( 2) |
| Stanford | | | | | | | 5 | ( 2) | 1 | | | |
| Wisconsin | | | | | | | 11 | ( 4) | | | 18 | ( 4) |
| Yale | 10 | (30) | 4 | (17) | 5 | (12) | 15 | ( 5) | 26 | (13) | 24 | ( 5) |
| Others[a] | 4 | (12) | 4 | (17) | 4 | (10) | 6 | ( 2) | 10 | ( 5) | 26 | ( 6) |
| Totals | 33 | | 23 | | 41 | | 310 | | 203 | | 472 | |

Note: Percentages do not always total 100 because of rounding.
[a] See note a, table 3.

163

Table 5
Number of American Articles Published in Major Foreign Journals

**Physicists**

| Journal | 1870-93 N | 1870-93 % | 1894-1914 N | 1894-1914 % |
|---|---|---|---|---|
| Ann. Physik. | 11 | (8) | 28 | (9) |
| Astr. Nach. | 12 | (8) | 0 | |
| Brit. J. Photog. | 17 | (12) | 0 | |
| Comptes Rendus | 16 | (11) | 10 | (3) |
| Nature | 21 | (15) | 7 | (2) |
| Phil. Mag. | 39 | (27) | 162 | (49) |
| Physic. Ztschr. | 0 | | 52 | (16) |
| Others[a] | 38 | (19) | 76 | (23) |
| Totals | 154 | | 335 | |

**Mathematicians**

| Journal | 1878-90 N | 1878-90 % | 1891-1915 N | 1891-1915 % |
|---|---|---|---|---|
| Astr. Nachr. | 4 | (10) | 0 | |
| Comptes Rendus | 2 | (5) | 29 | (10) |
| Copernicus | 2 | (5) | 0 | |
| Crelle J. Math. | 3 | (8) | 1 | |
| Jahr. Deutsch Math. | 0 | | 14 | (5) |
| London Math. Soc. Pro. | 2 | (5) | 37 | (12) |
| Math. Ann. | 3 | (8) | 41 | (14) |
| Mess. Math. | 3 | (8) | 9 | (3) |
| Nature | 3 | (8) | 0 | |
| Palermo Cir. Mat. | 5 | (13) | 24 | (8) |
| Phil. Mag. | 6 | (15) | 15 | (5) |
| Quat. J.P.A. Math. | 1 | (2) | 41 | (14) |
| Others[c] | 5 | (13) | 92 | (30) |
| Totals | 39 | | 303 | |

**Chemists**

| Journal | 1879-91 N | 1879-91 % | 1892-1914 N | 1892-1914 % |
|---|---|---|---|---|
| Ber. D. Chem. Ges. | 73 | (54) | 115 | (29) |
| Comptes Rendus | 10 | (7) | 1 | |
| J. Prakt. Chem. | 24 | (18) | 34 | (9) |
| Liebig's Ann. Chem. | 1 | | 24 | (6) |
| Ztschr. Anor. Chem. | 0 | | 69 | (17) |
| Ztschr. Physik. Chem. | 0 | | 81 | (20) |
| Others[b] | 26 | (19) | 76 | (19) |
| Totals | 134 | | 400 | |

Note: Percentages do not always total 100 because of rounding.

[a] Others include Annales, Chemis, Arch. Sci. Phys., Gen., Bohm. Ges. Wiss. Abhand., Brit. Assoc. Report, Cambridge Phil. Soc. Proc., Carl's Rep., Elect. Mag., Exner Rep. Phys., Himmel und Erde, Jahr. Drahtl. Teleg., Jahr., Radioakt. Elekt., Japan Univ. Mem., J. Physique, Il Nuovo Cimento, Kolloidztschr., Le Radium, Lond. Phys. Soc. Proc., London Roy. Inst. Proc., Lond. Roy. Soc. Proc., Lond. Roy. Soc. Trans., Meteor. Ztschr. Wien, Mon. Scient., Neues Jahr. Mineral., Oest. Meteor., Ges. Ztschr., Paris Soc. Phys. Sean., Photog. Mittheil., Quat. J.P.A. Math., Rev. Scien., Spectro. Ital. Mem., Verh. Phy. Ges., Ztschr Anorg. Chem., Ztschr. Elekt., Ztschr. Instrum., Ztschr. Phys. Chem., Ztschr. Wiss. Photog.

[b] Others include Ann. Phys., Archiv. Pharm., Arch. Sci. Phys. Nat., Brit. Assoc. Rep., Bull. Soc. Chim. Paris, Chem. Zeitung, Edin. Roy. Soc. Proc., Gazz. Chem. Ital., Jahr. Radioakt. Elekt. J. Chimie Phys., J. Physique, Landw. Vers. Stat., London Chem. Soc. J., Lond. Roy. Soc. Trans., Lond. Roy. Soc. Proc., Nature, Phil. Mag., Phys. Ztschr., Rev. Scien., Tokyo Coll. Sci. J., Ztschr. Anal. Chem., Ztschr. Ver. Rueben-Ind.

[c] Others include Acta Math., Ann. Math. Brioschi, Archiv. Math. Phys., Bibl. Math., Coll. Sci. Mat. Loria, Bordeau Soc. Sci., Brit. Assoc. Rep., Bruxelles Acad. Mem., Bull. Soc. Math. France, Cambridge Phil. Soc. Proc., Cambridge Phil. Soc. Trans., Edin. Math. Soc. Proc., Edin. Roy. Soc. Trans., Gior. Mat. Battag., Gött. Nachr., J. Reine Angew. Math., J. Math. Liouv., Lond. Phys. Soc. Proc., Manchester Lit. Phil. Soc., Mitt. Natur. Gesell., Monat. Math. Phys., Nouv. Ann. Math., Phys. Ztschr., Re. Mois, Rev. Inter. L'Enseign., Roma Lin. Rend., Tohuku Math. J., Torino Atti. Acad. Sci., Venezia Inst. Atti. Ztschr. Bauwes., Ztschr. Math. Phys., Zurich Vierteljahr.

Table 6

Major Countries of Foreign Publication for Productive Groups

| | First Period | | | | | | Second Period | | | | | |
|---|---|---|---|---|---|---|---|---|---|---|---|---|
| | Physicists 1870–1893 | | Mathematicians 1878–1890 | | Chemists 1879–1891 | | Physicists 1894–1914 | | Mathematicians 1891–1915 | | Chemists 1892–1914 | |
| Country | N | % | N | % | N | % | N | % | N | % | N | % |
| Germany, Austria, Switzerland | 37 | (26) | 11 | (28) | 109 | (81) | 132 | (40) | 85 | (28) | 357 | (89) |
| England, Scotland, Ireland | 82 | (57) | 19 | (49) | 10 | ( 7) | 186 | (56) | 123 | (41) | 26 | ( 7) |
| France, Belgium | 22 | (15) | 2 | ( 5) | 13 | (10) | 15 | ( 4) | 43 | (14) | 17 | ( 4) |
| Italy | 1 | | 6 | (15) | 1 | | 1 | | 47 | (16) | | |
| Others[a] | 2 | ( 1) | 1 | ( 3) | 1 | | 0 | | 5 | ( 2) | 0 | |
| Totals | 144 | | 39 | | 134 | | 334 | | 303 | | 400 | |

*Note*: Percentages do not always total 100 because of rounding.

[a] Others include Japan and Sweden.

## Table 7
### Distribution of Employment

| | First Period | | | | | | Second Period | | | | | |
|---|---|---|---|---|---|---|---|---|---|---|---|---|
| | Physicists 1870–1893 | | Mathematicians 1878–1890 | | Chemists 1879–1891 | | Physicists 1894–1915 | | Mathematicians 1891–1915 | | Chemists 1892–1915 | |
| Employer | N | % | N | % | N | % | N | % | N | % | N | % |
| Amherst | 1 | ( 2) | | | | | | | | | | |
| Arizona | | | | | | | | | 1 | (1) | | |
| Armour | | | | | | | | | | | | |
| Berkeley | 1 | ( 2) | 2 | ( 5.0) | | | 3 | ( 2) | 2 | (2) | 4 | ( 2.0) |
| Brown | | | | | | | 1 | ( 1) | | | | |
| Bryn Mawr | | | 1 | ( 2.5) | | | 1 | ( 1) | | | 4 | ( 2.0) |
| Carnegie Inst. | | | | | | | 2 | ( 2) | 1 | (1) | 1 | ( 0.5) |
| Case | 1 | ( 2) | | | | | | | | | 1 | ( 0.5) |
| Catholic Univ. | | | | | 1 | (1) | | | | | | |
| Chicago | | | | | 1 | (1) | 2 | ( 2) | 8 | (8) | 5 | ( 2.4) |
| Cincinnati | | | 1 | ( 2.5) | 2 | (3) | 3 | ( 3) | 1 | (1) | 2 | ( 1.0) |
| CCNY | 1 | ( 2) | | | 3 | (4) | | | 1 | (1) | 2 | ( 1.0) |
| Clark | | | 2 | ( 5.0) | | | 2 | ( 2) | | | 1 | ( 0.5) |
| Columbia | 2 | ( 3) | 1 | ( 2.5) | 1 | (1) | 2 | ( 2) | 4 | (4) | 8 | ( 4.0) |
| Cornell | 1 | ( 2) | 1 | ( 2.5) | 2 | (3) | 8 | ( 7) | 6 | (6) | 4 | ( 2.0) |
| Dartmouth | 1 | ( 2) | | | | | 1 | ( 1) | 3 | (3) | | |
| Georgia | | | | | | | | | | | 1 | ( 0.5) |
| Georgia Tech. | | | | | | | | | | | | |
| Geo. Washington | | | | | | | | | | | | |
| Goucher | | | | | | | | | | | | |
| Harvard | 5 | ( 8) | | | 5 | (7) | 10 | ( 8) | 6 | (6) | 5 | ( 2.4) |
| Haverford | | | | | 1 | (1) | 1 | ( 1) | 2 | (2) | | |
| Hopkins | 2 | ( 3) | 11 | (31.0) | 3 | (4) | 2 | ( 2) | 6 | (6) | 6 | ( 2.9) |
| Idaho | | | | | | | 1 | ( 1) | | | | |
| Illinois | | | | | 1 | (1) | 5 | ( 4) | | | 8 | ( 4.0) |
| Indiana | | | | | | | 2 | ( 2) | 4 | (4) | | |
| Iowa State | | | | | | | | | | | 1 | ( 0.5) |
| Kansas | 2 | ( 3) | | | | | 1 | ( 1) | 1 | (1) | 2 | ( 1.0) |

| Institution | n | (%) | n | (%) | n | (%) | n | (%) | n | (%) | n | (%) |
|---|---|---|---|---|---|---|---|---|---|---|---|---|
| Knox | | | | | | | 1 | ( 1) | | | | |
| Lafayette | | | | | | | 1 | ( 1) | | | | |
| Lehigh | | | | | | | | | | | | |
| Maine | 3 | ( 5) | | | 2 | ( 3) | 2 | ( 1) | 3 | (3) | 8 | ( 4.0) |
| MIT | | | 1 | ( 2.5) | 1 | ( 1) | 5 | ( 1) | 2 | (2) | 6 | ( 3.0) |
| Michigan | 1 | ( 2) | | | | | 5 | ( 4) | | | 3 | ( 1.4) |
| Minnesota | | | | | 1 | ( 1) | 3 | ( 3) | 2 | (2) | | |
| Missouri | 1 | ( 2) | | | | | 1 | ( 1) | 1 | (1) | 2 | ( 1.0) |
| Mt. Holyoke | | | | | | | 1 | ( 1) | 1 | (1) | 2 | ( 1.0) |
| Nebraska | | | | | 1 | ( 1) | 2 | ( 2) | | | 2 | ( 1.0) |
| New Hampshire | 1 | ( 2) | | | | | | | | | 3 | ( 1.4) |
| NYU | | | | | | | | | | | | |
| N. Carolina | 1 | ( 2) | 1 | ( 2.5) | 1 | ( 1) | 2 | ( 4) | 4 | (4) | 2 | ( 1.0) |
| N. Dakota | | | 1 | ( 2.5) | | | 5 | ( 4) | | | | |
| Northwestern | | | | | 1 | ( 1) | | | 3 | (3) | 2 | ( 1.0) |
| Ohio State | 2 | ( 3) | | | 1 | ( 1) | | | 1 | (1) | 3 | ( 1.4) |
| Oklahoma | | | | | | | | | | | | |
| Oregon | 2 | ( 3) | 1 | ( 2.5) | 1 | ( 1) | 5 | ( 4) | 9 | (9) | 1 | ( 0.5) |
| Pennsylvania | 1 | | 2 | | 1 | ( 3) | | | 1 | (1) | | |
| Penn. State | | | | | | | | | | | | |
| Pittsburgh | 1 | ( 2) | | | 1 | ( 1) | 2 | ( 2) | 2 | (2) | 2 | ( 1.0) |
| Princeton | 2 | | | | | | | | 1 | (1) | 1 | ( 0.5) |
| Purdue | | | | | 2 | ( 3) | 1 | | 1 | | | |
| Rice | | | | | 2 | ( 3) | 2 | | 2 | (2) | 1 | ( 0.5) |
| Rutgers | | | | | | | 1 | ( 1) | 1 | (1) | | |
| Smith | 2 | ( 5.0) | 2 | ( 3) | 2 | | 1 | | 1 | (1) | | |
| Stanford | 1 | ( 2) | 1 | | 1 | ( 1) | 1 | ( 1) | 2 | (2) | 1 | ( 0.5) |
| Stevens | | | | | | | | | 1 | | 2 | ( 1.0) |
| Syracuse | | | | | | | | | 2 | (2) | | |
| Tennessee | | | | | | | | | | | | |

*(continued)*

167

Table 7 (continued)

|  | First Period | | | | | | Second Period | | | | | |
| Employer | Physicists 1870–1893 | | Mathematicians 1878–1890 | | Chemists 1879–1891 | | Physicists 1894–1915 | | Mathematicians 1891–1915 | | Chemists 1892–1915 | |
|  | N | % | N | % | N | % | N | % | N | % | N | % |
| Wash. & Lee |  |  |  |  | 1 | (1) | 1 | (1) |  |  |  |  |
| Wellesley |  |  |  |  |  |  |  |  |  |  |  |  |
| Wesleyan | 1 | (2) |  |  | 1 | (1) |  |  |  |  | 2 | (1.0) |
| W. Reserve |  |  |  |  | 1 | (1) |  |  | 2 | (2) |  |  |
| West Virginia |  |  |  |  |  |  | 1 | (1) | 1 | (1) |  |  |
| Wisconsin | 1 | (2) |  |  | 1 | (1) | 3 | (3) | 1 | (1) | 4 | (2.0) |
| Worcester | 10 | (17) | 1 | (2.5) |  |  | 3 | (3) | 3 | (3) |  |  |
| Yale | 4 | (7) | 1 | (2.5) | 4 | (6) | 2 | (2) | 5 | (5) | 7 | (3.5) |
| Observatories |  |  |  |  |  |  | 1 | (1) |  |  |  |  |
| High Schools |  |  |  |  | 1 | (1) | 1 | (1) |  |  | 1 | (0.5) |
| Agricultural Colleges |  |  |  |  | 2 | (3) |  |  |  |  | 1 | (0.5) |
| Agricultural Expt. Stns. |  |  |  |  | 2 | (3) |  |  |  |  | 16 | (8.0) |
| Medical Colleges & Hospitals |  |  |  |  | 2 | (3) |  |  |  |  | 3 | (1.4) |
| Other Colleges & Universities | 4 | (7) | 4 | (11.0) | 1 | (1) | 18 | (15) | 6 | (6) | 21 | (10.0) |
| Rockefeller Inst. |  |  |  |  |  |  |  |  |  |  | 1 | (0.5) |
| Smithsonian |  |  |  |  |  |  |  |  |  |  |  |  |
| Coast Survey | 1 | (2) | 3 | (7.5) | 1 | (1) |  |  |  |  | 2 | (1.0) |
| Geological Survey | 4 | (7) | 1 | (2.5) | 1 | (1) | 3 | (3) |  |  |  |  |
| Bureau of Standards |  |  |  |  |  |  |  |  |  |  | 3 | (1.4) |
| Bureau of Mines |  |  |  |  |  |  |  |  |  |  |  |  |
| Agricultural Dept. |  |  |  |  | 2 | (3) | 1 | (1) |  |  | 18 | (9.0) |
| Weather Bureau |  |  |  |  |  |  | 1 | (1) |  |  |  |  |
| Army | 3 | (5) | 1 | (2.5) |  |  |  |  |  |  |  |  |
| Navy | 2 | (3) |  |  |  |  |  |  |  |  |  |  |
| State & Local Health Depts. |  |  |  |  | 2 | (3) |  |  |  |  | 2 | (1.0) |
| Misc. State & Local Agencies |  |  |  |  |  |  |  |  |  |  | 4 | (2.0) |
| Misc. Federal Agencies |  |  |  |  | 1 | (1) |  |  |  |  | 9 | (4.0) |
| Business & Industry |  |  | 1 | (2.5) | 4 | (6) | 8 | (7) | 1 | (1) | 13 | (6.0) |
| Independent | 3 | (5) | 2 | (5.0) |  |  |  |  |  |  | 3 | (1.4) |
| Totals | 60 |  | 39 |  | 67 |  | 121 |  | 101 |  | 208 |  |

Note: Percentages do not always total 100 because of rounding.

Table 8
Contributions to Journals by Local Faculty or Doctorate Recipients

| | | Faculty or Ph.D.'s in Discipline | | | Contributions to Journal Edited at Local School | | |
| --- | --- | --- | --- | --- | --- | --- | --- |
| Period | School | Discipline | Number | Percentages of Total[a] | Publication | Number of Articles | Percentages of Total |
| First Period (1870–1893) | Yale | Physics | 11 | 22% | Am. J. Sci. | 114 | 21% |
| | Hopkins | Chemistry | 6 | 8 | Am. Chem. J. | 87 | 18 |
| | Hopkins | Mathematics | 11 | 37 | Am. J. Math. | 61 | 53 |
| Second Period (1891–1915) | Cornell | Physics | 19 | 21 | Phys. Rev. | 208 | 35 |
| | Hopkins | Chemistry | 25 | 16 | Am. Chem. J. | 383 | 45 |
| | Hopkins | Mathematics | 8 | 11 | Am. J. Math. | 41 | 17 |

[a] The total is of productive practitioners.

Table 9
Doctorates Awarded in the United States

| Institution | Physics | | Mathematics | | Chemistry | | Total | |
|---|---|---|---|---|---|---|---|---|
| | To 1897 | 1898–15 | To 1897 | 1898–15 | To 1897 | 1898–15 | To 1897 | 1898–15 |
| Berkeley | 0 | 4 | 0 | 1 | 1 | 16 | 1 | 21 |
| Brown | 1 | 2 | 0 | 0 | 0 | 0 | 1 | 2 |
| Bryn Mawr | 0 | 2 | 0 | 2 | 0 | 0 | 0 | 4 |
| Chicago | 2 | 26 | 2 | 42 | 9 | 44 | 13 | 112 |
| Clark | 4 | 8 | 5 | 7 | 0 | 8 | 9 | 23 |
| Columbia | 2 | 19 | 3 | 8 | 10 | 41 | 15 | 68 |
| Cornell | 8 | 49 | 3 | 15 | 0 | 42 | 11 | 106 |
| Harvard | 6 | 17 | 4 | 15 | 22 | 39 | 32 | 71 |
| Hopkins | 25 | 32 | 16 | 19 | 27 | 61 | 68 | 112 |
| Illinois | 0 | 10 | 0 | 2 | 0 | 9 | 0 | 21 |
| Iowa | 0 | 2 | 0 | 0 | 0 | 0 | 0 | 2 |
| Lafayette | 0 | 0 | 0 | 0 | 0 | 1 | 0 | 1 |
| MIT | 0 | 2 | 0 | 1 | 1 | 11 | 1 | 13 |
| Michigan | 1 | 12 | 0 | 1 | 4 | 9 | 5 | 22 |
| Minnesota | 0 | 5 | 0 | 0 | 0 | 1 | 0 | 6 |
| Missouri | 0 | 0 | 0 | 0 | 1 | 16 | 1 | 16 |
| Nebraska | 0 | 0 | 0 | 2 | 0 | 0 | 0 | 2 |
| NYU | 0 | 2 | 0 | 0 | 0 | 9 | 0 | 11 |
| North Carolina | 0 | 0 | 0 | 0 | 2 | 8 | 2 | 8 |
| Pennsylvania | 0 | 12 | 0 | 3 | 1 | 38 | 1 | 53 |
| Princeton | 2 | 10 | 4 | 7 | 1 | 9 | 7 | 26 |
| Stanford | 0 | 5 | 0 | 1 | 0 | 0 | 0 | 6 |
| Wisconsin | 0 | 11 | 1 | 0 | 0 | 18 | 1 | 29 |
| Yale | 16 | 14 | 7 | 20 | 14 | 15 | 37 | 49 |
| Others[a] | 6 | 8 | 11 | 4 | 8 | 24 | 25 | 36 |
| Totals | 73 | 252 | 56 | 149 | 101 | 419 | 230 | 820 |

[a]Others include Basel, Berne, Cambridge, Christiana, Geneva, Jena, Paris, St. Andrews (Scotland), St. Petersburg, Upsala, and Vienna.

Table 10
Doctorates Awarded Abroad

| Institution | Physics | | Mathematics | | Chemistry | | Total | |
|---|---|---|---|---|---|---|---|---|
| | To 1897 | 1898–15 | To 1897 | 1898–15 | To 1897 | 1898–15 | To 1897 | 1898–15 |
| Berlin | 13 | 8 | 3 | 0 | 7 | 1 | 23 | 9 |
| Bonn | 1 | 0 | 0 | 1 | 0 | 0 | 1 | 1 |
| Bordeaux | 0 | 1 | 0 | 1 | 0 | 0 | 0 | 2 |
| Edinburgh | 1 | 1 | 1 | 1 | 0 | 0 | 2 | 2 |
| Erlangen | 0 | 0 | 1 | 1 | 0 | 0 | 1 | 1 |
| Freiburg | 0 | 0 | 0 | 0 | 8 | 9 | 8 | 9 |
| Giessen | 0 | 1 | 0 | 0 | 1 | 0 | 1 | 1 |
| Göttingen | 6 | 6 | 10 | 8 | 30 | 2 | 45 | 16 |
| Heidelberg | 6 | 3 | 5 | 2 | 18 | 1 | 29 | 6 |
| Leipzig | 8 | 3 | 5 | 2 | 26 | 9 | 39 | 14 |
| London | 0 | 2 | 2 | 0 | 0 | 0 | 2 | 2 |
| Marburg | 1 | 6 | 0 | 0 | 0 | 0 | 1 | 6 |
| Munich | 0 | 3 | 0 | 1 | 9 | 0 | 9 | 4 |
| Strasburg | 3 | 0 | 0 | 2 | 0 | 0 | 3 | 2 |
| Tubingen | 1 | 0 | 0 | 0 | 3 | 0 | 4 | 0 |
| Wurzburg | 3 | 1 | 0 | 0 | 2 | 0 | 5 | 1 |
| Zurich | 0 | 1 | 0 | 0 | 9 | 1 | 9 | 3 |
| Others[a] | 1 | 1 | 4 | 1 | 3 | 9 | 7 | 11 |
| Totals | 44 | 37 | 31 | 21 | 116 | 32 | 189 | 90 |

[a] Others include Basel, Berne, Cambridge, Christiana, Geneva, Jena, Paris, St. Andrews (Scotland), St. Petersburg, Upsala, and Vienna.

## Table 11
### Characteristics of Professional Society Officers

| Characteristics | American Chemical Society 1879–1891 | | Productive Chemists 1879–1891 | American Chemical Society 1892–1914 | | Productive Chemists 1892–1914 | American Mathematical Society 1892–1915 | | Productive Mathematicians 1892–1915 | American Physical Society 1899–1915 | | Productive Physicists 1894–1915 |
|---|---|---|---|---|---|---|---|---|---|---|---|---|
| | N | % | % | N | % | % | N | % | % | N | % | % |
| Officers Listed | 61 | | | 166 | | | 91 | | | 40 | | |
| Officers with Information[a] | 38 | | | 145 | | | 91 | | | 40 | | |
| Ph.D.'s | 21 | (55.3) | 46 | 100 | (68.9) | 71 | 69 | (75.8) | 93 | 31 | (77.5) | 96 |
| Foreign Ph.D.'s[b] | 12 | (57.1) | 25 | 47 | (47.0) | 23 | 28 | (40.6) | 28 | 12 | (38.7) | 18 |
| Foreign Study[c] | 16 | (42.1) | 51 | 77 | (46.3) | 40 | 51 | (56.0) | 45 | 22 | (55.0) | 39 |
| Average Productivity Rate[d] | 0.75 | | 1.03 | 0.55 | | 1.32 | 0.71 | | 1.13 | 0.72 | | 1.12 |
| Publishers[e,c] | 37 | (60.5) | — | 121 | (72.9) | | 66 | (72.5) | | 37 | (92.5) | |
| Employment Characteristics | | | | | | | | | | | | |
| Total Positions | 50 | | | 191 | | | 101 | | | 45 | | |
| Total Institutions | 41 | (1.22)[f] | | 123 | (1.55)[f] | | 40 | (2.52)[f] | | 31 | (1.45)[f] | |
| High Claim Institutions[g] | 0 | | 0 | 11 | (24.6) | | 10 | (56.5) | | 1 | (9.9) | |
| Positions in: | | | | | | | | | | | | |
| Academic Institutions | 26 | (52.0) | 75 | 141 | (59.7) | 73 | 96 | (95.0) | 98 | 38 | (84.4) | 89 |
| Public | 7 | (14.0) | | 54 | (28.3) | | 23 | (22.8) | | 10 | (22.2) | |
| Private | 19 | (38.0) | | 60 | (31.4) | | 73 | (72.3) | | 28 | (62.2) | |
| Ag. Expt. Stns. | | | 3 | 4 | (2.1) | 6 | | | | | | |
| Medical Institutions | 2 | (4.0) | 3 | 9 | (4.7) | 2 | | | | | | |
| Federal Agencies | 3 | (6.0) | 7 | 16 | (9.4) | 11 | 3 | (3.0) | 1 | 6 | (13.3) | 5 |
| State & Local Agencies | 3 | (6.0) | 3 | 4 | (2.1) | 1 | | | | | | |
| Business & Industry | 11 | (22.0) | 8 | 35 | (18.3) | 5 | 2 | (2.0) | 1 | 1 | (2.2) | 6 |
| Independent | 5 | (10.0) | | 9 | (4.7) | 1 | | | | | | |

[a] Information was obtainable for some officers who did not publish in the journals surveyed.
[b] Percentages as total of Ph.D.'s.
[c] Percentages as total of group.
[d] Calculated for professional career (see text).
[e] Means listed among the publishers designated as productive. For the case of the later chemists, those not listed were checked against the total group from which the sample was drawn and entered if found there.
[f] Positions per institution.
[g] Institutions with four or more positions. Numbers in parentheses are total positions held in these institutions. The percentages are of total positions.

# The Transformation
# of a Science: T. H. Morgan
# and the Emergence of a New
# American Biology

### GARLAND ALLEN

During the last decades of the nineteenth century, biology underwent a major transformation in the scope of its subject matter and in its methodology. In the earlier decades of the century, most biology was concerned with descriptive studies of natural history: the study of anatomy, biogeography, paleontology, and what today would be called ecology and embryology. Prior to the publication of Darwin's *Origin of Species* in 1859, such descriptive studies were directed toward cataloging organisms and demonstrating their position or role in the economy of nature. After 1859, such studies increasingly focused on the solution of evolutionary problems, particularly the tracing of phylogenetic histories. However, during the 1880s and 1890s many younger biologists began to tire not only of asking phylogenetic questions but of using exclusively descriptive methods. Some, especially embryologists, saw that their field posed intriguing questions of its own, such as determining the factors that lead to embryonic differentiation. They began to revolt against the dominance of the aims and methods of descriptive biology to pose new questions and to develop new techniques for answering them.

Of chief importance among the new methods was the emphasis that the younger workers placed on experimentation and the use of exact, quantitative data. By employing the experimental approach, many younger biologists sought nothing less than to place biology on an equal footing with the physical sciences. They felt that the time had come to make biology a rigorous science, based not on speculation and fancy but on measurement and experimentation.

Instrumental in promoting the new wave of experimentalism in biology was Thomas Hunt Morgan (1866–1945), recognized as one of America's leading biologists and the recipient of the 1933 Nobel Prize in Physiology and Medicine for his work on the chromosome theory of heredity. Trained in embryology under W. K. Brooks at Johns Hopkins, Morgan was steeped during his graduate days, in both the concept and the methodology of the descriptive, naturalist tradition. His transition from primarily descriptive to primarily experimental biology was the result of several influences: his exposure to the experimental approach of H. Newell Martin at Johns Hopkins; his friendship with Jacques Loeb, beginning in 1891 at Bryn Mawr; and his experience in 1891 and 1895 at the Naples Zoological Station, in particular his close association with embryologist Hans Driesch. Morgan imbibed the new experimentalism and applied it first to problems of regeneration and embryogenesis and later, in his laboratory at Columbia University, to the study of heredity. Morgan's work in heredity in particular came to be viewed by the younger generation of biologists as the crowning example of the advances biology could make if workers employed a quantitative and experimental approach.

This paper will focus on the work of Thomas Hunt Morgan as an illustration of the factors that influenced the transformation of biology from a largely descriptive to an increasingly experimental science between 1890 and 1920. Morgan was both typical and atypical of the new mood in biology. He was typical in that he voiced concerns and ideas that were prevalent among younger workers in particular around the turn of the century. He was atypical in that he saw more clearly, and voiced more strongly than many, the need for radical change in areas of concern and methodology within the life sciences. Although much of the following discussion focuses on Morgan, it should be kept in mind that no single individual directly stimulated or caused the changes that biology underwent. Many workers played a part, some larger and more easily traced, some smaller and less easily traced, but all were involved and in various ways left their mark.

## The Naturalist-Experimentalist Dichotomy

The career of Thomas Hunt Morgan cannot be understood apart from the historical struggle that came to a head within the biological community in the last decades of the nineteenth century—the struggle between the naturalist and the experimentalist traditions. The naturalist and experimentalist traditions within the biological sciences represent different viewpoints about organisms and the methods for studying them. Both have existed in one form or another during most of the history of biology, but the naturalist tradition was the dominant view from ancient times through most of the nineteenth century, when it received its greatest stimulus from the work of Darwin.

Characterized by a number of different but interconnected concepts and practices, the naturalist tradition involved an interest in whole organisms as opposed to their isolated parts, and was concerned largely with form or structure as opposed to function. It took its cue from field naturalists, who were concerned with organisms in their natural state, while at the same time it encompassed museum studies of preserved specimens with an emphasis on taxonomy and classification. In the post-Darwinian period, natural history came to focus on historical questions: How did the variety of living forms, particular adaptations, or particular ecological interrelationships come to exist? Methodologically, the naturalist tradition has been largely descriptive in orientation, whatever the subject; its data have been qualitative and primarily observational.

In contrast, the experimentalist tradition, from its conscious inception in biology in the late seventeenth century, was characterized by a strong interest in function as opposed to structure. It thus found particular expression in the study of animal and plant physiology. The experimental approach was tied much more closely to the laboratory than to the field and often viewed organisms wholly removed from their natural surroundings. With its emphasis on controlled conditions, the experimental approach tried to reduce the number of variables operative in a particular situation at any one time; consequently, experimentalists often investigated only a single process in isolation from others. But physiologists assumed that the principles of function determined in experiments with isolated parts (e.g., organs) could be applied to an understanding of the organ's function within the intact animal.

By definition, experimentation meant the imposition of unnatural conditions upon a system. Experimentalists persisted in the assertion that the response of the system under artificial conditions reveals a great deal about its function under normal conditions; they further maintained that the data obtained from laboratory experiments can be validly extrapolated to the field situation. The experimentalist tradition emphasized the rigorous approach to scientific problems that meant, among other things, the posing of hypotheses in such a way that rival views could be distinguished from one another by an appropriate experiment and by the collection of quantitative, rather than qualitative, data. From the very earliest days, experimentalists in biology often attempted to model their methodology on the physical sciences. Many experimentalists had as their stated aim to make biology as "scientific" as physics and chemistry.

From the viewpoint of contemporary philosophy, there is no necessary contradiction between the experimentalist and naturalist approaches to biological problems. Each deals with different levels of organization or with different kinds of problems. However, through much of the history of nineteenth- and twentieth-century biology, the two views were often very much in conflict. The clash was open and conscious in the minds of many workers, who often came to view themselves as belonging to one or the other camp. Naturalists accused experimentalists of seeing only one part of a system and generalizing from it to the whole. Experimentalists accused naturalists of drawing, from merely descriptive observations, speculative conclusions that they felt could have no relation to normal life processes; moreover, they saw in the naturalists' endless descriptions no information that led beyond trivial, individual problems.

The naturalist-experimentalist dichotomy was amply characterized by a number of writers in the late nineteenth century, including William Bateson and E. B. Wilson. In his 1894 book, *Materials for the Study of Variation,* Bateson wrote:

[The data of variation] attract men of two classes, in tastes and temperament distinct, each having little sympathy or even acquaintance with the work of the other. Those of the one class have felt the attraction of the problem. It is the challenge of nature that calls them to work. But disgusted with the superficiality of "naturalists" they sit down in the laboratory to the solution of the problem, hoping that the closer they look the more truly will they see. For the living things out of doors, they care little. Such work to them is all vague. With the other class, it is the living thing that attracts, not the problem. To them the methods of the first class are frigid and narrow. Ignorant of the skill and of the accurate final knowledge the method has bit by bit achieved, achievements that are the real glory of the method, the "naturalists" hear only those theoretical conclusions which the laboratories from time to time ask them to accept. With senses quickened by the range and fresh air of their own work, they feel keenly how crude and inadequate are these poor generalities and for what a small and conventional world they are devised. Disappointed with the results, they condemn the methods of the others, knowing nothing of their real strength. So it happens that for them the study of the problems of life and the species become associated with crudeness and meanness of scope. Beginning as naturalists, they end as collectors, despairing of the problem, turning for relief to the tangible business of classification, accounting themselves happy if they can keep their species apart, caring little how they become so, and rarely telling us how they may be brought together. Thus each class misses that which in the other is good.[1]

Bateson's description indicates how much hostility and even bitterness attended the dichotomy between the naturalist and experimentalist traditions. This was due in part to the fact that the naturalist tradition, predominant in the pre-1880 period, had begun to lose ground to the experimental by the 1870s. The long-established private Eastern universities as well as the major new institutions founded in the latter part of the nineteenth century—Johns Hopkins, Clark, Cornell, and Chicago—established programs in experimental biology. Even Harvard's distinguished tradition in natural history gave way in the 1890s to courses in experimental biology.[2] Henry Fairfield Osborn, a paleontologist at the American Museum of Natural History and Adjunct Professor of Zoology at Columbia, complained that by the early 1920s natural history was in such disfavor that it was difficult to obtain money for research and teaching positions in paleontology and other related areas.[3]

A quick survey of articles published in *The American Naturalist* over a twelve-year period (1900, 1906, 1912) shows a significant change in the percentage of articles dealing with natural history subjects on the one hand and experimental on the other. Somewhere between 1906 and 1912 a dramatic drop occurred in the number of papers devoted to natural history, while a corresponding upsurge is noted in the number of experimentally oriented works.[4] In a very interesting and revealing article written in 1901, "Aims and Methods of Study in Natural History," E. B. Wilson echoed Bateson's observations. Wilson captured particularly well the psychological milieu in which the dichotomy was perpetuated:

I shall never forget the impression made on me many years ago, shortly after returning from a year of study in European laboratories [including the Naples Zoological Station], by a remark made to me in the friendliest spirit by a much older naturalist, who was one of the foremost systematic and field naturalists of his day, and enjoyed a wide reputation. "I fear," he said, "that you have been spoiled as a naturalist by this biological craze [experimentalism] that seems to be running riot among the younger men. I do not approve of it at all." I was hardly in a position to deny the allegations; but candor compelled me to own to having had a suspicion that while there might have been a moat [*sic*] in the biological eye, a microscope of sufficient power might possibly have revealed something very like a beam in that of the systematist of the time. However that may have been, it is undeniable that at that period, or a little later, a lack of mutual understanding existed between the field naturalist and the laboratory workers which found expression in a somewhat picturesque exchange of compliments, the former receiving the flattering appellation of the "bug hunters," the latter the ignominious title of the "section-cutters," which on some irreverent lips was even degraded to that of the "worm-slicers".... I daresay there was on both sides justification for these delicate innuendos. Let us, for the sake of argument, admit that the section-cutter was not always sure whether he was cutting an *ornithorhynchus* [duck-billed platypus] or a Pearly Nautilus and at times perhaps he did lose sight of out-of-doors natural history and the living organism as he wandered among what Michael Foster called the "pit-falls of carmine and Canada balsam" [a stain and preservative material, respectively, used in preparing and staining sections of organs and tissues for microscopic observation]; but let us in justice mildly suggest that the bug hunter, too, ... was sometimes a trifle hazy as to whether the cerebellum was inside or outside the skull, and did not sufficiently examine that hoary problem as to whether the hen came from the egg or the egg from the hen, and by what kind of process.[5]

The tension between the naturalist and the experimentalist in American science is perhaps nowhere better illustrated than in the career of Thomas Hunt Morgan.

### Early Training of Thomas Hunt Morgan: Morphology and W. K. Brooks

In 1866, the same year that Gregor Mendel set forth his theory of heredity in the *Proceedings of the Brünn Natural History Society,* Thomas Hunt Morgan was born into genteel and gracious, if not extravagant, surroundings in Lexington, Kentucky. Early in his life, Morgan developed an interest in natural history that he sustained throughout his career, eventually publishing taxonomic studies on over fifty kinds of animals. During his college years at the State College of Kentucky, he studied anatomy, physiology, plant histology, microscopy, zoology, geology, and paleontology. Following graduation in 1886, Morgan spent the summer at the Marine Biology School at Annisquam, Massachusetts, which offered courses in marine biology and the natural history of marine organisms and provided Morgan with an opportunity to learn important collecting and handling techniques for live specimens.

In the fall of 1886, Morgan entered The Johns Hopkins University to study for a doctorate in zoology. In selecting Hopkins, Morgan was among the first generation of Americans to break with the tradition of seeking doctoral level training in Europe, particularly Germany. Hopkins was young in 1886, but its reputation had spread widely, and the challenge of attending America's first graduate university appealed to the energetic and ambitious Morgan.

As a student of William Keith Brooks at Johns Hopkins, Morgan was trained largely in the descriptive-naturalist tradition at a time when "morphology" was its dominant element. By definition "the study of form," morphology in the 1880s incorporated a number of disciplines that today would be considered independent fields of biology: comparative anatomy, embryology, paleontology, and cytology.[6] Although morphology had a long history, with goals and methods changing over the years, it took on a new importance in the post-Darwinian period and was understood to encompass three major aims: (1) to determine the basic unity of plan underlying the diversity of living forms; (2) to discover the common ancestor, the so-called "archetypal" form that related two or more divergent groups of organisms, or served as an ancient progenitor of a single modern line; (3) to reconstruct family trees or phylogenies of various animal and plant groups based on evidence from comparative anatomy, the fossil record, and a careful study of embryonic development.[7]

William Keith Brooks was a specialist on the embryonic development of marine invertebrates and a morphologist par excellence.[8] His influence on Morgan and other members of the younger generation was striking—as much for what he taught them not to do as for what he taught them to do. Brooks was educated at Williams College and in the fall of 1873 began his graduate studies under Louis Agassiz at Harvard's Museum of Comparative Zoology. Agassiz died that fall, but Brooks continued his work in descriptive morphology under Louis's son, Alexander. After receiving his Ph.D. (the third granted by Harvard University) in 1875, Brooks accepted Daniel C. Gilman's offer of a position at Hopkins, working under physiologist H. Newell Martin to train medical and graduate students in areas of descriptive natural history. Brooks remained at Hopkins throughout his academic career, rising to the position of chairman of the Department of Biology in 1893, a post he held until his death.

A confirmed Darwinian, Brooks felt that morphologists could most accurately come to understand the evolutionary significance of structures by studying their process of embryonic development. He felt it was possible to deduce, from studying larval or other embryonic stages of an organism, not only the evolution of structure but, more importantly, the evolution of the interaction of structure and function, i.e., the evolution of adaptions.

To Brooks, marine organisms provided the most valuable materials for morphological studies. Because he thought that competition and selective pressure had always been less in the oceans than in other ecological situations, he believed that marine forms had undergone less transformation in the course of their evolutionary history and thus retained many more of their primitive ancestral characteristics than did terrestrial or fresh-water forms. Furthermore, to Brooks, marine life was so diverse that evolutionary relationships could be seen more clearly than in land forms, where the diversity in any one area is often more restricted. In an effort to further morphological studies of marine life, Brooks was instrumental in founding the Chesapeake Zoological Laboratory of Johns Hopkins in 1878; in addition, he conducted summer courses at the biological stations at Beaufort, North Carolina, and Bermuda.

While focusing on such detailed studies, Brooks was also highly concerned with the larger problems of contemporary biology, particularly the mechanisms of heredity and embryonic differentiation. Evolution and adaptation figure prominently in Brooks's writing. His views on heredity were developed, as were those of many of his generation, in response to questions about the origin of variation that were raised, but not satisfactorily answered, by Darwin between 1859 and 1883.

Moreover, like most morphologists, Brooks did not refrain from speculation about the great biological issues of the day. He maintained that speculation was valid and even essential, especially in areas such as evolutionary history where direct verification was almost never possible. A complete series of fossil forms was almost the only definitive evidence of a particular line of development. Since such a series was seldom, if ever, obtained, the morphologists were forced to use their imagination. In fact, Brooks was skeptical about the value that experimental methods could ever have in such areas as evolution, phylogeny, or field natural history. As Brooks saw it, experimentation tended to isolate parts from wholes and thus to obscure the broad actions that were the key to life. Similarly, the tools of physics and chemistry appeared to him to be inappropriate for investigating the fundamental processes of living organisms. Toward the end of his life, Brooks wrote that one could achieve important discoveries and unravel the mysteries of life without grants of money, foreign travel, the latest equipment, and "above all, without undertaking to resolve biology into physics or chemistry."[9]

There is little doubt that Brooks's students numbered among the most original and influential biologists in the twentieth century. Aside from T. H. Morgan, they included Edmund Beecher Wilson (cytologist), Ross G. Harrison and E. G. Conklin (embryologists), and William Bateson (geneticist). A whole generation of young biologists, of which Morgan was a member, owed their biological heritage to Brooks.

Yet, despite Brooks's apparent success as a teacher, a number of his students have documented their exasperation with the aims and methods of morphology which he championed. To many of the younger biologists, much of morphology, particularly phylogeny, seemed a fruitless endeavor. The data were too circumspect and the conclusions too fanciful ever to be rigorously tested. One phylogenetic scheme seemed about as good as another, with often no way to distinguish between them. In a letter to his friend Hans Driesch in 1899, Morgan remarked about Brooks's new book, *The Foundations of Zoology,* "My old professor, Dr. Brooks, of Balto [*sic*] has published a book that you may have seen. A strange production in which are trotted out all the worn out themes of the metaphysicians.... Perhaps you may be interested in his theme that life is a response to nature. But his thought is vague and he fails to handle his subject or to tell clearly what he means."[10] Morgan and many of his fellow students at Hopkins felt that in the long run, Brooks's style of biology was not likely to lead to the solution of crucial biological problems. In fact, most of Brooks's students ended by working in areas quite different from that of their teacher; almost all became strong experimentalists and renounced both the methods and aims of morphology.

In a larger context, the conflict between the naturalist and experimentalist tradition was present at Hopkins from the inception of the university. H. Newell Martin was undisputed head of the biological sciences, particularly physiology. Brooks was hired explicitly as his younger assistant to handle the morphological subjects. Any hopes Brooks may have had of parity between physiology and morphology were dashed soon after his arrival in Baltimore. Martin was unequivocal about the dominant role of physiology in the new university. Physiology was to be queen, morphology her handmaiden. Moreover, because of the medical orientation of physiology, most of the graduate students in the first decade or so were M.D.'s interested in physiological research. In dedicating the new Biological Laboratory in 1884, Martin pointed out that morphology had had its day—it was time for the experimental side of biology (i.e., physiology) to come to the fore: "I think even the morphologists will admit that hitherto, and especially in the United States, they have had rather more than their fair share; numerous museums and laboratories have been built for their use; while physiology, if she got anything, had been usually allotted some out of the way room in an entirely unsuitable building, if no one else wanted it; and been very glad to get even that."[11] The experimental tradition was beginning to win out in its struggle against descriptive natural history. The relative positions of Brooks and Martin at Johns Hopkins clearly symbolized this development.

## The Revolt from Morphology

Morgan entered biology at a crucial transition period, and the transition greatly influenced the subsequent course of his biological work. His doctoral dissertation under Brooks concerned the embryology and phylogeny of a group of invertebrates known as *Pycnogonids* (the sea spiders). It was a sound, thorough, and well-reasoned piece of morphological work. Having thereby demonstrated his ability in this area, what factors led Morgan to revolt from morphology and to embrace enthusiastically the new wave of experimentalism? The change grew out of his skepticism about the future of the morphological tradition as exemplified in Brooks's work; and it flowed from his association with Jacques Loeb at Bryn Mawr, beginning in 1891, and his collaboration with Hans Driesch in Naples in 1895.

Even in Morgan's dissertation, the differences between his work and that of the old-style morphologists, such as Brooks, were clear. Morgan laid out neatly and clearly the conflicting opinions about the phylogenetic history of the *Pycnogonids* in an effort to provide observations on which of the hypotheses could be rejected. Brooks seldom presented his evidence in such a clear-cut manner nor did he attempt to consider and eliminate alternative hypotheses; rather he simply championed overtly the one or ones he favored. Second, there is in Morgan's thesis almost a complete lack of the kind of speculative suggestions characteristic of Brooks's writings; Morgan's thought processes already demonstrated a critical quality generally lacking in morphologists of the older generation.

With his doctorate in hand, in 1891, Morgan accepted a position as associate professor of biology at Bryn Mawr College. Bryn Mawr was a young and vigorous college for women, committed to providing full-scale graduate opportunities as well. Parallel in its principles and designs to its Baltimore model, it was often referred to as the "Jane Hopkins."[12] The Biology Department, of which Morgan became chairman, consisted of two faculty members, both new to the college and to each other. Morgan was to teach all the morphological subjects, and the German-born physiologist, Jacques Loeb, the physiological ones. Although their teaching duties appeared to perpetuate the experimentalist-naturalist split, Loeb and Morgan became quite close friends during their year together. Even after Loeb subsequently took positions at the University of Chicago, Berkeley, and finally the Rockefeller Institute, he and Morgan retained a life-long association that was rich and productive for both.[13]

Loeb's experimental work, carried out mostly in the United States, concerned problems in embryology and animal behavior. He found that he could cause an unfertilized sea urchin egg to begin dividing by pricking it with a needle or changing the salt concentration of the sea water in which it was cultured—a process known as artificial parthenogenesis.[14] His research on animal tropisms indicated that specific, quantitatively measurable responses could be produced by application of specific, quantitatively determined stimuli. From these various studies, Loeb developed what he termed "the mechanistic conception of life," a phrase that became the title of an article in 1911, and a collection of essays in 1912. In these essays, Loeb summarized his belief that all biological processes are at heart physical and chemical and that the proper method for studying these processes is quantitative experimentation. Rejecting speculation and metaphysical forces, Loeb became an enthusiastic and vocal proponent of the new experimentalism in biology.

Although his publications on the "mechanistic conception" came later, Loeb had already developed his basic philosophy by the time of his arrival in Bryn Mawr in 1891. Loeb was eight years older than Morgan and a man of forceful views. Although there is no direct evidence on this matter, Morgan could not have escaped being influenced by Loeb's attitude toward the values of experimental and mechanistic thinking.

Even more influential than his association with Loeb were Morgan's experiences at the Stazione Zoologica, a marine laboratory founded by Anton Dohrn in Naples in 1872. A student of the great Darwinian popularizer and morphologist, Ernst Haeckel, Dohrn was a zoologist of considerable skill and erudition who had pioneered in a number of studies of invertebrate morphology and phylogeny. By the early 1890s, his reputation as an outstanding biologist as well as his abilities as an organizer and administrator had made the Naples Station "the Mecca of the biological world."[15] Investigators from all over visited the station for a month, a summer, a year, or more, to carry out studies on a variety of topics from cell structure and function to embryology and natural history. The Bay of Naples was particularly rich in marine fauna; and it was the marine organisms (almost exclusively invertebrates) that formed the common denominator of all the research carried out at the Naples Station.

Morgan heard of the wonders of the Naples Station from several of his personal friends. E. B. Wilson had been the first American to work at the Station as far back as 1883; he returned there again in 1892, sending back glowing reports of the exciting research possibilities that Naples offered. Meanwhile, two other friends, George H. Parker and William Morton Wheeler, had both been to Naples in 1893. Use of the station was obtained by renting "tables" (research benches, equipped with running seawater tanks), one of which was supported by the Smithsonian Institution. Morgan applied to the Smithsonian for permission to work at its table. With permission granted, and a year's leave of absence (1894/95) secured from Bryn Mawr, Morgan left for Europe in June of 1894.

What Morgan found at Naples more than fulfilled his expectations. The physical plant as well as the personnel were enormously exciting to a home-trained American biologist. In the mid-1890s the United States was still relatively isolated from the great research centers of the world, and unlike many of his older colleagues, Morgan had not taken his doctorate in a foreign university. Morgan stayed at Naples through July of 1895, working on problems of experimental embryology that included a long study of the development of ctenophores (called by the popular name "comb jellies") in collaboration with Hans Driesch. Of all the friends he made among the regular workers at the Naples Station, Driesch was the one who most influenced the direction of his work in subsequent years. Morgan found both working with Driesch and being at the Naples Station one of the most exciting experiences of his life. No sooner had he returned to Bryn Mawr than he wrote to Dohrn: "My greatest wish is to return again to Naples. When I compare the freedom there with the artificial and busy life here, I am filled with a desire to go back."[16]

Although Morgan wanted to encourage as many Americans as possible to work at the Naples Station, it was obvious that no more than a handful (perhaps two or three) could conveniently do so in any one year. There was a need for a "Naples Station" in the United States, one that combined the availability of a variety of marine organisms with the benefits of a national (if not international) center for biological research. To Morgan, the most likely place to fill these demands was the already existing but small Marine Biological Laboratory (MBL) at Woods Hole. Prior to his year abroad, Morgan had already spent several summers doing research at Woods Hole. He was aware of its potential and was enthusiastic about the prospects of helping to build an American "Stazione Zoologica."

The Marine Biological Laboratory at Woods Hole grew out of several earlier, primarily summer, seaside stations on the northeast coast of the United States: Louis Agassiz's short-lived Anderson School of Natural History on Penikese

Island, founded in 1873, and the small station at Annisquam, Massachusetts (which Morgan had attended in the summer of 1886), supported by the Women's Education Association under the auspices of the Boston Society of Naturalists. The purpose of both was to provide instruction in marine biology for secondary and college teachers. The MBL was organized with the explicit aim of realizing both the best ideals of the wholly research-oriented Naples Station and the goals originally set out by the Anderson School and the Annisquam laboratory. The first director of the MBL, Charles Otis Whitman, stated at the founding of the laboratory in 1888: "Other things being equal, the investigator is always the best instructor. The highest grade of instruction in any science can only be furnished by one who is thoroughly imbued with the scientific spirit, and who is actually engaged in original work."[17] Organized on the "table system," as at Naples, the MBL thus attracted two groups of people: teachers seeking further instruction in modern (and especially marine) biology, and original investigators taking advantage of the abundance of organisms available in the Woods Hole area. The institution opened its doors in 1888 and by the mid-1890s had grown to seven buildings.

After his return from Naples, Morgan became an even more firm supporter of the MBL than he had been prior to departure. Although in its early days the MBL was populated largely by morphologically oriented workers, Morgan saw clearly after 1895 that it could be a center for the new experimental biology he had seen at Naples. The eggs of marine organisms such as the sea urchin offered ideal material for experimental studies of early embryonic development, and Morgan was more than anxious to develop this line of work at MBL. He also saw that in the scientific growth of the institution lay the prospect of establishing an international center as well-known as Naples. Consequently, his interests lay far more in the research, as opposed to the teaching, programs at the MBL. In these summers after 1895 when he did not return to Europe, Morgan carried out research on experimental embryology, particularly regeneration, and he worked on artificial parthenogenesis with Jacques Loeb, who also spent the summers in Woods Hole.

Morgan's move toward experimental work may have been influenced by another factor implicit in his work with Driesch at Naples: his contact with the new experimental approach to embryology called *Entwicklungsmechanik*. As a method of studying embryos, *Entwicklungsmechanik* represented a significant departure from earlier nineteenth-century studies in embryology, which had been largely descriptive in nature. The German embryologist Wilhelm Roux and others among the new experimentalists sought to learn from the embryo not what its phylogenetic history might have been but rather what factors *cause* embryos to differentiate during development. To find answers to that question, Roux resorted to modifying embryos in order to observe the resulting changes in their developmental form. He dared to interfere with development. In a word, he *experimented*.[18]

The work performed by Roux in 1888 led him into an intense controversy with Hans Driesch over the causal agents in embryonic development.[19] Yet despite their strong differences of opinion, both Roux and Driesch agreed substantially at this time (c. 1891) on the *methods* necessary to pursue embryological questions. Driesch considered himself a proponent of *Entwicklungsmechanik* and as much conveyed his enthusiasm for the new approach to Morgan.

In addition to experimentation, Roux's program emphasized the mechanistic philosophy that must underlie all work in the "new biology:"

Since, moreover, physics and chemistry reduce all phenomena, even those which appear to be most diverse, e.g., magnetic, electrical, optical, and chemical phenomena, to movements of parts, or attempt such a reduction, the older more restrictive concept of mechanics in the physicist's sense as the causal doctrine of the movement of masses, has been extended to coincide with the philosophical concept of mechanism, comprising as it does all causally conditioned phenomena, so that the words "developmental mechanics" agree with the more recent concepts of physics and chemistry, and may be taken to designate the doctrine of all formative phenomena.[20]

Thus, Roux tried to reduce the complex problem of differentiation, with its myriad component parts, into mechanical causes. In a very real sense, he created the field of experimental embryology by separating study of the causes of development from the more complex field of general morphology.

Although Morgan was familiar with the growing school of *Entwicklungsmechanik,* he had had little direct contact with experimental embryology prior to 1894. It was his stay at Naples in 1894/95 that brought him face to face with these new developments. It underscored what Morgan had already heard from Loeb about the importance of using the tools of physics and chemistry and the fundamental mechanistic basis of life. As a result of his close contact with Driesch, Morgan was immersed in experimental embryology from that time onward. Undoubtedly, the excitement emerging from the work of Roux, Driesch, and others following the tenets of *Entwicklungsmechanik* had much to do with catalyzing Morgan's turn from descriptive to experimental biology.

Once he had adopted experimental embryology, Morgan became a leader in the field. His books on *Regeneration* (1901) and *Experimental Zoology* (1907) established him as one of the principal experimental biologists not only of the United States but of the world. His appointment as professor of experimental zoology at Columbia in 1904 was tangible recognition of his accomplishments in this direction. By then he was an acknowledged expert on the development of sea urchin and frogs' eggs, as well as the most knowledgeable person in North America on the general problem of regeneration. From the turn of the century onward his interests lay increasingly in the areas of evolution, heredity, and sex determination.

## The Experimentalist's Approach to Evolution and Heredity

Two persistent problems stemming from the work of Darwin continued to plague biologists in 1900. One centered around the efficacy of natural selection itself: was Darwin's theory sufficient to account for the origin of the many intricate adaptations known to exist among plants and animals? The other problem focused on the issue of heredity. Which characteristics were inherited and which not? Were there any laws governing the transmission of inherited traits? And perhaps the most important of all to those concerned with the origin of species: how do new variations arise to provide the raw material for evolution? Through his work on regeneration, Morgan had become involved in the problem of the origin of adaptations; through his work in experimental embryology, he became fascinated with the problem of sex determination. The former brought him face to face with Darwinian evolution by natural selection and with De Vries' concept of speciation by large-scale "mutations"; the latter brought him into direct contact with the newly rediscovered Mendelian theory of heredity.

Morgan's views on both Darwinian and Mendelian theory offer considerable insight into his mode of approaching biological problems. Initially, he opposed both theories rather vigorously, for a short period of time embracing De Vries's mutationism as a viable alternative for understanding both heredity and evolution. Eventually, however, Morgan changed his mind and became a strong, even zealous, supporter of both Mendelism and Darwinism. Morgan's initial opposition to these theories, especially in the early 1900s, reflected his abiding distrust of broad, large-scale hypotheses.

Although an evolutionist from his earliest days, Morgan rejected Darwinism because he did not see how specific mechanisms of selection, acting upon very small individual, but supposedly inherited, variations could produce adaptative structures over numerous generations. To understand these objections, it is first necessary to understand Morgan's concept of species, for the view that a biologist holds about the nature of species will determine much of what he believes about the mechanism of evolution.

Like many other biologists at the turn of the century, Morgan held that species were only arbitrary units created for the convenience of taxonomists; the only real unit in nature, he contended, was the individual.[21] Morgan tended to see species in two contradictory ways. On the one hand, his experience with organisms in nature, particularly marine invertebrates, suggested that all forms exist in an infinitely graded series with no sharp lines between discrete groups. On the other hand, he also tended to see groups such as starfish and earthworms as types bounded by a limit on their range of variability. Morgan's inability to see species as real, natural groups, as modern taxonomists view them, prevented him from understanding the basic populational level on which natural selection inevitably works—evolution does not occur with individuals, only with groups.

Beyond this general confusion about the nature of species, Morgan's strongest criticism of Darwinism centered on methodology. Morgan believed that most Darwinians, past and present, had engaged in flights of fancy and speculation that had no basis in fact. In Morgan's view, a great offender along these lines was the German biologist August Weismann, who enjoyed a widespread popularity and enormous influence around the turn of the century. Weismann had tried to unite five important areas of biology—evolution, heredity, cytology, physiology, and development—into one comprehensive conceptual scheme that Morgan maintained was both speculative and fanciful.[22]

Weismann's and Morgan's conceptions of the role of theory in biology were direct opposites. To Weismann, working in the tradition dominated by Darwin's *Origin of Species,* a theory served primarily to gather the facts together in an umbrella fashion. To Morgan, on the other hand, a theory served mainly as a means of giving direction to further research; for a theory to be of any value, it had to be framed in such a way as to be subject to verification. It was on the nature of theory formation that Morgan leveled his most vehement attack on Weismann:

Weismann has piled up one hypothesis on another as though he could save the integrity of the theory of natural selection by adding new speculative matter to it. The most unfortunate feature is that the new speculation is skillfully removed from the field of verification and invisible germs (particles), whose sole functions are those which Weismann's imagination bestows upon them, are brought forward as though they could supply the deficiencies of Darwin's theory. That is, indeed, the old method of the philosophizers of nature. An imaginary system has been invented which attempts to explain all difficulties, and if it fails, then new inventions are to be thought of. Thus, we see where the theory of selection of fluctuating germs has led one of the most widely known disciples of the Darwinian theory.[23]

As an alternative to Darwinism, Morgan became, for a time, a strong proponent of Hugo De Vries' "mutation theory"—a particulate concept of heredity that accounted for the origin of new species by quick jumps instead of the minute gradation on which Darwin's theory was based.[24] The De Vries theory was intended to supersede the theory of natural selection in accounting for the origin of species and the Mendelian theory (of which De Vries had been one of the rediscoverers) in accounting for the inheritance of specific traits.

By and large, those favoring De Vries' theory were young experimentalists in universities and research institutes. Like Morgan, they found in De Vries one of the first examples of what they thought to be an experimental approach to evolution, a continuing commitment to the *Entwicklungsmechanik* tradition. Furthermore, most of those who favored De Vries were opposed to the old-style morphological speculation, and particularly to the work of taxonomists. Those opposing De Vries' theory included older workers, especially the strong neo-Darwinians (and even the neo-Lamarckians), many of whom were trained in the German tradition. Plant and animal breeders also constituted a significant portion of the opposition to De Vries. Most had gained their knowledge not through university training but through practical experience. Opponents of De Vries were generally unfavorable to any biological theories that attempted to reduce complex organic processes to the interaction of particles or to single mechanistic-type explanations (such as postulating a single, large-scale variation). Thus, support for or opposition to the mutation theory fell along the lines of the experimentalist and naturalist camps respectively. In many ways, the predispositions of the two groups determined the way in which members of each reacted to the new theory.[25]

Morgan's concern with the problem of evolution and particularly the mutation theory, coupled with his interest in the nature of sex determination, led him to give increasing attention in the early 1900s to the concept of heredity. The theory of heredity that Morgan ultimately did so much to establish after 1910 was a combination of two previously separate lines of thought: the chromosomal theory, which maintained that the cell structures known as chromosomes were directly involved in hereditary transmission, and the Mendelian theory, which postulated the existence of hereditary "factors" that segregate and assort themselves in the production of male and female parents. The chromosome theory was based on the extensive nineteenth-century studies of plant and animal cells. The Mendelian theory was based on analyses of breeding results and had grown out of a long tradition of plant and animal hybridization. Morgan's early views on these theories can be illustrated by a series of questions relating to the problem of sex determination. Is sex determination the result of internal factors established at the moment of fertilization or of external factors during embryonic growth (such as the amount of nourishment, temperature, etc.)? If sex is established at fertilization, by what mechanism does it occur? Is the egg or the sperm the most important germ cell in determining sex?

Morgan at first rejected both the internalist (chromosomal) and the externalist (environmental) theories of sex determination because he felt there was no evidence to support either case. One factor that gradually led him to accept the chromosomal theory was the cytological work carried out in 1904 and 1905 by Nettie M. Stevens, Morgan's former student at Bryn Mawr, and by E. B. Wilson, his colleague at Columbia. Working independently, Stevens and Wilson studied the so-called "accessory chromosome" and its relation to sex in a variety of organisms—mostly insects. (Today, the odd-shaped accessory chromosome for most species is called the $Y$-chromosome and is normally paired with a differently shaped chromosome, the $X$.) From their research, a pattern emerged: in certain insects, inheritance of two $X$ chromosomes produced a female, while inheritance of one $Y$ chromosome and one $X$ chromosome produced a male. In other groups of insects, the reverse was true. Morgan's letters at the time show his strong skepticism about Stevens's and Wilson's theory, but he did have to admit that there was some regularity between the determination of sex and the passage of specific chromosomes from parent to offspring.

Further evidence for acceptance of the chromosome theory came from Morgan's own exhaustive cytological investigation into how rotifers and aphids were able to reproduce parthenogetically under certain circumstances and sexually under others. He found, surprisingly, that the parthenogenetic generations were caused by the extension of a chromosome—one of the accessories—that invariably produced females, suggesting a parallel to Wilson's and Stevens' findings. By 1909 or 1910, Morgan was prepared to believe that the process of heredity could have some material basis in the cell structures known as chromosomes.

The second element in Morgan's concept of heredity was the newly rediscovered Mendelian theory of inheritance. In the years between 1900 and 1910, Morgan was among the strongest critics of Mendelism, expressing many of the same criticisms voiced by other skeptics of the period. As in the case of Darwinian theory, Morgan's overriding criticisms were rooted in problems of methodology. Morgan argued that the Mendelian theory was "preformationist." Popular in the seventeenth and eighteenth centuries, preformationism maintained that the individual adult organism was already "preformed" in either the unfertilized egg or the sperm. By simply positing a factor transmitted from parent to offspring, Mendelism did not consider what was to Morgan the most critical issue in biology—the *development* of adult traits. In Morgan's view, a Mendelian factor, *Anlage* (gene), could explain nothing of interest because it was a "black box."

More important, Morgan felt the Mendelian theory was too much like the older, speculative theories of heredity put forth by such nineteenth-century biologists as Weismann. In a seething attack in 1909, Morgan accused the Mendelians of simply creating or discarding factors at will in order to save their theory in any given instance.[26] He was referring to the work of William Bateson and his colleagues in England as well as to that of Charles Davenport, W. E. Castle, and others in the United States. To Morgan, there appeared to be no evidence that there were any such units, or hereditary particles, as those postulated by Mendel. Anyone could invent hypothetical particles to "explain" the outcome of one or another crosses, but to Morgan that was not legitimate. He looked for direct evidence that such particles existed—but prior to 1910, that knowledge was not forthcoming.

### *A Change of Views on Mendelism: The Beginning of the* Drosophila *Work*

Morgan's change of attitude toward the Mendelian theory was principally the result of his work with the fruit fly, *Drosophila melanogaster*. In an effort to determine whether De Vriesian mutations occurred in animals, Morgan began breeding *Drosophila* in his Columbia laboratory in the fall of 1908. For a year he obtained no satisfactory results. Then, early in 1910, Morgan observed a curious variation in one of his *Drosophila* stock bottles: a single male fly with white, rather than the normal "wild type" red eyes.[27] The eye color variation did not make the fly a new species but it was obviously a mutation—and, for Morgan, an enormously exciting discovery. Morgan bred this male with a red-eyed female and found that the first generation ($F_1$) produced all normal, red-eyed flies, suggesting that the white-eyed condition might be a Mendelian recessive. When he crossed some members of the first generation with each other, the white-eyed condition reappeared in a ratio of three red-eyed to one white-eyed fly. These results seemed to confirm the hypothesis that white-eye was a Mendelian recessive, since this is exactly the ratio that the Mendelian scheme would predict for a cross between two hybrid forms. However, Morgan noted something that was not in strict accordance with the Mendelian scheme: *all of the white-eyed flies were male!* The red-eyed flies were found to occur in a ratio of two females to one male. Still another cross of white-eyed males to $F_1$ red-eyed females produced both red-eyed and white-eyed progeny in equal ratios of male to female. The white-eyed condition was obviously a stable genetic variation—a small, discrete, Mendelian recessive that did not in any way make the offspring a different species from the parents.

The appearance of the white-eyed mutant shifted Morgan's immediate interest from evolution to heredity. What appeared to attract Morgan's attention was not simply that the white-eyed condition acted according to Mendelian laws, but that in some fundamental way it appeared to be associated with sex inheritance. Why, after all, should all of the white-eyed flies in the $F_2$ have been males? To explain these results, Morgan not only accepted the basic tenets of the Mendelian scheme, but combined these notions with the suggestions of Wilson and Stevens that the determination of sex had a chromosomal basis. In a now famous paper published in *Science* in July 1910,[28] Morgan refrained from claiming that the factor for eye color was definitely linked to the accessory chromosomes but he did try to explain his results by saying that both always segregated together. Given this conclusion, it was a small conceptual step to the linkage of certain Mendelian factors with the accessory chromosomes and the development of a comprehensive-theory of heredity. Morgan termed the white-eyed condition and other traits thought to be determined by factors on accessory chromosomes, "sex-limited characters."

Morgan was enormously excited about his results and the broadening horizons for further research that *Drosophila* represented. He discovered the original white-eyed male in early 1910, and in a letter to Driesch in November of the same year, he wrote that—although he had been overwhelmed by work, mostly breeding experiments with fruit flies—"it's wonderful material."[29] Already, Morgan claimed, he had more than a half-dozen mutants, some of which were sex limited and others were not. Morgan confessed to Driesch that the sex limited cases interested him most and "they may throw some further light on the process of heredity."[30] He saw quickly and clearly that *Drosophila* provided the basis for answering, in an experimental way, questions about the physical nature of the hereditary process.

Indeed, *Drosophila* proved to be an ideal laboratory organism for studies in heredity. It was easy to culture in quantities and, because of its short generation time—about two and a half weeks—it could produce over a dozen generations a year, providing Morgan with abundant data to analyze. In the five years following publication of the first *Drosophila* paper in 1910, Morgan and his coworkers obtained astonishing results in three directions. First, chromosome maps were constructed that indicated the position of the various Mendelian genes, relative to each other, along the chromosome. The mapping techniques allowed the Morgan group to elaborate what appeared to be a consistent picture of the architecture of the germ plasm. That picture, beginning as the simple concept of genes arranged in a linear fashion on chromosomes, was an essential first step to the development of a theory of how genes functioned and interacted. Second, as a result of extensive breeding experiments with *Drosophila,* some of the basic assumptions of Mendelism, such as random assortment and pure dominance or recessiveness that Morgan had earlier called into question, were shown to be too rigid and simple to apply to real-life breeding situations. Armed with this evidence, Morgan became prepared to accept the broad outlines of the Mendelian theory while admitting the necessity of extending and modifying some of Mendel's over-simplified conclusions. Third, the discovery of nondisjunction that pointed to the association of Mendelian factors with the *X*-chromosomes led not only to the first direct proof of the chromosome theory of inheritance but also, in later years, to new views on the determination of sex.[31]

Underlying all of these lines of work was the development of the basic structure of the Mendelian-chromosome theory. In its own way, each line of work contributed something in support of the idea that Mendelian genes were, in fact, arranged in a linear fashion on specific chromosomes. Each line of work also helped to expand the original Mendelian concept in a more comprehensive and sophisticated way. The chromosome theory of heredity as elaborated by the Morgan group was far richer in experimental and conceptual detail than the simplified scheme Mendel had reported in 1865.

## The Composition and Characteristics of the Drosophila *Group—1910–1920*

The development of Morgan's experimental work, and his ultimate success, owed much to the physical and social setting in which he carried out his research. At the time Morgan was beginning his *Drosophila* work, his long-time friend E. B. Wilson was chairman of Columbia's Department of Biology; Wilson had a strong interest in heredity and evolution and did everything possible to encourage Morgan. The physical facilities at Columbia's Schermerhorn Hall may have been primitive by modern standards, but Morgan was able to fashion his "fly room" out of a laboratory adjoining his office and to equip it with old tables and thousands of milk bottles for culturing *Drosophila.*

In addition to a relatively favorable research environment, Morgan also had an intelligent and enthusiastic group of students to aid his efforts. Prior to 1910, Morgan carried out most of his studies alone, or occassionally in collaboration with another worker. However, as the *Drosophila* work blossomed, he began to include others in his work. In the fall of 1909, Morgan taught the introductory biology course at Columbia for the only time in his career. Sitting in that class were two students: one a sophomore, Alfred Henry Sturtevant, and the other a freshman, Calvin Blackman Bridges. From the outset both students were intrigued by, and attracted to, Morgan's style.[32] To the student who possessed natural curiosity, Morgan conveyed a sense of excitement about the study of biological problems, and he attracted those who were eager to follow new leads in research. The appeal was all in Morgan's personality, for otherwise the introductory biology course in 1909/10 was rather traditionally organized (it consisted of a phylogenetic survey of animals). Ironically, Morgan did not discuss heredity in any organized way in the course; it was only later that Sturtevant and Bridges realized that Morgan himself was actively working in this field.

In the fall of 1910, both Bridges and Sturtevant asked Morgan if they could work in his laboratory. Sturtevant, the more advanced undergraduate (then a junior) was accepted as a research assistant, while Bridges was given a job washing bottles. But Bridges proved so expert in observing mutants in the cultures he was cleaning up that he was soon given an official position as researcher. Two years later, a third student, H. J. Muller, was formally incorporated into the group, although he had already been closely associated with much of the work during his junior and senior years (1908/10).

All three of these men received their B.A. degrees from Columbia and they all stayed on to earn their Ph.D.'s under Morgan's direction. In addition, many other investigators passed through the *Drosophila* lab between 1910 and 1920. Morgan's graduate students included Charles Zeleny, Fernandes Payne, Charles Metz, H. H. Plough, Franz Schrader, Donald Lancefield, Alexander Weinstein, and L. C. Dunn. Among those who worked for a year or more in the laboratory as research associates or postdoctoral fellows were Otto Mohr from Norway and Theodosius Dobzhansky from the Soviet Union. Although all of these workers made important contributions to the *Drosophila* work, it was Bridges, Muller, and Sturtevant who participated with Morgan in the most dramatically productive period of research between 1910 and 1920.

Since the "fly room" was physically small and crowded, Morgan was careful in selecting those who would have regular space in it. This was a practical necessity, but it was also part of Morgan's approach to research. He was intense about the progression of his work and had little or no time for those who did not share the same seriousness of purpose. It was a canon of Morgan's research spirit that hard work and complete devotion to the biological cause were virtual prerequisites to acceptance into the group. But Morgan was also wise enough to recognize his own limitations. He wanted to include among those working with him individuals whose abilities and personalities complemented his own. He chose wisely when he selected Bridges, Sturtevant, and Muller. Morgan's creative imagination ranged over so many new ideas that he was not always interested in, or able to work out, all the exact details of an idea at once, in the way Sturtevant did. In turn, Bridges was given great credit by Sturtevant for his almost endless, painstaking efforts to keep the "stock" strains of *Drosophila* "clean," a basic requirement for all the work.

In still another way, Morgan's original group complemented their teacher's abilities. Morgan had never been an outstanding student of mathematics; he had an exact mind, but not primarily a quantitative one. Sturtevant, Muller, and

Bridges were all more at ease with quantitative arguments than was Morgan. They were able to handle some of the complex reasoning that went into designing rigorous matings. Morgan would suggest what questions needed to be answered; but it was Sturtevant or Muller, most often, who would design the actual experiments.

In terms of personality, Sturtevant was slow and patient, quantitative and highly incisive. With Morgan he shared wide-ranging biological interests, including the topics of evolution, cytology, embryology, taxonomy, and many aspects of heredity. His major contributions over the years centered on the mapping of genes and the development of a picture of the architecture of the germ plasm through analysis of breeding results.[33] Calvin Bridges was both a unique personality and an extraordinary investigator. After receiving his Ph.D. under Morgan, Bridges remained at Columbia as a research associate of the Carnegie Institution of Washington, a position he continued to hold even after he moved with the group to California in 1928. He was the outstanding cytologist in the *Drosophila* group and his main attention was given to the study of chromosomes in cells from various offspring of *Drosophila* matings. It was largely Bridges' work that helped establish the close correlation between breeding data and chromosomal structures.[34] Hermann Joseph Muller, the son of a first-generation metal worker, entered Columbia on a scholarship. It was at a meeting of a biology club that Muller helped to organize for Columbia undergraduates that he met Bridges and Sturtevant who told him of Morgan and the "fly room." Unable to gain a space in Morgan's lab immediately, Muller entered graduate school in physiology, which offered the fellowships and teaching assistantships he needed to finance his studies. In 1912 he became a full-time student in the "fly room." Like Morgan, Muller had a broad interest in all aspects of biology, and his published writings consist of numerous articles on subjects ranging from the hazards of radiation to eugenics, science fiction, and evolution. Muller's main contribution to the *Drosophila* work in the years 1910 to 1916 lay in devising the precise experimental crosses that had to be made to test specific hypotheses that he or others proposed and in designing stocks of flies with specific "chromosome markers"—parts of chromosomes that could be observed visibly with the microscope—and thus followed from one generation to another.[35]

It was, to a very considerable extent, the variety and diversity of people involved that made the nuclear *Drosophila* group so effective. Another unique feature of the Morgan group was the atmosphere in which the major ideas were developed and worked out. There was constant conversation, infused with humor, complete devotion to work, and a sense of equality among the four central members. Sturtevant described the working atmosphere, emphasizing the integrity and interrelatedness of each individual with the rest of the group:

This group worked as a unit. Each carried on his own experiments, but each knew exactly what the others were doing, and each new result was freely discussed. There was little attention paid to priority or to the source of new ideas or new interpretations. What mattered was to get ahead with the work. There was much to be done; there were many new ideas to be tested, and many new experimental techniques to be developed. There can have been few times and places in scientific laboratories with such an atmosphere of excitement and with such a record of sustained enthusiasm. This was due in part to Morgan's own attitude, compounded with enthusiasm combined with a strong critical sense, generosity, open-mindedness, and a remarkable sense of humor. No small part of the success of the undertaking was also due to Wilson's unfailing support and appreciation of the work—a matter of importance partly because he was head of the department.[36]

The constant discussion within the group was crucial, for it was through such exchanges that the various interests and specialities of different members of the group could gain their input into the total program of work. New ideas were continually brought up for analysis and in many cases put into practice as one or another new experiment.

While Morgan knew the general outlines of the work that was going on, he increasingly left the members of his group alone to go their own way and work in a spirit of complete independence. After 1913 or 1914, it is apparent that most of the experiments and the plans were in fact laid by Sturtevant, Bridges, and Muller. Morgan had his mind on many problems, and the details very soon became less interesting to him than the broader picture.

Always a part of the *Drosophila* group, yet somewhat detached from it, Morgan was affectionately referred to as "the boss" by the others, and he referred to them as "the boys." Yet Morgan, like all people, had his likes and his dislikes, his stronger and weaker affections for those around him. Sturtevant was his closest associate, his "pet" as Muller described it. Bridges was well-respected but not as close personally to Morgan. Muller always stood further away from Morgan and from the group as a whole. Muller's sense of "outsideness" stemmed from several factors: he was not part of the *Drosophila* work during its first two years, and his personality was very different from that of Morgan. Even as a student, Muller occasionally criticized Morgan both in private and in public and often in a direct and aggressive way. Morgan and Muller came from widely divergent backgrounds and social classes. Morgan never thought of himself as aristocratic or aloof, and he never acted as such in any overt or conscious way. Nonetheless, aggressiveness was something he neither liked nor could understand. The world of the working class, immigrant New Yorker, which Muller represented, was about as far from his own experience as anything could have been.

Despite these difficulties, Morgan and his three principal coworkers remained a remarkably cohesive group. Especially valuable in terms of both advancing work and promoting social interaction were the summers that the group spent at Woods Hole. In mid-June all the *Drosophila* material was packed up into barrels, with several culture bottles of each strain of *Drosophila* left behind in New York to serve as reserve in case any of the specimens were damaged en route. At Woods Hole, the *Drosophila* group had ample opportunity to discuss their work with biologists from a variety of other fields and it was here, too, that Morgan gave several of the famous Friday Night Lectures in which he introduced the group's findings on *Drosophila* before results were formally published. The long-standing tradition of emphasis on rigorous quantitative experimental work that permeated the MBL in the summer, especially after 1910 or so, was highly conducive to the program of research upon which the *Drosophila* group was engaged.

## *Funding the* Drosophila *Work*

In an age of "big science," it is difficult to realize the simple and modest financial support on which much work in Morgan's era was based. In the first three decades of the twentieth century, there were no large foundations or government-supported research grants. Funds for scientific research were difficult to secure. In some cases, universities provided meager support, but except for a few large and comparatively wealthy schools, this was not a widespread practice. For certain areas of biology, state agricultural stations sometimes provided funds. On rare occasions, an entrepreneur such as Louis or Alexander Agassiz could secure private donations for the cause of scientific research, but this was not a resource open to most investigators. Morgan, like many of his contemporaries, had adapted to these difficulties by conducting research that did not depend on expensive specimens and equipment.

The *Drosophila* work could be carried out, at least initially, on a relatively modest basis. The flies were obtained in the wild at no cost. They were grown in milk bottles that Morgan collected from his friends and associates. The major expense was the *Drosophila* food that by 1915 was costing anywhere from $100 to $200 a year. In the early years between 1910 and 1915, the funding of the project was largely a cooperative enterprise financed by Morgan personally and, in a very limited way, by Columbia University. Graduate student support came from Columbia mostly in the form of teaching assistantships, and in a few cases as scholarships. The University also provided such basic equipment as magnifying glasses, binocular microscopes, glassware, etc. Most of the rest, however, came directly from Morgan's own funds. For example, in addition to furnishing a scholarship for Sturtevant for a semester (1912/13), Morgan also paid Bridges' salary as bottle washer that year. This is something that Morgan could afford largely because he and his wife had independent resources—a course not open to every biologist at that time.

After about 1915, however, additional expenses loomed on the horizon. Bridges required more sophisticated equipment in order to carry out his cytological work; more binocular microscopes were needed as the number of people working in the fly room increased, and it was necessary to hire assistants to help in the day-to-day preparation of food and the washing of bottles in the lab. Above all, steady salaries had to be provided for research associates, such as Bridges and Sturtevant who were not paid by Columbia University, and for the project's artist and administrative assistant, Edith Wallace, who made most of the drawings of *Drosophila* published by the Morgan group. If the new genetics was to fulfill its promise, additional financial support would have to be obtained. Morgan thus turned to the Carnegie Institution of Washington whose willingness to support basic research in heredity and evolution had been demonstrated in the establishment of the Cold Spring Harbor Laboratory under Charles B. Davenport in 1904.[37] The Carnegie Institution agreed to support the *Drosophila* work for an initial five-year period. Between 1915 and 1919 the Carnegie Foundation provided Morgan with an annual grant of $3,600, which was used solely to pay the salaries of Bridges and Sturtevant as full-time Carnegie Institution research associates. The remainder of the expenses, such as the salary of Edith Wallace, still came from Morgan's own pocket.

Given these circumstances, it was understandable that Morgan was "annoyed and flabbergasted" when he learned in 1919 that his former student Charles W. Metz was proposing to set up a large-scale *Drosophila* research program at the Carnegie Laboratories in Cold Spring Harbor and was asking for considerably more financial support than Morgan had received. Even more disturbing were Metz's suggestions that the Morgan group limit itself only to *Drosophila melanogaster,* leaving the Cold Spring Harbor group to study all other species; and his inquiry as to whether Bridges might not be able to carry out his work more effectively at Cold Spring Harbor than at Columbia. In the face of the possible loss of the work and the group he had developed, Morgan dispatched a long letter to Metz that was a masterful combination of practical reasoning, candor, and diplomacy.[38] He expressed his disappointment at the prospect of losing support for the same work to someone else; but he phrased it in terms of envy, and even willingness to aid Metz because after all, the most important thing was to get on with the work. At the same time, he argued against Metz's presumption that a division of labor as regards different species of *Drosophila* might be effected between the Cold Spring Harbor and Columbia laboratories. He pointed out that even Metz's most significant work (the parallelism in mutation and cross-over rates among different species of *Drosophila*) was only meaningful when compared to Morgan's *Drosophila melanogaster* data, which by that time was very extensive.

But it was at the end of the letter that Morgan made what was probably his most significant point: scientific work should not be conducted in an atmosphere of competition between two groups, each vying for the greater share of the resources or the results. As Morgan stated, "the best work can be carried out by constant cooperation between individuals working on the best materials obtainable, and . . . the moment they begin to appropriate special fields of influence, the work will suffer." In Morgan's view, the success of the *Drosophila* group was rooted in the constant interaction among its members, and in the fact that no individual specialized so heavily in one area of the work that he did not at all times know what was going on in others. What Metz was proposing seemed to Morgan to be scientific empire building, which he felt in the long run would be detrimental to the research as a whole.

Possibly as a result of Metz's proposition, Morgan entered into new negotia-

tions with the Carnegie that more than tripled its support in the following year—
1920. Furthermore, Metz's group was incorporated as part of Morgan's under a
funding arrangement from the Carnegie. As Morgan wrote, with some satisfaction, to Otto Mohr:

We have had quite a turn-over in our relationship with the Carnegie. We shall be much
better off than heretofore. The salaries of the boys will be considerably increased. I am to
have an artist and a technical assistant, with a fund for running expenses and another for
apparatus. Metz also is to have a similar group (if he can get as good a one) and next
winter, at any rate, the two groups will work here together in this laboratory. So if you
will come back again, you will find the flies humming.[39]

### *The Influence of the* Drosophila *Work*

By 1915, Morgan and his three young and enthusiastic workers had gathered
enough information to publish the first comprehensive statement of the chromosome theory of heredity. Because of the closely knit nature of the group, all
shared coauthorship in *The Mechanism of Mendelian Heredity.*[40] In the book,
Morgan and his associates showed the many ways in which the Mendelian
chromosome theory contributed to an understanding of general biological principles. By surveying data not only from *Drosophila* but from other animals and
many kinds of plants as well, they demonstrated clearly that Mendel's work was
applicable to a great variety of species. Further, they showed that in every case
that had been specifically studied, the Mendelian factor hypothesis could be
related to cytological data about chromosomes. Each factor was considered to be
a discrete physical unit that was located at a definite position on the chromosome
and could be physically separated from other factors around it by chromosome
breakage and recombination. By linking breeding results to the facts of cytology,
Morgan asserted that Mendel's factors had a distinct physical reality in the
structure of the germ cells.

Morgan's initial objections to Mendelism were based on his belief that it was
too speculative and hypothetical. What won him to its acceptance was a realization that it could be tied to material structures like chromosomes within the
organism. While there was no observational proof in 1915 that chromosomes
were in fact linear arrays of Mendelian factors, the varieties of evidence were
clear enough to Morgan to lead him to this hypothesis.

Science proceeds not only by the innovation of new ideas and techniques but
also by the influence of people and schools of thought. Morgan himself played a
key role in the dissemination of the Mendelian-chromosome theory. Through his
voluminous writings, his influential position in various professional societies and
on the editorial boards of journals, and his lecture tours through the United States
and Europe, the new discoveries of the *Drosophila* group became known. A
quick survey of Morgan's bibliography shows that between 1910 and 1915, he
published two books dealing solely with the new work in genetics[41] and fifty
journal articles. Between 1915 and 1930 he published an additional two books

devoted solely to the new genetics[42] and one on the relationship between genetics and evolution.[43] He also authored or coauthored another fifty articles dealing either with genetics alone or with the relationship between genetics and evolution or embryology. The *Drosophila* group as a whole (Morgan, Muller, Sturtevant, and Bridges) published a laboratory manual on *Drosophila* experimentation for college genetics courses.[44] Morgan's unusually lucid writing style made the new results with *Drosophila* eminently comprehensible to specialists and non-specialists alike. Furthermore, he wrote for a wide variety of journals whose audiences included a large percentage of the biological and scientific community at the time. His articles appeared in highly specialized journals, such as *Genetics, Proceedings of the National Academy of Sciences,* and *The American Naturalist;* in less specialized scientific journals, such as *Popular Science Monthly* and *Science;* and in publications for general readers, notably *Harper's* and *Atlantic Monthly.* He also wrote the article "The Theory of Organic Evolution" for the thirteenth edition of the *Encyclopedia Britannica* (1926).

Morgan's influential position in various professional societies and on the editorial boards of several journals was especially important in the early years before his younger associates had established their own reputations and developed their own channels for rapid publication. For example, when the National Academy decided to begin publication of a *Proceedings* in 1915, Morgan made certain that a report of the group's findings was published in the first issue. As a founder and member of the editorial board of two very important journals, *The Journal of Experimental Zoology* (founded in 1904) and *Genetics* (founded in 1916), he saw to it that the *Drosophila* work received its fair share of space. Morgan's personal connections also helped in this regard. He was a close friend of James McKeen Cattell, a long-time professor of psychology at Columbia and throughout the 1920s and 1930s the editor of *Scientific Monthly, The American Naturalist,* and *Science,* in all of which Morgan and his students published frequently.

Morgan was invited to give a number of special lectures throughout the United States and Europe between 1915 and 1930,[45] and he enjoyed considerable leeway in arranging programs for annual meetings of scientific societies. During the period of the *Drosophila* group's most rapid development, roughly between 1910 and the early 1930s, Morgan was president of the Society for Experimental Biology and Medicine (1910–1912), the National Academy of Sciences (1927–1931), the American Association for the Advancement of Science (1930), and the Sixth International Congress of Genetics (1932).

The influence of Morgan's students, subsequent to leaving the Columbia laboratory, was also an important factor in making known the new work in genetics. Those who worked in the "fly room" took positions in diverse geographic regions of the United States and Europe, thus ensuring that a wide range of new students were brought into contact with the *Drosophila* work. Muller was probably the most widely traveled; he taught at Rice University (Houston) and the University of Texas (Austin), held a Guggenheim fellowship at the Kaiser-

Wilhelm Institute (Berlin), spent three years in the Soviet Union, worked at the University of Edinburgh, taught at Amherst, and finally at the University of Indiana. In each place he built up a group of students devoted to the *Drosophila* work. Fernandes Payne spent his entire teaching career at Indiana University, and H. H. Plough at Amherst; Charles Metz spent fifteen years as a researcher at Cold Spring Harbor and subsequently taught at Johns Hopkins. Of those who came from abroad, Otto Mohr brought the new genetics back with him to Norway, while Theodosius Dobzhansky remained in the United States and led the *Drosophila* work in new and imaginative directions.

It should be pointed out that the influence that graduate students and postdoctoral investigators carried away from Columbia was not only Morgan's but also E. B. Wilson's. So similar were Morgan's and Wilson's ideas on many subjects, and so intertwined were their day-to-day associations, that both were strong influences, in different ways, on the younger workers in the laboratory. Morgan was a "romantic" personality who displayed a flair for new ideas, overt and visible excitement about his work, boundless energy, and a feel for the connection that could be made between breeding data and the biological phenomena of heredity in living organisms. Wilson's influence was in many ways less visible. He was the "classic" scientist: less overt, more patient, moving more slowly in a more calculated direction, fiery and intense in his own way, and above all, committed to the idea that the fundamental principles of biology can be discovered by analysis of details at the cellular level.[46] A basic aspect of the *Drosophila* work—the unification of the breeding tradition (concerned with whole organisms) and the cytological tradition (concerned with cellular events)—was personified in the work of Morgan and Wilson. Through their many students, the newly unified Mendelian-chromosome theory of heredity and the excitement surrounding a young field was communicated throughout the world.

Finally, as has been noted, the new genetics gained ground importantly as a result of the contacts between Morgan and his group and the many prominent investigators and graduate students who came to Woods Hole in the summer months. Morgan and his group spent every summer in Woods Hole from 1910 through 1919 and from 1922 through the early 1940s. Through these various channels, the *Drosophila* work was almost fully accepted throughout the biological community by 1920.

However, acceptance was not complete, and ironically the criticisms that were voiced were similar to the objections that Morgan himself had made against Mendelism prior to 1910. Perhaps most important was the assertion that the chromosome theory totally ignored physiology and development. The conflict between Morgan and his principal critics—William Bateson and Richard Goldschmidt, outstanding and well-respected embryologists trained in the old-style morphology—was rooted in the tendency of the latter to intermix vertical with horizontal concepts of heredity. A vertical concept of heredity is concerned with the transmission of hereditary elements between generations; a horizontal concept is concerned with the translation of those hereditary elements into adult characters. Embryologists tend to be interested largely in horizontal concepts, since their whole area of concern is the development of the fertilized egg into differentiated adult characters. Biologists involved in breeding experiments, on the other hand, tend to be more concerned with vertical concepts. Failure to distinguish between these two very different concepts of heredity led workers such as Bateson and Goldschmidt to expect too much from Mendelism. They looked to research on Mendelism, a vertical issue, to yield information about embryonic development, a horizontal issue. Like the old-style morphologists, they hoped that any theory of heredity would also explain development and evolution.

In contrast, Morgan's group rigorously distinguished between vertical and horizontal components and focused on the former. Neither Morgan nor any of his associates ever claimed that their work threw light on how genes functioned to produce adult characters. What the Morgan group did emphasize was that the mechanism of hereditary transmission was separable from that of gene function, at least at that time. There was a reason for this approach and in it perhaps lay Morgan's genius. The question of gene function in a biochemical or embryological sense could not be answered through experiments in 1915, whereas the question of transmission of genes and their physical relation to chromosomes could be approached experimentally and quantitatively. By centering their attention on the latter, Morgan and his group were able to develop a highly elaborate but consistent theory grounded in the newest results of cytology and the data from *Drosophila* breeding experiments.

Because of its focus largely on the Morgan group, the preceding discussion might suggest that no other groups contributed in any significant way to the growth of Mendelian theory in the early twentieth century. This, of course, is not the case. Active centers for genetic research existed throughout the world between 1915 and 1930, many long antedating the appearance of Morgan and *Drosophila* on the scene in 1910. In the United States alone, much important work in heredity was carried out using organisms other than *Drosophila*, and methods other than those developed by the Morgan group. Harvard had an active group of workers: W. E. Castle at the Biological Laboratories in Cambridge and E. M. East at the Bussey Institution in Jamaica Plain. Castle made significant contributions to the understanding of heredity in mammals, and East studied such crop plants as potatoes, corn, and tobacco. At Cornell, R. A. Emerson developed corn (maize) to the same refined position in the study of plant genetics that *Drosophila* held in animal genetics. Using maize, Emerson and his students led the way in developing hybrid corn and in demonstrating the cytological basis for crossing-over. At the Connecticut Agricultural Station in Storrs, Donald Jones (along with E. M. East, who worked at the station before going to the Bussey) developed ideas on inbreeding and outbreeding and coined the term "hybrid vigor." These and other centers contributed significantly to the growing body of genetic information between 1915 and 1930. Morgan and his students gained much from interaction with these groups; in turn, work with *Drosophila*, partly because of the rapidity with which the Columbia group achieved results, contributed significantly to the development of research along these different but related lines.

## Genes, Chromosomes, and Darwinism

Morgan's conversion to Mendelian genetics after 1910 was also a step toward his acceptance of the basic tenets of the Darwinian theory. A number of intellectual and social factors contributed to his change of attitude. The intellectual factors were associated with new biological insights into the evolutionary process gained by Morgan's own studies in heredity—i.e., the working out of the details of the Mendelian-chromosome theory. The social factors involved Morgan's colleagues and students who argued with him about Darwinism and the theory of natural selection.

Morgan's changed views were reflected in his first major publication on evolution since 1903, *A Critique of the Theory of Evolution,* which was based on a series of lectures presented at Princeton in 1916.[47] As these lectures reveal, through the work of his own group on *Drosophila,* Morgan was able to reconcile, slowly, the Darwinian notion of selection acting on small, individual variations with the Mendelian theory of discrete, hereditary units. The importance of this reconciliation cannot be overemphasized. In the latter part of the nineteenth and the early part of the twentieth century, the ideas of continuous and discontinuous variation had always been posed as mutually exclusive alternatives. Darwinians insisted that continuous variations were the important raw material of evolution; non-Darwinians maintained that discrete, discontinuous "mutations" or "sports" were the differences on which selection acted. Working out the details of the Mendelian theory began to show that there was no basic contradiction between these ideas, that, in fact, continuous variation as observed in a natural population can be obtained from discrete hereditary particles.

Morgan's acceptance of Darwinism stemmed from a number of factors. First, the new small-scale "mutations," such as white-eye in *Drosophila,* were within the limits Darwinians called "individual" or "fluctuating" variations; they were the small, individual differences on which Darwin had claimed selection most generally acted. The discovery that such variations, or "mutants" as Morgan termed them, were actually inherited in a Mendelian fashion demonstrated to Morgan that evolution did not depend upon large-scale, DeVries-type mutations or "sports" but could act on small-scale variations as well. Second, by 1912 DeVries' mutation theory had begun to come under serious attack. Primarily because of the work of Bradley M. Davis, it was becoming clear that the large-scale "mutations" observed by DeVries were not really species-level changes at all but were due to complex chromosomal changes that actually followed Mendelian principles when interpreted in conjunction with cytological observations. With the decline in validity of the mutation theory, Darwinism assumed a position of greater importance in Morgan's thinking.

A third factor that influenced Morgan was the idea of gene interaction that had begun to gain considerable support within the Morgan group by 1914 or 1915. The notion of "modifier genes" affecting the functioning of other genes meant that a much greater range of expressed variability was possible within a population than had been hitherto suspected. Moreover, since gene interaction meant quantitative variation in the strength of expression of a gene, it would be possible to obtain a virtually continuous range of variations for any trait that Darwinians (especially the biometricians in England) empirically observed in a population. Again, the small, individual differences on which Darwinian notions of selection were based could be viewed as distinctly hereditary along Mendelian lines. This insight also helped to explain how selection could produce a constant, gradual change over time, giving rise to an infinite variety of intermediate forms. Eventually, Morgan came to see that selection of interacting gene systems could give rise to the most diverse kinds of adult traits—there was, in fact, no limit to the adaptations selection could produce by acting on both gene mutations and groups of modifying factors.

A fourth and crucial element in Morgan's conversion to Darwinian theory was his slow, but increasingly profound, awakening to the difference between the *genotype* and *phenotype* of an organism. *Genotype* refers to the genetic composition of an organism: what genes it carries and can pass on to the next generation. *Phenotype* refers to how the organism looks—its visible (or measurable) adult character. The genotype-phenotype distinction was made explicit by Wilhelm Johannsen in *The American Naturalist* in 1911.[48] Johannsen gave a version of this paper at the 1910 meeting of the American Society of Naturalists in Ithaca—a meeting that Morgan attended. More important, Johannsen spent the winter term of 1911 at Columbia as a visiting lecturer, and it would be surprising if he and Morgan did not discuss their many areas of mutual interest: heredity, variation, and evolution.

The distinction between genotype and phenotype helped Morgan to understand the mechanism of natural selection. In Morgan's day, many biologists confused genotype and phenotype—a confusion that manifested itself in the failure to understand the difference between the gene that is passed on from parents to offspring and the adult character whose development is guided by that gene. Johannsen argued that selection acts directly on the phenotype, producing changes in the genotype over a number of generations. The phenotype represents the combined effect of many interacting genes with environmental factors. The environment selects, favorably or unfavorably, a particular phenotype; the result of selection is reflected in what the genotype of the next generation turns out to be.

To Morgan the embryologist, Johannsen's distinction showed that natural selection acts on neither the genotype nor the phenotype per se but rather on the developmental process—on the translation of genotype into phenotype. In effect, it enabled genotype and phenotype to be viewed as two aspects of a single, integrated phenomenon: embryonic development.

Among the external factors influencing Morgan's change of views on Darwin-

ian theory were his students, particularly Sturtevant and Muller. As undergraduates, both Muller and Sturtevant had taken E. B. Wilson's introductory
biology course and had read R. H. Lock's *Variation, Heredity and Evolution*,[49]
judged at the time to be the most up-to-date work relating evolution to concepts
of heredity (especially Mendelism). Lock tried to show how Mendelism and
Darwinian theory fitted together to form a complete mechanism for evolution.
Muller and Sturtevant imbibed this idea enthusiastically and argued with Morgan
about it at considerable length. Muller's reports on these discussions with
Morgan are most vivid. According to him, Morgan was stubborn: he would not
accept the idea that natural selection could create new species and continued to
regard it in the old, artificial way as a purely negative force. He also had
difficulty understanding that a recessive gene would not automatically (even
without selection against it) be reduced in frequency in a population over time.
Alexander Weinstein reports that Morgan submitted all his manuscripts on evolution to "the boys" in the lab for criticism and discussion. Over and over again
they corrected some of his misconceptions.

With the help of his students and colleagues, Morgan overcame at least some
of his obstacles to the most basic reconciliation of Mendelism with Darwinian
natural selection. The intellectual refinement of his ideas is evident in two
additional books: *Evolution and Genetics* (1925), and *The Scientific Basis of
Evolution* (1932). In the end, Morgan's own contribution to evolutionary theory
was slight but he did have a profound, if indirect, effect on the development of
evolutionary thought in the twentieth century. By elucidating the nature of
Mendelian variations, the process of transmission, and the structure of the germ
plasm, he laid the foundation for the quantitative, populational approach to
evoluation that was essential to understanding the dynamics of natural selection.

## Conclusion: Genetics and the New Biology

Morgan saw the value of the work of the *Drosophila* group stretching far
beyond the boundaries of genetics itself. Not only did it affect fundamental issues
in evolution and embryology, but it represented a new methodology—the quantitative experimental and physico-chemical approach—in biology. With Jacques
Loeb, Morgan became an outspoken advocate of "the new biology"—an extension to *all* fields of the methods and philosophy of *Entwicklungsmechanik*.

It was in large part Morgan's commitment to the new biology that led him to
accept the invitation of George Ellery Hale and Robert A. Millikan to found a
division of biology at the California Institute of Technology in 1928. At 62,
Morgan could well have rested on his laurels and remained at Columbia where he
had taught for 24 years. But that was not his nature. To establish biology as part
of an institute of technology, which for so long had been the home ground of only
the physical sciences, was an opportunity not to be missed.

At the California Institute of Technology, Morgan sought to give concrete
form to his philosophy of science in general and of biology in particular. To this

end, Morgan developed five major principles that were to guide the founding and growth of the biology division at Caltech. The first was that research, rather than teaching, should remain the major focus of the Institute.[50] Since Caltech sought to emphasize graduate education, teaching was to be more a matter of collaboration than of formal lecturing. Second, it was Morgan's belief that research at Caltech should focus on pure (basic), rather than applied, problems. It was for this reason, for example, that Morgan rejected the idea of building a hospital in conjunction with Caltech; he had no desire for the Division of Biology to become a resource for solving practical problems in medicine and agriculture.[51] Recognizing the threat posed to the Institute if it became primarily a technological research center tied to agricultural, medical, or industrial enterprises, Morgan argued that the principal job of Caltech was to push back the frontiers of basic knowledge; the applications of such knowledge would be carried out by others.[52] In his view, Caltech need not worry about developing research that was immediately useful, for all basic research could be beneficial for human needs; without basic knowledge, however, the solution of practical problems is impossible. As he wrote in his "program" of 1930, "the study of the metabolism of animals and plants is a typical example of the enormous unexpected benefits which have accrued from the development of pure science."[53] But the matter was more serious than simply a question of personal preference or the setting of priorities. To Morgan, programs for applied research had critical long-range implications for the future of the Institute; for instance, applied research programs could establish a pattern of funding for specific problems or projects that would be highly restrictive. Such programs could also create a distinction or division between two types of researchers; if this distinction were intensified by a differential availability of research funds, the Institute as a whole would suffer. Most important, Morgan considered it essential to convince benefactors and business leaders that their own long-term interests would best be served by generous financial support of basic rather than applied research.[54]

A third aspect of Morgan's program entailed the establishment of priorities with regard to those specific fields of biological research to be supported. It was impossible to develop all areas of biology at an equal rate, and Morgan felt it was necessary to concentrate on those areas in which physics, chemistry, mathematics, and biology could interact—this meant, at the most fundamental level, problems of a physiological nature. What Morgan meant by physiology was not simply human or vertebrate physiology as it was then practiced in biology departments or medical schools, but rather the study of functional problems, primarily at the cellular level.[55] In Morgan's view, it was such functional problems, approached from the physical, chemical (biophysical and biochemical), genetic, embryological, and evolutionary perspectives that should be encouraged in modern research. Morgan had no personal compunction to eliminate descriptive biology and morphology, including systematics, from the curriculum. Indeed, he found a convenient way of publicly rationalizing what might appear to be a one-sided approach to biology. As he wrote to Hale, "We can counter the argument that we are neglecting the old aspects of biology by saying that we are not trying to duplicate what is being done well elsewhere, but rather furnish the opportunity for new directions of research."[56]

Fourth, Morgan believed that biology at Caltech should be rigorous and analytical in character. With personnel trained in biophysics, biochemistry, and mathematics, biology would take its place beside physics and chemistry as a rigorous and quantitative science. The fifth and final feature of Morgan's program, upon which the realization of all the others in many ways depended, was the selection of personnel. It was Morgan's aim to gather together the best workers in every field and encourage their continual cooperation and interaction. Morgan informed Hale and Milliken that he had no interest in "bossing" the new Division of Biology, but only in coordinating the work of men who knew what they wanted to do.[57]

In setting forth his program, Morgan was adamant that the new organization at Caltech should not be divided into the traditional departments of botany and zoology but rather termed a division or department of *biology*. As he wrote, this insistence "calls for a word of explanation:"

It is with a desire to lay emphasis on the fundamental principles underlying the life processes in animals and plants that an effort will be made to bring together, in a single group, men whose common interests are in the discovery of the unity of the phenomena of living organisms rather than in the investigation of their manifold diversity. . . . It is true that, at what may be called the biological level, an immense diversity of form and function may manifest itself, but enough insight has already been gained to make evident that this diversity is in large part due to the permutations and combinations of relatively few fundamental and common properties. It is in the search for these properties that the zoologist and botanist may profitably pool their interests. The animal physiologist today who wishes to have a broad outlook over his field can as little neglect the physiology of bacteria, yeast, and higher plants as the bacteriologist and plant physiologist can ignore the modern discoveries in animal physiology. The geneticist who works with animals will know only half his subject if he ignores the work on plants, and both plant and animal geneticists will fail to make the most of their opportunities if they overlook the advances in cytology and embryology. It is, then, to bring together in sympathetic union a group of investigators and teachers whose interests lie in the fundamental aspects of their subjects, that a department of Biology will be organized.[58]

Along the same lines, Morgan suggested perhaps that the name of the division should be simply "The Biological Laboratory," rather than "Biological Department." Morgan was anxious that the program be set up with the greatest amount of flexibility and with the greatest scope and ambition. At the same time, however, he would not promise what could not ultimately be delivered. He was willing to proceed only along general lines, with no strings attached and no concrete promises as to the exact form and structure of the division and its program. The academic year 1927/28 was to be a time of planning and sifting through various proposals.

Morgan saw the research of the new division proceeding along five basic lines. The first area, genetics and evolution, was to embrace not only the work on the genetics of *Drosophila* but also the new fields of the genetics of viruses and bacteria. Furthermore, genetics and evolution were considered to be two sides of the same coin, interacting in Morgan's mind in a dialectical fashion: one preserving stability, the other promoting innovation. The second line, experimental embryology, would in Morgan's view focus on the cellular and subcellular events occurring in embryonic differentiation. Either by conscious or unconscious choice, it did not include, either in the initial planning stages or later, experimental work at the tissue and organ level. A third area, general physiology, included particularly the study of cell physiology and ranged through general plant and animal physiology. The fourth was biophysics, which meant to Morgan the study of such problems as the quantum absorption of plant pigments in photosynthesis and the response of plants and animals to light, an extension of Loeb's earlier work on phototropism. The fifth area, biochemistry, then encompassed not only the study of anabolic and catabolic reactions within cells but also, more specifically, the study of enzymes and their effects upon biochemical reactions. To Morgan especially, the analysis of enzymes and proteins in general was an important aspect of the new physico-chemical approach to biology.

An additional line of work, to be incorporated at a somewhat later date, was experimental psychology. Influenced by J. McKeen Cattell and some of the work that had emerged from Clark University's famed psychology department in the preceding several decades, Morgan felt that psychology and physiology should have a closer relationship in the future. However, Morgan felt it unwise to include psychology in the initial organizational plans, lest it appear that the Caltech program was betraying its stated high aims of pursuing quantitative science. Later, when the general biological disciplines were established in a rigorous fashion, experimental psychology could be brought in without jeopardizing the overall dedication of the Institute to rigorous and analytical science.

The five groups that Morgan envisioned were only guidelines for the types of work that he wanted to see carried out at Caltech. The areas of research that were ultimately pursued would depend in large part upon the personnel whom Morgan was able to attract to Pasadena. Morgan also recognized that the kind of work developed in one area, for example, physiology, would have definite implications for that carried out in others, such as biochemistry and cytology.[59] Thus, the program depended in large measure upon the interactions between fields that specific persons could engender.

In the end, the Division of Biology developed along the lines Morgan had envisioned. Aside from the *Drosophila* group (Bridges and Sturtevant) that came intact from Columbia, Morgan brought to Caltech—either as one- or two-year postdoctoral fellows, graduate students, or faculty—Boris Ephrussi, George Beadle, Max Delbrück, Theodosius Dobzhansky, Sterling Emerson, Frits Went, and Kenneth Thimann. The "unity" of the biology division provided continuous opportunity for interchange among these various workers; and as if to fulfill Morgan's highest aspirations, today Caltech has become a center of research in molecular genetics.

It is often said that the *Drosophila* work represented the end of the line for classical genetics—that the new biochemical and molecular genetics of the 1950s and 1960s evolved from a wholly different tradition and represented a separate and independent line of development. While there is some truth to that statement, it neglects the very real roots that biochemical and molecular genetics had in the classical *Drosophila* school. Morgan knew that there were no simple and obvious experimental tools with which to investigate the physiology—to him, the biochemical and molecular basis—of genetics. But he did realize that the most effective way to attack the problem was to bring together, in one institution, individuals who could approach heredity from different viewpoints and who could forge an intellectual relationship between studies concerned with the "structural features of inheritance" and those dealing with the "physiological aspects of heredity."[60] It was the scientists that Morgan brought to Caltech in the early and middle 1930s who gave the study of biochemical and molecular genetics its first experimental impulse.

At Caltech, Morgan put into a concrete form the ideas he had formulated forty years earlier at the Naples Station. The organization of the Division of Biology at Caltech gave the spirit of *Entwicklungsmechanik* a concrete basis. By 1928, experimentalism was well on the way to becoming a prominent part of modern biological research. The revolt from morphology that Morgan and his generation had initiated was beginning to bear fruit. Morgan's own work with the Mendelian chromosome theory was but one example of the way in which the new methods could yield startling results. He and his generation hoped, and expected, that these methods could be applied to all biological problems in the future.

## Notes

1. William Bateson, *Materials for the Study of Variation* (London: Macmillan, 1894), pp. 574–75.

2. Hamilton Cravens, "The Role of Universities in the Rise of Experimental Biology," *Science Teacher* 44, no. 1 (January 1977): 33–37.

3. H. F. Osborn to E. G. Conklin, 29 March 1921, Conklin Papers, Box 33, Osborn folder, Firestone Library, Princeton University, Princeton, N.J.

4. Journal articles classified by natural history and experimental subject orientation in *The American Naturalist:*

|  | Percent Papers | |
| --- | --- | --- |
| Year | Natural History | Experimental |
| 1900 | 89 | 11 |
| 1906 | 92 | 8 |
| 1912 | 47 | 53 |

For the purpose of this survey, "natural history" included articles dealing with: paleontology, invertebrate zoology (but not physiology), botany, descriptive embryology, and general field natural history; "experimental" included general physiology, heredity (where experimental breeding was involved), experimental embryology (including regeneration), and cytology. *The American Naturalist* is a journal with a natural history bias and was, therefore, chosen specifically to illustrate an upsurge in interest in experimental topics. The time shift, 1906–1912, does not apply in a general way to other journals in other fields.

5. E. B. Wilson, "Aims and Methods of Study in Natural History," *Science*, n.s. 13 (1901): 14–23; quotation from p. 19.

6. Today the term *morphology* is used almost synonymously with *anatomy*. Its meaning also encompasses the concept of developmental anatomy, that is, the developmental pattern of various structures. It is important to keep in mind that the term has a much more limited use today than in the 1880s and 1890s.

7. One of the most complete and concise accounts of the whole range of activities encompassed by morphology in the nineteenth century can be found in *Encyclopedia Britannica*, 9th ed., s.v., "Morphology."

8. See E. G. Conklin, "William Keith Brooks," *Biographical Memoirs, National Academy of Sciences* 7 (1910): 25–88.

9. W. K. Brooks, "The Lesson of the Life of Huxley," *Smithsonian Institution Annual Report*, 1900 (Washington, D.C.: U.S. Government Printing Office, 1902), p. 710.

10. Morgan to Driesch, 12 February 1899, Morgan-Driesch Correspondence (Leipzig: University of Leipzig Microfilm, courtesy of Professor Dorton Reinbard Mocek), p. 5.

11. *Johns Hopkins University Circulars* 30 (April 1884): 87.

12. Hugh Hawkins, *Pioneer: A History of the Johns Hopkins University, 1874–1889* (Ithaca, N.Y.: Cornell University Press, 1960), pp. 265 ff.

13. For more detail on Loeb, his background and influence, see Donald Fleming, "Introduction," to the reprint edition of Loeb's *The Mechanistic Conception of Life* (Cambridge, Mass.: Harvard University Press, 1964), pp. vii–xli; Garland E. Allen, "T. H. Morgan and the Emergence of a New American Biology," *Quarterly Review of Biology* 44 (June 1969): 168–188; and idem, "Philosophy and Biology: The Mechanistic Materialism of Jacques Loeb" (in press).

14. Parthenogenesis is the process whereby an unfertilized egg undergoes normal embryonic development. In a number of invertebrate species, this process occurs normally. It can be induced by special physical or chemical processes in a number of other species, producing adult organisms derived only from the female hereditary material.

15. Charles A. Kofoid, *Biological Stations of Europe*, United States Bureau of Education, Bulletin no. 4 (Washington, D.C., 1910), pp. 1, 9.

16. Morgan to Dohrn, 5 October 1895, p. 3. From the Dohrn Archives, Stazione Zoologica, Naples, Italy. I am grateful to Dr. Isabel M. Mountain, Morgan's youngest daughter, for a xerox copy of this letter.

17. E. R. Lillie, *The Woods Hole Marine Biological Laboratory* (Chicago: University of Chicago Press, 1944), p. 38. Lillie's book remains to date the only history of the founding and historical development of the MBL.

18. A detailed discussion of the many influences leading to the establishment of Roux's experimental embryology can be found in Frederick Churchill, "Wilhelm Roux and A Program for Embryology" (Ph.D. diss., Harvard University, 1968), esp. chap. 11. Some of this information is also contained in Churchill's "Chabry, Roux and the Experimental Method in Nineteenth Century Embryology," in *Foundations of Scientific Method: The Nineteenth Century*, eds. R. N. Giere and R. S. Westfall (Bloomington, Inc.: Indiana University Press, 1973).

19. Roux's experiment performed in 1888 involved killing (with a hot needle) one of the two blastomeres produced when a fertilized frog's egg makes its first division (cleavage). He noted that the subsequent embryonic development produced only a *half-embryo*, as if each blastomere contained determinants for only one-half of the embryo. Roux reasoned that with each subsequent cell division, determinants were parceled out in a more and more specific way so that by the time an adult organism was produced, each type of cell (muscle, nerve, skin, etc.) contained determinants for *only* that cell type. The embryo was thus a "mosaic" of hereditary determinants, parceled out in increasingly specific ways during embryogenesis.

Hans Driesch tested Roux's results on a different organism, the sea urchin, which was plentiful in Naples. In 1891 he published results that contradicted Roux's mosaic concept. Driesch allowed fertilized sea urchin eggs to divide once, producing a two-cell stage embryo (two blastomeres). Instead of killing one of the blastomeres, Driesch separated the two cells by shaking them. He found that each blastomere developed into a full adult, though of slightly smaller size. Driesch concluded that the embryo was capable of enormous internalized self-adjustment—it was not a mere machine as Roux's theory suggested.

The apparent contradiction between the Roux and Driesch experiments was the result of differences both in the experimental techniques used and in the species of organism involved. Several years later other embryologists showed that if the one punctured blastomere in Roux's frog embryo were removed from physical contact with its partner, the latter would develop into a full-fledged, viable embryo. The physical contact between the injured and the normal blastomere appeared to alter the developmental process. In addition, the different results seem also to have been to some extent the result of differences between the sea urchin and frog embryo. The important point here is not which now is most correct but the fact that the question being asked could be approached by experimentation, and did not have to remain subject only to speculation.

20. W. Roux, "Beitrage zur Entwickelungsmechanik des Embryo. Ueber die kunstliche Hervorbringung halber Embryonen durch Zerstorung einer der beiden der fehlenden Korperhalfte," *Virchow's Archiv pat. Anat. u. Physiol. u. kl. Med.* 114 (1888): 113–53; quotation, p. 150. This classic article is translated and reprinted in B. H. Willier and J. Oppenheimer, eds., *Foundations of Experimental Embryology,* 2d ed. (Englewood Cliffs, N.J.: Prentice-Hall, 1974).

21. T. H. Morgan, *Evolution and Adaptation* (New York: Macmillan, 1903), p. 33.

22. See, for example, Morgan's article, "Regeneration and Liability of Injury," *Science* 14 (1901): 235–48; also "The Origin of Species Through Selection Contrasted with Their Origin Through the Appearance of Definite Variations," *Popular Science Monthly* 67 (1905): 54–65, and *Evolution and Adaptation* (New York: Macmillan, 1903): 126–63.

23. *Evolution and Adaptation,* pp. 165–66.

24. Hugo DeVries, *Die Mutationstheorie,* 2 vols. (Leipzig: Von Veit, 1901–1903). In English, J. C. Farmer and A. D. Darbishire, trans., *The Mutation Theory* (Chicago: Open Court, 1910).

25. The opponents of DeVries' mutation theory were to have their heyday beginning shortly after 1910. Bradley M. Davis, in particular, in a series of papers between 1910 and 1912, showed that the so-called mutations of the evening primrose, *Oenothera,* were actually the result of an unusual hereditary pattern that basically followed Mendelian laws. In 1914, Renner showed specifically that Oenothera was a permanent heterozygote between two complexes, the pure homozygotes failing to survive. For a summary, see A. H. Sturtevant, *A History of Genetics,* (New York: Harper and Row, 1965), pp. 63–64. By 1915 the mutation theory, especially as it was put forth in its original form, had passed out of serious biological literature.

26. T. H. Morgan, "What are Factors in Mendelian Inheritance?" *American Breeder Association Report* 5 (1909): 365–368.

27. The term *wild-type* is used by geneticists to refer to the predominant phenotype (appearance) in a population for any given trait. Most fruit flies found in the wild have red eye color as well as long wings that fold back horizontally over the body. These two hereditary forms are referred to as the wild-type condition in regard to eye color and wing shape and position. Almost every heritable characteristic has a wild-type form, as well as a large number of variant, mutant forms.

28. T. H. Morgan, "Sex Limited Inheritance in *Drosophila,*" *Science* 32 (1910).

29. Morgan to Driesch, 23 November 1910, p. 2, Morgan-Driesch Correspondence.

30. Ibid., p. 2.

31. Nondisjunction is a process by which two homologous chromosomes fail to separate in meiosis, thus remaining together in one-half the gametes produced from the original parent germ cell.

32. Sturtevant, *History of Genetics,* p. 46.

33. L. C. Dunn, *A Short History of Genetics,* (New York: McGraw-Hill, 1965), pp. 144ff.

34. For a brief biographical account, see A. H. Sturtevant, "Calvin Blackman Bridges," *Dictionary of Scientific Biography,* 14 vols. (New York: Scribners, 1970), 2:455–57; a more complete account is T. H. Morgan, "Calvin Blackman Bridges, 1889–1938," *Biographical Memoirs, National Academy of Sciences* 22 (1941): 31–49. An anonymous manuscript, "The Boyhood and Family Background of Calvin Blackman Bridges" is located in the Archives of the American Philosophical Society, Philadelphia.

35. For biographical detail, see E. A. Carlson, "Hermann Joseph Muller," *Yearbook of the American Philosophical Society* (1967), pp. 137–42; idem, "H. J. Muller: A Memorial Tribute," *The Review,* Indiana University Alumni Publication no. 2 (Bloomington, Ind.: Indiana University Press, 1968), pp. 1–48; and idem, "H. J. Muller," *Genetics* 70 (1972): 1–30; Mrs. Tove Mohr has written a short, insightful account, "Hermann J. Muller, 1890–1967," *Journal of Heredity* 63 (1972): 132–34. E. A. Carlson is currently preparing a full-scale biography of Muller. For a discussion of Muller's interest in political and social aspects of biology, see his book, *Out of the Night: A Biologist's View of the Future* (New York: Vanguard Press, 1935); and G. E. Allen, "Science and Society in the Eugenical Thought of H. J. Muller," *BioScience* 20 (1970): 346–52.

36. A. H. Sturtevant, "Thomas Hunt Morgan," *Biographical Memoirs, National Academy of Sciences* 33 (1959): 295.

37. For Davenport's role in the founding of the Cold Spring Harbor Laboratory, see E. Carlton

MacDowell, "Charles Benedict Davenport, 1866-1944: A Study in Conflicting Influences," *Bioscience* 17 (1946): 3-50, esp. pp. 15-24. See also Charles E. Rosenberg, "Charles Benedict Davenport and the Beginning of Human Genetics," *Bulletin of the History of Medicine* 35 (1961): 266-76. As reflected in their support of the eugenics movement, the wealthy "robber barons" of the early 1900s had much to gain by supporting research into the question of heredity (especially human heredity). The conditions of deprivation and poverty found among the poor immigrant and working-class elements of society could be explained in one of two ways: such conditions were caused by unequal distribution of wages; or degradation and poverty were innate in the hereditary material of the "lower classes." Obviously the financial elite favored the second alternative since it provided not only a justification for their own present position at the top of the social and economic pyramid, but could also be used to counteract welfare programs and other social reforms that might cut into their large profits. The economic basis of support for such theories of biological determination has been extensively discussed by Richard Hofstadter in *Social Darwinism in America* (Boston: Beacon Press, 1964).

38. Morgan to Metz, 26 February 1919, Morgan Papers, Catalog no. BN 824, American Philosophical Society, Philadelphia.

39. Morgan to Otto and Tove Mohr, 6 March 1919, Morgan Papers, Catalog no. BM 824.

40. T. H. Morgan, A. H. Sturtevant, B. J. Muller, and C. B. Bridges, *The Mechanism of Mendelian Heredity* (New York: Henry Holt, 1915; reprint ed., New York: Johnson Reprint, 1972).

41. T. H. Morgan, *Heredity and Sex* (New York: Columbia University Press, 1914); and Morgan et al., *Mechanism of Mendelian Heredity*.

42. T. H. Morgan, *The Physical Basis of Heredity* (Philadelphia: Lippincott, 1919), and idem, *The Theory of the Gene* (New Haven, Conn.: Yale University Press, 1926).

43. T. H. Morgan, *A Critique of the Theory of Evolution* (Princeton, N.J.: Princeton University Press, 1916), later revised as *Evolution and Genetics* (Princeton, N.J.: Princeton University Press, 1925).

44. T. H. Morgan et al., *Laboratory Directions for an Elementary Course in Genetics* (New York: Henry Holt, 1923).

45. Among these latter were the Lewis Clark Vauxeum Lectures at Princeton (on the relation of genetics to Darwinian natural selection, 1918); the Hitchcock Foundation Lectures at the University of California, Berkeley (on the same subject, also delivered in 1916); the Middleton Goldsmith Lectures (on genetics and pathology, 1922) (published as *Some Possible Bearings of Genetics on Pathology* [Lancaster, Pa.: New Era Printing, 1922]); the Croonian Lectures, before the Royal Society, London (on the basic mechanism of the Mendelian-chromosome theory, 1922) (published as "On the Mechanism of Heredity," *Proceedings of the Royal Society* B 94 [1922]: 162-197); the Mellon Lecture at the University of Pittsburgh Medical School (on human inheritance, 1924) (later published as "Human Inheritance," *American Naturalist* 58 [1924]: 385-409); the Silliman Lectures at Yale (a series of published lectures outlining the theory of the gene, 1926) (published as *The Theory of the Gene* [New Haven, Conn.: Yale University Press, 1926]); and ultimately, the Nobel Lecture, presented in Stockholm (on the relation of genetics to medicine, 1934) (later published as "The Relation of Genetics to Physiology and Medicine," *Scientific Monthly* 41 [1935]: 5-18).

46. The famous German chemist Wilhelm Ostwald in a book entitled *Grosse Manner* (Leipzig: Akademische Verlagsgesellshaft, 1909) classified scientists into two categories: romantic and classic. In 1936 the American embryologist Ross G. Harrison used Ostwald's classification to contrast the personalities of Wilson and Morgan. Ross G. Harrison, "Response on Behalf of the Medallist," *Science* 84 (1936): 565-67.

47. T. H. Morgan, *A Critique of the Theory of Evolution,* The Louis Clark Vauxeum Foundation Lectures, February-March 1916 (Princeton, N.J.: Princeton University Press, 1916).

48. Wilhelm Johannsen, "The Genotype Conception of Heredity," *American Naturalist* 45 (1911): 129-59.

49. R. H. Lock, *Variation, Heredity and Evolution* (New York: E. P. Dutton, 1907).

50. A. A. Noyes, Draft of paper explaining the purposes of Caltech, G. E. Hale Papers, ed. Daniel J. Kevles (Pasadena, Ca.: California Institute of Technology Microfilm Edition), reel 26. A complete holding of the microfilm edition of the Hale Papers can also be found at the American Philosophical Society Library, Philadelphia.

51. Morgan to Hale, 4 December 1930, Hale Papers.

52. Morgan's "Program for Biology," sent to Hale with a letter of 4 December 1930, Hale Papers.

53. Ibid.

54. Morgan to Noyes, 4 June 1928, Hale Papers.

55. See T. H. Morgan, "The Relation of Biology to Physics," *Science* 65 (1927): 213-20.

56. Morgan to Hale, 15 May 1927, Hale Papers.

57. Ibid.

58. T. H. Morgan, "Development of Biology at the California Institute of Technology." Draft of a paper sent to George Ellery Hale, Hale Papers. See also a printed version of this same quotation in T. H. Morgan, "A New Division of Biology," *California Institute of Technology Bulletin* (1928), pp. 16-17.

59. Morgan to Gary Calkins, 26 February 1930, L. C. Dunn Papers (Bi D917), American Philosophical Society, Philadelphia.

60. T. H. Morgan to Max Mason, 15 May 1933, Morgan Papers, Box 2, Rockefeller Foundation Folder, California Institute of Technology Archives, Pasadena, Ca.

# The Organization
# of the Agricultural Sciences

## MARGARET W. ROSSITER

The decades surrounding the turn of the century were an important transitional period for the development of the agricultural sciences in the United States. As the nation's natural fertility and geographic advantages diminished, farms came to depend increasingly on science and technology. At the same time, the processes of professionalization and specialization, evident in many diverse fields, began to appear in the agricultural sciences as well. An examination of the organization of the agricultural sciences between 1880 and 1920 casts light not only on these general processes but also on their specific form within the context of American agriculture.

Among the applied sciences, agriculture is especially interesting for several reasons: first, it lacked the earlier "professional" tradition of medicine or engineering and had to evolve a role of its own; second, unlike the physicians who were almost all in private practice and the engineers who were employed by private industry, practically all of the agricultural scientists at this time (with the notable exception of Luther Burbank) were full-time government employees working in bureaus, experiment stations, and agricultural colleges; and third, agricultural science is much more strongly tied to geographic and economic forces than are other sciences, including such applied sciences as medicine and engineering.

Although specialization in agriculture had been underway before 1860, with cotton, tobacco, wheat, hay, and other crops grown in particular parts of the East and Midwest, the process continued at an even faster pace after 1860. With the completion of an extensive nationwide railroad network, far-flung regions found themselves in competition for rapidly growing urban and foreign markets. As a result of the rapid commercialization of American agriculture, most of the specialized farming that we are familiar with today emerged in the period 1880 to 1920: the citrus fruit industries in Florida and California, dairy farming in Wisconsin and New York, wheat production in the Northern Plains and the rebuilding of Southern agriculture after the Civil War. Other new developments, such as the rise of a scientific poultry industry, were not limited to a single area.

The highly specialized and largely regional nature of American agriculture was evident in the existence or 2,400 agricultural societies in the United States in 1920.[1] Over 2,000 of these agricultural groups were either state or regional societies interested in promoting a particular product or crop, such as the Colorado State Poultry Association or the Georgia-Florida Pecan Growers Association. Another 300 were national organizations, either congresses or federations of smaller interest groups, or professional associations concerned with highly specialized areas of agricultural science.[2] These last—the professional societies—have been largely neglected in standard accounts of the history of agriculture, which concentrate instead on federal legislation and the achievements and administrative history of the United States Department of Agriculture (USDA), the experiment stations, and the agricultural colleges.[3] Yet they merit attention because they illustrate how knowledge was sought and organized during the significant transitional decades in the history of American agriculture.

Before examining in detail the development of the major subfields of the agricultural sciences, we should consider the principal factor underlying the growth of American agriculture in this period: the significant linkage of agriculture, science, and government. It is clear that the remarkably rapid specialization of American agricultural sciences was hastened by the input of large sums of government money. This phenomenon of "force-fed" specialization—in which the outside funding agency and the pressing social and economic problems it sought to solve directed the course of research and helped create new branches of science, perhaps before they would have emerged on their own—was unusual at the time, even for an applied science. However, farmers as a group were aware of both rising economic pressures and the practical advantages of scientific advice. Organized into interest groups, they took steps to secure the financial support and expert assistance they needed.

Agriculture (and agricultural science) in this period was unusual in its strong representation in the state and federal legislatures and its ability to extract large appropriations from them. In a time of rapid urbanization, agricultural interests were overrepresented in the U.S. Congress (in proportion to their share of the population); when farmers were organized into lobbies, they were particularly influential. By the late 1880s, agricultural leaders had demanded and won a vast infrastructure of one or more colleges in every state, agricultural experiment stations across the country (supported by a guaranteed annual appropriation of $15,000 for research), and a central agency with a staff of specialists in Washington, D.C. Not medicine, engineering, forestry, or any science—with the possible exception of geology under John Wesley Powell—could boast such massive funding on a guaranteed annual basis in the 1880s. In the late 1890s federal appropriations for agriculture jumped even higher as the USDA greatly expanded its bureaus in Washington. After 1900 and the passage of the Adams Act in 1906, the amount spent on both the stations and the USDA more than doubled again. Thus at a time when medical researchers received hardly any money from the federal government and hoped for a few hundred thousand annually from the Rockefeller charities, agricultural researchers already had millions and could count on strong government support for almost any worthwhile project they could devise.

But however much faith the farmers, their spokesmen, and congressmen might have had in the efficacy of science to improve agriculture, however much money and organization they could muster to solve their problems, and however many jobs they could create for experts to study them, there would have been few solutions without certain advances in the related sciences themselves. Fortunately, therefore, in the 1880s and 1890s, agricultural science experienced tremendous breakthroughs in the new and key sciences of bacteriology, virology, and genetics, and in several branches of botany. These developments transformed a number of older agricultural sciences (as dairying, breeding, and soils) and created several new ones. Emerging agricultural problems, such as plant and animal diseases, could be studied and "solved" as never before, and several even contributed new theoretical concepts to the "pure" side of the sciences (although such distinctions are not really valid in the agricultural sciences).

It was this fruitful interaction of massive funding and scientific breakthroughs that made the period 1880 to 1920 one of the golden ages of agricultural science in both an "internal" and an "external" sense. A few early successes whetted the farmers' appetite for more, and to a surprising extent the scientists were able to comply, thus making American agriculture the great success story it has since become, transforming the American diet into the science-dependent one we know today and leading most Americans to expect even greater miracles in the years ahead.

### Slow Beginnings, 1860–1890

1862 has been called the "annus mirabilis" of American agriculture because of the founding that year of the U.S. Department of Agriculture and the passage of the first Morrill Land-Grant Act.[4] Although these events and the subsequent founding of the first state agricultural experiment stations in the 1870s would later have wide-ranging effects, most historians agree that very little happened at these new agricultural institutions before the 1890s, when more funding, larger staffs, and a new problem approach were introduced. Thus, rather than recount once again the empty successes of the 1860s and 1870s, we will consider here the less heralded but more significant changes in governmental attitudes that took place between 1875 and 1890. It was in these years that the federal government adopted a highly favorable stance toward agricultural research and passed numerous funding bills to support it—the Hatch Act for the experiment stations in 1887, the second Morrill Act for agricultural colleges in 1890, and, beginning in the early 1880s, greatly increased appropriation bills for the USDA—all of which underlay much of the subsequent rise of agricultural science in the U.S.

In retrospect, this generous funding of agricultural research seems quite remarkable since during the 1870s and 1880s much of agricultural science was in the doldrums. Agricultural scientists were floundering intellectually in what was essentially a transitional period between the excitement over agricultural chemistry in the 1840s and 1850s and the bacteriological triumphs of the 1890s. The position of agriculture on college campuses in the 1870s and 1880s reflected this unhappy situation—the very low enrollments in agricultural subjects, the lack of trained professors, and the thinness of the curriculum. The chief activities of a professor of agriculture under such circumstances were to run field tests with various fertilizers and to maintain a model farm, preferably, but rarely, without financial loss.[5]

Given this situation, an inquisitive or suspicious congressman might well have wondered whether the Morrill money had been wasted and rather than finding new ways to spend even more on agricultural education and research, he might have started asking embarrassing questions, talked about cutbacks, or considered an investigation. But such doubts were never expressed. By the 1880s a new breed of lobbyist, the agricultural administrator, had arrived in Washington and was surprisingly successful in directing congressional attention away from this obvious lack of success on the campus and toward the tremendous potentialities agricultural science seemed to offer for the future.

The new agricultural lobbyist had generally served an apprenticeship in an experiment station. After the founding of the first state experiment stations in Middletown, Connecticut, in 1875 and Berkeley, California, in 1876, fledgling stations began to spring up in other states as well. Most were directed by agricultural scientists who became quickly dissatisfied with the way they were forced to spend their time. They felt that they and their small staffs should be doing more research rather than just responding to farmers' queries or testing fertilizers and seeds for frauds. But most state legislatures in the 1880s refused to support anything as vague and open-ended as "research," and only rarely would they fund even a short-term study of a specific problem.

As the number of disgruntled scientists and administrators began to grow in the early 1880s, they began to form various interest groups and societies. The first was the Society for the Promotion of Agricultural Science (SPAS) established at the meeting of the American Association for the Advancement of Science (AAAS) in Boston in 1880 by a group of horticulturalists. They thought that the formation of a select society of competent specialists who would criticize each others' papers would help raise the level of agricultural science in the country. They limited the membership at first to forty, then to fifty, and in 1892 to one hundred. For about twenty years the society was the most prominent group in agricultural science, but later its restrictive membership and its refusal to form sections on particular topics proved to have been fatal mistakes. During the late 1890s, the young scientists excluded from the SPAS gravitated toward other groups, especially the American Association for the Advancement of Science and the Association of American Agricultural Colleges and Experiment Stations (AAACES), which welcomed them and formed sections. After 1900, when these subgroups began to splinter into separate specialized societies, the SPAS found itself with an aging membership and without a function. It tried to take up the role of coordinating all the diverse new groups, but its offers of "affiliation" were ignored. Finally in 1920 the remaining members of the SPAS quietly merged with Section M (later O) of the American Association for the Advancement of Science. The failure of the SPAS after 1900 is strong evidence of the riskiness of maintaining a highly exclusive membership in a period of rapid growth.[6]

Another professional organization that grew out of these early contacts between the college and experiment station men was the Association of Official Agricultural Chemists (AOAC), established in 1880 and still in existence today. The purpose of this group, and the several others like it formed in other areas of agriculture,[7] was not to promote research but to standardize tests and measurements. Since most of the early stations were entrusted with the task of testing the fertilizers sold within their state for correct labeling and fair pricing, the agricultural chemists needed to coordinate their tests and methods and to work for uniform legislation. As the tasks entrusted to these chemists expanded in subsequent decades beyond agriculture and into the difficult and highly controversial realm of "pure foods and drugs," the association began to publish handbooks and field manuals that became essential references for all analytical chemists.[8]

But it was a third group and a third activity of the scientist-administrators that achieved the most success. In the early 1880s, the Secretary of Agriculture, George Bailey Loring, decided that the USDA ought to have closer ties with (some thought control of) the new experiment stations,[9] and in 1882 and 1883 he invited the station directors to Washington to a "convention" to consult with him about their relationship. Such national meetings of the agricultural leadership were not new, and several held in the early 1870s had been among the initial steps leading to the establishment of the first experiment stations. But when the dissatisfied scientist-administrators went to Washington in 1882, in 1883, and again in 1885 they were more numerous, sophisticated, and far more successful than they had been in the 1870s.

The administrators had not been in Washington long when they decided that funding of research at the state experiment stations should be the responsibility of the federal government. Quickly they went through the necessary motions of introducing bills to Congress, testifying at committee hearings, buttonholing congressmen, and flooding them with petitions of support. By 1885 they had convinced the Congress to support the agricultural experiment stations in some way but were still wrestling with the appropriate administrative arrangement. By 1886 the Hatch Bill, which promised each station $15,000 annually for research and established an Office of Experiment Stations within the USDA to coordinate their activities and receive their reports, had become the most popular compromise. It passed both houses and was signed into law by President Cleveland in March 1887.[10]

Why the agricultural administrators were so well received and so successful when their previous performance had led to so few practical results is hard to say. The numerous tests and researches the administrators promised in their various bills and hearings were no more worthwhile than those that had hitherto proven so fruitless. One can only conclude that the administrators found a fortunate set of circumstances in Washington and took full advantage of it: the Congress was besieged by various forms of agrarian discontent; the federal budget was showing a surplus; the administrators seemed like honest men who knew what they were doing; the congressmen had a strong faith in agricultural research; foreign competition was hurting American meat and wheat exports; plant diseases and insect epidemics were becoming increasingly frequent; and money spent on an experiment station in the home district had certain "pork barrel" advantages over a USDA appropriation. The more one thought about supporting the experiment stations, the more logical and appropriate such a bill apparently seemed, and the less one worried about the scientists' past failures. With the benefit of hindsight, passage of the Hatch Bill seems to have been a tremendous gamble but also a tremendous success.

As soon as the administrators had seen how fruitful their cooperative efforts in Washington could be, they voted to continue their annual meetings and to establish an ongoing organization: the Association of American Agricultural Colleges and Experiment Stations, mentioned before. This group has played a strong lobbyist role ever since in protecting the Washington interests of the land-grant colleges and the experiment stations.[11] During the 1890s, when the new experiment station workers sought a forum for their scientific researches, they turned to AAACES and its sections, which were often the birthplaces of the new professional societies.

### Rapid Growth, 1890–1920

After the passage of the Hatch Act in 1887, the Adams Act in 1906 (which increased the federal appropriation to each experiment station to $30,000 annually for research), and the sharp rise in the USDA budget after 1897, the number of agricultural scientists in the country increased greatly. As a result, the field, which had been almost dormant for decades and could barely support one professional journal, suddenly encountered many of the problems associated with rapid growth. Since the starting salary for a junior chemist or bacteriologist could be as low as $750 per annum, each station could now afford, even with minimal support from its own state legislature, to hire several young persons trained in the latest sciences. A chart prepared by A. C. True (table 1) shows the growth of fields and the emergence of whole new sciences at the experiment stations between 1889 and 1906.[12] The increase in the number of employees at the USDA between 1897 and 1912, as shown in table 2 was even more dramatic.[13]

Yet from the viewpoint of employers, whether station directors or bureau chiefs, there was, as happens in periods of rapid growth and sudden demand for trained personnel, a shortage of suitable candidates. The potential employer often had to make do with persons trained in the traditional academic sciences, such as

Table 1
Personnel of the Agricultural Experiment Stations

| Title* | 1889 | 1895 | 1900 | 1905 |
|---|---|---|---|---|
| Directors and assistant directors | 63 | 67 | 71 | 74 |
| Substation superintendents | 14 | 40 | 10 | 27 |
| Agriculturalists | 13 | 55 | 74 | 58 |
| Agronomists | — | — | — | 44 |
| Horticulturists | 40 | 61 | 75 | 82 |
| Viticulturists | 5 | — | — | — |
| Foresters | — | — | — | 4 |
| Animal husbandmen | — | — | 14 | 56 |
| Poultrymen | — | — | — | 12 |
| Dairymen | — | 11 | 30 | 39 |
| Veterinarians | 19 | 24 | 29 | 36 |
| Farm foremen | — | 25 | 24 | 30 |
| Chemists | 106 | 124 | 143 | 166 |
| Botanists | 30 | 36 | 55 | 56 |
| Plant pathologists | — | — | — | 11 |
| Mycologists | 2 | 7 | 17 | 4 |
| Bacteriologists | — | — | — | 18 |
| Entomologists | 29 | 43 | 50 | 65 |
| Zoologists | — | — | 6 | 4 |
| Biologists | 5 | 11 | 6 | 3 |
| Physicists | 3 | 3 | 7 | 5 |
| Geologists | 3 | 5 | 6 | 7 |
| Meteorologists | 10 | 15 | 16 | 8 |
| Irrigation Engineers | 1 | 7 | 7 | 3 |
| Librarians (1890) | 5 | 8 | 10 | 12 |
| Secretary-treasurers | 13 | 26 | 27 | 30 |
| Clerks | 16 | 27 | 51 | 46 |
| Miscellaneous | 17 | 28 | 30 | 54 |
| Total | 402 | 557 | 693 | 845 |

SOURCE: A. C. True, *A History of Agricultural Experimentation and Research in the U.S., 1607–1925*, USDA Misc. Pub. 251 (Washington, D.C., 1937), p. 137.
*In some cases, one person served in more than one capacity.

organic chemistry for soil science, zoology for entomology, and botany for agronomy, plant pathology, and bacteriology. The problem was intensified by expansion in other areas. The passage of the Smith-Lever Act in 1914 created a large number of new jobs in agricultural extension work, and many young scientists left their research positions because the extension jobs paid more than did some stations and seemed more immediately practical and satisfying than did research.[14] Moreover, the agricultural colleges were also expanding in this period and they had particular difficulty finding faculty qualified to teach the newest sciences. The founders of these new fields—such as Mark Carleton of agronomy, Erwin F. Smith of plant pathology, and Theobald Smith of animal pathology— often chose not to teach at an agricultural college but to stay on in a research capacity at the USDA or the Rockefeller Institute. Thus finding and retaining suitable staff was a continuing problem for agricultural administrators at all levels.

Although rapid growth was frustrating to the administrators, it presented excit-

*Table 2*
*Number of Employees, U.S. Department of Agriculture, 1897 and 1912*

| Department unit | 1897 | 1912 |
|---|---|---|
| Weather Bureau | 1,000[a] | 2,051 |
| Bureau of Animal Industry | 777 | 3,311 |
| Bureau of Plant Industry | 127 | 2,128 |
| Forest Service | 14 | 4,127 |
| Bureau of Chemistry | 20 | 546 |
| Bureau of Soils | 33 | 159 |
| Bureau of Entomology | 21 | 339 |
| Bureau of Biological Survey | 23 | 97 |
| Bureau of Statistics | 133 | 162 |
| Office of Public Roads | 7 | 163 |
| Office of Experiment Stations | 38 | 209 |
| Library | 6 | 29 |
| Division of Publications | 61 | 188 |
| Division of Accounts | 10 | 66 |

[a] Approximate number.
SOURCE: A. C. True, *A History of Agricultural Experimentation and Research in the U.S., 1607–1925*, USDA Misc. Pub. 251 (Washington, D.C., 1937), p. 190.

ing possibilities for the young scientist willing to enter a brand new field. He could find a job fairly easily with only a bachelor's or possibly a master's degree, and quickly found himself coping with problems on the frontiers of knowledge. This situation was not without its difficulties, however. Perhaps the specialty and interests of the young scientist would fit the problem at hand, but more likely he would have trouble adjusting. Even if the problems did suit his training, he would be working on them not because he chose to or thought them soluble with the existing tools, but because necessity or the station's appropriation required an attempt. The solution to some problems lay well beyond the current state of the field (as in virology), but for other problems, the solution might be tantalizingly close, so much so that if an investigator was lucky and had a certain drive and imagination, he might not only solve the problem but make a notable advance in the science as well, or even, like some of the leading men in the field, found a whole new science.

The frontiers of the new agricultural sciences were everywhere and anywhere—in cornfields, fruit groves, livestock pens, at home or abroad—and the heroic tales of discoveries by the "great men" in the field, who were essentially just young fellows, were enough to fire most imaginations. The scientists to whom these special opportunities came most often were either those situated in the USDA, where there existed the effective combination of expertise and colleagues in Washington and opportunities for interesting field work throughout the country; or those employed at the more prominent stations, as Wisconsin and Connecticut, where long range research on basic problems in bacteriology or biochemistry was underway. The other scientists, by far the majority in the field, were destined to work on problems without glamor or potential glory and perhaps without solutions, however "successful" the station director might portray their "progress" in his annual report.

Whatever his employment situation, the young scientist in a rapidly growing field was faced with the frustrating realization that vast new areas were opening up of which he knew nothing, that current work elsewhere in the nation (no longer abroad) might be especially useful for his own researches, and that whatever station bulletins or bureau publications he might manage to find and read would already be out-of-date and not tell him enough of the very things he most wanted to know—the informal comments, the hunches and hints of fellow workers in the same field. When an isolated and perhaps discouraged investigator learned around 1905 or 1910 that roughly 50 to 150 other persons were working on similar problems at other experiment stations or on other campuses, a certain pattern of events would ensue. A few leading figures in the field (usually at the USDA in Washington) would write to the others throughout the country inviting them to attend a special session at the next meeting of a relevant parent group— such as the American Association for the Advancement of Science, the Association of American Agricultural Colleges and Experiment Stations, or the Botanical Society of America—for the purpose of forming a separate professional society devoted to their mutual interest. When the new group assembled it would select its new leaders, plan future meetings, and discuss the publication of a separate journal. Sometimes it had also to justify its formation to the parent group (the Botanical Society was particularly sensitive), and thus one of the first tasks that unified the new group was the need to explain how, for example, agronomy or phytopathology differed from traditional botany. But the chief synthesizing force for a new organization was usually its journal, which only the larger and more stable of the groups were able to establish. It took on the role of a symbol or banner for the field, serving to identify it, make it visible to others, and define its subject matter and methodology.[15] (The establishment of a popular journal with which to communicate with farmers or laymen was rarely even discussed by these professional groups.)

In a period of growth and massive funding, such as the early 1900s, most of these groups flourished, and a scant ten years after their founding, many of their charter members were already historical figures. Members of these new groups felt a certain esprit de corps and pride in their new field and organization. Now if a professor of the classics or someone in "pure science" claimed that agriculture was not a science or lacked rigor, the new breed of young scientists had strong evidence to the contrary. But such accusations were also less common after 1900. The new agricultural scientist was employed in a separate station, at the USDA, or if at a land-grant university, in a newly-expanded agriculture college where a whole department was devoted to his specialty; he no longer came into contact with skeptical people from other fields, or if he did, he was no longer so marginal and vulnerable as his predecessors had been in the 1870s and 1880s. He was off in his "island empire,"[16] but for him it was a tremendous improvement over the past—at last he felt adequately recognized and supported.

Thus by 1890 the agricultural scientists were not only "professional" in the sense that they were employed by the government and trained by the universities and agricultural colleges, but they were also feeling greatly increased intellectual and social pressure for even more "professionalization" in the form of new organizations. Although most of these new societies had a long prehistory as sections of parent groups, better communication, especially necessary in a period of rapid growth, was usually the stated reason for a separate association. Yet the societies also performed an additional important function in helping to overcome some of the frustrations of working in an imperfect bureaucracy often riddled by local politics. For example, a devoted researcher who was éclipsed daily by the more aggressive and assertive bureau chief or station director (who might be a former politician or editor untrained in the sciences) might hope to get the recognition that he felt his work deserved from colleagues within the society. Here a youngster with a fresh idea for new work on a problem could seek advice from more experienced people in his own field, and of course, an encouraging word from Erwin Smith or Mark Carleton would do a lot to overcome the tedium of research.[17]

This brief overview of the general characteristics of the period can only suggest some of the forces at work within the agricultural sciences. The following survey of six major subfields—economic entomology, horticulture and breeding, animal nutrition, agronomy, plant and animal pathology, and soil science—will describe some of the more specific circumstances that affected particular specialities.[18]

## Economic Entomology

Economic entomology—the study of the control of insect pests—was the first agricultural science in the United States to be called upon to solve the new agricultural problems arising after the Civil War and to feel the effects of specialization. As farmers of the Reconstruction Era attempted either to reuse their soil in old ways or to introduce new crops, especially delicate semitropical fruits, the number of insect epidemics increased rapidly. The resulting crises and subsequent federal funding created the field of "economic" entomology, which had formerly been a neglected area of science.

To a large extent, economic entomology was an American creation or, more specifically, a product of the USDA. Unlike such fields as soil science, which flourished in Russia, economic entomology had no equivalent abroad. Moreover, perhaps because of its emergence at the end of the 1870s when the experiment stations were still quite weak and perhaps because of the vigorous actions of its bureau chiefs, C. V. Riley and L. O. Howard, economic entomology remained more centered at the USDA than did most of the other agricultural sciences. However, as the field evolved from a minor, neglected subject into a highly funded and increasingly arrogant specialty, certain border problems arose involving the more traditional entomologists. Finally, it should be noted that while scientists in the field were able to end some epidemics and prevent others, their success seems to have come not from major breakthroughs in scientific theories but rather through the empirical development of new insecticides, especially Paris green, arsenite of copper, and kerosene emulsions.

Although more than 70 percent of all the species on our planet are insects and their study dates back at least to Aristotle, the science of entomology was still a marginal pursuit in America as late as the 1870s. Louis Agassiz and H. A. Hagen at Harvard University trained some of the pioneers of American entomology—A. S. Packard, S. H. Scudder, A. E. Verrill, and A. J. Cook—but academic jobs did not exist for such specialists, and the field remained largely in the hands of amateurs who were, usually, self-trained collectors and taxonomists who belonged to local natural history and entomological societies. Through penury and self-sacrifice, they spent their lives building up complete sets of exotic specimens but were only rarely interested in the destructive agricultural pests nearer home.

In early America, with its diversified and cold climate, the economic importance of losses caused by insect epidemics was relatively limited. Later, between 1840 and 1875, when such problems as the wheat midge, Hessian fly, and the potato bug became increasingly bothersome, a local amateur such as T. W. Harris, Benjamin Walsh, or Asa Fitch might be hired by the state government or agricultural society to collect specimens and suggest a remedy or by an agricultural editor to write a few short articles for a farm journal. However, such studies were infrequent and the interest short-lived. It was only when the insect problem had become persistent and economically threatening that any government, state or federal, took action.

When the USDA was founded in 1862, its original legislation called for a botanist, a chemist, and an entomologist, a selection that epitomized the state of agricultural science in the 1860s. In the 1870s, however, a terrible epidemic of locusts or "western grasshoppers" afflicted the homesteaders in the Territory of Colorado, and in 1877 the Congress formed the temporary Rocky Mountain Entomological Commission to investigate. In the next few years there was a serious outbreak of scale insects in Southern cotton, and, not surprisingly, Congress decided to increase the commission's budget and establish a permanent Division of Entomology within the USDA. Although the number of entomologists at the experiment stations increased rapidly after the passage of the Hatch Act in 1887, the vigorous leaders of the division continued to send teams of experts to investigate local epidemics. In 1911 the division even established a series of "field stations" and "field laboratories" throughout the country, largely because many of the states, including some of the most prosperous and highly agricultural ones, either refused or were unable to solve their own entomological problems.

The situation in California in the 1870s and 1880s may serve as an example of how one state was unable (or unwilling) to deal with its own agricultural problems, despite the presence of many amateurs, an agricultural college, and an experiment station, and how the USDA capitalized effectively upon this inaction. Although the California Academy of Sciences—established in 1853, shortly after the Gold Rush—had from its start attracted a number of entomologists, apparently none of them was interested in studying the state's numerous agricultural pests. However, with the large number of new plants introduced into California and the beginnings of a commercial fruit industry, the insect problem increased and threatened serious economic repercussions. In 1875, when Eugene W. Hilgard, primarily a geologist and chemist, arrived at the California College of Agriculture, the young wine industry was suffering severely from phylloxera, a disease of the grape vine caused by aphids in the roots. Hilgard quickly put to use publications by C. V. Riley on a similar disease that had occurred elsewhere and published a booklet describing all known remedies for phylloxera but would do nothing more without a special appropriation from the state legislature.

In the late 1870s, when the dreaded San Jose scale was detected on fruit trees throughout the Santa Clara Valley, the California State Viticultural Board requested the Board of Regents of the University of California to hire an entomologist. The regents agreed, on the condition that the state legislature appropriate $2000 for the purpose, but the legislature refused. In 1882, however, Charles H. Dwinelle, a young agriculturalist already on the staff of the California State Agricultural Experiment Station at Berkeley gave some special lectures on entomology. Over the next several years Hilgard repeatedly urged, without success, that an entomologist be added to the College of Agriculture. Finally in 1888, when an outbreak of the cottony cushion scale became particularly severe, Hilgard again turned for assistance to C. V. Riley, who had just been renamed head of the Division of Entomology at the USDA. It was Riley who first had the ingenious idea of studying the scale's natural predators and then managed to have Albert Koebele (who had been sent to Australia on other business) ship back to California thousands of Australian lady-bird beetles (*Vedalia*), which in a few months consumed the scales. This experiment, one of the first in the "biological control" of insects, was a highly dramatic success story and quickly became one of the much vaunted triumphs of the USDA.

Still the University of California did not hire a full-time entomologist until 1891 when, with its Hatch money or with the new Morrill Act funds, it appointed C. W. Woodworth of the Arkansas station. Woodworth became an assistant professor of entomology, an assistant at the station, the first trained entomologist in the state, and subsequently the director of both the program at the university and the station (he held the latter position for thirty-nine years). In sum, California, whose rapidly developing wine and citrus fruit industries were highly vulnerable to insect epidemics, gladly used the free expertise of the USDA's Division of Entomology but refused to support its own entomologist until the 1890s, and even then probably did so with federal funds.[19]

If this was the situation in one of the richest agricultural states, it is easy to see why the entomology division at the USDA offered the most interesting and most stable career for a young economic entomologist in the 1870s and 1880s, and why the pioneers of the science, including C. V. Riley, L. O. Howard, and the Comstocks, congregated there. With the number of entomological problems increasing greatly in the 1890s—the boll weevil in the South, the gypsy moth in the Northeast, the San Jose scale in Virginia, the chinch bug in Kansas, and the mosquito everywhere—and Congress's proven interest in making appropriations for their control, the division was assured of a continuing and prosperous future, to a far greater degree than the universities and agricultural colleges of the time.

With the expansion in the number of young entomologists at the division and the stations in the late 1880s, the workers began to feel the need for a professional organization. The first to take action was L. O. Howard, then assistant chief of the division, who together with the president of the Entomological Club of the AAAS issued a call for the new society to be formed at the AAAS meeting in Toronto in 1889. Only eleven persons attended this first meeting of the Association of Economic Entomologists, but thirteen others were later added to a retroactive list of "charter members." At first the USDA assisted the organization by publishing the proceedings of the association's annual meetings in its series of bulletins, but in 1907, when the membership was more than 200, the association started its own journal. By 1928, L. O. Howard was proud to report that the membership was over a thousand. Meanwhile Howard, an active propagandist for the field, was making a career of "Fighting the Insects," as he entitled his autobiography, and writing widely on the "insect menace," a problem that after the discovery of the role of insects as carriers of disease came to include household as well as agricultural pests.

At the same time that Howard was making his heroic efforts to bring economic entomology to the public mind, academic entomology was also growing and organizing itself into a professional field. For a brief period in 1879 and 1880, John Henry Comstock, a Cornell University instructor in zoology specializing in entomology, replaced C. V. Riley as head of the Division of Entomology; when Comstock returned to Cornell in 1881, he keenly felt the loss of the funds and resources of the division. By comparison, Cornell offered an entomologist very little and Comstock could only hope that someday a chair in his field might be added to the department. In retrospect, Comstock's ambitions were modest, for by the time he retired in 1914 he was the chairman of one of the most prominent entomology departments in the country, with an entire classroom building devoted to his field and a separate laboratory (or "insectary") for his own studies of the life-cycle of insects. In the same period, Comstock's wife, Anna Botsford Comstock, a noted naturalist who had assisted her husband at the entomology division, became the first woman to attain professorial status at Cornell.[20]

By the early years of this century, the noneconomic entomologists had moved beyond their local societies and formed the Entomological Society of America in 1906 with John Henry Comstock and William Morton Wheeler of the Bussey Institution of Harvard as its first presidents. This organization, which numbered 500 persons in its first year, greatly overshadowed Howard's group. Moreover, its members did not view insects as a "menace" but as beautiful complex creatures, most of which are beneficial to man and from whose highly developed social patterns and lengthy stay on earth humans have much to learn. Admitting that the control of insects might on occasion be necessary, they considered further research on insect physiology or other studies preferable to the rather brutal methods of the economic entomologists. As Wheeler said in 1917: "The economic entomologist, like the physician, should strive to make himself unnecessary by prophylactic measures, or perhaps I should say that he should prevent plant diseases rather than spend his time studying symptoms and applying remedies to diseases after they have become established."[21]

L. O. Howard and his contemporaries were aware of this criticism but attributed it to certain class differences between the pure and applied entomologists. Howard noted in his autobiography that at international congresses in entomology attention was rarely given to applied subjects, which apparently interested only Americans. But, in referring to a 1912 meeting at Oxford, he inadvertently revealed what had probably been an even more bothersome problem over the years: "Practically down to that time [1912] the so-called economic entomologist, devoting himself almost entirely to agricultural entomology, has been considered by the university laboratory men, by the museum men, and by the amateurs interested wholly in Taxonomy, as a sort of farmer, with nothing like the same scientific standing as themselves... I am inclined to rate the Oxford Congress as a high point in the progress of applied entomology in the esteem of other branches of science."[22] The whole science of economic entomology seems therefore to have grown up in the United States as a result of rather unusual conditions—the economic threat posed by insect epidemics, the funding provided by the federal government, the vigor of USDA administrators, and the number of young scientists attracted by opportunities in the field.

## Horticulture, Breeding, and Genetics

Unlike economic entomology, which was largely dominated by the USDA and Comstock's graduate program at Cornell University, the field of horticulture was one of the few sciences ignored by the USDA and was instead led primarily by Luther Burbank of Santa Rosa, California and Liberty Hyde Bailey of Cornell. The careers of these two men illustrate that horticulture grew up in a lay and almost quack tradition and then had to fight to prove itself worthy of being considered a "science."

This horticultural tradition was already strong in the United States before 1860, and horticulture was one of the first agricultural specialties to form its own societies. The first national group, the American Pomological Society established in 1848, held annual exhibitions at which competitors could show off their products and creations. Occasionally an invited expert, as an editor or master grower, would deliver a speech or read a paper in the tradition of the agricultural fairs. These societies did little else, however, in the way of supporting the "science" of horticulture.

With the rise of the commercial fruit industry in New York, Florida, and California in the late nineteenth century, the field of horticulture began to move from its amateur past into a professional future. It received a popular boost, but a professional threat, in 1875 when Luther Burbank of Massachusetts moved to Santa Rosa, California and entered the nursery business, catering to the fledgling

California fruit and vegetable industry. Although Burbank had no training in botany beyond reading Darwin on variation in plants, he demonstrated unusually great skill in practical breeding and horticulture. He decided, after a few orders from ambitious growers for thousands of prune trees, that it would be commercially feasible to undertake plant experimentation on a grand scale. Over the next fifty years he created or improved on over 800 plants, a "conservative estimate," according to a recent biographer. His much publicized and dramatic creations as the spineless cactus, the Shasta daisy, and various plums and roses aroused wide popular and professional interest in the United States and abroad. Burbank's products were often so much more profitable than the traditional varieties (they extended the California growing season by three to four months) and were so numerous and so seemingly automatic that they appeared to be the result of a scientific method.

Burbank's work, however, received a mixed response from professional botanists and agricultural scientists. Since Burbank was not a government employee, whose creations were given to the public free of charge, but a businessman in a highly risky field, and since there was not until 1931 a patent law protecting plant creations (as there had long been for other inventions), Burbank tried to recoup the cost of his experimentation by selling contract rights to his new creations to selected nurserymen. Burbank was also enough of a showman to know that the more dramatic or unusual his creations were, the more sales and free publicity he would get. These circumstances and his money-making schemes opened Burbank to charges of quackery from suspicious persons, especially the professional in the USDA and the nearby experiment station at Berkeley. The criticisms increased when it became known that few other persons could duplicate his results, that his methods were largely intuitive, and that he took few field notes, which well-trained scientists thought essential. After the rediscovery of Mendel at the turn of the century, several interested scientists, including David Starr Jordan, Vernon Kellogg, David Fairchild, Hugo De Vries, and L. H. Bailey, visited Burbank, and most pronounced his methods "legitimate" but certainly amazing. In 1905, which seems to have been the peak of Burbank's career, the Carnegie Institution hired George Shull, later a geneticist at Princeton, to take notes on Burbank's methods, but despite months of effort, Shull could never get Burbank to explain his work. Thus, the scientists were puzzled by Burbank and he, though craving their respect, had little he could pass on except his results. However, his work made horticulture an exciting science to the American public and did much to give it a place at the experiment stations. If Luther Burbank, an untrained "wizard," could make so many dramatic and useful varieties, could not a trained scientist do even more? The answer would soon be apparent, for when the field began to develop as a science, Burbank was not at the center.[23]

In the early 1880s, at about the time Burbank was beginning his work in California, a Michigan farm boy and a graduate of the Michigan Agricultural College (now Michigan State University) went off to study botany with Asa Gray at Harvard University. But Liberty Hyde Bailey's real ambition and interest was in the field of horticulture, and when his alma mater offered him a job as professor of that subject in 1885, he accepted it eagerly. In 1888 Bailey moved to Cornell University where he became a popular teacher, prolific writer, highly successful administrator, and a pioneer in scientific horticulture.

Shortly after 1900, perhaps because of the public interest created by Burbank's creations and perhaps also because of the rediscovery of Mendel's ideas, Bailey became dissatisfied with the traditional horticultural societies that were still doing very little to support horticultural science. Although a certain amount of research was being done on plant varieties in the United States, it was scattered in so many odd places that Bailey thought a new society was needed to bring it all together for closer scrutiny by competent persons. Therefore, in June 1903, S. A. Beach of the Geneva, New York experiment station issued an open letter inviting interested persons to meet at the American Pomological Society in Boston the following September. The 30 persons who appeared formed the American Society for Horticultural Science and elected Liberty Hyde Bailey as the first president. By 1907 the society had 82 members, by 1914, 172, and by 1953, when it celebrated its fiftieth anniversary, over 1700 members, including over 200 from foreign countries, making it the largest society in its field in the world. Despite the society's subsequent success, the early years were rather bleak, and Liberty Hyde Bailey practically alone carried the society forward, each year giving an uplifting address that predicted the field's promising future if scientific methods were developed.[24]

In contrast with Bailey's modest success in organizing horticulture on a scientific basis, the early efforts to organize animal breeding had a much more dramatic and unstable history. Animal breeders were the only group to try to capitalize on their wide popular appeal, start a journal for laymen, and seek to combine popular and professional interest in one organization. However, this proved a dangerous game, and the eugenics forces ran away with their society in 1912. Not until 1931 was another professional society of plant and animal geneticists formed in the United States.

It was the excitement over Luther Burbank's work in plant breeding in the 1890s that convinced James Wilson, secretary of the USDA, and Willet M. Hays, director of the Minnesota Experiment Station (later assistant secretary of the USDA), that a society of scientists and breeders might stimulate similar work in animal breeding. Wilson suggested that the new group hold its first meeting at the December 1903 session of the AAACES in St. Louis. Some forty to fifty people appeared, named the group the American Breeders' Association, and elected Hays, who had come prepared with his presidential address, as their first chairman. Almost immediately Hays revealed that his conception of the group's role and future was different from that of the other professional agricultural societies founded about this time. More of a "booster" or "hustler" than the leaders of similar groups, Hays was determined to differentiate the role of the American Breeders' Association from that of other professional agricultural societies. In 1905, after announcing that the group already had 726 members, he set forth the goal of increasing the total to several thousand as soon as possible. In January 1906 Hays, now the perpetual secretary, announced a grandiose plan to encompass all future work in breeding within a single overarching society; forty-three committees of the association were formed to cover all aspects of plant and animal breeding: dairy production, meat production, insects, eugenics, poultry, citrus fruits, wild birds, cereals, corn, cotton, tobacco, coffee, vegetables, and several kinds of horses. In the end, many of these committees never met, and others very quickly split off and went their own way. In 1910 Hays, responding to a poll of the membership, added a section on eugenics to the association with David Starr Jordan and C. B. Davenport as leaders. This addition was very popular and quickly increased the membership to 1267.

At the peak of the society's influence in 1910, Hays launched the association's long-awaited popular journal, *The American Breeders' Magazine,* confidently expecting that, despite the society's limited membership, the magazine would soon be the equivalent of the *American Forester* with its 12,000 subscribers or perhaps the *National Geographic* with its 60,000. Meanwhile, the association had been meeting at various Midwestern universities with such related groups as the National Corn Exposition, and some of the papers presented at these meetings were justifiably published in the association's proceedings. But the purpose of one such meeting at which fifteen members of the association gave public lectures on breeding to about 3,000 persons attending the Exposition, was clearly popularization rather than informed communication among members.

In 1912 and 1913, with the change in political administrations and the resignation of secretaries Wilson and Hays, the association went into a serious crisis. Hays' grandiose plans were not working out, and if the society and magazine were to survive they would require a major overhaul. A steering committee consisting of William E. Castle; Alexander Graham Bell, founder of the *National Geographic*; and his son-in-law David Fairchild, a prominent plant explorer at the USDA, reorganized the society in several ways—they discontinued the meetings and professional papers, changed the name to the American Genetics Association (the word "breeders" could not be used in mixed company), and recast the publication as the *Journal of Heredity,* which they hoped would not only appeal to the wider public but would also provide solid scientific leadership in eugenics—a field they feared was on the verge of being "captured by sentimentalists and propagandists with slight knowledge of its biological foundation." The revised association and its journal, which had found a new purpose, new leadership, and a new clientele, are still in existence today.[25]

The success of the eugenics forces meant that the professional geneticists were left without a society in 1912, although the old breeders' group had not really suited their needs for several years. Their attempts to form a more suitable journal and society were to extend over several more years. In 1916 George Shull and nine other prominent geneticists formed the professional journal *Genetics.* In 1921 the sections on genetics in the American Society of Zoologists and in the

Botanical Society of America met at the AAAS meeting in Toronto to form a "Joint Genetics Section" that met annually until 1931, when with its combined membership of 289 the group formed its own separate Genetics Society of America—today the prominent professional group in the field.[26]

It is hard to analyze what went right and what went wrong in the emergence of the breeding and eugenics groups. Certainly Hays was overly optimistic, carried away by Burbank's successes and other highly publicized triumphs in cotton, citrus fruits, and corn. When it became apparent that the hopes for similarly rapid advances in animal breeding far outran the actual scientific accomplishments, the American Breeders' Association became more of a one-man show than a decentralized professional group. A greater error than seeking to popularize animal breeding was Hays' effort to use the society to create communication—and a science—that did not yet exist. It was not until the 1920s that the geneticists themselves felt the need for a professional society of their own and were strong enough to hold it from the eugenicists. But Hays' plans for the society were not toally misguided, for some of the committees he had formed so hastily in 1906 did have something to discuss and within a few years established separate professional societies of their own.

## Animal Nutrition and Husbandry

The splintering and regrouping of the animal sciences in the period 1900 to 1920 demonstrates two almost contradictory tendencies at work at the same time. On the one hand, what had formerly been "animal nutrition" or the study of foodstuffs and animal metabolism, one of the leading research areas at the experiment stations in the 1890s, was becoming absorbed around 1905 into the more medically oriented science of biochemistry, which continued to study nutrition, especially vitamins and minerals, but with smaller laboratory animals and in a university or medical school setting. This move left the study of the more "practical" aspects of animal husbandry to station men who stumbled along trying to standardize practices and collect data, seemingly unaware of the great triumphs taking place in vitamin research between 1910 and 1920. On the other hand, two applied fields that had been rather dormant before 1905, poultry and dairy husbandry, flourished under changing economic conditions and became the focus of a cluster of subsciences (such as the bacteriology, biochemistry, engineering, and economics of egg and milk production) ready to serve the needs of their particular industries. Practically all of these developments took place at the experiment stations and agricultural colleges and not at the USDA, despite the existence of a Dairy Division in its Bureau of Animal Industry.

The fact that American biochemistry had its roots in both agriculture and physiology is sometimes overlooked.[27] When the American Society of Biological Chemists (ASBC) was formed in December 1906 by the chemical members of the American Physiological Society, four of its twenty-four charter members, T. S. Osborne, F. G. Benedict, H. C. Sherman, and H. P. Armsby, had backgrounds in agricultural institutions. They all had very strong ties to Wilbur O. Atwater, a European-trained chemist who emphasized the agricultural tradition in his metabolism and nutrition studies at Wesleyan University and during his service as first director of the Office of Experiment Stations in the early 1890s. In addition, four of the eight new members elected to the ASBC in 1908 were from the USDA: Harvey Wiley, Mary Pennington, Oswald Schreiner, and Albert C. Crawford. Although the long-range trend was for biochemistry to become increasingly medically oriented, it started, and at Wisconsin remains to this day, in the agricultural colleges and the experiment stations.

The formation of the ASBC in 1906 led Armsby, director of the Pennsylvania Experiment Station, and others to move toward the formation of a society of practical animal nutritionists that would encourage research on livestock and large animals in the Atwater tradition. Their chance came in July 1908 at one of the graduate summer schools in agricultural science sponsored by the USDA and held at Cornell University. These summer schools proved to be, with the meetings of the AAAS and AAACES, one of the more active spawning grounds for new agricultural societies of the period. After a few weeks together, the specialists in a field would often decide to establish a professional society to continue such interaction in the future. In the spring of 1908, Armsby issued an open letter to the members of the summer course and other interested persons; in July, thirty-two charter members from thirteen stations and the USDA formed the American Society of Animal Nutrition with Armsby as president. At their first official meeting, at the Chicago stockyards in November 1908, the organizing committee reported that the essential purpose of the society was to further animal research, especially by encouraging cooperative projects and standard methods of recording data. Despite the fact that the society's membership grew to one-hundred the second year and changed its name to the American Society of Animal Production in 1912 (in order to include the breeders who had been dropped from the eugenics group), its goals and the content of its meetings remained stagnant and the field became a scientific backwater.

In 1913, President E. B. Forbes of the Ohio station suggested that the society no longer meet at the Chicago stockyards but move downtown to one of the hotels and meet with the AAACES, SPAS, and other agricultural groups. He also revealed that only eleven papers had been read to the society in the five years of its existence. By 1920, the membership had grown to two hundred, but not until 1942 did the society establish its *Journal of Animal Science* and begin to show any sign that the scientific study of livestock required a combination of biochemistry, genetics, physiology, veterinary medicine, agronomy, and economics.[28]

By 1920, two other more specialized areas of animal husbandry had already taken the path "animal science" was to follow in the 1940s. While "animal science" was in a period of quiescence, economic, technological, and dietary changes were bringing forth new industries that would require other new applied sciences. The growing urban market, the rise of refrigeration, and the changing

American diet—with its stress on vitamins, minerals, and proteins—transformed the old dairy farms and backyard chicken coops into major industries with larger units of production, more efficient processes, and healthier animals. To overcome their numerous problems, these new industries needed selected aspects of many different sciences that, when combined, would transform the old fields of dairy husbandry and poultry husbandry into the new applied sciences of "dairy science" and "poultry science."

The first persons in dairy and poultry husbandry to sense the new directions their fields were taking were the instructors at agricultural colleges. Aware of the need to discuss ways of dealing with the changes brought about by growth and diversification, they sought to encourage dialogue and coordinate efforts through the formation of associations of dairy and poultry "instructors and investigators." In July 1906, W. J. Fraser of the University of Illinois called the first meeting of a group, later known as the National Association of Dairy Instructors and Investigators, at Champaign; only 17 persons attended and became "charter members." In 1917, when the membership reached 145, the society changed its name to the simpler and broader American Dairy Science Association and started its *Journal of Dairy Science.*[29]

In 1905, W. R. Graham of the Ontario Agricultural College made the first attempt to form an association of poultry teachers by suggesting a meeting at the next Madison Square Garden Poultry Show, but only four persons appeared and the attempt was abandoned. In July 1908, however, during the same summer graduate course at Cornell at which the Society of Animal Nutrition had been formed, Professor James Rice of Cornell issued a second call for a society. The International Association of Instructors and Investigators in Poultry Husbandry (later the American Poultry Science Association) was quickly formed with W. R. Graham as chairman and twenty-five charter members (including one woman). In 1914, the association started its journal, changing its name to *Poultry Science* in 1921.[30]

By 1920, the animal sciences had split into a variety of new fields and new settings. Some had moved into medical schools and left agriculture behind, while others were moving rapidly into the new world of agribusiness.

## Plant and Animal Pathology

Plant and animal pathology was another area transformed by significant developments between 1870 and 1920. Pasteur's work on sheep anthrax, silkworm diseases, and canine rabies revolutionized basic concepts of animal pathology, and subsequent discoveries by several Americans created similar breakthroughs in plant diseases. Although both new fields had immediate application in the American fruit and livestock industries and led to new bureaus in the USDA, the two sciences came to be organized and institutionalized in different ways. Animal pathology was easily absorbed into the veterinary medical tradition, but plant pathology, which lacked such a professional role, was caught between botany and bacteriology and only later established itself as a separate field with its own society.

In animal pathology, Pasteur's work, coupled with the numerous unsolved diseases that plagued the American livestock industry, led to the formation of the Bureau of Animal Industry at the USDA in 1884 and to an era of well-publicized triumphs there—the eradication of pleuropneumonia and bovine tuberculosis from American cattle, Theobald Smith's masterful study of the Texas fever, and Marion Dorset's work on hog cholera. The work of Smith and Dorset brought important new concepts to bacteriology and medical research—Smith showed that insects could transmit a protozoan disease in animals, Dorset that an animal disease could be caused by a filtrable virus as well as a bacterium. Considering how basic a change these discoveries made in understanding the nature of animal disease, it is surprising in retrospect how slowly they were absorbed into the everyday practice of veterinary medicine and veterinary education, which remained in many parts of the country in an apprenticeship system after 1900.

Similarly, the new bacteriology did not lead to the formation of a new society of scientific veterinarians. An attempt to start such a group in 1898 proved abortive. Those persons in the United States doing research in animal diseases were forced to work through the American Veterinary Medicine Association (established in 1863) or the largely medical Society of American Bacteriologists (founded in 1899). This failure to form a separate society may have stemmed from the fact that veterinary research was even smaller and more centralized than other sciences at the time. Although some research was done at the experiment stations, most of it was conducted at the USDA, where the experts clustered, sending teams of investigators into the field for particular epidemics. Few of the veterinary colleges were able to support research, and after 1915, as tractors and automobiles replaced horses and mules, enrollments in veterinary medicine dropped off drastically. Many schools fought for their survival until the late 1920s, when supply and demand stabilized once again. Meanwhile animal pathology remained an example of a new science that might have, but seemingly did not, lead to a new specialty. Instead it was absorbed into the mainstream of the medical and veterinary medical traditions.[31]

The quiet assimilation of the new bacteriology into animal pathology makes the situation in plant pathology, a seemingly close relative, appear rather unusual. In fact, plant pathology followed the development pattern typical for most agricultural sciences. There were no known remedies for diseases classified as "rusts," "blights," "smuts," "mildews," and the like until the 1870s, when botanists discovered that fungi and bacteria were the causes of many plant diseases, and the 1880s when the new fungicide of Alexis Millardet, the famed "Bordeaux mixture" of lime and copper sulphate, provided a highly effective spray for plant diseases. With these discoveries, the subsequent development of lime-sulphur about 1910, and improvements in spraying apparatus, a new era in plant pathology began.

In 1884 a committee of five botanists of the AAAS urged Congress to create a section of mycology within the USDA's Division of Botany for the purpose of studying fungus diseases. A year later, the department hired F. Lamson-Scribner as its first mycologist. Within fifteen years this section would grow tremendously and become one of the strongest divisions within the USDA, as Congress and all the industries afflicted with plant diseases voted ever larger appropriations. The section, later to be a division, became famous for the high quality of its staff members, both men and women.

In 1888 Beverly T. Galloway succeeded Lamson-Scribner as head of the Division of Mycology. Galloway's career at the USDA seems quite reminiscent of L. O. Howard's exploits there in economic entomology. In fact the two were rather strong rivals, with Galloway often winning out. In 1901 Galloway achieved the bureaucrat's dream of first consolidating his division with several others into one major Bureau of Plant Industry and then being promoted to bureau chief. Galloway became, like Howard, a major spokesman for his field and continued even into his retirement to write historical articles on the triumphs of his field and his bureau.[32]

The first courses on plant pathology taught in the United States began in the late 1870s at the University of Illinois with Professor T. J. Burrill and at the Bussey Institution of Harvard University with Professor W. G. Farlow. In 1907, as part of the expansion and reorganization of Cornell's College of Agriculture, Liberty Hyde Bailey established the first separate department of plant pathology with H. H. Whetzel as chairman. By this time the field was expanding rapidly with numerous jobs in both government and industry.

In their effort to build a professional organization, both the botanists and the bacteriologists faced numerous difficulties during the 1890s. American botanists were still a rather small group in this period, with perhaps as few as fifty trained professionals. Yet unlike the veterinary researchers whose work was concentrated at the USDA, the botanists seemed to break up into geographic units, separate specialties (as taxonomists and physiologists), and rival organizations (as section G of the AAAS and the American Society of Naturalists). The resulting fragility of all the groups caused the leading botanists to worry about the frequent "secessions" of the new specialties of horticulture, mycology, bacteriology, and forestry. Despite the merger of several of the rival groups in December 1906 into the Botanical Society of America (BSA), the leaders were still concerned about the new groups that continued to form outside them. Their fears were probably justified since it was 1915 before they were able to start their own journal, the *American Journal of Botany.*[33]

However, the plant pathologists were not happy in either the new BSA or the older Society of American Bacteriologists. In 1908, C. L. Shear of the Bureau of Plant Industry talked to a few colleagues about forming a separate society for plant pathologists and called an open meeting for the next AAAS session in December in Baltimore. Fifty-four persons appeared at this first gathering of the American Phytopathological Society, but so many others wrote to express interest that 130 were considered "charter members." Several speakers were fearful that a separate group would weaken the BSA, but enthusiasm for the organization ran high, forty-five papers were presented, and plans were made to launch a separate journal, *Phytopathology,* as soon as possible. *Phytopathology* began publication in 1911 and remains today the leading international journal in its field. By 1920 the American Phytopathological Society numbered 500 members and had taken its place as one of the strongest agricultural science societies in the United States. The field had a long prehistory, but its rapid emergence in the early twentieth century and its overshadowing of the parent field of botany was due largely to the encouragement and support of the USDA, the Congress, and the highly specialized nature of American agriculture.[34]

## Agronomy and Regional Development

Although some of the new agricultural sciences at the USDA prided themselves on having a wide and diversified clientele, the development of the new field of agronomy (agrostology or the study of grasses, as it was called initially) was very closely tied to the economic development of one major region of the United States, the Great Plains, in the decade between 1900 and 1910. Working in the humid Northeast, the nation's first farmers had taken their native forage of timothy and clover for granted. But on the semiarid Plains, the vast "empty" space north of Texas up to Montana and the Dakotas, rainfall was so slight that only grasses would grow; thus the hardiness and even the very existence of these crops assumed much greater economic importance. For several decades, livestock had roamed freely in the region, but by the 1880s the area had been so badly overgrazed that stockmen began to ask Congress to do something to protect their free fodder. In 1895 their efforts were finally rewarded, and the USDA created a Division of Agrostology to investigate the grasses of the Great Plains.

The division quickly established several field stations to study local conditions, but its most dramatic and successful work involved sending several "plant explorers" to other parts of the world to collect new grasses and other drought-resistant crops. Most notable of this group was Mark A. Carleton, an assistant botanist at the Kansas station who came to the USDA in 1894 to study cereal rusts. In the course of these studies he discovered that some strains of wheat were more resistant to disease than others, and in 1898 and 1899, the secretary of the USDA, James Wilson, sent him to Russia and Siberia to collect these rust- and drought-resistant grains for trial in the United States. As a result of his and N. E. Hansen's travels, the USDA introduced to the Great Plains such new grains as the Swedish Select and the Sixty-Day oats, the Kharkov and hardy red wheat, and several varieties of durum wheat. Carleton and others also worked at the field stations to develop new methods of "dry-farming" (i.e. without irrigation) for those farmers willing to take up the new crops. Moreover, the USDA and the experiment stations imported or developed their own new strains of corn, alfalfa, sorghum, barley, flax, and millet for the Plains region. The result was that much of the area became suitable for certain types of restricted farming and the grain line, the western limit to grain production, moved about 300 miles farther west.

Agronomy's success in recovering worthless land and making it yield a profitable crop led to a situation not encountered in the other agricultural sciences. The idea that new grasses and methods of cultivation would make grazing land profitable appealed to land speculators who often, to the horror of the scientists at the local station or the USDA, distorted their cautious statements into guarantees and strong endorsements of the value of the new miracle grasses, some of which had yet to be tested or even discovered. Eventually, however, despite several incidents of swindling, much of the northern Plains regions (including Canada) did become productive of various wheats and grasses.

The Division of Agrostology thus proved itself highly successful in just a few years of existence. In 1901, when the USDA was breaking up its old "divisions" into "offices" and recombining them into "bureaus," Mark Carleton was placed in charge of the new Office of Grain Investigations (later Cereal Crops and Diseases) with a staff of agronomists within the Bureau of Plant Industry. Several other "offices," including those of Forage Plants, Dry Land Agriculture, and Western Irrigation Agriculture, also hired numerous agronomists for their Washington and branch stations. The specialty grew so rapidly that the number of agronomists at the USDA increased from three in 1900 to ninety-nine in 1908 and at the experiment stations from zero to at least forty-four by 1905. And there were probably many more, since agronomists were often employed under the old titles of "agriculturalist" or "botanist."

Agronomy also began to be taught at the agricultural colleges after 1900, and separate departments were established at Cornell, Wisconsin, and other midwestern universities. However, the status of these departments lagged behind that of others in the agricultural sciences; not even the Wisconsin department hired a Ph.D. until 1930. At Nebraska, agronomy was closely tied to the botanical field of plant ecology as pioneered by Professor Charles E. Bessey, and his students Frederic and Edith (Schwartz) Clements and H. C. Cowles, who are all now counted among the founders of ecology. The Nebraska group was indirectly influential in founding the Ecological Society of America in 1915.[35]

By the turn of the century, the very rapid and somewhat decentralized growth of the field led, as it had in the other agricultural sciences, to the formation of a separate professional society and journal. In November of 1907, Mark Carleton and four colleagues addressed an open letter to the other members of the field suggesting a meeting at the next AAAS convention to consider the formation of a separate society of agronomists. In December, 43 people appeared and formed the American Society of Agronomy (ASA) with Mark Carleton as its first president. During the next several months additional members were recruited: by July 1908 the group could boast of 101 charter members; by 1910 the number had grown to 176 and by 1917 to 652. The society published its own proceedings until 1913 when it combined them into its quarterly journal. The rather large size of the

ASA was partly due to its ability to capture a group of soils men in the Midwest who had been planning to form their own group but joined the ASA when it promised to form a special section on crops and another on soils. After the new journal *Soil Science* was established in 1916, the membership of the ASA fell sharply to 436 in 1920, but it rose again in the 1920s.

The ASA also had border problems with the botanists who were in 1907 still concerned about the new fields of applied botany. Mark Carleton's 1907 presidential address on "The Development and Proper Status of Agronomy" indicates the existence of such tensions. Carleton asserted that although agronomists must consider botany, especially plant ecology, to be "indispensable," they must also know a great deal about the chemistry, geology, physics, and bacteriology of the soil of the region. In addition, agronomists must study plants even more intensively than the botanists because they are dealing not with species but with varieties, such as spring and winter wheat, and must know the needs and characteristics of each. If, in 1907, Carleton was anxious to show that agronomy was different from and even superior to botany, it may have been because the field was made up of a motley collection of old-time agriculturalists, former botanists, and former fertilizer chemists. By 1914, this earlier attitude was changing and the journal's editor openly set forth a more mature view of "mutual appreciation" and recognition that botany was essential and closely related to good agronomy. The ASA and the BSA had learned to coexist and go their separate though related ways.[36]

## Soil Science

The final science that merits consideration here—but strangely more for what did not happen than for what did—is agricultural chemistry or soil science, a field that had formerly been one of the leading sectors of agricultural science.

At the outset, it should be noted that soil science did not lack important breakthroughs in this period. There were, in fact, two new currents in the field in the 1880s and 1890s—soil bacteriology and pedology. The field of soil bacteriology originated in the work of two German experiment station scientists, Hermann Hellriegel and Hermann Wilfarth, who showed in 1886 that nitrogen-fixing bacteria (*Azotobacter*) in the roots of legumes could turn atmospheric nitrogen into useful nitrates within the soil. For reasons not entirely clear, the United States government took only a minor interest in this new field, which would seem to have offered many potential applications. As a result, work on soil bacteriology proceeded so slowly in the United States that some twenty years later Jacob Lipman at the New Jersey experiment station at Rutgers University and his brother, Charles Lipman at the University of California, were still among the first Americans to study the subject.

In 1915 Jacob Lipman, by then director of the New Jersey station, attended the meeting of the Society of American Bacteriologists at which the decision was made to begin publication of the *Journal of Bacteriology*, primarily because of the war-time break in communication between American bacteriologists and their European colleagues. For this reason and also because the reports of soil re-searches were scattered in a wide variety of publications, Lipman returned to New Jersey determined to start his own journal, *Soil Science,* with the help of his bright assistant, Selman Waksman, but without the support of any society. Al-though the journal's emphasis was largely microbiological, it interpreted "soil science" broadly and filled an important international need, since the only other publication devoted to any kind of soil research at the time was the Russian journal, *Pedology.*

Because of his journal and his researches on *Azotobacter* and ammonification, Jacob Lipman assumed a prominent position in the international world of soil science. In 1924 he was elected president of the newly formed International Society of Soil Science and placed in charge of the First International Congress of Soil Science that was held in the United States in 1927. Lipman remained active in several international groups until his death in 1939, but it was the 1927 congress and its carefully arranged postconvention tour of United States and Canadian soils that was remembered years later as a high point in the history of soil science and one of Lipman's great contributions to the field.

Lipman, however, never did find himself the center of a burgeoning field within the United States. Like bacteriology in general, soil bacteriology re-mained a largely European specialty into the 1920s with particular strength in France at the Pasteur Institute, in Britain at the Rothamsted Agricultural Experi-ment Station, and in Holland at M. W. Beijerinck's laboratory at Delft. It was the coming of World War I and the use of nitrates as an essential ingredient in explosives and artificial fertilizers that taught the American government how myopic its neglect of soil bacteriology had been. In 1916 the War Department started some preliminary investigations and then in 1919 formed the Fixed Nitro-gen Laboratory to produce this much-needed product artificially.

The field continued to grow, but it is difficult to know how rapidly. By the mid-1920s at least twenty-five experiment stations could report projects under-way in soil bacteriology, but few of these employed a full-time microbiologist. It was not until the late 1930s and early 1940s, when Rene Dubos of the Rockefeller Institute and Selman Waksman of the Institute for Microbiology at Rutgers discovered the first antibiotics in soil bacteria, that the commercial and medical possibilities of soil microbiology suddenly made it a popular area for applied research.[37]

The other and largely unrelated area of soil science that emerged in this period was pedology, or the classification of soil, including soil mapping. Unlike soil bacteriology, pedology was considered the mainstream of soil science; it was of major interest to the USDA and was pursued by several major scientists, but in an atmosphere of considerable controversy.

In the 1870s and 1880s the chemical analysis of soils had been one of the chief tasks of the chemical division of the USDA, even though opinion among the leading soil chemists of the time, Eugene Hilgard of California and Samuel

Johnson of Connecticut, was divided as to the usefulness of such analyses. Hilgard, familiar with the arid climate and alkali soils of the West, thought them essential, but Johnson and other eastern scientists, whose experience was limited to their area's humid climate and resultingly acid soils, maintained that such chemical tests did not distinguish adequately between fertile and barren soil. For the latter the new frontier was in soil physics—the texture and porosity of the different soils as well as their ability to absorb and retain water.

Hilgard and Johnson clashed firmly but politely over the issue in the 1870s and 1880s, but in subsequent decades the dispute widened and became more heated. In 1892 Milton Whitney, formerly of the Maryland station but then an employee of the Weather Bureau within the USDA, published a report that attributed soil fertility solely to physical features; Hilgard promptly denounced him in *Agricultural Science*. However, the outburst did no harm to Whitney whom secretary James Wilson placed in charge of a new Division of Agricultural Soils within the Weather Bureau in 1894 and promoted to chief of the USDA's newly formed Bureau of Soils in 1901. As a result, Harvey Wiley, whose Bureau of Chemistry had formerly conducted the department's soil work, became thoroughly alarmed. When, in 1902, Whitney's bureau published its controversial Bulletin 22, *The Chemistry of the Soil as Related to Crop Production,* Wiley, Hilgard and several others opposed to Whitney entered the fray, firing strong letters off to *Science* and *Nature,* writing their own bulletins in rebuttal, and doing their political best to have Whitney unseated. But he remained entrenched, largely, his enemies asserted, because of his strong friendships with secretary Wilson and chief B. T. Galloway of the Bureau of Plant Industry, rather than his own scientific merit. Perhaps they were right, for although Whitney held on until his normal retirement in 1927 and his bureau made important contributions to soil science, Whitney himself conspicuously lacked the professional honors and attention normally accorded bureau chiefs at the USDA.

While this controversy raged, quiet progress was being made in another area of pedology. The idea that soil formation was closely related to climate was becoming increasingly accepted by soil scientists in this period; indeed it underlay most of the work being done by Hilgard, Whitney, and two Russians: Glinka and Dokuchaiev. To develop a system of soil classification, however, required thousands of soil samples from a great variety of soil formations. In 1898 Whitney was greatly impressed by a soil map made by a USDA man in Montana that had such a small scale that one could identify individual farms on it. Whitney thought such maps would have practical value and, though many of his colleagues were skeptical, he convinced Congress to create the Soil Survey to prepare similar maps for the entire United States. The idea appealed to the pork barrel nature of American politics and was soon generously funded. Whitney hired a large staff, and made the inspired decision to place geologist Curtis F. Marbut, a former professor at the University of Missouri, in charge. Marbut was an outsider and a "loner" who strongly disliked the cliques and attitudes of his fellow workers in the Bureau of Soils, and they in turn ridiculed his work, asserting that he would be better off in the U.S. Geological Survey. To avoid such unpleasantness, Marbut spent most of his time in the field. Over the years, as he handled and mapped innumerable soil samples and absorbed the latest writings of Hilgard and the Russians, Marbut evolved his own ideas of how soils had been formed and his own system of classification by soil "types." Eventually in the 1920s when the results of his work were becoming known, Marbut became an international celebrity, with his work greatly acclaimed at the international congresses, a reception that reportedly astounded many persons at the USDA. Years later the soil mapping project is still not complete, but the systems in use today date back to Marbut's classifications.[38]

Despite the work of such giants as Lipman, Hilgard, and Marbut, soil science failed, for a variety of reasons, to coalesce organizationally and to become a leading sector of agricultural science in the United States between 1880 and 1920. It was divided into subspecialties, some of which were undermanned, and beset by factions. Much of the problem seems traceable to Milton Whitney and the scientific and political squabbling that his reports and administration of the Bureau of Soils aroused. Though in retrospect his bureau and especially the Soil Survey produced much valuable work, the field was so wracked by scientific differences and personal animosities that no society was established and soil researchers were left to join the agronomists' association instead. The usual model of initiative and leadership by the bureau chief at the USDA or by a prominent figure at an agricultural college failed to take hold. When a society finally did appear in 1924, it was distinguished by its international rather than American orientation, its leadership by a station man rather than the USDA, and its stress on soil bacteriology rather than on soil mapping or pedology. In comparison to the dramatic growth in the other sciences between 1880 and 1920, the serious problems and relative stagnation of soil science provide an interesting example of how personalities and controversies can hinder the organization of a science.

Henry Menard maintains that such squabbling and long-term controversy are typical of slow-growing (or declining) fields of science. Whitney's bureau (table 2, p. 218) may exemplify this assertion, for although it increased in size between 1897 and 1912, it did not grow as rapidly as many of the others, and the field did not really exist at the experiment stations as late as 1905 (table 1, p. 217). The difficulty was not only Whitney's personality, which made him singularly unsuccessful in attracting the cooperation of colleagues, but the fact that soil science itself experienced a generally erratic development. Although its roots went back to the 1840s and 1850s, it stagnated for many decades thereafter. Hilgard, Wiley and the staff of the Bureau of Chemistry were among the very few concerned with soil science in the 1880s. When the field did begin to grow again in the 1890s, it had to work around the old guard and its institutions and the result was continued division. Moreover, by 1920, it was the agronomists and the soil men in the American Society of Agronomy who were solving the farmer's day-to-day problems with fertilizing and tillage. Soil science had become a remote and abstract taxonomical science with practical benefits only in long-range planning and land usage. Even one of Marbut's soil maps required an extension worker to explain it.[39]

## Conclusion

From this overview of the major subfields of agriculture in the period 1880 to 1920, it is apparent that although the agricultural sciences as a whole underwent tremendous growth in these years, not all branches were equally successful or developed in quite the same way. Some "took off" and grew dramatically, such as economic entomology, agronomy, and plant pathology; others, such as horticulture and animal nutrition, limped along, and still others, notably soil science, had a hard time even getting started. Some sciences were closely related to the development of a particular region; others claimed to be useful everywhere. Some were tied to the development of particular industries; others were of use to any and all. Some were, for better or worse, heavily centered in the USDA; others developed primarily within experiment stations. And others, like soil science, had no single base.

All, however, exhibited in one form or another the effort to establish a professional organization. By 1920 a family of professional agricultural societies had sprung up in America. Most had been formed since 1900, or even 1905, and most still exist today as the major professional society in their field.

With the sudden appearance of so many new and specialized professional societies, the need arose for some means of coordinating their activities and keeping them in communication. As mentioned earlier, in 1909 the Society for the Promotion of Agricultural Science tried to project itself into a position of leadership by inviting thirteen new groups to "affiliate" with it. The animal nutritionists voted to send two delegates to a planning session, but only the agronomists really cooperated and ran joint meetings with SPAS for a few years. This was largely because Thomas F. Hunt, president of the SPAS from 1909 to 1910, was a prominent agronomist who had been urging the organization to adopt a more aggressive role since at least 1907. Other societies, such as that of the plant pathologists, which had been in existence only one year in 1909, thought it better for their own "autonomy" to bypass the SPAS offer.

Most of the new societies, however, did affiliate with the new Section M of the AAAS established for the agricultural sciences in 1913 and chaired in its first year by Liberty Hyde Bailey. Since Bailey later became president of the AAAS and L. O. Howard was its perpetual secretary until 1920, the agriculturalists were well represented at the highest levels, but most of them had been attending AAAS meetings for years anyway, had formed their societies there, and these in turn had grown up with the AAAS. They all felt at home at the AAAS and knew they could trust its large, receptive and relatively loose confederation to respect their independence more than they could the elitist and perhaps overbearing SPAS.[40]

Another attempt to coordinate the various agricultural fields was the establishment in 1917 of the Agricultural Committee (later the Division of Biology
and Agriculture) of the newly formed National Research Council. Its first chairman was Vernon Kellogg, a Stanford entomologist and Herbert Hoover's assistant food administrator in 1917 and 1918. The division's greatest accomplishments, large interdisciplinary projects such as the NRC fellowships in biology
and agriculture and the *Biological Abstracts,* began in the 1920s.

With this survey of the organization of the agricultural sciences as background, it is possible to make some limited generalizations about the nature and
broader effects of professionalization and "force-fed" specialization in the agricultural sciences. Aside from the fact that members of agricultural societies
were largely government employees and more often farm boys with midwestern
masters degrees than Ivy Leaguers with German doctorates, these organizations
carried out functions surprisingly similar to those of professional groups in other
less "applied" fields—the holding of meetings and the support of a journal. In
fact the notion of "applied" science, though convenient, is not really accurate
to describe the work of most agricultural scientists. They dealt with practical
problems that arose in certain economic contexts, but they were not really "applying" well-established theoretical principles to practical problems. Instead they
were discovering new ideas and principles that were also highly useful, such as
the life-cycles of insect pests or the inheritance of certain traits in poultry. Some
contemporaries, usually those in bordering fields less favored by the government, were highly critical and scornful of the agricultural men. But from the
perspective of the work they did and the societies they formed, rather than in
terms of certain elusive social class differences, the agricultural scientists could,
by 1920, have been any other group of professional specialists.

There was also more variety and fluidity within these agricultural groups than
the term "applied science" suggests. Each field had a slightly different setting
with its own problems, opportunities, and traditions that affected the subsequent
organization of the specialty—the chemists' regulatory work, the horticultural
tradition, the veterinary medical setting, the eugenics movement, and the new
agribusinesses. By 1920 when these traditions had sorted themselves out into
distinct fields and specialties, American agricultural research had shown itself to
be a fertile ground not only for numerous agricultural specialties but also for
basic research in the equally new biological fields of biochemistry, genetics,
plant physiology, and parts of bacteriology and plant ecology.[41]

How else can one assess the results that were achieved? Was the congressmen's faith in agricultural research justified after all? Isolating the effects of
science, as separated from technology and the other economic forces in the
period, is difficult, but several general trends can be suggested.

First of all, as the skyrocketing budgets readily attest, the new science created
a demand for even more science. The immediate results were visible and advantageous enough for each bureau chief and station director to be able to write a

self-congratulatory annual report full of "successes" and "progress" accounts of diseases cured, crops "saved" and others "improved," often with an estimated cash value attached. But despite all these triumphs, there always remained other and more expensive problems that would require even larger appropriations. Practical results and the accompanying favorable publicity seemed to sustain Congress's faith in the scientists and built up the belief that whatever agricultural problem might arise, the United States government would spend money on it and there would be an eventual solution. This belief was so strong as to border on an addiction and created a dependency among the farmers for more and more science. Hardly anyone before 1920 questioned the value of ever more science in agriculture, or even questioned where the money was coming from. Governmental science seemed a free and highly beneficial commodity, and farmers wanted more and more of it, even to the point of overproduction and agricultural depression in the early 1920s.

Second, all this research, especially after the passage of the Adams Act in 1906, created an equal and opposite reaction in the demand for more extension work by farmers. As early as 1908 the AAACES began lobbying for federal support of extension activities. In 1914 Congress passed and President Wilson signed the Smith-Lever Act giving each agricultural college $10,000 (to be matched by the state) plus a supplement based on its rural population for home economics and other extension work, especially local demonstrations by county agents. These new funds created a sudden demand for home economists and county agents, but again these amounts were never enough, and like the funds spent on research, had to be greatly increased later. Widespread extension work also created new interest in the problems of rural poverty and the new subjects of rural sociology and farm economics, two fields that would be among the first agricultural social sciences.[42]

One gets the general feeling, however, that despite the activities of the extension service, the overall effects of most of this science were not neutral or "value-free" but "conservative" in helping the richer farmers, the owners, and the growers rather than the sharecroppers, tenants, and small farmers to become even more prosperous and to drive the smaller, less efficient, poorly capitalized ones out of business. Of course, the rich farmers tended to be the ones who supported the various lobbies, took the chances, invested their capital, read the USDA bulletins, and generally used the government to further their own needs. Thus in a sense they were the most deserving of prosperity, although not all achieved it. But even assuming that government agencies were biased in their favor, the economic effects of scientific research seem to have been less the result of a deliberate policy to help certain classes and more the consequence of supposedly neutral improvements that inevitably had an unbalanced economic impact. For example, the discovery and development of a new fungicide or insecticide would seem like a useful step that would help all farmers, large and small alike, but in fact it helped the large, specialized farmers more by taking some of the risk out of their ventures. Plant epidemics had been great equalizers, and possibly even advantageous for smaller diversified farmers who could ride out a disease in one crop by relying on others to pull them through. Diversification was one form of insurance against such disasters, but once the spray can or the resistant variety took much of the risk out of large-scale specialized crops, the small diversified farmers lost their comparative advantage and were less able to compete.

Finally, the development of large-scale, government-financed agricultural research appears to have been primarily an American phenomenon not readily copied abroad. Germany, which had led the field in the mid-nineteenth century with the first experiment stations, was not much heard from after the 1880s and 1890s. France had certain established agricultural societies, such as the Societé Entomologique and three agricultural scientists—Jean-Baptiste Boussingault, Louis Pasteur, and Alexis Millardet—who would have been a credit to any experiment station, but the government seems never to have felt the need for large-scale bureaus. In Britain, John Bennet Lawes founded his own private experiment station at Rothamsted in the 1850s for fertilizer experiments. It later received government support, but even then, its efforts were largely limited to soil studies.[43] Japan seems to have had experiment stations in the 1890s, but we know little about them except that they were well funded.

Thus the rise of agricultural science in the United States between 1880 and 1920 was in one sense a success story on a grand scale but in others a more debatable achievement whose social and economic effects were widespread but hard to isolate and evaluate. The overall achievement seems to have depended on numerous factors: the large and diverse agricultural base of the American economy, its extensive transportation network and refrigerated railroad cars, the mechanization of the farms, the strong political force of the farmers, the generosity of Congress, the general belief in the value of science and technology, market incentives for particular innovations and economies of scale, as well as the numerous breakthroughs in the sciences. These may have been a unique set of conditions that did not exist abroad around 1900 or even in the United States in the other applied sciences. But rare as they would seem to be, most Americans confidently took them for granted and fully expect such agricultural triumphs to continue regularly into the future.

## Notes

1. United States Department of Agriculture (USDA), Office of Farm Management and Farm Economics, *Directory of American Agricultural Organizations, 1920* (Washington, D.C.: U.S. Government Printing Office, 1920).

2. Roughly eleven "professional" associations to promote agricultural science sprang up in most fields between 1880 and 1920. They were the Society for the Promotion of Agricultural Science (SPAS) (1880), the Association of Official Agricultural Chemists (AOAC) (1880), The Association of Economic Entomologists (AEE) (1889), the American Society for Horticultural Science (1903), the American Breeders' [later Genetics] Association (ABA) (1903), the American Dairy Science Association (1906), the American Society for Agronomy (1907), The American Society of Animal Nutrition (1908), the American Phytopathological Society (1908), the American Poultry Science Association (1908), and the International Society of Soil Science (1924). These groups, together with

such related groups as the American Veterinary Medicine Association (1863), the American Pomological Society (1848), the Association of American Agricultural Colleges and Experiment Stations (AAACES) (1887), the Botanical Society of America (1892), the Society of American Bacteriologists (1899), and the Entomological Society of America (1906) form a fairly distinct family of professional societies designed to promote and further the largely governmental field of agricultural science.

3. The only previous article I have found is by the prolific A. C. True of the USDA's Office of Experiment Stations. See "Scientific and Technical Societies Dealing with Agriculture and Related Subjects," *Proceedings of the Association of Land-Grant Colleges and Universities* 42 (1928): 37–58, which describes twenty-nine groups. The most useful material here has been found in the publications of the scientific societies themselves—the editorials, the presidential addresses, and the historical accounts on twenty-fifth and fiftieth anniversaries. Other helpful material has been: A. H. Dupree, *Science in the Federal Government: A History of Policies and Activities to 1940* (Cambridge, Mass.: Belknap Press of the Harvard University Press, 1957), chap. 8; idem, *Science in the Emergence of Modern America, 1865–1916* (Chicago: Rand McNally, 1963), pt. 3; the numerous articles of Charles Rosenberg cited below; T. S. Harding, *Two Blades of Grass* (Norman, Okla.: University of Oklahoma Press, 1947); Gould P. Colman, *Education and Agriculture, A History of the N.Y. State College of Agriculture at Cornell University* (Ithaca, N.Y.: Cornell University Press, 1963); A. C. True, *A History of Agricultural Experimentation and Research in the U.S., 1607–1925*, USDA Misc. Pub. 251 (Washington, D.C., 1937); Fred A. Shannon, *The Farmer's Last Frontier: Agriculture, 1860–1897* (New York: Farrar & Rinehart, 1945) and the USDA *Yearbook for 1899*, which contains several historical articles on the agricultural sciences. Unfortunately the last two items end just before the period of greatest activity. Useful bibliographies are John T. Schlebecker, *Bibliography of Books and Pamphlets on the History of Agriculture in the U.S., 1607–1967* (Santa Barbara, Calif.: ABC-Clio, 1969); Carroll Pursell, Jr., and Earl M. Rogers, eds., *A Preliminary List of References for the History of Agricultural Science and Technology* (Davis, Calif.: Agricultural History Center, 1966); and Joseph Kiger, *American Learned Societies* (Washington, D.C.: Public Affairs Press, 1963).

4. André Mayer and Jean Mayer, "Agriculture: the Island Empire," *Daedalus* 103 (Summer 1974): 88.

5. This lack of subject matter led to a generally low morale among agricultural workers in these decades. Isaac P. Roberts, professor of agriculture at Cornell in the 1870s, complained in his autobiography that he had to suffer daily the snubs and "social neglect" from his fellow professors in the liberal arts. (Isaac P. Roberts, *The Autobiography of A Farmboy* [Albany: J. B. Lyon, 1916], p. 177, 196–7.) Charles Rosenberg has elaborated on this malaise among experiment station workers, relating it more, however, to frustrations with the unprofessional setting than to the intellectual poverty of the sciences. (Charles Rosenberg, "Science, Technology, and Economic Growth: The Case of the Agricultural Experiment Station Scientist, 1875–1914," *Agricultural History* 45 [1971]: 1–21.) Even L. O. Howard, later the outspoken, self-congratulatory chief of the Bureau of Entomology at the USDA, intimated that he had had certain feelings of inferiority when he first went into economic entomology in the 1870s and 1880s, a field that was then held in low esteem by other entomologists but which was at the same time among the most active and successful of the agricultural sciences. Later, in the 1920s, he was surprised when young economic entomologists not only did not have similar feelings but wondered what he was talking about. (L. O. Howard, "The Rise of Applied Entomology in the United States," *Agricultural History* 3 [1929]: 132.)

6. A. C. True, "Scientific and Technical Societies," pp. 37–38; "The Origin and History of the Association," *Proceedings of the 1st, 2nd and 3rd Meetings of SPAS* (1883), pp. 9–11; occasional items in Byron D. Halsted, "The Society's Progress," *Proceedings of SPAS* 19 (1898): 17–49; and *Proceedings of SPAS, 1880–1920*, 41 vols. See also Richard A. Overfield, "Charles E. Bessey: The Impact of the 'New' Botany on American Agriculture, 1880–1910," *Technology and Culture* 16 (1975): 162–81.

7. Interstate Association of Livestock Sanitary Boards (1897), Association of Official Seed Analysts of North America (1908), Association of Feed Control Officials of the United States (1909), and International Association of Dairy and Milk Inspectors (1911).

8. A. C. True, "Scientific and Technical Societies," pp. 39–41. There does not seem to be any other history of the AOAC.

9. The relations between the stations and the USDA would require a paper in itself. Some stations found the relations fruitful, were highly cooperative and proud of it (as Wisconsin—W. H. Glover, *Farm and College: The College of Agriculture at the University of Wisconsin* [Madison, Wis.:

University of Wisconsin Press, 1952], pp. 240–92). Others were highly critical and very distrustful, as Illinois, which withdrew from the federal soil program in 1903 and rejoined only in 1943 (Richard G. Moore, *Fields of Rich Toil: The Development of the University of Illinois College of Agriculture* [Urbana, Ill.: University of Illinois Press, 1970], 164n). Eugene Davenport of Illinois was a frequent critic of the USDA's treatment of the stations; see especially "The Relations Between the Federal Department of Agriculture and the Agricultural College and Experiment Stations," *Proceedings of AAACES* 27 (1913): 121–33 and subsequent discussion; and idem, "Obstacles to Progress in Agricultural Science," *Proceedings of SPAS* 33 (1912): 11–17.

10. True, *History of Agricultural Experimentation,* 118–30. For later developments see also Charles Rosenberg, "The Adams Act: Politics and the Cause of Scientific Research," *Agricultural History* 38 (1964): 3–12.

11. For example, when in 1916 George Ellery Hale and his newly formed National Research Council added an amendment to the Newlands Bill that would channel appropriations for engineering experiment stations through the National Bureau of Standards rather than the land-grant colleges, the AAACES and its experienced Executive Committee swung into action and had the bill defeated (*Proceedings of AAACES* 30 [1916], especially 223–31; ibid. 32 [1917]: 234–35, 236–37, 240). See also Daniel Kevles, "Federal Legislation for Engineering Experiment Stations: The Episode of World War I," *Technology and Culture* 12 (1971): 182–89. A full history of the AAACES has not been written.

12. True, *History of Agricultural Experimentation,* p. 137. Interestingly, no geneticists or soil scientists appear.

13. Ibid., p. 190.

14. Davenport, "Obstacles," p. 14.

15. Various bureaus of the USDA helped the early professional societies by publishing the proceedings of the annual meetings as part of their bulletin series; the Bureau of Entomology published the AEE proceedings until 1906, the Bureau of Chemistry the AOAC proceedings until 1912, and the Office of Experiment Stations the AAACES proceedings until 1909. This last—having the government publish the proceedings of a meeting of lobbyists—would seem to show how close was the relationship between the AAACES and the USDA.

16. Mayer and Mayer, "Agriculture: the Island Empire."

17. One particularly difficult problem in the early days of the USDA that still rankled decades later was the frequent allocation of credit for a bureau scientist's research or writing to his chief. Decades later the younger men still felt they had been abused. (L. O. Howard, *Fighting the Insects: The Story of An Entomologist* [New York: Macmillan, 1933], pp. 29, 32–33; Claude E. Dolman, "Texas Cattle Fever, A Commemorative Tribute to Theobald Smith," *Clio Medica* 4 [1969]: 1–31.)

18. The related areas of forestry (or applied botany) and agricultural technology are omitted from this analysis. It must be admitted, however, that to most contemporaries, the development of the gasoline tractor between 1900 and 1920 must have seemed a much more visible and dramatic demonstration of the new usefulness of "science" on the farm than all the other developments combined. This whole section is an impressionistic mixture of the ideas of Henry Menard, *Science: Growth and Change* (Cambridge, Mass.: Harvard University Press, 1972); E. Davenport, "Obstacles," and David Fairchild, *The World Was My Garden: Travels of A Plant Explorer* (New York: Charles Scribner's Sons, 1938). Fairchild was a bright young man at the USDA in the 1890s who knew most of the people mentioned in this paper. His autobiography is an informed inside account of the Bureau of Plant Industry.

19. Entomology in California is discussed in E. O. Essig, *A History of Entomology* (New York: Macmillan, 1931); L. O. Howard, *A History of Applied Entomology (Somewhat Anecdotal),* Smithsonian Miscellaneous Collections 84 (1930): 151–58, and Ralph E. Smith et al., "Protecting Plants from Their Enemies," in *California Agriculture,* ed. Claude B. Hutchison (Berkeley: University of California Press, 1946), pp. 239–315. Other useful sources on the history of entomology in the United States are: L. O. Howard, "Rise of Economic Entomology"; Herbert Osborn, *Fragments of Entomological History* (Columbus, Ohio: private, 1937), and idem, *A Brief History of Entomology* (Columbus, Ohio: Spahr & Glenn, 1952); Gustavus A. Weber, *The Bureau of Entomology* (Washington, C.C.: Brookings Institute, 1930). Some helpful contemporary articles are: F. M. Webster, "The Relation of the Systematist to the Economic Entomologist," *Proceedings of the 16th Annual Meeting of the AEE,* Bureau of Entomology Bulletin 46 (1904): 40–41, A. L. Quaintance, "Some Present-Day Features of Applied Entomology in America," *Proceedings of the 17th Annual Meeting of the AEE,* Bureau of Entomology Bulletin 52 (1905): 5–25; W. J. Holland, "The De-

velopment of Entomology in North America," *Annals of the Entomological Society of America* 13 (1920): 1–15; C. Gordon Hewitt, "A Review of Applied Entomology in the British Empire," *Annals of the Entomological Society of America* 9 (1916): 1–34. Of even greater interest, especially for what can be read between the lines, are L. O. Howard, *Fighting the Insects,* Anna Botsford Comstock, *The Comstocks of Cornell* (Ithaca, N.Y.: Comstock Publishing Associates, 1953), and Mary Alice Evans and Howard E. Evans, *William Morton Wheeler: Biologist* (Cambridge, Mass.: Harvard University Press, 1970).

20. James G. Needham, "The Lengthened Shadow of a Man and His Wife," *Scientific Monthly* 62 (1946): 140–50, 219–29 includes a history of the Cornell entomology department. Initially Anna Botsford Comstock was named an assistant professor in the College of Agriculture at Cornell in 1899. However, as a result of opposition to female professors voiced by certain conservative trustees, her rank was changed to lecturer in 1900. She was again made an assistant professor in 1913 and became a full professor in 1920. Edward T. James, ed., *Notable American Women, 1607–1950,* 3 vols. (Cambridge, Mass.: Belknap Press of the Harvard University Press, 1971), 1:367–69.

21. Evans and Evans, *William Morton Wheeler,* p. 180. Wheeler was also critical of Howard's *History of Applied Entomology,* p. 311.

22. Howard, *Fighting the Insects,* p. 205.

23. There are numerous biographies of Luther Burbank. The two used here are Ken and Pat Kraft, *Luther Burbank: The Wizard and the Man* (New York: Meredith Press, 1967) and Walter L. Howard, *Luther Burbank: A Victim of Hero Worship,* Chronica Botanica, vol. 9 (Waltham, Mass.: Chronica Botanica, 1945). See also David Fairchild, *The World Was My Garden,* 263–66.

24. Biographies of Bailey include: Andrew D. Rodgers III, *Liberty Hyde Bailey* (Princeton: Princeton University Press, 1949) and Philip Dorf, *Liberty Hyde Bailey* (Ithaca, N.Y.: Cornell University Press, 1956). The early days of the ASHS are touched on briefly in Freeman S. Howlett, "The American Society for Horticultural Science," *Science* 118 (1953): 617, and "In Recognition of our Fiftieth Anniversary," *Proceedings of ASHS* 62 (1953): 1–3. Horticultural science in Britain is discussed in T. Wallace and R. W. Marsh, eds., *Science and Fruit* (Bristol: University of Bristol, 1953).

25. The confusing history of the breeding and eugenics groups is best pulled together from the ABA's own publications. However, W. E. Castle, "The Beginnings of Mendelism in America," *Genetics in the Twentieth Century,* ed. L. C. Dunn (New York: Macmillan, 1951), 59–76; Fairchild, *The World Was My Garden,* 294, 403–4, 423–24; and Robert Bruce, *Bell* (Boston: Little, Brown, 1973), 417–18 are also useful. See also, C. E. Rosenberg, "Factors in the Development of Genetics in the United States" Some Suggestions," *Journal of the History of Medicine* 22 (1967): 27–46.

26. "History and Organization," *Records of the Genetics Society of America* 2 (1933): 5–8 and "Addenda to History," *Records of the Genetics Society of America* 3 (1945): 5.

27. There are two differing accounts of the origins of biochemistry in the United States. Russell Chittenden of the Sheffield Scientific School at Yale has given it a decidedly Yale and New York medical flavor by limiting his accounts to "physiological chemistry" and the formation of the American Society of Biological Chemists, while overlooking the agricultural tradition exemplified by the work of Atwater. The alternative view of biochemistry in this period by Elmer V. McCollum of the Wisconsin experiment station and later Johns Hopkins University deemphasizes this New York orientation and sees most of the important work done in the history of nutrition, especially in his specialty, the vitamins, as taking place in an agricultural chemistry tradition. However many of the papers he cites, even by workers at experiment stations,were published in the *Journal of Biological Chemistry,* established by Chittenden's group in 1906. See Russell H. Chittenden, *The First Twenty-Five Years of the American Society of Biological Chemists* (New Haven, Conn.: American Society of Biological Chemists, 1945) and *The Development of Physiological Chemistry in the United States* (New York: Chemical Catalog, 1930); Elmer V. McCollum, *A History of Nutrition* (Boston: Houghton Mifflin, 1957).

28. For the history of the American Society of Animal Nutrition (Production), see C. S. Plumb, "History of the Society," *Proceedings of ASAP* 25 (1932): 377–79; J. R. Wiley, "The Growth of Our Society," *Proceedings of ASAP* 23 (1930): 9–13; E. B. Forbes, "The Past and the Future of the American Society of Animal Production," *Proceedings of ASAP* 6 (1913): 109–14; and W. H. Peters, "President's Address," *Journal of Animal Science* 1 (1942): 52–56; selected other items in the early volumes of the *Proceedings of ASAP;* Raymond W. Swift, "Henry Prentiss Armsby," *Journal of Nutrition* 54 (10 September 1955): 3–16.

29. Most useful for the history of dairy science are E. E. Lampard, *The Rise of the Dairy Industry*

*in Wisconsin: A Study in Agricultural Change, 1820–1920* (Madison, Wis.: State Historical Society of Wisconsin, 1963). Edward Beardsley, *H. L. Russell and Agricultural Science in Wisconsin* (Madison, Wis.: University of Wisconsin Press, 1969); John T. Schlebecker, *A History of American Dairying* (Chicago: Rand-McNally, 1967); Wilber J. Fraser, "The Formation of the American Dairy Science Association," *Journal of Dairy Science* 16 (1933): 583–86; various items in *Journal of Dairy Science* 1 (1917), and the fiftieth anniversary issue, 39 (1956): 619–908.

30. For poultry science, see the six historical articles on the fiftieth anniversary of the American Poultry Science Association in *Poultry Science* 37 (1958) and M. A. Jull, A. R. Lee et al., "The Poultry Industry" in USDA *Yearbook, 1924,* 377–456. The meetings of this society, as described by one of the former participants, seem to have been much more informal and frolicsome than those of the AAAS or the AAACES. Since the society was largely made up of young men recently off the farm and usually met in the summer on a university campus, the papers were supplemented by baseball games (the Thins vs. the Fats), track meets and various pranks. In 1920, a men's fraternity was started (the "Yellow Dogs") and in 1925 a ladies' auxiliary was added ("Yellow Cats," later "Pink Kittens") for female investigators, wives, and "sweethearts" who often came, since many young couples attended the meetings on their honeymoon. The women also elected the handsomest man present (the same one every year). Socially, the poultry men were a long distance from Russell Chittenden and the New York medical men. See also American Poultry Historical Society, *American Poultry History, 1823–1973: An Anthology Overview of 150 Years of People, Places and Progress* (Madison, Wis.: American Printing and Publishing, 1974), a useful compendium.

31. Since animal pathology did not succeed in forming a separate professional society and had rather colorless bureau chiefs at the USDA, the writings on its history are quite limited. There are two essays on it in the USDA *Yearbook, 1899,* and J. F. Smithcors, *The American Veterinary Profession* (Ames, Iowa: Iowa State University Press, 1963), the standard and very comprehensive history of the field. Other sources are obituaries and biographies of T. Smith and M. Dorset, especially Claude Dolman, "Texas Cattle Fever: A Commemorative Tribute to Theobald Smith," *Clio Medica* 4 (1969): 1–31; and the "Proccedings of the Second Annual Meeting of the Association of Experiment Station Veterinarians," Bureau of Animal Industry *Bulletin* 22 (USDA, 1898).

For Great Britain, see Ministry of Agriculture, Fisheries and Food, *Animal Health: A Centenary, 1865–1965* (London: Her Majesty's Stationery Office, 1965).

32. B. T. Galloway came to the USDA in 1887 to work on mycology but his studies were quickly lost in the haze that surrounds the early work of successful administrators. Other botanists who worked at the USDA include Erwin F. Smith who had a distinguished career starting with his studies of peach diseases in 1886. W. T. Swingle and H. J. Webber came in 1891 and 1892 and devoted their lives to citrus diseases; Mark Carleton worked briefly on the cereal rusts; and M. B. Waite studied the pear blight and other fruit diseases. The division was also famous for the number of women botanists it hired and for their able work on the fungi: among the most important were Effie Southworth (later Spalding) who studied the anthracnose diseases and Flora W. Patterson who directed the fungus herbarium.

33. Oswald Tippo, "The Early History of the Botanical Society of America," in *Fifty Years of Botany,* ed. William C. Steere (New York: McGraw Hill, 1958), 1–13 is a very helpful summary.

34. For plant pathology, see John A. Stevenson, "The Beginnings of Plant Pathology in North America," and S. E. A. McCallan, "The American Phytopathological Society—The First Fifty Years," both in *Plant Pathology: Problems and Progress, 1908–1958,* ed. C. S. Holton et al. (Madison, Wis.: University of Wisconsin Press, 1959); C. L. Shear, "First Decade of the American Phytopathological Society," *Phytopathology* 9 (1919): 165–70; Erwin F. Smith, "Plant Pathology: A Retrospect and Prospect," *Science* 15 (18 April 1902): 601–12; and idem, "Fifty Years of Plant Pathology," *Proceedings of the International Congress of Plant Sciences* 1 (1926): 13–46 with numerous plates; B. T. Galloway, "Plant Pathology: A Review of the Development of the Science in the United States," *Agricultural History* 2 (1928): 49–60; John A. Stevenson, "Plants, Problems, and Personalities: The Genesis of the Bureau of Plant Industry," *Agricultural History* 28 (1954): 155–62; Andrew D. Rodgers, *Erwin Frink Smith: A Story of North American Plant Pathology,* Memoirs of the American Philosophical Society 31 (1952); L. R. Jones, "Biographical Memoir of Erwin Frink Smith, 1854–1927," *Biographical Memoirs of the National Academy of Sciences* 21 (1941): 1–71; Herbert Hice Whetzel, *An Outline of the History of Phytopathology* (Philadelphia: W. B. Saunders, 1918); Herbert J. Webber, "History and Development of the Citrus Industry," in *The Citrus Industry,* 3 vols., eds. Walter Reuther, H. J. Webber et al. (Berkeley: University of California Press, 1967) 1: 1–37; plus obituaries of B. T. Galloway, Flora W. Patterson, and other workers at the

Bureau of Plant Industry, and historical prefaces to textbooks. A recent work by I. L. Conners, ed., *Plant Pathology in Canada* (Winnipeg, Manitoba: Canadian Phytopathological Society, 1972) is also suggestive.

35. "The Organization of the Ecological Society of America, 1914–1919," *Ecology* 19 (1938): 164–65; Richard A. Overfield, "Charles E. Bessey;" C. E. Bessey was also a strong administrator at the University of Nebraska in its formative years (Robert N. Manley, *Centennial History of the University of Nebraska,* 2 vols. [Lincoln, Neb.: University of Nebraska Press, 1969] vol. 1).

36. Most useful for the history of agronomy and the ASA are T. Lyttleton Lyon, "History of the Organization of the American Society of Agronomy," *Journal of the American Society of Agronomy* 25 (1933): 1–9 and "Notes on the History of the Society," ibid. 23 (1931): 1035; R. I. Throckmorton, "Origin, Aims, and Organization of the American Society of Agronomy," ibid. 33 (1941): 478–9 and "History of the American Society of Agronomy," ibid. 1135–40. C. W. Warburton, "A Quarter Century of Progress in the Development of Plant Science," ibid. 25 (1933), 25–36; "Agronomy and Botany," ibid. 6 (1914): 89–90; F. Lamson-Scribner, "Progress of Economic and Scientific Agrostology," USDA *Yearbook, 1899,* 374–76; Fred W. Powell, *The Bureau of Plant Industry* (Baltimore: Johns Hopkins Press, 1927); Mary W. M. Hargreaves, *Dry Farming in the Northern Great Plains, 1900–1925* (Cambridge, Mass.: Harvard University Press, 1957), especially chap. 8; Carl F. Kraentzel, *The Great Plains in Transition* (Norman, Okla.: University of Oklahoma Press, 1955); J. E. Weaver, "Some Ecological Aspects of Agriculture in the Prairie," *Ecology* 8 (1917): 1–17; and various obituaries of Mark Carleton. "The History of Western Range Research," *Agricultural History* 18 (1944): 127–43 by the Division of Range Research, Forest Service, USDA discusses the area that did not become farmland.

37. For soil bacteriology, see: Selman A. Waksman, *Jacob G. Lipman: Agricultural Scientist, Humanitarian* (New Brunswick, N.J.: Rutgers University Press, 1966), "The Background of Soil Science," *Soil Science* 101 (1966): 6–10, and "Soil Microbiology in 1924: An Attempt at an Analysis and a Synthesis," ibid. 19 (1925): 20–46; P. E. Brown, "The Beginnings and Development of Soil Microbiology in the United States," ibid. 40 (1935): 49–58; and Alexis A. J. deSigmond, "Development of Soil Science," ibid. 77–86.

38. The best sources on the history of soil science are: Charles E. Kellogg, "We Seek; We Learn," in USDA, *SOIL: Yearbook, 1957,* 1–11; A. G. McNall, "The Development of Soil Science," *Agricultural History* 5 (1931): 43–51; Harvey W. Wiley, "The Relation of Chemistry to the Progress of Agriculture," USDA, *Yearbook, 1899,* 201–58; Gustavus A. Weber, *The Bureau of Chemistry and Soils* (Baltimore: Johns Hopkins University Press, 1928); Margaret Rossiter, *The Emergence of Agricultural Science: Justus Liebig and the Americans, 1840–1880* (New Haven, Conn.: Yale University Press, 1975). For the Hilgard-Whitney controversies, see Hans Jenny, *E. W. Hilgard and the Birth of Modern Soil Science* (Pisa, Italy: Agrochimica, 1961), especially chap. 4; Eugene W. Hilgard, *Soils* (New York: Macmillan, 1906), especially chap. 18, and n. 39 below. Obituaries of Whitney are brief and uninformative. For C. F. Marbut, see Soil Science Society of America, *Life and Work of C. F. Marbut: A Memorial Volume* (n.p., n.d. [c. 1940]). The California soils proved especially difficult and long eluded even Marbut's classification (Hans Jenny et al., "Exploring the Soils of California," in *California Agriculture,* ed. Hutchison, p. 334). Soil science in Britain is discussed in Sir E. John Russell, *The Land Called Me: An Autobiography* (London: George Allen & Unwin, 1956).

39. Henry Menard, *Science: Growth and Change;* Rossiter, *Emergence of Agricultural Science,* 122–23; Samuel W. Johnson, "Agricultural Chemistry—Soil Analysis," *American Journal of Science* 32 (1861): 233–52; Eugene W. Hilgard, "The Objects and Interpretations of Soil Analysis," ibid. 22 (1881): 183–97; "On Soil Analyses and Their Utility," ibid. 4 (1872): 434–45.

40. I have found no history of Section M of the AAAS, but *Science* 41 (26 February 1916): 330–32 describes its first meeting. See also L. O. Howard, *Fighting the Insects,* 228–29.

41. Whether basic research in the agricultural sciences would have fared better in privately endowed institutions than it did in governmental ones was occasionally discussed, as in Raymond Pearl, "The Need for Endowed Agricultural Research," *Science* 37 (1913): 707–9. Plant physiologists in the 1950s were still complaining that though their field was very well supported in the United States, much of the work was agriculturally oriented (F. W. Went, "Fifty Years of Plant Physiology in the U.S.A.," in *Fifty Years of Botany,* ed. Campbell Steere [New York: McGraw-Hill, 1958], p. 623), although the Boyce Thompson Institute for Plant Research in Yonkers, N.Y. had been established in 1922 to overcome this limitation.

42. For the history of extension work in the United States, see A. C. True, *A History of Agri-*

*cultural Extension Work in the U.S., 1785–1923* (USDA, 1928); Gladys Baker, *The County Agent* (Chicago: University of Chicago Press, 1939), and most recently Roy V. Scott, *The Reluctant Farmer: The Rise of Agricultural Extension to 1914* (Urbana, Ill.: University of Illinois Press, 1970). But the impact of federal support of extension work on certain fields, as home economics, seems not to have been studied. One other response of the USDA to the clamor around 1912 for more intelligible bulletins was to create in 1913, in collaboration with the AAACES, the *Journal of Agricultural Research*. This serial was rapidly made superfluous by the rise of more specialized professional journals, and though it lasted into the 1940s, its support from the USDA was endangered as early as 1919 and its prospects discussed annually at the AAACES meetings. See especially Raymond Pearl, ''The Publication of the Results of Investigations Made in Experiment Stations,'' *Proceedings of the AAACES* 29 (1915): 186–91, plus discussion.

    43. Additional items on British agricultural science (see nn. 19, 24, 31, and 38) are: E. John Russell, *A History of Agricultural Science in Great Britain, 1620–1954* (London: Allen & Unwin, 1966); J. A. S. Watson, *History of the Royal Agricultural Society of England, 1839–1939* (London: Royal Agricultural Society, 1939); P. J. Perry, ed., *British Agriculture, 1875–1914* (London: Metheuen, 1973); Christine Orwin and Edith H. Whetham, *History of British Agriculture, 1846–1914* (London: Archon Books, 1964); and G. B. Masefield, *A Short History of Agriculture in the British Colonies* (Oxford: Clarendon Press, 1972). A. C. True and D. J. Crosby, *Agricultural Experiment Stations in Foreign Countries,* USDA Office of Experiment Stations Bulletin 112 (1902, rev. ed. 1904) has data on 750 stations in 40 countries.

# The Application
# of Science to Industry

*JOHN RAE*

The interrelationship of science, technology, and industry is taken for granted today—summed up, not altogether accurately, under the rubric "research and development." Yet historically this widespread faith in the economic virtues of science is a relatively recent phenomenon, dating back in the United States about 150 years, and in the Western world as a whole not over 300 years at most. Even in this current era of large-scale, intensive research and development, the interrelationships involved in this process are frequently misunderstood. Until the coming of the Industrial Revolution, science and technology evolved for the most part independently of each other. Then as industrialization became increasingly complicated, the craft techniques of preindustrial society gradually gave way to a technology based on the systematic application of scientific knowledge and scientific methods. This changeover started slowly and progressed unevenly. Until late in the nineteenth century, only a few industries could use scientific techniques or cared about using them. The list expanded noticeably after 1870, but even then much of what passed for the application of science was "engineering science" rather than basic science.[1]

Nevertheless, by the middle of the nineteenth century the rapid expansion of scientific knowledge and of public awareness, if not understanding, of it had created a belief that the advance of science would in some unspecified manner automatically generate economic benefits. The widespread and usually uncritical acceptance of this thesis led in turn to the assumption that the application of science to industrial purposes was a linear process, starting with fundamental science, then proceeding to applied science or technology, and through them to industrial use. This is probably the most common pattern, but it is not invariable. New areas of science have been opened up and fundamental discoveries made as a result of attempts to solve a specific technical or economic problem. Thermodynamics grew out of a search for methods of determining the efficiency of a steam engine, and Louis Pasteur began the study of microorganisms when he was commissioned to find a way to improve the quality of French beer. Conversely, William Thompson (Lord Kelvin) made his reputation with basic research in thermodynamics and electricity: he also augmented his income handsomely as a consultant, conspicuously on the Atlantic cable and on the Niagara Falls power project. In sum, the science-technology-industry relationship may flow in several different ways, and the particular channel it will follow depends on the individual situation. It may at times even be multidirectional.

## The American Background: Preliminary Steps

In its science, technology, and industrial development, the United States has been an integral part of Western civilization, and in its attitude toward and utilization of science it has basically reflected the general pattern of Western culture. However, there have been variations and adaptations. Since America was a new country, rapidly expanding both physically and economically, there was normally more work to be done than there were hands available to do it. There was therefore a premium on devising techniques or gadgets that supplemented labor. It was important to be able to make devices that worked, but it was not important to know why they worked. The main goal was to get things done. In addition, colonial America, and the United States until late in the nineteenth century, lacked the well-established universities of Europe or any considerable body of "gentleman scientists" free to indulge their intellectual curiosity. Thus, what American tradition there was minimized the pursuit of science for its own sake and magnified, quite out of proportion, the untutored but ingenious gadgeteer.[2] As one consequence, advocacy of support for such science as existed in early- and mid-nineteenth-century America was markedly utilitarian in its nature.[3]

One reason for the glorification of the cut-and-try tinkerer was that the technical needs of America, unlike those of Eruope, were not filled by trained craftsmen. There were craftsmen in America, and good ones, but there were never enough, and American society was too fluid for European craft traditions to take root. In any case there was no reason why a tradition that was already on the decline in the Old World should flourish in the New.[4] In early America much of the work that in Europe would have been done by trained craftsmen was of necessity performed by self-taught handymen—hence the strength of "cut-and-try." The ingenious tinkerer enjoyed an astonishing longevity as an American folkhero, reaching an apex in fact in the twentieth century with Thomas A. Edison and Henry Ford—though Edison depended far more on a well-equipped laboratory and a scientifically trained staff than his popular image suggested.

Yet even while "cut-and-try" was dominant, there was continued urging that America should exploit the utilitarian benefits of science. The Franklin Institute as early as the 1830s had as one of its announced functions the education of mechanics who would be able to apply science to their work.[5] This was not a program for educating engineers, but for giving some scientific background to practicing artisans. This urging became more persuasive as subsequent developments brought science and industry into closer relationship—e.g., industrial applications of chemistry in mining and metallurgy, petroleum, and the chemical industry itself and the emergence of electric power.

It was one thing to proclaim the utilitarian values of science, quite another to implement them. The effective application of science to industry required an institutional structure that the United States and almost all other countries except Germany lacked until late in the nineteenth century. American industry was quite willing to use the resources of science and even to support research when it was perceived to be advantageous to do so, but the initial efforts were matters of individual relationships, some of them reasonably substantial but none resulting in any permanent organization. Before 1870 the longest-lasting such relationship was Samuel L. Dana's service as chemist for the Merrimack Manufacturing Company of Lowell, Massachusetts from 1834 to 1868. Dana was a physician in Waltham, Mass., who became interested in textile chemistry, especially dyeing, and established a laboratory in Waltham in 1826 for analysis and testing.[6] He was frequently called to Lowell as a consultant and finally, after two years' study in Europe, was invited to move there on a regular appointment by the company.

Lowell also provided the setting for the experimental work of James B. Francis and Uriah Boyden on water turbines.[7] The promoters of Drake's oil well in 1859 sought advice from Benjamin Silliman, Jr., Professor of Chemistry at Yale, regarding the commercial possibilities of petroleum, and the most eminent American chemists and geologists were consulted freely during and after the 1850s by Western mining enterprises. Silliman himself earned $50,000 on a consulting tour of the West in 1864.[8] Thus over a span of years there was an accumulation of individual contributions to the application of science and scientific methods of industry. These individual steps laid the foundation for the acceptance of organized industrial research.

## The Creation of Institutional Structures

After 1870 institutional structures for promoting scientific research and its application to industry developed on an extensive scale and in time effectively replaced the individual, ad hoc arrangements of the past. The first and most obvious focus for the development of these institutional structures was the engineering profession. At the end of the American War of Independence, George Washington urged the creation of a military academy with the training of engineers as one of its principal functions. This institution attained its full stature after the War of 1812 when it was, for a generation, the only college of engineering in the United States. Its curriculum was organized by Claudius Crozet, a graduate of the French Ecole Polytechnique who became West Point's first professor of engineering. He modeled the education of engineers on his own training in France, which stressed a foundation of basic sciences and mathematics.

Even in these early years, West Point contributed only about 15 percent of the country's engineers, but because of their academic training, their influence was far out of proportion to their numbers.[9] Their obvious value in nonmilitary work may well have saved the Military Academy from extinction at the hands of egalitarian enthusiasts during the Jacksonian period.[10] Before 1860 most other American engineers were self-taught and trained on the job; the Erie Canal and the early railroads provided the training grounds for a number of distinguished figures—John B. Jervis and Moncure Robinson, for instance.

By the 1850s this situation was perceptibly changing, clearly indicating that on-the-job training was becoming increasingly inadequate. Other institutions for engineering were gaining stature: Rensselaer, founded in 1824 but offering only a one-year program until about 1840; Norwich University in Vermont; the Naval Academy; the Lawrence and Sheffield Scientific Schools at Harvard and Yale (despite their names, they were schools of engineering). Moreover, engineering courses were being added to the curricula of existing colleges and universities, especially the new state universities, which were less inhibited by the classical tradition.

This process accelerated after 1860. The Massachusetts Institute of Technology was founded in 1861, and a year later Congress passed the Morrill Land-Grant College Act, which provided for the establishment in every state of at least one institution committed to higher education in, among other things, "the mechanic arts." In 1900 the list of privately supported engineering colleges included Case, Carnegie, Stevens, Worcester Polytechnic Institute, and the precursors of the Illinois and California Institutes of Technology.

By the 1880s, earlier than has previously been assumed, academically educated engineers outnumbered the self-taught, trained-on-the-job products of earlier years.[11] The engineering students of the period were the products of middle-class families, concentrated primarily at the lower rather than the upper end of the class.[12] Yet they came from environments in which education was considered to have value—even if it was frequently a monetary value—and in which there was some recognition of the kind of abstract thought required in science. It was predominantly through these engineers that science was transmitted to industry. The transmission occurred, as a rule indirectly, through the engineering sciences; however, it did occur—more and more superseding the "cut-and-try" methods of earlier years.

The college-bred engineers of the late nineteenth century were generally well equipped to use the sciences. The French model of engineering education, initially introduced at West Point, remained a powerful influence in America, so that although curricula were likely to be strongly "practical"—courses in surveying, engineering drawing, machine shop practice, etc.—they always contained a substantial amount of mathematics and the physical sciences. The leading institutions like MIT also provided instruction in English, foreign languages, and economics.

Coupled with the expansion of engineering education was the founding of professional engineering societies, reflecting both a rise in professional consciousness and an accelerating complexity of technology that fragmented engineering into more and more specialized segments.

The American Society of Civil Engineers was formed in 1852, after several earlier unsuccessful attempts. At that time, the term "civil engineer" in the United States still included all but strictly military engineers. In Great Britain civil and mechanical engineers had separated ten years earlier, less because of professional necessity than because of the refusal of the Institution of Civil Engineers to admit George Stephenson to membership—a reflection of rivalry between the older generation of highway and waterway engineers and the new breed of railway engineers.

The American situation was different. It is illustrative of the way the American economy expanded and of the most urgent pressures on American technology at the time that the first separation in the engineering profession occurred with the formation of the American Institute of Mining Engineers in 1871. Between that time and 1920, practically all the principal engineering societies in the United States were established, reflecting in their proliferation the expansion of the economy and an accompanying growth in the variety of its technical needs. As examples, the American Society of Mechanical Engineers (1880) was formed in response to the demands of intensive mechanization in industry and transportation; the Institute of Electrical Engineers (1884), now IEEE to include electronics, followed close on the heels of the commercial application of electricity for power and light; the Society of Naval Engineers (1888) coincided with the revival of American naval power after its post–Civil War stagnation; the Society of Automotive Engineers (1904) was an obvious response to the rapid growth of motor vehicle manufacturing; and the American Institute of Chemical Engineers (1912) symbolized the elaboration of chemical manufacture and the developments in petroleum refining created by the mounting demand for automotive fuels. The centrifugal effect of this trend toward specialized organizations was partially offset by the founding of the United Engineering Societies in 1904 and the Engineering Foundation ten years later.

Concurrent with the expansion of organization came a significant increase in the total number of engineers—from about 7,300 in 1870 to 136,000 in 1920, according to the Bureau of the Census.[13] In the words of Raymond H. Merritt, "Technology brought into history a momentous power, which centered in the capacity to utilize mechanical strength in the production and distribution of material goods. . . . The engineering profession was primarily responsible for nineteenth century American technological growth."[14]

As has been mentioned, the engineering profession was, and is, the principal agency for the transmission of the findings of science to industry. There have been several channels for this transmission. One must point, in the first instance, to the large number of engineers in industry, not only in the aggregate but in proportion to the total work force. The ratio of engineers per thousand workers rose from 0.4 in 1880 to 2.4 in 1920.[15] To this must be added the high proportion of engineers in industrial management—a phenomenon that was peculiar to American industry during this period, or at least more pronounced in American industry than elsewhere.[16] Recalling his enrollment as a student at MIT, Paul W. Litchfield, former president and board chairman of the Goodyear Tire and Rubber Company, observed:

Harvard men used to say the Tech would turn out engineers but that the nation would turn to Harvard for the heads of business. Some of the men who were in school with me, however, got along all right, and I got a little satisfaction out of it as Alfred P. Sloan, class of '95, became head of General Motors, Gerard Swope, also '95, head of General Electric, Irenée du Pont, class of '97, was made head of that great company, and Roger Babson, class of '98, became a world-famous economist.[17]

The impact of this influx of engineers in both technical and managerial roles was accentuated by changing conditions in industry. More complex technologies demanded people with systematic training in the application of scientific principles, a development that, among other things, handicapped the bench-trained engineer in competing with the academic product.[18] The development of electric power and electronic communications affords a conspicuous example, since electricity is not readily susceptible to "cut-and-try." It is not, however, the unique and exclusive example as suggested by a biographer of Peter Drucker:

Engineers had been associated with coal and soot, with grease and lampblack. With the coming of electricity there appeared a new breed of engineers, cleaner and more scientific. They were socially on a higher level, and the whole world of industry became more worthy of study. Just as scientific agriculture began with the invention of gumboots— without which the scientist never went beyond the farm gate—so the science of management began with the electrical plant, which was clean enough for the theorist to explore.[19]

This quotation admittedly relates to the "science of management" rather than to the strictly technical aspect of industrial operations, but it is still an exaggeration. There was indeed "a new breed of engineers," but they were coming from the engineering colleges and did not owe their existence to electricity alone. The scientific approach also emerged in the soot and grease atmosphere of steel and petroleum, and this approach included managerial problems. Industrial engineers, concerned with improving the techniques of production, were the principal contributors to the development of cost accounting in the late nineteenth century.[20] And Frederick W. Taylor, the founder of "scientific management"— not necessarily identical with the "science of management" but certainly closely related—began his work in the machine shop of the Midvale Steel Company, outside Philadelphia. Taylor was a mechanical engineer and a graduate of the Stevens Institute of Technology. Frank Gilbreth, who with his wife Lillian was Taylor's chief competitor in the development of scientific management, was also an engineer. Mrs. Gilbreth was a psychologist, and in their collaboration, the Gilbreths made what was probably the first application of the social sciences to industrial management, at least in the United States.

Finally, the engineering societies provided outlets for the dissemination of technical information, much of it consciously intended for industrial application. They all had (and still have) proceedings, journals, and transactions through which technical papers were published and circulated to members, who in turn transmitted the appropriate items of information to their respective industrial firms.

This function of the engineering societies was augmented by the engineering colleges, where laboratory work, supplementary to the instructional program, was undertaken in response to industrial needs. The pioneer of this activity was Robert L. Thurston, a graduate of a Brown University program that included civil engineering, the physical sciences, mathematics, history, languages, and literature.[21] After service in the Navy during the Civil War and later on the faculty of the Naval Academy, he went to the newly founded Stevens Institute of Technology in 1871 to organize its program in mechanical engineering. He recognized that there were technical problems in industry that required properly organized research laboratories for their solution and that industry itself did not yet possess such facilities. Consequently, he persuaded the trustees of Stevens to establish a laboratory in 1874, the first of its kind in the United States, in which mechanical engineering students would work on industrial problems as part of their regular instruction. Thurston's own description of the program states:

The opportunity thus came to us at once to secure opportunities to investigate previously unstudied problems, and to introduce scientific methods of research and investigation of professional problems, while, at the same time, securing some pecuniary return that might be made use of effectively to help in building up my department ... This was the first time, so far as I know, that this now general and recognized essential of an engineering program was made an integral part of any school of engineering.[22]

Thurston became Director of the Sibley College of Engineering at Cornell University in 1884 and there instituted a similar but larger-scale program that included electrical as well as mechanical engineering.

Scientific societies, like engineering societies, also grew rapidly between 1870 and 1920. In an intriguing parallel, just as the specialized engineering societies branched off from the American Society of Civil Engineers, so many of the scientific societies were spin-offs from the American Association for the Advancement of Science. The reason was the same: the fast-growing body of scientific knowledge demanded more highly specialized organizations.[23] However, these societies were less directly concerned with industrial applications than were the engineering organizations. In fact, because of the increasing emphasis on basic science strongly reflected in the growth of graduate research programs in American universities, there was even some disposition to avoid strictly practical problems.

This development was underlined by Joseph Henry's policies as head of the National Academy of Sciences. The Academy was founded in 1863 for the publicly expressed purpose of marshaling the nation's scientific talent to aid in the prosecution of the Civil War. Yet the Academy contributed little of practical significance to the war effort and in 1867 its new president, Joseph Henry, set forth a major plan of reorganization. Original research became the primary qualification for Academy membership, thereby shifting "the emphasis in the purpose of the Academy from practical service to the government to the recognition of 'abstract science.' "[24]

Nevertheless, the prevalent American attitude, shared by the scientific community itself, continued to emphasize the pursuit of science for useful and beneficial applications. Despite his policies at the National Academy, Henry himself applied his knowledge by giving advice to Alexander Graham Bell, as he had earlier done to S. F. B. Morse. In any event, the dissemination of scientific knowledge, especially in fields like chemistry, electricity, and geology, of necessity opened new possibilities for industrial application, and the scientific societies were the primary agents of this dissemination. A conspicuous step in this direction was the founding of the *Journal of Industrial and Engineering Chemistry* by the American Chemical Society in 1909.

Although the period between 1870 and 1920 saw the emergence of a large number of trade associations, a natural accompaniment of rapid industrial growth, their role in fostering research and the application of science seems limited. They were essentially promotional organizations, chiefly concerned with collecting and distributing data on business matters—markets, prices, and so on. Yet they were disseminators of information and in many industries some of this information was technical. Four of the associations founded in this period have been singled out as important contributors to industrial research: the National Federation of Textiles (1872), the American Paper and Pulp Association (1878), the Steel Founders Society of America (1902), and the National Association of Manufacturers (1895).[25] The list should also include the American Iron and Steel Association (1866), whose bulletin was a prolific publisher of technical papers.

The automobile industry produced a special situation. The famous, or notorious, Selden patent came under the control of an organization called the Association of Licensed Automobile Manufacturers (ALAM), formed for just this purpose in 1903.[26] The ALAM collected a small royalty on every car licensed under the patent, and as part of its operations maintained a testing laboratory in Hartford, Connecticut and supported a program for technical standardization. When in 1911 the Selden patent was held "valid but not infringed" (by the Ford Motor Company), the ALAM was dissolved. It was replaced in 1914 by the National Automobile Chamber of Commerce, precursor of the Motor Vehicle Manufacturers' Association, which in 1915 became the administrative agency for an agreement on cross-licensing patents that would prevent the industry from being constantly entangled in litigation. The standardization program of the ALAM was taken over by the Society of Automotive Engineers, which still carries it on. Until 1920 this was the only serious research program associated with the automobile industry, which then and indeed for long after remained strictly "cut-and-try." Charles F. Kettering and Thomas F. Midgley began their research on automotive fuels (resulting in ethyl gasoline) in 1916, but in cooperation with Indiana and Jersey Standard rather than the automobile manufacturers.[27]

Finally the role of the government in the support of identifiably useful scientific activities in this period must not be overlooked. As A. Hunter Dupree points out in his major study of *Science and the Federal Government,* it was the Civil War and

the peculiarly public and centralized nature of military problems that ineluctably forced the government into the business of using experimental science to evaluate technology. In these research efforts, spasmodic and on the fringes of the great organizational accomplishments of the war, a consistent relation between science and technology appears for the first time. This new union, of course, far exceeded the bounds of the war effort, because it was one of the most significant changes of the nineteenth century—the one in which the popular mind eventually linked science with the production of material wealth... Sometimes technology benefited directly by the application of a principle discovered in the general pursuit of knowledge. More often science entered technology in the guise of replacing cut-and-try with more orderly forms of experiment.[28]

Given this attitude, governmental sponsorship of scientific activities (it is not really accurate to designate them all as "research") was bound to accentuate the utilitarian bent of American science. This was certainly true of agricultural research which until the First World War was by far the largest field for government-supported science. In other areas, the establishment of the United States Geological Survey in 1879 exemplified the effort to incorporate science into the structure of the American government. Its first director was John Wesley Powell, a geologist with little formal training, an explorer of the Colorado River, and the first person to point out forcefully and vigorously that a land system designed for the well-watered East was quite unsuited for the arid and semiarid regions west of the 100th meridian. It can be reasonably argued that the Geological Survey was created for Powell and very largely by him.

Defining the functions of the Geological Survey, Powell spelled out the prevalent approach to science: "The statesmen of America who compose and have composed our National Legislature have been not averse to the endowment of scientific research when such research is properly related to the industries of the people. The endowment of science should be very limited and scrupulously confined to those objects of research which... could not be undertaken by individuals."[29] In its operation, the Geological Survey has adhered to Powell's goal of utility, but it has not by any means restricted itself in the way he proposed. It has produced a vast amount of information on mineral and other natural resources, and this information has, of course, been freely available for industrial use.

The founding of the Bureau of Standards illustrates even more forcefully the accepted belief that the government should employ science to promote the economy. Pressure for such an organization began in the 1880s with agitation for the establishment of national standards of electrical measurement.[30] This task was initially assigned to the Office of Weights and Measures of the Coast and Geodetic Survey (the name was changed from Coast Survey in 1878), but the arrangement was unsatisfactory, and the Bureau of Standards was created in 1901. In addition to serving as the custodian of and testing agency for scientific and technical standards, the Bureau was charged with investigating properties of materials "when such data are of general importance to scientific or manufacturing interests." In short, service to industry was one of the primary motives for the creation of the Bureau of Standards.

This service role was still more pronounced in the Bureau of Mines, which was established in 1910 to assume a function that had originally been performed by the Geological Survey—the testing of fuels and the investigation of mine explosions. In addition, the Bureau of Mines was commissioned to study mining technology with a view to promoting safety and improving mining conditions. Three years later the Bureau's scope was expanded to include "scientific and technological investigations, the promotion of safety and efficiency, the study of economic conditions affecting the industry, and the conservation of mineral resources."[31]

Comparable activities developed in other governmental agencies during the late nineteenth and early twentieth century. In this period, the Smithsonian Institution, together with the National Academy of Sciences, was the home of what little basic research—in the current sense of the term—was supported by the federal government. Yet the Smithsonian also engaged in application by becoming the sponsor of Samuel P. Langley's aeronautical experiments. It was not a successful application, but research, whether basic or applied, is bound to have failures as well as successes, and the failure may be just as important for the diffusion of knowledge.

## The Establishment of Industrial Research

The culminating stage in the application of science to industry in the United States was the systematic organization of industrial research, by which is meant research consciously and specifically directed to the utilization of scientific knowledge and scientific methods for discovering new products, improving or finding new uses for existing products, and devising new or improved techniques and processes for production, transportation, or communication. Industrial research was not an American innovation. It was firmly established in Germany earlier than in any other major industrial country and was in fact a vital contributor to the phenomenal growth of German industry after 1870. American and British businessmen of this period were constantly being exhorted to imitate the German example or risk falling behind.

It would be possible, but rather unrewarding, to argue the question of priority. Analytic and consulting laboratories can be identified in the United States as far back as the 1830s.[32] None, however, had a discernibly significant effect on industrial development. A more definite beginning can be seen in the iron and steel industry during the period of the introduction of the Bessemer and

Siemens-Martin processes for making steel. The Bessemer process, as is known, was independently discovered in the United States by William Kelly, but Kelly himself failed to develop his discovery, in large part because he did not understand the chemistry involved and could not control the quality of the product.[33] However, when a steelworks with rights to Kelly's patents was built at Wyandotte, Michigan in 1863, it included a laboratory to determine the quality of the pig iron that was used—the first such laboratory to be linked with an American iron- or steelworks.[34] The Bessemer process proper was brought to the United States in 1865 by a brilliant engineer, Alexander L. Holley, a product of the same Brown University program that Thurston had attended. Holley and his associates bought the American rights to the Bessemer patents and transplanted the technology; a year later, they and the Kelly group pooled their patents. In 1872, William F. Durfee, the chemist in charge of the Wyandotte plant, went to the Midvale Steel Company when problems developed in its open-hearth (Siemens-Martin) process. Durfee and an associate, Charles F. Brinley, a metallurgist, analyzed the plant's raw materials, kept records of trial runs, and after repeated efforts managed to get the process functioning successfully.[35]

The critical need for accurate control of materials in the manufacture of steel led to other steps. In 1866 the Iron and Steel Association promoted an "Ironmasters' Laboratory" in Philadelphia in order to "encourage the development of workable bodies of iron ore and to inform producers of the quantity and quality of the metal they would yield."[36] In its early years the Carnegie firm also discovered the utility of chemists:

Companies producing steel were beginning to state their requirements in chemical terms, the principal one being that the metal should contain not more than 1/10 of one per cent of phosphorous. For every increase of 1/100 of one per cent of phosphorous, the companies deducted 25 cents per ton from the price they would pay. Also at a critical period the Lucy furnace suffered a "chill" upon the substitution of high-grade Lake Superior ores for the low-grade ores on which it had been running well. As a result the company hired a German chemist, Dr. Fricke, and in the words of Andrew Carnegie, "Great secrets did the doctor open to us. Iron stone from mines that had a high reputation was found to contain ten, fifteen, and even twenty per cent less iron than it had been credited with. Mines that had hitherto had a poor reputation were found to be yielding superior ore. Nine-tenths of all the uncertainties of pig-iron making were dispelled under the burning sun of chemical knowledge."[37]

Such operations were limited to the testing of ores and furnace runs, but they were recognition that certain aspects of science had industrial value. If they were not as yet industrial research, they were at least a prelude.

By an odd quirk of history, the first important industrial laboratory was organized in Menlo Park, New Jersey in 1876 by Thomas A. Edison—the personification, in his public image at any rate, of the ingenious self-taught tinkerer. Yet here was acknowledgement by the master cut-and-try genius of his day that this time-honored technique was no longer adequate for dealing with the complexities of contemporary industry or even for producing usable inventions. The

Menlo Park laboratory has been termed "perhaps Edison's greatest invention."[38] In its early years it was the only full-time industrial research organization in the country with both excellent physical equipment and a talented staff, such as Francis R. Upton, an electrical engineer who had spent a year in Berlin studying under Hermann von Helmholz. Interestingly enough, the founding of Menlo Park came before the industrial achievements of late-nineteenth-century Germany were widely known and the contributions of research to them fully understood.

Edison intended the laboratory to make studies of specific projects that would yield patentable discoveries and profits. It did so very successfully, and its success, coupled with Edison's reputation, was undoubtedly of material assistance in persuading the leaders of industry that scientific research had something to offer them. A second type of industrial research was exemplified by the founding, in Boston in 1886, of the Arthur D. Little research laboratories which undertook industrial research on a consulting basis. The advantages of this kind of research organization were twofold: it offered research facilities to small companies that could not afford their own laboratories; and it permitted greater leeway in approaching problems than would have been acceptable in the few existing company laboratories while, at the same time, providing an atmosphere somewhat more appreciative of industrial requirements than was likely to be found in a university science laboratory of that period.

A third method of associating industry and the independent research laboratory was the nonprofit research institute, which seems to have originated in observations of the mutually advantageous relationships that existed between industry and the universities in countries like Germany and France. The most prominent pioneer in transplanting this system to the United States was Robert Kennedy Duncan, professor of industrial chemistry at the University of Kansas. After extensive travel in Europe to study industry-university cooperation, Duncan in 1907 initiated industrial fellowships at the University of Kansas, a system whereby a company could establish a temporary fellowship for the study of a specific problem.[39] Shortly afterward his ideas came to the attention of Andrew W. Mellon, who was so impressed with their potential that in 1911 he and his brother, Richard B. Mellon, arranged for Duncan to organize an enlarged program of industrial fellowships at the University of Pittsburgh. In 1915, a year after Duncan's death, the program was endowed and formally constituted as the Mellon Institute of Industrial Research. Although it initially continued to be associated with the University of Pittsburgh, it was later separately incorporated and subsequently merged with the Carnegie Institute of Technology as Carnegie-Mellon University. Other such organizations followed—but all after 1920.

However, the most striking and unquestionably the most significant development of the period from 1870 to the outbreak of the First World War was the growth of company-owned research laboratories. Growth was slow and on a moderate scale for the first twenty years; in fact the laboratories established prior to 1890 were for the most part analytical and testing rather than research organizations. One such laboratory attained quite impressive proportions for its time. In

1875 a chemist, Charles R. Dudley, was appointed to do advanced testing for the Pennsylvania Railroad. By the end of the century Dudley had thirty-four chemists working for him, and a program that had begun with the chemical composition and physical properties of steel rails had extended to axles, springs, paint and varnish, dyes, and coal.[40] Strictly speaking this was not a research laboratory, but it would be difficult to determine exactly where testing and analysis stopped and research began.

The 1880s saw preliminary moves toward what would eventually become major industrial research structures. In 1885 Hammond Hayes began to do experimental work for the American Bell Telephone Company in Boston. This activity grew to sufficient proportions for Theodore N. Vail to organize a central research and experimental division in American Telephone and Telegraph in 1907,[41] but it was not until 1925 that Bell Laboratories attained its independent status. Meanwhile, two of the most important early technological advances came from outside the organization: Michael Pupin's loading coil (1900), developed at Columbia University, and Lee de Forest's audion, produced in the traditional manner by an inventor working on his own.[42]

As we have seen, the petroleum industry had sought advice from chemists since its earliest days. This procedure became more important as the industry expanded. In the later 1880s, the Standard Oil Company found itself with ample new supplies of oil in the Lima-Indiana field, but the crude oil was so heavily sulfurated that it could not be made usable through existing techniques. The company invoked the assistance of a German-born chemist, Hermann Frasch (the inventor of the process that bears his name) for mining deep deposits of sulfur. Frasch went to work for Standard Oil in the summer of 1886, and after two years of experimentation, including several false starts, successfully solved the problems of "sour crude." This operation is regarded as the first large-scale application of chemical and engineering research to a refining problem in the United States.[43]

Frasch's status was that of an independent consultant. The institutionalization of chemical research within the petroleum industry actually began with Standard Oil's appointment of William H. Burton in 1889. Burton was a recent Ph.D. in chemistry from Johns Hopkins who went to Standard Oil somewhat to the dismay of his Hopkins mentor, Ira Remsen, who felt that a research chemist should not go into industry.[44] But Burton was a Clevelander who had grown up in a petroleum-laden atmosphere. His family lived near the Rockefellers and he had been introduced to chemistry at Western Reserve University by Edwin W. Morley, best known as A. A. Michelson's associate in the famous ether-drift experiments of 1887 and later.

Burton's first assignment was to assist Hermann Frasch, but after a very short time he was transferred to the new refinery at Whiting, Indiana—without equipment or quarters, or any definite mission except to work on quality control.[45] He was given his first laboratory building in 1895, by which time similar operations were being conducted at the Bayonne, N.J. and Point Richmond, California, refineries. At each of these installations, experiments beyond routine testing were undertaken as opportunities arose, but Burton's laboratory outstripped the others: "Especially between 1902 and 1907, the Whiting Refinery was the acknowledged center of research in petroleum chemistry, not only in the Standard Oil group but in the United States."[46] A few years later (1913), the value of this kind of research was fully demonstrated when a research team led by R. E. Humphreys, under Burton's supervision, developed the high-pressure gasoline cracking process that bears Burton's name.

The chemical industry might have been expected to take the lead in organizing American industrial research, particularly in view of the conspicuous example of the German chemical industry. That it did not was due to a special set of circumstances. The American chemical industry was dominated for an entire generation, from the Civil War until his death in 1889, by General Henry DuPont, president of the country's largest chemical company. DuPont devoted his quite considerable talents to the creation of a combination for restricting competition in the manufacture of explosives (the "Powder Trust"), but he ruled his own company as an absolute autocrat and resisted change stubbornly.[47] For example, he would have nothing to do with nitroglycerin and dynamite.

Nephew Lammot DuPont was a different type. In 1882 he organized the Repauno Chemical Company in New Jersey to manufacture nitroglycerin and included a small laboratory for his own research. He was killed, in fact, when carelessly handled nitroglycerin exploded in this laboratory. But he represented a new era. By the 1890s the Du Pont organization had come to recognize that powder-making could no longer be learned entirely on the powder line; a sound technical education was required.[48] Thus when the company was taken over and reorganized by Lammot's son, Pierre S. DuPont, along with his cousins Alfred and Coleman, Repauno became the site of a laboratory for research on explosives (1902).[49] A year later another laboratory, called the Experimental Station, was established near the company's headquarters in Wilmington, Delaware. The Experimental Station was consciously directed toward future growth; its staff was "to regard DuPont not as a producer of explosives alone, but as a chemical manufacturer ready to venture wherever its logical chemical interests might lead."[50] Although the initial interest was in products of nitrocellulose—lacquers, plastics, and photographic film—there was little development along this line for some time. The Experimental Station was a harbinger of the future; until after the First World War, DuPont remained primarily a manufacturer of explosives.

The most immediately successful work on synthetics in America in this period was done by Lee H. Baekeland, a Belgian chemist who came to the United States in 1890. After a variety of experiments in various areas of applied chemistry, Baekeland, working on his own, developed the plastic known as Bakelite. A far more successful chemist was Charles Martin Hall, coinventor of the Hall-Héroult electrolytic process for reducing aluminum. When the Pittsburgh Reduction Company, now the Aluminum Company of America, was formed in 1888 with Mellon support, Hall supervised its experimental work until his death in 1914.[51]

There was, however, no central research laboratory at Alcoa until after the First World War.

In its initiation of formal research, Eastman Kodak antedated DuPont by a year or two. In 1886, George Eastman appointed a chemist, Henry M. Reichenbach, expressly to do research on photographic film. A laboratory building was constructed at Kodak Park in Rochester in 1893, and in 1919 it was enlarged to facilitate research on any questions of a scientific nature that might have application to the photographic industry. Its director, appointed in 1912, was Dr. C. E. Kenneth Mees, an Englishman with training in both chemistry and physics who had been a manufacturer of photographic plates.[52] Mees is an interesting figure in that most of the scientists involved in industrial research at the time were chemists; Mees was one of the few representatives of physics. There were not many American physicists available, and most of the physics applied to industry was done so by engineers.

It was General Electric that founded the best-known of the pioneering American industrial research laboratories at Schenectady in 1900. Edison's laboratory at Menlo Park was one of its models; more directly it was inspired by the individual research and experimentation carried on for G.E. and its predecessors by Elihu Thomson, Charles P. Steinmetz, and Frank J. Sprague.[53] Thomson was directly responsible for the appointment of Willis R. Whitney, another chemist, with a Ph.D. from MIT, as the laboratory's first director. Thomson and Steinmetz envisioned a laboratory "free from production worries and able to pursue fundamental experimental investigations,"[54] and Whitney managed very capably to combine this goal with the need to justify the laboratory's existence by demonstrating that its work was valuable to the company. He also succeeded in recruiting a brilliant staff, notably William D. Coolidge and Irving Langmuir who were both, like himself, physical chemists. Langmuir would later win a Nobel Prize (1932) for research done at the laboratory on surface chemistry, research that grew out of studies on the incandescent lamp. While the Schenectady laboratory was not the first American industrial research laboratory, it was the first to demonstrate so effectively the wisdom of recruiting the best possible talent and giving it freedom to pursue its individual interests.

Westinghouse kept pace with its big competitor, opening a research laboratory in Pittsburgh in 1903. However, as with American Telephone and Telegraph, Westinghouse's outstanding application to science in this period occurred earlier and came from an external source, specifically Nikola Tesla's development of the polyphase current motor. Westinghouse bought Tesla's patents and took over the company Tesla had formed to exploit them. The commercial success achieved by Westinghouse was enhanced by Thomas A. Edison's repugnance for alternating current in any form, which reduced competition materially.[55]

Several other large corporations established laboratories in the years between the turn of the century and the First World War, but there is no need to enumerate them. Most were still organized for analysis and testing, or for working on specific problems that arose in the day-to-day operation of the business. However, they also contrived to find opportunities for longer-range studies, and they were increasingly encouraged to do so by management. Industrial research was still a minor element in the total structure of American industry, but if the age of "R. and D." was some distance in the future, at least the seed had been planted.

## The Influence of the First World War

When the First World War broke out, it became evident that American industrial research, corporate and otherwise, was still embryonic, certainly by comparison with what the science-oriented industries of Germany had accomplished. When Allied sea power cut off trade with Germany, shortages of dyes and other chemicals appeared immediately, and it was clear that the Germans had a marked qualitative edge in such areas as pharmaceuticals and optical instruments. It was also obvious that, in the country where powered, heavier-than-air flight had first been achieved and where people prided themselves on technical ingenuity, so little research and development had been done since the Kittyhawk flights that American aviation in 1916 was a joke and not, under the circumstances, a particularly humorous one.

Yet the spell of "cut-and-try" and the national faith in the inspired gadgeteer showed an astonishing ability to survive. When the Naval Consulting Board was created in 1915, Thomas A. Edison was made its chairman as a matter of course. Even though Edison was nearing seventy and had badly impaired hearing, the manifest expectation was that a stream of miracle weapons would be forthcoming under his leadership. And according to James B. Conant, when the United States entered the war, the American Chemical Society promptly offered the services of both the organization and its members to the government. The offer was declined, with thanks, by the War Department on the grounds that the department already had a chemist.[56]

But the needs of the situation were against the old tradition. As it was finally constituted, the Naval Consulting Board was composed predominantly of trained scientists and engineers, rather than cut-and-try inventors.[57] Only four of the twenty-two members did not hold degrees in science or engineering, and one of the four, Elmer L. Sperry, affords a striking example of the decline of "cut-and-try." Basically a self-taught inventor, although with some formal training in chemistry and physics, Sperry, like Edison, had come to appreciate the need for systematic research and experimentation. By 1914 he was advertising that his company had "a large experimental staff"—actually five engineers.[58] At the end of the war this number of engineers working on electrical control systems, gyroscopes, and the other areas of Sperry's interest had grown to twenty.

Two other organizations were created to marshal the nation's scientific and engineering talent in the war effort. In 1916 the National Academy of Sciences formed the National Research Council (NRC) in order to reach out beyond the somewhat restricted membership of the Academy, and a year earlier the National

Advisory Committee on Aeronautics (NACA) was organized to provide a research base for the much needed advancement of American aviation.[59]

Although it can scarcely be regarded as an achievement of American industrial research, one other phase of the scientific conduct of the war should be noted. At the instigation of Francis P. Garvan, the government established the Chemical Foundation, to administer some 4,500 German patents that had been taken over by the Alien Property Custodian under wartime legislation. The conscious hope was to aid American industry to remedy some of the deficiencies the war had revealed.[60] The function of the foundation was to use the income derived from licensing these patents to foster research in chemistry.

Both the NACA and the NRC would become distinguished research agencies in the future, but neither they nor the Naval Consulting Board contributed significantly to the war effort. Organized research was very much a novelty in the American experience. It took time to organize these agencies and put them into operation. Moreover, neither the Naval Consulting Board nor the NRC had clearly defined missions or adequate funding.[61] By the time they had resolved their internal problems and begun to work on viable projects, the war was over. Yet this was not wasted effort. Even though it contributed little to the immediate prosecution of the war, the NRC demonstrated enough promise to justify its establishment on a permanent basis. The Naval Consulting Board never progressed much beyond screening a mass of largely impractical inventions submitted by misguided amateurs, but its advocacy of a research laboratory led to the establishment of the Naval Research Laboratory in 1923. The NACA, of course, remained in existence to become one of the world's great centers of research in aerodynamics, eventually becoming the core of the National Aeronautics and Space Administration.

There was also an indirect long-range gain from these efforts. For the first time in American experience, scientists and engineers from industry, government, and the academic world came together to work cooperatively in group research. The National Research Council included distinguished professors of physics such as Michael Pupin of Columbia, Albert A. Michelson of Chicago, and Robert A. Millikan, then at the University of Chicago and later president of Caltech; John J. Carty, head of research at AT&T; Gano Dunn, president of the J. D. White Engineering Corporation; Charles P. Walcott, secretary of the Smithsonian Institution, and Samuel W. Stratton, director of the Bureau of Standards. It does not matter that their achievements were limited, indeed trivial when compared with what was done in World War II. There was a lesson to be learned—and it was. When the country returned to peacetime activity, it was ready for a new stage in the utilization of science by industry. There was a deepened realization by leaders of both industry and government that organized research had become not just a potential source of profit but a vital national need. It was by no means a universal realization, and its growth had been distinctly uneven. In the half-century from 1870 to 1920, the application of science through organized and systemic research was fully accepted by the chemical, electrical equipment, electrical communications, petroleum, and photographic industries—all with a recognizable dependence on science. Iron and steel used scientific advice to a somewhat lesser degree, and other industries virtually not at all—"cut-and-try" died hard. Yet the example had been set and its success confirmed by substantial results in those areas where industrial research was effectively employed. Gradually other industries became part of the pattern, leading to the great blossoming of applied science during the Second World War.

## *Notes*

1. Edwin Layton, "Mirror Image Twins: The Communities of Science and Technology," in *Nineteenth Century American Science: A Reappraisal,* ed. George Daniels (Evanston, Ill.: Northwestern University Press, 1972), pp. 214–22.

2. Some of the principal folk heroes of early American technology, like Whitney, Morse, Fulton, and Goodyear, were certainly ingenious but hardly untutored.

3. This attitude is amply documented in *The Pursuit of Knowledge in the Early American Republic,* eds. Alexandra Oleson and Sanborn C. Brown (Baltimore: The Johns Hopkins University Press, 1976).

4. The decline of the European craft tradition is brought out in A. Rupert Hall, "The Changing Technical Art," *Technology and Culture* 3 (Fall 1962): pp. 501–15.

5. Bruce Sinclair, "Science, Technology, and the Franklin Institute," in *The Pursuit of Knowledge,* ed., Oleson and Brown, p. 195.

6. Howard R. Bartlett, "The Development of Industrial Research in the United States," in *Research—A National Resource,* 3 vols., Report of the National Research Council to the National Resources Planning Board, December 1940 (Washington, D.C.: U.S. Government Printing Office, 1941), 2:25. See also, *National Cyclopedia of American Biography,* 30 vols. (New York: J. A. White, 1924), 8:167.

7. Edwin Layton, "Scientific Technology, 1845–1900: The Hydraulic Turbine and the Origins of American Industrial Research," (Paper presented at the bicentennial meeting, Society for the History of Technology, Washington, D.C., October 17, 1975); James B. Francis, "Lowell Hydraulic Experiments," in *Lowell: An Early American Industrial Community,* eds. L. S. Bryant and J. B. Rae (Cambridge, Mass.: Technology Press, 1950), pp. 66–74.

8. Carroll Pursell, "Science and Industry," in *Nineteenth Century American Science,* ed. Daniels, pp. 241–45.

9. The data on American engineers come from John B. Rae, "Engineers Are People," *Technology and Culture* 16 (July 1975): 404–18.

10. Daniel H. Calhoun, *The American Civil Engineer* (Cambridge, Mass.: Technology Press, 1960), pp. 164–65.

11. Rae, "Engineers Are People," p. 415.

12. Ibid., p. 416.

13. E. L. Brown, *The Professional Engineer* (New York: Russell Sage Foundation, 1936), p. 60.

14. Raymond H. Merritt, *Engineering in American Society* (Lexington, Ky.: University Press of Kentucky, 1969), p. 2.

15. W. H. G. Armytage, *The Rise of the Technocrats* (Toronto: University of Toronto Press, 1965), p. 172.

16. See for example, J. B. Rae, "Engineering Education as Preparation for Management," *Business History Review* 29 (March 1955): 64–74 and idem, "The Engineer as Manager," *Journal of Engineering Education* 48 (October 1957): 25–31.

17. P. W. Litchfield, *Industrial Voyage* (Garden City, N.Y.: Doubleday, 1954), p. 55.

18. This conflict as it relates to mechanic engineers is described in Monte Calvert, *The Mechanical Engineer in America* (Baltimore: The Johns Hopkins Press, 1967).

19. John J. Tarrant, *Drucker: The Man Who Invented the Corporate Society* (Boston: Cahner's, 1976), pp. viii–ix.

20. S. P. Garner, *Evolution of Cost Accounting to 1925* (Montgomery: University of Alabama Press, 1954), p. 346.

21. W. F. Durand, *Robert Henry Thurston* (New York: American Society of Mechanical Engineers, 1929), p. 15.

22. Ibid., p. 71.

23. For the creation of scientific societies during this period, see Ralph S. Bates, *Scientific Societies in the United States*, 3d ed. (Cambridge, Mass.: MIT Press, 1965), pp. 85–136; and Daniel J. Kevles, "Physics, Mathematics, and Chemistry in America, 1870–1915. A Comparative Analysis," in this volume.

24. A. Hunter Dupree, *Science in the Federal Government: A History of Policies and Activities to 1940* (Cambridge, Mass.: Harvard University Press, 1957), p. 147.

25. Bates, *Scientific Societies in the United States,* p. 107.

26. J. B. Rae, *American Automobile Manufacturers* (Philadelphia: Chilton, 1959), p. 75.

27. Ibid., p. 155.

28. Dupree, *Science in the Federal Government,* pp. 121–22.

29. Powell quoted in ibid., pp. 206–7.

30. This account of the founding of the Bureau of Standards is based on ibid., pp. 272–77.

31. U.S. Congress, Senate, Investigation of Executive Agencies of the Government, *Senate Report No. 1275,* 75th Congress, 1st Session, 1937.

32. Kendall Birr, *Pioneering in Industrial Research* (Washington, D.C.: Public Affairs Press, 1957), p. 7.

33. W. Paul Strassman, *Risk and Technological Innovation* (Ithaca, N.Y.: Cornell University Press, 1959), pp. 30–31.

34. Bartlett, "Industrial Research," p. 27. Elting E. Morison, *Men, Machines, and Modern Times* (Cambridge, Mass.: M.I.T. Press, 1966) p. 140.

35. Strassman, *Risk and Technological Innovation,* pp. 38–39.

36. Bartlett, "Industrial Research," p. 27.

37. Ibid., pp. 27–28.

38. Matthew Josephson, "The Invention of the Electric Light," *Scientific Technology and Social Change: Readings from "Scientific American"* (San Francisco: W. H. Freedman, 1974), p. 130.

39. This account is based on Bartlett, "Industrial Research," pp. 71–72.

40. Ibid., pp. 26–27.

41. *A History of Engineering and Science in the Bell System: The Early Years (1875–1925)* (Murray Hill, N.J.: Bell Telephone Laboratories, 1975), p. 887; John Brooks, *Telephone* (New York: Harper and Row, 1976), pp. 129–31.

42. Brooks, *Telephone,* pp. 131–37. De Forest was educated at Yale's Sheffield Scientific School and so cannot be classed as an untutored genius.

43. R. W. and M. E. Hidy, *Pioneering in Big Business* (New York: Harper and Row, 1955), pp. 160, 163–65, 168.

44. Paul H. Giddens, *Standard Oil Company (Indiana)* (New York: Appleton-Century-Crofts, 1955), pp. 6–7.

45. Hidy and Hidy, *Pioneering in Big Business,* pp. 437–38.

46. Ibid., p. 441.

47. See W. S. Dutton, *DuPont* (New York: Charles Scribner's Sons, 1942), pp. 113–25.

48. Ibid., p. 150.

49. Ibid., p. 184.

50. Ibid., p. 185.

51. Bartlett, "Industrial Research," p. 33.

52. He later was coauthor of a treatise on industrial research: C. E. K. Mees and J. A. Leermakers, *The Organization of Industrial Scientific Research,* 2d ed. (New York: McGraw-Hill, 1950).

53. Birr, *Pioneering in Industrial Research,* pp. 30–31. For the development of the electrical industry before 1900, see H. C. Passer, *The Electrical Manufacturers, 1875–1900* (Cambridge, Mass.: Harvard University Press, 1953).

54. Birr, *Pioneering in Industrial Research,* p. 31.

55. Passer, *Electrical Manufacturers,* pp. 277–82.

56. James B. Conant, *Modern Science and Modern Man* (Garden City, N.Y.: Doubleday, 1952), p. 18.

57. A good description of the Naval Consulting Board is Thomas P. Hughes, *Elmer Sperry: Inventor and Engineer* (Baltimore: The Johns Hopkins Press, 1971), chap. 9.

58. Ibid., p. 158.

59. Jerome C. Hunsaker, "Forty Years of Aeronautical Research," *Smithsonian Report, 1955,* no. 4237 (Washington, D.C., 1956), is a first-hand account of the organizing of the NACA.

60. Bartlett, "Industrial Research," p. 36.

61. Dupree, *Science in the Federal Government,* pp. 302–25.

# The American Economy
# and the Reorganization of the
# Sources of Knowledge

*LOUIS GALAMBOS*

I

The major sources of formal knowledge in America experienced a fundamental reorganization during the second half of the nineteenth century.[1] The processes of change were extremely complex: they took place on several levels of American society, sometimes generating contradictory results, often bringing unanticipated consequences, and frequently producing conflict over the means as well as the ends of social development. In spite of these complexities, however, certain general trends stand out, and the article that follows explores some of the economic consequences of these major patterns of change. My principal concerns are the aggregate or macro-effects, in particular, those effects that had some relationship to the institutional setting in the American economy during the early part of the twentieth century.

One of the most obvious trends was an acceleration in the process of social differentiation. The systems that produced formal knowledge in America fractured into a multitude of new and more specialized units. While this type of institutional development had been going on for a long time before 1870, the process of change clearly accelerated in the latter part of the nineteenth century. In engineering, for example, the profession broke into a number of new subdisciplines, each with its own organization, elite, modes of communication, and special body of knowledge.[2] The same pattern could be seen within universities and colleges, where new departments arose and specialists began to supplant professors of such catchall subjects as natural philosophy. The sciences and social sciences followed similar developmental paths between 1870 and 1920; the number of practitioners increased sharply as did the degree of specialization.

Social differentiation was accompanied by a rapid, almost revolutionary, expansion in the output of formal knowledge in the United States. The transformation was especially marked in science and technology. A recent quantitative study of physics suggests that by international standards, this branch of American science was growing very rapidly at the turn of the century; among the leading nations of the world, for instance, only Germany enjoyed a faster rate of growth in the output of scientific papers. There were over two hundred physicists in academic posts in the United States. American expenditures for laboratories were large and were also increasing faster than those of most nations; an average of over two hundred thousand dollars a year was being spent to build new laboratories for this particular discipline.[3] Another indicator of the expansion taking place was the growth in journals dedicated to the emerging specialties. While one might argue about the precise nature of the relationship between these various indicators and the state of knowledge in the disciplines, the transformation during these years was of such magnitude that the existence of a secular, upward trend in the output of formal knowledge seems beyond question. In chemistry, for example, there were no well-established, specialized media for publication of research results in the United States before the 1870s; by the mid-1890s, American chemists were supporting two journals and in subsequent years founded several more catering to subdisciplines.[4] In this and in other branches of science, new publications, new organizations, a rapid increase in expenditures and in the number of practitioners were accompanied by a significant growth in the body of formal knowledge.[5]

## II

This growing fund of theory and data and the personnel and organizations producing it offered opportunities for those who could muster the capital and labor needed to apply new ideas in the economy. The nineteenth-century United States seems always to have had an abundance of entrepreneurs eager to perform this function, and the impact of their activities can be seen in the data on the nation's economic growth. At the beginning of our time period, America was just entering a cycle of unusually rapid growth. Indeed, the rate of expansion of national product in these years was as high as it had ever been and higher than it would be at any time in the nation's subsequent history.[6] Central to this great economic surge was the railroad, an innovation that accounted for a significant percentage of the capital formation in America during the years 1869 to 1882 and enabled expansion to continue even during the serious depression of the 1870s.[7] Manufacturing and agriculture were both growing at impressive rates. Immigration provided much of the additional labor needed in the nation's new factories, and despite the rapid growth in population that this occasioned, Gross National Product (GNP) per capita increased at a very respectable pace.

During these years—and, to a lesser extent, during the next growth surge that began in the late nineties and lasted for about a decade—the American economy had certain advantages that it would gradually lose after the turn of the century. For one thing, new factor inputs—capital, people, land, and other new resources—were responsible for much of the economic growth experienced in the nineteenth century; after 1900, however, Americans would no longer be able to depend to the same extent upon new inputs as the major impetus for growth.[8] In that sense, the economy was becoming more dependent on increases in productivity, on its ability to employ the new specialists and to tap the new bodies of formal knowledge for agriculture and industry. Of course, Americans had been doing that during the nineteenth century, and part of the country's spectacular increase in GNP could be traced to technological change. The task of converting ideas into viable economic undertakings in that setting had, however, been relatively simple. As Nathan Rosenberg has explained, "The industrialization of the American economy in the nineteenth century focused strongly upon the development of a machine technology. The invention of new machines or machine-made products . . . involved the solution of problems which required mechanical skill, ingenuity and versatility but not, typically, a recourse to scientific knowledge or elaborate experimental methods."[9] These conditions changed radically in the twentieth century as the job of applying new ideas became far more complex and expensive. The formal knowledge and the new force of scientific and engineering personnel that were emerging could not be used in the traditional ad hoc manner; institutions that could sustain joint efforts on a long-term basis were needed as were administrators who could cope with large-scale organizational problems. Thus, just as the economy was becoming more dependent upon productivity-enhancing innovations, the task of innovating was becoming more expensive and difficult.

How well did the economy meet these dual challenges? The available data suggest that, over the long run, American businessmen and farmers successfully exploited the rapid expansion in the production of formal knowledge that began in the postbellum years. In the long period from 1889 to 1957, America's real net national product per capita increased four fold, and about three-quarters of this can be attributed to advances in productivity.[10] A substantial part of the improvement in productivity can, in turn, be traced to increases in "society's intangible capital," including what we have called formal knowledge.[11] While GNP grew at a slower pace than it had in the previous century and while the rate of population increase fell even more sharply, Americans could take solace in the fact that GNP per capita was actually increasing faster than it had in the nineteenth century. The modern American economic system had many serious flaws, but its record on converting new knowledge into successful innovations was very respectable.

There was, however, a transitional phase—a twenty-year period of institutional adjustment—when the U.S. economy's performance was not very impressive. Between 1899 and the end of the First World War, when farmers and businessmen might have been harvesting a rich crop of new ideas in science, social science, and technology, the rate of productivity change was actually lower than it had been in the previous decade and considerably below the average for the years following 1919. After the war there was a "pronounced acceleration in productivity advance to an annual rate of 2.1 per cent;" for the years 1899–

1919, by contrast, the annual rate was only 1.1 percent.[12] This is the period upon which we will focus. Our task is to explain why American firms and farms did not in these years take full advantage of their unusual opportunities to innovate.

III

For small economic units facing competitive markets, the explanation doubtless rests in the major expenditures and substantial risks associated with any investment aimed at exploiting the modern sources of formal knowledge. The information costs involved in utilizing the new scientific and technological concepts were rising in the late nineteenth century. Part of this increase was attributable to the labor costs of employing persons with specialized training in fields such as chemistry. By this time, specialization had gone so far in America that academic appointments were being made in such subdisciplines as organic chemistry.[13] In industry, however, very few companies hired even a single chemist with good professional credentials; in 1900, one scholar estimates that in the United States there were only 276 chemists working on a full-time basis in the entire chemical industry.[14]

One could hardly have expected much else from small firms. And in agriculture the constraints on innovation were even more severe. This was the case even when farmers could look to other agents for commercially feasible ideas. During these years an impressive series of institutions were established to produce and distribute new knowledge of the sort that promised increased agricultural productivity. Margaret Rossiter's chapter in this volume describes the several professional associations that were organized to promote special branches of this diverse discipline. Their efforts were closely linked to the activities of a complex governmental and quasi-governmental delivery system that included experiment stations, agricultural colleges, the county agent network, and various state and local organizations. Public funds kept the entire system running: indeed, by the standards of that period, farmers were particularly favored by the government and millions of dollars went into the effort to develop new ideas and to see to it that farmers actually used them.

Yet the immediate results were disappointing. Productivity in the agricultural sector as a whole actually declined in the first two decades of the twentieth century. While the total output of American farms was increasing, the output per unit of labor input showed no improvement, and output per unit of capital input fell during this period.[15] Farmers were prosperous in the years immediately prior to the First World War but their good fortune was not a consequence of innovations tied to the new delivery systems or the burgeoning agricultural sciences. At best one could say that a backlog of formal knowledge was being built up and an institutional pipeline for distributing the ideas was being constructed—all for use at a much later date when unusual economic conditions would finally persuade farmers to do what neither the U.S. Department of Agriculture nor their private associations could convince them to do in the years 1899 to 1919.[16]

Businessmen were not much more successful than farmers in improving the efficiency of their operations in the period under consideration. Of course, business—unlike agriculture—was not favored with a government-funded system for generating and distributing new ideas, and this was a substantial handicap for small firms facing sharp competition.[17] In addition to labor costs, those businesses that wanted to take advantage of the new sources of formal knowledge and new personnel had to anticipate substantial expenditures for equipment. When General Electric founded a research laboratory at the turn of the century, the company spent over one hundred thousand dollars to develop an effective factory process for manufacturing tungsten filaments for lamps; later, in 1914, when GE built a new laboratory, it spent about this much on equipment alone.[18] In Germany, a Badische firm had expended a million pounds sterling by 1897 to discover a synthetic indigo for commercial dyes.[19] By current standards the sums involved may seem small, but in the late nineteenth and early twentieth centuries, the cost of even the most rudimentary industrial research and development represented a substantial barrier for most American businesses.

It is important to remember that before the merger movement of the late 1890s, most industries remained relatively competitive and most firms relatively small. In the chemical industry, single-owner businesses and partnerships were the rule. Although the industry experienced rapid growth in the second half of the century, the typical business continued to serve a local or at best a regional market and to depend for innovations on ideas developed outside of the company—often outside of the country. A number of the major changes that were made involved improvements in production techniques that merely applied already known principles in new and more efficient ways.[20] A firm's expertise in science was normally provided entirely by the owner or partners rather than by staff members hired to specialize in research. In this setting, one can hardly fault American chemical manufacturers for not incurring the additional costs of industrial research: serving as they did a highly competitive market and operating as they did with relatively small capitalization, they and their counterparts in similar business enterprises could not be expected to assume the risks of an ongoing investment in research.

However, in the period that is of particular interest to us, 1899 to 1919, small firms gave way in many American industries to large corporate enterprises. As late as 1897, large combines were still the exception in most industries. In oil and in transportation, in meat packing and in the electrical industry, a few corporate giants had carved out secure economic positions and, in doing so, had aroused public animosity toward all trusts and combines.[21] Antitrust measures notwithstanding, a wave of mergers swept through American industry between 1897 and 1903. The chemical industry produced its first major combination during these years—the General Chemical Company in 1899—and in 1901, the United

States Steel Company brought together, under a one billion dollar corporate roof, most of the productive capacity in the vital iron and steel industry. By 1903, the majority of America's leading industries had been reorganized and were dominated by a few leading combines.[22]

For giant corporations of this sort, the costs of hiring research personnel or building a laboratory were not prohibitive, and indeed one might have expected such companies to be quick to exploit the advantages inherent in their greater capitalization and freedom from short-run competitive pressures. We associate a long-range managerial viewpoint with corporations of this ilk, and that too seems consistent with an ongoing investment in research and development.[23] During the first two decades of the twentieth century, however, America's largest firms were slow to seize this opportunity. Most of the major combines in manufacturing were no more innovative in this regard than the smaller companies they had replaced or absorbed. Indeed, there is some reason to believe they were actually less interested than were small and middle-sized firms in drawing upon the new personnel and new ideas in science, social science, and technology.

This was particularly true in the manufacturing sector in which total factor productivity increased only 0.7 percent per year between 1899 and 1909 and fell to an annual average of 0.3 percent in the following decade. The performance of different industries varied considerably. A few compiled impressive records: printing and rubber products, for example, enjoyed significant increases in productivity; and among the public utilities, the new electrical industry achieved annual increases of 5.2 and 8.2 percent during these same two decades. On balance, however, U.S. manufacturers (and mining companies as well) were increasing the productivity of their plants at a rate substantially below the figure they had achieved in the years before 1899.[24] If private firms were innovating along these new lines, the results were not evident in the aggregate data on productivity in American industry.

Indeed, the early history of scientific or systematic management suggests that large corporations were slow in seeking productivity-enhancing innovations throughout this transitional phase from the late nineties to the end of the First World War. In the nineties, Frederick W. Taylor had begun to publicize his ideas about ways to improve the efficiency of labor and capital through new methods of organizing, rewarding, and evaluating work; by 1911, when Taylor published his book *The Principles of Scientific Management,* there was a Taylor Society that discussed and propagated his ideas. In the next few years, Taylor's disciples gave wide currency to his basic concepts and made important additions to this new approach to administration. After Louis D. Brandeis popularized the new method in the famous Eastern Rate Case of 1910 and 1911, "an efficiency craze hit America."[25]

Yet, during the years 1899 to 1919, the managers of most of America's largest companies seem to have been largely oblivious to the Taylor movement. Taylorism—unlike contemporary developments in the physical sciences, for example—did not involve very high information costs. Expensive scientific personnel were not needed. Laboratories were unnecessary. Furthermore, the relationship between systematic management and existing business situations was fairly obvious. Nevertheless, the companies that first experimented with Taylorism were, for the most part, small or middle-sized firms. Not until the 1920s did many of America's corporate giants begin to explore the possibilities of this new and promising method of increasing organizational efficiency.[26] Their failure to move more quickly was symptomatic, I believe, of a general unwillingness on the part of the corporate leaders of these years to seek means of exploiting the new sources of formal knowledge.

To explain this period of corporate conservatism, we must look more closely at what was happening inside the newly merged combines and at their relationships with their competitors. When a new corporation brought together all or most of an industry's productive capacity, the process of organizational evolution did not suddenly stop. Combination was normally followed by a long period of experimentation, as the combine's leaders sought effective means to achieve control over their new industrial holdings. Apparently there was little communication between the organizers of corporate mergers in different industries; each seems to have approached the problem of centralization as if it had arisen for the first time.[27] Thus new statistical reports and committee structures were introduced in one industry after another with little regard for past experience. America's railroads had been dealing with these problems since the 1850s and Standard Oil's innovations in corporate consolidation dated back to the 1880s, but business leaders in the early 1900s did not draw upon this rich fund of information. There were as yet no media for communicating such experiences; administration had not yet become a recognized profession, and the idea that each separate industry had unique problems imposed a serious constraint on the imagination of the business elite. One result was a long postcombination siege with the problems of centralization—a phase of business development that seems to have dominated the years from 1897 through the First World War.[28]

The managers of the nation's largest corporations were preoccupied with the need to consolidate their firms and stabilize their companies' positions in their respective markets. From our vantage point, the difficulties of stabilizing market shares, prices, and profits do not look very great—the outcome seems assured. We have forgotten the combines that failed. We are accustomed to thinking of so-called center firms that have successfully weathered depressions and seem assured of a dominant position in their industries for at least the forseeable future.[29] It is difficult for us to imagine how problematic General Motors' future was in the years 1910 through 1920, and it is instructive to read Arthur Stone Dewing's *Corporate Promotions and Reorganizations* for its contemporary account of mergers that failed.[30] Most, of course, did not fail, but the possibility was real enough to keep corporate managers obsessed with the problems of solidifying their oligopolistic market positions. The rewards for a successful performance were great and the risks far less than they were for ventures along new technological paths. One can hardly fault the managers for their sense of priorities during these years. One consequence of their long bout with the problems of centralization and consolidation, however, was a phase of business development in which the majority of America's most important firms failed to take advantage of their unusual opportunities to draw upon the new sources of formal knowledge evolving outside the business system.[31]

This is not to say that managers completely ignored immediate opportunities to improve the efficiency of their corporations. One of the first major actions after merger was normally the elimination of inefficient plants and the concentration of production in a few sites; this doubtless lowered unit costs, although the savings were probably less than either the ex ante estimates of corporate promoters or the ex post calculations of business historians. That, at least, is the conclusion indicated by the aggregate data on productivity increases. Where management fell short, however, was in areas of innovation that required new institutional structures and a distinctly different bundle of administrative talents within the firm.[32]

The record of the United States Steel Corporation is instructive. This awesome holding company brought together most of the large corporations in an industry that had already undergone a long period of horizontal and vertical integration. Initially, the central office of the corporation did little more than collect standardized statistical reports and prevent member firms from competing with each other.[33] Stabilization of prices was not an automatic consequence of concentration, and the company's stock was so heavily watered that management could ill afford to ignore the problems of price competition in the short run.[34] It was some years, in fact, before the firm even started to achieve thoroughgoing centralization. One can understand, then, why the U.S. Steel Corporation was not a particularly aggressive firm, at least during this phase of its development. Its managers were content to stabilize the industry even though that meant gradually losing part of their control of the market to smaller and more aggressive rivals. U.S. Steel did not invest heavily in industrial research; it was not an innovative company.[35] It represented the type of industrial combine that was more concerned with centralization and consolidation than with innovations leading to improved productivity in the transitional years through 1919.

All of the nation's giant corporations were not as slow as U.S. Steel to take advantage of the revolutionary developments in the sources of formal knowledge. Fortunately, we already have several studies of more innovative firms and of their pioneering efforts in research and development. Kendall Birr's volume on the General Electric Research Laboratory describes a company at the opposite pole from the Steel Trust.[36] GE represented an industry that was itself the product of nineteenth-century science and advanced technology.[37] In the company's earliest years (1892–1900), however, the special characteristics of the electrical industry did not prompt GE to put much money into research; indeed, the two combines that came to control the market in this industry were at first actually less innovative than the smaller firms they had absorbed. GE—like U.S. Steel and other combines—was for a time more concerned with consolidation than with innovation, more worried about protecting its share of the market than achieving growth through technological change.[38] Not until the prosperous years at the beginning of the twentieth century did GE move—at first hesitantly and then decisively—into industrial research and development.[39] By 1906 the GE Research Laboratory had a staff of 102. Eleven years later, it had 298 employees, many with advanced degrees and some with substantial reputations in science and engineering, and was carrying out important research in several fields, including electric lighting, X-rays, metallurgy, and radio.[40]

In the course of this research, however, the corporation kept in mind its primary goal of maintaining a stable oligopolistic position in the markets it served, and patent rights were a crucial means of achieving that end. Birr credits GE, quite appropriately, with significant advances in research on vacuum tubes and radio transmission, and these innovations were protected by the patent system; without patent rights, the research might not have been undertaken.[41] Birr neglects, however, the other side of this coin, giving less attention to the manner in which the results of that research were shaped by the intricate negotiations involving three major firms that were concerned, above all, with economic stability. As a recent study demonstrates, GE, American Telephone and Telegraph, and Westinghouse used patent rights—either purchased or stemming from their own research—in an elaborate chess game entailing control of the radio industry and of telephone communications as well. A substantial amount of the research done in the labs of these companies—all leaders in the field of industrial research—was directed toward the goal of protecting an oligopolistic order instead of promoting productive innovation.[42] To the extent that this was a common practice, even the research efforts of the most advanced corporations must be partially discounted as a spur to increased productivity.

Furthermore, corporations such as GE were, between 1897 and 1919, the exception and not the rule. If one arrays the largest enterprises in America during these years on a scale extending from U.S. Steel on one extreme to General Electric on the other, the median firm is far closer to the steel combine than to G.E. Only a few leading corporations concentrated in a limited number of industries—including DuPont in chemicals and the firms mentioned above in electrical products—were making significant investments in research and development before World War I. Even highly conservative companies could innovate, of course, by buying ideas from individual inventors or from erstwhile competitors; as late as 1916, about three-quarters of the patents in the United States were still issued to individuals as opposed to companies.[43] But the failure of these businesses to invest directly in "R and D" reflected, I think, a general managerial orientation that militated against even the least expensive means of acquiring and applying new ideas from outside the firm. Corporate concern with the profits to be realized from stability at the industry level and control within the company were thus partly responsible for the relatively poor performance of the American economy in achieving higher levels of productivity in the years 1899 through 1919.

## IV

These conditions did not change significantly until the First World War. By that time, relatively innovative firms such as GE and DuPont had demonstrated the value of company investments in "R and D"; the wartime mobilization program had popularized these efforts and wartime profits gave firms the leeway to experiment with new programs. By the early 1920s, most of the combines organized at the turn of the century had also solved their internal problems and stabilized their positions in the market. Their managers could afford to think more about innovation and to consider changes that required large investments and new administrative structures within the firm.[44] Many large corporations began to implement programs in systematic management. "R and D" spread to a variety of industries that had heretofore been satisfied to purchase patent rights for new processes and products; even U.S. Steel ventured into the field. For the economy as a whole, "R and D" expenditures grew much faster than did the net national product, and, as subsequent studies have shown, such investments have been an important source of productivity gains.[45] The interest of corporate management in research was, furthermore, symptomatic of a fundamental shift in managerial attitudes, a transformation that affected a broad range of business policies and contributed to the successful performance of the economy in the 1920s.

In the decade following the First World War, American corporations adopted a variety of innovations that improved the efficiency of their operations. In manufacturing the rate of productive change jumped to 5.3 percent annually for the years 1919 through 1929. The institutional developments described here were of course only one of the factors contributing to this general improvement; even in agriculture—where there was still little evidence that the government-funded research system was producing results—the rate of productivity change went up in the twenties. The most dramatic improvements were, however, in industry. Corporate managers experimented during these years with a variety of new ways of improving the efficiency of their work force and their plants; these efforts were successful enough to yield an average annual improvement of 5.6 percent in the productivity of labor and 4.3 percent in the productivity of capital.[46] Efficiency is not the only measure of economic success, and there were certainly economic problems in the twenties: the rate of growth of GNP was slower than it had been in the nineteenth century; and labor's share of national income was declining.[47] But in terms of its ability to draw upon the reorganized sources of formal knowledge that had developed since 1870, the American economy had clearly entered a new and more successful phase.

### Notes

I would like to thank the many scholars and students who read earlier versions of this chapter and gave me the benefit of their criticism. Their ranks include the contributors to this volume, the participants in seminars at Columbia University and The Johns Hopkins University and other thoughtful friends too numerous to list.

1. The adjective *formal* is used to distinguish this body of knowledge from the larger collection of ideas sometimes identified as the "state of knowledge." See Jacob Schmookler, "Changes in Industry and in the State of Knowledge as Determinants of Industrial Invention," in *The Rate and Direction of Inventive Activity: Economic and Social Factors,* National Bureau of Economic Research (Princeton: Princeton University Press, 1962), p. 195. "Formal knowledge" is in this usage slightly more restrictive than "science and technology," because I intend to deal only with concepts and theories that were generated and transmitted as part of the activities of ongoing social systems in the scientific, engineering, and general academic professions. Thus I am leaving out the random tinkering that frequently seems to have had significant economic results but that did not directly experience the reorganization analyzed by the several contributors to this volume. I am including systematic management, however, because this body of ideas became associated with the types of organized, professional activities discussed above.

2. I have described these developments in *The Public Image of Big Business in America, 1880–1940: A Quantitative Study in Social Change* (Baltimore: The Johns Hopkins University Press, 1975), pp. 8–14.

3. Paul Forman, John L. Heilbron, and Spencer Weart, *Physics circa 1900: Personnel, Funding, and Productivity of the Academic Establishments* (Princeton: Princeton University Press, 1975), pp. 5–9, 101, 115–19.

4. Edward H. Beardsley, *The Rise of the American Chemistry Profession, 1850–1900,* University of Florida Monographs, Social Sciences, no. 23 (Gainesville, 1964), pp. 34–42. See also Williams Haynes, *American Chemical Industry: Background and Beginnings,* 6 vols. (New York: D. Van Nostrand, 1954), 1: 397–98.

5. Aaron J. Ihde, *The Development of Modern Chemistry* (New York: Harper & Row, 1964), chap. 27, discusses the growth of the profession and the "explosion of chemical literature" since 1900. As Ihde points out, the American Chemical Society had only 2,000 members in 1900 and had grown to 15,000 by 1920. See the papers by Daniel J. Kevles and John Rae in this volume. My concern here and throughout is with "the growth of the body of science" and not with particular discoveries. As Jacob Schmookler points out, that body of ideas helps create a certain "inventive potential," and the "potential of any period may not be fully realized. Men may not make some of the inventions that they think of because they find more profitable uses for their resources." *Invention and Economic Growth* (Cambridge, Mass.: Harvard University Press, 1966), pp. 15, 200. My primary interest is in the institutional setting in which the forces of supply and demand for innovations intersect; on the need for such analysis, see Nathan Rosenberg, "Science, Invention and Economic Growth," *The Economic Journal* 84 (March 1974): 90–108.

6. Alfred H. Conrad, "Income Growth and Structural Change," in *American Economic History,* ed. Seymour E. Harris (New York: McGraw-Hill, 1961), pp. 26–64. See also, Robert E. Gallman, "Gross National Product in the United States, 1834–1909," in *Output, Employment, and Productivity in the United States after 1800,* Conference on Research in Income and Wealth (New York: National Bureau of Economic Research, 1966), pp. 8–10. For different interpretations see the following: Thomas C. Cochran, "The Paradox of American Economic Growth," *Journal of American History* (March 1975): 925–42. Jeffrey G. Williamson, *Late Nineteenth-Century American Development: A General Equilibrium History* (Cambridge: At the University Press, 1974).

What is especially impressive about American growth during the years 1869–1882 is the manner in which GNP per capita increased while the country's population was growing at a high rate; later, when the population and the GNP were both growing more slowly, the increase in GNP per capita would actually be higher. See Simon Kuznets, "Notes on the Pattern of U.S. Economic Growth," in *The Nation's Economic Objectives,* ed. Edgar O. Edwards (Chicago: University of Chicago Press, 1964), pp. 15–35.

7. Since the publication of Robert W. Fogel's *Railroads and American Economic Growth: Essays in Econometric History* (Baltimore: Johns Hopkins Press, 1964), economic historians have given less emphasis to the role of the railroad in promoting growth than was formerly the case. Albert Fishlow's *American Railroads and the Transformation of the Ante-Bellum Economy* (Cambridge, Mass.: Harvard University Press, 1965), offered an important corrective to Fogel's estimates for the 1850s, but a far stronger case for the railroads' impact—especially on capital formation—can be made for the postwar years. I am indebted to Naomi R. Lamoreaux, "Schumpeter and Beyond: A Comparative Study of Two Phases of Rapid Growth, 1869–1882 and 1897–1907" (unpublished ms.) for an excellent discussion of this problem and the relevant literature.

8. Robert E. Gallman, "Capital Formation and Capital Allocation: Comments on the General Report," (paper delivered at the Sixth International Congress on Economic History, Copenhagen,

1974). See also Gallman's chapter, "The Pace and Pattern of American Economic Growth," in *American Economic Growth: An Economist's History of the United States,* ed. Lance E. Davis et al. (New York: Harper & Row, 1972), especially pp. 33–40.

9. Nathan Rosenberg, *Technology and American Economic Growth* (New York: Harper & Row, 1972), p. 54.

10. John W. Kendrick, *Productivity Trends in the United States,* National Bureau of Economic Research Publications no. 71 (Princeton: Princeton University Press, 1961), p. 3. See also Moses Abramovitz, "Resource and Output Trends in the United States since 1870," *American Economic Review, Papers and Proceedings* 46 (May 1956): 5–23, and Robert M. Solow, "Technical Change and the Aggregate Production Function," *Review of Economics and Statistics* 39 (August 1957): 312–20.

11. Solomon Fabricant, "Basic Facts on Productivity Change," in Kendrick, *Productivity Trends,* p. xliii. See also, Moses Abramovitz and Paul A. David, "Reinterpreting Economic Growth: Parables and Realities," *American Economic Review* 63 (May 1973): 428–39. For different approaches to measurement and different conclusions about productivity change, see Laurits R. Christensen and Dale W. Jorgenson, "U.S. Real Product and Real Factor Input, 1929–1967," *Review of Economic Studies* 34 (July 1967): 249–83. These latter studies have raised some serious questions about the size of the residual that is labeled "productivity change," but to date at least the position advanced above—the Kendrick-Abramovitz-Solow-David position—still seems to this author to be intact and worthy of the role I have given it in this essay.

12. Kendrick, *Productivity Trends,* pp. 65–71, 126. As should be obvious to the reader, I am dealing with only a few of the elements that seem to have contributed to shaping these trends; for a discussion of the data and other causal factors, the reader should refer to Kendrick's volume and to the other sources mentioned in notes 11 and 12, above. The wartime experience influenced the trends I am discussing; productivity gains were lower after 1914 than they were before the war. Even if one disregards the war years, however, there was a transitional phase—characterized by a lower rate of increase in productivity—during the years following 1899.

13. Beardsley, *American Chemistry Profession,* pp. 48–49.

14. Ibid., pp. 60–62. For a more optimistic view, see Kendall Birr, "Science in American Industry," in *Science and Society in the United States,* ed. David Van Tassel and Michael Hall (Homewood, Ill.: Dorsey Press, 1966), pp. 52–62.

15. Kendrick, *Productivity Trends,* pp. 152, 166. See also Harold Barger and Hans H. Landsberg, *American Agriculture, 1899–1939: A Study of Output, Employment and Productivity* (New York: National Bureau of Economic Research, 1942), pp. 247–54.

16. Wayne D. Rasmussen, "The Impact of Technological Change on American Agriculture, 1862–1962," *Journal of Economic History* 23 (December 1962): 578–91; Kendrick, *Productivity Trends,* pp. 152, 157–60.

17. We have become accustomed to thinking of businessmen as the primary recipients of government largess in the late nineteenth and early twentieth centuries; in the matter at hand, however, farmers fared much better than businessmen in their efforts to tap public funds.

18. Kendall Birr, *Pioneering in Industrial Research: The Story of The General Electric Research Laboratory* (Washington, D.C.: Public Affairs Press, 1957), pp. 39, 53. As Birr points out, when GE hired William D. Coolidge, who was an assistant professor of chemistry at MIT, the company doubled his salary and allowed him to spend half his time on his own research—using GE's equipment. Small companies could certainly not afford to be so magnanimous, ibid., p. 37.

19. Ihde, *Modern Chemistry,* p. 458.

20. Haynes, *American Chemical Industry,* 1: 239–51.

21. Alfred D. Chandler, Jr., *The Railroads: The Nation's First Big Business* (New York: Harcourt, Brace, and World, 1965); "The Beginnings of 'Big Business' in American Industry," *Business History Review* 33 (Spring 1959): 1–31; and "The Coming of Big Business," *The Comparative Approach to American History,* ed. C. Vann Woodward (New York: Basic Books, 1968), pp. 220–37.

22. Ralph L. Nelson, *Merger Movements in American Industry, 1895–1956* (Princeton: Princeton University Press, National Bureau of Economic Research, 1959), pp. 1–70.

23. These arguments have been advanced by Joseph A. Schumpeter, *Capitalism, Socialism and Democracy* (New York: Harper & Brothers, 1942), pp. 87–106; and more recently in John K. Galbraith, *The New Industrial State* (New York: New American Library, 1967), pp. 23–45.

24. Kendrick, *Productivity Trends,* pp. 136–37. The figures for 1909 and 1919 are biased by the

excess capitalization (i.e., watered stock) resulting from the mergers and by the wartime experience; the biases do not, however, appear to be large enough to change the longrun trends. See Daniel Creamer et al., *Capital in Manufacturing and Mining: Its Formation and Financing* (Princeton: Princeton University Press for the National Bureau of Economic Research, 1960), pp. 14–15, 44–45.

25. Samuel Haber, *Efficiency and Uplift: Scientific Management in the Progressive Era, 1890–1920* (Chicago: University of Chicago Press, 1964), pp. 30–74. See also, Joseph A. Litterer, "Systematic Management: The Search for Order and Integration," *Business History Review* 35 (Winter 1961): 461–76; and the same author's, "Systematic Management: Design for Organizational Recoupling in American Manufacturing Firms," ibid. 37 (Winter 1963): 369–91.

26. Haber, *Efficiency and Uplift*, pp. 160–67. Daniel Nelson, "Scientific Management, Systematic Management, and Labor, 1880–1915" *Business History Review* 48 (Winter 1974): 479–500.

27. The early development of Standard Oil is described in Ralph and Muriel Hidy, *Pioneering in Big Business: The Standard Oil Company (New Jersey) 1882–1911* (New York: Harper & Brothers, 1955), pp. 14–75. On the sugar trust, see Alfred S. Eichner, *The Emergence of Oligopoly: Sugar Refining as a Case Study* (Baltimore: The Johns Hopkins Press, 1969).

28. Alfred D. Chandler, Jr., *Strategy and Structure: Chapters in the History of the Industrial Enterprise* (Cambridge, Mass.: MIT Press, 1962), pp. 383–90. Also see Chandler, *The Visible Hand: The Managerial Revolution in American Business* (Cambridge, Mass.: Harvard University Press, 1977), for a far more positive view of the accomplishments of big business during these years.

29. Robert T. Averitt, *The Dual Economy* (New York: Norton, 1968), pp. 1–2.

30. Arthur Stone Dewing, *Corporate Promotions and Reorganizations*, (Cambridge, Mass.: Harvard University Press, 1914). See also, Richard C. Edwards, "Stages in Corporate Stability and the Risks of Corporate Failure," *Journal of Economic History* 35 (June 1975): 428–57.

31. Gabriel Kolko, *The Triumph of Conservatism: A Reinterpretation of American History, 1900–1916* (New York: Free Press of Glencoe, 1963), pp. 11–56, advances a somewhat similar argument to explain why corporate leaders turned to the federal government for solutions to their problems. While agreeing that businessmen were concerned with the need for stability, I cannot accept Kolko's evidence on two points: that the companies failed in their private efforts to achieve satisfactory resolutions of their major problems; and that most of them looked upon the federal government as a reasonable means of reaching their goals.

32. Edith Tilton Penrose, *The Theory of the Growth of the Firm* (New York: John Wiley, 1959), pp. 43–80, 112–16. An interesting and informative exception to my general statement about innovations and big business is provided by developments in cost accounting. In this case, large firms were clearly the first to adopt advanced techniques. The innovations in this instance were, however, integral to the very process of administrative consolidation that we have been describing.

33. Chandler, *Strategy and Structure*, pp. 333–34.

34. Henry R. Seager and Charles A. Gulick, Jr., *Trust and Corporation Problems* (New York: Harper & Brothers, 1929), p. 260.

35. Gertrude G. Schroeder, *The Growth of Major Steel Companies, 1900–1950* (Baltimore: The Johns Hopkins Press, 1953), pp. 43–45.

36. Birr, *Pioneering in Industrial Research*.

37. This is the type of invention excluded by Schmookler, "Changes in Industry," p. 206.

38. Harold C. Passer, *The Electrical Manufacturers, 1875–1900* (Cambridge, Mass.: Harvard University Press, 1953), comes to this conclusion about the combines.

39. As Birr points out, the company had by this time undertaken the type of consolidation I have been discussing above: the firm's officers "installed new cost accounting methods and a more functional organization. Efficient production methods and improved business conditions were reflected in rapidly rising sales and profits and in the absorption of several smaller firms." Birr, *Pioneering in Industrial Research*, p. 30.

40. On the early development of this institution, see ibid., pp. 31–66. Thomas P. Hughes has kindly shared with me some of the conclusions of his current research on GE; among other things, he has found that a substantial amount of the firm's "R and D" was done outside of the GE Research Laboratory. To the extent that this was true, my paper understates the company's contributions because my focus is entirely upon the latter institution.

41. For a discussion of the patent problem and the relevant literature, see Wayne D. Collins, John A. Ferejohn, and Daniel J. Kevles, "Patent Policy, Technological Innovation, and Government Contracts: A Selective Critique," California Institute of Technology, Social Science Working Paper 56 (Pasadena: 1974).

42. Leonard S. Reich, "Research, Patents, and the Struggle to Control Radio," *Business History Review,* 51 (Summer 1977): 208–35. Reich quotes an AT&T internal memorandum that commented on the company's radio research as follows: "If we never derive any other benefit from our work than that which follows the safe-guarding of our *wire interests* we can look upon the time and money as having been returned to us many times over." Italics mine. See also, Birr, *Pioneering in Industrial Research,* pp. 42–48, 97–103.

43. Schmookler, *Invention,* p. 26, table 1. George S. Gibb and Evelyn H. Knowlton, *The Resurgent Years, 1911–1927* (New York: Harper & Brothers, 1956), pp. 520–69, describe Standard Oil's experience. As the authors point out: "Jersey's Manufacturing Committee was predominantly concerned with the immediate problem of coordinating refinery schedules with other phases of the business and getting the most out of the existing plant. In 1918 neither the men nor the organizational devices were at hand to effect the drastic technological revitalization which was necessary. In greater or less degree this same stagnancy pervaded many other oil companies. Pure research on petroleum refining processes was confined largely to university laboratories and to the workshops of independent chemists" (p. 520).

44. According to figures compiled by Leonard S. Reich, who drew upon J. McKeen Cattell and Dean R. Brimhall, eds., *American Men of Science* (Garrison, N.Y.: Science Press, 1921), the number of scientists with Ph.D. degrees working in American industry was small and increasing very slowly from 1885 through about 1909; the rate of increase was higher from 1910 through 1914, and substantially higher for the years 1915 to 1920. After the war the cycle of inflation and deflation in 1920 and 1921 may also have been an important spur to some major firms; see the discussion of DuPont's structural innovations in Chandler, *Strategy and Structure,* pp. 96–113.

45. One estimate puts "R & D" expenditures at $59 million (0.08 percent of NNP) in 1920 and at $166 million (0.21 percent of NNP) ten years later. Kendrick, *Productivity Trends,* p. 109. A useful survey of developments in the twenties is available in George Perazich and Philip M. Field, *Industrial Research and Changing Technology,* Work Projects Administration, National Research Project, Report no. M-4 (Philadelphia: January 1940). Nestor E. Terleckyj, "Sources of Productivity Advance: A Pilot Study of Manufacturing Industries, 1899–1953" (Ph.D. diss., Columbia University, 1960), especially pp. 80–108. On subsequent relationships between "R and D," productivity, and profitability, see Jora A. Minasian, "The Economics of Research and Development," in *Rate and Direction,* National Bureau of Economic Research, pp. 93–141. See also, Richard R. Nelson, "The Economics of Invention: A Survey of the Literature," *Journal of Business* 32 (April 1959): 101–27.

46. Barger and Landsberg, *American Agriculture, 1899–1939,* pp. 247–87. Kendrick, *Productivity Trends,* pp. 136, 152, 166. Readers who are interested in the other factors should turn to ibid., especially pp. 177–88; and Terleckyj, "Sources of Productivity Advance." At this point in the analysis of the problem, I am satisfied to identify an institutional factor that seems to have had a significant impact on the trends in productivity change; I cannot place that factor in rank order with what Kendrick identifies as the "pervasive forces" (e.g., economic growth itself) or the "forces with differential impact" (e.g., cyclical fluctuations in industrial output).

As Robert E. Gallman has suggested, however, there may well be a significant relationship between the patterns of business behavior I have identified and the fact that the years 1906–1920 were characterized by troughs in the Kuznets cycles for a number of the relevant series. See Moses Abramovitz, "The Nature and Significance of Kuznets Cycles," *Economic Development and Cultural Change* 9 (April 1961): 231. During such a trough, one would expect managers to concentrate more heavily on strengthening the position of their combines and stabilizing their markets than on innovating along the lines I have been discussing.

47. Kendrick, *Productivity Trends,* pp. 136, 157. See Robert R. Keller "Factor Income Distribution in the United States During the 1920s: A Reexamination of Fact and Theory," *Journal of Economic History* 33 (March, 1973): 252–73, for a corrective to George Soule, *Prosperity Decade: From War to Depression: 1917–1929* (New York: Rinehart, 1947), pp. 121–24.

# The Institutional Context
# of Learning

# University Identity: the Teaching and Research Functions

## HUGH HAWKINS

In defending a dictionary definition of "university" that he wrote in 1891, Charles S. Peirce argued that a university had nothing to do with instruction.[1] His negation fit the research emphasis that had spurred the university movement in the United States. Dedicated teachers sometimes approached the opposite extreme and denigrated research as an institutional irrelevancy. But those academics who labored to fulfill both roles—researcher and teacher—were truer representatives of the new and newly shaped institutions that revolutionized American higher education in the last third of the nineteenth century. Even the two universities at which the research ethos was clearly dominant—Johns Hopkins and Clark—stressed the advanced level of their students, never proposing scholarship in isolation from instruction.

This essay seeks to place universities in the context of other institutionalized efforts to preserve, increase, and apply knowledge. Above all else, what distinguishes universities among knowledge-oriented organizations is their persistent concern with forming links between other allegiances to knowledge and the function of teaching. Members of a learned academy do at times speak of educating each other, directors of libraries sometimes see themselves promoting a general process of self-education, and scientists in industrial laboratories occasionally bring in apprentices, but none of these knowledge-centered institutions approaches the schooling responsibilities of universities. Indeed, the builders of universities took pride in providing an apex for the nation's incomplete school system. They often indicated that nurturing creative scholarship made universities superior to other schools, but when speaking with other learned associations in mind (usually avowing shared purposes while denying redundancy), university spokesmen gained firmest ground by stressing the effects of university teaching. Teaching, it was said, preserved the accumulated body of learning by passing it on to successive generations, provided a seedbed for future creators of new knowledge, and enhanced the contributions students would make to society. Such intertwining of teaching with the university's other knowledge-serving functions has been both its glory and its shame. Here is a case in which institutional purposes support, but also threaten, each other. The conflicts and compromises engendered by the simultaneous presence of teaching obligations and research-mindedness in the rising American universities will form the central thread of the account that follows. Attention will also be paid to the "external" aspects of teaching-research tensions, specifically to their relationship to the social setting of universities. The ability to shift the balance between these functions was part of the flexibility that helped win support for universities in a nation that often seemed too democratic and too utilitarian to nurture the life of the mind.

Definitions of the university were often only implicit in the presidential inaugural addresses that mark the emergence of the American university. At newly founded Cornell in 1868, President Andrew D. White foresaw an institution giving equal respect to liberal and practical studies in a widely inclusive curriculum, granting unusual curricular freedom to students while remaining denominationally unattached. He directed the faculty not to the challenge of discovering new truth, but to the satisfactions of helping to educate distinguished alumni. A year later, when he began his forty-year presidency of Harvard, Charles W. Eliot placed similar stress on curricular inclusiveness, student freedom to elect courses, and equal status for newer studies. Although he believed that "the strongest and most devoted professors will contribute something to the patrimony of knowledge," he reminded the faculty that except for the observatory, "the University does not hold a single fund primarily intended to secure to men of learning the leisure and means to prosecute original researches."[2]

No one was better aware than Daniel Coit Gilman of earlier struggles to attain university ideals in America. When, as president of the new Johns Hopkins University in 1876, he referred to previous efforts, he could draw on his administrative work at Yale's scientific school in the 1850s and 1860s, his friendship with White, and his three years in California as president of a state university receiving federal land-grant aid under the Morrill Act of 1862. Academic legend, accurately reflecting the major influence of the Johns Hopkins experiment in American higher education, sees Gilman as nailing the banner of research to the mast of the new enterprise in Baltimore. But in his inaugural Gilman cited the university's teaching function as its first priority. The elevated level of students seemed the most distinctive element in his plan: "The University is a place for the advanced and special education of youth who have been prepared for its freedom by the discipline of a lower school." He spoke of the university's "freedom" to investigate, but of its "obligation" to teach.[3]

Gilman differentiated the university, where "teaching is essential, research important," from the academy or learned society, where "research is indispensable, tuition rarely thought of." He included complimentary references to two Baltimore learned institutions, the Maryland Academy of Sciences and the Peabody Institute (a unique blend of library, lyceum, and music conservatory), and for good measure cited eleven "powerful instruments for the advancement of science, literature, and art" in nearby Washington, ranging from the Smithsonian Institution to the Corcoran Art Gallery. When he chose a metaphor, however, he made the university the sun, the other learned agencies the planets.[4]

Perhaps no inaugural ever expressed the research ideal as boldly as did G. Stanley Hall's address at Clark University's first-year opening exercises in 1889. Hall had earned a Ph.D. at Eliot's Harvard and held a professorship at Johns Hopkins before being called to head the new university in Worcester, Massachusetts. His design for the institution showed the prestige of investigation at a high point, and Clark opened with provision for admission of graduate students only. Hall's pristine conception was suggested in his comment that the university "should be financially and morally able to disregard practical application as well as numbers of students . . ., and the increase of knowledge and its diffusion among the few fit should be its ideal." Faculty members should be "absorbed in and living only for pure science and high scholarship." They could best serve those few fit students by following the example of a German professor Hall described who set a newly arrived American college graduate to work on one muscle of a frog's leg, thus giving him "the invaluable training of abandoning himself to a long experimental research upon [a] very special but happily chosen point." With a faculty of eighteen, Clark in its first year had thirty-four students, all of them seeking advanced work, and twelve already holding Ph.D.'s.[5]

The opening of Clark preceded the founding of two other new universities, Stanford (1891) and Chicago (1892) by only a few years. Whereas Clark's striking concern for advancing scholarship was symbolized by its omission of undergraduates, these two universities provided space for research in much more complex institutions. Although passages in the inaugural of David Starr Jordan, the Cornell alumnus who was Stanford's first president, raised images of character-building and kindly paternalism of the Mark Hopkins-and-the-log variety, it also reflected the importance of research. He identified the heart of a university as "personal contact of young men and young women with *scholars* and *investigators*"; indeed, "a professor to whom original investigation is unknown should have no place in a university."[6]

The University of Chicago summed up the major developments in higher education of the previous three decades. In addition to a graudate school of arts and sciences, it included an undergraduate program, professional schools, an extramural adult education division, a university press, a spate of specialized journals, and a moral-competitive athletic program in which football held the star role. More striking than their existence in a single institution was the care with which these parts were organized. William Rainey Harper, Chicago's genius president, who had earned his Yale Ph.D. at the age of eighteen, had a penchant for organization. This trait made him a fit representative of a time when specialization seemed to have created a disarray that called for institutional reordering. His elaborate plan, largely drawn up before the hiring of his faculty, revealed a compulsive structuralism that led to the establishment of twelve faculty ranks, four equal quarters, a division of undergraduate work into junior and senior colleges, and a subordinating affiliation of small colleges with the university.[7]

Concentration on structure and management was evident also at older universities, where the rise of electives and the increasing autonomy of departments had brought fears of institutional incoherence. In 1890 Harvard turned its formerly amorphous graduate program into the Graduate School of Arts and Sciences, and Columbia began a reorganization that balanced its School of Political Science with Schools of Philosophy and of Pure Science. In 1896 both Columbia and Princeton signaled a sense of expanded function by adopting the name "university," often believed to symbolize unity amid diversity.[8]

In the new concern for carefully rationalized structure during the 1890s, teaching and research were not severed. The fact that its professional knowledge-creators were teachers still distinguished the university most sharply from other learned organizations. The early stress on teaching in presidential statements was, however, moderated by assertions that other functions were equally essential. In 1891 Eliot envisioned universities as having three principal functions. "In the first place they teach; secondly, they accumulate great stores of acquired and systematized knowledge in the form of books and collections; thirdly, they investigate." Research, he insisted, was "quite as indispensable" as the other two purposes. Gilman, abandoning the circumspection of his inaugural, could in 1896 glimpse a utopian future for universities, in which dedication to creating new knowledge overshadowed the teaching function. Other presidents, especially those at state universities, increasingly included public service as a principal university characteristic. Teaching no longer held place as uniquely essential. But even though the hierarchy might change and the lists lengthen, the persisting definitional functions of universities remained teaching and investigation, two elements that could follow each other tidily in a statement of purpose, but were daily entangled in relationships of considerable ambiguity.[9]

For the dedicated discoverers of truth, scarcely any place in America offered as good a haven as did universities. That much was admitted by even the devoutly research-minded. But universities, which in the 1880s had moved to lighten the burdens that older college patterns had placed on investigators, came gradually to pose new difficulties. Complaints varied with time and place, but it seems fairly accurate to schematize them as shifting from the unsympathetic environment set by a democratic society (1880s) to interference by business power (1890s), and from the distraction of faculty administrative duties (1890s) to administrative imposition from above (1900s). Accompanying these were more or less constant complaints that the teaching function itself hindered the university's ability to serve as the setting for productive scholarship.

The research-teaching conflict was matter of factly put by President Jacob Gould Schurman of Cornell in 1906: "It must, I think, be admitted that most university teachers, at least in the scientific departments, have chosen their profession not so much from the love of teaching as from the desire to continue the study of their specialty. While the number of those who have a positive distaste for teaching is small, there are many whose interest in teaching is secondary to their interest in investigation." But Schurman failed to convey the

passionate elevation of research above teaching in the self-images of some professors. From the highest of the twelve ranks at the University of Chicago,
William Gardner Hale, a Latinist, saw the advance of civilization dependent on
the research ideal. After suggesting the distress of a professor who foresaw his
epitaph as recounting merely, "He learned much that other men had discovered,
and conveyed much of this to others," Hale declared: "Had such a statement
been always the best that could be said of any man, our science today would still
be that of the primitive cave-dweller. It is the minds that have advanced *beyond*
what they have received from others that have brought us to the point where we
are. It is to the *discoverers,* in far greater measure than to the transmitters, that
the world is under obligation." But assertions of the excellence of research were
not always grounded in a theory of social progress. For some, its value transcended social experience. There were professors who associated the quest for
new knowledge with untainted motives and "sacred fire." "Remember the
research ideal, to keep it holy!" adjured Professor Albion Small of Chicago.
Research could be imagined as transforming the individual and elevating him,
not merely by its advancement of the nation or mankind, but through a merging
with ultimate reality akin to that of the Emersonian Genius.[10]

Professors with an eye to their own research sometimes protested the "democratic average" that was increasingly welcomed into university student bodies,
but even more troubling than quality were the quantity of students and the
amount of time that the faculty were obliged to spend teaching them. As if
regularly enrolled students were not burden enough, administrators sensitive to
calls for public service began in the 1890s to urge that professors involve themselves in the newly invented snares of summer school and extension lecturing.

Faculty resentment of distractions from research had grown acute by 1906,
when a survey by David Starr Jordan brought long, reflective responses. One
pointed to the importance of not disrupting "that unconscious cerebration which
is one of the most important factors in working out scientific results." Another
argued that the leisure of its greatest scholars was the university's most precious
asset: "We should count it a sin to require such a man to 'cover the ground.' We
should sacrifice the catalogue, make it thin and full of holes, confine the students
to a narrow range of typically good choices, and by these inconsequential sac-
rifices preserve for the great man his chance to do the work which he alone can
do." When it came to respect for the professor's leisure, European models were
found inadequate, although they were still cited as superior to those of the United
States. "America, it would seem," wrote one of Jordan's respondents, "has
combined the English way of keeping its instructors occupied all day with the
German idea of extending the working year over three-quarters or more of the
solar year."[11]

A survey of assistant professors at various universities taken in 1909 found
them evenly divided on the question of whether their conditions of employment
reasonably favored "carrying on advanced work and intellectual growth."
Among the complaints of the fifty-one who were dissatisfied, excessive or

elementary teaching duties overshadowed other problems (such as committee work, inadequate libraries, and low salaries). Hours of scheduled teaching ranged from occasionally below ten to as high as twenty, with fifteen being "not uncommon."[12]

The distractions of the teaching commitment seemed to reappear constantly in new guises. Trustees and patrons of universities sometimes sympathized with student complaints about faculty disinterest in teaching and sometimes asked for proof of direct practical results, which the seekers of new truth could not give. But faculties won some distinct successes for the research ideal. In a regent-faculty confrontation of 1909 at the University of Wisconsin, an ad hoc faculty committee charged the regents with placing undue emphasis on introductory courses and with belittling research outside the applied sciences. The controversy had been brought to a head by Frederick Jackson Turner's resignation. A major motive for Turner's decision had been his wish to expose what he regarded as an assault on humanistic research: the regents, after agreeing to free him from every other semester of teaching, had sided with students who complained of his inaccessibility. After an exchange of views between representatives of faculty and regents (which involved other issues beside research), the faculty won the regents' formal assent to its position.[13]

Some university insiders punctured high-minded objections to the interference of teaching by insisting that absence of creative scholarship on the part of a faculty member could be traced to either inherent incapacity or dislike of hard work.[14] But the more common counter argument presented teaching and research as mutually supportive. Both administrative officers and professors joined in this interpretation, and although it became a commonplace of discourse about universities, its interior logic is not without interest.

The subordinate part of the argument declared that teaching improved the quality of research. Gilman spoke of investigators who, being also teachers, gained from "the incitement of colleagues, the encouragement of pupils, and the observation of the public." The case was put more forcefully by his successor as president of Johns Hopkins, Ira Remsen, who had been the university's first professor of chemistry. Looking back over the experimentation during the university's formative years, Remsen recalled examples when relief from teaching had proved disastrous to men who were primarily researchers, because it had deprived them of stimulus.[15] The benefit teaching could bring to research was clearest in a setting like Johns Hopkins or Clark, where advanced students offered comradeship in investigation and enlightened appreciation of achievement. At these two universities, and in research-oriented departments elsewhere, the relationship between faculty and students often resembled not so much the tutelage of apprentice by practitioner as the bond among those in an evangelical college who had experienced salvation. But even elementary teaching was said to clarify the mind of the professor and keep him conscious of fundamentals.

The reverse proposition—that research was of benefit to teaching—was the major element in the case for linking the two functions. It became a staple of prouniversity rhetoric, though not many were as emphatic as the university man who maintained in 1906 that the teacher who was not a scholar was "likely to be a self-constituted oracle whose dilettantism is quite patent to the average undergraduate." Lecturing was best, the classicist Basil L. Gildersleeve believed, when the professor enhanced the material "by the living, plastic forces of personal research and personal communion with the sources." Evoking what has elsewhere been called the "dualistic" professor, President Charles R. Van Hise of the University of Wisconsin saw creative scholarship as essential to a university faculty member, crucial to his work with graduate students, but also enriching to undergraduate instruction. He made his position unusually explicit in 1916, when he called for each Wisconsin faculty member "to resolve that he will become a recognized scholar in his field and begin at once some piece of productive work."[16]

While assertions of the beneficial effect of research on teaching were sometimes motivated by a desire to promote research, they focused on the nature of the university as fundamentally a teaching institution and thus tended to undercut the most profound dedication to investigation. Sometimes this tendency was made explicit. President Jordan was one who could bluntly subordinate research to teaching, as when he said, "for the rank and file of our university men, teaching is the main function, and investigation receives its first value from the fact that adequate teaching is impossible without it." Occasionally warnings came from professors, including active researchers, that the teaching-research interdependency was being overstated. Harvard economist Thomas Nixon Carver recalled a faculty member whose efforts at productive scholarship were failures, but who still proved extraordinarily effective in teaching advanced students and directing their research. A classicist put the matter with surest restraint: "True, an able explorer may be an indifferent teacher; a good teacher may not have the spirit of initiative which leads to successful investigation; but the two faculties, though not always in perfect balance, are seldom wholly divorced, and a university professor should possess both."[17]

The organizational elaboration of universities can be variously explained, for instance, as simply a response to problems of size or as an expression of pervasive rationalizing tendencies of modern society. But at least some light is thrown on this complexity of design when it is seen as working out tensions between the teaching and research functions. The rise of the Ph.D. degree was one product of this functional interconnectedness. Etymologically, the Doctor of Philosophy was a teacher of the love of wisdom, and most early Ph.D.'s became professors. Yet the standards for the degree called for a rigorous devotion to investigation for its own sake and to knowledge justified by the way it extended previous learning, without regard to any pedagogical promise of the recipient. This degree, first earned in America at Yale in 1861, became the hallmark of Johns Hopkins, which awarded the highest number of Ph.D's in the 1880s and 1890s. In succeeding years, Harvard, Columbia, and Chicago demonstrated their eminence as universities partly by leading in the number of Ph.D.'s granted.[18]

It was primarily concern over the reputation of an American doctorate that brought about the formation of the Association of American Universities in 1900. All twelve original members had graduate schools and conferred the Ph.D. All of them were concerned that the degree be distinguished as one based on formal pursuit of nonprofessional learning beyond the bachelor's. Although there was sympathetic response when William James in 1903 branded the Ph.D. a symptom of "the Mandarin disease," observing that it offered no guarantee that its recipient would be an effective teacher, the degree remained firmly established. Its special aura symbolized both a high standard of scholarly investigation and the identification of the university with research. Yet partly because university rhetoric had so successfully intertwined teaching and research functions, the Ph.D. was desired by those seeking careers as teachers in colleges. Efforts to restrict such candidates to the master's degree failed, as did proposals to create a higher degree, comparable to the French Doctorat d'Etat. For a time, the honorary Ph.D. threatened to become the D.D. for college professors, but by 1910 the unearned Ph.D. was little more than a bad memory from a benighted academic past. The Ph.D. was unshakeable, even though one had to admit that it "really covers a multitude of things."[19]

Faculty rank was another device sometimes used to clarify relationships between teaching and research. As late as 1830 at Yale, and later elsewhere, a tutor was associated with a particular entering class, teaching it in a variety of subjects, whereas a professor was identified with a field, in which his knowledge might lead to his making scholarly contributions. In the university era, even younger faculty members were unlikely to accept a drillmaster's role, and some of them were expected to make investigation their chief concern. The wish to provide berths for young scholars who would do some teaching for little or no pay while actively pursuing their researches, led to various efforts to import the German position of Privatdocent. It was apparently an abortive program at Johns Hopkins in the late 1880s that inspired the creation of the position of docent at Clark, where it was held initially by no less a scholar than Franz Boas. Its occupants, generally just launching their careers, were expected to give only a single advanced course of lectures annually. By 1904 Hall described the rank as distinguished by its temporary nature, its independence of departmental authority, and its lack of salary. At Chicago, where the rank of docent specifically provided for half-time research and half-time advanced instruction, with payment from student fees only, President Harper declared the position to have lost its importance by 1904, though it sometimes provided a waiting niche for an aspirant to higher rank.[20]

Various plans to enable professors to pursue research, free of teaching responsibilities, trace back to Harvard's creation of the sabbatical year in 1880, a move timed to win Sanskritist Charles R. Lanman away from Hopkins. This expensive innovation had few early imitators, although by 1900 eleven colleges and universities granted sabbaticals.[21] Proposals for a more selective granting of research time through research professorships were under lively consideration by 1906.

President Arthur Twining Hadley of Yale, predicting that research professorships would bring decay of teaching power and breed envy, suggested an alternative that kept research tied to instruction; under his plan, any faculty member would be allowed to give one course of his own choosing close to his investigative concerns. It was generally considered a "first" when Cornell established a distinct research professorship in 1909 for psychologist Edward B. Titchener, though in fact he continued to teach a few graduate students. The step was part of an invigorated concern for research on the Ithaca campus. President Schurman, who had earlier stressed undergraduate liberal education and complained of the narrowness of premature specializers, now declared that "the future of the American university is with the graduate school or department of research." The recurrence of schemes to free faculty time for research suggests how strong teaching obligations remained. When both teaching and research were supposed to be underway, teaching generally got the lion's share of the faculty member's attention.[22]

Although the origins of the department system at the University of Virginia and Harvard in the 1820s lay mostly in concern for the student's opportunity to choose and to specialize, the spread of departmental organization during the university era increasingly represented the faculty's research specialization—its loss of concern for a realm of established knowledge that all educated persons should share. Terminology remained hazy for some time. Until at least 1890, the term "academic department" was often used to designate that part of an institution where studies for the Bachelor of Arts were pursued, as compared to the medical school, for instance. In the early days of Johns Hopkins, Gilman used a qualifying phrase—"of work" or "of science"—when speaking of "departments" in the newly emerging sense. The reorganization of the Harvard catalogue in 1870-71, which arranged courses by field rather than by the class of students who were allowed to take them, helped establish departmental identity, but not until the 1890s was there the clarity of organization that gave the term "the department" the precise referrent that it has today. With the opening of the University of Chicago, the view that departments were indeed a requisite organizational form for a university faculty seemed ratified. By the end of its first year, Chicago had twenty-seven departments, including neurology, elocution, and physical culture, each with its "head."[23]

The emergence of the departmental system can be used as evidence of over-compartmentalization in institutions becoming too structure-conscious. Still, in a period when intensified specialization tended to leave each faculty member isolated amid his research concerns (so narrow that one scarcely dared bore a colleague with what seemed in the isolation of the study to be a momentous breakthrough), departments helped hold together colleagues in danger of estrangement. In the enlarging faculties of universities, the alternative path of having each member identified with a fully differentiated specialty might well have led to an amorphous body of individuals deprived of the stimulation of small-group identity. One Harvard professor likened departments to "little

Faculties,'' reporting that they ''hold many and hotly contested meetings; they issue pamphlets; they edit publications; they examine candidates for honors and higher degrees.'' Although departments sometimes became self-aggrandizing entities that worked against broader institutional purposes, they did more good than harm. They offered both a focus for concerns about how a student could best pursue a subject and a body of research-judging peers more accessible than fellow specialists in other places.[24]

Doubtless there were occasions when university presidents thought of departments chiefly as a way of keeping the faculty under control. But in time it became clear that departments exerted institutional power that few professors could have attained as individuals. Some presidents came to worry about dictatorial attitudes of senior professors within departments, as Eliot did. The shift at Chicago in 1911 to elected chairmen indicated reaction to this concern, and something more. What could have been little more than a functional differentiation within a large organization had become a collegial, self-governing body. In Germany, by contrast, full professors—limited to one per subject—dominated academic governance.[25]

The tendency of departments to create artificial boundaries in the pursuit of knowledge was partially countered by the appearance of other intrauniversity organizational units. ''Divisions'' were more likely to be curricular abstractions than functioning bodies of colleagues. More significant was the emergence of superdepartments called ''schools,'' for which Columbia's School of Political Science (1880) early set the pattern. Such schools within the university were clearly teaching bodies. They revealed not only specialization but strivings for programmatic coherence and academic and public visibility akin to those of the older professional schools. It was not enough for Richard T. Ely in making his move to Wisconsin to be called to head a department. He had to be assured that he would be director of the ''School of Economics, Political Science, and History'' and that the position was equivalent to the headship of the observatory. Calling schools of political and social science a necessity, President George E. MacLean of the State University of Iowa in 1904 stressed their direct utility to the public, since they pursued studies ''in connection with the men of affairs and business institutions.'' A later development, the university research institute, sometimes associated with interdepartmentalism, sharply diverted faculty from teaching. Although such institutes were essentially a post–World War I development, they were predicted as early as 1903.[26]

With particular aptness, graduate students symbolized the dual commitment of the university. Not only were they the objects of teaching, they were also neophyte researchers. As an early official statement from Johns Hopkins put it, ''The instruction is carried on by such methods . . . as will encourage the student to become an independent and original investigator.'' Hopkins's first faculty member, Henry A. Rowland, satirized the usual mode of undergraduate teaching when he boasted that his scientific equipment was ''for investigation and [not] for amusing children.'' Asked what he would do with the students who had gathered in his laboratory at Hopkins, he responded, "I shall neglect them." But Rowland's "neglect" was part of an atmosphere of scholarly production that stimulated students as well as professors.[27]

With so much of institutional purpose focused on graduate students, there was a tendency to defend the university by idealizing them and their work. G. Stanley Hall felt that a thesis which was only "a very small brick in the great temple of human knowledge" needed no apology, and he found even more admirable the transforming effects of research on the student himself. For the young graduate student to grapple with the unknown and get "ever so tiny a result" was "an experience of epoch-making importance." Speaking on behalf of publication of theses, sociologist Albion Small was equally sanguine. What mattered, he said, was "the revolution of mental and moral attitude which publication of the results of one's first serious investigation marks. The young man discovers for himself that the thing can be done. The men who write books are no longer a superior species. They are merely elect through consecration of the same powers of which he begins to be aware. He enters their ranks feeling some of the sense of responsibility with which we like to believe other men assume holy orders." Although some professors exploited graduate students, setting them to work on narrow topics in order to get data for their own researches, both Hall and Small emphasized how much freedom students were given in choosing the subjects of their dissertations, especially if American practices were compared to German. Even while criticizing much about modern universities, the classicist Paul Shorey attributed a transforming effect to graduate study, from which even a "littérateur" could gain "the scholar's conscience and a clear conception of the difference between first-hand and second-hand knowledge."[28]

The fellowship as an award to attract resident graduate students (rather than a way for colleges to send their graduates elsewhere—usually abroad) was probably the crucial institutional invention that brought success to the early Johns Hopkins. In spite of grumblings from President Eliot and others about "hiring students" and cautionary analogies with theological schools whose subsidies for students were said to attract those with corrupt motives, the fellowship system was widely imitated. The proper arrangement for fellowships was among the questions most often discussed by the Association of American Universities. The growing propensity to utilize fellows as teaching assistants remained controversial. In 1912 President A. Ross Hill of the University of Missouri, true to the earlier vision, condemned the label "research fellowship" as a term that would once have been a redundancy and that reflected an undesirable conception of most fellows having to render an immediate return through some form of instruction. "Is not investigation," he asked, "if it is worthwhile at all, a service to the university, the fellow students of the incumbent, and the larger purposes for which the university exists?" In 1920 Dean Alfred H. Lloyd of the University of Michigan urged similar preservation of the standard: the fellowship, like the university professorship, "should mean complete freedom as well as distinct ability of mind."[29]

As graduate programs expanded after the turn of the century, the quality of students allegedly declined, but it was partly because these programs had been so freighted with institutional ideals that complaints over inferior graduate students arose. Graduate students were branded "children," mediocrities who were working off requirements, or mere "clever intellectual artisans." The brightest undergraduates were observed to be going into professional schools rather than graduate schools. Even the aging Gilman warned of useless and repetitive work from unguided graduate students. As horrible examples were exchanged, one account described a newly minted Eastern Ph.D. who, when told he would not be retained in his instructorship at the University of Michigan, replied, "Well, anyway I can drop into the ministry." In the aftermath, it was recounted, he dropped "heavily into and rapidly even through the ministry, his end being . . .in a small mercantile clerkship."[30]

One result of this post-1900 disillusionment with graduate students and alarm at perfunctory dissertations was an effort to spread into graduate programs the spirit of liberal culture that was then reviving in the colleges. Nowhere was this movement carried further than at Princeton, where both President Woodrow Wilson and Dean Andrew F. West, although divided over the graduate school's location, did agree on the name "Graduate College" and on applying the English residential pattern to graduate students. Both the surface appeal of Princeton's approach and its underlying organizational weakness were displayed at the 1913 meeting of the AAU. Wilson's successor, John G. Hibben, cited the dangers of narrowness and pedantry in graduate work as generally pursued. He spoke of the need for a sense of proportion, for human sympathy, and for linking the student's special subject with other kinds of knowledge. He wanted to insure a "humanistic strain" even in students pursuing the natural sciences. In a sharp departure from the established meaning of the Ph.D., Hibben expressed his doubts about current notions of research:

It is not absolutely essential that in the studies of a scholar some new discovery should be made. The progress of scholarship is often along the lines of rediscovering for himself that which has been known to the world of thought. The main question . . . is this, Does a scholar's research furnish a new center of illumination to lighten the path of his progress? Is his increasing knowledge a lamp to his feet? . . . The exclusive desire to discover something new and in an original way has its dangers and may lead to purely mechanical methods of investigation. And our studies will become mechanical unless we bring to our task a richly furnished mind.[31]

Hibben's audience, including the president of the University of Wisconsin, a University of Illinois professor of chemistry, and a Johns Hopkins professor of economics, expressed high admiration for his views. But subsequent discussion of his address revealed the unlikelihood of any significant change in the epistemological narrowing that accompanied the research orientation of graduate schools. Attempting to combine continued insistence on original investigation with Hibben's humanism, his auditors focused their attention principally on alternative organizational devices to add to an already highly bureaucratized institution. They proposed requirements that graduate students pursue a minor subject, maintain a longer period of residence, major in a division rather than a department, and—fatefully—that the degree itself be subject to "more administrative thoroughness." Predictably, graduate study at most universities would remain centered on specialized individual research, but another suggestion, participation of graduate students in actual teaching, showed the survival of older notions that teaching was innately humanistic and drew on the general belief that teaching and research were mutually enhancing.[32]

For all their pride in the institutions they were building, university leaders did not forget that universities existed among other institutions dedicated to the advancement of knowledge—at first, learned academies and government agencies, later also research foundations and business laboratories. With its almost reverential mention of the "academy," Gilman's inaugural had suggested fruitful interchange between the university and the established learned societies of Europe and America. Government bureaus were regarded as a source of financial support and ideas for research, not only at Johns Hopkins, where the staff was alert to the capital's scientific community, but also at Western state universities, where federal and state geologic surveys proved particularly important as research models. An exemplary institutional collaboration was the relationship between the University of Wisconsin and the State Historical Society, which furnished quarters for the university library for many years.[33]

Granting the frequency of mutual assistance, universities were still in competition with other learned organizations for personnel, funds, and authority. In such situations, one principal weakness of the universities was the tendency of teaching responsibilities to deflect faculty from original research. In language foreshadowing that of Adolf von Harnack three years later, Robert S. Woodward, head of the Carnegie Institution, argued in 1906 that research grantees who tried to remain in part-time teaching usually found their time consumed not only by teaching but by committee work. He implied that the university setting was appropriate for limited research efforts but that major projects belonged more properly in organizations such as his. Meanwhile, Remsen was grumbling that Woodward's Carnegie Institution and another new foundation, the Rockefeller Institute, were depriving universities of needed investigators. Worse yet, Schurman could foresee a grave threat to university autonomy posed by powerful, self-perpetuating trustees of wealthy foundations with sweeping purposes to serve "civilization."[34]

Sometimes university spokesmen directly attacked competing knowledge-producing bodies: learned academies were said to be fossilized, research foundations inexperienced, governmental bureaus given over to routine and subject to political whim, and business laboratories deflected from truth-seeking by economic motivation. But the university was on firmest ground when it stressed what was, from some vantage points, a weakness—its obligation to combine teaching with creative scholarship. This very duality gave the university a unique importance. Versions of the "mutual support" argument were brought forward, with emphasis placed on the stimulation that teaching gave researchers through a return to first principles and the process of encountering the fresh queries of the younger generation. "The big man in the university," Van Hise declared, "goes broadly over his subject, in an elementary course, thinks ahead over his special lines, and puts those additional thoughts in their relations with the older ideas, and so advances his subject in a broader way than do most men in the [government] bureau. I think, if we compare a half-dozen universities with a half-dozen scientific bureaus, we shall find that, so far as great ideas are concerned, the advantage is upon the side of the university." Examining a list of the most important contributors to the fields of electricity and radioactivity, physicist Ernest G. Merritt of Cornell found that it included only professors, evidence for his assertion that nearly all major discoveries of pure science came from universities. Not only its transforming effect on research, but teaching itself was put forward as a defense of the university's importance for the increase of knowledge. The presence of disciples was sometimes called essential for productive scholarship. Only the university was designed to guarantee transgenerational continuity, and if no new scholars were trained, the learned enterprise would founder.[35]

Coinciding with the rise of American universities was the appearance of such organizations as the American Philological Association, the American Chemical Society, and the American Economic Association. The new scholarly groups differed from earlier learned academies in their emphasis on specialized fields of knowledge. Although admission did not confer the honor accorded by membership in such bodies as the American Philosophical Society and the American Academy of Arts and Sciences, the newer organizations were powerful vehicles of professional status, stressing the value of trained expertise. Since universities gained their reputation by having a professionalized faculty, their leaders were on the whole sympathetic to the emerging specialized scholarly associations. Gilman, whose reform efforts as president of the American Social Science Association appeared to convince him of its hopeless stodginess, encouraged his faculty to take the initiative in forming such groups, and Eliot (never dreaming of the epithet "slave market") praised them for giving universities valuable opportunities to discover talented candidates for their faculties. On the grounds that the associations counteracted provincialism, President W. H. P. Faunce of Brown justified his institution's financial support of attendance at annual meetings. By offering scholars extramural visibility, the associations further helped to counter the tendency of teaching to overshadow and sometimes obliterate the value of research. If students did not flock to a professor's classes, recognition from colleagues within his specialty at other institutions might more than compensate. Rather than competing, the associations helped universities in their formative years to develop an identity as institutions defined by more than the teaching function.[36]

Knowledge-oriented organizations seemed benign colaborers compared to social groups that judged universities by bald utilitarian or ideologically puristic standards. Practical men of the nineteenth century had often seemed to expect the work of the university to lead more or less directly to the production of tangible goods. Although there is evidence that industrial leaders were rather slow to see universities as a source of technological advance, farmers with complaints about hog cholera and businessmen who associated sound money with morality and free trade with the devil applied pressure to bring universities into line. When the Populists won power in Kansas, they proved no better than their Republican predecessors at tolerating truthseekers of another economic persuasion in the State Agricultural College. The defense of the classics in the Yale Report of 1828 found echoes a half-century later as universities sought to justify the pursuit of esoteric truth in the face of accusations of uselessness, unorthodoxy, and elitism.[37]

At Cornell, the founder believed that the dignity of labor, the reduction of expenses, and the advantages in "learning a trade" dictated a Voluntary Labor Corps for students. Obliged to cooperate, President White rationalized that the shop and farm work would prove educationally illustrative and that repetitious production could be avoided. The emphasis on the major-subject system at Stanford derived in part from founder Leland Stanford's insistence on preparing students for useful lives. As president of the University of California in the early 1870s, Gilman, who had warned against dilution of the university possibilities created by the Morrill Act, found himself the target of vitriolic attacks from farm and labor organizations when he resisted using land-grant funds to give instruction in shop mechanics and basic farming techniques. Expecting to escape such pressures in Baltimore, he found that there too proponents of bread-and-butter education could be vocal, even within the circle of the Johns Hopkins trustees. One of that body, dubious about professional abstraction, insisted that the greatest discoveries always came from those involved in matters of practical application. In many ways, the new Massachusetts Institute of Technology and technically oriented Lehigh University were truer to the mood of the Flash Age than was Johns Hopkins. Eliot brought some of the MIT ethos with him to Harvard, where he had a standing disagreement with the chemistry professors over their resistance to applied courses. In 1881 he assured the American Bell Telephone Company that professors would be allowed to use Harvard's new Jefferson Laboratory in work for private corporations.[38]

State universities, which in their earliest form had been elitist classical colleges, avoided being reduced to trade schools but were increasingly obliged to demonstrate that they not only turned out students who could get jobs but were "good for the state" in the sense of helping develop resources. Geology and engineering, with their tangible contributions to industrial advance, were favored fields in the state university expansion of the 1880s. A representative of the University of Georgia recounted to a meeting of the National Association of State Universities that, given the importance of the Georgia peach, an entomological program had been particularly effective in loosening legislative pursestrings. Increasingly, state universities were expected to keep their agriculture programs

open to students who were not high school graduates. But through their preparatory departments, their power to accredit high schools, and their determination
to raise admission standards for their liberal arts programs, state universities
managed to counter pressures that might have adulterated their work. At the same
time, they created an educational ladder that appealed to ideals of equal opportunity. Not many argued that the state university should be all-inclusive, but the
public expected ''sensible'' results from those who did attend. The down-to-
earth educational philosophy of Booker T. Washington sounded like good sense
not only for freedmen's offspring, but for any young person being supported by
society while extending formal education into early adulthood. It grew ever
harder to recall the almost superstitious awe of elegant learning that had once
kept large audiences sitting through day-long commencement exercises that included addresses in Greek and Latin.[39]

Universities that had scorned the ''pork-chop'' practicalism of the nineteenth
century often embraced a high-brow ''service'' orientation that focused principally upon governmental achievement. This view, recognizable as a factor in
university reform as early as the post–Civil War decade, was salient during the
Progressive Era, affecting the newly professionalized social sciences more than
any other part of the university. The Johns Hopkins economist Jacob Hollander,
noting in 1915 that ''every American university has to an increasing extent
felt . . . pressure—emanating from federal, state, and municipal governments . . . —for the services of members of its staff expert in economical and
social affairs,'' granted certain benefits in these relationships but warned of
deflection from both teaching and research. Indeed, as economists found themselves able to exert direct influence on those in power through their role as
experts, their concern for teaching noticeably declined.[40]

The effects of these two phases of utilitarianism—economic practicalism and
government service—can be traced at the University of Wisconsin, the state's
sole recipient of its Morrill funds. The biology department was early steered
toward practical problems of medicine, agriculture, and fisheries, and the geology program toward mining. It seemed in the early 1890s that the state's businessmen might be similarly served by a program modeled on the Wharton School
at the University of Pennsylvania, but the effort was sidetracked by the restructuring necessary to attract Richard T. Ely to head the school. Yet Ely was far
from shunning social utility. He and his associates sought to make the School of
Economics, Political Science, and History a ''West Point for civil life.'' The
practical bent of the new program forecast the later emergence of ''the Wisconsin
Idea,'' when the activities of professors and graduates in aiding the legislative
and regulatory agencies would make the university's name an international
byword for government by expert. In his inaugural in 1904, Van Hise had called
for an eclectic ''combination university,'' insisting that it must support disinterested scholarship in every field. He argued that there was no real conflict with
utility: ''It cannot be predicted at what distant nook of knowledge, apparently
remote from any practical service, a brilliantly useful stream may spring. It is

certain that every fundamental discovery yet made by the delving student has been of service to man before a decade has passed.'' This interpretation was common among university presidents, though Van Hise suggested an unusually speedy rate for delivery of practical applications. Although the scholarly might find it preferable to belong to an institution whose practical bent was toward general social welfare rather than business, and whose presidents recognized the difficulties in predicting ultimate utilities, it was still true that the increasing service orientation of the university drew glamour away from nonapplied research.[41]

After hearing Van Hise in 1905 predict a future of power and wealth for state universities, President Hall was worried, and not just about the status of endowed universities. Recalling that a generation earlier the uselessness of a piece of research had placed it ''a little at a premium,'' he gently questioned the feeling, however nonmercenary it might be, ''that the usefulness of a discovery is the best and most legitimate motive for the investigator of the future.'' Nonetheless, programs that academic purists feared were corrupting sometimes turned out to be supportive of their ideal of knowledge for its own sake. The state universities' involvement in nonutilitarian research often derived from the status originally given research programs in applied fields under the Hatch Act of 1887. When a wealthy dairyman on the Wisconsin Board of Regents attacked the policy of granting time off from teaching in the College of Letters and Science for research that he felt led nowhere, Van Hise was able to respond with an argument for fairness, since comparable research opportunities were firmly established in the Colleges of Agriculture and Engineering. The Wisconsin Idea might deflect some professorial experts from teaching, but ideals of intrainstitutional comity kept professors of philology within the range of prerogatives granted professors of public administration.[42]

To the challenge for justification of the privileges claimed by universities in a democratic society, ''we teach'' was perhaps the principal response. To the inquiry as to how such teaching benefitted the everyday citizen who would never set foot on university grounds, the answer sometimes was that university representatives would reach these people through extension services. The answer could also be that the university prepared the teachers of the all-inclusive public schools. In fact, that task was more often carried out by normal schools that university builders regarded as separate and inferior institutions; there was nevertheless a persistent effort by even the most research-oriented universities to reach public school teachers. Johns Hopkins appointed a professor of psychology and pedagogy in 1884, and Clark University was the home of the journal *Pedagogical Seminary*. In 1890, when Massachusetts seemed likely to raise teacher preparation to postsecondary status and to create in Boston a ''Normal College'' with a postgraduate course, Eliot showed surprising alacrity in creating a new faculty post that made preparation for secondary school teaching careers more readily available to students at Harvard.[43]

Alternatively, ''we teach'' might imply that the university taught all those young people who proved themselves capable by ascending the educational ladder to its doors. The last quarter of the nineteenth century saw sustained efforts by colleges and universities to regularize admission requirements and to establish close links with public high schools as well as private preparatory schools. The movement for upgrading high schools through inspection by state universities in the West, the creation of standardized admission examinations in the East, and the development of regional accrediting associations made up of high schools and colleges—all these lent credibility to the university's claim that its teaching stood for democratic openness. Mounting enrollment statistics in institutions of higher education—from 52,000 in 1870 to 355,000 in 1910—bespoke a trend toward greater inclusiveness.[44]

As a response to social queries about the usefulness and democracy of universities, "we teach" was not a fully satisfactory answer. The persistent critic could always point out that the vast majority of "college-age" Americans were not being taught and could quickly discover examples of impractical or abstruse subjects on which good money was being "wasted." But the public was not generally unfriendly to universities. After all, Americans had long supported the recondite fields of theology and astronomy, noted for neither utility nor democracy. Prouniversity rhetoric seems to have reached a broad public; in any case, university presidents became well-known figures through newspaper interviews and public addresses, and the five-foot bookshelf that "Dr. Eliot" recommended sold beyond the publisher's most optimistic estimates. The case for universities was laid before the country with enough success that on the whole these creations of the last third of the nineteenth century were nurtured, survived, and grew.

But to the extent that university spokesmen emphasized teaching in response to challengers, they subtly undermined those who made the creation of knowledge a defining characteristic of universities and whose primary allegiance was to research. If the university rested its case before society solely on its role as teacher, then by implication other institutions might as well control the search for new truth. To emphasize teaching was especially risky after 1900 because the goals of teaching itself had undergone a revitalization independent of research. The integral student mind began to be seen as a ground on which to recreate the institutional coherence undermined by increasing specialization. This renewed concern for students focused attention on undergraduates not graduates, ideals not facts, and humane wholeness rather than specialized innovation by experts. This movement for liberal culture, recognizable in the 1890s, grew increasingly vocal after 1900. Although it was strongest in small liberal arts colleges, it is only a slight exaggeration to say that it captured control of Harvard when A. Lawrence Lowell succeeded Eliot as president in 1909.[45]

Some of these counterrevolutionaries (who were, ironically, among the most effective academic innovators of the twentieth century) branded as myth the widely accepted generalization that investigation led to better teaching. To the contrary, they challenged, did not the concentration essential to original investigation deprive teaching of reach, connectedness, philosophy, and links to humane and social concerns? To the extent that students also wanted to specialize, the investigator-professor met their need. But was it not better to protect students against any tendency toward early narrowing? More and more, it was argued, whether they liked it or not, students were being drawn toward the professional scholar's stance at its worst. Undergraduate "research papers" were said to reveal formalized pedantry as often as understanding. Research-minded professors were accused of thinking that "showing them how to be like me" was the essence of good teaching.

Andrew F. West, a power at Princeton, spoke out for the nonproductive professor who could still be "a well of knowledge for everybody." (He himself apparently never published a piece of research-based work.) In this spirit, certain professors of the humanities were calling in 1906 for the creation of specifically nonresearch professorships to be held by teachers who unembarrassedly accepted results of others' investigations and dedicated themselves to education for undergraduates. Some professors even insisted that it was impossible to teach well *if* one did research, and Professor Fred Lewis Pattee of Pennsylvania State, satirizing the decline of teaching, urged that higher education "bring back Mark Hopkins." Anyone reading Edwin Slosson's description of the lecture method as he found it operating during his explorations of 1909 could easily believe something was drastically amiss: "It would be well if the teachers did not know quite so much, if they knew how to tell what they did know better. . . . In many cases it has seemed to me that the instructor has come into the room without the slightest idea of how he is to present his subject. He rambles on in a more or less interesting and instructive manner, but without any apparent regard to the effect on his audience or the economy of their attention." Perhaps things went better in the laboratories.[46]

What the overspecialized, "Germanized" professors who had shaped the universities had tended to forget, it was said, was "culture." "A wide vision of the best things which man has done or aspired after" was proposed as an educational goal superior to "competence" or "expertise." Culture stood for standards, connectedness, balance, and keeping nature in its place. Although it would be a distortion to reduce this attitude to a desire for social status, it is fair to say that the new rationale for academic social ascendancy, based on specialized knowledge and expert service, had failed to satisfy either the intellectual or social aspirations of some who harked back to an older ideal, that of an aristocracy of culture. Some spokesmen for a revival of culture argued in language that included graduate students as well as undergraduates, but the younger students were the usual object of concern. Unless something was done, warned Harvard's Irving Babbitt, "the A.B. degree will mean merely that a man has expended a certain number of units of intellectual energy on a list of elective studies that may range from boiler-making to Bulgarian."[47]

Attitudes at the University of Wisconsin suggest common ambivalences toward the effect of research on undergraduates. There Frederick Jackson Turner had said in 1892 that the best seniors were quite ready to pursue original investigation, and soon the research ethos had captured the annual "joint debate" between the two literary societies. This Wisconsin tradition, with its emphasis on rhetorical skill and esprit de corps, had long seemed the essence of collegiatism. Under the stimulation of Ely's applied empiricism, however, it became a major investigative venture into a selected social problem, followed by publication of accumulated findings. In fact, the research techniques practiced became the model for the state's pioneering Legislative Reference Library. But the very legislature that gained international repute for its reliance on scholarly investigation was concerned that excessive faculty involvement in research could hurt students, especially undergraduates. In 1906 a legislative committee urged that faculty research be encouraged "only so far as that can be done without detriment to the instruction to which students are entitled." The *Wisconsin Alumni Magazine* echoed the concern, deprecated the attention given graduate students, who tended to be out-of-staters, and urged that teaching should be the criterion for promotion. Shortly thereafter, the regents reined in the university's research-advocating president by voting that investigative ability, if not combined with teaching skill, should not be an adequate basis for hiring or promoting faculty. It was not merely in the small colleges or the older Eastern universities that researchism was challenged by demands for "good teaching."[48]

Although it is easy to exaggerate the importance of wars as turning points in academic history, it is still true that World War I was a test for American universities that left their relation to the world of knowledge significantly changed. Professors eagerly sought ways to join the "real world" of the war, and service to the state in its pursuit of military victory swept other ideals aside. Only an exceptional few preserved a stance of critical independence.[49] Actions taken with passionate certitude were later recalled with shame, though the record of violations of academic freedom has never been fully traced. War disrupted customs and ideas about status that had somewhat protected the university from the rest of society. Basic research in wartime appeared almost unpatriotic. Teaching took on an immediacy that pulled it toward training and indoctrination. When there was opportunity for stock-taking, however, the wartime experience appeared to have strengthened the university's identity as a knowledge-creating institution. At the same time, the rise of other research agencies had lent new urgency to putting forward the case for the special merit of research pursued in a teaching institution.

After initial alarms over the sharp drop in enrollments early in the 1917–18 school year, universities and colleges found themselves nearly swamped with students in 1918, as the Students' Army Training Corps set up programs on 525 campuses. The American Council on Education and the Bureau of Education had propagandized to get young men into the program, and some who had never intended to go to college found themselves there as a patriotic duty. Not only were a number of students academically ill-equipped, but the course of instruction set up for the SATC was designed "to develop as a great military asset the large body of young men in the colleges." The classics, for instance, were excluded, and faculty members found themselves teaching the rudiments of fields far from their areas of specialization. After the war, enrollments did not drop back. It became increasingly common for young Americans to attend college, and complaints mounted concerning poorly prepared students, overcrowded classrooms, and overburdened teaching schedules. It was not new to hear American professors say that their heavy teaching assignments kept them from their "own work." But for some, the situation now appeared so hopeless that in fairly good conscience they could settle for perfunctory teaching and escape into studies and laboratories. Honors programs, partly justified as rescuing the gifted from the sea of ordinary students, gave the investigative ideal a new hold on undergraduates.[50]

The liberal culture critics of research-mindedness had suffered a check by the quantity, quality, and motives of the new wave of students. Yet for humanists too there had been a gain. At Columbia, the interdisciplinary "war issues" course required by the SATC quickly developed into an introductory course in contemporary civilization. It was intended, in the words of Columbia's Dean Frederick J. E. Woodbridge, to "give to the generations to come a common background of ideas and commonly understood standards of judgment." Many other institutions also continued variants of the wartime course.[51]

As the war brought students flooding in, faculty were pouring out—none in greater numbers than scientists with research backgrounds. Some in fact had left before America entered the war, to work in industries stimulated by the cut-off of German dyes, drugs, and optical glass. After April 1917, they left for a range of duties—expanding food supplies for the Allies, setting industrial allocation procedures, manufacturing poison gas. Fears that the best might never return to academic life proved ill-founded: most did return, and most were still devoted to investigation. Yet wartime experiences had modified some attitudes. Now universities often seemed rather too placid. "The ideal dedicated investigator no longer stood alone on a high pedestal," James Bryant Conant recalled of his feelings on returning to the Harvard faculty after service in the Chemical Warfare Service. "I recognized that there were other fascinating ways of using one's energies."[52]

"Pure" research in particular was undercut during the war. Wisconsin reported to the Bureau of Education that almost all scientific research had been shifted into "war channels," and at Cornell war conditions had led to dropping "twenty-seven different lines of investigation." Research work in psychology was reported to be down by seventy-five percent. Like the plowman seizing his musket, the dwellers in libraries and laboratories had proved their patriotism and their versatility. Hailed for wartime services, the universities emerged with a fund of public respect. How was this new prestige to be used? It could conceivably increase autonomy and allow reaffirmation of the goal of discovering truth without regard to utility. In this season of reassessment, antiutilitarian investigators were sometimes most forcefully represented by the humanists. Dean Woodbridge, whose own works of scholarship centered on Aristotle, urged universities to strive for "the philosophical spirit . . . the interest, poise, and sense of power which come only from the consciousness that a particular thing which one may be engaged in doing is part of a commanding whole." The experimental method, in contrast (and here he resisted the flexibility praised so heavily during the Progressive Era and the war), had led to "a readiness to attack any problem without preparation," a tendency found at its worst in the social sciences.[53]

Skepticism about the German university pattern had grown up in America well before the war. The peak decade for American students in Germany had been the 1880s, and by 1900 it was generally believed that America had created a worthy university establishment of its own. It was nevertheless a shock to American academics to have Germany emerge as the enemy in war, and many who had praised German academic achievement felt themselves contaminated. A desire to purge and purify helps explain the series of incidents of intellectual chauvinism in universities. German language courses were dropped, German-born or pro-German professors fired, and German universities bitterly identified with autocratic callousness. Yet the upshot was not a rejection of the research motive. A generally accepted interpretation among the research-minded pictured German universities as betraying or forced to violate their own ideals. Some argued that the United States had now replaced Germany as the world's most favorable setting for universities that sought truth for its own sake. In any case, German universities appeared so badly weakened by the war and subsequent economic catastrophe that American scholars imagined themselves seizing the torch from a fallen leader and taking on responsibility for the highest university ideals.[54]

During and immediately after the war, the American learned enterprise produced a new array of knowledge-oriented organizations. Particularly challenging to universities were industrial research programs, thriving in businesses that had witnessed the wartime effectiveness of research teams. This increased competition, sharpened by industry's larger salaries, forced universities to review their relation to utilitarian purposes. In the heady materialism of postelection 1920, President Hadley of Yale could project the happiest symbiosis of social utility and university purpose. Whereas industry sought to secure "gainful knowledge," he explained, universities had as their object the promotion of "useful knowledge," and given the overlap of these two aims, it was appropriate to welcome outside stimuli that could make a student learn more efficiently. Involvement in industrial programs was a justifiable "means for giving the student a motive in the way of personal advantage to himself in the solving of a problem." Michigan's graduate dean saw great benefit in the fact that graduate schools now included more students planning nonacademic careers. With the intentions of students becoming so varied, he maintained, "teaching can only gain, not lose; . . . becoming at once more vigorous and more nobly serviceable. After all, it is from teaching and the teacher that interpretation and appreciation of life and the facts of life must come. Yet these things are . . . bound to be feebly done, unless teachers meet on their own solid ground those who are making so much of science and nature in the practical exploitation of life and its facts." A similar feeling for solid ground and practical exploitation underlay the remarks made at about the same time by Professor Henry P. Talbot of MIT before the American Chemical Society. To improve teaching, he suggested, "pedagogues" should consider spending occasional summers in industrial plants.[55]

All this was a far cry from the old-fashioned research purism expressed by Frank Baldwin Jewett, chief engineer of the Western Electric Company who, at the same gathering that Hadley addressed, saw the university as "primarily concerned with the mental side of the advancement of human beings and only incidentally with the material side. Its whole organization is one designed to transmit accumulated knowledge and methods of acquiring knowledge from one generation to the next, and to explore unknown fields for the purpose of extending the stock of accumulated knowledge. Its whole being is governed by a code of ethics based on the idea that the acquisition and dissemination of exact knowledge is the central force of its existence." A university leader like Hadley was not going to have his institution turned into any such fortress of abstraction. Yet it was on grounds close to Jewett's position that the universities could best justify themselves in a world in which industrial leaders had decided to foster investigation. Universities were the matrix, it could be maintained, from which knowledge-makers were produced. Without universities, other research organizations would soon dwindle for lack of personnel. Rather than taking advantage of university weakness, "raiders" should help see to it that academic salaries and other conditions did not fall too far behind those of business research organizations. Further, industrial laboratories might support some basic research, but they would remain in the shadow of a profit-making organization. Universities could by comparison justify themselves as the home of pure, theoretical—the "highest"—research.[56]

Since it was not only industry that now vied with the universities for leadership in knowledge-creation, there was good reason for university rhetoric to remain multiform. The air was full of proposals for "exclusively research institutes" in addition to the older Carnegie Institution and Rockefeller Institute.[57] Researchers in institutes were generally freer of external concerns than those in either industry or academic life. Against these competitors, accordingly, the logic of the universities' argument was reversed. Foundations were pictured as too selective to keep knowledge growing as it should; they were even thought to be unhealthily divorced from social concerns. The same university spokesmen who warned of the practicalist bias in the industrial laboratory could caution against the isolationism of the independent research institute.

For the universities, the new coordinating bodies that developed as a result of the war, the National Research Council and the American Council of Learned Societies, did not represent a particularly new or unwelcome phenomenon. If anything, they were viewed as too inactive.[58] University leaders themselves had launched the Association of American Agricultural Colleges and Experiment Stations, the National Association of State Universities, and the Association of American Universities. The rationale for these groups fit the new councils as well: in a nation where the government was relatively unconcerned with science and education, voluntaristic organizations with institutional members could discourage redundancy and uphold standards. Similarly, the scholarly professional organizations had bred a good deal of sophistication about how other loyalties could support rather than undercut university purposes. In effect, spokesmen for universities could accept the new coordinating bodies, grant them their due, and yet insist that finally, so far as the creation of new knowledge and the developing of creators of new knowledge were concerned, "it happens here."

American universities of world importance, the dream of a few frustrated academics when the Civil War broke out, were firmly established by the onset of post–World War I normalcy. It had happened within a single human lifespan. The written history of these universities, blessed with a wealth of preserved documents, has been crippled by the institutional parochialism that has made many a centennial history a catch-all of who came and went. To what purpose did they come and go—the presidents, the professors, the students? That question should not go unasked. In the congeries of individual motives, it is possible to discern that what held them together, what made them part of an institution, was a concern for knowing. Yet the goal of helping someone else know something (or how to do something) that he or she did not know before sometimes contradicted the goal of making known something never known before. The many facile denials of such conflict did not prevent its persistence. These two versions of the pursuit of knowledge underwent manipulations that had more to do with immediate situations of institutional stress than with a genuine sense of what was involved in embracing such ideals, and both were reshaped by the demands of a democratic, industrializing society. The presence of these social pressures helped force into alliance teachers and researchers (and teaching and research tendencies within individuals). The university's flexibility and its bureaucratic elaboration made room for both functions, even when their antagonism could not be disguised or removed.

## Notes

1. John Jay Chapman to Mrs. Henry Whitman, 12 August 1893, in *John Jay Chapman and His Letters,* ed. M. A. DeWolfe Howe (Boston: Houghton Mifflin, 1937), pp. 96–97.

2. Andrew Dickson White, "Inaugural Address," in *Builders of American Universities: Inaugural Addresses,* ed. David Andrew Weaver (Alton, Ill.: Shurtleff College Press, 1950), pp. 248–49, 255–56, 268; Charles William Eliot, "Inaugural Address as President of Harvard College," in *Educational Reform: Essays and Addresses* (New York: Century, 1898), esp. p. 27.

3. Daniel Coit Gilman, "The Johns Hopkins University in its Beginnings," *University Problems in the United States* (New York: Century, 1898), p. 13.

4. Ibid., pp. 14, 15, 31–32; J. Thomas Scharf, *The Chronicles of Baltimore . . .* (Baltimore: Turnbull, 1874), pp. 395–96.

5. Dorothy Ross, *G. Stanley Hall: The Psychologist as Prophet* (Chicago: University of Chicago Press, 1972), chap. 11, esp. p. 202; Hall, "Address at Opening Exercises," in *Builders of American Universities,* ed. Weaver, pp. 370, 373, 375–376.

6. Jordan, "Inaugural Address," in *Builders of American Universities,* ed. Weaver, pp. 353 (italics mine), 356.

7. Laurence R. Veysey, *The Emergence of the American University* (Chicago: University of

Chicago Press, 1965), pp. 371–72; Richard J. Storr, *Harper's University: The Beginnings* (Chicago: University of Chicago Press, 1966), esp. pp. 61–62. See also, Thomas Wakefield Goodspeed, *A History of the University of Chicago Founded by John D. Rockefeller: The First Quarter-Century* (Chicago: University of Chicago Press, 1916).

8. Hugh Hawkins, *Between Harvard and America: The Educational Leadership of Charles W. Eliot* (New York: Oxford University Press, 1972), pp. 72–73; Nicholas Murray Butler, *Across the Busy Years: Recollections and Reflections*, 2 vols. (New York and London: Charles Scribner's Sons, 1939–40), 1:136–46; Thomas Jefferson Wertenbaker, *Princeton, 1746–1896* (Princeton: Princeton University Press, 1946), pp. 368–69.

9. Eliot, *Educational Reform*, p. 225; Gilman, "The Future of American Colleges and Universities," *Atlantic Monthly* 78 (1896): 179; George E. MacLean, "The State University the Servant of the Whole State," *Transactions and Proceedings of the National Association of State Universities* 2 (1904): 33 (hereafter cited as *NASU Transactions*).

10. Jacob Gould Schurman, "The Reaction of Graduate Work on the Other Work of the University," *Journal of Proceedings and Addresses of the Association of American Universities* 7 (1906): 60 (hereafter cited as *AAU Journal*); William Gardner Hale, "The Doctor's Dissertation," ibid., 3 (1902): 16–17 (italics in original); Veysey, *Emergence of the American University*, p. 150; Joseph Ames's remark, quoted in "The Degree of Master of Arts," *AAU Journal* 12 (1910): 45; Small, quoted in Storr, *Harper's University*, p. 159.

11. David Starr Jordan, "To What Extent Should the University Investigator Be Relieved from Teaching?" *AAU Journal* 7 (1906): 30, 34, 42.

12. Guido Hugo Marx, "The Problem of the Assistant Professor," *AAU Journal* 11 (1910): 28. This survey of younger faculty may reflect the sort of restiveness that led in Germany to one formation of the Junior Faculty Association. See Fritz Ringer, "The German Academic Community," in this volume.

13. Merle Curti and Vernon Carstensen, *The University of Wisconsin: A History, 1848–1925*, 2 vols. (Madison, Wis.: University of Wisconsin Press, 1949), 2:59–62; Ray Allen Billington, *Frederick Jackson Turner: Historian, Scholar, Teacher* (New York: Oxford University Press, 1973), pp. 292–97, 303–5.

14. Anon. remark, quoted in Jordan, "The University Investigator," p. 41.

15. Gilman, *University Problems*, p. 19; Ira Remsen's remark, quoted in "Discussion of the Opportunities for Higher Instruction and Research in State Universities," *AAU Journal* 6 (1905): 66.

16. Anon. remark, quoted in Jordan, "The University Investigator," p. 41; Hugh Hawkins, *Pioneer: A History of the Johns Hopkins University, 1874–1889* (Ithaca, N.Y.: Cornell University Press, 1960), pp. 222–23; Curti and Carstensen, *Wisconsin*, 2:47; Steven Turner, cited by Ringer in his essay in this volume, p. 413.

17. Jordan, "The University Investigator," p. 25; Basil L. Gildersleeve, quoted in Hawkins, *Pioneer*, p. 217. Cf. Joseph Ben-David, *American Higher Education: Directions Old and New* (New York: McGraw-Hill, 1972), p. 113.

18. Frederick Rudolph, *The American College and University: A History* (New York: Alfred A. Knopf, 1962), p. 335; Henry James, *Charles W. Eliot: President of Harvard University, 1869–1909*, 2 vols. (Boston: Houghton Mifflin Company, 1930), 2:345; Hawkins, *Pioneer*, p. 122.

19. "Second Day's Proceedings," *AAU Journal* 1 (1900): 14–15; Veysey, *Emergence of the American University*, pp. 175–76; James, "The Ph.D. Octopus," *Harvard Monthly* 36 (1906): 1–9; Joseph Ames's remark, quoted in "The Degree of Master of Arts," *AAU Journal* 12 (1910): 45–46; George E. Vincent, "The Granting of Honorary Degrees," ibid. 16 (1914): 27–34; "Discussion of the Granting of Honorary Degrees," ibid., pp. 34–41; Charles H. Haskins, quoted in "The Degree of Master of Arts," p. 46. See also, Edward Delavan Perry, "The American University," in *Monographs on Education in the United States*, 2 vols., ed. Nicholas Murray Butler (Albany, N.Y.: J. B. Lyon, 1904), 1:296.

20. Rudolph, *American College and University*, pp. 162–63; Hawkins, *Pioneer*, pp. 127–28; Ross, *G. Stanley Hall*, p. 197; Hall's remark, quoted in "Discussion of the Actual and the Proper Lines of Distinction Between College and University," *AAU Journal* 5 (1904): 34–36; William Rainey Harper's remark, quoted in ibid., p. 36.

21. Hawkins, *Between Harvard and America*, pp. 67–68; John S. Brubacher and Willis Rudy, *Higher Education in Transition: A History of American Colleges and Universities, 1636–1963*, rev. ed. (New York: Harper & Row, 1968), p. 386.

22. Arthur T. Hadley, "To What Extent Should the University Investigator be Relieved from

Teaching?" *AAU Journal* 7 (1906): 45; Morris Bishop, *A History of Cornell* (Ithaca, N.Y.: Cornell University Press, 1962), p. 358. David Starr Jordan opposed a separate rank but was willing to establish research years in addition to the regular sabbatic program (Jordan, "The University Investigator," p. 29).

23. Veysey, *Emergence of the American University,* pp. 320–24; Hawkins, *Pioneer,* pp. 90, 91; Storr, *Harper's University,* p. 75n.

24. Albert Bushnell Hart, "University Happenings," *Harvard Graduates' Magazine* 5 (1896–97): 389; Brubacher and Rudy, *Higher Education in Transition,* p. 117; E. Benjamin Andrews, "Current Criticism of Universities," *NASU Transactions* 3 (1905): 28. Josiah Royce, "Present Ideals of American University Life," *Scribner's Magazine* 10 (1891): 386. Cf. Laurence R. Veysey, "Stability and Experiment in the American Undergraduate Curriculum," in *Content and Context: Essays on College Education,* ed. Carl Kaysen (New York: McGraw-Hill, 1973), pp. 32–34.

25. Mark Beach, "Professional versus Professorial Control of Higher Education," *Educational Record* 49 (1968): 267–68; Hawkins, *Between Harvard and America,* p. 75; Goodspeed, *History of the University of Chicago,* p. 151. On Germany, see Ringer, "German Academic Community," in this volume, pp. 420–21.

26. Raymond M. Alden's remark, quoted in "Discussion of the Type of Graduate Scholar," *AAU Journal* 15 (1913): 31; John W. Burgess, *Reminiscences of an American Scholar: The Beginnings of Columbia University* (New York: Columbia University Press, 1934), pp. 187–90; Curti and Carstensen, *Wisconsin,* 1:635; MacLean, "State University the Servant," pp. 35–36; Veysey, *Emergence of the American University,* p. 177.

27. Hawkins, *Pioneer,* pp. 46, 90, 218.

28. Hall, "What is Research in a University Sense, and How May it Best be Promoted?" *AAU Journal* 3 (1902): 46–48; Small, "The Doctor's Dissertation: Selection of Subject, Preparation, Acceptance, Publication," ibid. 9 (1908): 50, 54; William A. Noyes's remark, quoted in "Discussion of the Type of Graduate Scholar," p. 29; Paul Shorey, "American Scholarship," *Nation* 92 (1911): 467.

29. Hawkins, *Pioneer,* pp. 79–81; idem, *Between Harvard and America,* p. 57; Benjamin Ide Wheeler's remark, quoted in "Economy of the Time in Education," *AAU Journal* 16 (1914): 70; Hill, "The Influence of Graduate Fellowships and Scholarships upon the Quality of Graduate Study," ibid. 14 (1912): 31; Lloyd, "Fellowships—with Special Consideration of Their Relation to Teaching," ibid. 22 (1920): 90.

30. Franklin H. Giddings's remark, quoted in "Discussion of the Social Environment of the Graduate Student," *AAU Journal* 22 (1920): 78; Charles H. Haskins's remark, quoted in "Discussion of the Type of Graduate Scholar," p. 30; Arthur T. Hadley, quoted in "Discussion of the Organization of Research," *AAU Journal* 21 (1919): 45–56; Veysey, *Emergence of the American University,* pp. 178–79; Gilman, *The Launching of a University and Other Papers: A Sheaf of Remembrances* (New York: Dodd, Mead & Co., 1906), p. 243; Alfred H. Lloyd, "Fellowships," p. 84. Cf. Edwin E. Slosson, *Great American Universities* (New York: Macmillan, 1910), pp. 492–94.

31. Veysey, *Emergence of the American University,* pp. 244–48 (see also idem, "The Academic Mind of Woodrow Wilson," *Mississippi Valley Historical Review* 49 [1963]: 613–34); Hibben, "The Type of Graduate Scholar," pp. 27–28.

32. "Discussion of the Type of Graduate Scholar," pp. 29–31.

33. Gilman, *University Problems,* pp. 15, 31–32; Hawkins, *Pioneer,* pp. 99, 144; Curti and Carstensen, *Wisconsin,* 1:359–60; Walter Muir Whitehill, *Independent Historical Societies: An Enquiry into Their Research and Publication Function and Their Financial Future* (Boston and Cambridge: Boston Athenaeum, distributed by Harvard University Press, 1962), pp. 256–57.

34. Harnack founded the Kaiser-Wilhelm-Gesellschaft in 1911 (see the Ringer essay in this volume, p. 421); Woodward's remark quoted in Jordan, "The University Investigator," p. 43 (cf. *AAU Journal* 8 [1906]: 46–47); Ira Remsen's remark quoted in "Discussion of The University Investigator," p. 49; Jacob Gould Schurman, "The Policy of Incorporating Such an Organization as the Rockefeller Foundation," *NASU Transactions* (1910) 8:287–88. See also the essay by Nathan Reingold in this volume.

35. David Prescott Barrows's remark, in "Research Professorships," *AAU Journal* 22 (1920): 51; Charles R. Van Hise's remark, in "Discussion of to What Extent Should The University Investigator be Relieved of Teaching," p. 51; Merritt's remark, in "Discussion of the Organization of Research," *AAU Journal* 21 (1919): 48–49.

36. Charles W. Eliot, *University Administration* (Boston: Houghton Mifflin, 1908), pp. 91–93,

151; W. H. P. Faunce, "Annual Report to the Corporation of Brown University for 1919-20," quoted in *American Association of University Professors Bulletin* 8 (1922): 254 (hereafter cited as *AAUP Bulletin*); Rudolph, *American College and University*, pp. 403-4. For a skillful interpretation of the rationale of these new scholarly organizations, see Thomas L. Haskell *The Emergence of Professional Social Science: The American Social Science Association and the Nineteenth-Century Crisis of Authority* (Urbana, Ill.: University of Illinois Press, 1977).

37. See the essay in this volume by Louis Galambos, whose general argument agrees with my impression that business pressures on universities in the nineteenth century more often sought ideological and economic orthodoxy than direct economic contributions. Allan Nevins, *The State Universities and Democracy* (Urbana, Ill.: University of Illinois Press, 1962), pp. 53-60; Edward Danforth Eddy, Jr., *Colleges for Our Land and Time: The Land-Grant Idea in American Education* (New York: Harper, 1957), p. 73; Rudolph, *American College and University*, p. 256; Hawkins, *Between Harvard and America*, pp. 216-18; Richard Hofstadter and Walter P. Metzger, *The Development of Academic Freedom in the United States* (New York: Columbia University Press, 1955), pp. 422-25.

38. Bishop, *Cornell*, pp. 126-28; Orrin Leslie Elliott, *Stanford University: The First Twenty-Five Years* (Stanford, Ca.: Stanford University Press, 1937), pp. 24, 512; William Carey Jones, "California," in Fabian Franklin et al., *The Life of Daniel Coit Gilman* (New York: Dodd, Mead, 1910), passim; Hawkins, *Pioneer*, pp. 19, 23, 305; Rudolph, *American College and University*, p. 246; Hawkins, *Between Harvard and America*, pp. 213-15.

39. Nevins, *State Universities*, pp. 85-90, 46-47, 91-92; Henry C. White's remark, quoted in "Discussions," *NASU Transactions* 2 (1904): 79.

40. John G. Sproat, *"The Best Men": Liberal Reformers in the Gilded Age* (New York: Oxford University Press, 1968), pp. 7, 17-18; John Higham, *History* (Englewood Cliffs, N.J.: Prentice-Hall, 1965), pp. 8-11; Daniel J. Kevles, "On the Flaws of American Physics: A Social and Institutional Analysis," in *Nineteenth Century American Science: A Reappraisal*, ed. George H. Daniels (Evanston, Ill.: Northwestern University Press, 1972), pp. 137-38; Jacob Hollander's remark, quoted in "Discussion on Outside Remunerative Work By Professors," *AAU Journal* 17 (1915): 64-65; Robert L. Church, "Economists as Experts: The Rise of an Academic Profession in America, 1870-1917," in *The University in Society*, ed. Lawrence Stone (Princeton: Princeton University Press, 1974), pp. 571-609. Cf. Veysey, *Emergence of the American University*, pp. 124-25.

41. Curti and Carstensen, *Wisconsin*, 2:354-56, 1:630-32, 2:87-88; Benjamin G. Rader, *The Academic Mind and Reform: The Influence of Richard T. Ely in American Life* (Lexington, Ky.: University of Kentucky Press, 1966), pp. 112, 128, 162; Charles R. Van Hise, "Inaugural Address," *Science* 20 (1904): 203, 204.

42. G. Stanley Hall's remark, quoted in "Discussion of the Opportunities for Higher Instruction and Research in State Universities," p. 64; Eddy, *Colleges for Our Land and Time*, pp. 97-100; Charles R. Van Hise, "The Opportunities for Higher Instruction and Research in State Universities," pp. 52-53; Curti and Carstensen, *Wisconsin*, 2:38-40.

43. Eddy, *Colleges for Our Land and Time*, pp. 104-7; Edward Potts Cheyney, *History of the University of Pennsylvania, 1740-1940* (Philadelphia: University of Pennsylvania Press, 1940), pp. 347-49; Curti and Carstensen, *Wisconsin*, 1:711-14, 721-28; Hawkins, *Pioneer*, p. 202, n. 68; Ross, *G. Stanley Hall*, pp. 211-12; Arthur G. Powell, "The Education of Educators at Harvard, 1891-1912," in *Social Sciences at Harvard, 1860-1920: From Inculcation to the Open Mind*, ed. Paul Herman Buck (Cambridge: Harvard University Press, 1965), pp. 226-29.

44. Edward A. Krug, *The Shaping of the American High School* (New York: Harper & Row, 1964), pp. 151-53; Hawkins, *Between Harvard and America*, pp. 178-80; U.S. Bureau of the Census, *Historical Statistics of the United States: Colonial Times to 1957* (Washington, D.C., 1960), p. 211. As a percentage of eighteen to twenty-one year olds in the population, these figures represent 1.68 percent in 1870 and 5.2 percent in 1910. For 1920 the enrollment was 598,000 (8.09 percent). The count includes all enrolled students, not just undergraduates. For an instructive caution against interpreting increased enrollments as democratic, see the Ringer essay in this volume, p. 418. On shifting notions of whether or not college enrollment should be maximized, see Harold S. Wechsler, *The Qualified Student: A History of Selective College Admission in America* (New York: Wiley, 1977).

45. Veysey, *Emergence of the American University*, pp. 233-59. See Ringer, "German Academic Community," in this volume for an account of even stronger concern among German

academics over the disappearance of values and integrative world-views from specialized scholarship.

46. Andrew F. West's remark, quoted in "Discussion of the Opportunities for Higher Instruction and Research in State Universities," p. 67; Jacob Gould Schurman, "The Reaction of Graduate Work on the Other Work of the University," *AAU Journal* 7 (1906): 59; Herbert F. Davidson, "The Puzzled Professor," *AAUP Bulletin* 8 (1922): 399–402, reprinted from *School and Society;* Pattee, "The 'Log' Unseats 'Mark Hopkins'," ibid. 9 (1923): 309–13, reprinted from *Nation;* Slosson, *Great American Universities,* p. 517.

47. Matthew Arnold, quoted in Veysey, *Emergence of the American University,* p. 186; Hawkins, *Between Harvard and America,* pp. 264–65; Charles Eliot Norton, "Harvard University," in *Four American Universities* (New York: Harper, 1895), p. 12; Irving Babbitt, "The Humanities," *Atlantic Monthly* 89 (1902): 773.

48. Curti and Carstensen, *Wisconsin,* 1: 433–38; 2: 49–50, 98–99; Rudolph, *American College and University,* p. 451.

49. Carol S. Gruber's *Mars and Minerva: World War I and the Uses of the Higher Learning in America* (Baton Rouge, La.: Louisiana State University Press, 1975) is the fullest treatment available.

50. *Report of the Commissioner of Education* (Washington, D.C.: 1918), p. 14; ibid. (1919), pp. 6–7; Parke Rexford Kolbe, *The Colleges in War Time and After . . .* (New York: Appleton, 1919), p. 201; Swarthmore College Faculty, *An Adventure in Education: Swarthmore College under Frank Aydelotte* (New York: Macmillan, 1941), pp. 81–88; Veysey, "Stability and Experiment in American Undergraduate Curriculum," pp. 11–12.

51. *Report of the Commissioner of Education* (1919), p. 9; Gruber, *Mars and Minerva,* pp. 238–45.

52. Kolbe, *Colleges in War Time,* chap. 7; James B. Conant, *My Several Lives: Memoirs of a Social Inventor* (New York: Harper & Row, 1970), p. 52, chap. 5.

53. Kolbe, *Colleges in War Time,* pp. 203–204; *Report of the Commissioner of Education* (1918), p. 15; Frederick J. E. Woodbridge, "The Social Environment of the Graduate Student," *AAU Journal* 22 (1920): 73–75.

54. Jurgen Herbst, *The German Historical School in American Scholarship: A Study in the Transfer of Culture* (Ithaca, N.Y.: Cornell University Press, 1965), chap. 1; Hofstadter and Metzger, *Development of Academic Freedom,* pp. 368, 495–506; Curti and Carstensen, *Wisconsin,* 2: 323–24, 114; Louis G. Geiger, *University of the Northern Plains: A History of the University of North Dakota, 1883–1958* (Grand Forks, N.D.: University of North Dakota Press, 1958), p. 286; James Gray, *The University of Minnesota, 1851–1951* (Minneapolis, Minn.: University of Minnesota Press, 1951), pp. 245–49; Carol S. Gruber, "Academic Freedom at Columbia University, 1917–1918: The Case of James McKeen Cattell," *AAUP Bulletin* 58 (1972): 297–305; Arthur O. Lovejoy, "Annual Message of the President," ibid. 5 (1919): 33–35. I also draw here on a wide range of correspondence between Americans who had studied in Germany and their German mentors, notably in the papers of Ernst Ehlers, Manuscript Division, University Library, Göttingen.

55. A. Hunter Dupree, *Science in the Federal Government: A History of Policies and Activities to 1940* (Cambridge: Belknap Press of Harvard University Press, 1957), pp. 315–25; Arthur Twining Hadley's remark, quoted in "Discussion of Co-operation in Research with Private Enterprises from the Standpoint of Industry," *AAU Journal* 22 (1920): 70; Alfred Henry Lloyd, "Fellowships—with Special Consideration of Their Relation to Teaching," ibid., p. 87; Talbot, quoted in John Johnston, "Co-operation Between Universities and Industry," ibid., p. 57.

56. Frank Baldwin Jewett, "Co-operation in Research with Private Enterprises from the Standpoint of Industry," *AAU Journal* 22 (1920): 64; David Prescott Barrows's remark, quoted in "Research Professorships," ibid., p. 51. Cf. Ben-David, *American Higher Education,* p. 103.

57. James Rowland Angell, "The Organization of Research," *AAU Journal* 21 (1919): 33.

58. James R. Angell's remark, quoted in "Discussion of the Organization of Research," ibid., p. 44; Charles H. Haskins's remark, quoted in ibid.; Haskins, "Co-operation in Research in the Humanities," ibid. 22 (1920): 37–40; William Morton Wheeler, "The Dry-Rot of Our Academic Biology," *AAUP Bulletin* 9 (1923): 119, reprinted from *Science.*

# National Science Policy
# in a Private Foundation: The Carnegie
# Institution of Washington

## NATHAN REINGOLD

### Introduction

Within a small circle near the end of 1901 there was much excitement. A great gift to American intellectual life was coming from the Laird of Steel, Andrew Carnegie. In December 1901 the transfer of ten million dollars in United States Steel Corporation bonds to the newly formed Carnegie Institution of Washington (CIW) was publicly announced and tension spread widely within the communities of American scientists and scholars who might potentially benefit. A distinguished Board of Trustees was designated by Carnegie, and Daniel Coit Gilman, lately retired from the presidency of Johns Hopkins University, was named the Institution's first president.[1]

To aid them in wisely disbursing Carnegie's gift, the trustees appointed committees of experts to deliberate and to advise on which intellectual fields should be supported and how each of these areas could best be advanced. These reports were supplemented by solicited and unsolicited advice of individuals given in print, correspondence, and conversation. The committee reports are curious reading today, being a presumably authoritative survey of the state of many disciplines in America and their future needs. They range from the detailed to the laconic, from modest reasonableness to the rodomantade of special pleading. For example, the anthropologists' committee, which included Franz Boas, gave as one of the aims of the field "to discover the principles and laws of human development with the view of utilizing them to regulate the present and to mould the future of the race." With such advice, a wide variety of options were open to the trustees.[2]

Today, some seventy-five years later, the Carnegie Institution of Washington is a private center for research in the physical and biological sciences; its divisions include a department of terrestrial magnetism and a geophysical laboratory in Washington, D.C.; a department of plant biology at Stanford, California; a department of embryology at Baltimore, Maryland; a genetics research unit at Cold Spring Harbor, New York; and the Hale Observatories (owned and operated jointly with the California Institute of Technology).

Unlike such European countries as France, Germany, and the Soviet Union, America has relatively few independent institutions devoted solely to basic research. In the United States, most research establishments are associated with, or exist in juxtaposition to, larger entities in government, medicine, industry, agriculture, and higher education. In whole or in part, their research is justified by such missions as national defense, public health, agricultural and industrial production, or even popular enlightenment (in the case of museums). Thus, the process by which the Institution established its purpose and determined its future is of particular interest to historians.

Retrospection coats events in the Institution's development with a patina of inevitability. In fact, great uncertainty about its nature and function existed from the formal launching until well into the administration of its second president, Robert S. Woodward (1904–1920).[3] Conceptual issues, personalities, ideologies, institutional rivalries, and many other factors openly entered into the discussions of the trustees and their interchanges with interested parties outside the Institution.

When the Carnegie Institution was established at the turn of the century, there were no governmental bodies with wide concern for intellectual life; thus CIW necessarily dealt with what are now considered to be national policy questions, principally the establishment of priorities for the support of research areas. The Rockefeller philanthropies were then largely involved with public health and medical research. Only toward the start of World War I did they edge into the broad concerns manifested so significantly between 1920 and 1940. Nor did such programs as the Guggenheim fellowships exist in 1902. In the absence of alternative bodies, the support not only of science but of research in the broadest terms became the concern of the officers and trustees of the Institution. Perhaps this is what Andrew Carnegie really wanted, but the record of his motivations is quite obscure.

Emphatically, Carnegie asserted that the first aim of the new body was the promotion of original research, in which the country was so deficient. Clearly, he was reacting to the turn-of-the-century literature about American indifference to basic research.[4] But Carnegie's assertion left much unanswered; quite deliberately, the formal founding papers were both sweeping in their statements of scope and obscure in their particulars. For the purposes of this chapter, the origin of the gift and the nature of Carnegie's views are of interest only insofar as they entered into the policy discussions. Fiduciary responsibility led the trustees to invoke their interpretation of Carnegie's intentions from time to time; the possibility of increased endowment was ever present in the early days, possibly influencing solicitude for the founder's motives. Once the Institution was established, Carnegie was rather conscientious about letting the trustees manage it. When Gilman in 1903 asked Carnegie to confirm that the funds could support non-Americans, Carnegie agreed, but added it was not proper for him to interfere.[5] Only two instances of Carnegie's pressure on the Institution are known to me. In 1910 Carnegie tried unsuccessfully to have Woodward use simplified spelling in Institution publications.[6] More significant is his role in the case of Luther Burbank, an important incident dealt with later.

The Gilman administration was marked by a highly interesting clash between the president and two influential trustees, C. D. Walcott, then the head of the U.S. Geological Survey and the secretary of the Carnegie Institution, and John Shaw Billings, who early became chairman of the Board of Trustees. A physician, Billings is best known as the man who developed two great libraries, the Surgeon General's Library, now the National Library of Medicine, and the New York Public Library. Ostensibly, the dispute was on questions of governance, the president vs. the trustees, or more specifically, the Executive Committee dominated by John Shaw Billings.[7] However, more than administrative prerogatives were involved; as will be evident, Gilman, Walcott, and Billings had strong differences on matters of policy.

As far as governance is concerned, Gilman's successor, Robert S. Woodward, achieved the strong executive leadership Gilman sought but could not attain. Woodward came to the Institution from Columbia University where he was Dean of Pure Science. Originally trained as an engineer, Woodward was an old Washington hand with service in the Lake Survey of the Corps of Engineers, the Coast and Geodetic Survey, the Geological Survey, and the Naval Observatory. From the pre-graduate school era, Woodward was a highly competent applied mathematician or classical physicist who saw the Earth as *the* great object of study. His principal scientific work occurred during his years with the Geological Survey, notably a finding contrary to Kelvin's estimate of the age of the Earth. After three years with the Coast and Geodetic Survey, Woodward became Professor of Mechanics and Mathematical Physics at Columbia University in 1892; in 1895 he was named Dean of its College of Pure Science.

Billings and Walcott knew Woodward from his days with the surveys. Before his elevation to the presidency of Carnegie, Woodward headed two of the advisory committees. When Billings saw that Walcott and other favored candidates were not acceptable for the position of president, he pushed Woodward forward, confident in having a willing collaborator.[8] As president, Woodward quickly and smoothly edged Walcott away from control of the paperwork that constituted much of the vital life of the organization.[9] Smoothly but not so quickly, Woodward reduced Billings and the Executive Committee to a subordinate role. In the last years of Billings' life, a bitter enmity existed between the two men,[10] and an observer in the Rockefeller Foundation could write of the autocratic control in the Institution.[11] Whether this characterization is true or not, Woodward evolved a policy uniquely his own—with points of agreement and disagreement with Gilman, Billings, and Walcott.

Certainly the most fundamental issue in the early history of the Carnegie Institution was its relationship to the university world. At the first meeting of the trustees, both Andrew Carnegie and Daniel Coit Gilman presented statements identifying the Carnegie Institution of Washington as a research organization, distinguishing between the Institution and a university, and very carefully disentangling the new body from its origins in the national university idea and in the movement to aid graduate students coming to Washington.[12] The concept of a national university was not new, of course; its lineage traced back to George

Washington. In the decades before the turn of the century, the national university was pushed with great vigor by John W. Hoyt. Although he succeeded in gaining considerable support, Hoyt's moves were frustrated, first by the obvious disinclination of some to increase federal activities and second by the opposition of those in higher education who claimed their institutions now filled many of the roles destined for the national university and looked with trepidation on a possible federally funded rival. Still others, eager to expand research and advanced training, had qualms about the ambitious but vaguely defined institution being promoted by Hoyt. Such individuals, including key scientists and educators, wanted suitable action on a national level.[13] Among these were the president of Cornell Andrew D. White and Daniel Coit Gilman.

According to standard accounts, the origin of the Carnegie Institution was a conversation in Scotland in the spring of 1901 during which White and Carnegie discussed the possibility of a national university.[14] Hoyt had previously raised the issue with Carnegie with no success. On Carnegie's return to America, Gilman took up the task of promoting the idea.

Simultaneously, a sequence of related events occurred. Apparently independent of Hoyt, a group of women formed the George Washington Memorial Association before the turn of the century with the avowed purpose of establishing in the District of Columbia "a Washington Memorial University." So far as one can judge from a distance, the women were sincerely motivated by a combination of patriotism and a desire to advance education. In the years 1900 and 1901, the Association worked out a promising alliance with a group of influential scientists and educators.

In 1898 the Washington Academy of Sciences came into existence. Despite its name, the Academy aspired to a national role and was so viewed at least by some outside its ranks. (The National Academy was in a quiescent state.) Leading the Washington Academy in these early years was C. D. Walcott, John Wesley Powell's successor as director of the U.S. Geological Survey. Connecting the Washington learned community with institutions of higher learning in the country was a major point in Walcott's program for the Academy. That point fitted in well with the inclinations of a number of educators like Nicholas Murray Butler; they wanted to avoid a national university while obtaining access for their students to the facilities and resources of the Washington area.[15]

Shortly afterward (May 20, 1901), the Washington Academy and the George Washington Memorial Association joined forces to incorporate the Washington Memorial Institution; its purpose was to bring students to the nation's capital to utilize its scientific and cultural resources. To house the Institution, the George Washington Memorial Association hoped to construct an edifice which would be suitable as the administrative headquarters of the national university that would hopefully emerge from this nucleus. Walcott and his female allies turned to Andrew Carnegie to give substance to their blueprint.[16]

By the fall of 1901, however, Carnegie was definitely not interested in any university but in aiding research and in developing exceptional men. Despite the opinions of other historians, I doubt Carnegie's interest in the national university was more than a momentary one or ever at a high voltage. At the November 16 morning meeting of Carnegie, Gilman, and Billings that launched CIW, Gilman still urged a national university in Washington. In contrast, Billings "advised instead of a university [that] the institution be founded for the promotion of original research, advanced teaching, etc., to be located in Washington, to be so original as not to interfere with the work of any existing university, but on the contrary to assist them, and to grant scholarships, etc., for work in laboratories and institutions outside of Washington as well as in it." Billings prevailed, and the resulting plan of November 20 won Carnegie's assent two days later.[17]

Gilman had no illusions about the fate of the national university and the Washington Memorial Institution. Writing C. W. Eliot on December 3, 1901, he thought the Carnegie gift killed both.[18] Nor did the women of the George Washington Memorial Association have any doubts about the effect. CIW was "exactly along the lines with identical aims, and with a charter embodying the very same features" as their proposals: CIW "rendered forever impossible of fulfillment our purpose that there should be here a worthy memorial of Washington's deep interest in science and learning. . . ."[19]

No doubt Gilman sincerely wanted to help the universities, but, in general, there was an aloofness from, or a coolness to, the university world on the part of Carnegie and the trustees—an aloofness rooted in the determination of CIW's leaders to separate teaching from research. Today, universities are generally regarded, in the words of the title of a recent book, as "the home of science."[20] Yet Walcott, Billings, and Woodward did not accept that view. Their governing model was not the German or some other form of university but the Royal Institution of Davy and Faraday. In a February 1902 memorandum, Billings called for the establishment of laboratories like those of the Royal Institution, adding "they do no teaching." The only other precedent cited by Walcott and Billings in those early days was that of the Smithsonian Institution.

Given the spectacular personalities and the fascinating byplay between them, there is a strong temptation to structure historical explanations in terms of human dramas: in the beginning, Carnegie coyly playing off Andrew D. White and Gilman against Billings and Walcott, then Walcott teaming with Woodward against Billings, with Woodward first using Billings and Gilman to supplant Walcott and later isolating Billings with the help of William H. Welch, Dean of the Johns Hopkins Medical School. And there are others in the cast—members of the Carnegie Board of Trustees including the banker Henry L. Higginson, the lawyer Elihu Root, and, toward the end, the senator Henry Cabot Lodge—not to mention such extraordinary concerned outsiders as the astrophysicist George Ellery Hale and James McKeen Cattell, the psychologist who edited *Science*. But the participants' continuing explicit awareness of issues renders quite suspect explanations largely in terms of dramaturgy.

The tension between teaching and research, between the concept of the university and that of the research institute was a pervasive factor underlying the three areas of contention that dominated the formative years of the Carnegie Institution: the support of individuals, the allocation of funds among intellectual fields, and the relation of the Institution to higher education. Quite often, disputes in one area were linked to differing viewpoints in another, but all of the disputes occurred more or less simultaneously.

## *"The Exceptional Man"*

Following the primary objective—support of original research—the deed transferring $10 million of United States Steel Corporation bonds to the newly formed Carnegie Institution of Washington gives as the second aim of the trust: "To discover the exceptional man in every department of study whenever and wherever found, inside or outside of schools, and enable him to make the work for which he seems specially designed his life work."[21] Billings, Gilman, and Walcott undoubtedly agreed with that aim, even though they knew exceptional men were not always readily found. Being scientists with university connections, they assumed exceptional men were largely at or from universities, so the "inside or outside" phrases did not, at first, appear vexing. But they and their fellow trustees quickly took a step that was to have serious consequences for universities. By the time of the first annual meeting of the trustees on November 27, 1902, there was agreement with Billings's general principle of aiding individuals, not institutions, in the conduct of research.[22] With this seemingly modest act, universities were cut off from direct aid.

Even before the formal launching of CIW, the leading figures were seeking and receiving advice on this question. Billings, who was intent on aiding individuals, received two letters in January 1902 from The Johns Hopkins University that are a good introduction to the problems discussed by the trustees over the next decade or so. The author of the first letter, William H. Welch, would become a CIW trustee in 1906; in 1902 he wrote from the perspective of a trustee of the newly founded Rockefeller Institute as well as Dean of the Hopkins Medical School. Although the Institute was initially giving research grants to investigators, Welch looked toward a general policy of concentrating on in-house research—exactly what occurred in the Carnegie Institution of Washington. As to fellowship recipients, Welch saw two categories: those with demonstrated ability and those recommended by laboratory directors to work under their supervision. Better still, freeing established men from the burden of teaching would increase the output of American laboratories. But the number of those with "any real fitness for original research is small, and these are likely to come to the front under any circumstances." On the other hand, Welch saw a danger—not from CIW—"of encouraging those who have no genuine capacity for such work and who had better be at something else."[23]

Gilman's successor at Hopkins, the chemist Ira Remsen, agreed that only a few individuals were capable of significant research and not many of these were languishing for want of funds. The few really good men were snatched up by the universities. Referring to large-scale investigations requiring substantial funding, he stated, "I do not think there are many such." (That presumably meant the kind of installations CIW did fund subsequently.) "What we lack is men," wrote Remsen who doubted CIW could enlarge the supply of exceptional men. Instead he urged CIW to increase the efficiency of the demonstrably productive men in universities by providing funds for research assistants. As to fellowships for the untried, "that is now overdone . . . the danger in it is that it tends to develop a lot of men up to a certain point and then drop them" Only a few fellowships were needed for those with clear signs of an ability to carry out independent research.[24]

Billings, Gilman, and the other trustees agreed to aid individuals immediately and not wait for the careful formulation of a program based on the reports of the expert advisory committees. At the outset, at least, Billings and Gilman were in agreement on the two principal forms of aid: what we would now call fellowships to as yet unrecognized individuals and what we now designate as project grants to the more established investigators. By the end of 1905, Woodward could inform Nicholas Murray Butler, the president of Columbia University, that 260 individuals in 89 institutions had benefitted from CIW funds.[25]

Right from the outset, two semantic problems were created for the Institution, most likely by Walcott—not the most auspicious move for a future secretary of the Smithsonian Institution and a future president of the National Academy of Sciences. Much to Billings's distress, the young investigators were tagged with the title of "research assistants." Billings had originally suggested "junior associate." Walcott's term immediately confused those young neophytes being tested "in special lines of work, for which they profess to have a special aptitude," with assistants provided to a professor as "a careful, accurate, serviceable human tool."[26] That confusion only confirmed the fears of some that professors would use the "research assistants" to do their drudge labor, not to launch careers. To some of the young investigators, the term carried unflattering connotations.

The second semantic problem arose from Walcott's attempt to distinguish between the two principal objects of research that fell within the purview of CIW. In his 1902 instructions to the advisory committees, he differentiated between objects of broad scope for the discovery and utilization of new forces to benefit man—exemplified by the CIW laboratories—and objects of lesser scope such as filling gaps in known areas, acquiring knowledge of specific phenomena, or undertaking research in restricted fields.[27] Given Walcott's personal support of laboratories over short-term research grants, perhaps there was a pejorative connotation from the start. More likely, the choice of the term "minor grants" to identify the latter category was unfortunate; it clearly lacked an inspirational ring. Yet a harassed Robert S. Woodward later would point out that T. W. Richards of Harvard received America's first Nobel Prize in chemistry for the kind of work supported by his minor grants.

The Institution advertised the research assistantships. Applications were sent to "expert advisers" for report and awarded on the judgment of the Executive Committee. Billings pointedly called attention to the geographical diversity of the research assistants and their origin in small colleges as well as large universities; "their connection with this place or that" was not to be the determining factor. Awarding minor grants was more vexing, given the difficulty of evaluating the competing projects. A Charles Sanders Peirce did not impress the Executive Committee. Despite grants to the "wrong men" or grants "used not to a very good purpose," the Executive Committee was satisfied in 1903 to have found "about a dozen really exceptional men." Observing the proceedings, Carnegie expressed great gratification: "As the Chairman [Billings] has said, if you have three or four exceptional men, that is a great deal. We do not judge by the number that do not produce, we judge by the number that are successes."[28]

Enter the Dean of Pure Science, Robert S. Woodward, filled with ideas for cooperation in science and somewhat leery of the founder's "happy phrase" about the exceptional man (the characterization is Woodward's). To his dismay, some scientists accepted Carnegie's formulation. Richards of Harvard, for example, doubted the value of cooperation in physics and chemistry, whatever the merits in astronomy:

> On the other hand it seems to me that the making of a great original discovery is not unlike the writing of a great poem or the painting of a great picture. The thought and its execution must be hammered out by genius alone. . . . I agree with Mr. Carnegie entirely in his belief that from the individual exceptional man alone is any great addition to be expected to the sum of our original conceptions. Who can imagine Faraday as cooperating? In short it seems to me that cooperation may be highly productive of routine work and of a general rounding off of already acquired knowledge; but might be equally destructive of great advance in entirely new directions.[29]

Within less than a year after Richards wrote, Woodward and the trustees began wrestling with an exceptional man, quite unlike Michael Faraday, who found cooperation very difficult—the horticulturalist Luther Burbank. In 1904 the Executive Committee tried to have the Department of Agriculture examine and report on the methods and results of Burbank. Popularly acclaimed as a "wizard," Burbank was the object of considerable contention in the scientific community and among his fellow horticulturalists. CIW had given funds to Burbank and wanted to place before the public and its own biological stations the knowledge acquired by this extraordinary man who kept few, if any, records. In Woodward's words: "He is like a mathematician who never has to recur to his formulas; all information he possesses he can summon in an instant for his use." Complicating the task of extricating Burbank's "formulas" from his mind was the problem of commercial rivalry with competing horticulturalists. Nevertheless, Woodward was impressed with the man, his work, and the potential benefit to humanity:

> A word or two as to his [i.e., Burbank's] personality. He is not a trained man of science; he lacks knowledge of the terminology of modern science. He often expresses

himself in a way quite offensive to many scientific men, if due allowance is not made; but he is a man who unconsciously works by the scientific method to most extraordinary advantage. I think anybody who goes to his orchards and sees what he has produced and who studies Mr. Burbank as I have done will admit at once that he is a most unusual man. But along with his unusual abilities he has unusual peculiarities. Let any ordinary man of science go to his orchards and enter into a discussion with him and they will be at loggerheads in fifteen minutes. It is our duty to make allowances for these things. If we can make such allowances then what we can get out of Mr. Burbank will be extremely valuable to humanity; if we cannot make that allowance we shall fail.[30]

With those words in the trustees' meeting of December 12, 1905, Woodward precipitated unusually animated exchanges. His idea was to place one or two bright young scientists with Burbank to extract the underlying findings and general method. The subsequent discussion took an unexpected antiscientific turn that Woodward would implicitly counter in later years. First, Carnegie worried about men of science interfering with the workings of a genius: "a body of professors acting in a professorial role will look askance at the idea of such a man . . . revolutionizing us . . . with his experiments." Like Carnegie, a number of the trustees had some reservations about science, its methods, and its practitioners. Elihu Root contrasted Burbank's "extraordinary and exceptional faculty" with the "careful, scientific way." Billings observed, "The scientific language is rubbish; plain simple language is what is needed." As to whether Burbank is in accord with Darwin, Mendel, or DeVries, Billings thought "it is of no importance. . . ."[31]

Only S. Weir Mitchell expressed doubt about the nature of Burbank's work. The argument in support of Burbank "has taken a very practical turn. We did not quite begin that way." Although Mitchell supported Woodward's proposal, he differed from him in regarding Burbank as no more than "an exceedingly careful observer." Woodward was right, in Mitchell's opinion, in seeking the laws underlying Burbank's work.[32] On July 26, 1906, CIW's young scientist, George Harrison Shull, completed a report on Burbank and his work. Fascinated by Burbank, even fond of the man, Shull's report clearly indicated the limits of Burbank's empiricism.[33] But CIW continued Shull's work with Burbank; as late as 1911, it still hoped to publish his full study.[34] By one of the ironies that makes history interesting, Shull was one of the generation of pioneer geneticists who played an important role in the development of hybrid corn.

In 1908 the trustees once more clashed over Luther Burbank. Woodward now spoke quite differently: "It should be understood also that from a scientific point of view there is nothing mysterious or occult in the work of Mr. Burbank. His methods are as a rule neither unique nor unknown, and his work turns out to be of less value to biological science than is generally supposed." Having translated Burbank's work into scientific language, its stature was diminished. Woodward— despite bad publicity and despite Burbank's commercializing of his findings— recommended continuing support of Shull's work and of Burbank's. At the same time, however, he indicated that "much to our disappointment, our association

with him [Burbank] does not appear to have been at all effective in raising him
to the level he might deservedly occupy . . .'', that is, Burbank did not wholly
appreciate the possibility of becoming a scientist.[35]

Shortly afterward, Andrew Carnegie made one of his few incursions into the
proceedings:

Will you let me interrupt you, gentlemen, for just a moment? Would you like the view
of a rank outsider, and a most ignorant man compared with you learned people? My friend
here [Woodward] said the only thing we expect is a scientific report, and my other friend
here [John L. Cadwalader, a trustee] said that the only thing we would get would be an
economic result from Mr. Burbank. I would like to know what our scientific reports avail
us if the end be not economic gain, that we shall get plants which will yield revenue,
which are now useless. If we can sustain Mr. Burbank in his work so that in the end we
will have economic gain, I would be in favor of increasing the amount given him.

Although Woodward and Carnegie prevailed, this was one of the rare occasions
in which some trustees voted in the negative.[36] By 1909, the Institution withdrew
further support ''to avoid entangling alliances with Mr. Burbank and his numerous exploiters.''[37]

Shortly after Woodward began his disillusioning relationship with Burbank, he
declared open war against the two principal CIW mechanisms for aiding individuals, the research assistantships and the minor grants. One aspect of his
hostility remains shrouded in obscurity. In print in the Institution's *Yearbooks* in
1905 and in 1911, Woodward leveled serious charges against the programs. In
the first year he condemned them as a scientific ''spoils system''; in 1911 he described at least some participants as motivated by ''dreams of avarice.''[38] Writing in 1920 to his friend, the geologist T. C. Chamberlin, Woodward referred
cryptically to the ''sinister aspects'' of the Institution's history,[39] presumably a
reference to the ''spoils system'' and to the ''dreams of avarice.'' To the best of
my knowledge, these words were never challenged in print nor were they elaborated on by Woodward. If true, they not only involved applicants for funds but
also distinguished referees. More important, implied is the involvement, know-
ingly or unwittingly, of the Executive Committee, which up to 1905 meant
Billings and Walcott.

Opposition to the minor grants and the research assistantships did not merely
spring from maladministration, real or alleged. Woodward favored support of
research, certainly over any educational function. And the best way to advance
research was by supporting proven people, either in CIW laboratories or in their
home institutions. Such a policy avoided sheer waste (which had not bothered
Carnegie) and the danger of involvement with cranks.

At the trustees' meeting of December 11, 1906, Woodward outlined his reasons for opposing the existing program: ''At least three quarters of my time is
absorbed by the business appertaining to these small grants and to the business of
research-assistantships. . . . At present we are conducting a species of Havana
Lottery, with monthly drawings, in which the inexperienced and the inexpert

man is almost as likely to receive a prize as the expert and the experienced man.''[40] Further in the meeting, Woodward asserted that only one in seven of the research assistants produced results worthy of publication. In the next year, similar statements about the unproductiveness of the short-term minor grants would embroil Woodward in a dispute with his former colleague, James McKeen Cattell.

What Woodward proposed instead was a system of research associateships: commitments of long-term support to proven investigators who could remain at their universities. The research associates would also serve as expert advisers to the president in their areas of competence. S. Weir Mitchell, speaking for himself and for Billings, defended the original program as in accordance with Carnegie's intention:

... I wish to say that in Mr. Carnegie's original gift to us he especially dwelt on the desirability of experimenting on the finding of competent men. He did not expect to do what the President desires to have done, to limit our gifts only to those who had through years proven their capacity.... I will say also that his request for research associates and none others, to have these grants, would be cutting off a certain amount of valuable future human material. I feel strongly about this subject and Dr. Billings and I have gone over the statistics of success and failure in these minor grants and we believe that we have had a sufficient amount of success in these gifts to entitle us to continue for some years longer this search for competent men. I feel very strongly in regard to it, because there have been times in my young life when certainly, under the President's rule, I would not have been a proper person to give a grant to... and when I should have longed to have one, and applied to institution after institution without getting it.[41]

Although Woodward did not prevail in 1906, in time his views became accepted. The pressure of inflation was on his side, not only the economic kind, but the steadily rising demands of the successful departments and laboratories. And such great scientists as Thomas Hunt Morgan became CIW research associates. Persistence also paid off. Recognizing the key role of the relationship with universities in the minor grants and research assistantships, Woodward told the trustees in 1906 that he had in the past two years had more than 2,000 interviews on the subject. Methodically, he would delimit the contacts with higher education. Just as methodically, he would review the support of fields of learning and of the "exceptional man." Between 1906 and his retirement he carefully restated again and again what amounts to a theory of research, not very original but striking in its certitude.

As to the "exceptional man," by 1916 he had clearly become the proven specialist within an established discipline. As Woodward noted, "It has been very commonly supposed... that the chief business of your humble servant should be hunting by means of a lantern in the bushes and the tall grass for exceptional men. That happy phrase of our Founder has worked out very unhappily for the Institution... we have had our experience with wizards— and... that Burbank was by no means the only one, nor the worst of them.''[42] Yet many people continued to think otherwise. Woodward characterized Edison's Naval Consulting Board in the World War I period as the mobilization of genius "and that meant, if it means anything, the stimulation of cranks." In Woodward's view, science was not a matter for abnormal minds, and Woodward's friend Richards agreed, forgetting his earlier comment on the artistic genius theory of scientific advances.[43] In 1918 Woodward reiterated his belief in supporting scientists of proven ability by contrasting the work of the Naval Consulting Board, now out of Edison's control, with that of George Ellery Hale's National Research Council:

> On the one hand, the National Research Council has proceeded on the supposition that discoveries and advances may be most reasonably expected to arise with those who have already shown capacity to make them. The theory of the Council has been that the best advice to the Government in cases of emergency is most likely to come from experts of repute in their various fields of research. The initial theory of the Naval Consulting Board, on the other hand, was that discoveries and advances are about as likely to come from untrained as from trained minds and that, since the number of amateurs is very large, the best way to secure advances is to set experts at work examining the suggestions and inventions of inexperts. In addition, initially, the Naval Consulting Board was also encouraged to believe that discoveries and advances are developed chiefly by abnormal minds and that it is therefore worthwhile to set men of proved efficiency and capacity at work scanning the horizon for the scintillations which might otherwise emanate unperceived from exceptional men, who are supposed to be in hiding, or at best more or less concealed behind books and bottles in dingy laboratories. . . .
>
> Happily for the reputations of the members of the Naval Consulting Board, this initial and popular theory was subjected to the tests of plain experience, which proved what is well known in the history of science and what has been demonstrated on a grand scale in the experience of the Institution, namely: first, that revolutionary discoveries, advances, and inventions do not arise suddenly or in necromantic fashion; and, secondly, that the poetic process of winnowing vast quantities of intellectual chaff with the hope of securing good grains of truth is the sheerest of futilities.[44]

## Intellectual Fields

While the search for the exceptional man was difficult, choosing fields for support was a deeper, more fundamental problem. The sums in the control of the trustees were finite; the demands seemingly infinite. Each time a choice was made—laboratories rather than minor grants, this field rather than another—the Institution made enemies among the disappointed. Supporting every field, no matter how worthy, was impossible. Somehow, priorities had to emerge.

After Billings met with Carnegie and Gilman on November 18, 1901, a memorandum was prepared on the nature of the proposed institution. Its subject scope obviously included science "in the ordinary sense of the word." To this was added history, political science, economics, philology (especially "Chinese and Oriental"), and library economy and management. (The last clearly reflected Billings's devotion to developing great libraries.) After listing a number of topics in the physical sciences, the text surprisingly called attention to the need for instruction in statistics and actuarial sciences and in Chinese and other Oriental languages; it also noted the importance of establishing an advanced school of bibliography and related topics. Nowhere else in the CIW context did Billings suggest support of teaching programs; in fact, teaching programs vanish from the surviving record of later discussions. A further Billings memorandum of February 1, 1902 noted that the objective of CIW was the same as that of the Smithsonian: "the increase and diffusion of knowledge, not limited to any field of inquiry."[45]

No doubt Gilman agreed with these sentiments. But by the first annual meeting of the trustees on November 27, 1902, Billings was qualifying his Smithsonian-like scope. Medical research was excluded, being a territory occupied by the Rockefeller interests. Despite that limitation, Billings's influence resulted in CIW support of *Index Medicus* from 1903 through 1926. Billings purged literature, music, and the fine arts from the Institution's purview. At least publicly, Gilman agreed. Emphatic as usual in his views, Billings was quite unimpressed by the nonscientific applicants: "We have had a number of requests for funds, to enable a man to abandon all his other business and write a treatise on logic or a treatise on philosophy, or a treatise on the history of religion, or a treatise on some particular points in theosophy or metaphysics. I have not considered that the urgency of those demands or that the character of the men who proposed to do it was so exceptional."[46] But where the exceptional man existed, like Ewald Flügel, the Middle English scholar at Stanford, the trustees provided support. Perhaps more important, the "Bureau," later the Department of Historical Research, was organized in 1903. The Department of Economics and Sociology became active in 1904. Individual archaeologists and anthropologists, like Raphael Pumpelly, received CIW funds.

Despite these actions, the bulk of CIW support went to science "in the ordinary sense of the word." Twelve of the eighteen advisory committees were concerned with scientific fields; of the remainder, engineering was not viewed as an applied field and the rest—economics, history, psychology, anthropology, and bibliography—were as far as the trustees cared to venture outside the established physical and biological fields.

In the sciences proper, the Institution encountered considerable skepticism and even hostility. Doubts were rampant about the ability of the trustees to act wisely. For example, in correspondence with George Ellery Hale, the astronomer Lewis Boss expressed reservations about the trustees' interest in big reflectors: "Dr. Walcott is an old friend of mine. I have known him ever since you were a small boy. . . . But I cannot bring myself to attach much weight to his judgment upon a technical matter in astronomy."[47]

Distrust of the trustees, largely nonscientists, produced the one major set-back of the Institution's early years. After a majority of the trustees of the Woods Hole Marine Biological Laboratory voted to join CIW in August 1902, C. O. Whitman, its director, mustered enough support to thwart the merger. Whitman believed scientists should run their own institutions.[48] That experience, plus some relations with universities, undoubtedly hardened CIW's belief in the need to have its own laboratories.

Woodward and Walcott had key roles in this development, perhaps best illustrated by the fate of the advisory committee reports on geophysics, physics, and chemistry. Woodward chaired the first two committees. Serving also with him on both were the physicists A. A. Michelson and Carl Barus. Joining these three on the geophysics committee was the entire geology advisory committee: T. C. Chamberlin, C. R. Van Hise, and C. D. Walcott. Chamberlin and his colleagues maintained that since geology was in good shape, the future was in geophysics. Woodward produced two symmetrical reports, calling for a special research laboratory in geophysics and another in physics.

What followed was probably Walcott's greatest moment as a policy-maker in CIW. Word of the reports of the various advisory committees spread quickly in 1902. By late summer and early fall, James McKeen Cattell, the Columbia psychologist and editor of *Science,* was on the attack, particularly against the geophysical laboratory. Earlier, he had given the trustees unsolicited advice; at Woods Hole, Cattell had sided with Whitman against absorption by CIW. Cattell favored laboratories for physics, chemistry, and psychology in addition to a very liberal program of fellowships and grants. He was decidedly against tying up an appreciable portion of Carnegie Institution funds for geophysics. No amount of assurances by Chamberlin, Walcott and, presumably, Woodward could convince him the subject merited so much cash.[49] In addition, Cattell was against the growing inclination of the trustees to favor the expensive plans of the astronomers, notably those of George Ellery Hale to construct an observatory on Mount Wilson.

In 1902, Walcott purposefully moved to commit CIW to a program of laboratory construction. Locating tracts of land in Washington, he presented plans to the trustees on November 25. One hundred and ten acres seemed excessive before the Institution had decided on its policy: as Billings declared, "that is practically an endorsement of the centralized large laboratory scheme for Washington." Following that assertion, the trustees had a heated, if rambling, debate. Putting resources into land and then into bricks outraged those interested in finding and developing the exceptional man. To others, a good buy in real estate was simple prudence looking to the future. Alexander Agassiz wavered, tempted by the possibility of a biological laboratory in northwest Washington. Still others argued for giving the exceptional men physical homes for their talents. Walcott's particular site proposal failed, but the net effect was to harden opinion among the trustees for acquisition of land in Washington, particularly for a geophysical laboratory.[50]

Woodward's other proposed laboratory scheme for physics quietly expired. No exceptional man appeared, at least not one interested in leaving academe. Presumably, if someone like Michelson had evinced interest, then the Institution might have erected another laboratory in Washington to go along with those for geophysics and terrestrial magnetism. Significantly, the trustees, including

Woodward himself in later years, made no effort to find such an exceptional investigator. By 1906 at least some leading physicists were convinced CIW support for their field was a lost cause.[51]

The advisory committee on chemistry submitted majority and minority reports. Remsen of Johns Hopkins chaired a committee of three that included T. W. Richards and E. F. Smith. The majority favored giving funds to established chemists at universities so they could hire suitable research assistants. Yet in their initial concept of research assistantships, the trustees in effect disregarded the substance of the majority report.

The attitude of T. W. Richards regarding CIW support of chemistry is of particular interest. While signing the majority report, Richards issued a minority report calling for an alternative rejected by his two colleagues—the establishment of Carnegie Research Professorships "to relieve university professors from part of the routine work which they are now doing." Richards and Woodward tentatively considered forming a laboratory of physical chemistry, but their idea foundered on the ambiguous attitude of the trustees toward universities. In general, however, Richards' views on the pursuit of science differed significantly from those of Woodward and other trustees. For example, when Woodward's appointment was under discussion, Richards initially opposed it because, in his view, chemistry had greater possibilities of promoting the "welfare of mankind" than physics or astronomy. On the basis of no evidence known to me, Richards stated that Carnegie favored experimental work over mathematical or abstract investigations. Science, Richards asserted, is more likely to advance along inductive rather than deductive lines. Yet Woodward himself had no doubt that he was an inductive scientist; his own work included instances of careful observation and experimentation.[52]

With the exception of the abortive merger of CIW and Woods Hole, the biological sciences did not represent an area of contention within the Carnegie Institution. The Desert Laboratory opened in 1903; the Station for Experimental Evolution and the Department of Marine Biology were established in 1904; the Nutrition Laboratory followed three years later; and the Department of Embryology in 1914.

By contrast, the Carnegie policy toward the "newer" sciences led to several disputes, with Catell once again at the center of the opposition. Beyond Cattell's great skepticism of the need for a research facility for geophysics was a strong desire to obtain funds for experimental psychology. To him the issue was favoritism for older established fields over the newer ones. As Hale's plans progressed, Cattell shifted his criticism from geophysics to astronomy. His way of looking at the matter was quite different from that of Hale, Woodward, and the trustees. In 1905 he wrote Hale: "Any distribution of the funds of the Carnegie Institution is likely to cause criticism. . . . As a psychologist I naturally feel that we are as much in need of money as the astronomers, and I do not see just how the account can be settled, except on the assumption that as there are about an equal number of workers in astronomy and psychology, they should receive equal consideration.''[53] Assuring Cattell of his desire to advance psychology, Hale argued that his proposals were unique, valuable, and timely.

Cattell's criticism roused Woodward, particularly when points made in correspondence subsequently appeared in print. Being a methodological and conscientious person, Woodward thought out and presented an answer. After citing ''the practical and commercial value'' of astronomy, he cited ''a still higher value'':

> Astronomy, for example, has done more than all the other sciences put together up to date to straighten out the kinks in the minds of human beings, to remove superstition and to enable us to think straight on questions in general. . . . It is much easier in general to get money to carry on astronomical researches than to carry on other researches. . . . There is good reason for it. Many people have asked me how it is that, if we speak of shares amongst the different sciences, astronomy is getting the lion's share. I have tried to find out why it is, and it is this: It is the oldest and most highly developed science. . . . Look over the applications we have for projects [and] you will find that the certainty, the definiteness of these applications is almost directly proportionate to the age of the sciences represented. Roughly speaking, the order of precedence, which is fixed not by us but by nature, is this: Astronomy, chemistry and physics second, and zoology third. . . . One of the aims [of CIW] should be to bring up the other sciences to the level of the older sciences.[54]

Woodward's certainty about the order fixed by nature arose from the clear, self-evident truths of the history of science—at least as seen by him.

Given the limited funds, the trustees understandably favored the more established sciences. Being sympathetic with his former colleagues, Cattell and Franz Boas, Woodward was not wholly comfortable with his position and the prejudices of his trustees:

> It is not alone sufficient to show the possibility of taking up work in new directions. This is in fact the least of the difficulties. The greatest difficulty is to overcome the prejudice and inertia of the society in which we live. Some lines of work which appear to me to be of the greatest importance to the future of humanity are looked upon with unmitigated contempt by many of our most eminent contemporaries. The Institution is severely criticised for pursuing the obviously advantageous sciences. What could be the stream of criticism and abuse received if we were to take up work in lines less obviously advantageous?[55]

An outsider like Cattell did not realize that Woodward and the trustees were often genuinely interested in moving into new fields. As proposals for new thrusts encountered the limitations of funds, they reacted sometimes out of prejudice, sometimes with genuine concern to think out issues and do right. The openness to expansion of the Institution's scope is well illustrated by the new departments that were under consideration in 1907: municipal government, classical philology and archaeology, legal research, hydromechanics, and anthropology. While Woodward's sole reservation on the five was fiscal, only anthropology became a research area of the Institution.[56]

Despite Woodward's interest, he was very cautious about entering into anthropology. His 1901 presidential address to the American Association for the

Advancement of Science spoke approvingly of science entering and exploring "the domain of manners and morals."[57] Woodward had great respect for Franz Boas, his former colleague at Columbia, and consulted with him on this issue. Boas's initial training was related to Woodward's, and one can speculate that he might have served as the "exceptional man" in anthropology. But Boas preferred to remain at Columbia. In correspondence with Cattell in 1906, Woodward summed up his problem with the field: "The fact that there are numerous tribes of the human race now rapidly disappearing has been stated to me at least once a day on the average during the past year, and yet I fear we could hardly get two men to agree on a practicable method of dealing with the problems presented by these tribes."[58] Woodward was noting the absence of a consensus, one of the characteristics of a science, a point later rediscovered by Thomas Kuhn.

These misgivings aside, by 1911 Woodward seemed ready to find an exceptional man for a department of anthropology. One of the trustees, William Barclay Parsons,[59] avidly pushed Central American archaeology, and other trustees enthusiastically supported him. But at the next annual meeting, Woodward balked. In his view, there was still no single person exceptional enough to take a broad view of the entire field. Instead, he recommended going forward in human embryology, "a field which lies at the basis of anthropology." For Woodward, Central American archaeology was too narrow, yet Parsons persisted. The result was that, in 1914, CIW began support of Sylvanus G. Morley's archaelogical work in Central America. Eventually, a separate program for the study of Central American archaeology was developed.

The Carnegie Institution's experience with two other social sciences, economics and sociology, was completely different. The Department of Economics and Sociology was organized in 1904—one of the earliest to be established in the Institution. It differed from the other CIW departments in two respects. First, its director from 1904 to his death in 1909 was Carroll D. Wright, a statistician and one of the trustees.[60] Perhaps for that reason, little attention was paid to the department at trustees' meetings during Wright's lifetime.

After Wright's death, Woodward and the Executive Committee looked carefully into the work of the department and were appalled. Wright had ambitious plans for a series of studies constituting a comprehensive social and economic history of the United States.[61] Yet despite sizeable allocations by the standards of the day, few results were produced nor was there optimism about future works reaching CIW for printing. At fault, in Woodward's opinion, was a totally pernicious manner of organization unlike that of any of the other operating departments of the Institution. Woodward pointedly reminded Billings that the defective procedures were specifically approved by the Executive Committee in January 1904.[62] But he was careful to point out, at a trustees' meeting in December 1909, that the faults were not inherent in economics[63] and in sociology:

It appeared, moreover, that most of the work which has been done under the auspices of this department had been carried on or executed by young men or women who were, at the time, candidates for the higher degrees in colleges and universities. It appeared, on further examination, that many of these candidates for degrees had been supported in going through colleges and universities, and had actually had their dissertations and other papers printed at the expense of the Institution. . . . It appeared from the confessions of these collaborators of Colonel Wright, all very able and eminent men, that nearly all of the work which had been collected by their assistants was regarded as untrustworthy, defective, much of it defective to such an extent that it could not be used at all.[64]

To Woodward, it was vindication for his belief in the full-time pursuit of knowledge. By 1916, he was more than a bit smug in reminding the trustees of his opposition to assistantships and to minor grants and how opinion inside and outside the Institution opposed him by a margin of six to four, the majority preferring to aid university men.

With the discovery of conditions following Wright's death, Woodward tried to rescue something from the debacle. To the trustees he displayed, on December 11, 1916, "the first fruits from that department." It was too late; the trustees voted for its abolition. Woodward hoped to revive the group in five years when funds might become available, but this proved impossible.[65] In retrospect, the department did achieve a measure of success; its products eventually included important contributions, some not wholly supplanted by later work.[66]

At the same trustees' meeting that revealed the bad news about Carroll Wright's creation, a pointed question was asked about the quality of the work carried out by the Department of Historical Research. Staunchly defending the department, Woodward pointed to its productivity—a result of full-time devotion to research so unlike the university-type arrangement in Wright's group. While the Department of Historical Research survived from 1903 until 1930, its career within CIW was not always smooth. Walcott and Billings strongly opposed it. In 1903 Walcott decided to remain on the Executive Committee "to prevent any development of the Institution on the lines of an educational organization. I fear we are drifting into it in the historical work."[67] A number of years later, Billings unsuccessfully attempted to abolish the Department of Historical Research.[68] Woodward stopped that move and in 1916 defended the department, then under John Franklin Jameson, against the charge of not producing history but simply "materials for historic research" in the form of guides, catalogs, and indexes.[69] The products of Jameson's group were valuable and influential in their day; in addition to guides to sources, a number of important documentary collections eventually appeared.[70]

Full-time professionalism rated high in Woodward's scale of values. That concept had much to do with the demise of CIW support of a program in classical archaeology and philology. At the very same trustees' meeting of December 13, 1904, in which Woodward was elected president, Gilman introduced an appeal for funds for the schools of classical studies in Athens and Rome. The sum was modest, $3,300, and the sponsors impeccable—T. D. Seymour of Yale, James R. Wheeler of Columbia University, and Andrew F. West of Princeton. Billings voiced his objections; the work was not under the direction of CIW but of outside organizations. Gilman prevailed largely because many of the trustees regarded the schools as admirable examples of self-help.[71]

Woodward was also sympathetic. Linking classical studies to his support of anthropology, he observed in 1908:

It seems to me that it would be quite practicable now to raise classical philology and archaeology from the plane of amateurism and dillettantism on which they have rested, perhaps for centuries, to the plane of anthropology. The ablest philologists and archaeologists, I think, in this particular field are engaged in work which is as truly scientific as that carried on in the physical sciences. It should be remembered that a very large majority of our fellow citizens of the world, especially among educated men, are men whose education and whose interests are almost wholly confined to those lines of work, and it appears to me that one of the best ways to get them to appreciate other lines of work, which now certainly receive the preference in educational institutions and in the world generally, would be to give our classical friends an opportunity to come in on the same ground with the physical sciences.[72]

But in 1912, Woodward withdrew CIW support for the American School of Classical Studies in Rome: "I visited it last summer, spent nearly a month in Rome, and looked into it very carefully. . . . [It] is an admirable school for elementary education, or perhaps for the dilettante or amateur who aspires to a modicum of culture; it is a school . . . somewhat of the character of an international afternoon tea . . . but it does not lead to research." Loath to desert the field, Woodward made two scholars from the Rome School research associates: Elias A. Lowe (later at the Institute for Advanced Study) and Esther Boice Van Deman. Unfortunately for the humanities, Woodward's observations of "an international afternoon tea" occurred in the period when he and CIW were under pressure to expand into that intellectual area.[73]

At the same meeting of December 14, 1909 in which Woodward disclosed the shortcomings of the Department of Economics and Sociology, the trustees received a petition fron ten national societies calling for a redress in the balance of CIW funding for science and the humanities.[74] The petition was endorsed by the presidents and former presidents of nine universities. Although it was sent to the Executive Committee for consideration, no significant change occurred in CIW's allocation among fields. Despite Woodward's sympathetic words a year earlier, neither he nor the trustees were inclined to adopt a change in policy, especially in view of a fairly tight budget.

What the petition did cause was a reexamination of the status of the humanities within CIW, a topic that concerned Woodward almost to the end of his tenure. Earlier in his presidency, Woodward sided with Gilman against Billings and Walcott on support of the humanities but with only modest effects.[75] After the receipt of the 1909 petition, Woodward began a systematic study of how CIW "may best promote research and progress in the humanities." Naturally, the results confirmed his long-held beliefs. "About thirty distinguished authors" replied to a circular letter. Very little agreement existed as to the definition of the humanities; asked to indicate which CIW publications were in the humanities, the respondents reached no consensus.[76]

Woodward had no qualms about where he stood. While sympathetic to the humanities, he regarded science as both intellectually and morally superior. In public addresses while Dean of Pure Science at Colombia, he made his position quite explicit. In his presidential address of August 27, 1901, before the American Association for the Advancement of Science, he sketched a scheme for the history of science which was, to him, *the* history of mankind. To extend the sway of man and to diminish the scope of the supernatural, three distinct methods were developed in the past and applied down to the present: the a priori, the historico-critical, and the scientific.

> The second . . . depends, in its purity, on tradition, history, direct human testimony and verbal congruity. It does not require an appeal to Nature except as manifested in man. . . . And in the serenity of his repose behind the fortress of "liberal culture," the reactionary humanist will prepare apologies for errors and patch up compromises between traditional beliefs and sound learning with such consummate literary skill that even "the good demon of doubt" is almost persuaded that if knowledge did not come to an end long ago it will soon reach its limit. In short, we have learned, or ought to have learned, from ample experience, that in the search for definite verifiable knowledge we should beware of the investigator whose equipment consists of a bundle of traditions and dogmas along with formal logic and a facile pen; for we may be sure that he will be more deeply concerned with the question of the safety than with the question of the soundness of scientific doctrines. . . . I would not disparage the elevated aspirations and noble efforts of the evangelists and the humanists who seek to raise the lower to the plane of the higher elements of our race; but it is now plain as a matter of fact, no matter how repulsive it may seem to some of our inherited opinions, that the railway, the steamship, the telegraph, and the daily press will do more to illuminate the dark places of the earth than all the apostles of creeds and all the messengers of the gospel of "sweetness and light."[77]

Two years later Woodward tilted at the humanities in a commencement address:

> Thus, even at the present day, many of the older schools of education hold, tacitly, if not openly, that studies may be divided into sharply defined categories designated as "liberal," "humanistic," "scientific," "professional," "technical," etc.; and men and women are said to have had "a liberal training," "a professional training" or "a technical training," as the case may be. They say, by implication at least, that mathematics, when pursued a little way, just far enough to make a student entertain the egotistic but erroneous notion that he knows something of the subject, is an element of liberal training. On the other hand, if the student goes further, and acquires a working knowledge of mathematics, his training is called professional or technical. Similarly, studies which include the memorabilia of Xenophon and Caesar, the poetry of Homer and Virgil and Dante and Shakespeare, or, in short, the so-called polite literature of ancient and modern times, are said to lead to breadth and culture; while studies which include the works of Archimedes, Hipparchus, Galileo, Huygens, Newton, Laplace and Darwin are said to lead to narrowness and specialism; as if the first class of authors were somehow possessed of humanistic traits, and the other class of demoniacal tendencies. So far, indeed, are

these distinctions carried that higher moral qualities are not uncommonly attributed to the young man who studies Latin and Greek in order that he may earn a living by teaching them than are attributed to the young man who studies engineering in order that he may earn a living by building bridges which will not fall down and kill folks.[78]

Above all, the attribution of "higher moral qualities" to humanists outraged Woodward. For example, in 1906 he had a dispute about John Tyndall with one of T. W. Richards' Harvard colleagues, C. L. Jackson. Woodward's defense of Tyndall unexpectedly brought in the humanities:

We Americans, I think, are especially indebted to Tyndall for helping us to get a start in our colleges for the pursuit of postgraduate studies. We should remember also that while Tyndall left the proceeds of his "Lectures in America" to found fellowships at Harvard, at Columbia, and at the University of Pennsylvania, the prince of humanists, Matthew Arnold, refused to go on the lecture platform in some instances before receiving a check in payment for his address.[79]

In addition to the claims of the academic humanists, Woodward had to consider the views of a number of his lay trustees, some of whom favored support for poetry. As Senator Lodge stated: "Literature and the humanities are pretty nearly dead, science has pretty nearly killed them, but I would like them to live and I would like to see something done to keep them alive." One gathers that there was little sympathy among the trustees for Woodward's attempt to convert the humanities into research fields.[80] His last public words on the subject were: "It appears to be the duty of the Institution to proceed . . . in a spirit of sympathy and equity based on merit toward all domains of knowledge, with a full appreciation of the necessary limitations of any single organization and with a respectful but untrammeled regard for the views, the sentiments, and the suffrages of our contemporaries."[81]

Here George Sarton's dedication to volume three, part one of his *Introduction to the History of Science* becomes a clue to Woodward's behavior. Extravagantly, it calls Woodward the "second author" of the work, pointing up a bookish, learned element in the man who wanted Archimedes, Hipparchus, Galileo, Huygens, Newton, Laplace, and Darwin to be part of liberal training. Such a man gloried in the publication of a translation of a revision of Ptolemy and could proudly call attention to the publication of the Vulgate version of the Arthurian romances, Charles W. Hodel's translation of the "Old Yellow Book," and concordances to Spenser, Horace, and Keats. And he could even approve the publication in 1913 of Morgan Calloway's statistical study, *The Infinitive in Anglo Saxon*.

If one looks at the pattern of CIW support of fields of learning as a whole—not only at the areas of contention—two factors emerge as decisive for a major commitment of its funds. In each and every case there was an exceptional man (in the eyes of the trustees) and a field already familiar to the American scene. Where a field, such as physics or chemistry, was marginally established in the hands of a small number of university practitioners, even eminent ones like A. A.

Michelson, CIW support of a laboratory was most unlikely. Even the two nonscientific departments, History and Economics and Sociology, represented activities and intellectual styles already familiar to Americans with any reasonable cultural awareness. Walcott and Chamberlin properly stressed the originality of the proposed geophysical research. Concern with the physical and chemical properties of the earth's constituents was, nevertheless, an intrinsic part of a widespread, successful research enterprise in geology in nineteenth-century America. A special laboratory was a logical extension of this tradition. Terrestrial magnetism had attracted American physical scientists in the nineteenth century. The early interests of Ferdinand Rudolph Hassler and Alexander Dallas Bache embedded the subject in the Coast and Geodetic Survey. By 1900 Americans had invested considerable intellectual and economic capital in astronomy; even the newer specialty, astrophysics, was fully assimilated.

Much the same pattern exists within the biological installations; the Station for Experimental Evolution (later the Department of Genetics), the Desert Laboratory (later the Department of Plant Biology), and the Department of Marine Biology all had American antecedents. At first glance the Nutrition Laboratory (1907) and the Department of Embryology (1914) do not quite fit the pattern. Both had exceptional men as directors, Francis G. Benedict and Franklin P. Mall, respectively. Yet the fields are not part of the conventional historical landscape of the sciences in America. If, however, one remembers R. H. Chittenden's history of physiological chemistry in America and the earlier work of Wilbur Atwater, the Nutrition Laboratory does fall within the pattern.[82] On the other hand, Franklin P. Mall's focus on human embryology required a fetus collection analogous to the anatomical and pathological collections of the Army Medical Museum. I am inclined to view CIW's interest in embryology as an outgrowth of concern with medical pathology and histology, now extended to include physiology.

Citing the impact of precedent and of exceptional men is not to deny nor to diminish the value of the research issuing from CIW installations. Quite often the laboratories and the Mt. Wilson Observatory did fresh and influential work. What is at issue here is the range within which the trustees were willing to make long-term obligations in contrast to short-term fellowships and specific grants. Understandably, even enlightened laymen would hesitate about venturing too far from the familiar. Moreover, the scientific trustees were not the sort likely to lead the CIW into revolutionary ventures. Billings and Mitchell were elderly physicians not inclined to stray from the safety of the reports of expert advisers. A great paleontologist, Walcott's intellectual scope was limited; after the Geophysics Laboratory was assured, his influence diminished. As a man from a rising, bustling university, Woodward was more knowing and sympathetic to new trends; countering that characteristic were his administrative caution and his ideological set. Yet, despite this cautionary approach, CIW in its early years was a notable increment to the intellectual life of the United States.

### Higher Education and the Carnegie Institution

After support of original research and the discovery of exceptional men, the trust deed establishing the Carnegie Institution of Washington set forth three aims related to institutions of higher learning:

3. To increase facilities for higher education.
4. To increase the efficiency of the Universities and other institutions of learning throughout the country, by utilizing and adding to their existing facilities and aiding teachers in the various institutions for experimental work, in these institutions as far as advisable.
5. To enable such students as may find Washington the best point for their special studies, to enjoy the advantages of the Museums, Libraries, Laboratories, Observatories, Meteorological, Piscicultural, and Forestry Schools, and kindred institutions of the several departments of the Government.[83]

These three aims plus the two prior ones could easily lead to the conclusion that the bulk of the Carnegie gift was destined for universities, their faculty members, and their students. Indeed, many drew that conclusion—to their bitter disappointment as the Institution's program unfolded. Despite the promising language of the trust deed, the origins of aims three, four, and five practically guaranteed only limited aid to higher education, either directly by grants to institutions or indirectly to faculty and students. To this birth defect (from the standpoint of the universities) must be added the resolve of Carnegie and the trustees (with the notable exception of Gilman and White) to avoid the enmeshment of CIW with the world of higher education.

As has been shown in the preceding pages, evidence of this determination to keep a careful distance from the university world became increasingly apparent as the Carnegie program developed. But even in the very beginning there were indirect indications of this intent. For example, a letter from Henry Smith Pritchett, then president of the Massachusetts Institute of Technology, reveals that in the early planning stages of CIW, five of the trustees were to have come from institutions of higher learning.[84] Yet when the Institution actually came into existence, an unwritten rule barred active university administrators and faculty from the Board of Trustees. President Charles W. Eliot of Harvard was asked to join only after his retirement; Welch of Johns Hopkins was the first to breach the rule. University men by definition were interested parties. The trustees feared their funds might blight the initiative of the universities; they also worried about the diversion of funds to support routine educational activities, not research or outstanding individuals. When a revision of the CIW charter occurred in 1904, the trustees, without any qualms, dropped those clauses on education objected to by the Congress.[85] Finally, innumerable encounters with university men seeking funds only strengthened an existing bias for in-house research. Writing to Billings only a few months after Woodward assumed office, Walcott was "somewhat amused to hear of the experiences Dr. Woodward is having with university and other men. I told him it was a duplication of what you and I have been through and that he would probably come to the same conclusions before long."[86]

At the very end of his tenure as president of the Institution, Woodward was still complaining that university men misunderstood the nature of CIW. They disbelieved or resented the effort to make the Carnegie Institution more than a mere "disbursing agency," in fact, a real participant in research. Nor was Woodward wholly successful in conveying his rationale, even though he wrote several statements on his "theory of research" in the Institution's *Yearbooks,* emphasizing his belief that research should be conducted on a full-time basis at an institution designed specifically for that purpose.[87]

A good example of this lack of successful communication can be found in Woodward's long and friendly relationship with T. W. Richards. Despite an extensive exchange of correspondence over many years, neither really understood the other nor succeeded in convincing the other. As late as 1914, after Richards had spent several years as a CIW research associate, the gap was still wide. As a notable researcher and a university man, Richards continued to favor the endowment of research professorships at universities to relieve outstanding faculty from the routine of teaching. Although the possibility of a CIW laboratory for physical chemistry came up several times, Richards always insisted that the laboratory be at Harvard.

Richards' reasons for endowing professorships and building laboratories at universities were in part highly practical. Using existing staff, buildings, and funds at universities would enable CIW funds to go further. In addition there was the "great mass of advanced students ... held partly by their desire for the degree ... and by sentimental considerations ..." available as cheap labor. This argument based on economy was flatly opposed by Woodward; CIW experience was to the contrary. In addition he pointed to the irritations and frictions almost invariably arising between grantor and grantee. Nor was Woodward impressed by Richards' call for CIW to expand the small portion of funds available for research at Harvard.

The raising of the flag for the universities by Richards brought forth rebuttal from Woodward:

Curiously enough, it seems to be tacitly assumed by many eminent men that there is something about a university that will prevent investigators from stagnating more completely than similar influences in institutions organized for the express purpose of research. This argument applied to the Royal Institution of London, for example, would lead us to suppose that Davy, Faraday, Tyndall, and Dewar ought to have undergone deterioration immediately on being given life positions for the purpose of devoting their entire energies to investigations.

An eminent man of science wrote me a few days ago that he viewed "with alarm" the tendency of our institution to build departments of work, for ... the men at work in these departments will tend to stagnate. . . . Everyone knows . . . that most men tend to stagnate rather early in life; but I fail to see why picked men should tend to stagnate in an institution whose atmosphere is that of research, any more than men in academic institutions, who are, as a rule, to a much less extent subject to stimulus to original productivity.[88]

That elicited an interesting rejoiner from Richards: "What I meant to say was this:—no man can predict what a man is going to do in the future; some increase in productiveness; others diminish. If a research institution engages a man in a life position, and his originality diminishes, both the institution and the man are in an unfortunate position. If the university does the same thing, the man may throw his energies into teaching."[89]

In the 1912 *Yearbook* of the Institution, Woodward gave a number of "inductions" from CIW experience in supporting research. Full-time professionalism loomed large. One induction was aimed at the universities. "Many investigations of real scope require men untrammeled by other occupations. . . . The common notion that research demands only a portion of one's leisure from more absorbing duties tends to turn the course of evolution backwards and to land us in the amateurism and the dilettantism wherein science finds its beginnings."[90]

Walcott and Billings supported Woodward in his determination to create an organization devoted purely to research. Although so different in personality and intellectual interests, the three men shared at least two experiences. First, since they entered science before the widespread establishment of graduate education, they had followed other career routes. Walcott never went to college, being largely trained by apprenticeship and self-study. He is probably the last American scientist of consequence to lack formal academic training. Billings (if viewed as a scientist) entered the world of research from medical school, a path fairly common in America during the first half of the century before the growth of science in the liberal arts colleges, in the scientific schools, and in the graduate schools. And Woodward was a mathematically talented engineer who turned to pure science. Not having passed through a graduate school, they did not consider the university as necessarily the site of research. What they saw was some research conducted at a few of the outstanding schools and very little investigation, indeed, performed at the mass of colleges and universities.

A second point in common was a career in the federal service. Each had engaged in full-time professional work in the government. Their support of an independent installation specializing in research was a reasonable extension of their personal experiences. In no way could they agree with the tacit assumption of their critics that persists to this day: the support of research must be necessarily linked to the support of higher education. By implication, Walcott, Billings, and Woodward were advocating policies at the Carnegie Institution of Washington that called for universities to specialize in teaching. Lurking among the minutes, memoranda, and correspondence of the Carnegie Institution of Washington may be a moral.

Yet even at the founding, such a moral was futile because it came too late.

The Carnegie Institution was not alone in attempting to separate teaching from research. In the same period, similarly motivated organizations appeared in the United States and in Europe—the Rockefeller Institute for Medical Research in New York, the National Physical Laboratory in England, the Kaiser-Wilhelm-Gesellshaft in Germany.[91] However, by the turn of the century the leading American universities, as well as those institutions just below the first rank, had come to include research in their definition of the essence of higher education. Perhaps as important, universities and colleges with pretensions to excellence scrambled down the same path. As circumstances permitted, university after university with little hesitation and considerable support from their faculties incorporated more and more aspects of the research institute. A T. W. Richards of Harvard, after all, vied with Woodward, Billings, and Walcott in his admiration for the Royal Institution of Michael Faraday. And there was no shortage of university faculty who regarded students as obstacles to the pursuit of knowledge.

## Notes

1. By far the best account of the founding of the Carnegie Institution is in chapter 9 of Howard S. Miller's *Dollars for Research: Science and Its Patrons in Nineteenth-Century America* (Seattle, Wash: University of Washington Press, 1970). The latest biography of Carnegie, Joseph Wall, *Andrew Carnegie* (New York: Oxford University Press, 1970), pp. 858–63, adds only a few details. A valuable article bearing on the founding is David Madsen, "Daniel Coit Gilman at the Carnegie Institution of Washington," *History of Education Quarterly* 9 (1969): 154–86.

2. Carnegie Institution of Washington, *Yearbook* 1901, Appendix A, pp. 1–238.

3. S. V. "Woodward" in the *Dictionary of Scientific Biography,* in press at this writing.

4. Nathan Reingold, "American Indifference to Basic Research: A Reappraisal," in *Nineteenth-Century American Science: A Reappraisal,* ed. George H. Daniels (Evanston, Ill.: Northwestern University Press, 1972), pp. 38–62.

5. Gilman to Carnegie, April 13, 1903, with reply of Carnegie. Carnegie Institution of Washington Archives (hereafter CIW).

6. Woodward to Billings, November 30, 1910, Billings Papers, New York Public Library.

7. As this matter is adequately handled in Madsen, "Daniel Coit Gilman," it will not be discussed in detail here.

8. Billings to H. L. Higginson, November 23, 1904, Billings Papers, and Woodward to T. C. Chamberlin, July 11, 1904, Chamberlin Papers, University of Chicago.

9. Billings to Walcott, October 25, 1905, Billings Papers, in which Billings agrees to Woodward acting as secretary of the Executive Committee.

10. W. H. Welch to Woodward, November 30, 1911, and Woodward to Welch, December 21, 1911, CIW.

11. File DR 75, May 24, 1916, p. 3, Record Group 3, Series 915, Box 1, Folder 6, Rockefeller Archive Center.

12. While Carnegie's remarks are in the trustees' minutes, Gilman's are not but survive separately at CIW.

13. The standard account is David Madsen, *The National University: Enduring Dream of the U.S.A.* (Detroit, Mich: Wayne State University Press, 1967). Chapter 5 deals with Hoyt.

14. For White's optimistic reaction, see his letter to Gilman of June 21, 1901, CIW.

15. An 1892 statute had opened government facilities to students and investigators for institutions incorporated by Congress or under the laws of the District of Columbia. In March of 1901, this privilege was extended to all.

16. Miller, *Dollars for Research,* has a good account of the events. In the Walcott Papers, Smithsonian Archives, are Walcott's files on the Association and the Institution. An interesting account in the context of the later events is Philip C. Ritterbush, "Research Training in Gov-

ernmental Laboratories in the United States," *Minerva* 4 (1966): 186–201. Walcott hoped to have Gilman head the Washington Memorial Institution. Walcott to Gilman, November 18, 1901, CIW.

17. Billings's memo of the meeting, dated November 22, 1901, is in Box A of his papers in the folder "Memos-Bibliographies."

18. Gilman to Eliot, December 3, 1901, CIW.

19. In the Walcott file cited in n. 16. See also Trustees' Minutes, 1 March 1902, 12f, and the undated letter (1902) of Walcott to N. M. Butler about CIW developing as a research institute rather than "education in the usual sense." Walcott Papers. Butler headed the Washington Memorial Institution in these early days. By 1903 it was fading; Walcott thought that Columbian University in Washington would take up the function by becoming purely a graduate organization. But although Columbian changed its name to George Washington University, nothing came of this. Walcott to Billings, July 13, 1903, Billings Papers. As to the Memorial Association, almost down to World War I, it persisted in trying to get a memorial hall constructed suitable for a national university.

20. Dael Wolfle, *The Home of Science* (New York: McGraw-Hill, 1972).

21. *Yearbook,* 1902, p. xiii.

22. Billings' copy is in Box A of the Billings Papers.

23. Welch to Billings, January 16, 1902, Billings Papers.

24. Remsen to Billings, January 24, 1902, Billings Papers.

25. Woodward to Butler, November 23, 1905, Butler Correspondence, Columbia University Archives.

26. Billings to Walcott, December 10, 1902, CIW.

27. Walcott's memo, dated May 28, 1902, is in the Billings Papers.

28. Trustees' Minutes, December 8, 1903, pp. 167–8, 179–80, 216. The Carnegie quote is from the last.

29. T. W. Richards to Woodward, March 28, 1905, Richards Papers, Harvard Archives.

30. Trustees' Minutes, December 12, 1905, pp. 470–71.

31. Trustees' Minutes, December 20, 1905, pp. 445, 452, 469–71, 474, 486.

32. Ibid. Mitchell was referring to the stress on the practical application of Burbank's work. But Woodward, who later usually noted that practicality should never be raised in considering the best research, also noted at that meeting the possible application of the work in geophysics.

33. Shull's report, dated July 26, 1906, is in the Shull Papers, Library of the American Philosophical Society.

34. Trustees' Minutes, December 15, 1911, p. 210.

35. Trustees' Minutes, December 8, 1908, pp. 736, 754–56, 761–63.

36. Ibid. Carnegie quotation appears on p. 761.

37. Trustees' Minutes, December 14, 1909, pp. 25–9.

38. The first is on p. 29; the second is on p. 6 of the respective *Yearbooks*.

39. Woodward to Chamberlin, July 10, 1920, Chamberlin Papers.

40. Trustees' Minutes, December 11, 1906, pp. 581–2. A statement of Woodward's views is in his letter to George Ellery Hale, December 12, 1906, Hale Papers, California Institute of Technology Archives. See also Hale's reply of December 20, 1906, Caltech Archives. For an exchange on minor grants, see Woodward to Cattell, March 6, 1907, and Cattell to Woodward, March 9, 1907, Cattell Papers, Library of Congress.

41. Trustees' Minutes, December 11, 1906, pp.

42. Trustees' Minutes, December 15, 1916, pp. 611–2.

43. Woodward to Richards, March 22, 1918, and Richards to Woodward, April 6, 1918, Richards Papers.

44. This discussion, including a restatement of Woodward's "theory of research," is in the Trustees' Minutes of December 13, 1918, pp. 759, 760–1.

45. Both memos are in the Billings Papers.

46. Trustees' Minutes, December 8, 1902, pp. 192–5.

47. Lewis Boss to Hale, August 27, 1902, Hale Papers.

48. In addition to the references in the Trustees' Minutes to Woods Hole, there is a very interesting run of letters of E. B. Wilson to Billings in the Billings Papers, as well as a scattering of related letters in the same collection.

49. Walcott to Cattell, September 17, 1902, and Chamberlin to Cattell, September 10, 1902, Cattell Papers, Library of Congress.

50. Trustees' Minutes, November 25, 1902, pp. 63–8, 86–106, 113–9, 127–8. Before the organi-

zation of the Geophysical Laboratory in 1906, CIW supported the researches of the Geological Survey's George F. Becker (an old school chum of Henry Adams and C. S. Peirce) and Arthur L. Day. Under the latter's directorship, the Geophysical Laboratory had a notable record in research.

51. E. P. Rosa to A. G. Webster, March 12, 1906, Webster Papers, Archives, University of Illinois (Urbana).

52. Richards to Higginson, December 1 and December 3, 1904, Richards Papers.

53. Cattell to Hale, April 15, 1905; Hale to Cattell, May 2, 1905, Hale Papers.

54. Trustees' Minutes, December 12, 1905, pp. 471–3.

55. Woodward to Cattell, February 2, 1906, Cattell Papers.

56. Woodward to Billings, October 18, 1907, Billings Papers.

57. "The Progress of Science," *Science,* n.s. 14 (1901): 305–15. The reference to anthropology is on p. 312.

58. Woodward to Cattell, January 24, 1906, Cattell Papers.

59. Parsons (1859–1932) was an eminent civil engineer. Woodward apparently regarded the proposed archaeological program as too much like a conventional museum program. In modern terms, he leaned to a more "behavioral" approach. Trustees' Minutes, December 15, 1911, pp. 206–7, 250–5; December 13, 1911, pp. 301–5, 333–9.

60. From 1885 to 1905 Wright (1840–1909) headed the Bureau of Labor, the predecessor of the Department of Labor.

61. Wright to Billings, February 26, 1904, Billings Papers. Billings was concerned that the products have more than data and be analytical.

62. Woodward to Billings, April 15, 1909, and February 14, 1910, Billings Papers.

63. For example, see Woodward to E. R. A. Seligman, April 28, 1908, Seligman Papers, Columbia University Library, with its discussion of aid to economics in the context of Woodward's opposition to minor grants and aid to universities.

64. Trustees' Minutes, December 14, 1909, pp. 16–18; December 15, 1911, pp. 202–3.

65. Trustees' Minutes, December 11, 1916, pp. 540–1, 666.

66. For example, Emory Johnson et al., *History of Domestic and Foreign Commerce of the United States,* 2 vols., Publication No. 215A (Washington, D.C.: Carnegie Institution of Washington, 1916); Victor S. Clark, *History of Manufacturers in the United States,* 3 vols., Publication No. 215B (Washington, D.C.: Carnegie Institution of Washington, 1916–1929); Balthasor Meyer et al., *History of Transportation in the United States,* Publication No. 215C (Washington, D.C.: Carnegie Institution of Washington, 1917); P. W. Bidwell and J. I. Falconer, *History of Agriculture in the Northern United States to 1860,* Publication no. 358, series 2 (Washington, D.C.: Carnegie Institution of Washington, 1933).

67. Walcott to Billings, July 13, 1903, Billings Papers; Trustees' Minutes, December 14, 1909, pp. 25–6.

68. Woodward to Welch, December 2, 1911, CIW.

69. Trustees' Minutes, December 11, 1916, p. 542.

70. For example, only recently have historians picked up the work done in the 1920s on cases involving slavery and on the African slave trade.

71. Trustees' Minutes, December 13, 1904, pp. 452–9.

72. Trustees' Minutes, December 8, 1908, pp. 736–7.

73. Trustees' Minutes, December 13, 1912, pp. 336–7.

74. Trustees' Minutes, December 14, 1909, pp. 29–32.

75. Gilman to Woodward, November 16, 1906, CIW.

76. Referred to in the *Yearbook,* 1917, pp. 19–20. The correspondence apparently no longer exists.

77. "The Progress of Science," *Science,* n.s. 14 (1901).

78. "Education and the World's Work of Today," *Science,* n.s. 18 (1903): 161–9. The quotation is from p. 163.

79. Woodward to C. L. Jackson, June 29, 1906, Richards Papers.

80. Trustees' Minutes, December 15, 1916, pp. 544, 608–9, 666–75.

81. This is from a discussion of the "claims of humanists" in the 1917 *Yearbook,* pp. 16–21.

82. Russell Henry Chittenden, *The Development of Physiological Chemistry in the United States* (New York: Chemical Catalog, 1930).

83. The text of the trust deed and the original articles of incorporation appear both in the *Yearbook* for 1902 and the minutes of the first meeting of the Trustees on January 29 and 30, 1902.

84. Pritchett to Carnegie, December 13, 1901, Carnegie Papers, Library of Congress.

85. Madsen's article (''Daniel Coit Gilman'') is quite good on this point.

86. Walcott to Billings, May 26, 1905, Billings Papers.

87. A convenient summary of this view is in Woodward's address, ''The Needs of Research,'' *Science,* n.s. 40 (1914): 217–29. See the *Yearbooks* 1912, pp. 11–12; 1914, pp. 16–17; 1915, pp. 11–17; 1917, pp. 21–26.

88. Woodward to Richards, March 30, 1906, Richards Papers.

89. Richards to Woodward, April 2, 1906, Richards Papers.

90. *Yearbook,* 1912, pp. 11–12.

91. This is discussed in Loren R. Graham, ''The Formation of Soviet Research Institutes: A Combination of Revolutionary Innovation and International Borrowing,'' *Social Studies of Science* 5 (1975): 303–29, particularly, pp. 303–6.

# The National Academy
# of Sciences and the American
# Definition of Science

## A. HUNTER DUPREE

The National Academy of Sciences today calls itself a private cooptative society of distinguished scholars in scientific and engineering research. It still celebrates as its charter the Act of Incorporation passed by the U.S. Congress and signed by Abraham Lincoln during the Civil War. However, its modern form more nearly resembles a government agency than a learned society. It has associated with it the National Academy of Engineering and the Institute of Medicine. Its administrative arm, the National Research Council, has a large number of permanent employees and is divided into an array of assemblies and commissions. Even the critics of the Academy attest to its power by comparing it to a large consultative research organization such as the Rand Corporation and calling it the "brain bank of America." Yet the present conspicuous position of the National Academy of Sciences does not necessarily deny an essential unity between the imposing structure of today and the struggling organization of the late nineteenth century.

Founded a hundred years too late to be the American Philosophical Society and eighty years too early to be the Office of Scientific Research and Development, the Academy has had a life as mysterious as its birth.[1] Both the intentions of its founders and the success with which those intentions were carried out have been called into question by historians. Much of the scholarly discussion of the origin of the Academy and of its early years has centered around the quiet, not to say conspiratorial, maneuvers that marked the events of the evening of March 3, 1863 and the efficacy of the Academy in carrying out its statutory function to "whenever called upon by any Department of Government, investigate, examine, experiment, and report upon any subject of science or art..." for which "the Academy shall receive no compensation whatever...."[2]

The role of Louis Agassiz, Alexander Dallas Bache, Benjamin Peirce, Benjamin Apthorp Gould, and their circle of friends who put together the original list of fifty scientists named in the organic act has come in for special attention. That a small group drew up the original list is beyond doubt, as is their identity. In retrospect the maneuvers of the group, referred to in the literature as the scientific

Lazzaroni,[3] were not unlike those of any organizing committee. The makeup of the original group was determined in part by who was in Washington in the spring of 1863, and the list they decided on was a product of their institutional affiliations, their friendships, and their enmities. Alexander Dallas Bache of the United States Coast Survey and Louis Agassiz of Harvard University were the shapers of the list. Joseph Henry, Secretary of the Smithsonian Institution and a close associate of Bache, was temporarily out of touch with the organizers because of his reservations about the tactics of asking for immediate federal legislation. Therefore, Agassiz secured the services of Senator Henry Wilson of Massachusetts to push through a bill without discussion. The names of fifty individuals were written directly into the legislation to make up the self-perpetuating membership. The Lazzaroni as a completely informal and changing group of friends nevertheless had enough cohesion to perform the one act that gave the Academy structure—naming the fifty incorporators.

The National Academy of Sciences thus formed had what I have called some "flaws in the foundation."[4] The secret and irresponsible nature of the original selection process seriously undermined the relationship of the Academy to the government. Indeed, an examination of the role of the Academy during its first fifty years as advisor to the government yields little of note. On those few occasions when an important scientific problem came to the Academy, it soon found its way into stronger hands. The Academy's brief and unsuccessful attempt to enter the field of military research in 1863 and 1864 gave way to the far more substantial work of the Permanent Commission of the Navy Department.[5] In 1878 the Academy was asked to review the organization of government-sponsored surveys, only to have the matter resolved by the creation of the United States Geological Survey and the appointment in 1884 of a congressional investigatory commission.[6] A study of forest reserves in the 1890s gave the Academy only a temporary involvement in federal science activities.[7]

At the source of the Academy's modest efforts in government service was the key question of accountability. In American political theory, power resides ultimately in the people, and some chain of representation must stretch back from the group on which authority is temporarily conferred to the ultimate sovereign. The creation of a perpetual corporation of fifty individuals, appointed for life with the exclusive right to select their successors, sealed the Academy off in perpetuity from any constituency at all. The problem has remained a real one for the Academy: for this reason, both Franklin D. Roosevelt and Harry Truman balked at the idea of appropriating public funds directly to the Academy through a Research Board for National Security. The doleful word "quasi-governmental" does little to assuage those who wish to hold the Academy accountable.

The National Academy has, however, a significance beyond its role as scientific advisor to the government. Its organic act could be conceived, at least potentially, as a permanent rallying point for American science.[8] This aspect of the Academy merits serious examination since it bears directly on the hard question about the history of the institution: How, despite its demonstrable flaws, did the National Academy manage to survive to the time of the First World War and, indeed to the present day, essentially on the basis of the 1863 organic act? The question is not how an irresponsible Academy survived in an America alien to its nature, but rather what in the nature of the Academy allowed it to survive as a permanent American institution and what that survival says about the nature of institutions of knowledge in the United States? A first step in answering such a question might be to view the National Academy as a social unit—a system concerned with the gathering, processing, and dissemination of information—and to examine its function from four points of view: (1) as a community, an aggregate of people; (2) as a polity, a group that mobilizes power and even invokes sanctions; (3) as a mobilizer of resources; and (4) as the exemplar of a value system exhibited both locally and globally through symbolic acts.[9]

In his 1851 presidential address before the American Association for the Advancement of Science, Alexander Bache pointed to improvements in methods of communication and the rapid growth of the scientific community as forces that would bring about a changed environment for the production and dissemination of knowledge in America—a change reflected in the drive toward specialization. Bache not only challenged the AAAS to respond to these forces but also called for the creation of a national academy that would be limited in membership and tied to the government. In fact, however, the increasing specialization of the sciences led not to a centralization of information networks but rather to what I have termed a "new kind of pluralism." The disciplines themselves came to form the boundaries that channeled the information flow. Given this new environment, it was unclear which way a national academy would go in the period following the Civil War.

As an information system, the National Academy did not function well after the Civil War. As a group it was not representative of the larger scientific community nor did it provide a unique setting for discussion and experimentation. It had trouble deciding whether it should always meet in Washington or journey, from time to time, to such rustic locations as Northampton, Massachusetts. Asa Gray suggested that it conform to the European practice by adding to its name the phrase "in Washington" so that it would be viewed as the equal of other local societies whether in London, Paris, Philadelphia, or Boston.

As a polity, the Academy gathered significant power neither in the general society, nor in the scientific community as a whole, nor even within its own membership.[10] Its lack of success in the role of advisor to the government has already been noted. Moreover, it turned its back when it was afforded the opportunity to become a tribunal for the ethics of science. The seriocomic story of Josiah D. Whitney's effort to drive Benjamin Silliman, Jr., out of the Academy and ultimately out of academic life is instructive here.[11] The Academy took the charge under consideration but then allowed it to lapse without decision in 1875. However, the incident did draw from James D. Dana a statement of principle: "I am strongly of the opinion . . . that Academies of Science have nothing to do with the moral delinquencies of their members. It is an immense calamity to Science if they are courts for the trial of their members. It would tend to fill the ranks of Science with quarrels and bitterness, making individual hostilities, hostilities of parties."[12]

As a mobilizer of economic resources for its members, the National Academy proved almost totally ineffective. To protect the Academy from charges of political corruption, direct congressional appropriations were ruled out as a source of compensation for research by members. Although in the early years Benjamin A. Gould talked of an appropriation for travel to meetings and for support of the cost of publications, others objected to even this amount of government subvention. When he died in 1867, Bache left his estate to the Academy, but by 1914 the endowment was only enough to offer a few modest prizes. The Smithsonian provided a kind of subsidy by allowing meetings to take place in the Museum, but the Academy still lacked a central office and adequate space to store its records—a circumstance that is painfully evident to the historian examining the thin archives of the Academy for this early period. In summary, a functional view of the Academy shows it to have been strikingly ineffective just at the time when the government, the universities, and the great foundations were all learning not only to support science but to grant the scientific community a measure of autonomy.

Before characterizing the academy as an insignificant institution, however, its role as a repository of the values of the scientific community and as the creator of symbols signifying those values must be considered. This function is not manifest either in the Academy's abortive activities or in the stereotyped speechifying of its officers on those rare occasions when anyone outside the fellowship even heard or read their words. The Academy's sole function was *to exist*. The population inside its boundaries—a population selected from the larger scientific community—was in itself the sole symbol. Becoming a member of the Academy meant that an individual was given a special position in addition to all the essential supports and connections derived from his own career. Once selected, a member had only to exist until he died. His sole function as a member was to belong to a body that perpetuated itself. Thus sovereignty lay in the body of the Academy itself. Once set in motion the body was immortal. Small wonder that it did not adapt to the forces shaping other institutions of learning in late-nineteenth-century America.

The founders themselves recognized that the boundaries of the Academy were the means of symbolization. In the very beginning, Louis Agassiz established an important limit with a grand plan drawn from European precedents: the National Academy of Sciences would be matched by an Academy of Letters and an Academy of Moral and Social Sciences. It was Agassiz's intention to group "all the eminent men in the country" into some society. Clearly "Sciences" in the title of the Academy did not embrace the whole of knowledge as the founders understood it.

The theoretician of the founding group, and the youngest of the organizers, was Benjamin Apthorp Gould. Following a struggle over control of the Dudley

Observatory in Albany that left him without a permanent post, Gould had more time to devote to the founding than Bache, Peirce, Agassiz, or Admiral Charles H. Davis.[13] On April 9, 1863, less than a month after the passage of the organic act and before the first meeting of the Academy in New York, Gould drafted a lengthy letter to Bache on the organization of the National Academy.[14] Although it never became fully operative, this plan makes clear the boundaries under discussion within the founding group.

Gould began by pointing to the conditions imposed on the organization by the American environment:

From its intrinsic nature the National Academy will have one peculiarity distinguishing it from all other learned institutions of a similar character, and one which, while attended with serious disadvantage, may of course be made productive of advantage also . . .—I mean the wide geographical distribution of its comparatively few members—rendering frequent meetings difficult, but probably entailing the necessity of annual or semi-annual sessions protracted over several days. How far this peculiarity may yield good fruit I cannot tell, but as the universe is a series of compensations and balanced forces—I am anxious that the favorable features which must exist be studied out and made available for the scientific progress of the Academy and the nation.

In addition, Gould perceived the necessity of sealing off the Academy from politics:

There is no thinking American who has not felt the serious evil attendant on all our political and executive institutions from the grasping spirit of bad men who leave no avenue unexplored which may afford an orbit for their fingers into the public treasury. School committees are elected by the intrigues of publishers who wish to introduce some particular book,—public edifices are destroyed and rebuilt to suit the joint convenience of those who have the power to grant and the desire to receive contracts. Even our sacred struggle for nationality, for republican institutions, and for human rights is profaned and desecrated by the polluted hands which coin lifeblood and heartstrings into lucre. And it seems to me that one of the most serious dangers to which our young Academy is liable in the future is from these sources.

This stark appraisal of the political climate surrounding the Academy led Gould directly to the crucial role of the selection of members:

And although the fact that elections are to be made by the Academy itself without any external nominations or confirmations is a great safeguard, yet even this will not suffice unless other safeguards are gradually introduced as opportunity may offer. We all know the meaning of the deep significance of the phrase 'external pressure.'—I am therefore most anxious that in the details of organization and fundamentals laws,—obstacles be thrown in the way of any and all persons who may at any future time desire to make use of the Academy for partisan or pecuniary motives.

In order to control the widely scattered Academy, Gould envisaged a small, strong council consisting of the principal officers and "one delegate representing each of the principal sciences. . . . The internal equilibrium of the Academy would thus depend not only on the outer boundaries but on the internal partitions among the disciplines,'' As Gould stated:

a pretty thorough canvass of the names mentioned in the law shows the feasibility of a tolerably equal division into sections thus—by a system of classification which seems to me as applicable to the future as to the present.

| | |
|---|---|
| Mathematics | 7 |
| Physics | 6 |
| Astronomy | 5 |
| Chemistry | 4 |
| Zoology & Comp Anat | 5 |
| Geology & Mineral. | 6 |
| Botany | 3 |
| Geography & Naviga. | 5 |
| Mechanics & Engineer | 4 |
| Industrial Arts | 5 |
| | 50 |

Gould had but to look at the list to see that his classification reflected not only scientific but political considerations: instead of creating equal sections he gave the physical sciences a strong numerical advantage—in terms of both members and sections—over botany, the despised descriptive pursuit of Asa Gray, who was the main opponent of all Lazzaroni schemes in Cambridge and the thorn in Agassiz's side. Gould justified this inequality on the basis of the relative maturity of the various branches of science in the young nation: ''I think that in the present development of sciences in America it would be unwise to insist Procrustes-like on an equality of members either in the different sections or in the same sections at different times, as has been found expedient in older and maturer nations.''

The connection between sections and elections was a close one in Gould's mind. ''The election of members to fill vacancies ought to receive the endorsement of the section to which they would belong if elected, and also of the Academy independently.'' In this balance-and-compensation model both the judgment of the section and the judgment of the general Academy would be consulted. But since the nominations would arise from within the sections, the debate would not transcend the boundaries of the sections in each individual case. Gould envisaged an elaborate sectional organization with separate officers, meetings, and journals. The discipline rather than a region would thus provide the subdivisions within the Academy. These plans, like those for governmental appropriations for the support of research, never bore fruit.

To Gould the criterion for membership was clear:

It ought to be distinctly understood that scientific achievements constitute the evidence of eligibility, and power of scientific investigation forms the qualification,—subject to the sole condition of moral integrity. A man whose character is acknowledged to be unworthy ought not to compete *ex aequo* with an upright and honorable man. With this one limitation, the principles should be adopted that the capacity and likelihood to enlarge the domain of natural and physical science constitute the qualification for membership, and that the best *a priori* evidence of what a man can do is what he has done.

Since, for Gould, the Academy was so intimately tied to a spirit of nationalism, he shifted the standard for the election of "foreign members" or "associates." They would be "elected chiefly as a mark of honor, and this honor must have reference of course solely to the past;—so that old men who have won their title to our gratitude by enlarging the boundaries of science would possess a higher claim than younger men whose strength and vigor entitles us to expect more from them hereafter."

The fifty were thus the heart of the Academy. Gould's depth of feeling on this point emerges clearly when he contemplates the possibility of the election of subordinate members, allowed by the wording of the organic act:

It appears to me that the establishment of such a class would lead to infinite harm. It would create an invidious distinction likely to produce very uncomfortable social effects, and would open the door for the access of that class of men whose connection with the Academy would bring with it the greatest danger... Let us be on our guard against intrusting any portion of the influence or reputation of the Academy to the keeping of persons who are not adjudged worthy to be made full members.

Finally, the difficulty of finding worthy replacements for members suggested to Gould the desirability of a steady state: "Until Science has taken a more vigorous growth than is now manifested among us, we cannot expect proper candidates to arise much more rapidly than the order of nature and the possible resignations will create vacancies."

Gould's formulation of the purpose of the Academy is consistent with the concept of the learned society as an information system. The "ends for which it will have been incorporated and organized . . . are the making and stimulating of scientific researches and the communication of the results to the government or to the world." The Academy should indeed make reports to the government and furthermore should publish them as transactions or memoirs. "But the fundamental principle ought never to be lost sight of, that the primary function of the Academy is to *investigate* rather than *describe,* is scientific, rather than historical." One thing is certain: the Academy has always been true to the principle of not viewing anything, even itself, historically.

Gould was equally prophetic in suggesting that while publication should be the end-product of the Academy's deliberation, secrecy should guard its functions.

. . . I would urge that for the first years at least, until the Academy shall have become in all measures consolidated, shall have begun to show its value by good works and services rendered,—and shall have brought itself to public notice and regard by its intrinsic dignity and power,—its sessions be private and conducted with as little notoriety as possible. In a country like ours where it is already the fashion, even among the well meaning people, who ought to know better—to antithesize between theory and practice, between 'book-learning' and experience, the true functions and value of a National Academy are by no means understood or appreciated.

Since Gould lived until 1896 and was never far from the inner circle of the Academy, his opinions had a marked influence on its workings.

For historians, Gould's exposition on the outer and inner boundaries of the Academy is of particular interest. The scientific community has long resisted precise mathematical modeling, but the boundaries of the Academy are so clear that one can conceive of matching a person to a membership within the Academy in much the same way that Harrison White matches persons to jobs in his study of occupational mobility.[15] Indeed White himself calls for the application to our case:

A new perspective is required by vacancy models. . . . Each man may scheme and gossip about building a career, getting ahead through credentials, 'know-how,' and 'know-who.' A system evolves by its own logic, neither controlled by putative central authorities nor amenable to manipulation by its members. Even the boundaries for a system of interrelated men and jobs evolve, much of the time, out of sight and control, although they are recognized from time to time in reorganizations, mergers, splits, *formation of professional societies,* creation of specialized journals and the like[16] [emphasis added].

*Table 1*
*Total Membership with Elections and Deaths, National Academy of Sciences, 1863–1912*

| Year | Number Elected | Number Died | Academy Figure[a] | Year | Number Elected | Number Died | Academy Figure[a] |
|------|------|------|------|------|------|------|------|
| 1863 | 50 | 1 | 47 | 1888 | 3 | 3 | 100 |
| 1864 | 4 | 3 | 47 | 1889 | 5 | 5 | 100 |
| 1865 | 4 | 1 | 51 | 1890 | 5 | 3 | 101 |
| 1866 | 4 | 1 | 51 | 1891 | 0 | 4 | 97 |
| 1867 | 0 | 2 | 49 | 1892 | 2 | 7 | 93 |
| 1868 | 7 | 0 | 56 | 1893 | 0 | 2 | 91 |
| 1869 | 3 | 1 | 58 | 1894 | 0 | 2 | 89 |
| 1870 | 0 | 1 | 57 | 1895 | 4 | 3 | 89 |
| 1871 | 0 | 2 | 55 | 1896 | 2 | 4 | 87 |
| 1872 | 22 | 2 | 78 | 1897 | 4 | 6 | 85 |
| 1873 | 11 | 6 | 81 | 1898 | 0 | 2 | 83 |
| 1874 | 5 | 1 | 84 | 1899 | 5 | 2 | 86 |
| 1875 | 4 | 1 | 89 | 1900 | 4 | 2 | 88 |
| 1876 | 11 | 0 | 100 | 1901 | 5 | 5 | 88 |
| 1877 | 4 | 4 | 100 | 1902 | 5 | 5 | 87 |
| 1878 | 3 | 2 | 103 | 1903 | 5 | 3 | 87 |
| 1879 | 4 | 0 | 106 | 1904 | 4 | 1 | 89 |
| 1880 | 2 | 5 | 104 | 1905 | 5 | 2 | 91 |
| 1881 | 2 | 1 | 103 | 1906 | 3 | 2 | 95 |
| 1882 | 1 | 7 | 95 | 1907 | 4 | 1 | 97 |
| 1883 | 5 | 5 | 95 | 1908 | 9 | 3 | 99 |
| 1884 | 5 | 3 | 96 | 1909 | 10 | 2 | 106 |
| 1885 | 5 | 1 | 100 | 1910 | 7 | 6 | 112 |
| 1886 | 0 | 1 | 99 | 1911 | 9 | 4 | 113 |
| 1887 | 3 | 2 | 99 | 1912 | 8 | 3 | 117 |

[a] Includes active members and honorary members as of December 31 until 1902; as of April thereafter ("Minutes of the Academy," 1863–1901; "Report of the Home Secretary," in NAS, *Annual Reports,* 1902–).

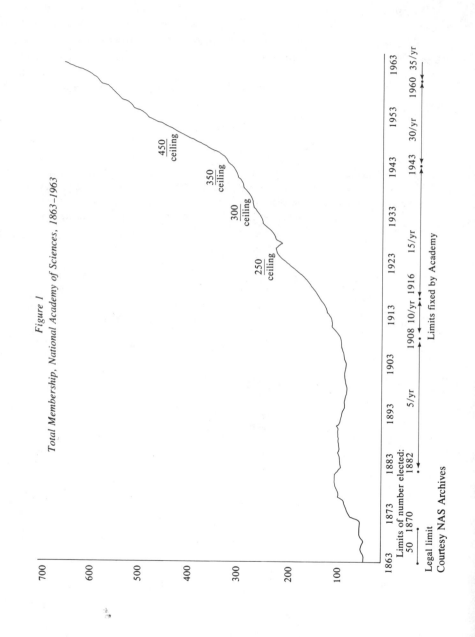

Figure 1

*Total Membership, National Academy of Sciences, 1863–1963*

Courtesy NAS Archives

In the case of the Academy's first fifty members, each membership slot and each person were matched one-to-one. When U. A. Boyden refused membership, when John A. Dahlgren soon resigned, and when J. S. Hubbard, one of the youngest members died, vacancies were created. An election was then possible: a person on the outside was paired with the vacancy, extinguishing it and creating an incumbency which that person occupied until his own death.

The membership of the Academy for the years 1863 to 1912, including deaths and elections, is shown in table 1. The equilibrium represented by the total number in the Academy (column 3) is stable at approximately 50 until 1872, when the 22 appointments—followed by 11 in 1873, 5 in 1874, 4 in 1875, and 11 in 1876—established a new equilibrium at 100, a figure not quite maintained until 1899. A slight expansion again became evident at the end of this period, when the total reached 117 in 1912. Most of the vacancies were created in the death column and extinguished by elections. (Figure 1 shows the total membership of the Academy, 1863–1963.)

The input (election) and output (death) of persons, and the pattern of vacancies within the Academy's population thus determined the boundaries between the Academy and its external environment. The criteria for selection of persons from the outside population were the controlling factors in formulating the definition of science embodied in the population of the Academy.

It was precisely this subject of the criteria of selection that Joseph Henry addressed when he came to save the Academy in 1867. With Bache on his deathbed, the divisions within the Lazzaroni grew more severe and the literal breakup of the Academy was a possibility that members and outsiders at the time contemplated, talked about, and took definite action to accomplish.[17] In these troubled circumstances, Henry put strong emphasis on the importance of maintaining high standards for the selection of new members:

It was implied in the organization of such a body that it should be exclusively composed of men distinguished for original research and that to be chosen one of its members would be considered a high honor, and consequently a stimulus to scientific labor, and that no one would be elected into it who had not earned the distinction by actual discoveries enlarging the field of human knowledge.

The names of the fifty original members were included in the act of organization and were chosen from among those of the principal cultivators of science in this country. For the appointment of these members the Academy itself is not responsible. It is, however, responsible for those who have since been and are still to be elected; and I am happy to say that in filling the large number of vacancies which have been occasioned by death and resignation since the original organization, the principle before mentioned has been strictly observed, and no one has been admitted except after a full discussion of his claims and a satisfactory answer to the question, 'What has he done to advance science in the line of research which he has specially prosecuted?'

The organization of the Academy may be hailed as marking an epoch in the history of philosophical opinions in our country. It is the first recognition by our government of the importance of abstract science as an essential element of mental and material progress.[18]

Whatever the uncompromising nature of Henry's criteria did to the ability of the Academy to offer scientific advice to the government, it greatly enhanced the Academy's image as a repository for a symbolic definition of science.

The internal boundaries among the disciplines within the Academy provided an added dimension to the definition of science beyond those signaled by the outer boundaries. Table 2 shows the breakdown of the Academy's membership by sections and classes. If one assumes—and there is plenty of indication of it—that each class had a tendency to become a vacancy chain, then the members of each class became a nominating committee that claimed precedence over the rest of the Academy in filling a vacancy resulting from the departure of one of their own. Thus the marked imbalance between the class of mathematics and physics and the class of natural history tended to be highly resistant to change. In addition, this imbalance strongly reflected the political structure of Bache's friendships. The only important naturalist among the Lazzaroni group was Agassiz, who courted disaster at the meeting of the Academy in New Haven in 1864 by trying to block the appointment of Spencer F. Baird, director of the National Museum and assistant secretary of the Smithsonian, on criteria that would have sparked a large number of resignations from among the existing members. In 1865 a provision of the constitution allowed a member of one section to be elected an honorary member of another. This provision produced the distribution for 1865 shown in table 3. While the honorary members had no added voting rights, they can only have solidified the class of mathematics and physics further.

Several other reforms put forth by Henry also had an important influence on the definition of science implicit in the Academy. It was Henry who went to

*Table 2*
*Classes and Sections in 1864, National Academy of Sciences*

| Class of Mathematics and Physics | Number of Members | |
|---|---|---|
| Sect. 1. Mathematics | 6 | |
| Sect. 2. Physics | 6 | |
| Sect. 3. Astronomy | 9 | |
| Sect. 4. Mechanics | 6 | |
| Sect. 5. Chemistry | 3 | |
| Total | | 30 |
| *Class of Natural History* | | |
| Sect. 1. Mineralogy & Geology | 6 | |
| Sect. 2. Zoology | 5 | |
| Sect. 3. Botany | 1 | |
| Sect. 4. Anatomy & Physiology | 2 | |
| Sect. 5. Ethnology | 0 | |
| Total | | 14 |
| Grand Total | | 44 |

SOURCE: F. W. True, *A History of the First Half-Century of the National Academy of Sciences, 1863–1913* (Washington, D.C.: National Academy of Sciences, 1913), p. 26.

Table 3
Classes and Sections in 1865, National Academy of Sciences

| Class of Mathematics and Physics | Number of Members | Honorary from within Class | Honorary from Outsiders |
|---|---|---|---|
| Sect. 1. Mathematics | 6 | 2 ( Sect. 3) | 0 |
| Sect. 2. Physics | 6 | 1 ( Sect. 5) | 0 |
| Sect. 3. Astronomy, Geography & Geodesy | 8 | 3 ( Sect. 1) | 0 |
| Sect. 4. Mechanics | 7 | 4 (2 Sect. 1) | 0 |
|  |  | (2 Sect. 2) | 0 |
| Sect. 5. Chemistry | 3 | 0 |  |
| Total | 30 |  |  |

Class of Natural History

| | | | |
|---|---|---|---|
| Sect. 1. Mineralogy & Geology | 5 | 0 | 1 (Sect. 3) |
| Sect. 2. Zoology | 6 | 0 | 0 |
| Sect. 3. Botany | 2 | 1 ( Sect. 1) | 1 (Sect. 5) |
| Sect. 4. Anatomy & Physiology | 1 | 0 | 0 |
| Sect. 5. Ethnology | 1 | 0 | 0 |
| Total | 15 |  |  |

SOURCE: *Annual of the National Academy of Sciences* for 1865 (Cambridge, Mass.: 1866), pp. 23–25.

Congress for legislation to remove the fifty-member ceiling on Academy membership,[19] thereby opening the way for the Academy's expansion in the early 1870s. This move not only discouraged the growth of rival academies by enabling the National Academy to elect some of its most vocal critics, but it also provided a measure of stability by limiting to five the number of new members to be elected at any one session of the Academy.

Less noticed among Henry's reforms was the complete abolition of sections and classes. In the context of sweeping generalizations about the increasing specialization of science in late-nineteenth-century America, such action might appear to be counter to the trend of the times. However, the fact that the abolition lasted for more than a quarter of a century—until 1899—suggests that it embodied a deeper logic. First, Henry realized that unless the influence of mathematics and physics was reduced, the outer boundaries of science itself would contract as the existing, powerful special ties entrenched their control over the vacancy chain. Second, he was aware that as scientists looked to the outside world, they felt the unity of science more deeply than its diversity. Although most of them thought of science as a hierarchy with mathematics at the top and botany at the bottom and although there were occasional disagreements over the appropriate position for individual fields, it was clear that these hierarchical considerations existed only for purposes of internal stratification.[20] Unless every Academy member acknowledged that every other member was a scientist of equal distinction, it would be possible for the outside world to divide the scientific community by playing on its exposed structure of hierarchical prejudice. Hence the abolition of the sections can be interpreted as an important and possibly even necessary survival maneuver.

Although there was no difference in procedure, the elections held after the abolition of sections and classes did show clear evidence of a significant shift in the balance among fields. The thirty-three new members elected in 1872 and 1873 cannot, of course, be directly classified according to the old divisions. However, some of them lived beyond 1899 and were assigned to sections then, while most of the others can be effectively assigned a field. As indicated in table 4, the once favored fields of mathematics, physics, astronomy, and mechanics accounted for only ten of the thirty-three new members elected in 1872 and 1873, while chemistry gained five. Natural history gained dramatically with eleven in geology and zoology alone.

Yet the power of processes already in motion could not be denied. The bastion sections of the Lazzaroni were by no means overwhelmed by the new natural history members further down the line. The ten places were enough to maintain their lead, especially if one remembers that five of the balancing elections went to the relatively weak chemistry section of the mathematics and physics class.

On the natural history list, the predominance of zoology and, to a lesser extent, geology reflected the hierarchical values of Agassiz. The weakness of botany, however, is partly attributable to Asa Gray's deliberate policy of ignoring the Academy. Despite the abolition of sections, members of a discipline lacking the numbers and interest to work for new members did not get them.

At two points the innovators of 1872 and 1873 tested the boundaries of science itself. In naming James B. Eads and John Ericsson, the Academy recognized a new kind of activity that might be called engineering and invention. However, Ericsson declined membership and a group of inventors and engineers capable of electing Thomas A. Edison did not develop before World War I. Likewise, the election of J. J. Woodward, a doctor whose specialty was medicine, foreshadowed the ambivalence of the Academy toward medicine. The fault line along which the National Academy of Engineering and the Institute of Medicine were later to develop had already appeared. To most in the hard core disciplines, engineering and

*Table 4*
*Section Breakdown (if there had been one) for NAS Members*
*Elected 1872–73*

| Section | 1872 | 1873 | Total |
|---|---|---|---|
| Mathematics | 2 | 1 | 3 |
| Physics | 2 | 1 | 3 |
| Astronomy, Geography, & Geodesy | 2 | 2 | 4 |
| Mechanics | 1 | 1 | 2 |
| Chemistry | 5 | 0 | 5 |
| Mineralogy & Geology | 2 | 2 | 4 |
| Zoology | 5 | 2 | 7 |
| Botany | 0 | 1 | 1 |
| Ethnology | 1 | 0 | 1 |
| (Engineering & Invention) | 2 | 0 | 2 |
| (Medicine) | | 1 | 1 |
| Total Members Elected | | | 33 |

medicine could not be accepted as part of the Academy's definition of science, yet the ties were too close for the fault not to recur.

In 1876, eleven new members were elected to the Academy, bringing the total membership to nearly 100; it remained at that level until 1890 when it began a distinct decline. To understand the changes of the 1890s, one must view them in the context of a contemporary movement to reinstate the disciplinary subdivisions within the Academy.

An attempt to revive the sections appeared briefly in 1885, when a four-section proposal was rejected.[21] It reemerged with greater strength in 1890 when the organization of the Academy again became the consuming interest of Benjamin Apthorp Gould—along with Wolcott Gibbs—a survivor of the old Lazzaroni. Gould was still brooding about what had gone wrong in the 1870s:[22]

The National Academy was at first organized in this way, by the accordant action of its original members; and the practical working of the organization appears to have been advantageous and satisfactory in all respects save one. It was then required that all nominations for membership should emanate from that section to which the candidate, if elected, would belong. And since the number of members in several of the sections was small,—the total membership of the Academy being limited to fifty,—difficulties and embarrassments arose on this account, which led to the discontinuance of the system.

Gould advocated a sectional organization for the purpose of separate meetings, discussions and publications. The academies of Europe found sections useful, and "the somewhat limited number of institutions . . . in this country" that had classifications found them helpful:

With the growth of modern science, the tendency of all organizations for its advancement is toward specialization in research; and the same ends which were sought a century ago by the formation in this country of societies for scientific enquiry now demand joint action in special directions of research. . . . This object may be largely attained within the Academy by incorporating in its organization some classification . . . which shall not in any way weaken the bond that unites all the members as representatives of scientific investigation in general.

Heeding the lessons he learned in the early days, he insisted there be no change "affecting in any way the present mode of election."

The ten sections set forth in Gould's 1890 manuscript read as follows:

| | |
|---|---|
| 1. Mathematics. | 6. Geology. |
| 2. Physics. | 7. Botany. |
| 3. Astronomy. | 8. Zoology. |
| 4. Geodesy & Mechanics. | 9. Anthropology. |
| 5. Chemistry & Mineralogy. | 10. Political Economy & Statistics. |

Wolcott Gibbs could not tolerate Gould's proposal to move mineralogy to chemistry and, in the report, mineralogy appears after geology in Gibbs's handwriting. Someone, possibly Ira Remsen, opposed the whole idea and ran rough pen strokes across the entire section.

The boundaries of science defined here are, not surprisingly, almost identical to those of 1864 with the one exception of "Political Economy and Statistics."[23] By favoring the inclusion of the social sciences, the Lazzaroni survivors had suggested the first major external boundary extension in the Academy's history. Their acceptance of statistics was a sign that American scientists saw, in the application of mathematics, common ground with certain aspects of social science. Unlike engineering and medicine, the social sciences were not a fault that would ultimately defy clear definition, but an extension that would find itself, at long last, inside the boundary in 1972 when a section of "social, economic, and political sciences" was formed. As for Gould's report of 1890, it had no effect on Academy policies.

In 1892 Gould made another bid to change the shape of the Academy membership. In his view, the way to clearer definition was to cut the size of the Academy. The increase in the number of scientists in the United States was to him not a signal to expand but to shrink the size of the anointed population so that they could elevate the standards of the whole community. Since restriction is a fundamental process in all elites, Gould was merely making explicit a tendency that less candid theorists in America often seek to conceal. The sole survivor of that meeting at Bache's house in 1863 where the original list of fifty had been drawn up was still true to the principles of the founders. Their conception of the Academy was deeply considered and worked out by Gould to a logical conclusion.

Although sincere in his desire to advance the Academy, Gould sometimes employed dubious methods to achieve his goals. In 1892 he tried to get his way by purchase. In a letter to O. C. Marsh, president of the Academy, dated March 3, 1892, Gould made the following proposition:[24]

A friend of the National Academy, who wishes to contribute to its welfare and influence, yet wishes that his name shall not be known, has the idea of making a large donation, sufficient to afford an income of at least $1,500 a year, for the purpose of defraying a portion of the expenses to which members are subjected in attending the meetings. He has given me his views freely, and wishes me to act as his organ of communication with the Academy, which I gladly do. . . .

Being well acquainted with European academies of science, and hopeful that ours may follow a similar line of usefulness, he shares the feeling that there is danger of the number of our members being too large for the best attainment of the influence which the National Academy ought to exert in scientific affairs, believing that a smaller number, even though above the original 50, would for many reasons be desirable, provided a larger proportion than in recent years could attend the meeting. . . .

[A] controlling element in his motives is that the gift may be a means of gradually reducing the number of members, in such a way as to insure a high standard in future elections, and at the same time increase the participation of members in the Academy's work. . . .

The losses which the Academy has recently suffered have reduced the number of its members to 90. . . . And as the scientific growth of the country seems not likely to offer, for some years to come, an equal number of persons who can be regarded as leaders of their respective sciences, the present time appears favorable for any action by the Academy, in the direction hoped for by the intending donor. . . .

I am persuaded that the adoption of any definite policy which would be likely to reduce the membership to the vicinity of say 70 within a few years, and keep it there, would be followed at once by the gift. . . .

The record does not indicate whether the gift was accepted, but the numbers in table 1 show a decline in membership to a low of 83 in 1898. Gould's policy thus had real effect.

The members of the committee to which Gould's letter was referred were of a far different generation than the founders. The chairman, T. C. Mendenhall, aged fifty-one, had been elected in 1887 as had Henry P. Bowditch, aged fifty-two. W. H. Brewer, aged sixty-four, was a botanist and thus had only been elected in 1880. Charles A. Young, some six years younger than Brewer, had come into the Academy in the rush of 1872. On receiving Gould's letter in 1892, the committee polled the Academy concerning the optimal size of membership but received only seventeen answers. On this basis they concluded:[25] "There is a decided opposition to increase the regular membership of the Academy, and to the addition of a separate class of members from which selections for full membership may be made. There is divided opinion upon the desirability of decrease in membership, with a preponderance of belief that on the whole the present limit, which is practically one hundred, is about right." The committee went on, however, to identify a ground-swell of sentiment in favor of a revival of sections. "The plan of dividing the membership into classes according to the various branches of science represented, essentially that of the French Academy, is apparently looked upon with favor by many members as offering a means of securing a more judicious selection and a fairer distribution of the honors among the different classes of scientific workers." That sentence marked an epoch in the history of the Academy. Classification was not for the purpose of "socialization," as Gould would have had it, but for elections. If this principle were adopted, the Academy would ultimately become more responsive to growing specialization and the increasing size of the scientific community.

The Mendenhall Committee proposed seven section divisions, fewer than either the 1864 or the 1890 lists had included:

1. Mathematics, including Astronomy and Geodesy.
2. Physics.
3. Engineering, including Civil, Mechanical, Electrical, Hydraulic, etc.
4. Chemistry, including Applied Chemistry.
5. Geology, including Mineralogy, Paleontology, etc.
6. Biology.
7. Anthropology, including Sociology, Economic Science, etc.

The bow to the social sciences may have been a courtesy to Francis A. Walker, an honored member, while the inclusion of engineering reflected recent developments in the world outside the Academy. With these exceptions, the Mendenhall Committee maintained the external boundaries of science as they had been traditionally embodied in the Academy. In terms of election procedure, the report assigned considerable power to the sections: "A physicist must receive the approval of at least one-third of the physicists of the Academy. He cannot be elected without it, but may not be elected with it."

Before the principles of the Mendenhall report could take effect, the Academy had to find a successor for its third president, O. C. Marsh. In 1895 it turned to the venerable survivor of the founders, the seventy-three-year-old Wolcott Gibbs, whose appointment to Harvard in 1863 had been a high point in Lazzaroni influence. The addresses of the outgoing and incoming presidents were so unsettling that the Academy had them printed but marked confidential and distributed only to members.

In his presidential address,[26] Gibbs promptly raised a question that had been virtually unmentioned since before the establishment of the Academy: "Is it wise to attempt to increase the number of branches of knowledge which the Academy should embrace within its sphere of activity?" He knew, of course, where the Academy had always stood. "At present we include only the physical and so-called natural sciences, and by no means all of these, so far at least as a full representation is concerned."

Among the excluded studies "which deserve our respect and must assuredly be considered as branches of science" he listed "History, Philology, Anthropology in its widest sense, including Ethnology, Geography, Agriculture, and Political Science." Although it sounds as if Gibbs favored expansion of boundaries, a close examination of his words reveals otherwise. He only asked for "consideration which is justly their due. There may of course be reasons why, independently of the character of a particular subject as such, it would be wisest not to give it a place in the organization of the Academy." Indeed there was precedent for the inclusion of philology and ethnology in the person of William D. Whitney. The combination of history, geography, and agriculture is reminiscent of the interests of James Hammond Trumbull, elected in 1872 and still alive when Gibbs spoke, while political science could easily be linked to Francis A. Walker. However, once he had stated the question—and without so much as tipping his hand—Gibbs moved abruptly on to pure mathematics, a subject that "can hardly be said to be represented at all in the Academy as now constituted." Hence Gibbs seems to have raised the issue of expansion of boundaries with fanfare only to present a devious defense of the status quo.

Gibbs also outlined ten sections very much on the model of the 1864 plan, and his proposals for the election of members amounted to no more than simplifying the procedures for the general canvass, pointedly ignoring any tie between the election process and the sections. The Academy of the founders had had its last salute.

A committee to consider the addresses of the presidents reported on April 22, 1896.[27] Gould, just seven months from death, was a member of the committee together with Alexander Agassiz, John Shaw Billings, and Francis A. Walker. They gave short shrift to any idea of "an increase of the branches of knowledge embraced." They could not "but feel that the welfare and influence of the Academy might be imperiled by any change of this sort at present, or until the relations of the Academy to the government had been more distinctly emphasized by usage and experience." The threat that the inclusion of the social sciences posed to the political viability of the Academy was already recognized.

The committee wanted sections but shied away from a list and counseled "vagueness" for the titles. Much of the rhetoric sounds like Gould's, but one paragraph looked back to the Mendenhall report and forward to the practice of the future:

The reestablishment of [sections] will greatly facilitate the most desirable selection of new members. For, if the fitness of candidates could be passed upon, as a preliminary, by the members of those sections which represent the fields of research to which the investigations of the candidates have been chiefly devoted, a great gain would probably result in guiding the suffrage of members not versed in those special studies.

From this point on, the revision of the constitution moved steadily forward. A division into committees on nominations of new members under the proposed amendment appeared in the *Report* for the year 1898.[28] From 1899 onward the list of members was regularly broken down into committees on nominations. These sections were strikingly unadventurous, appearing until 1911 as follows:

1. Mathematics and Astronomy.
2. Physics and Engineering.
3. Chemistry.
4. Geology and Paleontology.
5. Biology.
6. Anthropology.

As the years of the first decade of the twentieth century passed, some strains developed both on the external boundaries and on the internal partitions. Medicine, although not recognized as a separate committee and denied position as a separate profession, came to be represented by the new generation of medical scientists headed by William H. Welch. Lacking any specific home, they tended to pile up in anthropology. At the same time, with the election of Franz Boas in 1900 and James McKeen Cattell in 1901, a proper start had been made for both anthropology and psychology. In 1908 John Shaw Billings asked the council to restructure the anthropology committee.[29]

In 1911 the constitution was amended, rearranging committees five (biology) and six (anthropology) into four groups:

5. Botany.
6. Zoology and Animal Morphology.

7. Physiology and Pathology.
8. Anthropology and Psychology.

Most of the medical scientists moved into committee seven, clearing the way for a full development of anthropology and psychology. But gone was any hint of a social science beyond that boundary.

The total number of Academy members reached only 117 in 1912, but with the limit on the number elected annually raised to ten in 1908, the curve of member-ship moved steadily upward. For the first time, the Academy's demographic patterns shifted into phase with those of the scientific community generally. Since university departments and government laboratories could maintain vacan-cies indefinitely and also retire scientists before their deaths, the Academy still had a built-in lag in comparison with the larger scientific community. But unlike the ideal of B. A. Gould, which called for restricting Academy membership as the number of American scientists grew, this Academy slowly moved to conform to the dynamism of American life.

The new Academy was the one that the astronomer George Ellery Hale under-took to reform in 1913. Following his election in 1902, Hale grew increasingly concerned with the need to transform the Academy into a vital scientific organi-zation. His ideas for reform were set forth in an address presented at a meeting of the Academy in Baltimore in November 1913.[30] One of Hale's primary concerns was the pressure of specialization:

Specialization is inevitable in the maze of modern progress, and the narrowing effect of constant devotion to a single subject must become still more apparent as science ramifies further. A general academy, by insisting on the importance of large relationships, by demonstrating the unity of knowledge, by recognizing the fact that fundamental methods of research, whenever developed, are likely to be applicable in more than one department, can do much to broaden and to stimulate its members.

Whatever its shortcomings, the National Academy that Hale was criticizing had at least some virtues when viewed as a foe of specialization:

We are thus led to the conclusion that the functions of a National Academy should be of the broadest character, and that the advantage of sharing in the results of all its depart-ments should belong to every member. Thus the policy of our National Academy of avoiding division into separate sections, (except for voting purposes) and of bringing papers on the most diverse subjects before the entire body, is fundamentally sound and should be maintained.

Hale's efforts in 1913 were focused on raising the publications of the Academy to the level of highest distinction—an old idea of Gould's—and on launching an evangelical campaign to attract the attention of the general public—an idea that bore the stamp of Hale. The conversion of American business to the gospel of industrial research was another of Hale's goals. If one follows this last reform seriously to its conclusion, however, one can see that Hale would either have to change the Academy he had already pronounced fundamentally sound, or he would have to add to it an operating arm not hampered by the stability built into the Academy structure through the historical process. Hale opted for the latter course when he took the lead in the movement to establish the National Research Council.

With the outbreak of World War I, the question of the Academy's role as advisor to the government reemerged. Although the size of the Academy increased during the war period at about the same rate as in 1912 and 1913, its members were generally considered too old and too narrowly restricted by field to contribute effectively to the war effort. In addition they were prevented from receiving direct compensation by the terms of the organic act. Motivated by a concern for preparedness, an intense enthusiasm for the Allied cause, and a genuine desire to serve the government, Hale and his group turned to an entirely new mechanism to meet the emergency. In 1916 the Academy voted to recommend to President Woodrow Wilson the creation of the National Research Council. This organization would be an arm of the Academy deriving its authority from the organic act of 1863 but would not be composed entirely of members and thus would be free to employ younger scientists as well as those whose specialties were relevant to the specific tasks set by war, including engineers who had not been effectively represented in the Academy.

The National Research Council of 1916–1918, headed by the physicist Robert A. Millikan, was much more effective than the National Academy of 1863–1865 in organizing scientists into research teams around such problems as the detection of submarines and the development of offensive and defensive chemical warfare. Yet it fell far short of its World War II counterpart, the Office of Scientific Research and Development, in "organizing scientific research for war." Most of its scientists, including Millikan himself, had to be put into uniform in order to be paid. The result was a loss of autonomy and an inability to control the programs of the research teams. Indeed, the period of full activity for the wartime National Research Council, with its professor-administrators and its funding in large part from private foundations, was actually less than two years.

In May of 1918, with the end of the war still several months away, an executive order by President Wilson created a permanent National Research Council that derived its congressional sanction from the Act of 1863. The peacetime National Research Council was empowered to stimulate research, to survey the larger possibilities of science, to promote cooperation in research at home and abroad, to involve outside investigators in the solution of problems of the War and Navy departments and other branches of the government, and "to gather and collate scientific and technical information at home and abroad."[31] By this time George Ellery Hale was more concerned with perpetuating the wartime alliance into the postwar future by means of the International Research Council, which ultimately became the International Council of Scientific Unions. Soon after the armistice, the National Research Council dropped its direct ties with weapons development in the government and concentrated on becoming a clearing house for the exchange of scientific information among national professional societies and by means of international congresses.

The postwar National Academy differed from the prewar National Academy in two important respects. First, it had developed a bureaucracy in the form of the staff of the National Research Council. Second, its symbolic function became much more visible with the completion of a building in Washington. Since Hale was instrumental in raising the money, the building can be regarded as his last great gift to the Academy. Whether or not an Egyptian temple is a fitting symbol for American science, the structure on Constitution Avenue gave the bureaucracy some offices and the Academy a mailing address.

Looking back at the functions of the Academy as a social unit, it is possible to identify some accomplishments in the period from 1863 to 1918. As a community, the Academy was much more aware of itself in 1918 than it had been in the last decades of the nineteenth century. As a polity, it demonstrated during World War I that it had considerable potential for mobilizing power even though it always fell far short of invoking the kind of sanction that a government agency could employ. As a mobilizer of resources, however, the Academy had shown only limited potential. Indeed the sectors of support for science within American society—the government, the universities, industry, the foundations—had used the Academy as a conduit of resources to only a minor extent. Finally, as an exemplar of value systems, the Academy by its structure and membership had become a respected voice if not the final arbiter in determining the boundaries and directions of the sciences.

If, in the prewar period, the members conferred as much prestige on the Academy as the Academy did on them, the postwar Academy was better positioned to serve the hopes of the founders. Nonetheless, its major function remained the definition of science by its very existence.

## Notes

1. The standard official history has long been Frederick W. True, *A History of the First Half-Century of the National Academy of Sciences 1863–1913* (Washington, D.C.: National Academy of Sciences, 1913). A reinterpretation of the story of the founding was put forward in 1956 by A. Hunter Dupree, "The Founding of the National Academy of Sciences—A Reinterpretation," *Proceedings of the American Philosophical Society* 101 (1957): 434–40. The same story appears in A. Hunter Dupree, *Science in the Federal Government: A History of Policies and Activities to 1940* (Cambridge: Belknap Press of Harvard University Press, 1957), pp. 135–48; and idem, *Asa Gray, 1810–1888* (Cambridge: Harvard University Press, 1959), pp. 313–24. With some changes and elaborations the basic thrust of the reinterpretation has been accepted by a number of scholars, among them, Edward Lurie, *Louis Agassiz: A Life in Science* (Chicago: University of Chicago Press, 1960), pp. 331–44; Nathan Reingold, ed., *Science in Nineteenth Century America: A Documentary History* (New York: Quadrangle, 1964), pp. 200–225. The most recent acceptance of the basic thesis is Philip Boffey, *The Brain Bank of America: An Inquiry into the Politics of Science* (New York: McGraw-Hill, 1975), p. 5. I wish to thank Jean St. Clair and Paul McClure of the National Academy of Sciences Archives for making materials in the archives available to me. Janice F. Goldblum, records analyst at NAS, read an early draft of this paper and made helpful suggestions.

2. Quoted in True, *First Half Century*, p. 352.

3. Edward Lurie played a leading part in uncovering the role of the Lazzaroni. In addition to the above citations, additional material on the Lazzaroni appears in Mark Beach, "Was There a Scientific Lazzaroni?" in *Nineteenth Century American Science: A Reappraisal*, ed. George H. Daniels

(Evanston, Ill.: Northwestern University Press, 1972), pp. 115–32. Edward Lurie, "The History of Science in America: Development and New Direction," in ibid., pp. 3–21, contains an answer to Beach. The two views are not mutually exclusive.

4. Dupree, "Founding of the National Academy," p. 438.

5. Nathan Reingold, "Science in the Civil War: The Permanent Commission of the Navy Department," *Isis* 49 (1958): pp. 307–18.

6. Dupree, *Science in the Federal Government,* pp. 204–31.

7. S. B. Sutton, *Charles Sprague Sargent and the Arnold Arboretum* (Cambridge: Harvard University Press, 1970), pp. 159–70.

8. Dupree, "Founding of the National Academy of Sciences," p. 438.

9. A. Hunter Dupree, "The National Pattern of American Learned Societies, 1769–1863," in *The Pursuit of Knowledge in the Early American Republic,* eds. Alexandra Oleson and Sanborn C. Brown (Baltimore: The Johns Hopkins University Press, 1976), pp. 21–32.

10. For a statistical profile of the Academy that extends beyond the limits of this paper, see Raymond Pearl, "Vital Statistics of the National Academy of Sciences," *Proceedings of the National Academy of Sciences* (hereafter cited as *Proceedings of the NAS*) 11 (1925): 752–68; ibid., 12 (1926): 258–61.

11. Gerald T. White, *Scientists in Conflict: The Beginnings of the Oil Industry in California* (San Marino, California: Huntington Library, 1968), pp. 177–206.

12. Quoted in ibid., p. 201.

13. Even Mark Beach, who doubts the influence of the Lazzaroni beyond the individual importance of its members, concedes that Gould had some sense for keeping the group together. See Beach, "Was There a Scientific Lazzaroni?" in *Nineteenth Century American Science,* p. 132.

14. Draft of Letter to Professor Bache on the organization of the NAS, (9 April 1863), Archives of the National Academy of Sciences, Washington, D.C.

15. Harrison C. White, *Chains of Opportunity: Systems Models of Mobility in Organizations* (Cambridge: Harvard University Press, 1970).

16. Ibid., p. 317.

17. James Dana resigned the vice-presidency of the Academy; Agassiz and Peirce had withdrawn from active participation to contemplate other troubles. Jeffries Wyman and Asa Gray both resigned from the Academy in 1867. Gray, then president of the American Academy of Arts and Sciences, believed that the established societies were sufficient. John W. Draper, one of those passed over for membership, was busy organizing a rival in New York. If Joseph Henry had not committed his reputation and position to the task of reviving the Academy, its replacement by regional academies would have been a distinct possibility. Its "survival" might then have been as a local society in the place soon occupied by the Washington Academy of Sciences.

18. U.S. Congress, Senate, National Academy of Sciences, Report for 1867, 40th Cong., 2d Sess., 1968, Senate Misc. Doc. No. 106, pp. 1, 2, as quoted in True, *First Half-Century,* pp. 13–14.

19. True, *First Half-Century,* pp. 37–38.

20. This hierarchy, which had already cropped up in B. A. Gould's plan, had by 1872 become painfully and obviously institutionalized in the sections. Agassiz argued that physiology ranked above descriptive natural history, and Joseph Henry agreed with him in principle although not in practice.

21. *Proceedings of the NAS* 1, pt. 3 (April 1885): 264.

22. MS Report, dated April 1890, in B. A. Gould's handwriting and signed by him and Wolcott Gibbs, with Ira Remsen's name marked out. Gould folder, NAS Archives, Washington, D.C.

23. The anthropology section can be considered a descendant of the old ethnology section.

24. National Academy of Sciences, *Report for the Year 1892* (Washington, D.C., 1893), pp. 12–13.

25. "Special Stated Session, November 2, 1892," *Proceedings of the NAS* 1 (1895): 373–75.

26. "Address of President Wolcott Gibbs," 30 October 1895 (privately printed) pp. 7–8, NAS Archives, Washington, D.C.

27. Minutes of the Council of the National Academy of Sciences, Washington, April 22, 1896, NAS Archives.

28. NAS, *Report for the Year 1898* (Washington, 1899), pp. 25–26.

29. Minutes of the Council, 23 April 1908, NAS Archives, Washington, D.C.

30. George Ellery Hale, "The Future of the National Academy of Sciences," reprinted in *The Legacy of George Ellery Hale,* eds. Helen Wright, Joan N. Warnow, and Charles Weiner (Cambridge, Mass.: MIT Press, 1972), pp. 177–91. Quotations from pp. 179–80.

31. NAS, *Annual Report for 1918* (Washington, D.C., 1919), pp. 40–41.

# Storehouses and Workshops: American Libraries and the Uses of Knowledge

*JOHN Y. COLE*

In 1880 Samuel L. Clemens sent his nephew to the Library of Congress to spend a day "burrowing" in that "grand literary storehouse."[1] Thirty years later, New Jersey Governor Woodrow Wilson was but one of several prominent figures who urged the Library of Congress to establish the specialized reference service known as a legislative reference bureau, a new function that would make the Library a true "legislator's workshop."[2] The altered perception of the Library of Congress, from Mark Twain's "storehouse" in 1880 to Woodrow Wilson's "workshop" in 1912, was a transfiguration experienced by most American libraries. This redefinition of American libraries and American librarianship between the Civil War and World War I was part of a general restructuring of American institutions and intellectual life, and a change directly related to similar developments in education, scholarship, government, and science—as well as in the American publishing industry. The common denominator was the rapid expansion and the increasing specialization of knowledge. The purpose of this essay is to examine how the growth of a new American faith in the power of knowledge and its specialized uses transformed American librarianship.

## The Age of Accumulation

On the eve of the Civil War there were few libraries in the United States that might be considered research institutions. The first libraries, the subscription or social libraries, were declining in number. The direct descendant of the subscription library, the public library, was still in its infancy. College libraries and scientific societies generally had meager library collections. The activities of most historical societies were of an antiquarian nature and rarely could their libraries be used for scholarly research. The largest government library was the Library of Congress, but its collection was weak and unbalanced. In 1862 Ralph Waldo Emerson visited the Library, then in the Capitol, and was told by one of the assistants that the medical and theological collections were huge but that the collection of modern literature was "very weak," a situation the assistant attributed to the domination of the Library by southern congressmen.[3] In truth, disproportionately large theological and medical collections were also common in many college libraries.

If the book collections of most American institutions were small and inadequate, the private libraries of many individuals were not. The enormous personal libraries of men such as George Bancroft, George Ticknor, and Francis Parkman were also the libraries that provided these historians with the research materials for their books. In 1850 the librarian of the Smithsonian Institution, Charles Coffin Jewett, pointed out that George Ticknor could not have written his monumental *History of Spanish Literature* (1849) without using his personal 13,000-volume collection; in Jewett's words, the work "could be written, in this country, only by one who was able to procure for himself the necessary literary apparatus." Similar stories comparing the inadequacies of American library resources to the rich collections of Europe were common in mid-nineteenth-century America. Perhaps the best known was the assertion that Gibbon could not have written *The Decline and Fall of the Roman Empire* utilizing research materials available only in the United States.[4]

Realization of such inadequacies stimulated a new nationalism among American intellectuals who eagerly promoted the development of an American culture that would be independent of European traditions and institutions. A primary goal was the accumulation and preservation of large collections of books and research materials in the United States for American use. Such patriotic appeals helped stimulate the American library movement; in fact, two of the founders of the Boston Public Library, Edward Everett and George Ticknor, were among the most prominent of these scholar-nationalists.

The establishment of the Boston Public Library between 1850 and 1854 is generally considered as the beginning of the public library movement since that institution was the first large tax-supported municipal library in the United States. The motivating factors that led to the establishment of public libraries throughout the United States in the latter half of the nineteenth century were complex and varied considerably among different cities and townships; they included a commitment to popular education and the expansion of educational opportunities, an elitism that often emphasized the search for an acceptable means of social control, a growing belief in the power of reading and books— especially "good books"—and a healthy dose of local pride. Finally, and of particular interest in examining the development of the "storehouse" concept of libraries, there was the need to accumulate and preserve materials to be used for historical research, especially the study of the American past.[5] The origins of the Boston Public Library provide a good illustration of the mixture of motives behind the library movement.

By 1850 Edward Everett had completed several careers: congressman, governor of Massachusetts, ambassador to Great Britain, and president of Harvard College; all contributed to his concern for the collection and preservation of historical materials. When serving in Congress from 1825 to 1835, Everett was chairman of the Joint Library Committee and tried, unsuccessfully, to persuade both his colleagues and the Librarian of Congress to build comprehensive research collections. In 1850, as public interest in the establishment of a free public library in Boston increased, Everett offered his personal collection of public documents and papers to the city as a nucleus for the library. He asserted in a letter to Boston mayor John Bigelow that his collection of over one thousand volumes, carefully acquired over the past thirty years, would be an appropriate foundation for a public library. George Ticknor supported his friend Everett's plan and shared his belief that such an institution would put the "finishing hand" on Boston's already admirable system of public education. Ticknor, however, also argued in favor of the widespread circulation of new and popular works by the library, claiming that what the city really needed was "an apparatus that shall carry this taste for reading as deep as possible into society." Everett, who had originally conceived of the library as "a quiet retreat for persons of both sexes who desire earnestly to improve their minds," admitted that he had not thought much about the circulating library notion; nevertheless, he accepted it, rationalizing that it would "apply only to a particular class of books, and does not contemplate the unrestrained circulation of those [books] of which the loss could not be easily replaced." When it opened in 1854, the Boston Public Library incorporated both the preservation and research purpose of Everett and the popular library function advocated by Ticknor. The accumulation and preservation of its collections dominated the first half-century of the institution's history, however. In 1868 the new superintendent of the library, Justin Winsor, found that the 144,000-volume collection was second only to the Library of Congress in size and in offering to the student "the largest collection of valuable books on the American continent."[6]

New York City's Astor Library, an endowed library established by John Jacob Astor in 1848, was opened to the public in 1854. Founded primarily for research purposes, the collection rapidly expanded under librarian Joseph Cogswell, who had advised and persuaded Astor to create the library in the first place. Cogswell, who had studied in Germany with Ticknor and Everett earlier in the century, shared the cultural nationalism of his Boston friends.

The Astor Library and the Boston Public Library were hardly typical, but the desire to accumulate and preserve sizeable collections of knowledge in central locations was an important stimulus to the creation and growth of public libraries in many states. By 1876 a total of 188 tax-supported public libraries existed throughout New England and the Midwest; 127 of them were in Massachusetts, 14 in Illinois, 13 in New Hampshire, and 9 in Ohio. Free municipal libraries had been established in Cincinnati (1856), Detroit and St. Louis (1865), Cleveland (1869), Louisville (1871), Indianapolis (1872), and Chicago (1873).[7]

The post–Civil War growth of libraries was closely related to the remarkable expansion of the publishing industry during the same period. The common denominator was the gradual development of a mass audience for books as well as for magazines and journals. The general educational level of Americans was increasing, stimulated by compulsory school attendance laws in most states, and the new popularity of reading created a demand for books that both publishers and librarians had a difficult time satisfying.

American publishers had experienced prosperous periods before but most of them had been short-lived. The first "paperback revolution" occurred in the 1830s and early 1840s, but it was insignificant compared to the next one, which began in the 1870s and lasted for the next two decades. Dime novels, juvenilia, and inexpensive pirated novels from England dominated the paperbound book market which was stimulated even further by a decrease in the price (as well as the quality) of paper and the introduction, in 1879, of pocket-sized books. According to *Publisher's Weekly,* the number of new titles published in the United States increased sixfold between 1880 and 1910, from approximately 2,000 books a year to over 13,000. Furthermore, between 1865 and 1885, the number of periodicals published in the United States increased fivefold.[8]

The periodical press, in fact, dominated the book publishing industry during these years; in order to survive, most of the major publishers also produced magazines. Firms diversified by publishing various types of books—economics, law, science, reference books, even textbooks—in addition to their fiction lines. The reason was that, until the international copyright law of 1891, foreign fiction in cheap paperbound editions dominated the American fiction market. The important hardbound sales lines of American publishers before 1891 were nonfiction—sociology, economics, law, and an increasing number of self-help and home improvement books. For example, "house pattern" books, explaining how to build a house, etiquette books, and beginning in the 1870s, books about accounting, statistics, and business methods were popular. The rise of the novel and the short story in American publishing, as well as in American literature, occurred between 1890 and 1910. In 1880, only about 300 novels were published by American firms; by 1890 the figure was 1,100 and the next year it jumped to an all-time high of 2,234, according to *Publisher's Weekly.*[9]

These trends in the publishing industry clearly indicate that while American higher education, scholarship, and librarianship were becoming more specialized, the American publishing industry was diversifying. Although some smaller publishers did specialize, most of the larger houses, centered in New York, Boston, and Philadelphia, expanded and became general publishers. This broadening of publishing activity by the established publishing houses, e.g., Harper's, Putnam's, and Scribner's, facilitated the development of the university presses, which specialized in scholarly works that appealed to a limited readership. The origins of the university press movement in the United States can be traced to Harvard in the 1870s, even though Harvard University Press itself was not founded until 1913. Other early university presses evolved as the new graduate schools were established: the Johns Hopkins Press was founded in 1878 and published its first book in 1887; the University of Chicago Press was established in 1892, the Columbia University Press in 1893, Princeton in 1905, and Yale in 1908.[10]

In its annual book trade statistics, the editors of *Publisher's Weekly* often commented on changing trends in book production. In 1885, they noted that "libraries, hitherto satisfied in finding material in the field of fictitious literature, invaded the more serious lines of reading and embraced in their issues representative works of history, travel, biography, literary history, and poetry."[11] The question of how libraries dealt with "the field of fictitious literature" is an interesting example of how librarians struggled with pressures for increased use of their collections in an age of accumulation and preservation. Most librarians viewed themselves primarily as cultural custodians and concentrated their efforts on the careful selection of books that would properly educate the users of the library; the accessibility and use of a collection was of less importance than its steady and careful accumulation. The debate over fiction in public libraries slowly altered that emphasis, but the transformation was a difficult one, since the basic controversy focused on the purpose of the public library: was its prime objective educational or recreational?

The first professional library organization in America was established in Philadelphia in 1876, and that meeting provoked two decades of lively discussion about the role of fiction in public libraries. There was no particular problem regarding the acceptability of books by such "classic" authors as Dickens, Scott, Cooper, and Thackeray. Most librarians also agreed that "sensational" literature and dime novels should be excluded, even though there were many disputes about what books should be considered sensational. The fundamental controversy centered on the works of such "popular" authors as Emma D. E. N. Southworth, Louisa May Alcott, Thomas Hardy, Lew Wallace, Horatio Alger, Mark Twain, and Stephen Crane. Many library boards and librarians felt that works by popular authors simply had no place in an institution with an educational function. This point of view was explicitly stated in the 1875 Boston Public Library annual report: "Notwithstanding many popular notions to the contrary, it is no part of the duty of a municipality to raise taxes for the amusement of the people . . . the sole relation of a town library in the general interest is as a supplement to the school system; as an instrumentality of higher instruction to all classes of people."[12]

There were three basic arguments favoring the inclusion of more fiction in public libraries. The first was that it would attract patrons who were needed to ensure the survival of the public library. At the 1876 convention of librarians, Samuel S. Green of the Worcester Public Library bluntly articulated this theme: "The people do not demand vicious literature, but they do demand exciting stories; and neither citizens nor city government will support a library generously that does not contain the books they and their families want." The second theory, advocated by William Frederick Poole of the Chicago Public Library, was that popular novels at least provided a starting point for the gradual elevation of public taste. Poole was only one of several scholarly librarians who favored the generous inclusion of fiction in libraries, even though the Chicago librarian proclaimed: "We must interest the reader before we can educate him; and, to this end, [we] must commence at his own standard of intelligence." Librarian William I. Fletcher had a more picturesque way of describing this approach. He felt that librarians should lure readers by following the old recipe for cooking a hare, which began "first catch your hare." The final justification advanced for including fiction in public libraries was, quite simply, that it satisfied a recreational need in life for most adults by providing wholesome relaxation.[13]

It is interesting to note how the organization of the book collections in most public libraries contributed to the controversy. Fiction was kept together as a separate class and was easily identifiable—often with the so-called recreational objective of the public library. Nonfiction, however, fell into its appropriate subject classification; thus, many librarians felt that it had a serious educational objective and was perfectly suited for collection and dissemination by a public library. By the turn of the century, most public libraries had achieved a balance or accommodation that permitted the acquisition of the popular fiction that was in the greatest demand—provided, of course, that it was within the bounds of taste as defined by the library board and often by the librarian. In the first decade of the twentieth century, as the recreational objective of the public libraries gained acceptance, so did popular fiction. The question was then no longer whether popular fiction should be included, but how much.[14]

The greatest stimulus to public library development at the turn of the century was a single individual—Andrew Carnegie. In one sense, Carnegie's expenditures for public library buildings were but an expansion of the philanthropic tradition that had already brought so much to American librarianship in the form of the gifts of John Jacob Astor, James Lenox, and Samuel Tilden to the city of New York, of Walter L. Newberry to Chicago, and of George Peabody and Enoch Pratt to Baltimore. Carnegie's philanthropy, however, was on a grander scale and of greater significance. After three decades of rapid collection growth, many public libraries were out of space; Carnegie's new buildings were essential for the continued momentum of the library movement. Between 1890 and 1917, Carnegie contributed over forty-one million dollars for the construction of over 1,600 library buildings throughout America—but primarily in the West and Midwest. He never considered his buildings outright gifts and indeed in one sense they were not, for communities were required to provide books and maintenance costs for the buildings. This procedure was a fundamental part of Carnegie's philosophy concerning libraries and American society; he viewed libraries as democratic institutions that would promote progress primarily through community and individual self-improvement.[15]

The Carnegie buildings enabled libraries to expand their collections even further and gradually to introduce more specialized services. New types of reference assistance were added, services that usually were justified as an extension of the educational role of the public library. In many states special services to immigrants contributed significantly to the "Americanization" of new citizens. Programs for children were also inaugurated. Public libraries in many cities began to establish "book deposit stations" that soon became full-fledged branches. Finally, state libraries gradually extended services into rural areas, even though the rural library movement did not truly flourish until after World War I.

There is common agreement that the college library did not even begin its full development—in terms of both collection building and services—until the 1870s. All too often it fit a characterization offered by President James Canfield of Columbia University in 1902:

Fifty years ago, the college library was almost an aside in education. Indeed, it was like the sentence which we enclose in brackets; to be read in a low tone, or to be slurred over hastily, or even to be entirely omitted without making any serious change in the sense. With rare exceptions, the position of the librarian was a haven for the incompetent or the decrepit. The appropriations for maintenance were pitifully meager. The expenditures for expansion were even less worthy. The efficiency, or inefficiency, was, naturally, quite proportionate.[16]

In this age of accumulation, the collection-building fervor shown by many public libraries, but especially the Boston Public Library and the Astor Library, put their academic counterparts to shame. In fact, the principal college and university libraries did not even begin the rapid rate of collection growth already underway in several other depositories until the turn of the century, as illustrated in table 1.

John Langdon Sibley, librarian of Harvard College from 1856 to 1877, is the subject of a well-known anecdote often used to demonstrate the passive and possessive nature of college libraries and their librarians. As related in a 1912 issue of the *Bulletin of the American Library Association:* "Having once completed an inventory of the library and, when seen crossing the yard with a particularly happy smile, Mr. Sibley was asked the reason for this pleased expression. 'All the books are in excepting two,' said he. 'Agassiz has those and I am going after them.'" This story is probably true, for there is an entry in Sibley's official journal dated July 16, 1858 that states: "The Library Committee met at Gore Hall and examined various part [sic] of the Library. All the books were returned except one charged to Prof Agassiz & another to Prof Gray."[17] The journal entry demonstrates that an annual inventory of the volumes in the collection was a practice expected by the faculty library committee to whom the librarian was responsible. In this sense, the Sibley anecdote illustrates not the librarian's personal attitude, but the attitude of an age.

### The American Library Association and the Organization of Knowledge

Symbolically, at least, the age when librarians were concerned almost exclusively with the acquisition and preservation of knowledge came to an end in 1876. The establishment of the American Library Association (ALA) in October 1876 signified a new approach to books and knowledge on the part of American librarians, an approach that emphasized the efficient *use* of the collections in

Table 1
Collection Growth in Selected American Libraries, 1858-1913[18]

| | Number of Volumes | | | |
| Library | 1858 | 1876 | 1891 | 1913 |
| --- | --- | --- | --- | --- |
| Harvard (1638) | 74,000 | 154,000 | 292,000 | 1,083,000 |
| Yale (1701) | 36,000 | 78,000 | 185,000 | 1,000,000 |
| Philadelphia Library Company (1731) | 65,000 | 104,000 | 165,400 | 240,200 |
| Princeton (1746) | 11,000 | 29,500 | 84,200 | 308,000 |
| New York Society Library (1754) | 40,000 | 65,000 | 90,000 | 100,000 |
| Columbia (1763) | 18,000 | 18,700 | 135,000 | 580,000 |
| Brown (1767) | 29,000 | 45,000 | 71,000 | 200,000 |
| Library of Congress (1800) | 63,000 | 300,000 | 660,000 | 2,100,000 |
| Boston Atheneum (1807) | 70,000 | 105,000 | 173,800 | 254,000 |
| New York Mercantile Library (1820) | 51,000 | 160,600 | 240,000 | 243,000 |
| Philadelphia Mercantile Library (1821) | 16,500 | 125,700 | 166,000 | 211,000 |
| Surgeon General's Library, Washington, D.C. (1836) | 1,500 | 40,000 | 104,300 | 170,000 |
| University of Michigan (1838) | 7,000 | 23,000 | 77,700 | 322,000 |
| *Astor Library, New York (1848) | 80,000 | 152,500 | 239,000 | |
| University of Wisconsin (1850) | 3,000 | 6,400 | 22,800 | 210,000 |
| Boston Public Library (1852) | 70,000 | 300,000 | 556,300 | 1,050,000 |
| Cincinnati Public Library (1856) | 2,000 | 71,400 | 156,600 | 426,200 |
| Department of Agriculture Library, Washington, D.C. (1862) | | 7,000 | 20,000 | 127,800 |
| Detroit Public Library (1865) | | 22,900 | 108,700 | 278,000 |
| Cornell University (1868) | | 39,000 | 111,000 | 378,800 |
| University of California (1868) | | 12,000 | 48,200 | 265,000 |
| Cleveland Public Library (1869) | | 24,000 | 67,000 | 500,000 |
| *Lenox Library, New York (1870) | | 15,000 | 65,000 | |
| Chicago Public Library (1873) | | 48,100 | 175,800 | 614,000 |
| Johns Hopkins University (1876) | | | 55,000 | 175,200 |
| Enoch Pratt Free Library, Baltimore (1882) | | | 106,700 | 301,000 |
| Newberry Library, Chicago (1887) | | | 79,000 | 342,000 |
| University of Chicago (1891) | | | 380,000 | 532,500 |
| John Crerar Library, Chicago (1895) | | | | 360,000 |
| New York Public Library (1895) | | | | 2,100,000 |
| Totals | 637,000 | 1,946,800 | 4,635,500 | 14,471,700 |

*Collections merged into New York Public Library.

their care. The founding of The Johns Hopkins University in the same year is usually considered the birth of the modern American university and it was an event that had important consequences for the college library as well. For the public librarian, there were two other occasions in that eventful year that had a more tangible and immediate impact: inauguration of the *American Library Journal,* the official ALA journal; and publication of the U.S. Bureau of Education's 1,100-page *Public Libraries of the United States of America; Their History, Condition, and Management.* This survey, containing thirty-nine articles that describe all phases of library work and management, was essential reading for all librarians. The first edition of Charles A. Cutter's *Rules for a Printed Dictionary Catalogue* was published as a separate part of this remarkable volume. Finally, it should not go unnoticed that publication of the first edition of Melvil Dewey's decimal classification and subject index occurred in 1876.

The important events of 1876 in the American library world were also significant in Great Britain. The public library movement in both England and the United States started in the 1850s. While the Americans were still behind Europe in collection building, they took the initiative in organizational matters, and the British Library Association was founded in 1877 as a direct consequence of the establishment of the American Library Association. Moreover, in 1877 the *American Library Journal* changed its title to *Library Journal* and until 1883 was the official organ of both the American and the British Library Associations.

The most important personality behind the founding of the American Library Association was probably Melvil Dewey, a brash young librarian from Amherst College. Dewey successfully convinced his elders, particularly William Frederick Poole of the Chicago Public Library and Justin Winsor of the Boston Public Library, to support the establishment of the new organization. The other principals were Frederick Leypoldt, editor of *Publisher's Weekly,* and his partner, Richard R. Bowker. Leypoldt and Bowker were also the publishers of *American Library Journal;* their roles in the creation of the association cemented a partnership between the library and publishing worlds that continues to exist with beneficial consequences for librarians and scholars alike.

The creation of a professional association for American librarians was itself part of a post–Civil War trend toward the establishment of professional societies, including the American Philological Association (1869) and the Modern Language Association, the American Historical Association, and the American Economic Association—all founded between 1883 and 1885. The association of librarians, however, had characteristics that differentiated it from the other organizations. In the first place, the librarians, by the nature of their profession, were middlemen. In theory at least, the collections they accumulated were for the benefit of others: the public, college and university students, and even other professional associations. Secondly, the librarians were not subject specialists—also a consequence of the nature of their profession. This fact had both its advantages and disadvantages: the advantage was a freedom and variety not permitted other professions, the disadvantage a perennial label of "technician" and a systematic denial of professional status in the academic world.

The first graduate school for librarians was established by Melvil Dewey at Columbia in 1887. While the school itself met with acclaim from students and librarians alike, Dewey's forceful personality soon alienated both administrators and his fellow faculty members. For example, he openly defied the Columbia trustees by admitting a predominance of women to the school. Forced to resign in 1888, he took his graduate school of library economy with him to Albany where he became secretary of the state Board of Regents and the state librarian.

The most important inducement to the formation of a professional association of librarians was the need to establish cooperative cataloging methods and to discuss mutual cataloging and classification problems. In its fundamental sense, however, the great emphasis that librarians placed on cataloging and classification during the last quarter of the nineteenth century was rooted in a growing concern for improving the access to the knowledge housed in their libraries. Greater accessibility to collections was a prerequisite to developing the specialized reference services that soon were demanded of all librarians. It was this demand for improved access that prompted librarians to take a new approach to their collections at every level of library work. For example, in the view of Melvil Dewey: "The value of any collection depends quite as much on the classification, catalogues, and indexes as on the books themselves, for these are useless unless they can be found when wanted."[19]

A movement toward greater accessibility of collections paralleled the improvements in bibliographic accessibility. Both public and academic libraries extended their hours of opening; some even included Sundays. Collections on open shelves slowly became accepted practice. American libraries, unlike their European counterparts, emphasized the speed of book delivery to readers. The gradual development of interlibrary loan systems in the 1880s was part of the same trend. But first came changes in the library catalog.

Prior to the Civil War, printed book catalogs were predominant in American libraries. These bulky catalogs, with their periodic supplementary volumes, were adequate for the task until the transformation of American scholarship during the last decades of the nineteenth century made them obsolete. In his *The Printed Card Catalogue in American Libraries: 1723–1900,* Jim Ranz lists the following factors as principal contributors to the demise of the book catalog: the growing insistence on a subject approach to books; the rapidly increasing size of library collections, which made up-to-date supplements nearly impossible to maintain; the high costs of preparing and printing catalogs; and the inadequate financial support received by most libraries. While the idea of a catalog of cards was not new, it does not seem to have been successfully implemented until 1861, when assistant Harvard librarian Ezra Abbot began a public card catalog. Two years later, the Visiting Committee of Overseers proclaimed that "the new Catalogue on cards . . . has been making much progress and has been so constantly in use, during the past year, that experience has dissipated all doubts as to its intrinsic *practical* value."[20] In 1877, the Visiting Committee held that "the chief point to be considered is that the catalogue, whether of authors or of subjects, is a time-saving, labor-saving device, which a great library with a large circulation, or wishing to acquire a large circulation, can no more dispense with than it can dispense with sufficient shelf-room, with book numbers, or with runners to get the books."[21] The time-saving and labor-saving features of the card catalog gradually found favor with administrators, scholars, and librarians, and in 1901, when the Library of Congress began to sell its printed catalog cards, the public card catalog firmly achieved its dominance.

The debate between advocates of the classified approach to catalog arrangement and those who favored the dictionary approach was a related topic of interest during this period. Once again, the matter was finally settled on the side of maximum flexibility and accessibility. The dictionary approach was characterized by the interfiling of author, title, and subject entries, and the subject entries were much more specific and useful than the traditional, broad class entries. The great and unique value of the dictionary catalog was that it could be used immediately and easily without the need to learn the intricacies of a particular classification scheme. The 1861 Harvard card catalog, which incorporated features from earlier catalogs published by Charles Coffin Jewett and William Frederick Poole, was a major step toward the dictionary catalog. However it was the 1874 dictionary card catalog of the Boston Atheneum, prepared by Charles A. Cutter, that convinced librarians of the advantages of the dictionary arrangement. In an article in *Nation,* published in 1877, Cutter defended the new catalogs and catalog arrangements then gaining in popularity and summed up the new attitude of most librarians when he declared: "To assist those who come to the library in finding what will suit their needs is the librarian's highest work; and his best tool in doing this is a good catalogue."[22]

The establishment of the American Library Association was a pivotal event in the gradual specialization of the uses of knowledge, for the Association encouraged new approaches to the development and utilization of collections that were soon found indispensable in libraries everywhere. In effect, the Association played the principal role in the transformation of the "apparatus" as well as the molding of a new profession. Melvil Dewey, of course, was urging, leading, and proclaiming this revolution all at the same time. In 1876, on the eve of the ALA organizational conference, he asserted: "The time *was* when a library was very like a museum, and a librarian was a mouser in musty books, and visitors looked with curious eyes at ancient tomes and manuscripts. The time *is* when the library is a school, and the librarian is in the highest sense a teacher, and the visitor is a reader among the books as a workman among his tools."[23]

## The Age of Use

The development of a more liberal attitude toward collection use was the most important force in the evolution of the concept of the library as a workshop, or of the reader "as a workman among his tools." The new reference services, like the cataloging and classification apparatus, were the result of a fundamental change in American society: a growing belief that knowledge itself should be and could be used more efficiently. One of the most direct pressures on libraries came from the changing nature and increased specialization of American scholarship. As Arthur Bestor has documented, before about 1875, productive scholarship in the United States was rarely connected with college teaching or with college libraries.[24] The establishment of Johns Hopkins University in 1876 changed this situation radically, and American scholarship and scientific activity soon reorganized itself around the university and its library. The new professional societies and associations rarely formed their own collections and instead relied on established libraries. Increasing specialization among learned societies and college faculties as well as the development of university presses helped create a new professionalized attitude toward knowledge and even encouraged a trend toward cooperative scholarship. Libraries at all levels began to concentrate on the uses and the users of the knowledge that was accumulating in their collections.

Justin Winsor, the scholar-librarian who served as the first president of the American Library Association, was an influential advocate of the so-called doctrine of use. Winsor was superintendent of the Boston Public Library from 1868 until 1877, when he became librarian at Harvard. During his first year at Boston, Winsor undertook a nationwide survey of library collections and services as well as a detailed examination of the types of books being circulated and the interests of individual readers. Besides initiating circulation studies, he replaced the book catalog with a card catalog, reduced the age limit for borrowers, opened the library for an increased number of days per year—including Sundays—and established six branch libraries. To Winsor's satisfaction, the number of volumes circulated increased dramatically during his administration from 175,000 in 1868 to over 1,000,000 in 1877. In his first annual report at Harvard, Winsor articulated his basic philosophy: "Books may be accumulated and guarded, and the result is sometimes called a library; but if books are made to help and spur men on in their own daily work, the library becomes a vital influence; the prison is turned into a workshop."[25]

Winsor's "workshop concept," however, was not as successful at Harvard as it had been at the Boston Public. The notion that the library should make a concentrated effort to help readers took roughly a quarter of a century to become accepted practice, and public libraries were more amenable to the idea than their academic counterparts. There was one major exception—Columbia University— but for the most part, the constraints of the academic situation kept the concept of reference work from being fully accepted in colleges and universities until after the turn of the century. Indeed, continued emphasis on acquisitions and collection-building, on the part of both faculty members and college librarians, was the rule, so that collection size soon became equated with library excellence.

There were other factors that impeded reference work in college libraries. Many librarians were so firm in their commitment to the new catalogs, especially the subject catalogs, that they felt further aid to readers was unnecessary; many scholars not only agreed but were insulted by the suggestion that they needed assistance. Even the development of departmental libraries, formed in accordance with new organizational patterns in higher education, usually did not provide successful examples of specialized reference work. The physical dispersal of collections and the decentralization of administrative control frequently were viewed as threats, not opportunities, by the college librarian. Furthermore, once the libraries were under departmental control, they were often treated as departmental, if not personal, enclaves. Finally, the professional librarian with a subject specialty acceptable to a college faculty was a rarity.

The first explicit proposal for a program of aid to readers was made at the 1876 American Library Association meeting by Samuel S. Green of the Worcester

Public Library. Green's conference paper was entitled "The Desirableness of Establishing Personal Intercourse and Relations Between Librarians and Readers in Popular Libraries"; when published in *American Library Journal,* the title was shortened to "Personal Relations Between Librarians and Readers." At this meeting Professor Otis Robinson of the University of Rochester expressed his agreement with Green's objective, indicating that it would be especially appropriate in a college library, where "a librarian should be much more than a keeper of books; he should be an educator."[26]

By 1883 many public libraries were providing personal assistance to readers. In a report to the ALA convention on "Aids and Guides," William E. Foster of the Providence Public Library expressed his feeling that "it is certainly one of the most gratifying evidences of the gradual lifting of the level of library work that never before has there been anything like the degree of personal assistance reported from various libraries all over the country." In the 1880s, that aid still had its limits, however. In the Boston Public Library's Lower Hall, considered the "popular library," a full-time staff member provided reader assistance, but in Bates Hall, frequented by the more scholarly class of users, it was felt that readers could take care of their own bookish needs.[27]

Columbia University was an exception to the slow acceptance of reference work by academic libraries and the reason was, once again, Melvil Dewey. In 1884, Chief Librarian Dewey issued a circular on behalf of his library and its undergraduate school of library economy. In it, he reiterated his concern for the use of books and for the reader:

The Library is not content to accumulate and safely store many thousands of volumes. Nor is it sufficient to have carefully classified and fully catalogued its treasures. With the limited time at the command of students and investigators, and the immense amount of material with which the individual must often deal, the aid of someone fully acquainted with the resources of the library . . . and at hand to impart the desired help, becomes imperatively necessary.

The same year Dewey formally established a "reference department" consisting of two staff members, one "in special charge of law, political science, and history," the other in charge of "sciences, arts, and serials." By 1886 he claimed that it was "perhaps the most important single department."[28]

The "doctrine of use" gained acceptance among librarians alongside the growing tendency for subject specialization. Moreover, reference work was frequently most successful in highly specialized institutions like Chicago's John Crerar Library, a science library established in 1894. One reason for this can be found in a growing debate among librarians regarding the nature of the assistance to be offered. Should the librarian just point the way for the reader, limiting his help to suggesting useful sources, or should he actually do the work and answer the questions for the reader? In general, the more specialized the collection and the more specialized the librarian, the greater the degree of reference assistance offered. One of the reasons that Dewey's reference department at Columbia succeeded was probably the specialization of his librarians. At John Crerar, the reference librarian from the outset was a specialist in science and technical publications. After 1895, the growth of specialized departments at the New York Public Library brought about many successful examples of reference work, and a similar situation developed at the Library of Congress after it occupied its new building in 1897.

College and university library collections also became more specialized—a development that had been foreseen as early as 1874 by John Sibley of Harvard. Sibley felt that the new facilities for printing, the passion for reading in America, and the establishment of the new public libraries would make it necessary "both to use books to advantage and to keep library buildings within convenient limits as to size and attendants, to adopt quite generally a system of libraries for specialties or particular subjects." Writing thirty years later, Dewey noted that "as demand and income warrant, we shall have reference librarians each limited to history, science, art, education, or some other topic till we shall have in the library, as in the university, a company of men each an authority in his own field."[29]

The need for highly specific reference work was at the core of the "special libraries" movement that took place in the first decade of the twentieth century. In the forefront was the development of legislative libraries at the state level, but business, industrial, and technical libraries also came to be considered "special libraries." The specialized purposes of these libraries demanded a particular type of reference service, one that went beyond the assistance being offered even at such libraries as John Crerar, the New York Public Library, and the Library of Congress. William P. Cutter of the Engineering Societies Library in New York went so far as to describe a special library as "one that serves the people who are *doing* things, while a reference library is one that serves people who are *thinking* things." In 1915, Ethel M. Johnson, librarian of the Women's Educational and Industrial Union in Boston, reported that "the most distinctive feature of the special library is not so much its subject matter as its service. Before everything else, it is an information bureau. The main function of the general library is to make books available. The function of the special library is to make information available."[30] The special libraries movement, as well as the cultural developments that brought it about, also had an important impact on the public library. Municipal reference bureaus, for example, often took the form of a city hall branch of the public library.

The special libraries movement had a profound effect on the library profession as well. The American Library Association (ALA) had been established in 1876 to bring librarians together to discuss common problems, approaches, and philosophies. As library collections became more specialized, so did librarians, and those librarians who worked in the legislative, municipal, and business libraries soon felt that the ALA was not catering to their particular needs. The result was the formation in 1909 of the Special Libraries Association, which soon created subject committees that described the range of its concerns: agriculture, commerce, insurance, legislative and municipal reference, public utilities, sociology, and technology. It should be noted, however, that the Special Libraries Association was not the first fragmentation of the American Library Association. Between 1876 and 1915 the organization of the library profession, like that of other professional societies, became increasingly specialized. The Special Libraries Association was preceded by the National Association of State Libraries (1889), the American Library Trustee Association (1890), the Medical Library Association (1898), the Bibliographical Society of America (1904), and the American Association of Law Libraries (1906); it was followed, during the period under consideration, by the American Association of Library Schools (1915) and shortly thereafter by the Catholic Library Association (1921).

During the same period, yet another type of special library proliferated—the government library. Between 1865 and 1915, the federal government gradually assumed an important role in the library world as it did in almost every phase of American life. As the government grew and became more departmentalized, so did its libraries. They developed collections and performed reference work within the subject confines of the areas they served, whether it was the State, Treasury, Agriculture, or Interior Department, or perhaps the office of the Surgeon-General, or the Superintendent of Documents, the Patent Office, or the Bureau of Education. A survey taken in 1857 estimated that the collections of all federal libraries in Washington totaled about two hundred thousand volumes; two decades later, in 1876, that number had tripled, and by 1908 the estimate was over three million volumes.[31]

## Accumulation and Use at the Library of Congress

There was one governmental library that assumed dominance among American libraries in the decades following the Civil War—the Library of Congress. In 1867 it became the largest library in America; by 1900 its collections totaled over one million volumes. In no other library is it possible to delineate so clearly the "storehouse" to "workshop" transformation.

The Library of Congress assumed the role of principal government library only after the Smithsonian Institution voluntarily relinquished it. Between 1847 and 1854, Smithsonian librarian Charles Coffin Jewett, with the strong support of several members of Congress, tried to turn the Smithsonian into a national library and bibliographic center. There were four principal components in Jewett's plan: (1) a comprehensive collection of all American publications, accumulated through the copyright laws and generous expenditures of the Smithsonian endowment; (2) a general catalog of the holdings of all American libraries, made possible by reproducing cataloging information for individual titles on stereotyped blocks; (3) a uniform set of cataloging rules; and (4) the assumption by the Smithsonian of a leadership role among American libraries. Jewett's grand plans, however, came to naught when the Secretary of the Smithsonian, Joseph Henry, dismissed his librarian in mid-1854. Henry insisted that the proper role of the Smithsonian was the increase and diffusion of knowledge through scientific investigation and publication—not through the accumulation of a magnificent library at the expense of the Smithsonian fund. One can assume that Henry was in full agreement with a report from a special committee of the Board of Regents, prepared just before the Secretary fired his librarian, which proclaimed that the accumulation of a great library at the Smithsonian "would be the *hiving* of knowledge, not its increase or diffusion." It should be pointed out, however, that Henry in fact favored the development of a national library as long as it was not at the Smithsonian. The Secretary was an early proponent and ardent supporter of the development of the Library of Congress into such a national accumulator of books.[32]

Prior to the Civil War the functions of the Library of Congress were accurately described by its name: it served primarily as a legislative library for the American Congress. This situation changed dramatically after the Civil War, primarily at the urging of a new and ambitious Librarian of Congress, Ainsworth Rand Spofford, who took advantage of the favorable post–Civil War political and social climate as well as friendships with individual congressmen, to promote his cause of the Library of Congress as the national library. In this effort he also had the full support of Joseph Henry, who even arranged to have the entire Smithsonian library, consisting of over forty thousand volumes, transferred to the Library of Congress in 1866. The next year Spofford and Henry worked out an arrangement for the international exchange of public documents, whereby the Smithsonian, through its exchange system, would send surplus copies of U.S. public documents to foreign governments in exchange for their official publications, which would come to the Library of Congress.

Spofford's greatest collection-building feat, however, was the copyright law of 1870. Like Charles Coffin Jewett, Spofford realized that the best way to develop a comprehensive collection of American publications was through copyright deposit. Not only were all copyrighted items automatically included—and by 1870 this meant photographs, maps, and music, as well as books and pamphlets—but the service was free. In 1870, working through the proper legislative committees, Spofford single-handedly centralized all U.S. copyright registration and deposit activities at the Library of Congress. The new law required that two copies of all items registered for copyright be deposited in the Library as a condition of copyright. With the tremendous postwar expansion of American publishing, the Library was soon overflowing.[33]

Because of the overcrowded conditions in the west portion of the Capitol, the magnificent Americana collections of the Library were virtually unusable during the years in which they were being gathered. The approval of the copyright law of 1870 made a separate building for the Library an immediate necessity. Spofford asked for such a structure in 1872; in his annual report three years later he stated that all shelf space was gone and that if a new building was not imminent, he would soon be presiding over "the greatest chaos in America." The new building was authorized in 1886 but was not completed and occupied until 1897.

Spofford was the Library's great "accumulator," and the results of his efforts brought about dozens of congressional declarations about the great storehouse of knowledge under his supervision. In their rhetoric congressmen surpassed librarians and educators in espousing the "storehouse" theory of knowledge: as long as it had been collected, it was good. Many of the congressional statements were made in the debates regarding a separate Library building; for example, in 1884, Senator Justin S. Morrill of Vermont urged a new building because the Library was "the largest storehouse of human knowledge and of valuable materials for the use of scholars to be found in the United States."[34]

Spofford shared this view, and his emphasis on preservation and accumulation was typical of the librarians of his generation. But the Librarian of Congress was operating on a larger and more ambitious scale than his colleagues. For example, in his efforts to convince Congress to expand the Library, Spofford argued that a "great and monumental library" belonging to the American government was a necessity if the United States were ever to be "a nation claiming to hold a front rank in civilization. We ought to have one comprehensive library in the country, and that belonging to the nation, whose aim it should be to preserve the books which other libraries have not the room nor the means to procure." By 1891, when Spofford made the latter statement, many other librarians and university officials were in agreement. In ceremonies dedicating the new Cornell University Library, President Daniel C. Gilman of Johns Hopkins was already looking to the Library of Congress to perform precisely this function: "For the publications of a single country, it may be enough if there are one or two storehouses, like the Library of Congress, the British Museum, the National Library of Paris, and the like, where completeness is the aim. Among other libraries, some principle of differentiation may be worked out."[35]

In fairness to Spofford, it should be pointed out that, philosophically at least, he made the transition from accumulator to user. He stated, for example, that "my only conception of a useful library is a library that is used—and the same of a librarian. He should be a lover of books—but not a book-worm." He also held that "a library is an intellectual and material work-shop, in which there is no room for fossils nor for drones."[36] By the time the Library's new building opened in late 1897, however, there was a new Librarian of Congress.

A brief reference should be made to the way in which knowledge was organized in the Library of Congress during the nineteenth century. In 1815 Congress had purchased Thomas Jefferson's private collection which became the foundation of a new and expanded Library of Congress. With his collection, Jefferson sent his personal classification scheme, which was based on Bacon's classification of knowledge. Jefferson's scheme was utilized, with expansions, until the 1897 move into the new building. With the exception of one author catalog that Spofford managed to produce in 1864, all Library of Congress catalogs were arranged by class. Overwhelming accessions and the pressure of copyright business caused the system to break down in 1880; the last printed book catalog of the Library of Congress during the nineteenth century was published in that year, and it ended with the letter "C". When the new building opened, the size of the staff was doubled, and acknowledged experts in cataloging and classification were employed. A card catalog was started and a new classification scheme inaugurated—one that permitted the maximum degree of expansion and flexibility. The Dewey Decimal classification was rejected precisely because it was considered too narrow and inflexible for the needs of a major research library that housed nearly a million books.

The individual who developed the functions and services that turned the Library into a "workshop" was former librarian of the Boston Public Library, Herbert Putnam, who was appointed Librarian of Congress in 1899. Once again it is instructive to refer back to the scholar-accumulators of the mid-nineteenth century and particularly to the thwarted plans of Smithsonian librarian Jewett. If Spofford succeeded in accomplishing Jewett's first objective, the development of comprehensive Americana collections, by 1915 Putnam had fulfilled the other three as well as a fourth that was of crucial importance: provision for the specialized "interpretation" of the Library's massive collections. Putnam began by actively assuming leadership of the American library movement and soon made his institution a national center for cataloging and bibliographic services. In 1901 he inaugurated the sale and distribution of Library of Congress printed catalog cards to libraries throughout the nation, a sophisticated version of the centralized cataloging system Jewett had proposed a half century before. An interlibrary loan service also began in 1901. By 1908 the cataloging rules of the Library of Congress had been accepted as the standard by the rest of the American library community.

Putnam's greatest concern, however, was with the efficient and appropriate uses of the Library's collections. Nine months after taking office, he explained his idea of reader assistance: "Students with a purpose should receive at the hands of librarians not merely advice as to consulting the catalogues, but counsel as to the authoritative works on special subjects, and guidance as to unexpected sources of information." By 1901 his concept had expanded. In his annual report for that year, he described the reference functions of the various specialized divisions which by then included maps, manuscripts, prints, music, law, documents, and periodicals, as well as special services for the Smithsonian scientific collection and for the blind. With regard to the material in its custody, the Librarian explained, each division was "not merely to safeguard it, but to aid in the acquisition, to classify and catalogue, to make it useful to readers, and to answer inquiries which relate to it or may be answered effectively out of the special knowledge which its custody and administration involve."

The compilation of detailed bibliographies was considered one of the most important means for making the collections "useful to readers." In his next report, Putnam explained why he was hiring well-known subject specialists to aid in the "interpretation" of the Library's collections: "Such experts alone can realize the need of the inquirer, can assume for the time being his point of view, can translate the language of his science or art into the language of the classification and catalogue.'' Putnam's efforts to make the Library of Congress a national center for ''reader aid'' succeeded; by 1906, the Library was receiving annually over 10,000 letters of inquiry, most of which were answered by its loyal corps of ''interpreters.''[37]

In 1909 there took place a significant shift away from the concept of the Library of Congress as a comprehensive storehouse of knowledge. The general revision of the copyright law, approved on March 4, 1909, included authorization for the Librarian of Congress to dispose of copyright deposits as he saw fit: they could be added to the collections, exchanged, sold, or transferred to other agencies. This change was made at the request of the Librarian of Congress who regarded flexibility in the use of the Library's collections to be of greater importance than their comprehensive accumulation. With the copyright law of 1909, the Library of Congress deliberately abandoned any claim to being a complete archive or ''library of record'' for all American publications.[38]

In addition to providing specialized reference services to academic institutions and societies, government agencies, libraries, and the general public, the Library of Congress, beginning about 1911, evolved into the most efficient legislative reference library in the nation. That this function was worthy of a special effort is somewhat ironic, since the Library was always in the legislative branch and had as its prime purpose service to Congress. Since 1865, however, the ''non-Congressional'' or national services of the Library to other constituencies had been expanded to such an extent that it was time to correct the imbalance.

The legislative reference movement started in the states, most notably in the legislative reference libraries of Wisconsin and New York. In 1911, Wisconsin Senator Robert M. LaFollette began advocating a legislative reference service for the national legislature, and interest was evident in the House of Representatives shortly thereafter. Hearings were held and the advice of such authorities as James Bryce, author of *The American Commonwealth* and British Ambassador to the United States, and Woodrow Wilson, Governor of New Jersey, was solicited. Librarian Putnam carefully explained that the proposed service contemplated *research* rather than *reference* work, but that the Library would be delighted to undertake the reference service if Congress would authorize the necessary expansion. The testimony at the hearings provide ample demonstration of the firm ''Progressive era'' faith in the efficient and specialized uses of knowledge.[39]

The result, in 1914, was the creation of the Legislative Reference Service of the Library of Congress. The 1915 legislative appropriations act stipulated that the new service would ''gather, classify, and make available in translations, indexes, digests, compilations, and bulletins, and otherwise, data for or bearing upon legislation.'' A month later, Putnam reported that the service was anticipating requests from Congress concerning the most pressing public issues of the day: conservation, immigration, railroad securities, federal aid for road-building, a national budget system, and publicity regarding campaign contributions.[40]

In sum, the establishment of the Legislative Reference Service at the Library of Congress can be viewed as the culmination of fifty years of gradual specialization in the uses of knowledge among American libraries. Shortly after the Civil War, the Library of Congress became the largest American library, and in an "age of accumulation" there was no library more concerned with building large collections. From 1876 until the turn of the century, however, it was the American Library Association that provided the focal point for a reorganization of library catalogs, cataloging, and classification schemes. This reorganization, in turn, enabled libraries to respond to the specialized demands of scholars, the general public, industry, and government. Once it occupied its monumental new building, the Library of Congress assumed leadership not only in advancing the technical aspects of librarianship, but also in promoting the "uses" of its collections. Its reference services gradually were tailored to the needs of its own particular users as happened in libraries throughout the nation. Finally, with the advent of the Legislative Reference Service from 1911 to 1915, the Library of Congress and American librarianship began direct and highly specialized service to a client whose perceptions of the uses of knowledge have great importance for both scholarship and librarianship—the Congress of the United States.

## Notes

1. Samuel L. Clemens to Ainsworth R. Spofford, 11 March 1880, Spofford Papers, Library of Congress, Washington, D.C.

2. U.S. House of Representatives, Committee on the Library, *Hearings on Various Bills Proposing the Establishment of a Congressional Reference Bureau,* 26 and 27 February 1912 (Washington, D.C.: U.S. Government Printing Office, 1912), pp. 2–6 (hereafter cited as *1912 Hearings*).

3. Quoted in Edward Waldo Emerson and Waldo Emerson Forbes, eds., *Journals of Ralph Waldo Emerson,* 10 vols. (Boston: Houghton Mifflin, 1913), 9:395–96.

4. Smithsonian Institution, *Fourth Annual Report of the Board of Regents of the Smithsonian Institution... During the Year 1849* (Washington, D.C.: 1850), p. 41 (hereafter cited as *Annual Report of SI*). A detailed article on the "utility of large libraries" that repeats the Gibbon story is in the *North American Review* 45 (1837): 116–49.

5. Detailed examinations of the "causal factors" in public library development are found in Jesse H. Shera, *Foundations of the Public Library* (Chicago: American Library Association, 1949), pp. 200–248, and Sidney Ditzion, *Arsenals of a Democratic Culture* (Chicago: American Library Association, 1947), pp. 9–109. The major arguments in a new controversy on the same subject are outlined in Michael Harris, "The Purpose of the American Public Library: A Revisionist Interpretation of History," *Library Journal* 98 (1973): 2509–14, and Phyllis Dain, "Ambivalence and Paradox: The Social Bonds of the Public Library," *Library Journal* 100 (1975): 261–66.

6. The Everett and Ticknor correspondence is quoted in Walter Muir Whitehill, *Boston Public Library: A Centennial History* (Cambridge, Mass.: Harvard University Press, 1956), pp. 20–25. The results of Winsor's survey are reported in *Annual Report of the Trustees of the Public Library, 1869* (Boston, 1869), pp. 15, 71, 112–33. (hereafter cited as *Annual Report of the Boston Public Library*).

7. Robert Ellis Lee, *Continuing Education for Adults Through the American Public Library, 1833–1964* (Chicago: American Library Association, 1966), pp. 10–11.

8. John William Tebbel, *A History of Book Publishing in the United States,* 3 vols. (New York: R. R. Bowker, 1975), 2:22–33, 675–708.

9. Ibid., pp. 676, 683–84.

10. Hellmut Lehmann-Haupt, *The Book in America* (New York: R. R. Bowker, 1939), pp. 169–71, 217–19.

11. *Publisher's Weekly* 27 (31 January 1885): 93.

12. *Annual Report of the Boston Public Library, 1875,* p. 17.

13. Green and Poole made their comments at the first meeting of the American Library Association; see *American Library Journal* 1 (1876): 49, 99. Fletcher's statement is in his "Public Libraries

in Manufacturing Communities," in U.S. Bureau of Education, *Special Report on Public Libraries in the United States of America*, 2 pts. (Washington, D.C.: U.S. Government Printing Office, 1876), pt. 1, p. 410. The fiction controversy is thoroughly documented in Esther Jane Carrier, *Fiction in Public Libraries, 1876-1900* (New York: Scarecrow Press, 1965).

14. Lee, *Continuing Education*, pp. 24–27, 36–39.

15. George S. Bobinski, *Carnegie Libraries: Their History and Impact on American Public Library Development* (Chicago: American Library Association, 1969), p. 3. Carnegie's social theories are outlined in Peter Mickelson, "American Society and the Public Library in the Thought of Andrew Carnegie," *Journal of Library History* 10 (1975): 123–29.

16. Quoted in Kenneth J. Brough, *Scholar's Workshop: Evolving Conceptions of Library Service* (Urbana, Ill.: University of Illinois Press, 1953), p. 2. Brough's excellent volume is a rich source for the study of American college and research libraries.

17. Quoted in Brough, *Scholar's Workshop*, pp. 16–17.

18. Statistics are from the following surveys: William J. Rhees, *Manual of Public Libraries, Institutions, and Societies in the United States* (Philadelphia: J. B. Lippincott, 1859); U.S. Bureau of Education, *Special Report*, pt. 1; Weston Flint, *Statistics of Public Libraries in the United States and Canada*, U.S. Bureau of Education, Circular of Information no. 7 (Washington, D.C.: U.S. Government Printing Office, 1893); and *Public Society and School Libraries*, U.S. Bureau of Education, Bulletin no. 25 (Washington, D.C.: U.S. Government Printing Office, 1915).

19. Columbia College, *Annual Report of the Chief Librarian, 1884* (New York: Columbia College, 1884), p. 12 (hereafter cited as *Annual Report of Columbia Librarian*).

20. Jim Ranz, *The Printed Book Catalogue in American Libraries: 1723-1900*, Association of College and Research Libraries (ACRL) Monograph no. 26 (Chicago: American Library Association, 1964), pp. 76–78. The 1863 Visiting Committee report is quoted in Brough, *Scholar's Workshop*, p. 105.

21. Quoted in Brough, *Scholar's Workshop*, p. 109.

22. C. A. Cutter, "The Cataloguer's Work," *Nation* 22 (8 February 1877): 87. The controversy between the classified and dictionary approaches is thoroughly discussed in Ranz, *The Printed Book Catalogue*, pp. 62–75, 78–85.

23. Melvil Dewey, "The Profession," *American Library Journal* 1 (1876): 5–6.

24. Arthur E. Bestor, Jr., "The Transformation of American Scholarship, 1875-1917," in *Librarians, Scholars, and Booksellers at Mid-Century*, ed. Pierce Butler (Chicago: University of Chicago Press, 1953), pp. 9–15.

25. Winsor's accomplishments are outlined in Robert E. Brundin, "Justin Winsor of Harvard and the Liberalizing of the College Library," *Journal of Library History* 10 (1975): 57–70. Boston Public Library circulation statistics are summarized in Whitehill, *Boston Public Library*, p. 89. Winsor's first Harvard report is quoted in Samuel Rothstein, *The Development of Reference Services*, ACRL Monograph no. 14 (Chicago: American Library Association, 1955), p. 19. Rothstein's provocative study includes academic, public, and special libraries.

26. *American Library Journal* 1 (1876): 74–81, 123.

27. *Annual Report of the Boston Public Library, 1887*, p. 18; ibid, 1888, p. 6. Foster's report is in *Library Journal* 8 (1883): 241.

28. The 1884 circular is reprinted in Columbia University School of Library Service, *School of Library Economy, Columbia College, 1887-1889: Documents for a History* (New York: Columbia University, 1937), p. 31. Dewey's 1886 statement is in the *Annual Report of Columbia Librarian, 1886*, p. 39.

29. Sibley's views are quoted in Brough, *Scholar's Workshop*, p. 90. Dewey's statement is in his article on "The Faculty Library," *The Library*, n.s. 2 (1901): 239–40.

30. The quotation from Cutter, along with several other definitions of a special library, are in Miss Johnson's article, "The Special Library and Some of Its Problems," *Special Libraries* 6 (1915): 157–61.

31. Carleton B. Joeckel, *Library Service*, U.S. Advisory Committee on Education (Washington, D.C.: U.S. Government Printing Office, 1938), pp. 34–35.

32. The Special Committee report is in the *Annual Report of SI, 1853*, p. 83. An early example of Henry's support for the Library of Congress can be found in the *Annual Report of SI, 1851*, p. 20.

33. Copyright deposits as a means of building library collections is discussed in John Y. Cole, "Of Copyright, Men, and a National Library," *Quarterly Journal of the Library of Congress* 28 (1971): 114–36.

34. Congressional Record 15 (7 February 1884): 243.

35. The Spofford quotations are from the *Annual Report of the Librarian of Congress for 1875* (Washington, D.C.: U.S. Government Printing Office, 1876), p. 8 (hereafter cited as *Annual Report of LC*), and Spofford's "The Copyright System of the United States—Its Origin and Its Growth," in the *Proceedings of the Celebration of the Beginning of the Second Century of the American Patent System* (Washington, D.C.: Gedney & Roberts, 1892), p. 150. Gilman's statement is quoted in Brough, *Scholar's Workshop,* p. 91.

36. Ainsworth R. Spofford, *A Book for All Readers* (New York: G. P. Putnam's Sons, 1900), p. 274.

37. Herbert Putnam to Charles H. Hastings, 4 December 1899, Library of Congress Archives, Washington, D.C.; *Annual Report of LC,* 1901, p. 261; *Annual Report of LC, 1902,* p. 12; *Annual Report of LC, 1907,* p. 77.

38. U.S., *Statutes at Large,* vol. 35, p. 1075. Putnam's annual reports for 1905–1909 outline the dominant role played by the Library of Congress in the copyright revision.

39. House of Representatives, *1912 Hearings,* pp. 4–26. On 10 July 1913, the Senate Library Committee urged the creation of a legislative reference service "as quickly as possible . . . for, as pointed out in President Wilson's The New Freedom, great changes are to be made in the laws of the Nation affecting every special privilege." (U.S. Congress, Senate, Senate Library Committee, *Senate Report No. 73,* 63d Cong., 1st Sess., 1913).

40. Herbert Putnam, "Legislative Reference for Congress," *American Political Science Review* 9 (1915): 544.

# From Learned Society
# to Public Museum: The Boston
# Society of Natural History

### SALLY GREGORY KOHLSTEDT

*The Boston Society of Natural History was founded by "a few gentlemen, who were drawn together by a similarity of tasks and pursuits, for the purpose of increasing their own knowledge."* —Amos Binney, 1845

*"But it should also be taken into account that times have changed since then; public opinion which formerly sneered now applauds and therefore we should seize the work of the day and foster sentiment already in our favor; we should 'popularize science' —not by degrading it but by divesting it of its mysteries, by elevating the popular knowledge to our own standard."* —Samuel H. Scudder, 1870[1]

In the context of the late nineteenth-century professional societies, the Boston Society of Natural History (BSNH) appears the relic of an earlier period in the history of American learning—a period characterized by the appearance of provincial academies and learned societies organized by amateurs and reflecting a world of learning scarcely touched by intellectual fragmentation. With the rise of the university and the growth of specialized scientific and learned associations in the second half of the nineteenth century, many of these local, relatively broad-based societies disappeared, others went into decline, and a few—among them the BSNH—explored various new goals and functions in a determined effort to adjust to a rapidly changing society.

After the Civil War, the BSNH contributed only intermittently and indirectly to research and communication among scientists, yet it managed to survive well into the twentieth century as a viable community enterprise best known for its museum and public lecture series. The simple fact of survival would hardly justify an inquiry into the history of the BSNH, but the Society's continuous struggle to redefine itself, generation by generation, during a century of social and professional change, reveals much about the effect of professionalization on science and the influence of social attitudes on both the practitioners and the practice of natural history.

The social changes brought by urban growth, an industrial economy, and educational consciousness, as well as the more direct challenges posed by the emerging professional class of scientists, helped to underscore the feeling of uncertainty often expressed by the BSNH as attempts were made, at various intervals, to redefine the Society's function. On the one hand, a generation of practitioners had emerged that disdainfully rejected the general nomenclature of "natural history" in favor of biology, zoology, and entomology. They were balanced on the other side by a local public that increasingly sought a comprehensible and "democratic" science available to everyone. Confronted with this shifting pattern of expectations from membership and audience alike, the Society, throughout the late nineteenth century, reformulated its goals and devised new programs, cognizant that its very existence depended on the appropriateness of its activities to both constituencies. In the process, the Society lost much of its relevance for the productive scientific community, but it pioneered the development of a science museum and other activities designed to educate the public.

This chapter will not concentrate on the Society's withdrawal from the professional arena nor will it argue defensively that a museum by its nature attracts the unformed interests of students and thus helps youth aspire to a life in science—although this argument was quite explicitly advanced by BSNH leaders. Rather, this brief survey of the Boston Society of Natural History will consider the transformation of the organization in the late nineteenth century in order to demonstrate how changes in American society, and especially in science, affected at least one private, informal institution dedicated to learning.

The Boston Society of Natural History was founded in 1830, at a time when Bostonians were seeking to reassert the scientific and cultural leadership they had lost to Philadelphia.[2] It was not the first such effort. The American Academy of Arts and Sciences (1780) had earlier attempted to counter the influence of the American Philosophical Society by forming an organization modeled on both the French Academy of Sciences and the Royal Society of London. At the beginning of the nineteenth century, several Harvard graduates established a scientific club, the New England Society for the Study of Natural History.[3] As members of this society, such young wealthy Federalists as John Davis, William Emerson, and Josiah Quincy tried to duplicate classic experiments and form a collection of artifacts, but soon busy professional lives interfered and the organization was absorbed into the Boston Athenaeum. More promising was the Linnaean Society, founded in 1815 and composed primarily of medical practitioners.[4] This group undertook field trips to gather natural history and mineralogical specimens and became quite expert in the identification and classification of regional flora, fauna, and geological structure. However, it lacked sufficient financial support and leadership. In 1822 its collections were deposited with Harvard for proper maintenance, a symbolic gesture that marked the demise of the enterprise and proved a temporary caution to Bostonians interested in establishing another society in the 1820s.

Looking back on this failure in 1863, Augustus A. Gould, an early officer of the BSNH, noted that the relatively young members were so fully "engaged in professional pursuits" that they had neither the funds to hire a curator for their growing collections nor time to commit themselves.[5] A decade later, however, some of those individuals were well established in their careers, while changes in the curriculum at Harvard and other colleges provided additional graduates interested in avocational nature study.

The BSNH received a state charter of incorporation in early 1831. Like its predecessors, it was concerned primarily with the self-development of its members, although its founders hoped by vigorous activity to cultivate "a taste for natural history" in the community as well. Despite the fact that the Society was avowedly amateur,[6] its membership had professional and personal interests that suggested more than an offhand familiarity with science. Moreover, they had been involved in or were familiar with the problems of their predecessor societies, and they organized the Boston Society of Natural History fully determined that it would remain viable.

The early members rigorously studied natural history, were active discussants at regular meetings, and devoted considerable time to the organizational aspects of the Society as well. Almost all members had busy professional lives in medicine,[7] law, or business and were also engaged in other community projects.[8] One of the Society's early presidents, F. W. P. Greenwood, explained their dedication: "It is very true that most of us are so connected, in our several professions, with those to whom our first and chief attention is due, that we cannot lawfully be absorbed in pursuits which are extraneous to our immediate obligations;—but we can take a little from our leisure, and a little from our rest, and make our very amusement and healthful recreation contribute to the welfare and growth of this Society."[9] Through the efforts of members like Greenwood, the Boston Society equaled or surpassed similar societies in Philadelphia, Albany, and New York within its first decade of existence and became the most prominent scientific organization in New England.

The membership (118 members were listed by 1832) was dominated by old New England families. Most of its officers and curators were students of natural history with some, if minimal, expertise gained from college courses required for a medical apprenticeship. The dues-paying members and culture-minded local citizens, such as Ambrose Curtis who left a $10,000 legacy to the group, proved genuinely interested in promoting science and were generous in times of financial crisis.

The bylaws of the BSNH enumerated four functions analogous to those of natural history societies in other urban centers: holding regular meetings for discussion, sponsoring lectures for the public, maintaining a shared lending library, and gathering a collection of specimens. The substantial reference library of the BSNH was enriched by serial publications obtained through an international system of exchange. Equally important for the members' work was a museum of botanical, zoological, and geological specimens of the New England area. In the absence of any systematic survey of the region, this extensive cabinet provided the basis for study not only by local members but also by visiting naturalists from the South and West and from abroad. The geographical limitation enabled members to concentrate their skills and to work toward a systematic collection. A regional emphasis also meant that exhibits, lectures, and local tours could complement the personal experiences of members.

The BSNH was essentially a cooperative enterprise; the active members served as curators, reported on new books, and presented their own findings in the form of descriptions and specimens or publishable papers. The Society also benefitted from the state geological survey initiated under Edward Hitchcock and helped support its expansion to cover the topics of mineralogy, botany, and zoology.[10] Such success reinforced the members' assumptions that avocational researchers had a contribution to make to science. Thus the members of the Society looked upon the advancement of natural history as their first priority and initially a growing tendency toward specialization did not threaten them. In an address at the 1841 annual meeting, J. E. Teschmacher argued:

The process is clearly this: the great accumulation of facts in any science causes an absolute necessity for arrangement into divisions and subdivisions; the more extensive the knowledge and number of facts, the more natural, the more clearly defined and simple are these divisions, and each becomes the object of a separate study; hence, the subject is more easily mastered, more easily grasped by the mind, while the man of comparatively little leisure can undertake a single division and not only keep pace with discovery, but even add something to what is already known.[11]

Some Bostonians, content to attend lectures and peruse the Society's holdings, shared such optimism about the cumulative growth of knowledge but maintained a distance from the Society itself.

The initiative taken to present lectures and to make working collections available for general scrutiny indicated that the Society felt some sense of public responsibility. While the collections were open one or two days a week at no charge, the tickets to invited lectures by prominent scientists cost up to three dollars per person, an indication that an upper-class audience was anticipated. There was an unstated but growing awareness of different levels of public interest and background. The lectures, together with annual dues, provided an income sufficient for the Society to rent rooms at the Athenaeum by 1832.

The goal was always to present the best and most up-to-date interpretations in science. Lyceum-level lectures and public spectacles had no place. Unlike other societies that capitulated to "hokum,"[12] the Boston Society was delighted with the debunking given a sea serpent skeleton presented by a New York promoter. The enterprising entrepreneur had cemented together a "fossil" with head, teeth, ribs, paddles, and vertebrae entitled *Hydrarchus Sillimani*. The creature, which measured an impressive one hundred and fourteen feet, attracted large crowds. With little analysis Jeffries Wyman, anatomist at Harvard and later president of BSNH (in the 1860s), found that the vertebrae were not from one individual creature but belonged to many different ages, did not present any of the characteristics of an ophidian reptile, and had teeth that were probably those of a warm-blooded, mammiferous animal. Revelation of the hoax pleased members, who pointed out that they were a responsible group and would continue to introduce the often incredulous public to scientific truths, not spectacles and speculations.[13]

The meetings of the BSNH were serious occasions and when intense debate took place, it served only to reinforce the members' belief that their findings were serious business.[14] It was the organizing group of members who continued to dedicate their time and energy to the Society; for the most part the professionals who arrived in Cambridge in the following decades, including Asa Gray, Louis Agassiz, and William Barton Rogers, soon developed other priorities and responsibilities. As a young researcher in New York, Gray had used the Society's network of practicing naturalists to gather information more than he did as a fully established professor working locally at Harvard.[15] Similarly Agassiz presented new findings and worked actively with the Society during his first few years in Cambridge but his enthusiasm for voluntary groups waned over time.[16] Nonetheless the local scientists recognized the importance of such an organization and remained members, attending special meetings and nominating their promising students for membership. In 1859 Agassiz and Rogers used the Society as a forum at which to debate semipublicly Darwin's new theory on the origin of species.[17] The professionals also encouraged and contributed to the Society's *Journal,* established in 1834, because it provided an important supplement to Silliman's *American Journal of Science and Arts* as an outlet for new research. The BSNH publication specialized in botany and zoology and thus complemented the Philadelphia Academy of Natural Science's efforts in geology. After 1841 the Boston Society also published its *Proceedings* as a means of documenting the activities of the group as well as providing a place to credit contributors to their collection and demonstrate the quality of work prepared by members.[18]

Despite a prestigious and determined membership, the 1840s and 1850s were difficult decades for the Society. Locally there was competition for the responsibility assumed by, and the prestige that had earlier been accorded to, the Boston Society. When the Lowell estate established a public lecture series with sufficient funds to attract such internationally known figures as geologist Charles Lyell, attendance slackened at Society-sponsored events.[19] With the coming of Louis Agassiz to Harvard, his grand plans for the Lawrence Scientific School as well as his hopes for a research establishment diminished the Society's prestige and, perhaps, its sense of worth.[20] Community leaders who wanted informal, intellectual discussion turned to newly established clubs, especially the Thursday Club of John Collins Warren (founded in 1847), and later the famous fraternity of Oliver Wendell Holmes known as the Saturday Club (founded in 1855), both of which also absorbed the leisure time of leading local scientists. The clubs might discuss science, but their diverse fellowship assured that presentations would be comprehensible and even entertaining for an informed but nonprofessional audience. In this context science was promoted so that political leaders were apprised of new developments without any obligation to participate directly in the enterprise.[21] Nationally, too, challenges arose from large-scale enterprises. By comparison with the American Association for the Advancement of Science, first planned in Boston in 1847, and the Smithsonian Institution (1846), which served as a communications center for natural scientists, local activities seemed inconsequential. The results of the Wilkes Exploring Expedition, deposited in Washington, became the core of a collection with international significance dwarfing in scope, if not in content, all local collections. Retrenchment of smaller societies during the 1840s and 1850s was not uncommon; many, in fact, did not survive.[22] Those that did underwent considerable change in form and function. They sought to become more clearly defined in terms of local constituencies even as they reestablished their relationship to the body of knowledge and experts that gave their work contemporary significance.

To summarize, a personal enthusiasm for scientific investigation and a belief that individually and collectively they could contribute to science characterized the first generation of BSNH leaders. As local educational institutions and nationally based scientific organizations developed by mid-century, the Society's visibility and functions eroded. The relatively small cadre that constituted the pre–Civil War Society could not donate the time and money required to maintain a substantial library and research collection as emerging professionals turned to other institutional bases. Dramatic change or demise seemed the only alternatives.

Given its location in New England, it is not surprising that the Boston Society determined to adopt as its new goal the edification and education of a broader public than its earlier membership rules and lecture fees had permitted. Pioneering efforts to democratize education led to increasing literacy and a broader curriculum in Massachusetts schools and colleges by the middle of the nineteenth century.[23] As the BSNH shifted its concept of how it could advance science, it was cognizant of the growing interest in science in collegiate programs and hoped to attract a wider base of support from a more knowledgeable public. The old assumption had been that any person interested in natural history would seek out the Society; increasingly the BSNH found itself actively promoting study of the natural sciences.

In 1857 its leaders took a dramatic step in an effort to salvage their overcrowded and underutilized cabinet. They petitioned the Massachusetts legislature for a grant of land in the newly filled Back Bay area near Copley Square. William Barton Rogers, interested in the project as a component in his own effort to secure land for a technical school, helped write the request and publicize the efforts to create a new center for science in Boston (initially to house the Horticultural Society as well).[24] The legislature gave a grant of land to the BSNH and to the Massachusetts Institute of Technology, the latter being established with Rogers as its first president. The Society set about raising the funds necessary for a new building on their portion of the acquired land. Despite the difficult financial times and the interruption of the Civil War, the Society was invigorated by the activity required to plan the museum and accompanying lecture hall, to raise subscriptions, and to reformulate its program in terms of a new facility.

It was clear that when it opened in 1867 the stately Museum of the Boston Society of Natural History (so designated in 1864) symbolized a second phase in the Society's life.[25] The Society, like the Boston Public Library, also located in Copley Square, was, under the terms of the land grant, committed to public activity. The old enthusiasm for the advancement of natural history itself lost ground, and in its place the Society's leadership stressed its sense of obligation to educate the general public. Its commitment seemed vindicated by the more than 3600 visitors who came to the exhibit hall during the Museum's first year. Superficially, the new activity showed measurable success, with an increase in the number of persons at meetings, press coverage in local newspapers, and a series of afternoon and evening programs open to the public.[26]

A gala meeting, the centennial anniversary celebration of Alexander von Humboldt's birth, held in 1867, demonstrated that public interest attached most readily to scientific personality. Louis Agassiz's keynote address on the life of Humboldt attracted a crowd that filled every seat in Boston's Music Hall. Representatives from the literary, scientific, and civic leadership of Boston were there, including the mayor and governor. The Orpheus Musical Society, aided by various other German musical associations, entertained by presenting compositions by Bach, Beethoven, and Mendelssohn. Looking back at the contributions of Humboldt, a number of speakers found a model that aptly suited the style and intentions of the founders of the Society. Thomas Wentworth Higginson revealed his skepticism of new specialists by observing that, "Humboldt was not a mere scientist but one who loved beauty in nature and in art, and always recognized that side of culture."[27] Frederic H. Hedge asked, "And what better title can be conferred upon Humboldt? Master among them that know,—the master *savant*."[28] Eulogies came from transcendentalist Ralph Waldo Emerson as well as from Boston poet laureates, Oliver Wendell Holmes and Julia Ward Howe. These persons not only knew of Humboldt but also had respected friends like Agassiz who, to them, characterized the best kind of scientific generalist.

Yet, with a curious irony, it was decided at the conclusion of the ceremonies to establish a fund in the name of Humboldt, not to assist the Society but to aid Harvard students studying in the Museum of Comparative Zoology at Cambridge. Even as the contribution of Humboldt as scholarly generalist was celebrated, a new mode was coming to the fore. Systematic, scholarly training was required for the conduct of science in the latter half of the nineteenth century; the avocational interest, which was once sufficient to establish an individual as a credible researcher, was no longer adequate. The Boston Society confronted the reality that its former functions as a supporter of research and forum for researchers were being supplanted. Just in time, it turned its attention elsewhere.

In the years following the Civil War, the Society established for itself three major areas of activity: the museum and the lecture series, the library with its extensive periodical exchange, and the Society's regular meetings and publications intended "to sharpen mature minds and encourage the new student." The library received steady attention and its repetitive annual reports suggest that it was neither threatened nor encouraged—it was deemed essential to the Society and maintained at what the librarians felt was, at least, a minimal level. Attendance at the meetings of the BSNH was bolstered after the troublesome 1850s by the public attention given the museum and other new programs of the 1860s, but by the following decade it was again in decline.

Perhaps as significant as the pattern of attendance was the change in constituency. In the 1830s the Society passed an ambitious ruling, never carried out to the letter but indicating an aspiration, that all members should, at least once each year, present a paper or describe a specimen for the group. By the 1850s the requirement was not relevant. The medical practitioners, in prominent evidence at the time of the Society's founding, had been gradually displaced by a younger group of men, many of whom had undergraduate training in specific sciences at the new Massachusetts Institute of Technology or at Harvard University. There were no real research positions at the museum because each curator's time was spent in administration and the laboratories were designed for teaching rather than research. Indeed, the BSNH was peripheral to the research needs of local scientists. Professionalism proved strongest in core academic groups at neighboring universities, within research museums such as the Museum of Comparative Zoology or Asa Gray's herbarium at Harvard, and in national organizations. Because these individuals had specialized interests and a number of other affiliations to distract their attention and demand their participation, the concept of Society membership shifted.

A reorganization plan in 1870 invited all "scientific men, teachers, students, and amateurs, or those interested in science" to membership.[29] Some limits persisted—most notably sex—but the intention was to expand the roster and welcome any reasonably educated middle class male to join. Dues from members were still the largest income item in the treasurer's report. In the 1870s the corporate members numbered more than 400, although the average attendance at meetings was closer to 40 persons. Nominal membership was quite readily accepted, providing the person evidenced some interest in natural history.[30] By the end of the 1870s, after acrimonious debate, even women were admitted although only in a newly defined category of associate membership.

One of the key figures in redirecting the activities of the BSNH was Samuel H. Scudder (1837–1911), librarian and custodian of the Society's collections during the transition years from 1864 to 1870.[31] Scudder represented the second generation of leadership in the BSNH. He was not connected full time to the research community in science but had a substantial scientific background and worked well with popularizers like W. J. Youmans, editor of *Popular Science Monthly,* and Herbert Spencer. Scudder took a B.S. with Agassiz at the Lawrence Scientific School after graduation from Williams College and while a librarian at Harvard produced a number of catalogues, including a valuable compendium of scientific periodicals, in addition to numerous essays in entomology.

During his term of office at the BSNH, Scudder worked to develop a museum that directly reflected the Society's reordered priorities. The annual reports compiled by Scudder reflect his frustration with the limited research facilities and the apparent disinterest among most scientific leaders in Cambridge and Boston. On the occasion of opening a lecture hall, two exhibit rooms, and a second reading room in 1868, he decided to address the situation directly.[32] He pointed out that the older eclecticism in gathering and displaying specimens submitted by members meant that the time and energy of voluntary curators and paid assistants was often wasted handling duplicates and arranging them along the arbitrary lines of donation rather than in accordance with the integrative logic of science and the Society's total holdings. His speech signaled the end to the acknowledgment of "interesting" and "unusual" contributions in the *Proceedings*. While reluctantly agreeing that the Museum was not a research center, Scudder was determined that its staff and program be professionally competent. The amateur members began to withdraw as they found their work receiving scant recognition. Alternative sources of support were not immediately apparent. Scudder, a pragmatist, suggested that the government might be approached for ongoing financial backing, but the Society did not respond to his suggestion nor was such assistance forthcoming.

Scudder's hopes for the future were outlined explicitly when he left office in 1870, essentially turning authority over to his close friend Alpheus Hyatt. Candidly he noted the decline in membership attendance at meetings and in the number of papers presented. But he also suggested that the early days might not have been as golden as remembered:

Some have thought that the want of interest in our meetings was charged to those who have devoted themselves to pure science; that since their number has increased a feeling has arisen that only that which is new should be brought to the attention of the meetings. Yet I think two things will be found to be true: that our scientific quite as frequently as our nonscientific men speak of subjects which are not novel; and [from] those earlier days which we are told to look back upon with regret, we should find comparatively little left.[33]

He did not deny that the purposes of the founders had been quite different, citing founding member Amos Binney's often quoted goal of drawing men "together by a similarity of tastes and pursuits, for the purpose of increasing their knowledge by frequent intercourse." At that period, interest in the public had been tangential. By contrast, in the 1860s, a lecture series for local teachers and other public lectures overshadowed the BSNH's membership activity. Scudder argued that times had changed and that the Society must "popularize Science" (his own quotation marks indicated that the phrase was now more often used pejoratively) not "by degrading Science but by divesting it of its mysteries, by devoting the popular knowledge to our own standard."[34]

Given this shift in attention, Scudder urged that it was crucial for the museum to be seen differently. The idea of a museum for natural history was not unique—in fact, the first museum in America was founded nearly a century earlier in 1773 in Charleston for the purpose of "promoting the natural history of the province." Charles Wilson Peale, a taxidermist, had stressed natural history as well as art in his Philadelphia displays in the first half of the nineteenth century.[35] Such museums, however, were primarily demonstrational and eclectic: the BSNH hoped to be educational.

Alluding to the recently established Museum of Comparative Zoology in Cambridge, Scudder pointed out that an attempt to engage in competition for a research collection would squander the BSNH's resources. Instead he suggested that the Society try to maintain a popular museum aiming midway between entertainment and research. Its collection would display characteristic forms of organic life and inorganic matter didactically and would also offer a complete demonstration of local New England flora and fauna;[36] extraneous specimens and multiples were to be eliminated.

Scudder, like other young scholars educated at Harvard in the late 1850s and early 1860s, had come under the influence of the mellowing Louis Agassiz at a time when the statesman of science devoted much of his attention to educational projects. A number of Agassiz's students during this period devoted themselves to careers that combined their interest in science with organizational leadership. Several of Scudder's student colleagues, including Frederick W. Putnam, A. S. Packard, A. E. Verrill, and Edward S. Morse, became institutional leaders. Science museums in Chicago and Rochester as well as in nearby Worcester, Massachusetts, trace their origins to the enterprise of Agassiz and his students.[37]

One young student, Alpheus Hyatt, whose respect was so intense that rumor credited him with having memorized Agassiz's famous "Essay on Classification" by heart, shifted from engineering to natural history before graduating with a B.S. in 1863.[38] He joined Putnam at the Peabody Academy (later the Essex Institute) and helped found *The American Naturalist* in 1867, serving as one of its editors. In 1870 this relatively young naturalist was chosen to direct the activity of the BSNH on a regular basis as custodian, a position he held to his death in 1902. Hyatt's persistence helped stabilize the Museum.[39]

Given a changing membership roster and increasing administrative demands, the BSNH moved from volunteers to paid specialists for the day-to-day running of the museum. This change was justified by the need to make administration more efficient, but it also indicated that fewer members had the appropriate combination of leisure time and expertise to contribute to the organization and maintenance of a functional museum. Hyatt's appointment as professor of zoology and paleontology at the Institute of Technology, located conveniently next to the BSNH, formed a symbolic link between the two institutions. The bylaws explicitly placed the custodian in an ongoing supervisory position: "He shall have the immediate charge of the Museum and sole direction and supervision of the work of any person employed as an assistant therein." The council asked

Hyatt to report on the state of the museum and to provide a plan compatible with their desire to create a new public establishment. Within a few months Hyatt had not only reported back on intentions for museum display but had undertaken additional educational activities as well.

On July 6, 1870 Hyatt's "Proposed Plan of Organization" was adopted by the council. The plan stated that the museum was maintained "especially for the instruction of teachers, general students, and the public."[40] While the collections could still be used for research, they were to be displayed in an easily understood and developmental arrangement that demonstrated the nature of organic life. A wide-ranging collection with multiples for dissection was no longer the goal; rather Hyatt noted "to be strictly popular and educational, [the Museum] should be unencumbered by any very large collection."[41] In addition to its didactic display, which was intended to conform to evolutionary concepts without explicitly so stating, the museum would give the "greatest care and attention to the illustration of the Natural History of New England, and especially of the state of Massachusetts."[42] A major step had been taken in the field of museology. Earlier collections tended either to be entertaining and popular or to focus on research. Under Hyatt's leadership, the Boston Society pioneered in a new conception of a teaching museum. Ten years later in a speech accepting the presidency of the BSNH, Samuel Scudder could, with some justification, claim uniqueness for the museum: "This Society, like natural history societies everywhere, holds its stated meetings for discussions, and publishes the researches of its members; like most Societies in America it supports a museum. But its distinctive aim is educational."[43] Earlier Hyatt himself had indicated, "What we have been and are striving to do is as revolutionary in the management of museums as was the first attempt to open a circulating library for the public."[44]

Although Hyatt emphasized the museum ideal, he also pointed out the need for research facilities. He was personally skeptical about accepting full-time administrative responsibility (there was some discussion about consolidating offices and making a curator the full-time administrator) and he did not want to lose entirely his own opportunity for research. Yet he was a realist about the relationship between scientific researchers and curators producing displays. Throughout his tenure, Hyatt continued his own research and persuaded various patrons to underwrite minimal salaries for advanced students and two local women (Miss Carter and Miss Washburn) to keep the collections in order. In a letter to his friend Scudder in the early 1870s, he commented sarcastically on the expectation of a New York City museum to provide salaries and work space for specialists. In his observation was the seed of awareness that the BSNH had not been able to move simultaneously in two directions:

Doubtless he [the new director] is right to a certain extent, but then workers will be in a degree as little to be depended upon and as constantly changing as they used to be at our Society. It is the old plan, which all scientific institutions are so fond of, petting the scholar and starving the teacher, encouraging general scientific studies and throwing by their example and council insurmountable obstacles in the way of the special, professional student. What is one thing which makes Boston desirable [is that] science is no longer a show, and its followers can occupy themselves in real work without fear of displeasing the public upon whom they must depend even here.[45]

His observation held a hint of bravado since the public proved more fickle than he admitted.

As director, Hyatt did far more than reorder the collections. He actively engaged in educational programming, aiming for an audience that was neither the professional nor the curious public but rather the elementary and secondary educators teaching science in their classrooms. He credited Louis Agassiz with recognizing "that the future progress of science in this country must largely depend upon the good will of the people" and felt Agassiz had "created by his own efforts that popular respect for natural history which we now find throughout the country."[46] Turning aside a BSNH council decision of 1858 not to offer a lecture series, Hyatt planned a number of educational programs, pointing out to skeptics that an informal set of offerings in 1866 and 1869 had been highly successful.[47] Because the Society was operating on a tight budget, he arranged with the trustees of the Lowell Institute to sponsor four free science courses for local teachers. The following year, with financial assistance from a generous member and patron, John Cummings, the Teachers School of Science was formally put into operation. Local school masters and teachers were enthusiastic.

Seven hundred prospective registrants affixed their signatures to a circular describing the program. The timing was excellent. One principal, J. A. Page of the Dwight School, noted, "I felt a good deal of sympathy, having just read Herbert Spencer."[48] Darwin's controversial theory of evolution, tales of western geological exploration, and the establishment of an extensive public school system in Boston all reinforced support for the Society's new undertaking.

The twelve to sixteen week lecture series covered such topics as physical geography, mineralogy, zoology, and botany. The lectures were accompanied by laboratory work, and specimens were furnished to students whenever possible. The lecturers for the course were to be professors from the neighboring Institute of Technology, thus insuring high standards. At the same time, the circular promised that the scholars selected would be familiar with the "object method" of teaching and that their lectures would be "practical and familiar." In a letter to the committee of masters, Hyatt observed:

The diffusion of the knowledge of Natural Science among the people may be aided and assisted by public lectures on Science, but no very decided or permanent good can be anticipated, unless the minds of young people can be acted upon.

Success, therefore, in reaching the roots of all instruction which lie in our Primary and Grammar Schools, can only be satisfactorily attained when all the teachers of the Public and Private Schools join heartily in the enterprise.

Qualified scientific workers and lecturers are too few, and too much absorbed by strictly professional duties to act of themselves and directly upon the scholars; they must depend upon the teachers.[49]

Hyatt and the Society had not abandoned their goal of contributing to the advancement of science, but they were willing to acknowledge that they might have to take an alternative path to that end.

Measured by participation rates, the Teacher's School of Science was a success; however, in terms of financial support, its future was by no means secure. The Society felt that the lectures should be free of charge, but ongoing support proved difficult to arrange. John Cummings continued to underwrite the effort as did two "anonymous ladies"; intermittently, support came from the Lowell family trust funds. Lucretia Crocker (1829–1886), an early graduate of the Normal School at West Newton and supervisor of science for the Boston public school system, helped to raise money for the Teachers School (which she felt offered an essential supplement to typical normal school education in science), publicized its offerings, and did all the necessary paper work—in addition to her regular duties as teacher of mathematics, geography, and natural history.[50] Prominent Boston area women including Elizabeth Agassiz, Mrs. Quincy A. Shaw, and Mrs. John Forbes contributed substantially. In late 1878 when the School nearly died for lack of financial support, Crocker raised money from subscribers, primarily women whose individual donations were small but who collectively underwrote the program for nearly six hundred teachers the following summer; again Crocker did the necessary paper work to revive the School's operations.[51] The impecunious BSNH was concerned about public outreach yet reluctant to devote its own funds to support the various educational projects beyond the museum itself. The Society's commitment was changing but not transformed. Its preference was for mutual discussion with an educated, culturally atuned public rather than for education.

The Museum's laboratory was used not only in the teaching program but also by Institute of Technology students during the new college's "lean years" in the 1870s. After 1870, when Hyatt began teaching at Boston University, those students, too, were permitted to use the Society's facilities. Unencumbered by the professional pretentions that excluded women from the Institute, the supervisor of the Society's laboratory also allowed four women to work there, and the *Annual Report* for 1875–1876 stated that the laboratory "has been made useful to a very important and earnest movement for the diffusion of knowledge among women." Doubtless most of the persons attending the sponsored lecture series for teachers were also women. Without an alternative means for advanced study in science, they turned to Crocker who, in 1877, asked the laboratory director to teach the women zoology on a level appropriate for high school education.[52] This new Saturday laboratory program attracted nearly thirty local teachers each year. The teachers were a gratifying audience, one that was intermediate between researchers and the curious public.

The general public lectures, which had been a staple of the early Society, were virtually eliminated by 1877. The Society had found an alternative means of reaching the public through the museum and the teachers' training programs. As an alternative to public lectures the Society published a series of "Guides for

Science Teaching,'' as well as a number of general and special guides to the Museum itself. The printed word was a more effective teaching device for a public that wanted to wander through the Museum and absorb science at its own pace and inclination. Reviewing the Society's activity during the ten years of Hyatt's leadership, the Annual Report for 1881–1882 claimed, ''the Museum is capable of becoming an instrument of public culture unequalled in the power of awakening intellectual appreciation of the usefulness of its work in the minds of those visiting its collections.''[53] Public rather than scientific usefulness had become the new aim of the Society and it seemed, at least to Hyatt, that the BSNH had not only achieved a measure of success in this direction but was capable of much more.

By 1880, the Museum and the Teachers' School of Science were well established. However, an effort to make the Society's meetings more directly relevant to practicing researchers through special subsectional meetings in botany, entomology, and microscopy had been less effective. Again reordering seemed essential. Changes in the constitution and bylaws consolidated more authority under the custodian, whose title was changed to curator, and eliminated the largely honorary curatorial titles of some members.[54] Throughout the following decade, efforts were made to invigorate the Society, especially by advertising in advance topics to be presented at meetings. Prominent speakers still drew a good crowd from among the four hundred nominal members, but only a faithful few continued to participate regularly in meetings. Research efforts waned as the paid administrative staff (curators, librarians, and assistants) responsible for the Museum put its energy into arranging the collections and the educational programs.

In 1881, the Women's Education Association, noting as Crocker had earlier that several young women ''have made excellent progress and are prepared for more advanced study in the classes at the Society,'' offered to help underwrite a more intensive course to meet their needs. Hyatt, familiar with Agassiz's earlier experiment at Penikese Island, readily undertook the project, and a seaside laboratory was established at Annisquam in the summer of 1882. For the next six years the summer school was run primarily by G. H. Van Vleck, under the supervision of Hyatt. Since it supported only the experimental stages of the project, the Women's Educational Association called a meeting of biology teachers at the BSNH in 1887 to solicit an evaluation of the program and recommendations for the future. The teachers emphasized the importance of the summer sessions as a supplement to the normal school curriculum and recommended both the establishment of a marine biological laboratory and a drive to raise money for its independent foundation. Within a few years the Marine Biological Laboratory at Woods Hole was in operation. Its development into a well-recognized research center was quite different from the educational forum anticipated by some early supporters.[55] Once again, having identified and met a need, the BSNH was superceded by a more highly specialized institution.

An apparent opportunity to expand the Society's usefulness in the local com-

munity appeared in 1887 when the Park Commission of the City of Boston
inquired whether the Society was interested in participating in the proposed park
network initially designed by Frederick Law Olmsted.[56] For the next two years
the Society met regularly and considered various plans and the costs involved in
incorporating the museum ideal with outdoor parks. Finally, in December 1889,
the Society issued a narrowly circulated memorandum urging the formation of a
natural history garden and requesting two hundred thousand dollars for the project. The proposal excited the active members who hoped to take advantage of the
conservation movement in order to create "outdoor museums." The secretary of
the Society, J. Walter Fewkes, suggested that just as the Society in an earlier
generation had initiated a state natural history survey with public implications, so
in a later generation it was taking the lead in general scientific education.[57] The
second project was of more obvious and immediate public benefit.

The Society assigned a subcommittee to investigate how zoological gardens
were funded and administered elsewhere. The report indicated that the paternal
care that the French government offered the Jardin des Plantes was unlikely in the
United States, and that the zoological gardens in New York City's Central Park
experienced difficulty under local political control. It seemed that the Zoological
Garden in London, with its income from admissions, membership fees, and
bequests and with its professional museum staff, was the most realistic model for
Boston. Another subcommittee considered the scope and function of an outdoor
museum and drew up an elaborate tripartite plan to establish a marine aquarium
at City Point in South Boston and a fresh water aquarium and natural history
garden at Franklin Park. In an effort to raise funds, Samuel Scudder gave a
number of public speeches, including one subsequently printed for circulation
entitled, "Can We Have A 'Zoo' In Boston?" In his presentations, he attempted
to overcome a supposed conflict between the "scientific" and the "practical,"
arguing that the former often assisted the latter. Gone was his earlier assumption
that the larger society was eager and interested in learning and advancing science. Response to the publicity efforts underscored his increased awareness of
public apathy and skepticism.

Cautiously members agreed that they would begin the new program only after
raising half the required amount needed for support. A nationwide depression in
the early 1890s did not aid their efforts; nor did public assumption that the
Society was a group of rich old men who could themselves pay the costs. For a
number of reasons, the money was not raised and in December of 1893 William
Niles, president of the BSNH, reported to the Park Commission, "A vote has
just been passed to abandon, for the present, an effort to secure funds for the
establishment and support of Natural History Gardens and Aquaria."[58]

This effort proved the last grand scheme of the BSNH. Patrons were few and
the public was not interested. In 1891 the value of the Teachers' School was
reassessed and the school closed. In explaining the abandonment of a program
whose attendance had fallen dramatically, Hyatt began by noting that when the
school had been founded few teachers had any knowledge of natural history.

Twenty years later most teachers were too well-educated to need the general survey courses offered by the Society. The Saturday Laboratory courses continued and, in fact, were slightly increased in number, proving that the normal schools had not yet assumed responsibility for advanced science teaching. However, these supplementary courses were also eliminated within another decade.

A major donation of miscellaneous collections from the estate of Moses Kimball near the end of the century represented the last of the old eclecticism. The Society was given only three days to move the acquisitions and could not properly assess them in advance. Numerous problems were encountered, especially in transporting the stuffed elephants. The superintendent of police refused to allow them to be taken out and carried through the streets until after midnight. When they arrived at the Society, they could not fit through the doors and had to be hoisted through one of the front hall windows in the early hours of the morning.[59] Many events in the transfer were equally humorous but the gift only served to further dramatize the inadequacy of the Society's financial resources. It cost a thousand dollars to move and repair the collection. As in the past when money was tight, the Museum closed its doors from December to March because it could not afford to heat the massive building. A museum, as Scudder had predicted, could scarcely depend on private funding alone for its existence.[60]

Yet with membership and educational functions nearly eliminated by the turn of the century, the Museum had become the core of Society activity. A few dedicated members and staff sustained the two organizations in tandem until the end of the century. Hyatt died in 1902, and the annual reports slipped back to a compendium of donations received, combined with updated reports on each of the Museum's collections. As costs increased, there were also fewer scholarly publications and guidebooks; when a generous patron could not continue to underwrite the guide's salary, that project was ended as well. In an effort to pare down its responsibilities, the Society arranged to transfer all specimens in storage that were not relevant for display to the Museum of Comparative Zoology (MCZ) at Harvard and received in exchange some additional New England items for the museum. Its collections would, therefore, be primarily for teaching rather than the research conducted at the MCZ.

In the early decades of the twentieth century, the staff used a variety of tactics to expand the museum's visibility and usefulness, including field courses in structural geology and geography. It also conducted geological tours in the greater Boston area for local residents, sponsored Saturday morning activities for children, and presented "Natural History by Radio." Attendance at the museum remained steady year by year, increasing on days when admission was free.

While the Boston Society of Natural History temporarily expanded its membership in various recruitment campaigns, it never regained its momentum as an active society. Minutes suggest resignation rather than crises. There was neither the energy nor leadership necessary to reorganize an amateur society along the lines of such competing new groups as ornithological and conservation clubs. If in the nineteenth century the Society was a small natural history club, in the twentieth, it seemed most able to provide a casual meeting place for the general public. The *Proceedings* were replaced by a pamphlet *Bulletin* featuring popular articles and pictures. Any person interested in supporting the museum was welcome to join the Society; only a membership fee was required. The regular meetings of the Society were held in a newly refurbished hall and "light refreshments" were served to a socially compatible audience. The presentations were nontechnical and titles listed in the 1920s indicate that many were essentially travelogues, complete with lantern slide shows. Council records reflect an all-consuming concern with the finances of the Museum; Society members often had no special interest in natural history but were known for their intellect or their business acumen.[61]

The scientific society intended by its founders to advance the frontiers of science had been, in a hundred years's time, transformed into a public museum. In retrospect, the transformation was logical. Had the BSNH attempted to persist as a closed corporation of part-time nature lovers, it would certainly have failed to have any impact on science or the public. Its determination to limit activity and to shape its Museum for educational purposes, although reluctantly supported by many members, proved imminently practical in terms not only of survival but also of usefulness. The decisions of the Society's leaders were often ad hoc responses to specific requests or to an observed need. Sometimes the transitions in planning included the painful admission of earlier failure. Defensive explanations accompanied the description of new programs. In its uncertain search for a responsible role, the BSNH is an indicator of the awkward position of individual amateurs as they lost initiative and found themselves compelled to react to public as well as scientific expectation.

Yet, while the Society appears to run counter to the main current of professionalism, it was, in a curious way, in the vanguard. It provided a forum for discussion, a professional publication outlet, and a research collection at a time when older modes proved outdated and new techniques were still in the formative stages. Once other professional groups absorbed these activities, the BSNH moved into the arena of education, providing both laboratory space and supervision to college students from the Institute and Boston University as well as courses for public school teachers whose normal school training was inadequate in science. As educational institutions expanded their curricula and built appropriate facilities, the Museum, made functional for a general public, became the primary focus for the Society and remained a learning instrument—today the Boston Museum of Science—long after the Society itself faded from existence. Science had lost a cohort but it had gained an adept agent for popularization.

## Notes

Barbara Wiseman and Edward Pierce of the Boston Museum of Science Library were most helpful in giving me current information on Museum administration and allowing me the use of materials under their charge.

1. The two opening quotations are from Amos Binney, *Remarks Made at the Annual Meeting of the Boston Society of Natural History, June 2, 1845* (Boston: Freeman and Boyle, 1845), p. 8; and from Samuel H. Scudder, *Annual Report of the Boston Society of Natural History for 1869–1870*, p. 326.

2. Among the most important studies of colonial and early national science and scientific institutions are Max Meisel, *A Bibliography of American Natural History: The Pioneer Century, 1796–1865,* 3 vols. (New York: Hafner Press, 1924–26); Brooke Hindle, *The Pursuit of Science in Revolutionary America, 1735–1789* (Chapel Hill, N.C.: University of North Carolina Press, 1956); and Raymond P. Stearns, *Science in the British Colonies of North America* (Urbana, Ill.: University of Illinois Press, 1970). Most studies of local scientific institutions considered only the antebellum period when such groups enjoyed regional prestige and were productive for science. Thus, little has been written about the subsequent history of groups that were bypassed by emerging professionals.

3. Linda K. Kerber, "Science in the Early Republic: The Society for the Study of Natural Philosophy," *William and Mary Quarterly* 29 (1972): 279–80.

4. Aside from the reference in Meisel, *Bibliography,* the history of the society is best traced in a single bound volume kept by the secretaries, "Regulations and Records of the New England Society for the Promotion of Natural History established at Boston, December, 1814—the Linnaean Society of New England," which is in the library of the Boston Museum of Science (hereafter cited as BMS). The initial meeting of the Linnaean Society was held on December 18, 1814 at Dr. Jacob Bigelow's home; Dr. Walter Channing presided. The first roster lists nineteen members. The minutes suggest that the early years were spent recruiting new members and soliciting specimens for the cabinet. Attendance was promoted through a system of fines and elimination for nonattendance. The presentations given at meetings more frequently detailed excursions than presented a systematic analysis of findings. Although after 1817 the meetings were held at the Boston Atheneum, attendance declined until the group's demise in the early 1820s.

5. A. A. Gould's comments in the Boston Society of Natural History *Proceedings,* 4 (November 4, 1863): 335–40. The only narrative accounts of the Society were completed by members on anniversary occasions. Best is Thomas T. Bouvé (local clothing merchant and treasurer of BSNH), *Historical Sketch of the Boston Society of Natural History* (Boston: Boston Society of Natural History, 1880), which simply summarizes year-by-year activities and offers sketches of leading members. See also *The Boston Society of Natural History, 1830–1930* (Boston: Boston Society of Natural History, 1930). The BMS has an extensive collection of the printed and manuscript records of the Boston Society of Natural History (hereafter cited as BSNH) including its intermittant correspondence files from 1837 to 1883.

6. For an account of the amateur aspects of the BSNH's early years see Sally Gregory Kohlstedt, "The Nineteenth-Century Amateur Tradition: The Case of the Boston Society of Natural History," in *Science and Its Public: The Changing Relationship,* eds. Gerald Holton and William Blanpied (Dordrecht, Holland: D. Reidel, 1976).

7. In *Memorial Meeting of the Boston Society of Natural History, December 16, 1891* (Boston, 1892), the author of a eulogy on David Humphreys Storer noted that in 1831 six of seven officers and four of eight curators were physicians and that as late an 1855, six of seven officers and seven of eleven curators were doctors of medicine. As Joseph Lovering, a prominent methematician at Harvard, observed in his essay on "Boston and Science" for Justin Winsor's *Memorial History of Boston . . . 1630–1880,* 4 vols. (Boston: J. R. Osgood, 1880–81), 4:489–526, "a large part of the work done in science in every field has been accomplished by amateurs otherwise engaged in earning a support. In the last century and before, it was the clergy,—and at a later period it was the physicians,—who recruited the ranks of scientific men."

8. Many individuals like Walter Channing, George B. Emerson, Augustus A. Gould, and Amos Binney had established reputations for reform philanthropy or intellectual precocity in the Boston-Cambridge community.

9. F. W. P. Greenwood, "An Address Delivered before the Boston Society of Natural History," *Boston Journal of Natural History* 1 (1834–37): 12.

10. Edward Hitchcock was commissioned in 1830 to conduct the geological survey, which continued for three years and was renewed again in 1837. Copies of the reports and some specimens were deposited with the BSNH. See *Report of the Re-examination of Economical Geology of Massachusetts* (Boston: Dutton and Wentworth, 1838), p. 6.

11. J. E. Teschamacher, *Address Delivered at the Annual Meeting of the Boston Society of Natural History,* Wednesday, May 5, 1841 (Boston: Dutton & Wentworth, 1841), p. 5.

12. Although at times condescending in tone, Louis Leonard Tucker's "Ohio Show-Shop': The Western Museum of Cincinnati, 1820-1867" in *A Cabinet of Curiosities,* ed. Whitfield J. Bell, Jr. et al. (Charlottesville, Va.: University Press of Virginia, 1967) suggests in vivid terms the alternative path followed by some other societies.

13. *Proceedings of the BSNH* 2 (1845): 65. For an excellent discussion of the pattern of public enthusiasm in revealing a hoax, see Neil Harris, *Humbug: The Art of P. T. Barnum* (Boston: Little, Brown, 1973).

14. A. A. Gould's correspondence, preserved at the Houghton Library, Harvard University, suggests that Gould himself was often the center of controversy, especially with regard to the priority claims for identification of new specimens. See particularly Gould's correspondence with James G. Anthony of Cincinnati and Charles Baker Adams at Middlebury College, Middlebury, Vt.

15. A. Hunter Dupree, *Asa Gray, 1810-1888* (New York: Atheneum, 1968), p. 21.

16. Edward Lurie, *Louis Agassiz: A Life in Science* (Chicago: University of Chicago, 1960), p. 162.

17. Ibid., pp. 252-302.

18. Its printed publications are useful but of varying quality. In the 1830s some notices of meetings were printed in Benjamin Silliman's *American Journal of Science and Arts* and after 1841 a record of regular and annual meetings is found in the Society's *Proceedings.* An unpublished index for the *Proceedings,* 1841-1873, was prepared by Glover M. Allen and Harriet Biddle and is housed in the library of the BMS. Publications did not always appear regularly. In addition to the *Journal* and the *Proceedings,* the Society initiated *Memoirs* (1866-1947), which published highly specialized monographs on topics not necessarily related to New England, and a series of *Occasional Papers* (1869-1949), which covered topics of more local interest. In 1915 the *Bulletin of the Boston Society of Natural History* basically replaced the *Proceedings* (published intermittently to 1943) and was in turn supplanted by the *New England Naturalist* in 1938.

19. Margaret Rossiter, "Benjamin Silliman and the Lowell Institute: The Popularization of Science in Nineteenth Century America," *New England Quarterly* 64 (December 1971): 602-26.

20. For an excellent discussion of Agassiz's influence, see Lurie, *Louis Agassiz.*

21. Alexander W. Williams, *A Social History of the Greater Boston Clubs* (Barre, Mass.: Barre Publishers, 1970).

22. Perhaps the best single survey of scientific societies is Ralph S. Bates, *Scientific Societies in the United States,* 3d ed. (Cambridge: MIT Press, 1965), pp. 38-50. It documents the typical life-cycle of natural history societies as they flourished and declined along the Atlantic seaboard and then in the Midwest.

23. Michael B. Katz, *The Irony of Early School Reform: Educational Innovation in Mid-Nineteenth Century Massachusetts* (Cambridge: Harvard University Press, 1908). Katz's provocative study challenges the interpretation of the public school system as a movement toward democratic goals but underscores the availability of education in this period.

24. Council Minute Book for 1840-1861, BSNH mss., BMS. On December 7, 1857 the council voted to send a memorial to the legislature. A manuscript log containing the "Report of the Building of the New England Museum of Natural History at the corner of Berkeley and Boylston Street in the Back Bay of Boston" suggests that William Barton Rogers together with Drs. Cabot, Binney, and Kneeland were critical supporters of this move. In an effort to attract public attention to the proposals, Rogers spoke to a number of public audiences. Finally, the legislature did give a grant to the BSNH and to the Institute of Technology; the Horticultural Society withdrew from its earlier commitment because of the opposition of some of its members. The BSNH received a third of the total land grant.

25. For a popular account of the early Institute, see Samuel C. Prescott, *When MIT was 'Boston Tech,' 1861-1916* (Cambridge, Mass.: The Technology Press, 1954).

26. Although the BSNH has never had an archivist to manage its records, various officers apparently worked to preserve the manuscript records of the Society, and there also are a number of scrapbooks with newspaper clippings that record the public outreach in the 1850s, the 1870s, the 1880s, and the post-1890 period. In 1850 the BSNH council granted exclusive coverage rights to the *Boston Traveler,* but the scrapbooks indicate articles in the *Advertiser,* the *Journal* and the *Post* as well.

27. A summary of the activities are found with the printed version of Louis Agassiz, *Address Delivered on the Centennial Anniversary of the Birth of Alexander von Humboldt, under the Auspices of the Boston Society of Natural History* (Boston: Boston Society of Natural History 1869); the quotation is from p. 66.

28. Ibid., p. 68.

29. The "Plan of Organization" is found in the Minute Book of the Council, July 6, 1870, and was also separately printed by the Society as a pamphlet; the quotation is from the latter, p. 1.

30. A circular dated March 26, 1876, announcing changes in the bylaws regarding the membership of women and the two distinct categories of membership, admitted that the constituency had changed: "At present the membership of the Society included perhaps a large number who make no claims whatever to scientific knowledge; many of whom indeed, joined the Society by solicitation, simply for the Society's sake. The Society owes much of its usefulness to their pecuniary aid and moral support."

This cursory review does not do the Society full justice. During these intermediate years, some members continued to meet and to discuss research; the *Memoirs* and *Occasional Papers* were an important publication outlet, and the group cooperated with S. F. Baird at the Smithsonian Institution by sponsoring exploring expeditions and also worked with state and federal game and fish commissions to establish new policy regarding the preservation of certain species.

31. There is no full biographical account of Samuel Scudder, although he is included in most standard biographical dictionaries including, the *Dictionary of American Biography,* 20 vols. (1928–44), 16: 525–26. His private correspondence and entomological notes are deposited with the Boston Museum of Science.

32. *Annual Report of the BSNH* (1867–68), pp. 25–26. The annual reports, issued under various titles from 1864 to 1915, are bound as a series at the BMS. Pagination is not continuous because some reports are extracted from the *Proceedings of the BSNH* and some from separate publications. Subsequent references are to these volumes.

33. *Annual Report of the BSNH* (1869–70), p. 310.

34. Ibid., p. 326.

35. Alma Witten, *Museums: In Search of a Usable Future* (Cambridge: MIT Press, 1972), pp. 106–17.

36. The teaching museum was specifically designed to demonstrate Darwin's theory of evolution, but in order to avoid controversy, the Society decided not to use the term "evolution" in its descriptive material.

37. See Lurie's biography of Agassiz, and also Merrill E. Champion, "Edward Sylvester Morse with a Bibliography and Catalogue of his Species," *Occasional Papers on Mollusks* 1 (September 20, 1947): 129–44; and *Annual Report of the BSNH* (1873–74), p. 5.

38. The anecdote is recorded in the *Dictionary of American Biography,* 20 vols. (1928–1944), 9:446.

39. By the 1860s, a number of paid assistants worked in the library and with the collections. A member later recalled that in its "golden age" the "Society was . . . what might be called a delightful natural history club. . . . All the work upon the cabinets was done by members without pay. There may have been some neglect, but there was a vast amount of good work done in these days." *Memorial Meeting of the Boston Society of Natural History, December 16, 1891* (Boston: Boston Society of Natural History, 1892), p. 350.

40. The "Plan of Organization," p. 2.

41. Ibid., p. 5.

42. Ibid.

43. *Annual Report of the BSNH* (1879–80), p. 15.

44. Ibid. (1873–74), p. 3.

45. A. Hyatt to S. H. Scudder, n.d. and n.p., Scudder mss., BMS.

46. *Annual Report of the BSNH* (1873–74), p. 5.

47. The policy on public lectures was never clearly stated by the BSNH and such activity depended heavily on the Society's leadership at a particular time. A brief discussion of the two experimental lecture series are found in the annual reports for 1866 and 1870.

48. The letter dated October 27, 1871, is in the *Annual Report of the BSNH* (1871–72), p. 24.

49. Ibid., p. 27.

50. Edward T. James and Janet W. James, *Notable American Women,* 3 vols. (Cambridge: Belknap Press of Harvard University Press, 1971), 1: 407–8.

51. Ednah D. Cheney, *Memoirs of Lucretia Crocker and Abby W. May* (Boston, 1893). Although kept on the periphery, women made a substantial impact on the history of BSNH and, I suspect, of similar local societies. In a paper read at Harvard in May of 1974, I traced the movement for their membership in the BSNH, but the full extent of their participation merits further research.

52. *Annual Report of the BSNH* (1877–78).

53. Ibid. (1881–82), p. 1.

54. Ibid. (1880–82), p. 176. Hyatt noted, "The changes really occasioned no important revolution, and excited so little interest among the active members of the Society that the discussions with regard to them were wholly confined to technicalities." Also see *Constitution and Bylaws of the Boston Society of Natural History with a List of Officers and Members* (1883).

55. The statement of purpose is in a Women's Educational Association circular, undated, found in the BSNH scrapbooks. The Association, founded in 1871, helped sponsor the initial stages of projects that its members felt would advance women's educational opportunities. For a contemporary assessment of the program see Francis Zirngiebel, "Teacher's School for Science," *Popular Science Monthly* 55 (August and September 1899): 451–65 and 640–53. An ongoing account of the summer laboratory can be found in the BSNH *Annual Reports*.

56. A separate Minute Book records much of the Society's activity in relationship to the park proposal, including several subcommittee reports; the Minute Book of the Council is also helpful. In the early 1870s the BSNH had contemplated a zoological garden but determined that it was not economically feasible. Hyatt reported to Scudder that it was impossible because of the "universal system of doing everything on the free principle here in Boston" (1872 or 1873). Scudder mss., BSNH.

57. An updated pamphlet (probably 1891) entitled *Zoological Gardens and Aquaria for Boston: An Appeal*, (Boston: Boston Society Natural History), p. 6.

58. The wealthy industrialists had been supportive in the pre–Civil War period, and the Appletons, Lowells, and Cabots had helped support the young Society. The new wealthy classes were apparently disinterested in the older cultural organizations and the prominent Brahmin families that were concerned with public service after the war placed their energy and resources behind charitable institutions and schools. This shift in patterns of support for local science has never been systematically investigated, although Howard Miller, *Dollars for Research: Science and Its Patrons in Nineteenth-Century America* (Seattle, Wash., University of Washington Press, 1970) indicates that the newly wealthy interested in science sought to build monuments (observatories and research institutions) rather than support ongoing local efforts. A useful background discussion on Boston is found in Nathan Shiverick, "The Social Reorganization of Boston," in Williams, *Social History of Greater Boston Clubs,* pp. 128–43, and Frederick Jaher, "The Boston Brahmins in the Age of Industrial Capitalism," in *The Age of Industrialism in America,* ed. Frederick Jaher (New York: Free Press, 1968).

59. *Annual Report of the BSNH* (1893), p. 4.

60. Pride in private support persisted; as the centenary *Milestones* pointed out, "*In our hundred years of history, our Society has not made a public appeal for funds.*" (italics in text.)

61. The minute books taper in frequency and quality of entry through the 1920s; the last is dated 1932. In 1947 the Berkeley Street building was sold and the Society's trustees obtained a six-acre site on the Charles River Dam. At that time the name became the Boston Museum of Science in order to suggest a broader range of scientific display. The Society remained formally in existence until 1967 when the corporation of the Museum officially changed its own title to the Museum of Science but reserved the Society's name for future use.

# Comparison and Commentary

# The German
# Academic Community

## FRITZ K. RINGER

It has been generally held that German models played a significant role in the transformation of American higher education after 1865. Yet while certain conventional images of German learning were certainly invoked by academic reformers in the United States (and elsewhere) during the late nineteenth century, those images may have borne little resemblance to German realities.

In fact, as I shall try to show, the German universities of that time faced a series of practical and organizational problems that also arose in other Western societies, including the United States. Chief among these problems were the rapid advance of specialization and of applied study on the one hand, and the tension between research and teaching on the other. The issue of specialization became particularly serious in Germany and elsewhere during the decades around 1900 because an increasingly complex technology and social organization gave rise to an enlarged demand for educated specialists and for applied research. At the same time, the ancient tension between teaching and scholarship was heightened by rapidly rising enrollments, which were accompanied by limited but significant changes in the social origins of university students.

Yet while the American and German academic communities faced comparable problems, they apparently differed in their responses. In Germany, inherited ideals of learning as integral "cultivation" were distorted to accommodate, and simultaneously emphasized to repudiate, the realities of specialization and of applied research. An American observer of this process might interpret it in various ways. He might assimilate certain aspects of German academic rhetoric without following all its implications. Or he might be fascinated by the actual practices of German scholars and scientists in their seminars and institutes, while failing to comprehend either the ideological patterns in which these practices were understood or the wider system of social relations that helped to shape them. The invocation of German models by American academic reformers therefore cannot be accepted as full and accurate descriptions of German conditions and outlooks.

In reading some of the earlier chapters in this volume, particularly those by

Higham, Veysey, and Hawkins, I am struck by the extraordinary complexity of
the American university's responses to the problems and the often conflicting
demands it faced after 1865. Even when these problems had clear counterparts in
Germany, the responses took subtly different forms in the two societies. One of
the possible conclusions this suggests is that one can say very little about the
modern university in general, that one can talk intelligibly only about the
German university or the American university, recognizing that each is and has
been thoroughly rooted in its own social and cultural system. The other possible
conclusion, of course, is that we have scarcely begun to seek the insights that
might be derived from intensive cross-national comparisons in this field.


I

In comparable samples of the leading biographical encyclopedias for Germany, France, Britain, and the United States, the following percentages of male
biographees born between 1810 and 1899 were academics or other intellectuals:[1]

| Biographees | Germany | France | Britain | U.S. |
|---|---|---|---|---|
| | % | % | % | % |
| Academics | 45 | 16 | 20 | 15 |
| Clery | 4 | 7 | 8 | 8 |
| Artists, private scholars | 10 | 17 | 10 | 11 |
| Journalists, publicists | 3 | 7 | 7 | 11 |
| Total | 62 | 46 | 45 | 45 |

In the French sample, artists and private scholars were as numerous as university professors and related occupations. This in itself may shed light on certain
characteristics of French intellectual life. For the United States, the relatively low
share of academics is probably as revealing as the high percentage for journalists
and related occupations. But the outstanding numbers in the four distributions are
certainly those for Germany. Nearly two-thirds of all German entries were members of the intellectual occupations and not much less than half were academics.
It is hard to imagine a more graphic demonstration of the respect traditionally
accorded German professors and of the great importance of the universities in
modern German intellectual and social life.

Some of the general conditions that gave rise to the special vitality of the
German universities may be briefly considered. At bottom, they are closely
linked to Germany's distinctive road to modernity. Late industrialization combined with the survival of aristocratic dominance and of the bureaucratic
monarchy to create a middle class oriented less toward industry and commerce
than toward government service and the liberal professions.[2] Well into the
nineteenth century, as has often been noted, Germany remained an essentially
agrarian society. The influence of the landed aristocracy was extended through
its predominant role in the military and in other branches of the political system.

To the extent that modernization took place, it was the work less of private enterprise than of a rationalizing state bureaucracy. In the small provincial towns, a burgher stratum of artisans and petty tradesmen was no substitute for the entrepreneurial bourgeoisie of the more industrialized nations.

In these circumstances, higher education was in some ways the most visible path of upward mobility for a portion of the burgher stratum. Through higher education, the burgher could acquire the status of a notable. He might also come to share in the exercise of political power, at least in a subordinate way, by entering the state bureaucracy. Since higher education in fact became a prerequisite for entry into the civil service, a middle-class aristocracy of merit could compete with some success against the aristocracy of birth in the administrative system of the bureaucratic monarchy. Of course, state examinations also came to regulate access to the liberal professions. Theologians too were educated at the universities, and it must be remembered that the German *Aufklärung* did no significant damage to the cultural role of the Protestant pastorate. In short, there emerged in Germany a highly distinctive educated upper middle class composed of high government officials, liberal professionals, theologians, secondary teachers, and university professors. These occupations were sometimes called "academic," and they jointly made up the "educated" or "cultivated" stratum (*Bildungsschicht*), because their social distinction derived from learning rather than from birth or wealth. They held their place in German society during a period of transition when birth was no longer, and wealth was not yet, the chief determinant of social rank.

One way to describe the situation is to make use of Max Weber's distinction between class and status, in which class refers essentially to wealth and economic power and status to life style and social honor.[3] The fact is that status ranks, and education as a source of status, remained of considerable importance in early industrial Germany. It was only with the explosive industrialization of Germany after 1870 that the class society came to threaten the older status society and eventually to supersede it. But until the traditions of the status system were quite forgotten, the German university professor held a particularly eminent place in his society. He not only controlled admission to the civil service and to the "academic" professions generally; he also created and perpetuated the ideology of the educated elite, the symbols and instruments of its cultural leadership.

Among the tenets central to the ideology of the educated elite, the idea of *Bildung* should at least be touched upon. *Bildung* means education in the sense of "cultivation," the unfolding of a unique individuality through an integral engagement—not a merely analytical relationship—with a group of venerated sources, chiefly the classics. *Bildung* suggests something like a transfer of grace from the source to the learner. The cultivated man has the qualities of intellectual and spiritual aristocracy; he is a true rival and heir of the nobly born.[4]

Another element in what I have elsewhere called "mandarin ideology" is an emphasis upon the constitutive role of the human mind in the structure of the world as known. This is the Idealist element. In practice, it made German intellectuals particularly resistant to the fallacies of a doctrinaire positivism or scientism, and it also turned some of them against more consistently skeptical forms of empiricism. In any case, systematic knowledge or scholarship (*Wissenschaft*) in the Idealist sense must have a philosophical dimension. The particular must be studied and can be fully known only as an aspect of a totality. This is not to say, however, that German scholars could not perfectly well engage in highly specialized research. The Idealist impulse receded after 1830 and did not undergo a full-scale revival until after 1880. Nevertheless, the Idealist dimension always reemerged in some form when German academics became really self-conscious about their work and its meaning.

Finally, a word should be said about the traditional emphasis of German academics upon "pure" research and upon *Wissenschaft* for its own sake. This tenet was initially developed to ward off a danger that had been clear and present during the eighteenth century, and especially during the decades immediately before 1810. The danger was that the state, the universities' sole support, would insist on immediately practical learning, and that it would reduce the universities to mere training schools for higher officials. In response, the combination of research and teaching came to be regarded as essential to the character of the German university. Only contact with pure scholarship was thought to have the effect of *Bildung*. An animus developed, at least in principle, against applied research, and even the proverbial "freedom of *Wissenschaft*" was sometimes interpreted as though "pure" learning and "free" learning were essentially identical.[5]

Some of these axioms of the German academic ideology were first fully stated by Fichte, Schelling, Schleiermacher, and Humboldt during the decades preceding the founding of Berlin University in 1810. It has become customary to date the birth of the modern German university from the Prussian Reform Period and to regard the leading Idealists and neohumanists as its intellectual founders. That view may be chronologically too narrow and a little too personal as well. The most pertinent institutional innovations in Prussia extended from the 1780s to the 1830s. In addition to the measures that are usually mentioned, they included the introduction of a state examination that made secondary teaching a learned profession closely linked to the university faculties of philosophy. Other civil service and professional tests rounded out the state examination system. In the meantime, a series of regulations gradually elevated the classical *Gymnasium* above all other secondary schools. University matriculation was eventually reserved for those who had passed the leaving examination and earned the *Abitur* certificate from a *Gymnasium*. In this way, the educated elite defined itself and set itself off from the less qualified elements of the population.[6]

Among the academic disciplines, it was classical philology that defined new standards of scholarship and became the model of pure *Wissenschaft* in practice. The philological movement originated at Göttingen about 1750. It was decisively inspired by the neohumanist enthusiasm that swept the German literary and intellectual world toward the end of the eighteenth century. Friedrich August Wolf was in many ways the father of modern philological scholarship. But his interest in ancient Greek culture was comprehensive and historical, rather than narrowly textual or grammatical. As a pedagogue, he sought the perfect humanity and grace of classical Greece for his students. Both directly and through Humboldt, he contributed much to the emerging idea of *Bildung*. The classical *Gymnasium* and the new philologically oriented corps of secondary teachers probably owed more of their traits to Wolf than to anyone else.

The importance of Wolf's work lies in the fact that the development of philology paved the way for the emergence of a tradition of specialized empirical research in Germany by about 1830. Franz Schnabel was the first to point this out.[7] He believed that an ultimately romantic interest in the unique and the particular helped to lead German scholarship from the great Idealist systems to the critical methods and the detailed work of the later nineteenth century. He also noted that standards of exactitude in research that were transmitted from philology to other humanistic disciplines, especially to history, only gradually penetrated the natural sciences, which were the inexact and speculative disciplines of the early nineteenth century.

More recently, Steven Turner has traced the development of the modern "research imperative" to the German universities of the early nineteenth century, and to philology in particular.[8] According to Turner, the modern "dualistic" professor is more aware of the scholarly standards and demands of his fellow researchers in the discipline than of his teaching and other obligations to his local, collegial community. Turner further claims that the research imperative emerged first *in practice,* favored by specific institutional arrangements and by intradisciplinary developments in philology; only secondarily did it give rise to the first *theoretical* statement of the research imperative in the programmatic writings commonly regarded as the intellectual fundaments of the German university. It is an interesting hypothesis, but it may not do justice to those early proponents of the "research imperative" who were also passionate spokesmen for the theory of *Bildung,* the ideology of the emerging academic elite.

II

The dates of 1870 and 1920 do in fact mark important stages in the history of German universities and secondary schools. An early industrial phase in the evolution of German higher education gave way about 1860 to 1870 to a high industrial phase. The transition to a "postindustrial" phase is harder to date exactly, but about 1920 to 1930 is probably the most useful borderline. What has to be shown to justify the idea of three phases, of course, is that there were clear changes in the relationship between higher education and society about 1870 and again around 1920. Such changes can in fact be detected easily enough in the main quantitative characteristics of the German educational system, in the statistics on enrollments, on the social origins of students, and on the makeup and size of the faculty.[9]

Enrollments in German universities declined steadily and sharply throughout the later eighteenth and into the first decade of the nineteenth century. The recovery that followed became most rapid during the 1820s and culminated in an enrollment peak in 1830/1831. This high point, at about 0.5 students per thousand population, resulted in a much noted excess of graduates, some of whom were unable to find "appropriate" positions.[10] As might be expected, enrollments declined for a decade thereafter, settling finally on a stable plateau of about 0.3 to 0.4 students per thousand population, or around 0.5 percent of the age group in attendance at the universities. It seems reasonable to suggest that this plateau in university access between 1840 and 1870 reflected the real demand for graduates in the early industrial context. It is also worth noting that the variations in attendance at universities and academic secondary schools before 1840 stood in an inverse relationship to the economic outlook. So far as can be ascertained, university enrollments increased during recessionary cycles and decreased when business opportunities improved.

That in itself would suffice to characterize a distinctive early industrial phase in the history of German higher education. At least in the short run, there was at that point no positive correlation between industrial development and the growth of higher education. On the contrary, ambitious young men apparently decided to choose *either* education *or* business to get ahead in the world. In the long run, industrial development undoubtedly increased the demand for graduates even in the "nonproductive" occupations of lawyer, doctor, high official, and secondary teacher. But a really immediate and positive relationship between higher education and industrialization did not develop until after 1870. Before that time, the world of higher education was largely separated from the business world.

The exceptions, fortunately, prove the rule. In the 1860s and probably earlier, periods of prosperity were accompanied by growing enrollments in the nonclassical secondary schools and in the emerging technical institutes or their ancestors, the higher trade or polytechnical schools. Obviously, this sector of the educational system stood in a positive relationship to the economy. Its numerical significance before 1870, however, has been exaggerated. The German technical institutes enrolled less than 3,000 students in 1870, and almost 90 percent of secondary (*Abitur*) certificates were still conferred by the classical *Gymnasium* at that time. It was only at the nongraduate level that the modern secondary schools played an important role in early industrial Germany.

All this changed after 1860 and especially after 1870. During the closing decades of the century, the German economy not only expanded at unprecedented rates; it also came to involve advanced technology, and it therefore called for technically and scientifically educated men. The development of German higher education between 1870 and 1921 is summarized in the following percentages of relevant age groups who attended secondary schools, earned the *Abitur,* reached universities, or reached all university-level institutions:[11]

| Date | Secondary Students | Abitur Certifs. | University Students | All University Level |
|------|--------------------|-----------------|---------------------|----------------------|
|      | % | % | % | % |
| 1870 | 2.3 | 0.8 | 0.5 | 0.5 |
| 1900 | 2.7 | 0.9 | 0.8 | 1.1 |
| 1911 | 3.2 | 1.2 | 1.2 | 1.5 |
| 1921 | 6.0 | 1.3 | 2.0 | 2.7 |

A more detailed consideration of the evidence reveals that the growth in German secondary education after 1870 took place entirely in the nonclassical secondary schools: the *Realgymnasium,* the *Oberrealschule,* and their forerunners and affiliate institutions. As the *Gymnasium's* share of *Abitur* certificates fell to two-thirds by 1911, modern secondary graduates entered the technical institutes in growing numbers. They made their way even into the university faculties of philosophy (arts and sciences) toward the end of the century, and especially after 1900. In 1899, the technical institutes themselves became university-level institutions with the right to confer doctorates. By 1921, a further group of higher professional schools and academies could fairly be counted with the universities. In short, much of the growth in university-level education, along with the entire increase in secondary enrollments, was due to the addition of new institutions, subject areas, and groups of students.

One has the impression that a new system of education was simply superimposed upon an older one. The impression is confirmed by a look at the changing distribution of university students over the various fields of study. Between the early nineteenth century and the eve of the First World War, that distribution evolved roughly as follows, in rounded percentages by row:[12]

| Period | Theology | Law and Gov't. | Medicine | Humanities | Sciences | Minor Fields |
|--------|----------|----------------|----------|------------|----------|--------------|
|        | % | % | % | % | % | % |
| 1830–1860 | 30 | 30 | 15 | 15 | 5 | 5 |
| 1860–1890 | 20 | 25 | 20 | 15 | 10 | 10 |
| ca. 1911 | 10 | 20 | 20 | 25 | 15 | 10 |

More precise percentages would be useless; considerable short-term fluctuations in the figures would only obscure the more consistent long-term trends. These trends included the very marked decline in the number of students in theology and the slower reduction in the concentration in law. In general, the professional faculties lost ground to the humanities, to the natural sciences, and to other subjects taught in the faculty of "philosophy," which accounted for over half of university enrollment by 1911.

During the early nineteenth century, university study had been essentially a preparation for the clergy, the law, high officialdom, and medicine. Despite the intellectual founders' insistence upon the place of the "philosophical" faculty at the heart of the new university, few students entered the arts and sciences, and those who did were probably interested for the most part in secondary teaching as a career. All this changed after 1870 and especially around the turn of the century. Some of the increase in the size of the philosophical faculty may have been due to expanding opportunities in secondary teaching, and in the nonclassical schools above all. As of 1911, the natural sciences still enrolled a smaller portion of German university students than the humanities. Future secondary teachers of German and of modern languages probably made up a significant share of the humanities students. Still, the increase in the percentages for the sciences was certainly considerable, particularly since it was accompanied by the simultaneous growth of the technical institutes.

The figures strongly suggest, as a matter of fact, that a number of university graduates in the sciences and in other fields were beginning around 1900 to enter careers in business or in some of the newer professions, high white-collar, and service occupations. After the First World War, this happened with increasing frequency, and that is one reason to suspect that a new "postindustrial" phase in the history of German higher education opened around 1920.

It is worth outlining the main characteristics of this third, "postindustrial," phase, if only to set off the main traits of the second, high industrial, phase. First, there were further and rapid increases in enrollments per age group after 1920, which once again created an oversupply of educated men.[13] Apparently, an inherited sense that only certain specific occupations were appropriate for university graduates was being painfully altered. In the meantime, the old distinctions between the various streams or tracks within the educational system lost some of their former sharpness and significance. The Weimar Republic introduced the common school to age 10. The curricular differences that separated the *Gymnasium* from the other academic secondary schools were reduced, and statisticians actually began to ignore the old distinctions. Even the status gap between the universities and the technical institutes became more a memory and less a fact. As late as 1960, German enrollment ratios suggested nothing like "mass" secondary or higher education. Still, there was a sense from 1920 or 1930 on that a larger percentage of the population was being trained in a less compartmentalized system for a somewhat more inclusively defined set of positions in the emerging white-collar hierarchy.[14]

But that was a radical departure from the patterns prevalent between about 1870 and 1920. For the main characteristic of the second, industrial, phase was a sharp contrast between a traditional and a modern sector within the educational system. The modern secondary schools confronted, fought, and eventually outstripped the traditional *Gymnasium*. The technical institutes struggled for equality with the universities, and the arts and sciences challenged the hegemony of the older professional faculties. Taken as a whole, the process was an adjustment to the requirements of the high industrial economy. But it was a very painful adjustment, and one in which the new class society came in conflict with the status system that had reserved a special place for the "academic" stratum.[15]

A note on the social origins of German students will make this picture clearer.

It will also shed further light on the German universities' extraordinary vitality during the nineteenth century. One of the most fascinating surveys on the family background of German students lists fathers' occupations for the roughly eighty-five thousand graduates of all Prussian secondary schools between 1875 and 1899. It also reports on the occupational plans of the graduates themselves. This data permits us to compare the social origins (in) with the social destinations (out) of these students. In summary percentages by column, one obtains the following distributions:[16]

|  | Gymnasium | | Realgym-nasium | | Oberreal-schule | | All Schools | |
|---|---|---|---|---|---|---|---|---|
|  | In | Out | In | Out | In | Out | In | Out |
|  | % | % | % | % | % | % | % | % |
| "Academic" professionals | 21 | 75 | 7 | 26 | 5 | 12 | 19 | 68 |
| Military, lower officials, and teachers | 22 | 12 | 21 | 26 | 17 | 16 | 22 | 14 |
| Technical professionals or officials | 4 | 7 | 7 | 30 | 9 | 56 | 5 | 11 |
| Agriculture | 13 | 2 | 9 | 4 | 5 | 2 | 12 | 3 |
| Businessmen, artisans | 32 | 4 | 48 | 10 | 57 | 11 | 35 | 4 |
| Others, unknown | 8 | . . . | 8 | 4 | 7 | 3 | 7 | . . . |

The special prestige of the *Gymnasium* is reflected in its relatively high rate of recruitment from the "academic" professions: jurists and high officials, secondary and university professors, theologians, and medical doctors. The modern schools, and particularly the *Oberrealschule,* by contrast, proved most attractive not only to the sons of innkeepers and artisans but also to the offspring of merchants and industrialists. At the same time, the *Gymnasium* sent the vast majority of its graduates into the traditionally learned professions, whereas the modern schools prepared substantial contingents of its students for the technical professions, the technical branches of the civil service, and the world of commerce and industry.

This kind of social and curricular specialization in an educational system I would call "tracking" or "segmentation." What strikes me about the segmentation of the German secondary system is that it was "socially horizontal." It did not merely separate the higher from the lower strata on a presumably unilinear scale of social standing; it also marked a behavioral difference between the sons of industrialists and those of lawyers, or between the offspring of lower officials and those of merchants and innkeepers. In fact, it separated the economic from the noneconomic middle and upper middle classes. It revealed the difference between the traditional status system and the gradually emerging class society.[17]

During the last quarter of the nineteenth century, Prussian *Gymnasium* graduates still outnumbered modern school graduates by about seventy-one thousand to thirteen thousand. The distributions for all secondary schools in the table above therefore do not differ very much from the *Gymnasium* pattern. Moreover, most secondary graduates at that time went on to some form of university-level education. The tabulated distributions constitute a capsule description of German higher education at the opening of its high industrial phase.

Two features seem particularly worthy of emphasis. First, the system as a whole was oriented almost exclusively toward the civil service and the learned professions. When it recruited students from the world of the burgher artisans and shopkeepers, or even from that of the large merchants and industrialists, it almost always routed its charges away from the "productive" occupations. If that was true at the end of the nineteenth century, the pattern must have been truly remarkable before 1870. Second, there was a quite surprising amount of upward social mobility in the German educational system of the nineteenth century. What might be called the noneconomic lower middle class of petty officials and primary teachers accounted for a wholly disproportionate share of the secondary graduates. But the early industrial burgher class was quite well represented also. Of course there was a high rate of self-recruitment among the academic professions. But the educated elite also attracted new aspirants from other sectors of a social system in which industrialization was not yet the main motor of modernization and social mobility.[18]

There is no place in this summary essay for a more detailed discussion of social mobility in German higher education. The rather ample information on the fathers of university students is too complex to be briefly described. On the whole, however, it would merely qualify the conclusions derived from the data on Prussian secondary graduates. Near the beginning of the nineteenth century, it appears, roughly half of German university students had fathers in the learned professions. As might be expected, this highly indicative proportion then declined throughout the nineteenth century, falling to around 20 to 25 percent by the eve of the First World War. At first, before 1870, the lower officials and teachers made up most of the ground that was lost by the educated upper middle class. Especially after 1870, however, the commercial and industrial middle class significantly increased its representation. Around 1875, the whole world of commerce and industry still accounted for no more than 25 to 30 percent of the university students. By the eve of the First World War, however, the share of the business classes had reached some 33 to 40 percent, which surpassed the representation of the academic stratum. To understand the full meaning of this change, one must remember that the economic middle class of the early twentieth century had little left in common with the provincial artisans and shopkeepers of the decades before 1870. In Thomas Mann's phrase, the bourgeois had replaced the burgher.[19] Indeed, that was part of the process in which the class society came to challenge the inherited status system. It is not surprising that this changing of the guard was painfully felt in the German academic community during the decades around 1900.[20]

One of the most intriguing questions that remains to be asked in this whole area of social mobility through higher education is whether the recruitment of German university students became significantly more "democratic" between 1870 and 1920. One tends to assume that the increase in enrollments per age group must have had such an effect. Yet the evidence raises serious doubts about such an assumption; indeed, it suggests the contrary. There are great difficulties involved in comparing occupational classifications and distributions in a changing social environment. Even so, the best hypothesis would seem to be that German higher education was not unambiguously more "democratic" in 1920 than it had been a century earlier.[21]

The more cheerful of the two morals that can be derived from this hypothesis is clearly the one to emphasize. During much of the nineteenth century, before industrialization became an overwhelming competitor, higher education was a very important channel of upward mobility in Germany. Access to the universities was surprisingly open. Many an academic was the son of a provincial pastor, petty official, or small-town burgher. When I seriously ask myself about the vitality of German scholarship during the nineteenth century, I am frankly less inclined to speculate about the effects of intellectual competition than to imagine an early industrial or even preindustrial environment in which the exalted ideology of *Bildung* was a possibility, and in which talented young men really wanted to be poets and thinkers.

## III

The international reputation of the German universities reached a high point during the closing decades of the nineteenth century. Materially, too, the universities had never been better off—the German governments were spending huge sums to build institutes and to support an increasingly complex research apparatus.[22] Yet at the same time, the German academic community faced very serious practical problems of adjustment to the high industrial context. Moreover, a widespread sense of tension and uneasiness gave rise to the conviction that German *Wissenschaft* and German culture generally were in a state of crisis, perhaps even in a decline that could no longer be arrested.

Pressing practical problems arose most immediately from the rapid expansion of the student body. On one level, the German universities responded successfully to this challenge, for they managed to enlarge the total faculty almost as rapidly as enrollments grew. But senior appointments did not keep pace, so there was considerable change in the internal structure of the academic profession. In the table that follows, the total numbers of faculty teaching as of 1864 and 1910

| | 1864 | | 1910 | |
|---|---|---|---|---|
| *Field* | *Total Faculty* | *% Full Professors* | *Total Faculty* | *% Full Professors* |
| Theology | 184 | 67 | 277 | 65 |
| Law | 188 | 62 | 253 | 61 |
| Medicine | 322 | 42 | 1,012 | 24 |
| Humanities | 356 | 50 | 747 | 47 |
| Sciences | 258 | 52 | 680 | 35 |
| All fields | 1,468 | 49 | 3,807 | 32 |

in various fields are listed, together with the percentages of the totals who were full professors (*Ordinarien*). The overall situation at the German universities is described for "all fields" at the bottom of the table.[23]

Obviously, the full professors increased much less rapidly than the lower-ranking faculty. This was particularly true in medicine and in the sciences, where increasing numbers of instructors (*Privatdozenten*) worked as research assistants in institutes that were typically directed by a single *Ordinarius*. Neither the associate professors (*Extraordinarien*) nor the *Privatdozenten* participated in the collegial self-government that was the right of the several faculties in purely academic affairs. The full and associate professors were salaried state officials. The *Privatdozenten* were not officials, and they generally drew at most a meager stipend. In principle, they were meant to support themselves from what students' fees they received for the "private" courses they announced. One of their difficulties was that the full professors also gave most of their lectures "privately" and monopolized the large courses that were de facto prerequisites for the state examinations.

All this remained bearable as long as the instructors could expect to pass on, after a few years of honorable poverty, to a more secure position. But by 1907, the average age of German instructors was 32.5 years, that of associate professors was 46 years, and that of full professors was almost 54 years.[24] Alexander Busch has argued that the lengthening period of unpaid "apprenticeship" tended to introduce a "plutocratic" element into the selection for academic careers; one almost had to have a private income to survive as a *Privatdozent*.[25]

As a matter of fact, there was a change in the social origins of German academics during the later nineteenth and early twentieth century that paralleled the shift in the background of students. Comparing the fathers of faculty who taught at German universities as of 1859 with those that began to teach between 1890 and 1919, one obtains the following percentages by column:[26]

| Occupation | 1859 | 1890–1919 |
|---|---|---|
| | % | % |
| "Academic" professions | 62 | 49 |
| Military, lower officials, and teachers | 12 | 11 |
| Agriculture | 5 | 5 |
| Large businessmen, merchants, rentiers | 13 | 30 |
| Tradesmen, clerks, workers | 8 | 4 |

Obviously, the learned professions retained a much larger representation among the fathers of academics than among the parents of students. Just as clearly, though, there was a characteristic shift in favor of the economic upper middle class, and no evidence at all of a "democratic" trend.

During the first decade of the twentieth century, the lower-ranking faculty at German universities began to draw together in what eventually became a nation-wide Junior Faculty Association. What they petitioned for, above all, was some share in academic governance. They achieved no results until after the First World War, when the republican authorities tried, without much success, to support their cause against the senior professors. What these developments betray is a serious flaw in the fabric of academic collegiality and a crisis of authority that expressed itself in rather unpleasant personal confrontations as well.[27]

Another practical problem the universities faced was the rivalry of the technical institutes, which raised their academic standards even as their enrollments increased. The debate that ensued was an almost perfect echo of the simultaneous controversy between the defenders of the classical *Gymnasium* and the champions of the modern secondary schools. In both cases, the question was whether the newer curricular path should be accredited equally with the traditional one. In both cases, the issue was settled in favor of the modernists by the turn of the century. And in both cases also, the traditionalists fought their defensive battle in the name of "pure" *Wissenschaft*.

It is hard to know how seriously to take the slogans that were exchanged. One has the impression, for example, that very few of the spokesmen for the *Gymnasium* honestly still held the view of classical culture as a model for all time. They tended instead to recommend Latin as good exercise for the mind. Or they insisted, even less convincingly, that the ancient languages were pedagogically valuable precisely because they were practically useless. At this point in the argument, they could draw upon the antiutilitarian element in the ideology of *Bildung*. But they now used that ideology in a narrow defense of what had clearly become a routine source of social privilege.

The same false note was struck by the overwhelming majority of university professors in their battle against the technical institutes. They insisted that these younger institutions should not be allowed to confer the doctorate because their research was predominantly of the applied sort.[28] No one should be allowed to hold an academic degree, they argued, who had merely prepared for the exercise of a profession. They totally forgot that the vast majority of university students had always done just that, and that the universities' own involvement in specialized and applied research was increasing every day.

Nothing throws as much light on the ambiguities of this situation as the foundation of the Kaiser-Wilhelm Society for the Promotion of the Sciences in 1911.[29] The decisive impetus came from Adolf von Harnack, who worked out the basic scheme for the Society in a memorandum of 1909. In his text, Harnack explicitly rejected the traditional and more or less official thesis that research and teaching were optimally combined at the German universities. Instead he argued the need for highly specialized research institutes to be directed by leading scientists and staffed by scholars who would be free of any teaching duties.

Bringing forward a more weighty argument, Harnack insisted that German science had fallen behind its competitors in the United States, England, and France. His evidence on this score was rather impressionistic, but he was especially emphatic about what such private donors as Rockefeller and Carnegie were doing for American science. In an approach that has since become all too familiar, he saw a ''national political danger'' in the progress of science abroad. He described the proposed institutes as powerful forces in the ''battle'' to ''wrest nature's secrets from her'' and to attain ''predominance in scientific research.'' ''Military prowess and science,'' he said, ''are the two great pillars of Germany's greatness, and the Prussian state has the duty to insure the preservation of both.''[30]

The whole purpose of Harnack's recommendation was to attract private wealth, including donations from large industrial concerns, to launch his projected research institutes. The donors, including the corporate ones, would have the right to assign their contributions to specific purposes. Harnack believed that this posed no threat to the purity of *Wissenschaft,* as long as appointed scholars and officials prominently represented the state on the society's governing senate. The way Harnack thought about these problems was absolutely characteristic of his milieu. Like other German scholars, he was quite unable to imagine that privately funded scholarship could coexist with even a measure of academic freedom. He wanted to avoid any ''dependence of *Wissenschaft* upon cliques and upon capital.'' He called for the protecting ''hand of the state, which is still juster than that of any party.'' He sought a path that would avoid the ''tyranny of the masses and of bureaucracy'' on the one hand, and the influence of ''cliques and of the money bag'' on the other.[31] In the end, such leading industrialists as Thyssen and Siemens became members of the Society's governing senate. But Harnack was the Society's first President, and William II was its Protector. Harnack had solved his problem of governance by making most of the Society's important decisions subject to the Emperor's approval. Obviously, it was becoming increasingly difficult to manipulate the ideology of pure *Wissenschaft* and *Bildung* in the high industrial context.

## IV

The unifying theme that ran through many of the writings of German academics during the decades around the turn of the century was the anxious sense of a loss of authority. In politics, the contemporary scene seemed dominated by an unprincipled clash among contradictory interests, chiefly those of capitalists and those of workers.[32] As money competed for influence with masses of organized votes, political conflict took on a purely quantitative aspect. A flat utilitarianism appeared to be the only motive of all participants in an increasingly depressing contest. This was the kind of ''interest politics'' that made critics want to stand ''above parties,'' to be ''unpolitical,'' or to urge the cause of ''the whole'' against ''egotism'' and ''materialism.'' Most German university professors by that time were more or less conscious defenders of the bureaucratic monarchy and of the social status quo. For them the lost authority might be that of the nation as a supraindividual ideal or that of the bureaucracy as an agent of purposes that transcended the destructive conflict of the parties.

But even men who avoided such simplicities were deeply disturbed at the apparent spiritual vacuum in public affairs. The contrasts that suggested themselves were with the Era of Reform in Prussia after 1806, with the Wars of Liberation against Napoleon, or with the Revolution of 1848. In those earlier days, the very objectives of political discourse had apparently been higher than they were at present. The old doctrine of the *Rechtsstaat* had made positive law an instrument of justice and of progress in morals. The ideal of the *Kulturstaat* had grown out of the close link between the cultural revival and the national movement during the decades around 1800; it tied the legitimacy of states to the cultural life that they represented and sustained. It seemed a long step down from these Idealist principles to the Benthamite formulas implied by the new party politics.

Moreover, the deterioration in the very style of politics was apparently connected with the displacement of an older set of political leaders. The educated notables of the Frankfurt Parliament had the autonomy as well as the inclination to debate political principles for the entire nation.[33] Many a *Reichstag* deputy around 1900, by contrast, was a hired professional and a mere agent. He was explicitly or implicitly bound to represent only the immediate interests of his voters or sponsors. Summing up these changes, German academics tended to argue that the human mind and spirit had somehow lost control in the world of politics.[34] This was partly a complaint about the lack of principle in the new politics. But it also reflected a sense that the educated classes and particularly the academics had abandoned, or had been forced to abandon, the influential role they had once played in the political realm.

The famous crisis in the Social Policy Association (*Verein für Sozialpolitik*) around the turn of the century seemed to demonstrate that the loss of authority was partly a loss of intellectual coherence.[35] A pressure group as well as a scholarly association, the *Verein* brought together the most distinguished German economists and social scientists. In questions of scholarly method, most of the members continued the traditions of the German historical school. They disapproved of English classical economics because it abstracted timeless economic laws from specific historical settings and from the social and political context of economic activity. They also refused to assign anything but a strictly subordinate role to productivity, or to any other purely economic objective of individual or social life. Rejecting the implicit value judgments of many Manchesterite economists, they recommended an interventionist "social policy" in the name of the moral and cultural purposes of the national community. On the whole, they favored moderate reform to protect the work force and to ensure social harmony. Some of them also championed high tariffs, autarchy, and the particular protection of a "healthy" agrarian sector against the overly rapid and "unhealthy" development of the urban and industrial society.

From the late 1880s on, the theoretical work of the new Austrian school of economists challenged the historical approach favored by Gustav Schmoller and his followers in the Social Policy Association. The ensuing "methods controversy" served as a background to more practical disagreements that surfaced within the Association itself around the turn of the century. The dominant champions of bureaucratic paternalism, of agrarian and protectionist policies found it ever more difficult to contain dissent from colleagues who feared bureaucracy and the *Junkers* more than the trade union movement and the Social Democrats. Differences among factions within the *Verein* became at once more overt and more overtly political rather than scholarly. It became increasingly difficult to pretend that the scientific study of social questions *must by itself* produce unambiguous policy recommendations that no reasonable man could reject. After 1900 Max Weber drove the point home in his famous studies on the methodology of the social sciences. Of course his separation of scholarship from value judgment was meant to preserve the objectivity of scientific knowledge, but it also reduced the jurisdiction of science. It gave over to overt political conflict much that had previously rested in the realm of scholarly certainty. Particularly in the context of the Idealist tradition, this could easily appear a declaration of bankruptcy, a serious reduction in the authority of scholarship.

The relationship between science and value judgment also became problematical in the historical disciplines around the turn of the century. From the early 1880s on, the work of Wilhelm Dilthey reaffirmed and deepened the methodological preferences that had been characteristic of the German historical tradition since the later eighteenth century.[36] These preferences were closely related to the ideal of *Bildung* as integral immersion in the inherited sources. German historians traditionally insisted upon past-mindedness and upon the uniqueness of historical individuals, cultures, or epochs. Repudiating the application of timeless laws to the past, they stressed interpretation as the reconstruction of a unique constellation of meanings. Any particular element in such a constellation could be understood only in its relationships to the rest. The object of interpretation in the humanistic and historical disciplines was meaningful coherence rather than generality. After Dilthey, some of the leading figures in the neo-Kantian revival of the period emphasized the methodological differences between the humanistic disciplines and the natural sciences. In the meantime, the "Lamprecht controversy" began to agitate German historians during the 1890s. Karl Lamprecht was accused of "positivism" because he believed in (rather startling) laws of historical change. Most of his colleagues opposed him with a heightened commitment to neo-Idealist or neo-romantic conceptions of their discipline.

It was a difficulty inherent in these conceptions, however, that they bound all social norms and cultural values to their historical settings and epochs; the quest for timeless values was as hopeless as the search for timeless laws was misguided. That was the "problem of historicism."[37] A special form of historical relativism, it became more threatening precisely as the neo-Idealist movement in the humanistic and historical disciplines gained ground against more "positivist" approaches. Georg Iggers has rightly argued that the dangerous skeptical implications of German historicism were long hidden by the assumption of a divine transcendence.[38] Historically unique epochs—and values—were not disturbing as long as each was immediate to God. Cast loose from its religious moorings, however, the historicism of the decades around 1900 became increasingly problematical. There is some irony in that. The neo-Idealist revival, generally understood as a rebellion against mechanistic determinism or "materialism," was profoundly interested in ethics. Yet it aggravated the "problem of historicism," and it further undermined any hope of deriving valid norms from humanistic scholarship.

To express their sense that science or scholarship (*Wissenschaft*) was losing an authority it formerly had, German academics might say that it no longer produced the personal effect of *Bildung,* or that it failed to yield a *Weltanschauung,* an integral and partly evaluative orientation toward the world. The sociologist Georg Simmel, for example, spoke of a tragic disproportion between "objective" and "subjective" culture.[39] With the rapid accumulation of knowledge and of man-made objects generally, it became more and more difficult to attain the personal, "subjective," synthesis of "cultivation." Like the sorcerer's apprentice, the human spirit found itself overwhelmed by its creatures. Less subtle but probably more important than this neo-Idealist account of alienation was the frequent complaint that *Wissenschaft* was no longer productive of *Weltanschauung.* In part, this simply meant that science and scholarship sanctioned no value judgments; instead, they apparently led to relativism and skepticism.

At the same time, the disjunction between *Wissenschaft* and *Weltanschauung* was generally traced to the specialized character of modern scientific knowledge. And it was specialization and its consequences that became the central issues in most academic writings on the state of science and of learning.[40] The consensus was that a wave of increasingly specialized research and of thoughtless "positivism" had swept away the great Idealist systems about 1830 or 1840. The very considerable achievements of specialized scholarship fascinated German scientists and the German public until around 1880 or 1890. From that point on, however, the evils of specialization led to increasing dissatisfaction. Demands began to be heard for renewed efforts at synthesis, and for a revival of neo-Kantian and neo-Idealist philosophies that might tame the speculative outgrowths of rampant scientism. Neither the academic community nor the nation as a whole, the argument ran, could continue to endure the intellectual and spiritual vacuum created by excessive specialization and by "positivism."

No one ever specified exactly what positivism was and what was wrong with it. The attempt to transfer methods from the natural sciences to the humanistic disciplines was clearly positivist. So were any determinist, monist, or materialist systems that might serve as philosophical defenses of scientistic attitudes. Such systems, to be sure, were very rare in Germany. The repeated attacks upon "positivism" in the academic literature of the period therefore make sense only if "positivism" is equated with something like naive empiricism, or with the presumably unconscious philosophy of thoughtless specialists.

Thus the evils of specialization remained the real subject of most comments upon the state of German learning. The references to "positivism" merely indicate that "specialization" in turn meant more than the relative isolation of various disciplines or subdisciplines *from each other*. The real difficulty with specialization was taken to be its tendency to separate science and scholarship from a certain kind of integral philosophy. Specialized science lacked precisely the dimension that had connected Idealist *Wissenschaft* with *Bildung* and with *Weltanschauung*. The specialist was a mere expert; his knowledge was narrowly technical and dealt only with means. The revulsion against specialization was in effect a demand for wisdom, for reflection about ends, for the knowledge of the sage, the prophet, or the harmoniously cultivated man.

These associations linked the discussion of specialization with the more general theme of lost authority. For most of the typically nostalgic accounts of German Idealism and of its decline did not regret merely the kind of *individual* fulfillment suggested by Simmel's "subjective culture." They also made specialization responsible for a *social* condition of normlessness and spiritual poverty that in turn engendered all the evils of the age.[41] With the advent of specialization, in other words, the German intellectual elite lost its former authority and abandoned the spiritual guardianship of the nation. The people promptly fell prey to a vulgar utilitarianism or materialism. In a world without certain ends, public decisions were left to those who emerged temporarily victorious in the brutal strife among interest groups. The intellectual reduced to the role of expert had no more authority than any other merely technical adviser to business tycoons and party bosses.

Such were the anxieties current among large segments of the German academic community from around 1890 to the interwar period. The prospects of the modern specialist intellectual could probably have been assessed in less dismal terms. There are specialists in moral philosophy, mathematicians are not forbidden to read poetry, and even historians are sometimes moved by questions of general import. Though deprived of a pulpit—and of a kind of automatic respect—the modern scholar may yet see some relationship between his work and the general state of his culture and society. What he has been forced to tolerate is a great deal of indirection in that relationship, along with a disconcerting multiplicity of wisdoms and unwisdoms that compete with his own. But it is not surprising that German university professors around 1900 exaggerated the extent of the damage wrought by specialization. The German academic elite had long enjoyed an unusually secure and influential position, although for reasons that had less to do with intellectual matters than with certain social and political realities. When these realities changed, when the accustomed influence and status were threatened, German professors became particularly sensitive to the unpleasant prospects of the modern intellectual.

All of this is brilliantly reflected in Max Weber's two famous speeches of 1919, "Politics as a Vocation" and "Science as a Vocation."[42] Weber was aesthetically and morally repelled by the hysterical "prophets" among his colleagues who preached the German cultural mission during World War I and who then proceeded to launch a "spiritual" crusade against the Republic. Weber was also determined to make his student audiences face the truths that he himself had found most unpleasant. The universe of values is a pluralistic one; polytheism is the plausible religion. Science and learning do not dictate ultimate norms, or lead us to the highest good, or give a clear meaning to our lives. On the contrary, scientific progress has made the individual life cycle an absurdity while also giving man an environment his mind cannot master. Science and scholarship may evaluate the internal consistency of value systems, and they may answer limited causal questions, relating means to given ends. For the rest, individuals must make their own choices, and the paths to be taken by whole societies can be mapped only through overt political conflict. There is no escape from this situation. Only fools will be captivated by the search for privileged intuitions, by appeals to the irrational, by self-consciously manufactured new religions, and by the whole range of petty prophecies and intellectual patent medicines. Intellectual honesty is what Weber chiefly recommended, though he quickly added that the choice of reason too is a gratuitous one.

## Notes

1. *Neue deutsche Biographie*, 6 vols. (Berlin: Duncker & Humblot, 1953-64), N:2,953; J. Balteau et al., *Dictionnaire de biographie francaise*, 10 vols. (Paris, 1933-61), N:2,366; *Dictionary of National Biography* (London, 1917, with 5 supplements to 1959), N:1,001; *Dictionary of American Biography* (New York, 1928, with supplements 144, 1958), N:1,001. (Note: N = total number of entries in sample)

2. Fritz K. Ringer, *The Decline of the German Mandarins: The German Academic Community 1890-1933* (Cambridge, Mass.: Harvard University Press, 1969), pp. 1-25, and literature cited.

3. H. H. Gerth and C. Wright Mills, trans. and eds., *From Max Weber: Essays in Sociology* (New York: Oxford University Press, 1958), esp. pp. 192-94.

4. Ringer, *Decline of the Mandarins*, esp. pp. 86-87. The aristocrat is defined by what he is; the commoner, by what he can do. This sense of spiritual aristocracy is the utopian element, but also the source of the "class" connotation in most traditional definitions of liberal education.

5. Rene König, *Vom Wesen der deutschen Universität* (Berlin: Die Runde, 1935); Ringer, *Decline of the Mandarins*, pp. 102-13.

6. Lenore O'Boyle, "Klassische Bildung und soziale Struktur in Deutschland swischen 1800 und 1848," *Historische Zeitschrift* (December 1968), pp. 584-608; Ringer, *Decline of the Mandarins*, pp. 22-35.

7. Franz Schnabel, *Deutsche Geschichte im neunzehnten Jahrhundert*, 8 vols. (Freiburg im Breisgau: Herder, 1965), vol. 5, *Die Erfahrungswissenschaften*.

8. R. Steven Turner, *The Prussian Professoriate and the Research Imperative, 1760-1848*, forthcoming.

9. The following summarizes some sections of Fritz K. Ringer, *Education and Society in Modern Europe* (Bloomington, Ind.: Indiana University Press, 1979). The sources are principally German government publications and statistical surveys that cannot all be listed in a short note.

10. Lenore O'Boyle, "The Problem of an Excess of Educated Men in Western Europe, 1800-1850," *Journal of Modern History* 42 (December 1970): 471-95. O'Boyle explicitly recognizes the conventional element in any definition of the "demand" for educated men. It remains a problem for historians that there was apparently more such "demand" in Germany about 1700 than about 1800.

11. Enrollments in all grades of all secondary schools are stated as percentages of the nine-year age group, 11 through 19. Since there was a high rate of early leaving in the German system at the time, the results certainly understate the fraction of the age group that received any secondary education at all. Total university enrollments are stated as percentages of the four-year age group 20-23. Girls were just beginning to appear among German secondary and university students in the 1920s. The technical institutes are counted among university-level institutions from 1900, and a number of academies and higher professional schools are added in 1921.

12. Enrollment in the "faculty of philosophy" is broken down into humanities, natural sciences, and "minor fields"—chiefly pharmacy, dentistry, agriculture and (later) business studies.

13. Walter M. Kotschnig, *Unemployment in the Learned Professions* (London: Oxford University Press, 1937).

14. The National Socialist regime interrupted the expansion of German secondary and university education so that enrollments per age group in 1949 were about what they had been in 1931.

15. This is how I read the fierce conflict between classicists and modernists in secondary education and the reaction of the German academic community to the "mass and machine age." Ringer, *Decline of the Mandarins*, pp. 42–61. The basic idea, of course, is Weber's.

16. Calculations based on Wilhelm Ruppel, *Über die Berufswahl der Abiturienten Preussens in den Jahren, 1875–1899* (Göttingen: Fulda, 1904).

17. Of course I would not deny the central importance, even before 1870, of the basic class division in which those who had property or education confronted those who did not. In the same way, my emphasis upon the division between the classical and the modern secondary "tracks" is not to obscure the even higher social barrier that separated all forms of secondary education from the primary system.

18. One reason for the relatively high rate of social mobility through higher education before the middle of the nineteenth century was the "democratic" character of recruitment into the clergy and especially into the Catholic priesthood. Here was a very specialized form of "meritocratic" mobility, which had the advantage that it could be renewed in every generation.

19. In his *Gesammelte Werke*, 10 vols. (Berlin: Fischer, 1925), vol. 7, *Betrachtungen eines Unpolitischen*, pp. 115–18.

20. This seems to me one of the reasons for the popularity of so much German social analysis that dealt in romantic "estates," rather than "classes." Weber's class/status distinction took the wind out of those sails.

21. "Democratic" here refers to the extent of recruitment from the lower middle and lower classes, i.e., to the degree of opportunity. That usage will have to do for the present essay.

22. Frank R. Pfetsch, *Zur Entwicklung der Wissenschaftspolitik in Deutschland, 1750–1914* (Berlin: Duncker und Humblot, 1974). Unfortunately, I was able to obtain this highly informative book only after this essay was completed.

23. Computation in Alexander Busch, *Die Geschichte des Privatdozenten* (Stuttgart: F. Enke, 1959), p. 76, based on Helmuth Plessner, ed., *Untersuchungen zur Lage der deutschen Hochschullehrer* (Göttingen: Vandenhoeck & Ruprecht, 1956), vol. 3; Christian von Ferber, *Die Entwicklund des Lehrkörpers der deutschen Universitäten und Hochschulen 1864–1954.*

24. Franz Eulenburg, *Der akademische Nachwuchs* (Leipzig und Berlin: B. G. Teubner, 1908), pp. 80, 103–4, 118–19.

25. Busch, *Geschichte des Privatdozenten*, p. 123.

26. Calculations based on Ferber, *Entwicklung des Lehrkörpers*, pp. 177–78.

27. Ringer, *Decline of the Mandarins*, pp. 55–57; Felix Rachfahl, ed., *Der Fall Valentin: Die amtlichen Urkunden* (Munich: Duncker & Humblot, 1920).

28. Karl-Heinz Manegold, *Universität, Technische Hochschule und Industrie* (Berlin: Duncker & Humblot, 1970).

29. For the following, see *50 Jahre Kaiser-Wilhelm-Gesellschaft und Max-Planck-Gesselschaft zur Förderung der Wissenschaften, 1911–1961: Beiträge und Dokumente* (Göttingen: Max-Planck-Gesellschaft, 1961).

30. Ibid., pp. 80–94.

31. Ibid., p. 95.

32. For the following, see Ringer, *Decline of the Mandarins*, pp. 113–43.

33. Ibid., pp. 43–47 for a summary of actual changes in the personnel of electoral politics. Max Weber thought it important, in this context, to distinguish between an older amateur and a newer professional type of politician.

34. Aggravated after 1918, the sense of a divorce between *Geist* and politics was expressed again and again. Two particularly coherent variations upon this theme were written by Alfred Weber and Friedrich Meinecke. See Ibid., pp. 241–52.

35. Ibid., pp. 143–62.

36. Ibid., pp. 97–102, 302–4, 315–34.

37. Ibid., pp. 340–48. The translation of *Historismus* as "historicism" seems to have asserted itself despite the clear difference between *Historismus* and "historicism" as used by Popper. The

classics on *Historismus* are Ernst Troeltsch, *Der Historismus und seine Probleme,* Book 1: *Das Logische Problem der Geschictsphilosophie* (Tübingen: Mohr, 1922), and Friedrich Meinecke, *Die Entstehung des Historismus,* 2 vols. (Munich and Berlin: R. Oldenbourg, 1936).

38. Georg G. Iggers, *The German Conception of History* (Middletown, Conn.: Wesleyan University Press, 1968).

39. For example: Georg Simmel, "Der Begriff und die Tragödie der Kultur," *Philosophische Kultur: Gesammelte Essais* (Leipzig: W. Klinkhardt, 1911), pp. 245-47.

40. For the whole "crisis of learning" and its background: Ringer, *Decline of the Mandarins,* pp. 102-13, 243-69, 295-302.

41. Durkheim provides a fascinating contrast. Many German academics in effect blamed a certain kind of critical thought—and the consequent decline of Idealism—for an undesirable social condition. Durkheim not only insisted that Protestants sought enlightenment to compensate for a loss of religious conviction; he also treated religion principally as a social practice, not just a state of belief. He thus cut at two points the chain of causes that, for many German academics, linked "positivist" thought with social disorganization.

42. Gerth and Mills, *From Max Weber,* pp. 77-156.

# The Lamp of
# Learning: Popular Lights
# and Shadows

## NEIL HARRIS

The essays in this volume call attention to a set of interlocking institutions that developed in the United States between 1860 and 1920. They helped shape the world of knowledge from on high. But in addition to libraries, museums, laboratories, universities, and learned societies, an array of popular institutions also came into being. They have yet to receive much scholarly study. My essay aims not so much to redress the balance as to sketch the degree to which popular expressions of knowledge inspired, drew on, departed from, and clashed with the institutions and managers of high culture. As such its purpose is to suggest some directions for further research, rather than provide any definitive and conclusive answers.

The sparkling new campuses, libraries, and museums dominated the intellectual landscape. They housed objects, documents, and equipment; supported and stimulated research; certified researchers and codifiers; and refereed new knowledge and forms of classification. These functions acquired dramatic and ceremonial devices: convocations, congresses, exhibitions, and dedications. Their ongoing work identified colleagues, created a network of contacts, and permitted continuing participation by those whose profession or residence removed them from physical proximity to specific institutions.

But demands for participation in the dramatic expansion of consciousness were personal and subconscious, as well as scholarly and deliberative. If the professional approach to mastering data and technique was polished by new corps of teachers and managers, then the role of amateur participant, of ordinary witness (or victim) was also codified. The status of the layman was now defined in relation to congregations of the learned rather than congregations of the saints. The continuing demonstration during these sixty years that ideas had consequences transmitted itself to a public eager to replicate many of the characteristics of the learned institutions, or intent on developing independent (if similar) solutions to the problem of integrating experience and information.

There were, of course, continuities with the past. Since Gutenberg's day, printers had serviced a desire to absorb special skills and knowledge. In America from the eighteenth century on, carpenters and sculptors, engravers and gardeners, farmers, plumbers, and physicians exploited a wide selection of guides and manuals. The tradition of dispersed competence gained special strength during the Jacksonian period.

In the sixty years following the Civil War, the evolution of publishing mirrored the bewildering growth of knowledge. Because books were too static and final to serve as exclusive sources, periodicals developed which enlarged, amended, and reordered the knowledge that had appeared secure just a few months or years earlier. If chemists, psychologists, and historians had their journals, so did retail merchants, hardware manufacturers, and advertising agents. *Retail Druggist* (from 1893), *Plumbers' Trade Journal* (from 1881), *Restaurant Management* (from 1918), and *Advertising News* (from 1893)— these were among the hundreds of trade and occupational organs that passed on to co-workers advances in theory and practice. And some fields had many guides to browse. Innkeepers could read *Hotel Life* (established 1888), *Hotel Bulletin, Hotel Register,* and *Hotel World-Review*.

Some lore had been considered so permanent or so private that it could rely primarily on oral transmission. In the late nineteenth century, however, the mysteries of cooking, dressing, cleaning, bathing, and child rearing all received the attention of a group of experts who published their findings in a series of cookbooks, health tracts, etiquette manuals, and homemaking treatises. Again the tradition was older, but the twin thrust of the institutional story—specialization of interest and standardization of operation—was repeated on a more homely level.

Thus the subjects covered by writers like Maria Parloa, Ellen Richards, Juliet Corson, and Fannie Farmer (to remain in the area of homemaking) were ever more specific and detailed, supported by reservoirs of data obtained from travelers, journalists, and anecdotalists. And multivolume sets of rules and prescriptions, with ambitious attempts at comprehensiveness, regaled the reader with authoritative approaches to practically anything he or she wanted to know.

It was not that encyclopedias of knowledge were new. Rather, popular editors and compilers, understanding the powerful appeal of comprehensiveness, aped the encyclopedic style and were delighted to explain the histories, define the terms, and illustrate the mysteries of the mundane world. As Spencer and his American popularizers sought to synthesize sociology, anthropology, psychology, history, folklore, economics, politics, and art, so the household encyclopedias moved across their vast domains, touching on everything from the chemistry of cleaning and washing to the physiological meaning of nutrition and the role of dietetic planning.

With periodicals, textbooks, and encyclopedias to support them, a set of occupational (and gender) subcultures began to enjoy the dignity of conscious self-definition. An undifferentiated public continued to provide a growing market for novels, biographies, memoirs, general periodicals, and a series of other publications, but it is striking how energetically tradesmen, businessmen, bureaucrats, artists, and manufacturers utilized their own learned literatures and so furthered their own sense of identity.

Print was only one method of communication and mutual recognition. Another form of imitation was to create surrogates for the new, formal institutions or to penetrate them. Business colleges, for example, are one product of this period; their faculties granted degrees, held examinations, and debated standards, as did faculties of speech and rhetoric, drama, physical education, and home economics. The easiest way to popularize a skill and give it status seemed to be to establish a school, preferably a college. In the 1870s both the New York Cooking School and the Boston Cooking School were opened, training, among others, homemakers, teachers, nurses, and professional cooks. Some of these schools— cooking, stenography, home economics—were particularly concerned with such social issues as the character of urban poverty or the status of women in a hostile job market. Others existed to popularize products, line the pockets of promoters, or simply offer necessary vocational training. The constant repetition of the form, however, reveals the widespread assumption that the key to success in any field lay in disciplined organization, accumulation of a body of principles, careful instruction, testing, and good job placement. Vocational learning was wracked by debate and conflicts among leaders and major theories, just as the more dignified liberal arts and sciences were.

Publication and institution founding were supplemented by association: the formation of societies with common occupational or intellectual bases. It was the pursuit of information, and the sense that information contributed to performance, profits, and even reform, that characterized these assemblies. The growth of railroad networks and the standardization and expansion of hotels eased arrangements for annual conventions. While the American Historical Association or the Modern Language Association assembled its members yearly to present learned papers, aid the task of institutional placement, and debate current issues, American insurance salesmen, brewers, piano makers, and publishers held their periodic conferences to compare experiences and assess improvements. Of course, these meetings also served other very important functions—e.g., buying and selling, lobbying, price fixing—but bureaucratization had its expressive side as well. These annual encounters helped people feel like active participants in the improvement of their specialties.

Increasing organization was a response to new levels of size as well as to advances in technology and management methods. An outpouring of catalogues, directories, and compilations of standards formed a reference literature as crucial and complex in its own right as the texts of the new academic and professional disciplines. Economic and demographic growth, population dispersion, and specialization of function weakened the power of informal opinion and personal memory. Industrial leaders could no longer easily identify their counterparts in other cities, while celebrity itself was becoming so specialized that guides were necessary. *Who's Who in America* began publication in 1899, distinguishing itself from the many national encyclopedias by its exclusive attention to living Americans; *Polk's Bankers Encyclopedia* and the *Rand McNally Bankers Directory* go back to the late nineteenth century, as does *Who's Who in Railroading in North America.* The *Negro Year-Book* began in 1912; *Who's Who in Music and Drama* was launched two years later. The *American Catholic Who's Who* was only one of many religious directories to appear. For more general reading, there were *Distinguished Successful Americans of Our Day, Herringshaw's American Blue Book of Biography,* and *Men and Women of America,* all of which commenced publication between 1910 and 1912.

Collecting was another activity that reflected new specialization. Its progress during this period suggests the rise of knowledge communities whose interests were primarily recreational but whose organizations, once again, developed a superstructure that paralleled the procedures of the learned societies.

The earliest, largest, and most elaborate of these groups were the stamp collectors who formed societies and produced journals in the 1850s and 1860s. This pattern of collecting was somewhat different from anything that had gone before. For one thing it was a democratized form, open to sizable portions of the population. Large investments were not necessary, and the objects collected were inexpensive, numerous, and often quite recent. Indeed, one source of value was provided by the new industrial and bureaucratic processes themselves, for stamps with errors produced by faulty machinery were much more valuable than ordinary issues. Nevertheless, the excitement of discovering rare and costly examples formed only part of the collecting appeal. Another lure was the demonstration of mastery over this complex and numerous supply of objects, the exotic associations that foreign issues called to mind, the revelation of good judgment, discipline, and quick thinking that were vital to the creation of an impressive collection. And finally there was the fellowship and mental relaxation that accompanied the activity. Regional or local meetings, correspondence with fellow collectors, interest in post office operations, all enlivened the collector's art.

But the hobby itself was codified and academicized by a literature of commentary—the guides and the catalogues. To establish control over stamp lore required a good memory, a patient temperament, and a willingness to invest time and concentration. *Philatelic Monthly, Philatelic West, Philatelic World,* and *Philatelic News* were some of the many periodicals that serviced this market of trained experts, whose size and influence affected even the designing of new stamps. Their counterparts, the coin collectors, had a longer lineage, for numismatic study had traditionally formed part of classical scholarship. Here also one finds a similar network of societies, journals, and interest in the designs of the national government. A still greater expansion in American collecting habits would take place after World War I, but the pattern entrenched in stamps, coins, and antiques was well established by 1920.

The knowledge communities were able to utilize newly decentralized and dispersed facilities, particularly the museums and libraries that multiplied in this period. Andrew Carnegie spent over forty million dollars constructing almost

2,000 public library buildings and 100 college libraries throughout the United States. The New York City branch system alone involved eighty-one separate facilities that cost more than five million dollars. If the function of the Library of Congress and various specialty libraries created in this period—like the New-berry in Chicago—involved servicing the needs of specialists and academics, the public library systems handled middle-level inquiries and satisfied a thirst for recreation through the reading of fiction. Debates about whether municipal libraries should purchase modern novels were widespread in the late nineteenth century, but by 1920 modern fiction had secured its place. The public library did as much for popular recreation as for popular learning.

Nevertheless, the practice of solving disputes and revising judgments by calling on the resources offered by knowledge reservoirs—universities, libraries, museums—was new and important. Before the Civil War, public controversies had been dominated by personal arguments that drew upon individual resources of intelligence, learning, originality, or initiative. Wit and logic rather than sustained research or expert intervention dominated great public disputes. In this later period, however, when appeals to evidence involved methods and data outside the boundaries of personal experience, the work of the learned institution interacted more significantly with larger issues. One need only consider the range of arguments over immigration legislation, tariff reform, and social welfare, and compare the strategies of persuasion with their antebellum counterparts to see how striking a shift had occurred.

The importance of this intervention is connected with the larger notion of legitimacy. The empirical orientation of many American scientists and social scientists combined with their sense of intellectual accomplishment to project a self-confidence and assurance that was bound to affect many areas of popular belief. The growth of learning and its institutions did not, least of all in America, totally destroy a pattern of folk beliefs and uses that had a temporal priority. What it did, as in other areas, was stimulate mimicry of technique and organization. Institutional parallelism had a long record, if one examines the ancient intellectual wars against competing sects and societies. What was new was the creation of two kinds of communities, one legitimated by the new tests and institutions, the other suspect because of its failure to gain such legitimacy but continually seeking the approval of the newly prestigious certifiers.

In medicine, for example, the possession of certain credentials—attendance at renowned medical schools, service in teaching hospitals, election into colleges of specialists—was important for those able to select their practitioners. The credentials were advantageous because these new career patterns reflected the existence of a body of principles and practices worth knowing. General intelligence and a winning bedside manner were justifiably more persuasive to an earlier generation, when the medical schools and hospitals had less to offer in terms of differentiating their graduates and staff members from others. But increasing confidence in how to evaluate levels of expertise did not discourage the growth of new theories about the nurture of health, particularly the faith healing of sects like

Christian Science and New Thought. What scientific achievements did was to shape the vocabularies of the religious healers who transformed ancient impulses into properly up-to-date forms. Even so radical a position as the denial of physical death or disease sought to adopt science as a standard; specific conclusions were challenged, not the claims or vocabulary.

The prestige of the new university faculties and the progress of psychology and physiology were invoked by another group of enthusiasts extending the folk beliefs of an earlier day: the spiritualists. The first round of spiritualist activity in the 1840s had produced considerable interest among social reformers and some political leaders. But spiritualists of the 1880s were determined to storm the empire of academic science itself. Believers in mediumship, extraterrestrial life, and telepathic communication demanded the sympathy of prestigious scholars in England and America. One tactic was an appeal to popular opinion through university panels of trained experts who, it seemed, could evaluate the evidence more thoroughly and objectively than anyone else. A $60,000 legacy of Henry Seybert, a wealthy Philadelphia believer, established a chair at the University of Philadelphia upon the condition that the chair's incumbent "either individually or in conjunction with a commission of the university faculty will make a thorough and impartial investigation of all systems of morals, religion, or philosophy which assume to represent the truth, and particularly modern spiritualism."

The Seybert Commission, consisting of a group of distinguished academics and physicians, made only a preliminary report in 1887 and was generally negative about the truth of spiritualism. The commission examined slate writing, spirit rappings, materialization, telekinetic phenomena, and spirit photographs; it also contacted eminent scientists in Leipzig and Göttingen as part of its research. Its conclusions did not make happy reading for spiritualists who attacked the commission for alleged bias and hostility. Nonetheless, the effort to create within the academy a court of last resort for this controversial public question was a sign of how prestigious the mantle of learning had become for this generation.

The expert professor shortly became, in fact, a guest at many feasts, serving on governmental boards and commissions, testifying before legislative committees, offering advice to the public on child rearing, decoration, sports, civic improvements, military preparedness, foreign policy, food preparation, health, morals, and religion. The prestige of the expert, so large a theme in Progressive ideologies, was a by-product of the learning revolution that had enormous effects on daily life and ordinary persons. One reason for this clearly lay in the existence of new programs that trained the experts. Another lay in the complexities that outdistanced the practical skills of older civil servants and administrators. And still another was the novel character of work and leisure, exposing the public to risks and opportunities that experience alone did not permit it to assess. The hazards of life were quickly organized into statistical categories by expert actuaries who worked for insurance companies and whose mathematical skills and theories of probability were now accepted as hedges against risk.

Crime and deviance, apparently intensifying during this period, were also given up to learned students for analysis. For the first time students of genetics and anthropometry were able to present, through mathematical tables and photographs of bodily variation, apparently incontrovertible evidence about the causes and incidence of crime. Although, in some instances, the new expertise was only an older form of "folk wisdom," it was decked out in the new language of science, and ancient suspicions about physiognomy were given new legitimacy. Selective breeding and sterilization were among the solutions proposed for crime and hereditary insanity, and some of the legal and ethical implications of scientism would soon force themselves upon lawyers and laymen.

Physical labor and repetitive work were also captured as subjects by students whose careful experiments and observations attempted to rival, in persuasiveness, their counterparts in the science laboratories. Frederick Winslow Taylor's efforts to improve efficiency by breaking down the work process into component parts, and then revising the laborer's own habits, met with bitter resentment by workmen. But the new philosophy of efficiency, which Taylor insisted was not inherently antilabor, was greeted with delight by management and educators who found in other developments, like the objective measurement of intelligence in the new I.Q. tests, vast new opportunities for the manipulation of behavior. The classroom, as well as the factory, bore signs of the new confidence in objective experimental methods as the way to progress.

The power of the academies and the new learning rested also on the increasingly inscrutable character of some knowledge. Scientists and physicians had isolated microbes invisible to the naked eye and developed theories of disease that challenged old convictions. The production of electrical energy and its dispersion along a network of wires and cables was another such mystery. These wonders were now apparently the property of those willing to accept the special vocabularies and techniques of investigation necessary to their comprehension. Laboratories, libraries, and universities were not simply institutions for advancement or training in gentlemanly ethics. They were also temples of mystery; admission yielded not only jobs but also guides to read the contemporary world.

Popular interest in the new forms of information and classification was demonstrated most dramatically by the reception given the great expositions. From 1876 to 1915 they appeared in almost every geographical section of the United States. These fairs, as well as many other industrial, trade, and agricultural displays, paraded the extraordinary progress apparently being made in every branch of human achievement. Combined attendance at the fairs reached into the hundreds of millions; the White City at Chicago alone attracted more than twenty million. While the Pikes and Midways catered to sensual delights and exotic curiosities, inside the fair grounds were serious presentations of fields like mining and metallurgy, electricity, engineering and manufacturing, transport, anthropology, and agricultural science. According to journalistic observers and foreign tourists, American visitors seemed genuinely interested in studying the development of applied science and the progress of art. They used the expositions as adult education courses. Exhibits were crowded, lecturers were plagued with questions, and tourists returned again and again to stare at the maps, charts, models, and diagrams, many of which were planned by distinguished pedagogues and advertising specialists.

The fairs also permitted displays of academic virtuosity, featuring distinguished scholars in attendance from around the world. Seven miles to the north of the Columbian Exposition, in Chicago's new Art Institute building, the World Congress Auxiliary sponsored deliberations witnessed by some 700,000 spectators over a five-month period in 1893. More than 1,200 sessions were planned, and more than 6,000 papers or speeches delivered. Among the departments were Medicine, Engineering, Commerce, Music, Labor, Public Health, Women's Progress, Temperance, and Art. Groups like the American Philological Association, the American Historical Association, and the Modern Language Association arranged their annual meetings to coincide with this Congress. It was here that Frederick Jackson Turner delivered his famous paper on the passing of the frontier. And it was here that the World Parliament of Religions met—a gathering some insisted was the most important event in a thousand years.

The Louisiana Purchase Exposition, held at St. Louis eleven years later, featured an even more impressive assemblage of scholarly giants. With an administrative board that included Nicholas Murray Butler of Columbia, William Rainey Harper of Chicago, and Librarian of Congress Herbert Putnam, the Congress of Arts and Sciences attracted, in addition to distinguished American experts, Max Weber, Werner Sombart, Henri Poincaré, James Bryce, Adolf von Harnack, Otto Jesperson, and Carl Jung. The learned deliberations of the Congress were subsequently published in a multivolume set, as were the deliberations and proceedings of other fairs.

Here, in person and in print, was proof of the international character of the learned community, and its interaction with a broad, interested public. The ability to integrate popular amusement, instruction, art, and music at the expositions demonstrated a continuing affection for a universe that was unitary and had multiple activities still capable of clear organization and classification. The comprehensiveness of the fairs reminds us that specialization had not proceeded so far as to force Victorians to abandon the possibility of synthesis. While the energies of knowledge were expansive and occasionally disturbing in their force—as Henry Adams's famous comments at the Paris Fair of 1900 emphasized—the capacities of fairs, like those of universities, seemed equal to the task of making the sciences lie down with the humanities and bringing the artisan-inventor alongside the artist, to their mutual satisfaction. Tied to new learning through their congresses and demonstrations, the fairs also stimulated the creation of more permanent custodial institutions. In Philadelphia, Chicago, St. Louis, Seattle, and Buffalo, museums, public collections, and universities benefited from the expositions through the construction of new buildings and the suddenly aroused interest of potential patrons.

As one evidence of their sense of adventurous participation, American supporters of art, music, science, literature, and politics tried to enshrine their interest by creating canonized histories and heroes. The concert halls, museums, and libraries had the names of their imperishable masters carved in stone across their facades as if the very sight of Mozart, Goethe, Bacon, Newton, Raphael, or Shakespeare served to guarantee the respectability of the enterprise inside. Where more than usual disagreement might occur, recourse was made to the sentiments of the majority—within, of course, a properly selected electorate. Thus the old desire to create a national Valhalla was translated into the New York University Hall of Fame, where panels of eminent individuals, guided by elaborate rules, voted a specified number of Americans into immortality. Significantly, once again, the procedure was protected by the presence of a university and was administered by university officials. The judges were divided into four categories of twenty-five each; in addition to chief justices, editors, and authors, there were separate classes of university presidents and professors of science and history. Academicians were becoming national jurymen whose control of the learning process granted them special status in a world of new transactions.

But if the respectability of learning created new prestige, it also produced new degradation; legitimacy excited rebellion and heroes confronted outcasts. The requirements of special interests clashed with the dream of egalitarian democracy. Discrepancies could be partially resolved by the brilliant array of technocratic procedures and standardizing devices that proliferated in Victorian America, but they were never entirely obliterated.

Possession of learning now separated generations and occupations. It threatened equal and informal communication. Presidents and senators might hold Ph.D.'s or preside over learned associations, but this could not disguise the anger and anxiety. The self-confident I.Q. testers, who labeled almost half the population semi-imbecilic, faced resistant citizens not disposed to surrender older definitions of intelligence. Ethnic groups resented "objective" scientific research by anthropologists who concluded that racial safeguards were necessary for America's genetic future. Reformers quarreled with economists and sociologists who insisted that restrictions on property rights threatened the logic of evolution.

Angriest of all was the outcry of religious denominations. It is appropriate in this discussion of the power of learning to recall the outrage of fundamentalists, appalled by implications of the new scholarship. Such emotion fueled the legislation that provoked the Scopes case. For civil libertarians and the secularized majority, such legislation was obviously repressive, reactionary, and absurd. But its proponents felt too bitterly alienated from the world of the laboratory and the library to care. In the new learning and the bureaucratization of education they saw subversion. These parents and religious leaders knew that curriculum specialists and textbooks published in New York and Chicago would increasingly determine the values of their children, and they were unwilling to surrender their authority. Doomed to lose the fight by the power and prestige of the trained experts and the national temper itself, their bitterness continues through the present, as skirmishes about evolutionary theory persist.

In actual fact the victory of the textbook and the curriculum specialist was incomplete. For radio, film, and television would, in the next few decades, expand the frontiers of consciousness and the power of persuasion beyond the context favored by educators and scholars. Opposed to censorship and thought control, many in the educational establishment would nonetheless fight against the influence exerted by the mass media and against its effects upon personal morality, levels of violence, and patronage of the arts.

If limited, the hour of the scholar was intense. The dissatisfactions and anxieties had not yet reached cosmic levels. Gentility and prestige still clung to the mantle of the academic, providing him with social as well as intellectual status. The college president, the laboratory scientist, the museum curator, and the librarian had not yet accumulated the full range of hostile or patronizing images that fiction, drama, journalism, art, and politics would eventually fasten upon them. Protests were muted, if mordant. The eagerness with which the learning community—in the humanities and social sciences as well as the arts—adopted the patriotic slogans of World War I and tolerated the persecution of German scholars and artists, their efforts to demean or isolate the findings of German academicians, proved how little there was to fear from suggestions of disloyalty or deviance. Although radical leaders snorted with derision at the notion of socialist clubs at American colleges, a number were established, and faculties contained their share of political activists and dissenters. But colleges, museums, and libraries were still firmly committed to order, and the idea of continuity was stronger than any competing dreams of personal glory or revolution.

In the decades after 1920, trends that were held in uneasy balance earlier would disturb the peace of the knowledge institutions. Power and responsibility did not march along together, and the task of maintaining some sense of identity or self-confidence amid the expansion of research and the proliferation of specialties proved very difficult. In retrospect the period resembles a false dawn with a promise that could not be kept. But the energy and exhilaration of the adventure are still worth recalling.

# Toward an Ecology
# of Knowledge: On Discipline,
# Context, and History

## CHARLES ROSENBERG

America at the conclusion of World War I was vastly different from the nation that had stumbled through Reconstruction a half-century earlier. The present volume has sought to illuminate one aspect of the cultural revolution that took place in the half-century before 1918: the changing nature of organized knowledge and the contexts in which it was elaborated, transmitted, and used.

For at least a half-century, historians and sociologists have employed such terms as urbanization, industrialization, bureaucratization, and most recently the even more inclusive—if elusive—term modernization to describe the interrelated changes that brought the mid-twentieth century Western world into being.[1] Yet it is only within the past generation that American historians have sought to deal systematically with the multifaceted transformation of their society between the mid-nineteenth and early twentieth century—seeing it as a "response to industrialism" or a "search for order" in the phrases of two influential synthesizers.[2] American historians are thus belatedly orienting themselves toward a major question of social interpretation, one that has concerned European students of society for at least a century. Marx, Durkheim, and Weber—to cite only the most obvious examples—all sought to understand the institutional and even existential consequences of technological and economic change. Specialization of work, for example, or changing attitudes toward family and community have already attracted generations of social and historical speculation. Indeed, the term modernization implies—if anything—the necessity of integrating every aspect of a culture in attempting to understand social change.

This volume constitutes a pioneering attempt to survey our present understanding of a particularly significant period in the shaping of new relationships between knowledge and society. New kinds of knowledge, new institutions for the support of learning, new modes of education and certification all established themselves in the half-century between the Civil War and the First World War. In their diversity, the contributions that make up this volume indicate the difficulty of locating knowledge in society and the still tentative quality of our understanding; yet their very existence implies a new awareness that the ecology of knowledge does indeed constitute a significant historical concern. The following remarks attempt not to summarize the content of those pages which precede them, but to suggest some directions for further research, especially in areas not elaborated in these essays.

Intellectual history and the history of particular areas of pure and applied learning have a long and often distinguished tradition. Yet the bulk of this work has been undertaken by practitioners of the relevant mystery—physicians concerning themselves with the history of medical ideas, or philosophers with the geneology of particular philosophical problems. Not surprisingly, they have been comparatively unconcerned with the social and institutional context in which the ideas they study were elaborated, and demands for such research have sometimes been derided as an imposition of the trivial and temporal into a purer realm of thought. On the other hand, institutional and social historians concerned with learning or the professions ordinarily lack sufficient training in the relevant disciplines to allow them to explore fully the interactions between ideas and institutions. In recent years, however, this conventional division between the intellectual and institutional seems decreasingly tenable. It may describe much of an existing canon; it cannot dictate a necessary division of historical labor.[3] Virtually every contributor to this volume is a practicing historian and this constitutes in itself a significant reality; within the past decade, American historians have shown a steadily increasing interest in knowledge and its social context.

Indeed, something of a preliminary if informal consensus has emerged. We have become increasingly aware that even the internal logic of formal thought can be shaped by social needs and assumptions; the domain of seemingly value-free inquiry grows ever smaller.[4] We have become aware as well that specific institutional structures mediate the relationship between men of learning and the society that supports them. In sum, we have become conscious of the need to integrate knowledge into a more general understanding of organizational and attitudinal trends.

Yet such assumptions imply an interpretative challenge. These developing relationships cannot be understood by affixing to them neat labels such as specialization or professionalization. It is not that such terms are deficient in content; quite the contrary. They describe a significant social reality—but in a schematized and potentially misleading way. Insofar as we ask such ideal types to serve as both description and explanation of change, we have to some extent chosen to mislead ourselves. Such terms tend to incorporate a largely unexamined model of uniform institutional development, an evolution, moreover, whose end is the shape assumed in mid-twentieth century by such professions as those of medicine and law. But as Laurence Veysey has so forcefully argued in his contribution to this volume, most such definitions blur under careful historical scrutiny; diversity and inconsistency mark the professions and academic disciplines as much as commonality of value and institutional practice.[5]

Certainly one can find parallels in the development undergone by the several professions and learned disciplines in the half-century between 1865 and 1915, yet to dwell on these parallels is to obscure as much as to clarify. The terms that we habitually employ to describe these uniformities of development—specialization, professionalization, bureaucratization—tend like any such synthetic formulations to obscure the real differences that characterized change in the several areas of organized knowledge; the differences between academic disciplines or among professions are, after all, at least as instructive as their similarities.

It is no more than a truism to observe that social scientists are trained to discern and formulate patterns that can be expressed in general terms, while the historian is tied by sensibility and socialization to the particular. But this is as much the historian's advantage as his limitation—especially when we remind ourselves that no currently available formulation of the stages and characteristics of the professionalization of knowledge is based on adequate historical investigation.[6] To understand the relationship between knowledge and society, historians must move beyond the passive and taxonomic—are individuals professional or preprofessional? do they fulfill an appropriate number of characteristics in some sociologist's diagnostic checklist?—and try to understand the fine structure of interaction between knowledge and the society that supports its accumulators and practitioners. Generalizations about the characteristics of, let us say, professionalization might be likened to the bones that structure the body; they provide a necessary general framework. But to understand its anatomy and physiology—if I may be forgiven another biological metaphor—we must look at the flesh, the blood, and the connective tissue as well.

This is no utopian program. Formal thought is retrievable from surviving documents and its social context discernible with some precision (as is not the case with social values and attitudes, whose shifting forms and elusive social constituencies make the task of their would-be historian difficult indeed). The consumers and transmitters of academic and professional learning can be identified, their backgrounds evaluated, the formal content of their ideas retrieved from documents written with the specific intent of communicating these ideas. The place of knowledge in society is not only appropriate to the historian's concerns but clearly within the scope of his documentary resources.

Nevertheless, historians must accept several assumptions—at once of substance and method—if they are to systematically pursue the relationship between knowledge and its social setting. This is, after all, the central agenda of the present volume and a major theme generally in understanding the development of modern society. Let me mention each, then discuss them in somewhat greater detail. First, historians must assume that knowledge subsumes different kinds of relationships with society, that these are structured by diverse institutional contexts, that the interaction of discipline and context—be that context university, professional school, or applied research laboratory—is the stage upon which the needs of society interact with the specific norms and ideas of the several disciplines and professions. Second, knowledge itself must be seen as playing a significant *social* role within those institutions that shape the vocational lives of their members; specialized knowledge helps dictate the internal organization of academic disciplines and learned professions, defines needs, and rewards achievement. Third and finally, within the larger society, knowledge can define legitimacy, shape personal and vocational identity, imply and help to define social place. Individuals do not choose careers at random, nor does society support intellectual endeavor haphazardly. In a society like nineteenth-century America, moreover—undergoing rapid change and comparatively lacking in the sources of emotional reassurance available in traditional societies—the role of knowledge must be seen as potentially crucial, not only in bringing about social change, but in defining identities appropriate to a changed reality.

## I

In studying the institutionalization of knowledge in late-nineteenth-century America, perhaps the most useful distinction to be made is that between the professions and the learned disciplines.[7] Though the distinction cannot be defended as absolute, it is nevertheless useful not only because it reflects important substantive realities but because it implies differing strategies of historical analysis.

Probably the most important single distinction between the professions and academic disciplines lies in their relationship to the society that supports them. As they have grown in size and self-consciousness, in the past century, the learned disciplines have come to rely on indirect modes of support, primarily through universities but to some extent through foundations and private learned societies.[8] The professions have related far more directly to their supporting social substrate; even today the line between academic law and medicine and the world of practice is shifting and often ill-defined. To understand the social underpinning of a profession we must, to some extent at least, see it as a marketplace phenomenon—or, relatedly, as an object of government policy.[9] The contrast between, let us say, law and classical philology needs no elaboration.

This is not to suggest some absolute distinction between a university-based seeker after abstract knowledge and the more worldly professional. The various professions and academic disciplines might best be seen as occupying places along a continuum defined by the nature of their social support system. There are any number of ambiguous cases, each telling us something about the complexity of the relationship between ideas and society. Is an agronomist, for example, a professional or a member of an academic discipline? Or must one provide an answer depending on the agronomist's employer? Clearly the texture of interaction between his knowledge and the society that supports its accumulation is different from that confronting, for example, a professor of romance languages.[10] These two are perhaps extreme cases but represent in their diversity both the difficulty of defending an absolute distinction between discipline and profession and the complex social realities that must be faced by the would-be historian of knowledge in American society. The study of each discipline or profession implies a somewhat different research strategy.

Support for the learned disciplines is filtered through exterior priorities and assumptions, initially those that determine how generously the university and learning generally are to be supported. Then, within the university itself, an intervening layer of decisions and decision-makers interposes itself between the larger society and the department structure. Thus the historian of a particular discipline must, among other questions, deal with the exigencies of the departmental system and the priorities and perceptions that determine levels of support within the university. He must understand as well the division of authority between department and central administration. Who is to be hired or fired? What sorts of research are to be encouraged? How is teaching to be weighed against research? In each instance, the department plays a significant role, for it is the department that has come to mediate between the demands of the discipline and the realities of a particular university context. In some ways, indeed, the history of the university in the half-century between the Civil War and First World War is not only a history of growth in size and influence, but of a shift in structure—with the departments sharing power with a previously dominant executive.[11]

Historians have concerned themselves little with the department; insofar as individual departments have been studied it is ordinarily with the pious enthusiasm of the hagiographer. Yet it is the discipline that ultimately shapes the scholar's vocational identity.[12] The confraternity of his acknowledged peers defines the scholar's aspirations, sets appropriate problems, and provides the intellectual tools with which to address them; finally, it is the discipline that rewards intellectual achievement. At the same time, his disciplinary identity helps structure the scholar or scientist's relationship to a particular institutional context. His professional life becomes then a compromise defined by the sometimes consistent and sometimes conflicting demands of his discipline and the conditions of his employment.

The totality of any discipline or profession must be seen as a series of parallel intellectual activities being carried on in a variety of social contexts. Such rubrics as the "humanities", "life sciences", or "social sciences" mask diversity as much as they imply unity. A bacteriologist working at an agricultural experiment station or pharmaceutical firm deals with very different questions and in a very different work environment from a medical school bacteriologist or one attached to a research team at the Rockefeller University. At the end of the nineteenth century, indeed, bacteriology was not a field at all; it could be defined only in terms of botanists and mycologists, alert and ambitious pathologists, and employees of state and municipal departments of public health. To write a history of the origins of bacteriology would imply an evaluation of all these contexts and the specific influence they had in shaping the work and aspirations of would-be bacteriologists.[13]

In the opening years of the present century, to cite another example, American genetics grew as a discipline largely out of the work of biologists employed either by university departments of zoology or botany or in agricultural colleges and experiment stations (supported by an atypical federal commitment to the funding of farm-related research). Medicine had few resources to support laboratory investigation and little incentive to devote those it had to genetics, which seemed only marginally related to the physician's clinical realities.[14] As Garland Allen notes in his discussion of T. H. Morgan, however, an existing university-based experimental tradition with a well-defined interest in embryology and cytology proved a natural intellectual context for the elaboration of the "next step" in shaping a new science of heredity. Biochemistry, on the other hand, and at roughly the same time, found substantial support and encouragement in the world of medicine. Chemistry had proved itself relevant in pharmacology, in pathology, and in clinical diagnosis. It was only natural that many elite physicians were convinced that meaningful questions might indeed be asked in the laboratory, that they saw in chemistry a means of solving long-standing clinical problems. But biochemistry had roots outside as well as inside the medical school. When America's first professional biochemical society was founded in 1906, its charter members were drawn from a variety of contexts: industry, agricultural colleges and experiment stations, university departments of physiology and physiological chemistry as well as medical schools and hospitals.[15] Diversity of context is a characteristic of almost all learned disciplines in twentieth-century America—in particular the sciences.

Indeed, certain conventional disciplinary categories—chemistry for example—are almost too inclusive to be analytically useful. The American Chemical Society includes a host of individuals occupying very different social locations and making use of very different bodies of knowledge. Its membership includes men employed in the most routine quality control as well as the directors of lavishly funded research teams.[16] Nevertheless, scholars and scientists who identify themselves with a particular discipline, no matter how diverse their work places or marginal their commitment to the larger discipline, still feel some residual sense of common identity, still interact in professional associations, possibly even in editorial committees or positions of public responsibility. Even relatively small groups such as ecologists or limnologists may occupy radically different institutional positions, yet remain bound by an affinity growing out of a shared consciousness of disciplinary identity.

There are no simple cases. Even those disciplines with an almost exclusively academic setting may still be characterized by a complex and highly differentiated structure, differentiated not only in terms of varied institutional contexts—for even colleges and universities vary widely—but in terms of specialized intellectual relationships that create de facto subdisciplines. Research areas, that is, help shape a social as well as an intellectual identity; in many ways one's closest peers are the handful of individuals at work on the same or closely related areas of research. Each intellectual cluster of this type may constitute a distinct subculture within the larger discipline—plasma physics within physics, for example, or criminology within sociology—just as each learned discipline constitutes such a subculture within the world of learning generally.

A diversity at least equal characterizes the professions. Differing social functions imply differing patterns of organization, differing patterns of status and recruitment, and differing degrees of control over professional activities. The learned professions may all have traits in common, but clearly the differences between, let us say, medicine and engineering are no less enlightening than their similarities. Historically, most engineers have worked for large-scale enterprises, be it a canal, railroad, or industrial firm, and have to that extent been lacking in autonomy. Thus there exists a conventional wisdom among engineers which contends that in order to attain success the engineer must stop working as an engineer and instead use his credentials as an entrée to an entrepreneurial or administrative career. This realization would help explain the creation by engineers in the early twentieth century of an ideology of efficiency; this ideology, glorifying the engineer and his alleged problem-solving skills, reflected not a consciousness of social influence but of increasing marginality.[17]

American physicians, on the other hand, have always related directly to the consumers of their services. As they moved in the late nineteenth century into more institutionalized settings, physicians were able to retain, and indeed enlarge upon, that autonomy. With greater knowledge and a seemingly greater ability to heal, physicians began to control ever greater areas of their professional lives. A pattern of increasingly formal institutional ties coupled with greater control of their professional universe was consistent with organizational trends in society generally. In addition, the sacred, emotionally resonant quality of the doctor-patient relationship, its mediation at times of sickness and death, created another source of potential social leverage for the physician—one that other professions could not ordinarily draw upon in their claims to social autonomy.

Each profession constitutes a unique configuration of social need and intellectual and institutional tools, evolved through a unique historical development. Nursing, for example, failed to benefit to the same extent as medicine from the emotions surrounding sickness and death; other variables have shaped nursing as a social institution. Attitudes toward class, toward gender role, toward servile manual work, for example, as well as the very necessity for structured hierarchy implied by the need to work with medicine in the same social setting have all interacted to create a history of nursing very different from that which has shaped medicine. Indeed, knowledge itself has played a different role in nursing and medicine; nursing has never been clothed with the prestige-bearing mantle of innovation and the accumulation of esoteric knowledge.[18] Thus the historian must not only be aware of differences among the professions but of complex distinctions of function and status within each profession.

None of this is meant to deny the power of the professional model or the desire of occupational groups to see themselves and convince others that they are indeed a profession and entitled to its prerogatives. Librarians, teachers, optometrists, and undertakers, for example, have adhered as best they could to the program of professionalization, though with varying degrees of success. Would-be historians of knowledge must balance the general against the particular. They must, if I may be excused the analogy, commit themselves to an ethnology of knowledge—the unit of analysis being not the geographically isolated culture but the knowledge-defined discipline, subdiscipline, or learned profession. Like the ethnological field-worker, historians of knowledge must integrate formal intellectual content with social and institutional organization, systems of economic support, and finally, the values that sanction and reward the career choice of members of a particular intellectual subculture. Like ethnology itself at the beginning of this century, we must free ourselves from the domination of overschematized developmental models and seek to understand the specific forms of particular cultures.

## II

What the foregoing suggests is the necessity of seeing knowledge itself as a central element in shaping the structure of disciplinary cultures and subcultures. This is no more than common sense. The historian who hopes to study, let us say, late-nineteenth-century philosophy or chemistry must understand the ideas that scientists or philosophers regarded as the essential reality of their discipline. He must understand how such individuals evaluated the competence of their peers, how networks of personal and institutional relationships were predicated on shared goals and commonality of judgment. Without such intellectual competence, the historian can hardly hope to unravel the mechanisms through which status and power were distributed, or even the nature of institutional decision-making (why certain appointments were made, for example, or certain kinds of investigation underwritten) and the implications of such decisions for ultimate intellectual change.

The social contours of formal learning reflect not simply institutional arrangements—memberships in societies, editorships of journals and the like—but a less visible structure of group identity based on intellectual commitment. Ideas shape meaningful units of emotional identification: a sense of community based on common education, allegiance to the solution of parallel or identical problems with the same intellectual tools. The members of such groups are also likely to occupy similar positions and face parallel institutional problems. Despite the controversy surrounding Thomas Kuhn's much-debated term "paradigm," it is at the very least heuristically useful in pointing toward the need for disentangling such units of intellectual and institutional identity.[19] The fine structure of any twentieth-century discipline is a mosaic of such clusters, the precise configuration of which defines not only the discipline's intellectual profile but its social shape as well. Ideas must be taken seriously and they must be understood—even by scholars concerned primarily with questions of social organization or the social impact of knowledge.

On the other hand, historians concerned primarily with explaining intellectual innovation or the lack of it must, by the same token, become historical sociologists of knowledge. Understanding the intellectual options facing a particular scholar or scientist is a prerequisite to understanding his role as innovator; in order to reconstruct those options, the historian must necessarily study his protagonist's initiation into a particular discipline at a particular time. He must try to read the textbooks his subject used and recreate the atmosphere of the seminars he attended; he must understand the institutional pressures he experienced, be they for specific kinds of teaching or particular emphases in research. All of this may seem commonsensical, but it has all-too-rarely guided historians in their study of men of learning.

The needs of society can and do intrude even upon the internal texture of academic discourse. Those critical spirits who urge a demystification of the professions and learned disciplines are often correct in scoffing at the claims toward value-free neutrality that may embellish the social pretensions of such groups. But to concede the existence of an inevitable give-and-take between the realm of intellect and the needs of society is hardly to advance our intellectual awareness; the difficulty lies in understanding how and when such interactions take place. Each discipline presents a different potential for social relevance—and thus a different order of sensitivity to social pressure. Obviously the internal logic of ideas in quantum physics is less prone to reflect such social demands than their counterparts in political science or sociology. Yet it would be naive to assume that quantum physics has not had a significant social impact, though perhaps of a different kind from that exerted by political science. It would be equally naive to assume that even in many areas of physics social priorities and perceptions did not play some role in shaping research support and thus effecting the differential plausibility of research options. Most cases are even more ambiguous.[20]

Let me refer, by way of example, to an incident that took place in the years immediately preceding the First World War—an incident of both great practical and theoretical significance. Some years ago I was engaged in a study of American agricultural experiment stations before 1914 and was surprised to discover, in a generally undistinguished research canon, that two groups of American scientists had discovered vitamin A almost simultaneously. And this happened at a time when American agricultural research was notable more for assiduity in attracting support than eminence in achievement. How could this seeming anomaly be understood? The explanation is illuminating, for it illustrates nicely the interdependence of economic and social factors with intellectual and institutional ones.

The discovery of vitamin A grew out of the juxtaposition of a number of areas previously little-related; one was a sophisticated ability to work with the chemistry of proteins, another the use of small mammals as indices to the biological activity of chemicals of known composition, a third the skills of the pathologist. No existing discipline contained the configuration of tools and motivation appropriate to demonstrate that minute quantities of a previously unknown substance were necessary to the normal growth and development of men and animals. Protein chemists did not ordinarily work with the problems and tools of experimental pathology; agricultural scientists concerned with the comparative efficacy of diets lacked adequate biochemical skills; pathologists normally lacked the chemical skills and tradition of working in experimental situations (and were also distracted by an absorbing concern with the etiological role of microorganisms). Yet at both the Wisconsin and Connecticut agricultural experiment stations the force of economic necessity brought together an appropriate mixture of skills. Prodded by the need to contribute to the economic well-being of dairymen and cattle-raisers, research administrators at these experiment stations created a novel intellectual context by bringing the skill of protein chemists to bear upon the problem of explaining experimentally-demonstrated inadequacies in seemingly complete diets, thus transcending the limitations of conventional disciplinary training.[21]

In other fields, of course, the problems implied by the need to exist within society assumed different guises. The social sciences, for example, were shaped to a large extent in the half-century before 1920 by conflicting tendencies toward social intervention and reform, on the one hand, and a value-free, neutral stance on the other. Though some of the most prominent leaders in the formative decades of American social science were imbued with an almost evangelical desire to intervene righteously in society, it soon became clear that such intervention could be dangerous, not only to the individuals involved but to the disciplinary needs of the nascent social sciences. Certainly one of the characteristic themes in all of the social sciences in the last-quarter of the nineteenth century and first-quarter of the twentieth was this very conflict between social consciousness and academic cautiousness.[22] And social scientists did proceed with a growing caution in the twentieth century—or at least caution in expressing opinions potentially offensive to those who wielded social and economic power.

But how is one to interpret this shift? Were they paralyzed by a simple fear of reprisal from conservative trustees and administrators? Or were they intimidated instead by a growing respect for an increasingly complex body of empirical data and demands by their disciplinary peers for its mastery? Or did generational differences in recruitment imply a differing kind of vocational commitment among social scientists? Answers to such questions can never be one-dimensional or unambiguous, yet the questions must still be asked if we are to understand the evolution of the social sciences in America. For even if we do not concede a genuine decision-making power to the findings and deliberations of academic economists and sociologists, they nevertheless play a powerful legitimating role in society.

The humanities and social sciences have in some ways—as Dorothy Ross and

Laurence Veysey suggest—played very different roles. While social scientists have to some extent assumed the task of guiding society, the theologian and philosopher have played decreasingly prominent public roles. The philosopher's evolution from moral teacher to discipline-oriented academician is particularly striking and instructive. Moral philosophy was still central to the learned man's intellectual world in 1865; by the 1920s academic philosophy had turned away from consideration of those eternal human problems that philosophy had always addressed. The increasingly internal orientation of the philosopher has made the products of their scholarship well-nigh unavailable to the society that supports his linguistic, logical, or mathematical investigations. In some ways, the differentiation of the moral philosopher's subject matter into a half-dozen specialized descendants—among them philosopher, economist, psychologist, political scientist, sociologist—provides an exemplary paradigm for all those shifts that marked the changing context of knowledge in the half-century between the Civil War and World War I.[23]

## III

Thus far we have been discussing the role of knowledge within a particular discipline or profession. A second kind of question concerns the place of knowledge in the social order generally. What was the social value attached to the possession of knowledge? What did the mastery of a specific body of knowledge mean to its possessor? And how did his peers regard him? Such realities shaped not only recruitment into a particular discipline but also the willingness of society to accept that implicit evaluation and support its acolytes.

Laurence Veysey contends in his study of the humanities in this volume that one motivation for the embracing of humanistic knowledge was the status such a commitment implied to certain members of the older middle class. Such individuals, he maintains, found themselves sorely in need of the transcendence and moral stature implied by a seemingly selfless commitment to wisdom—not wealth.[24] These late-nineteenth-century academic humanists sought as well a collegial atmosphere of like-thinking peers whose devotion to the same scholarly vocation served to forge a bond of emotional affinity in a world frequently lacking in such ties for the sensitive and introspective. Even in an egalitarian and supposedly pragmatic society, the nurturance of a seemingly unselfish, and in that sense spiritual, orientation toward scholarship implied the kind of moral elevation that seemed necessary to at least some Americans as they sought to contend with their own desires for achievement in a context in which most kinds of distinction were tied to the sordid compromises of the marketplace.

This commitment to scholarship is intimately related to another central aspect of this period: the growth of the research ethos, a development touched upon by almost every essay in this volume and discussed in particular detail by Hugh Hawkins. Research and researchlike activities not only grew to play an ever-increasing role in the actual work of scholars but gained greater acceptance in the public mind as well. Though research seemed selfless, it was at the same time consistent with the urges of romantic individualism. The search for truth could thus channel and domesticate the emotional need of at least some ambitious young men. In certain areas, moreover, research promised painless conflict resolution in society—while providing new knowledge and serving as an agent of change.

Considerations similar to that of the spiritual value attached to the possession of knowledge help us to understand certain kinds of behavior among professionals that do not lend themselves to purely economic analysis. Why, for example, did nineteenth-century physicians publish, perform autopsies, work indefatigably to improve medical school curricula? Was it simply a need to provide a more prestigious product in competing for a limited stock of consumers? The truth is far more complex. Individuals crave moral legitimacy—and in medicine, legitimacy has traditionally implied mastery of a particular body of knowledge; that possession of such knowledge implies or might bring with it economic advantage (or social status) does not mean that the motivation for acquiring it can be understood in exclusively economic terms. One could argue indeed that the very materialism of most physicians motivated an idealistic and distinction-hungry minority to embrace the search for knowledge. To orient themselves toward the approval of their peers in Paris and Berlin was at once to remove themselves from the confining standards of their own community and, paradoxically, to elevate themselves within it. Could it be doubted that a physician who sought earnestly after intellectual enlightenment occupied a higher moral status than a contemporary who sought simply to increase his "business"? Both traditional religious values and the internal values of the profession endorsed many of the same kinds of behavior.

Though only a small percentage of American physicians may have sought such intellectual mastery, they nevertheless played a disproportionate role in bringing about the changes that were to reshape the institutional structure and public status of their profession between the Civil War and World War I. Learning, as measured in publication and membership in specialized societies, was close associated in late-nineteenth-century American medicine with status and influence—and in this association lay a structural basis for the leverage exerted by a comparatively small group of intellectual and institutional innovators. The desire to achieve intellectual distinction, to define one's aspirations in terms of the world of scientific medicine must be seen as a change agent in itself, a necessary ingredient not only in technical innovation but in the transmission of ideas such as the germ theory across the Atlantic. And it would be hard to overestimate the impact of such intellectual artifacts as the germ theory in ultimately reshaping the realities of even the humblest country practitioner; in this case, the link between high-culture ideas and their transforming social impact is unmistakable.

Of course, the status and emotional fulfillment implied by the possession of specialized knowledge served as a change agent in fields other than medicine.[25]

The motivations and activities of scholars and scientists and professionals are of significance not simply to a coterie of intellectual historians but to all who would understand the nature of American society in the twentieth century and the forces that brought it into being. To understand the developing ecology of knowledge is to understand a fundamental aspect of our world.

## *Notes*

1. In recent years the "modernization" concept has been subjected to much criticism, both in terms of its substance (or lack of it) and its political implications. For guidance to this literature, see L. E. Shiner, "Tradition/Modernity: An Ideal Type Gone Astray," *Comparative Studies in Society and History* 17 (1975): 245-52; Dean C. Tipps, "Modernization Theory and the Comparative Study of Societies: A Critical Perspective, ibid. 15 (1973): 199-225; S. N. Eisenstadt, "Studies of Modernization and Sociological Theory," *History and Theory* 13 (1974): 225-52.

2. I have referred to the titles of the two most widely cited syntheses: Samuel P. Hays, *The Response to Industrialism* (Chicago: University of Chicago Press, 1957) and Robert H. Wiebe, *The Search for Order, 1877-1920* (New York: Hill & Wang, 1967). In the last decade the literature exploring the implications of late-nineteenth-century structural change has become extensive.

3. The problem is not easily solved. The movement of historians into areas traditionally dominated by practitioners of a particular discipline or profession has tended to preserve this dichotomy in practice, though few would defend it in theory. For a more elaborate, and in retrospect perhaps overly optimistic, discussion of this point, see Charles E. Rosenberg, "On the Study of American Biology and Medicine: Some Justifications," *Bulletin of the History of Medicine* 38 (1964): 364-74, esp. 364-65; and idem, "On Writing the History of American Science," in *The State of American History,* ed. Herbert Bass (Chicago: Quadrangle Books, 1970): pp. 183-96.

4. For influential statements of the position emphasizing the culture-bound nature of knowledge, see Barry Barnes, *Scientific Knowledge and Sociological Theory* (London: Routledge and Kegan Paul, 1974); idem, *Interests and the Growth of Knowledge* (London: Routledge and Kegan Paul, 1977), and David Bloor, *Knowledge and Social Imagery* (London: Routledge and Kegan Paul, 1976). The literature in this area is, of course, extensive, including such recent contributors as Karl Mannheim, Michel Foucault, and Mary Douglas. For a criticism of certain aspects of such formulations, see Hugo Meynell, "On the Limits of the Sociology of Knowledge," *Social Studies of Science* 7 (1977): 489-500.

5. See the references and substance of Veysey's argument earlier in this book. For a recent discussion by a prominent contributor to the sociological literature see Elliot Friedson, "The Futures of Professionalization," in *Health and Division of Labor,* eds. M. Stacey et al., (London: Croom Helm, 1977), pp. 14-38. Friedson's essay includes an excellent bibliography.

6. Historians of organized knowledge have often accepted sociological ideal-type descriptions as given—rather than using their special competence to evaluate the adequacy of such formulations. Sociologists, on the other hand, are often casual and uncritical in their use of historical materials, both primary and secondary. For a much-quoted attempt to apply such sociological categories to understanding the professionalization of American science, see George H. Daniels, "The Process of Professionalization in American Science: The Emergent Period, 1840-1860," *Isis* 58 (1967): 151-66.

7. I have purposely avoided formulating a precise definition of the terms "discipline" and "profession"—since such definitional tasks provide an occasion for those very exercises in social taxonomy that lead so often to narrow and schematized visions of past reality.

8. Of course, the learned disciplines do offer products to society, even if these commodities are in some cases as intangible as social status, the satisfying of intellectual curiosity, or the palliation of a national insecurity. The marketplace is never removed entirely from the reality of even the most esoteric disciplines. But in most cases these relationships are indirect and cannot be studied as can explicit exchange of goods and services. Of course, the relationship between the professions and society also includes "noneconomic" elements; the marketplace must be seen as one in which multiple demands are made upon the professions by their particular constituencies—and the profession's ultimate shape incorporates a response to both economic and noneconomic demands.

9. For recent sociological analyses of the professions that incorporate such a point of view, see

Magali Sarfatti Larson, *The Rise of Professionalism: A Sociological Analysis* (Berkeley, Calif.: University of California Press, 1977); Jeffrey L. Berlant, *Profession and Monopoly: A Study of Medicine in the United States and Great Britain* (Berkeley: University of California Press, 1975); Paul Starr, "Medicine, Economy and Society in Nineteenth-Century America," *Journal of Social History* 10 (1977): 588–607; William Rothstein, *American Physicians in the Nineteenth Century* (Baltimore: The Johns Hopkins University Press, 1972). All of these studies demonstrate, to one degree or another, an uncritical faith in the existing historical literature.

10. The applied sciences have suffered a general neglect by historians. Margaret Rossiter's essay in this volume provides a significant introduction to the applied areas in agricultural science and their gradual differentiation into self-conscious disciplines. See also Charles E. Rosenberg, "Rationalization and Reality in the Shaping of American Agricultural Research, 1875–1914," *Social Studies of Science* 7 (1977): 401–23.

11. Much of our best historical investigation of higher education in late-nineteenth and early-twentieth-century America has centered on the role of the executive. See, for example, Lawrence Veysey, *The Emergence of the American University* (Chicago: University of Chicago Press, 1965); Hugh Hawkins, *Between Harvard and America: The Educational Leadership of Charles William Elliot* (New York: Oxford University Press, 1972); Richard Storr, *Harper's University: The Beginnings* (Chicago: University of Chicago Press, 1966).

12. There has, however, been a growing interest in the discipline as focus of investigation—though still more prominently among sociologists than historians. For an evaluation of current work in this area, see Gerard Lemaine et al, *Perspectives on the Emergence of Scientific Disciplines* (Chicago: Aldine, 1976), esp. "Introduction: Problems in the Emergence of New Disciplines," pp. 1–23. Thus far a good deal more attention has been paid to the sciences and social sciences than to the humanistic fields. The department structure and its evolution still await careful study, though there are a number of interesting case studies in the recent literature. Steven J. Diner, "Department and Discipline: The Department of Sociology at the University of Chicago, 1892–1920," *Minerva* 13 (1975): 574–653; Robert W. Seidel, "The Origins of Academic Physics Research in California," *Journal of College Science Teaching* 6 (1976): 10–23; John W. Servos, "The Knowledge Corporation: A. A. Noyes and Chemistry at Cal Tech, 1915–1930," *Ambix* 23 (1976): 175–86; Owen Hannaway, "The German Model of Chemical Instruction in America: Ira Remsen at Johns Hopkins," ibid. 23 (1976): 145–64.

13. There is no recent synthetic history of bacteriology in America, though there are many studies of particular individuals and innovations. Much valuable material is to be found in Paul Clark, *Pioneer Microbiologists of America* (Madison: University of Wisconsin Press, 1961).

14. This argument is presented at greater length in Charles E. Rosenberg, "Factors in the Development of Genetics in the United States: Some Suggestions," *Journal of the History of Medicine* 22 (1967): 27–46, and see also the appropriate references in Garland Allen's essay in this volume.

15. For a well-balanced evaluation of the history of biochemistry and its current status, see Robert E. Kohler, "The History of Biochemistry: A Survey," *Journal of the History of Biology* 8 (1975): 275–318; and idem, "Medical Reform and Biomedical Science: Biochemistry—A Case Study," in *Two Centuries of American Medicine,* ed. Morris Vogel (University of Pennsylvania Press, forthcoming).

16. Edward H. Beardsley, *The Rise of the American Chemistry Profession, 1850–1900,* University of Florida Monographs, Social Sciences no. 23 (Gainesville, Fla.: University of Florida, 1964); Anselm Strauss and Lee Rainwater, *The Professional Scientist: A Study of American Chemists* (Chicago: Aldine, 1962); the relevant sections in William Haynes, *American Chemical Industry: A History,* 6 vols. (New York: Van Nostrand, 1954); Herman Skolnik and Kenneth M. Reese, *A Century of Chemistry: The Role of Chemists and the American Chemical Society* (Washington: American Chemical Society, 1976); K. L. Taylor, "Two Centuries of Chemistry," in *Issues and Ideas in America,* eds. Benjamin J. Taylor and Thurman J. White, (Norman, Okla.: University of Oklahoma Press, 1976); pp. 267–84.

17. On the role of ideology in engineering, see Samuel Haber, *Efficiency and Uplift* (Chicago: University of Chicago Press, 1964); Edwin Layton, *The Revolt of the Engineers* (Cleveland: Press of the Case Western Reserve University, 1971); David Noble, *America by Design: Science, Technology, and the Rise of Corporate Capitalism* (New York: Alfred A. Knopf, 1977); William Akin, *Technocracy and the American Dream* (Berkeley, Calif.: University of California Press, 1977), and Charles E. Rosenberg, "Roles and Professions," *Science* 174 (15 October 1971): 280–81, a review of Layton. Within engineering itself, moreover, subfields have experienced quite different histories;

such differences have related both to technical and contextual factors. For examples, see Daniel H. Calhoun, *The American Civil Engineer: Origins and Conflicts* (Cambridge, Mass.: Harvard University Press, 1960); Monte A. Calvert, *The Mechanical Engineer in America, 1830–1910: Professional Cultures in Conflict* (Baltimore: The Johns Hopkins Press, 1967); Raymond H. Merritt, *Engineering in American Society, 1850–1875* (Lexington, Ky.: University Press of Kentucky, 1969).

18. The indispensable history of nursing is still that by Lavinia Dock and Mary Adelaide Nutting, *A History of Nursing*, 4 vols. (New York and London: G. P. Putnam's Sons, 1907–12). None of the recent synthetic histories of nursing (almost all aimed at a classroom audience) are entirely satisfactory, but see Richard H. Shryock, "Nursing Emerges as a Profession: The American Experience," *Clio Medica* 3 (1968): 131–47. For more recent and critical evaluations, see Amatai Etzioni, ed., *The Semi-Professions and their Organization: Teachers, Nurses, Social Workers* (New York: The Free Press, 1969); Jo Ann Ashley, *Hospitals, Paternalism and the Role of the Nurse* (New York: Teacher's College Press, 1976).

19. The debate surrounding Kuhn's term and its potential applicability is extensive, while attempts to apply it are even more abundant. See, for example, Imre Lakatos and Alan Musgrave, eds., *Criticism and the Growth of Knowledge* (Cambridge: At the University Press, 1970) and Kuhn's "Postscript—1969," in the revised edition of his *Structure of Scientific Revolutions* (Chicago: University of Chicago Press, 1970). For case studies attempting to incorporate the role of ideas and institutional factors in the shaping of a subdiscipline, see Nicholas C. Mullins, "The Development of a Scientific Specialty: The Phage Group and the Origins of Molecular Biology," *Minerva* 10 (1972): 51–82, and David O. Edge and M. J. Mulkay, *Astronomy Transformed: The Emergence of Radio Astronomy in Britain* (New York: John Wiley & Sons-Interscience, 1976). See also Diana Crane, *Invisible Colleges: Diffusion of Knowledge in Scientific Communities* (Chicago: University of Chicago Press, 1972). Daniel Kevles's essay in the present volume suggests the relationship between intellectual achievement and institutional status in those disciplines he treats.

20. For a diversity of insights into such relationships, see Daniel J. Kevles, *The Physicists: The History of a Scientific Community in Modern America* (New York: Alfred A. Knopf, 1978). Paul Forman's study "Weimar Culture, Causality, and Quantum Theory, 1918–1927: Adaptation by German Physicists and Mathematicians to a Hostile Intellectual Environment," *Historical Studies in the Physical Sciences* 3 (1971): 1–115 is a much-quoted case study of the interaction between physics and its cultural context. A parallel study emphasizing resources, support, and scale provides a useful perspective: Paul Forman, John L. Heilbron, and Spencer Weart, *Physics circa 1900: Personnel, Funding, and Productivity of the Academic Establishments,* constituting volume five of *Historical Studies in the Physical Sciences* for 1975. See also Russell McCormmach, "Editor's Foreword," ibid., 3 (1971): lx–xxiv.

21. Charles E. Rosenberg, *No Other Gods: On Science and American Social Thought* (Baltimore: The Johns Hopkins University Press, 1976), chap. 11, "Science Pure and Science Applied: Two Studies in the Social Origin of Scientific Research," pp. 185–95 and the references therein cited.

22. For illuminating case studies, see Mary O. Furner, *Advocacy and Objectivity. A Crisis in the Professionalization of American Social Science. 1865–1905* (Lexington, Ky.: University Press of Kentucky, 1975); Carol S. Gruber, *Mars and Minvera: World War I and the Uses of the Higher Learning in America* (Baton Rouge, La.: Louisiana State University Press, 1975); Robert L. Church, "Economists as Experts: The Rise of an Academic Profession in the United States, 1870–1920," in *The University in Society,* 2 vols., ed. Lawrence Stone (Princeton: Princeton University Press, 1974), 2: 571–609; Thomas L. Haskell, *The Emergence of Professional Social Science: The American Social Science Association and the Nineteenth-Century Crisis of Authority* (Urbana, Ill.: University of Illinois Press, 1977). So central was this dilemma that every biography of a significant American social scientist in this period contains at least some relevant material. For a guide, see the references in Dorothy Ross's essay in this volume.

23. The best case study of this evolution of the philosophical enterprise is Bruce Kuklick, *The Rise of American Philosophy: Cambridge, Massachusetts, 1860–1930* (New Haven: Yale University Press, 1977). See also: Wilson Smith, *Professors and Public Ethics: Studies of Northern Philosophers Before the Civil War* (Ithaca, N.Y.: Cornell University Press, 1956); Daniel Walker Howe, *The Unitarian Conscience* (Cambridge, Mass.: Harvard University Press, 1970); D. H. Meyer, *The Instructed Conscience: The Shaping of an American National Conscience* (Philadelphia: University of Pennsylvania Press, 1972); Gladys Bryson, "Comparable Interests of Old Moral Philosophy and the Modern Social Sciences," *Social Forces* 11 (1932): 19–27; Bryson, "The

Emergence of Social Sciences from Moral Philosophy,'' *International Journal of Ethics* 17 (1932): 304–23.

24. Scientists too could find spiritual transcendence and emotional assurance in choosing a life of the mind. I have made a related case study in attempting to interpret the motivations of a group of Americans who made the deviant career choice of studying chemistry in Germany in the 1850s (*No Other Gods,* pp. 135–52). This is not to contend that all mid-nineteenth-century Americans shared such views in regard to the worth of abstract knowledge and its pursuit (or that even those who held such positive views were entirely consistent). On the other hand, it seems clear that interpretations that emphasize a fundamental conflict between the pursuit of learning and an American society monolithically and implacably materialist and hostile to abstract learning are overstated. See, for example, the much-cited article by Richard H. Shryock, ''American Indifference to Basic Science during the Nineteenth Century,'' *Medicine in America. Historical Essays* (Baltimore: The Johns Hopkins University Press, 1966): pp. 71–89 (an essay originally published in 1948); and George H. Daniels, ''The Pure-Science Ideal and Democratic Culture,'' *Science* 156 (30 June 1967). For a recent study aggressively emphasizing the kinds of social and emotional aggrandizement possible in the creation of a professional career for middle-class Americans, see Burton J. Bledstein, *The Culture of Professionalism: The Middle Class and the Development of Higher Education in America* (New York: W. W. Norton, 1976). None of these studies, however, deals in a systematic fashion with the dissemination of either formal ideas in the culture or attitudes toward its possession.

25. I do not seek to underestimate an endemic skepticism toward new ideas and new techniques, as is emphasized by Louis Galambos in his essay in this volume.

# List of Contributors

Garland Allen is Associate Professor of Biology at Washington University. His principal area of interest is the history of genetics and evolutionary theory in the late nineteenth and early twentieth centuries, and he is currently at work on a history of eugenics. His publications include *The Study of Biology: Life Science in the Twentieth Century,* and *Thomas Hunt Morgan: The Man and His Science.*

John Y. Cole is Executive Director of the Center for the Book in the Library of Congress. He is the author of *For Congress and the Nation: A Chronological History of the Library of Congress.*

A. Hunter Dupree is George L. Littlefield Professor of American History at Brown University. He is the author of *Science in the Federal Government* and *Asa Gray* and the editor of *Science and the Emergence of Modern America.*

Louis Galambos is Professor of History at The Johns Hopkins University and editor of *The Papers of Dwight David Eisenhower.* He is an economic and business historian with a particular interest in large-scale organizations. He has served as a co-editor of *The Journal of Economic History* and recently published *The Public Image of Big Business in America, 1880–1940.*

Neil Harris is Professor of History at the University of Chicago and author of *The Artist in American Society* and *Humbug: The Art of P. T. Barnum.* His essays on cultural history include "All the World a Melting Pot," in A. Iriye, ed., *Mutual Images,* and "Museums, Merchandising, and Popular Taste," in I.M.G. Quimby, ed., *Material Culture and the Study of American Life.*

Hugh Hawkins is Anson D. Morse Professor of History and American Studies at Amherst College. He is the author of *Pioneer: A History of the Johns Hopkins University, 1874–1889* and *Between Harvard and America: The Educational Leadership of Charles W. Eliot.*

John Higham, John Martin Vincent Professor of History at The Johns Hopkins University, writes on American culture in the nineteenth century and on Ameri-

456

can ethnic history. He is co-editor, with Paul K. Conkin, of *New Directions in American Intellectual History;* co-author, with Leonard Krieger and Felix Gilbert, of *History;* and author of *Strangers in the Land: Patterns of American Nativism, 1860-1925* and *Send These to Me: Jews and Other Immigrants in Urban America.*

Daniel J. Kevles, Professor of History at the California Institute of Technology, is the author of *The Physicists: The History of a Scientific Community in Modern America.* He is working in the history of genetics and eugenics in the United States and Britain.

Sally Gregory Kohlstedt is Associate Professor of History at Syracuse University. Her current research interests are the development of American natural history museums in the late nineteenth century and the pattern of women's participation in scientific activity. Recent publications include *The Formation of the American Scientific Community: The American Association for the Advancement of Science, 1848-1866* and "Working in from the Periphery: Three Generations of Women in American Science, 1830-1880," *Signs* (1978).

Alexandra Oleson is Assistant Executive Officer of the American Academy of Arts and Sciences. She is editor of the *Bulletin of the American Academy* and co-editor, with Sanborn C. Brown, of *The Pursuit of Knowledge in the Early American Republic: American Scientific and Learned Societies from Colonial Times to the Civil War.*

John B. Rae is Professor Emeritus of the History of Technology at Harvey Mudd College. He is a former president of the Society for the History of Technology and is the author of *The American Automobile: The Road and the Car in American Life* and *Climb to Greatness: The American Aircraft Industry, 1920-1960.*

Nathan Reingold is Editor of *The Papers of Joseph Henry* at the Smithsonian Institution. He prepared *Science in Nineteenth-Century America, A Documentary History;* a twentieth-century successor is in press.

Fritz K. Ringer, Professor of History at Boston University, has worked in the history of higher education, scholarship, and particularly social thought in modern Germany and France. He is the author of *The Decline of the German Mandarins* and of *Education and Society in Modern Europe.*

Charles E. Rosenberg is Professor of History at the University of Pennsylvania. His publications include *The Trial of the Assassin Guiteau: Psychiatry and the Law in the Gilded Age; The Cholera Years: The United States in 1832, 1849, and 1866;* and *No Other Gods: On Science and American Social Thought.*

Dorothy Ross is Associate Professor of History at the University of Virginia in Charlottesville. She is the author of *G. Stanley Hall: The Psychologist as Prophet* and is at work on a study of the first generation of professional social scientists in America.

Margaret W. Rossiter, Research Associate at the Office for the History of Science and Technology at the University of California, Berkeley, is the author of *The Emergence of Agricultural Science: Justus Liebig and the Americans, 1840–1880*. She is completing a history of women scientists in the United States from 1830 to 1980.

Edward Shils is Professor of Sociology and Social Thought at the University of Chicago and a fellow of Peterhouse, Cambridge University. He is the editor of *Minerva* and the author of *The Intellectual between Tradition and Modernity* and *The Intellectuals and the Powers*.

Laurence R. Veysey, Professor of History at the University of California, Santa Cruz, writes on American social and intellectual history. His publications include *The Emergence of the American University,* and "Stability and Experiment in the American Undergraduate Curriculum," in C. Kaysen, ed., *Content and Context: Essays on College Education*.

John Voss is Executive Officer of the American Academy of Arts and Sciences. He is co-editor, with Paul Ward, of *Confrontation and Learned Societies* and, with Laurence Tribe and Corinne Schelling, of *When Values Conflict: Essays in Environmental Decision-Making*.

# Index

Abbot, Ezra, 373
Adams, Adeline, 87
Adams, Charles Francis, Jr., 73
Adams, Henry, 20, 340 n. 50, 437
Adams, Herbert Baxter, 76, 77, 99 n. 82,
99 n. 83, 99 n. 84, 99 n. 87, 113, 117,
134 n. 36
Adams Act, 24, 151, 212, 216, 241
Adams family, 70
*Advertising News,* 431
African art, 101 n. 109
Agassiz, Alexander, 178, 326, 359
Agassiz, Elizabeth, 398
Agassiz, Louis, 109–10, 178, 182–83, 221, 370;
and Boston Society of Natural History, 390,
392, 393, 395; and National Academy of Sciences, 342–43, 345, 346, 354, 363 n. 17,
363 n. 20; students of, 395
Agricultural experimental stations, 20, 23–24,
30, 211, 272; and agronomy, 233–34; association of, 216; in Europe, 236, 242; funding of,
213–14, 216, 445; and research, 448–49; and
science, 143, 145, 146, 151, 194, 199, 221,
228–29, 231; and soil science, 235; and U.S.
Department of Agriculture, 215–16, 221,
229, 231, 448–49
Agriculture, 211–48: associations, xiv, 212,
214–15, 219, 223–24, 226, 228–29, 230,
232–33, 234–35, 242–43 n. 1, 244 n. 15,
272; colleges of, 23–24, 211, 212–14, 215,
216, 217, 228, 229, 230, 234, 241, 272, 445;
and extension service, 241; and government,
24, 143, 151, 211, 212–14, 215, 221, 222–
23, 241, 242, 257; and politics, xvi, 216, 237,
238, 343; productivity in, 272–73; professionalization of, 211, 219–20, 239–42; and
research, 30, 151, 212–14, 218–20, 228, 242;
and science, 23–24, 213, 214–15, 216, 218–
20, 228–29; and social science, 241; and universities, 23–24, 219, 222, 223, 224, 226,
229, 232, 234, 299–300
Agronomy, 217, 229, 233–35, 239
Albany, N.Y., 373, 388
Alcott, Bronson, 80
Althoff, Friedrich, 43

Aluminum Company of America (Alcoa),
262–63
Alvarez, Luis, 147
Amateurs, xv, 19, 20–21, 58, 69; and learned
societies, 71, 72, 73, 386, 388, 394
American Academy of Arts and Sciences, 30,
298, 363 n. 17, 387; founding of, 97 n. 46;
*Proceedings,* 144
*American Art Annual,* 82, 84, 87, 102 n. 125
American Association for the Advancement of
Science, 3, 34, 197, 344, 391; and agricul-
ture, 24, 214–19, 229, 232; and natural sci-
ence, 140, 150, 151–52, 255, 332; and social
sciences, 108, 109, 328–29
American Association of Law Libraries, 378
American Association of Library Schools, 378
American Association of Museums, 82
American Breeders' Association, 226–27, 228,
242 n. 1
*American Breeders' Magazine,* 227
*American Catholic Who's Who,* 433
*American Chemical Journal,* 143, 144, 149, 156
American Chemical Society, 141, 150, 153,
155, 264, 298, 307, 445; growth of, 279 n. 5;
journal, 155–56, 256
*American Chemist,* 141, 143
American Council of Learned Societies, xiii, 56,
68, 90, 307
American Council on Education, 304
American Dairy Science Association, 230,
242 n. 1
*American Digest: Century Edition,* 14
American Economic Association, 110, 116,
124, 298, 372
American Federation of Arts, 67, 68, 82, 87,
97 n. 48, 101 n. 112, 102 n. 123
American Folklore Society, 76
*American Forester,* 227
American Genetics Association, 227, 242 n. 1
American Geographical Society, 26
American Historical Association, 59–60, 67, 69,
76–78, 94 n. 17, 97 n. 53, 108, 124, 373,
437; membership, 99 n. 84
American Institute of Architects, 82
American Institute of Chemical Engineers, 253

*The Johns Hopkins University Press*

*This book was composed in VIP Times Roman text and display type by The Composing Room of Michigan, Inc. It was printed on 50-lb. No. 66 Eggshell Offset Cream paper and bound in Holliston Roxite cloth by Universal Lithographers, Inc.*

*Library of Congress Cataloging in Publication Data*

Main entry under title:
The Organization of knowledge in modern America, 1860–1920.

  Includes index.
  1. Learning and scholarship—United States.
I. Oleson, Alexandra, 1939–    II. Voss, John, 1917–

AZ505.073   001.2   78-20521
ISBN 0-8018-2108-8